M000307620

ETIQUETTE

19TH
EDITION

MANNERS FOR TODAY

Also from the Emily Post Institute

Emily Post's Great Get-Togethers

Emily Post's Wedding Parties

Do I Have to Wear White?

How Do You Work This Life Thing?

"Excuse Me, But I Was Next . . ."

Emily Post's Wedding Planner, 4th Edition

Emily Post's Wedding Etiquette, 6th Edition

Emily Post's Wedding Planner for Moms

Emily Post's The Etiquette Advantage in Business, 3rd Edition

Essential Manners for Couples

Essential Manners for Men

A Wedding Like No Other

Emily Post's The Unwritten Rules of Golf

Mr. Manners: Lessons from Obama on Civility

Emily Post's The Gift of Good Manners

Emily Post's Teen Manners

Emily Post's Prom and Party Etiquette

Emily Post's Table Manners for Kids

Emily Post's The Guide to Good Manners for Kids

Emily's Everyday Manners

Emily's Christmas Gifts

Emily's New Friend

Emily's Magic Words

Emily's Sharing and Caring Book

Emily's Out and About Book

Emily Post's Manners in a Digital World

ETIQUETTE

19TH EDITION

MANNERS FOR TODAY

Lizzie Post ◆ Daniel Post Senning

Illustrations by Janice Richter

WILLIAM MORROW

An Imprint of *HarperCollins*Publishers

Emily Post is a registered trademark of The Emily Post Institute, Inc.

EMILY POST'S ETIQUETTE, 19TH EDITION. Copyright © 2017 by The Emily Post Institute, Inc. All rights reserved. Printed in the United States of America. No part of this book may be used or reproduced in any manner whatsoever without written permission except in the case of brief quotations embodied in critical articles and reviews. For information, address HarperCollins Publishers, 195 Broadway, New York, NY 10007.

HarperCollins books may be purchased for educational, business, or sales promotional use. For information, please email the Special Markets Department at SPsales@harpercollins.com.

Produced by Smallwood & Stewart, New York

Designed by Alexis Siroc

Illustrations by Janice Richter

Library of Congress Cataloging-in-Publication Data has cataloged the previous edition as follows:

Emily Post's Etiquette—18th ed. / Peggy Post . . . [et al.].
p. cm.
Includes bibliographical references and index.
ISBN 978-0-06-174023-7
1. Etiquette. I. Post, Peggy. II. Post, Emily, 1873–1960. Etiquette. III. Title: Etiquette.
BJ1853.P6. 2011
395—dc22

2010042228

ISBN 978-0-06-243925-3

17 18 19 20 21 QG/IND5 10 9 8 7 6 5 4 3 2 1

contents

Acknowledgments   ix

A Note to Readers   x

ETIQUETTE EVERY DAY

Part I Everyday Manners   3

CHAPTER 1   Guidelines for Living   5

CHAPTER 2   Essential Manners   8

CHAPTER 3   Common Courtesies   21

CHAPTER 4   The Art of Conversation   35

CHAPTER 5   Image and Attire   46

CHAPTER 6   Table Manners   56

Part II Out and About   77

CHAPTER 7   Living with Neighbors   79

CHAPTER 8   Around Town   91

CHAPTER 9   Dining Out   100

CHAPTER 10   Traveling Near and Far   119

CHAPTER 11   Sports and Recreation   136

CHAPTER 12   Attending Performances   155

CHAPTER 13   Tipping   165

CHAPTER 14   Volunteering   175

CHAPTER 15   Official Life   179

Part III Communication   195

CHAPTER 16   Notes and Letters   197

CHAPTER 17   Social Names and Titles   215

CHAPTER 18   Telephone Manners   221

CHAPTER 19   Personal Communication Devices   230

CHAPTER 20   Online Communication   237

Part IV Social Life   247

CHAPTER 21   Hosts and Guests   249

CHAPTER 22   Houseguests   261

CHAPTER 23   Invitations and Announcements   271

CHAPTER 24   Entertaining at Home   292

CHAPTER 25   Formal Dinners and Parties   314

CHAPTER 26   Celebrations Through Life   320

CHAPTER 27   Ceremonies and Religious Services   334

CHAPTER 28   Giving and Receiving Gifts   349

CHAPTER 29   Dating   370

CHAPTER 30   Life Online   383

LIFE IN THE WORKPLACE

Part V Getting the Job   393

CHAPTER 31   The Job Search   395

CHAPTER 32   The Job Interview   403

Part VI On the Job   409

CHAPTER 33   At the Office   411

CHAPTER 34   Workplace Relationships   428

CHAPTER 35   The Social Side of Business   442

LIFE STAGES AND SPECIAL TIMES

Part VII Home and Family Life   455

CHAPTER 36   Today's Home and Family   457

CHAPTER 37   Pregnancy, Birth, and Adoption   473

CHAPTER 38   Children and Teens   478

CHAPTER 39   Living with Others   490

CHAPTER 40   People Who Work in Your Home   500

CHAPTER 41   Separation and Divorce   511

CHAPTER 42   Elder Etiquette   520

CHAPTER 43   Illness   531

CHAPTER 44   Loss, Grieving, and Condolences   539

Part VIII Weddings   557

CHAPTER 45   The Engagement   559

CHAPTER 46   Trends and Traditions   567

CHAPTER 47   Planning Your Wedding   572

CHAPTER 48   Wedding Invitations
             and Announcements   597

CHAPTER 49   Wedding Attire   613

CHAPTER 50   Wedding Registries, Gifts,
             and Thank-yous   624

CHAPTER 51   The Big Day   634

CHAPTER 52   Remarriage   654

CHAPTER 53   A Guide for Wedding Guests   662

RESOURCES

Names and Titles   676

Official Forms of Address   678

Dressing for the Occasion   683

Sample Invitations and Announcements   685

Guide to Food and Drink   686

Wedding Budget Planning Chart   696

Wedding Budget Categories for Attendants   698

Index   699

*With love, gratitude, and great respect we dedicate the 19th edition
to the "fourth generation" of the Post family: Allen, Bill, Cindy, and Peter.
They have stewarded this tradition with such care and have made it
possible for us to carry on the family legacy.*

*We also dedicate this book to Peggy Post and Anna Post, whose thoughtful,
caring advice is reflected in the content of this book and whose years
of dedication and service to "Emily Post" has been of great
benefit to our family and our company.*

acknowledgments

Creating this book was truly a team effort, and it is with gratitude and deep appreciation that we thank the following for their contributions:

Tricia Post, who has edited and shepherded the 19th edition of *Emily Post's Etiquette* for the past two years; and Peter Post for his insights, advice, and keen eye.

Peggy Post, for her expert guidance and contributions, without which this book would not have been possible. With her twenty-five years of experience managing the brand both on her own and throughout its expansion, Peggy kept Emily Post alive and relevant, and made it possible for us to carry on our family legacy.

Anna Post, who over the last nine years has made significant contributions to the modernization of Emily Post etiquette. Anna's ability to see broadly the effect that our advice can have was invaluable in ensuring that Emily Post truly is for everyone.

Cindy Post Senning, for her patient guidance and for continuing to serve in an advisory capacity to The Emily Post Institute.

Steven Puettner and Susan Iverson at The Emily Post Institute, and Katherine Cowles, our agent, for their encouragement and moral support, as well as their creative ideas and assistance.

Our sincere thanks go to Emily Krump, our editor at William Morrow, who has a magical way of fine-tuning our massive tome to be accessible, relevant, and enjoyable. Thanks, also, to everyone at William Morrow who has supported and championed *Emily Post's Etiquette* in all its editions, including Liate Stehlik, Lynn Grady, Katherine Gordon, Andrea Rosen, Nyamekye Waliyaya, Andrea Molitor, Julia Meltzer, and Madeline Jaffe.

John Smallwood and Alexis Siroc of Smallwood & Stewart, whose elegant design continues to give the 19th edition a beautiful, easy-to-follow format, complemented by Janice Richter's charming and whimsical illustrations. Their work brings the written word to life.

Etiquette covers so many topics, and we are lucky to be able to draw on many generous sources. Not only do we value them for their expertise, but we consider them examples of best practice as well: Dr. Parveen Ali; Matt Bushlow; Cherlynn Conetsco; Nicole Dulac; Kris Engstrom; Dr. Manohar Singh Grewal and Mr. Ravinder Singh Taneja; Alka Gupta; April Harris; Anna Hart; Craig Iverson; Mac Keyser; Virginia Keyser; Mike Hakim; Deborah Jarecki; Britta Johnson; Adrea Kofman; Dale Loeffler; Barbara McDonald; Katherine Meyers; Owen Milne; John Parker; Peter Phillips; Thomas Pierce; Mauricia Rollins; Cindy Post Senning, Ed.D.; Kerin E. Stackpole, Esq., SPHR; and Samantha Wendel, B.A., CSA, CMC.

As this book is very much a reflection of the manners of today, we would also like to recognize the invaluable contribution of everyone who has sent us such interesting and challenging questions, in particular to the *Awesome Etiquette* podcast audience, and those who have reached out to us via social media. We are so grateful that you are not only interested in how your behavior affects others, but also are willing to share your questions and comments with our larger audience. Together we are building a nicer world and for that, we thank you.

a note to readers

In a world that is constantly evolving it's comforting to know that how we interact with one another still matters, and it is both rooted in tradition yet flexible enough to keep up with a rapidly changing and culturally diverse world. We want *Etiquette* to speak to traditional etiquette fans as well as those new to Emily Post—on the one hand reaffirming the values and manners of previous generations, while at the same time promoting the best practices of current society. We know that manners—the particular ways in which we show respect and consideration—change over time. Long gone are the 1st edition chaperone and the 12th edition ashtrays at the dinner table; they have been replaced by topics that have relevance to the daily lives of most Americans today, such as managing social media and mobile devices, having confidence at work, and navigating life at home.

The 19th edition of *Etiquette* reflects the different worlds we inhabit—our homes, communities, social circles, and workplaces. We examine the manners and considerations essential to building strong families, careers, friendships, and positive work environments. We cover all of life's stages—from birth or adoption, childhood, and adolescence to college, work, marriage, family, retirement, illness, and death. Often-accessed practical information, such as forms of address and attire charts, is grouped together in a ready-reference resource guide.

In our fast-paced, stressed-out world, is etiquette still relevant? We say yes: Etiquette is very much a topic of national conversation. At The Emily Post Institute, it's a rare day when we're not fielding media interviews on topics such as what's appropriate political conversation, what to register for when you already have the basics, whether it's okay to unfriend your ex but not his friends, guidelines for polite smartphone use, and how to handle dinner guests' myriad dietary restrictions. Emily Post has expanded its range from books, print columns, and a website to include a social media presence on Facebook, Twitter, and Instagram, as well as business etiquette training, seminars, and e-learning courses. Nothing illustrates the continuing relevance of etiquette more than the interactions we experience through the *Awesome Etiquette* podcast, hosted by Lizzie Post and Daniel Post Senning. They enjoy having a direct connection to their audience through the podcast. You, our readers, are also an essential part of those conversations. Your questions, feedback, suggestions, and etiquette salutes have further helped us to identify *What is American etiquette today?* It is clear to us through these interactions and conversations that etiquette still matters to Americans today.

As much as etiquette is about weddings and table settings and forms of address, at its most essential it's about relationships and communication. Knowing which fork to use will give you social confidence, but applying the principles of etiquette—consideration, respect, and honesty—will enhance every interaction. It's now not just possible but commonplace to connect with dozens, hundreds, even thousands of people at once through social networks, instant messaging, tweets, texts, and emails. Video calls have left the office and come home to the living room or out to the beach. This communications revolution offers so many beneficial opportunities, not just to connect offices and families, but to give each individual a voice. With this opportunity to voice our opinions and share our ideas comes the responsibility to do so civilly. Irresponsible rants and defamatory remarks are divisive and polarizing, and only serve to heighten anxiety and sow distrust. Used wisely, communication channels in all their forms can be powerful tools to build communities and foster civil discourse, cooperation, and positive outcomes. As our country faces the challenges of an increasingly complex and diverse world, civility becomes all the more critical to our success.

The 19th edition is fully integrated with The Emily Post Institute's website, **emilypost.com.** Readers can visit our site to get further information or the latest information on any subject from tipping to social networking. Simply use the URL found at the bottom of each page. Our mobile-friendly site is also home to our searchable database of advice and articles that puts Emily Post etiquette at your fingertips.

It is our fervent hope that you will turn to us not just for advice on planning your wedding or setting your dinner table, but as a trusted companion and guide, wherever your life's journey takes you.

We wish you all the best.

Sincerely,
Lizzie Post
Daniel Post Senning

Spring 2017

ETIQUETTE
EVERY DAY

Part I
everyday manners

CHAPTER 1 Guidelines for Living 5

CHAPTER 2 Essential Manners 8

CHAPTER 3 Common Courtesies .21

CHAPTER 4 The Art of Conversation 35

CHAPTER 5 Image and Attire 46

CHAPTER 6 Table Manners 56

guidelines for living

In this fast-paced world with its multiple demands, it's all the more important to be intentional about using common courtesies in our everyday interactions. Even though scientific and medical advancements have made life easier over the years, the stresses and strains that come with population density, technological advancements, 24/7 news and entertainment media, and a redefinition of the family have resulted in a whole new set of realities. People behave no worse than they used to, but with the pressures of modern life it can be more challenging to stay civil.

It's true that we take a more casual approach to dressing, communicating, and entertaining. But casualness, or informality, doesn't necessarily equate to rudeness. It's just as easy to be polite when wearing jeans to a party as when wearing a tuxedo to a wedding.

Etiquette and Manners

When Emily Post wrote her first etiquette book in 1922, she explained that etiquette, very simply, is a code of behavior based on consideration and thoughtfulness. The very word *etiquette* has an interesting derivation, originating with the French. During the reign of King Louis XIV, his gardener placed signs along the grounds and gardens of Versailles reminding visitors to "remain on the walkways," and to "keep off the grass and out of the flower beds." These little signs, called *etiquettes* or "tickets," instructed everyone on how to behave and to "keep within the *etiquettes*." The singular word *etiquette* evolved to become the instant definition of courtesy, thoughtful behavior, impeccable manners, dignity, and civility.

The philosophy of etiquette is timeless and everlasting, whereas *manners*—the ways in which we live out the code of behavior of etiquette—are ever changing. Manners, by their very nature, adapt to the times. While today's manners are often situational, tailored to particular circumstances and the expectations of those around us, they remain a combination of common sense, generosity of spirit, and a few specific guidelines or fluid "rules" that help us interact thoughtfully. And as fluid as manners are, they all rest on the same fundamental principles of etiquette: consideration, respect, and honesty.

Consideration. Consideration is being aware of and understanding how a situation affects everyone involved. The key to consideration is thoughtful behavior, which leads to actions that will affect others in a positive way. Consideration leads us to help a friend or stranger in need, to bestow a token of appreciation, to offer praise.

Respect. Respect builds on consideration by valuing the individuals involved, regardless of their background, race, or creed. Respect is demonstrated by actions, appearance, and words that honor and value others. It's demonstrated in all your day-to-day relations—refraining from demeaning others for their ideas and opinions, refusing to laugh at racist or sexist jokes, putting prejudices aside, and staying open-minded. Being inclusive is a way of being respectful—that is, making an effort to learn about and accept others whose backgrounds and cultures are different from one's own. We also show respect not just by what we refrain from doing but also by intentional acts, such as being on time, dressing appropriately, or giving our full attention to the person or people we're with.

Self-respect is just as important as respect for others. A person who respects herself isn't boastful or pushy but is secure in a way that inspires confidence. She values herself regardless of her physical attributes or individual talents, understanding that integrity and character are what really matter.

---

etiquette is . . .

FLUID . . . NOT A SET OF RIGID RULES.
Manners change over time and reflect the best practices of our times. Etiquette isn't a set of "prescriptions for properness" but merely the guidelines for doing things in ways that make people feel comfortable.

FOR EVERYONE . . . NOT SOMETHING FOR THE WEALTHY OR WELLBORN. Etiquette is a code of behavior for people from all walks of life, every socioeconomic group, and of all ages. Good manners are a valuable asset that cost nothing to acquire.

CURRENT . . . NOT A THING OF THE PAST. The bedrock principles of etiquette remain as solid as they ever were. Manners change over time and across cultural boundaries, but the principles are universal and timeless.

UNPRETENTIOUS . . . NOT SNOBBISH. A polite person doesn't try to be someone he's not, nor does he look down on others.

Honesty. Honesty is acting sincerely and being truthful. Honesty compels us to choose to act sincerely and with integrity in ways that honor and respect others. It's the basis of tact. Honesty allows us to apply empathy to find the positive truth and act upon it, without causing embarrassment or pain.

Two Other Essential Qualities

Graciousness and kindness are an integral part of courteous behavior. Graciousness is the ability to make other people feel welcome and comfortable in your world. Kindness is much like consideration but it also reflects the warmth in your heart.

Actions Express Attitude

Courteous people are empathetic—able to relate emotionally to the feelings of others. They listen closely to what people say. They observe what's going on around them and register what they see. Courteous people are flexible, willing to adjust their own behavior to the needs and feelings of others, while maintaining their integrity. Courteous people are forgiving, and understand that nobody is perfect. They would never embarrass or judge someone for a mistake in form, such as using the wrong fork or introducing people out of order. They don't keep an etiquette scorecard.

Why Etiquette Matters

Etiquette is the fuel that powers relationships. Emily Post said, "Etiquette is the foundation upon which social structure is built. Every human contact is made smooth by etiquette, or awkward by lack of it." Grounded as it is in timeless principles, etiquette enables us to face whatever the future may bring with strength of character and integrity. This ever-adaptive code of behavior also allows us to be flexible enough to respect those whose beliefs and traditions differ from our own. Civility and courtesy, the outward expressions of human decency, are the proverbial glue that holds society together—qualities that are more important than ever in today's complex and changing world.

2 essential manners

no one wakes up in the morning, looks in the mirror, and says, "I think I'll be rude today." Most of us think of ourselves as polite, but when we're in a hurry or dealing with strangers we don't always use the manners we know we should. Yet it only takes a moment to use the simplest courtesies, and what a difference that can make to our interactions. Good manners start with the famous "magic words." Greetings and introductions are important, too. *Please* make these fundamental manners a part of you. Using them sets the tone not just for a pleasant day, but for a civil society as well.

THE "MAGIC WORDS"

We learned them as children: "May I have a cookie, please?" almost always worked, while "I want a cookie" didn't get you a crumb. "Please," "Thank you," "You're welcome," "Excuse me," and "I'm sorry" are just as important for adults. These essential words are effortless to say but convey a wealth of meaning to others. They're powerful for their transformative ability to create positive interactions. "Thank you" shows that a gift or a favor is appreciated instead of expected. "Please" changes a demand into a request. "Excuse me" acknowledges your error and says your mistake wasn't intentional.

"Please"

As we tell children, "please" really is a magic word because it changes a command into a request. Using "please" expresses both respect and consideration for those with whom we're interacting, and it sets the tone for whatever follows. Along with "thank you," it is one of the two most important universal manners.

"Thank You" and "You're Welcome"

Most people know to express their thanks for gifts, favors, awards, and the like. But we sometimes fail to recognize and show appreciation for the everyday courtesies that come our way, such as when someone holds the door or lets us go ahead in line. Small kindnesses can go almost unnoticed if people are too busy or self-absorbed to care. Expressing thanks for these little services is a hallmark of civility.

When someone says, "Thank you," the best response is, "You're welcome" or, "My pleasure." Don't be bashful—accept the credit for your kindness. It's subtle, but an "It was nothing" or "No problem" is actually saying that you place no value on what you did. So don't brush off an expression of gratitude. By accepting thanks graciously you can also encourage the "thank-you" habit.

"Excuse Me"

"Excuse me," "Pardon me," and "I beg your pardon" all express your awareness that you've inconvenienced someone else. Bump into someone? "Excuse me" lets the person know that it wasn't intentional and calms the situation. Make it a habit to excuse yourself whenever you do the following:

◆ **Make a necessary interruption:** "Excuse me, but you have a phone call."

◆ **Make a request:** "Excuse me, but this is the non-smoking section."

◆ **Acknowledge an error:** "Excuse me. I didn't realize that you were already waiting in line."

◆ **Acknowledge a faux pas, such as burping:** "Excuse me."

◆ **Leave a conversation:** "Excuse me, I wish I could chat longer, but I have to leave now."

◆ **Get up from the table:** "Please excuse me."

"I'm Sorry"

Making and accepting apologies gracefully are acts of courtesy and maturity, and they are important for matters both big and small. How we handle our mistakes speaks volumes. Sincere apologies can defuse volatile situations; it's hard for most people to remain angry with someone who takes responsibility for his error and has a plan for amends. "Jennifer, I'm sorry. I shouldn't have borrowed your sweater without asking. I've had it dry cleaned."

"I'm sorry" is also one of the simplest and often kindest ways to express sympathy or regret. A job loss, an illness, a death in the family, or the loss of a pet are all times when you might say "I'm sorry." At these times, keep it simple—you don't need to elaborate. "I'm sorry you've had such a tough time. I've been thinking about you." (For more on expressing sympathy or condolence, see Chapter 44, "Loss, Grieving, and Condolences," page 539.)

The Courteous "No"

How do you politely turn down an offer, request, or invitation? It's amazing how often people are hesitant to say "no" when they really want to. Honesty is one of the bedrock principles of good manners. The simple "No, thank you" learned in childhood should be part of every adult's daily vocabulary. Everyone understands that "no" is a necessary answer sometimes, but *how* you deliver the message is what counts. Here are ways to help you say "no" considerately and effectively:

Count to ten. Take a moment to weigh your pros and cons, and evaluate your limits (time, money, interest). The result is that you'll have the power of your convictions, making the "no" easier to deliver and easier for the requester to accept.

Accompany a "no" with a positive comment. "No, but thanks for asking me," expresses appreciation for the person's thoughtfulness.

Give a good, honest reason when possible. "No, I'm swamped with my work schedule." "No, I give to other charities." "No, Joe and I have plans Friday, but maybe next time." Give a reason only if it's truthful and helpful to your response.

Avoid equivocating. A reasonable "no" isn't a cause for guilt, so don't hem and haw. "I don't think I can" or "I probably shouldn't" gives the impression that you haven't decided and leaves the door open for further persuasion. Failing to be definitive can prolong the discussion, to everyone's discomfort.

Don't open the door to future requests. Unless you'll welcome them, respond clearly: "No. With my work schedule, I really can't. I'll let you know if my situation changes." If you'd like to help in the future, say so: "No, I can't help this time, but please call me for the next project."

Beware of Traps!

It's okay to resist someone's campaign to change your mind:

Flattery: "Your pumpkin pies are so good. How about five for Thanksgiving dinner?" "I'm glad you like them but I only have time to bake two."

Bullying: "You've got to help out. Everyone else is calling two hundred names on the list." "Next time I'd be happy to, but right now it's not a possibility."

Making it your problem: "I'm so swamped! Could you just . . ." "I'm sorry you're swamped, but I have to meet my own deadline."

Is That Your Final Answer?

When someone says "no," turning down an invitation or request, it's important to respect his or her decision. Trying to cajole a "yes" or giving her the third degree and then arguing each excuse is both insensitive and rude. Of course, if the two of you have been trying to match your calendars for a dinner date, by all means propose an alternate. The invitation has already been tacitly accepted and you're both just trying to find the right time.

 **GREETINGS**

Greetings and introductions get things going, bringing people together in a positive way. From a casual wave to the most formal presentation, they're basic to civilized interaction in all societies, though the forms may differ. Every greeting and introduction is a chance to show your respect for others and to create a favorable impression of yourself. So the most important thing is to **do it**—make a conscious effort to say "hello" even when you feel a bit grumpy or shy, and make introductions even if you aren't quite sure of the finer points of who is introduced to whom.

The Essentials of Greeting Others

For most people, greeting others is so ingrained that they hardly notice doing it. Yet when a normally friendly person doesn't wave at her neighbor or say "good morning" to coworkers, they notice—and may think something's wrong. Usually, it's unintentional—the person is preoccupied, late for an appointment, or she just didn't see you. Still, people do notice and tend to assume the worst when we don't say hello.

The best place to cultivate the greeting habit is at home. It takes only seconds to acknowledge the people we live with, yet how often do busy families actually say "good morning" to one another? How frequently is someone welcomed home from work with a simple "Hi, how was your day?" which sets a positive tone?

Informal Greetings

An informal greeting may be spoken, gestured, or both. "Hello" and "Hi" (or the even more casual "Hey," "What's up?" or "How's it going?"), said with a smile and accompanied by the person's name if you know it, are the typical casual greetings. "Good morning," "Good afternoon," and "Good evening" are a little more formal, but also commonly used.

Saying "hello" doesn't obligate you to stop and chat, so don't hesitate to greet someone just because you're in a rush. If the person wants to talk, briefly explain your hurry and part graciously. It's only right to be courteous to people in general, so also don't forget to greet the people who serve you, such as cashiers and receptionists.

When someone's too far away to hear or when it would disturb others, a spoken greeting may not be possible. In that case, a smile and a nod or wave will do. During a religious service, lecture, or live performance where it could be distracting and disrespectful, just smile and save your "hellos" for later.

Formal Greetings

In certain situations the greeting is more formalized, such as at a business meeting with prospective clients, a formal event where participants may not know one another, in a receiving line, or at a state occasion. Instead of "Hi" use "Hello," "How do you do?" or "Good (morning, afternoon, evening)" along with the person's title and last name: "Hello, Mr. Carpenter" or "Good afternoon, Madam Secretary." "How do you do?" is another option. Formality is also conveyed by your tone of voice and even your posture. Make an effort to stand up straight, look the person in the eye, and speak clearly. Formal greetings should be pleasant and genuine, but not effusive.

Standing . . . or Not

Whether you're male or female, rising to greet someone who just entered a room is a time-honored display of respect. Old rules about men rising while women remain seated have gone by the wayside. Today, it's appropriate for a woman to stand and offer her hand in greeting to either a man or another woman, and it's the norm in business situations because they are gender neutral.

Standing to greet anyone instantly puts everyone on the same level, namely eye level. It's especially important to stand when the person you're greeting is

- older than you.
- senior to you in business.
- someone you're meeting for the first time.
- someone who is traditionally shown special respect, such as the head of a company, an elected official or a representative of a foreign country, or a member of the clergy or a religious order.

Hosts and hostesses should rise and go to greet all arriving guests at social events, but once the party is under way, it isn't necessary to stand every time someone enters a room.

It's okay **not** to stand when

- you have an injury or disability.
- you've already greeted everyone once.
- you're trapped at a restaurant table or booth.
- coworkers pop in and out of your office space.

If possible, make a "half up" gesture, a little rise out of your seat, signifying that you would stand if you could. While it's nice to meet on an equal level, when this isn't possible or practical keep a little distance so you don't tower over the seated person. Bending forward

a bit will help everyone hear the introduction in a noisy setting. (For more on business greetings, see Chapter 34, "Workplace Relationships," page 428.)

Handshaking

Ritual handshaking dates back at least to ancient Egypt and Babylon. An open right hand signified that you weren't carrying weapons and that you came in peace. Today, a handshake is a gesture of friendship and good faith (as when people seal a deal by shaking hands).

In the United States, a handshake, rather than a bow, *salaam, wai*, or kiss, is the way we greet others. Both men and women shake hands, and either may offer their hand first. There are four steps to a handshake:

1. Extend your right hand, thumb slightly separated, creating a V between the thumb and the forefinger. (It's fine to extend your left hand if you have an injury, infirmity, or don't have a right hand.)
2. Clasp the other person's hand, palm to palm with the V's interlocking.
3. Grip firmly—but not too hard!—and shake two or three times. Use about as much pressure as it takes to open a refrigerator door.
4. Release and lower your hand.

Remember, a handshake is an offer of friendship. If your grip is really weak (the "dead fish") you'll appear cold and disinterested. A bone crusher, however, can cause injury—hardly a friendly gesture. Don't exaggerate the shaking—it should move through a range of about 5 to 6 inches. Finally, don't place your free hand on top of the clasped hands or clasp the other person's wrist, as both of these gestures express dominance.

You can sense when offering your hand wouldn't be appropriate. Shaking hands will inconvenience a person who has a hand, arm, or shoulder injury, or who is carrying things in both hands. In some cultures, touching hands is offensive or may be prohibited between men and women. If this is the case, smile and use an alternative gesture, such as a slight bow of your head. Make sure you greet the person respectfully and with genuine enthusiasm. Convey with words what the handshake would have expressed: "I am so glad to meet you." (For more on greetings in other countries, see Chapter 10, "Traveling Near and Far," page 119.)

When Someone Doesn't Shake Your Hand

We're so accustomed to having the offer of a handshake accepted that when it's not reciprocated, it creates an awkward moment. Why isn't someone accepting my offer of friendship? Just lower your hand and ignore any awkwardness, even though offering your hand is correct.

When You Can't Shake Hands

There are times when it's legitimate not to shake hands: if you have an injury, disability, or a cold, for instance. If someone extends his hand, smile and say, "I'm sorry, I hurt my arm and can't shake hands right now, but I'm very pleased to meet you." Giving a reason lets the person know that it's not meant as an insult.

If someone has an obvious disability, such as a right hand or arm that is missing or in a cast, it's fine to shake his left hand with your left hand. A person with a chronic ailment, such as arthritis in their hands, may not want to call attention to their situation every time a handshaking opportunity arises. Receiving a firm handshake may be painful, but refusing without giving an explanation would most likely be seen as rude. A simple alternative is to grasp the extended hand with both hands and press as firmly as is comfortable while exchanging greetings. In this case, the two-hand clasp is acceptable.

four steps to a correct greeting

It's true: First impressions *do* count. The image you project when meeting someone for the first time can be permanent. If you smile and convey confidence and composure, you'll make a positive and long-lasting first impression.

STAND UP. If there's no room to stand, briefly lift yourself out of your chair, extend your hand, and say, "Please excuse me for not standing. It's nice to meet you."

SMILE AND MAKE EYE CONTACT. Your smile conveys warmth and openness; looking a person in the eye clearly shows that you're focused on them.

SAY YOUR GREETING. The direct "How do you do?" "Hello," and "It's a pleasure to meet you" are all good openers. Repeating the person's name also helps you remember it.

SHAKE HANDS. Grasp the other person's hand firmly, shake two or three times, let go, and step back.

Most times, it's unlikely that a handshake will expose a person to serious illness. If you're concerned about someone passing germs to you, you can always excuse yourself to wash your hands afterward. Regular hand washing—and more frequent hand washing when you have an illness or are traveling—should lessen the chance of spreading germs.

Should You Kiss, Hug, or Touch?

Comfort levels regarding physical greetings vary greatly, so rushing forward to kiss or hug a casual or new acquaintance might cause the person real discomfort. In a diverse society, it's also hard to know the many cultural and religious traditions and prohibitions involving physical contact—including restrictions based on gender. It's best to limit touching to the offer of your hand unless you're absolutely sure a person will welcome more intimate gestures. Other than handshaking, touching of any sort in business situations—especially between men and women and between superiors and subordinates—can be misinterpreted as harassment and have serious repercussions. While some people may regret the demise of the friendly pat on the back or the arm around the shoulder among colleagues, in today's world it's better to be safe than to risk reputation and career.

How do you avoid bumping heads when greeting with a kiss? There's a simple guideline for dodging a collision when greeting with a kiss: right cheek to right cheek. If you turn your head slightly to the *left*, the other person will instinctively follow suit.

Q: *When outdoors, does a person have to remove his gloves when shaking hands? By the way, where we live, the winter temperature is often below freezing.*

A: When you meet someone on the street in the dead of winter, you can leave your gloves on. In warmer weather, people normally remove their right glove to shake hands. If you're wearing heavy or soiled work gloves or padded sport gloves, like ski mittens, you may simply forgo handshaking. Except for very formal occasions and receiving lines, gloves are removed indoors.

How does the double or triple kiss work? Kissing both cheeks is a traditional greeting in many cultures. Some even go for the triple or quadruple kiss. Kissing is usually accompanied by an embrace, which may be close or involve only arm touching. While they are facing and hugging, each person turns his or her head a bit to the left and offers the right cheek, then the other. Usually, warm words are exchanged during the greeting. The cheeks don't actually have to be kissed with the lips (known as an "air kiss"); a cheek-to-cheek touch is common. To avoid an awkward accidental kiss on the lips when moving cheek to cheek, lean back slightly in the middle before leaning in to kiss the other cheek.

What about hand kissing? You may encounter hand kissing on occasion, though it's not customary

in the United States. A woman extends her hand palm down, and a man holds it lightly, bows, and quickly kisses the air just above the hand—without lip-to-hand contact.

How do you signal that you don't want to be hugged or kissed? You can extend your hand with a fairly stiff arm, shake hands, and then take a step back. Most people will respect the space you create with your body language. Sometimes you can't avoid the contact, and it's best to grin and bear it, backing away a bit once the person has released you.

The High Five and the Fist Bump

Not every greeting calls for a formal handshake. Among friends or peers informal greetings such as the high- or low-five palm slap are common. You'll often see athletes or friends high-five after scoring points or receiving news of a success. The fist bump or knuckle knock is when two people bump fists lightly. It's used as a greeting or in place of the celebratory high five. While fine to use among friends, stick to the tried-and-true handshake in business or when meeting someone for the first time.

Q: *I noticed a client sneezing into his hand. A few minutes later, my boss introduced me to him. I didn't want to shake his hand, but I did. Was there any other option?*

A: No, not really. Know that you did the right thing (assuming that your next stop was the restroom for a thorough hand washing with soap and hot water). If you didn't shake, the client would have wondered what was wrong with you, and your boss would have been embarrassed by your actions.

A Graceful Exit

When a greeting is followed by some conversation, departing requires more than a brusque "bye" or "see you." The traditional parting is still "good-bye," normally said with some pleasantry that winds the conversation down, such as "It's been so good to see you" or "I have to go now, but I'll call you next week."

INTRODUCTIONS

The only true breach of introduction etiquette is to fail to make one when you're with people who don't know each other. Making errors in the order of names, forgetting or mispronouncing a name, or using the wrong title is a minor mistake (and easily corrected) compared to the discourtesy of neglecting to make the introduction at all.

Before an event, do a little homework. For example, if you're planning to entertain and introductions will be required, brush up on pronunciations and correct titles before the party. If you're attending a meeting at which you are likely to be introduced, ask for a list of who will be there and familiarize yourself with names and titles in advance.

The following guidelines will help make introductions go as smoothly as possible for both parties.

When You Are Making the Introduction . . .

- **Look at the person you are speaking to first;** then turn to the other person as you complete the introduction.
- **Speak clearly.** A muffled or mumbled introduction defeats the whole purpose.
- **State your introductions courteously.** The basic language is well established: "I'd like to introduce . . . ," "May I introduce . . . ," "I'd like you to meet . . . ," or, more formally, "May I present . . ." It's considered impolite to make an introduction in the form of a command, such as "Harry, shake hands with Mr. Malone" or "Ms. Benson, come here and meet Mr. Simpkins."

THE ORDER OF INTRODUCTIONS

Before you begin, you'll need to identify who, for lack of a better description, is the more "important" person, or the person you'd like to honor. Address him or her first. Below are some examples:

TURN TO AND SAY THIS PERSON'S NAME FIRST . . .	THIS PERSON'S SECOND
Your grandparents, parents, or anyone older than you	Your contemporary (or younger)
Senator, Mayor, Judge, Colonel, nobility, Bishop, Reverend, Professor, Doctor, anyone senior to you (your boss, CEO)	Your contemporary (or younger)
A client	Anyone in your company, including your CEO
Your boss, or a higher-up	A person of lower rank in the company
Your friend	Another family member
An adult	A child
A woman	A man
Your guest of honor	Others attending the event

- **Introduce people by the names and titles they prefer.** In more formal situations or when there's an obvious age difference, it's best to use courtesy titles and last names: "Mrs. Miles, I'd like you to meet Mr. Akira." This allows Mrs. Miles to invite the use of her first name, if she chooses: "Please call me Judy." In casual settings or if the people are near in age and status, it's helpful to introduce them using first *and* last names: "Judy, this is Tom Akira. Tom, this is Judy Miles." You can also use a nickname if you know the person prefers it.

- **Teach children to use adults' titles** unless an adult specifically asks to use his or her first name: "Mrs. Miles, this is my nephew Benji Rose. Benji, this is Mrs. Miles." (For more on introduction etiquette for children, see Chapter 38, "Children and Teens," page 478.)

- **It's fine to skip last names when introducing your spouse and children.** Do include last names when your spouse or children have a different last name.

- **Introduce other family members by their full names** unless they request otherwise, and it's also nice to mention the family relationship. "Uncle Jonas, I'd like you to meet Matt Winnett. Matt, this is my great-uncle, Jonas Quinn."

- **Name group members first.** When introducing someone to a small group, this strategy is practical and gets the group's attention: "Louise, June, Will, I'd like to introduce Curtis Tyler. Curtis, I'd like you to meet Louise Oliver, June Weaver, and Will LaGasse."

- **Start a conversation.** Try to find some topic the two people have in common: "Sam, Roger is a NASCAR fan, so he might like to hear about your trip to Daytona."

When You Are Being Introduced . . .

- **Listen carefully and focus on names.** "It's nice to meet you, Liz" is an excellent way to cement the name in your memory. If you didn't catch a name, simply ask: "I'm sorry, but I didn't get your last name" or "Could you please tell me your name again?"

- **Respond graciously.** After a formal introduction, the traditional response is "How do you do?" But "Hello" and variants of "I'm pleased to meet you" sound less stilted and are suitable for both formal and casual situations. Using the person's name adds warmth to your response.

- **Use the names by which people are introduced.** If someone is introduced as "Peter," don't call him "Pete" unless he says to. If a person is introduced with a title, use it in your response. Always avoid familiar or sexist terms such as "sport," "buddy," "pal," "sweetie," and "honey."

- **It's okay to correct a mistake right up front.** If the person doing the introduction makes a mistake, you can graciously say, "Please, I go by Patti."

- **When you're repeatedly introduced incorrectly,** say by a title or nickname you don't like, take the person aside and tell him as nicely as possible: "I use Michael now. Would you introduce me that way?"

- **Wait until all introductions are complete before conversing.** Don't jump the gun and start talking before others in the group have been introduced.

- **Listen for conversational cues.** "My neighbor," "my sister," or a professional title can provide an opening for conversation.

When Someone Forgets to Introduce You . . .

The scenario: You're talking with someone when a third person approaches. The person with you greets the new arrival but doesn't introduce you. They start talking, and you feel like a third wheel.

Chances are the person who fails to introduce you assumes that you know the third person. Or she may have blanked on your name and is desperately hoping you'll speak up. When there's a little break in the conversation, address the newcomer with a pleasant "Hi, I don't think we've met; I'm Andrea Stein." Problem solved for everyone.

Self-Introductions

It may take a little courage to approach someone you don't know, but introducing yourself is really one of the easiest introductions. After all, you only have to remember your own name. At large social events, it's often impossible for the hosts to introduce everyone, so be prepared to introduce yourself. Even in the most formal setting, self-introductions are expected and relatively casual. "Hello, I'm Justin Vail" is usually enough to start. A simple reply, such as "Hi Justin, I'm Maria Fuentes. It's nice to meet you," and you can begin a conversation.

When introducing yourself to a group of people, wait for a natural break in their conversation. Then just say "Hello" and your name. You may want to explain your interest in the group: "Hi, I'm Justin Vail. This is my first Community Trails meeting and I was wondering about tonight's agenda." Asking for assistance or information

six introduction mistakes

Most introduction mistakes are the result of forgivable memory lapses or nervousness. But the mistakes below show insensitivity or tactlessness.

LOOKING AWAY. Eye contact is critical in an introduction. People who look over others' shoulders and around the room while involved in introductions are saying by their action that they really don't care.

MAKING TOO-PERSONAL COMMENTS. Divorces, bereavements, job losses, illnesses, and/or rehab history are topics too intimate to raise during an introduction.

INTERRUPTING. When others are engaged in serious conversation, don't break in to introduce someone else. Wait for a more convenient moment.

DEFERRING TO ONE PERSON AT THE EXPENSE OF THE OTHER. Be sure that both parties are included in any conversation that follows an introduction.

GUSHING. Most people are embarrassed by overly enthusiastic introductions.

MAKING SOMEONE WAIT TO BE INTRODUCED. When someone new joins a group already in conversation, put the conversation on hold and make the introduction. "Excuse me. Hi, Jane, nice to see you. Have you met Abby and Jack?"

when someone
introduces himself
to you

When someone who doesn't know you introduces him or herself to you, introduce yourself in return. There's nothing worse than introducing yourself, "Hi, I'm Debbie Porter," only to have the other person respond, "Hi." There's no way to gracefully start a conversation or find out the person's name except to ask, "And your name is?" How awkward!

name tags

Name tags are worn on the right-hand side of your shirt, sweater, or jacket. When you reach to shake someone's hand your eye is drawn to their right side, making a peek at the name tag more natural.

can be an effective way to join in the conversation. (See also "The Art of Small Talk," page 39.)

Handling Mistakes

Though it may be embarrassing to get a name wrong or draw a complete blank, such lapses aren't rude—just very human!

If you can't remember a name . . . Don't panic! Embarrassing as it may be to stumble over a name, don't fail to attempt an introduction. If the person is attentive, he may see your hesitation and cover for you by introducing himself. Just apologize quickly: "I'm so sorry—I've forgotten your name." And if you aren't sure of someone's last name just say so. The person should fill in the blank for you. And if someone's forgotten *your* name, do the kind thing. Help them out of their jam by extending your hand and saying, "Hello, I'm Kathy Smith. It's so nice to meet you."

If you get a title wrong . . . If you use an incorrect title, the person may make the correction during the introduction or tell you later. Apologize for your error and make an effort to remember the title in the future.

If you mispronounce a name . . . It's all right to ask someone to say their name in an introduction: "I'd like you to meet our new neighbor, Charles. Charles, would you please say your last name? I'm afraid I'll mispronounce it." When you mispronounce a name, apologize when the mistake is pointed out. When you know that you'll be expected to introduce a person whose name you aren't sure how to pronounce, ahead of time ask the person or someone else who knows.

DEALING WITH RUDENESS

One true test of good etiquette comes when grace and poise are challenged by inconsiderate behavior. Most people simply ignore rudeness, either because it happens so quickly they don't have a chance to react or because they wish to prevent a minor incident from escalating into a more serious confrontation. While you may think that pointing out someone's small error is no big deal, you never know how a stranger might react. Responding in kind is just as rude and can risk upping the ante. Give the person the benefit of the doubt: Most people don't intend to be rude. That doesn't mean you have to be a doormat, but before you say anything, size up the situation first:

- **Who is being rude?** Is the offender a stranger or acting aggressively? If the answer is yes, you're better off not responding than risk being a target of rage.

- **What's your point?** Pointing out a small error is fine: "Excuse me, but I think you're in my seat." However, it's not your job to correct a stranger's behavior: "Don't spit on the sidewalk—it's rude!"

- **Watch your tone.** If you do choose to say something, keep your voice pleasant and your remarks neutral: "Excuse me, but that's my shopping cart." "Would you mind taking off your hat? I can't see the screen."

- **Don't correct other people's children.** If there's a problem, talk to the parent: "I know it's tough for kids on airplanes, but could you ask your son to stop kicking my seat? Thanks."

- **Take it higher.** If your polite request isn't complied with, take it to a person in authority. For example, if the little boy continues to kick your seat, talk to a flight attendant.

And here are some other tips to help you keep your cool:

- **Don't take it personally.** Perhaps the offender is having a bad day.

- **Pick your battles.** Sometimes it's best to let it go. Will it accomplish anything to make a stink about the person who has 15 items in the 12-item line? Take a few breaths and ask yourself, "Is it really worth blowing my stack over this?"

- **Laugh it off.** Maintaining a friendly demeanor and sense of humor can help. Just chuckle and change the subject.

3
common
courtesies

sk a group of people if we are ruder today than ten years ago and the majority will answer with a resounding yes. Are we? In our hectic, crowded world it's easy to focus on our own particular agenda, oblivious to those around us. We forget that others can actually hear us talking on a cell phone or belting out a song while listening to music using earbuds. When we feel anonymous, it somehow gives us permission to behave less courteously than we would with people we know—making a rude gesture to someone who cuts us off, berating a slow cashier, screaming obscenities at a referee. We don't mean to be rude . . . we're just in a hurry.

Being courteous means taking personal responsibility for the way our actions affect others, showing respect for the space we share and the well-being of those we share it with. The small courtesies that we afford one another keep our interactions with strangers civil and even pleasant.

START WITH A SMILE

What little Orphan Annie said is true: "You're never fully dressed without a smile." A smile on your face and a positive attitude automatically improve the atmosphere wherever you are. Common courtesy starts with acknowledging those around you pleasantly. All it takes is a quick "Hi" to the bus driver, a "Good morning" to each person as you arrive at work, a "Hi, I'm home" to your spouse or housemates. Your tone of voice also projects courtesy. Being gruff or sarcastic robs any greeting of its sincerity.

COURTESY BEGINS AT HOME

It makes sense that the consideration, respect, and courtesy you show coworkers or even strangers should apply to your families and housemates. Adults who treat each other well are also setting an example for children.

- Greet your family or housemates each day—in the morning and when you return in the evening.

- Pick up after yourself.

- Don't leave routine chores for others. Empty the dishwasher when it's clean.

- Be on time for meals, activities, and appointments.

- Consult those involved before you make any social commitments. Your plans for a birthday bash at home may clash with your housemate's need to study for the bar exam.

- Avoid put-downs and discuss disagreements in private. Kids especially pick up on and are influenced by negative language and heated arguments.

- Notice, notice, notice. Say "thanks" when someone does you a favor and give compliments when you can: "Thanks, Hank, for emptying the dishwasher." "This chicken is awesome!"

- Respect each other's privacy.

- Respect each other's views, even if you don't share them.

BE ON TIME

It's never fashionable to be late whether it's for business or a social engagement. At the very least, lateness is a sign of disorganization; at its worst it screams, "I am more important than you or this occasion." In business, being late could cost you a job or a contract.

For a social invitation, always arrive at the time specified or within the next ten minutes, at most. It's awkward to arrive early because you'll interrupt your host, who may be finishing last-minute preparations. In business or for any appointment, it's a good idea to arrive a few minutes early so that you have time to freshen up and collect your thoughts. In either case, if you're going to be unavoidably late, call as soon as you realize the problem and give an ETA. (*Now* we love that cell phone!)

If you're the victim of a habitual latecomer, allow a fifteen-minute grace period, then go ahead with your program—serve the hot hors d'oeuvres or call everyone to the table. When Mr. Tardy arrives, greet him pleasantly and then serve whatever course is in progress.

HATS OFF

Removing your hat is a sign of respect that has a long history in Western culture. When a man of lesser rank entered the dwelling of a person of higher rank, he removed his hat or helmet. Baring his head was a sign of vulnerability and showed that he posed no threat, essentially acknowledging that the person of higher rank had power over him. If you followed up the hierarchy of rank, the only person left with a hat on was the king wearing his crown. Hats, including the king's crown, were removed in places of worship, acknowledging that spiritual authority outranked temporal authority.

Today, removing one's hat is more than a nod to tradition. It allows us better eye contact, which is a

HATS ON OR OFF?

	Men All hats	Women Sports cap	Women Fashion hat*
Outdoors	on	on	on
At athletic events (indoors or out)	on	on	on
On public transportation	on	on	on
In public buildings such as post offices, airports, train stations	on	on	on
In office and hotel lobbies	on	on	on
On elevators	on	on	on
While being introduced, indoors or out (unless it's frigid!)	off	off	on
In someone's home	off	off	on
Indoors at work, especially in an office (unless required for the job)	off	off	off
In a house of worship or at a religious service, unless a hat is required	off	off	on
In public buildings such as a school, library, courthouse, or town hall	off	off	on
At the table	off	off	on
In restaurants and coffee shops	off	off	on
At a movie or any indoor performance	off	off	on*
When the national anthem is played	off	off	on
When the American flag passes by, as in a parade	off	off	on

Remove a fashion hat anytime it blocks someone's view, such as at a wedding or in a theater.

sign of respect and acknowledgment. Men and women either remove or leave hats on depending on the place, whether they are in or outdoors, and in some instances depending on the type of hat itself.

Head coverings worn for religious or cultural reasons aren't usually removed indoors. If you're attending a religious service in a tradition outside your own, call ahead or check with someone of that faith about appropriate head wear and attire for visitors.

chemo caps

Cancer patients are exempt from hat rules. They may keep their hats on at all times if they wish.

[OUT IN PUBLIC]

You may feel anonymous, but you certainly aren't invisible, so give some thought to how others might see you.

Check your volume. Public places are noisy by nature, but don't add to the din by talking louder than you must.

Go easy on the cell phone. Try to find a more private place where your call won't disturb others.

Watch your mouth! Curse words that may not faze your peers are likely to offend those who overhear—and it's hard for people not to overhear. Be especially mindful when young kids are present.

If you need a mirror, find a restroom. Freshening lipstick is okay; otherwise do your grooming and makeup in private.

Chew gum unobtrusively. Cracking, smacking, or chomping away in a mechanical rhythm is unattractive.

Public displays of affection. Moderate displays of affection, such as holding hands, walking arm-in-arm, or exchanging a kiss, are okay; prolonged, passionate embraces and kisses or groping are not.

Keep it green. Throw *all* your trash into the nearest trash can or recycling bin. If you don't see a wastebasket nearby, hang on to your trash until you can dispose of it properly.

Don't spit. Spitting on the pavement is nasty, unhygienic, and rude.

Take care if you're a smoker. Only smoke in designated areas. Don't flick butts onto the street: They may be small, but they still qualify as litter. Avoid smoking in or near entryways.

Waiting in Line
"Next . . ."

It seems as if half our lives are spent waiting in line—at the grocery checkout, at the airport check-in, at the movies. Line manners are simple and they're the same ones you learned as a preschooler—one at a time; wait your turn; be patient; no pushing, shoving, or shouting; and no "cuts" or jumping ahead of people who arrived before you.

When you're stuck in a line, what can you do to pass the time? First, check to make sure that when it is your turn, you're ready with all the right documents, coupons, or payment. As long as you keep up with the line, it's okay to occupy yourself with activities that won't bother those around you: Text or email from your phone, read a book or magazine, listen to music with earbuds. It's even okay to strike up a casual conversation with your line mates as long as it's welcome and you keep the volume down. What's not okay?

◆ Making long or private calls on your cell.

◆ Racing to get ahead of someone who's about to get in line.

◆ Complaining out loud about the wait.

◆ Getting in the express lane when you clearly have more than "10 items or less."

◆ Holding space in a line for friends who are paying separately from you.

Of course, it's kind to let someone who has only one or two items or a quick question go ahead of you. And when it is your turn, take out your earbuds and greet the person helping you with a smile. It's not their fault the line is long. Complete your transaction as efficiently as you can.

THOSE WHO SERVE YOU

Salesclerks, cashiers, customer service representatives, flight attendants, taxi drivers, bus drivers, waitstaff, hotel staff, household help—there's no excuse for treating people who serve you rudely or disrespectfully. It's your responsibility to be courteous and respectful. You don't have to become best friends, but there's no doubt that a pleasant manner will make others feel better and it will get you better service. That's true whether your interaction is in person or on the phone. (See also "Running Errands," page 96.)

HOLDING DOORS

In the past, men showed deference to women with many of these small courtesies: holding doors and chairs or walking on the street side of the sidewalk. Following the women's movement in the late twentieth century, many women viewed such courtesies as condescending and demeaning—at the very least, unnecessary. What was a man to do? He was trapped in a double standard: a chauvinist if he held the door, an ill-mannered lout if he didn't. As with all manners, even the common courtesies get a makeover now and again. In this case, it isn't the manners themselves that have changed, but who is responsible for performing them.

Nowadays, everyone agrees that holding the door for the next guy is still a "nice thing to do," and that *all* able-bodied people, regardless of gender, should do so as a matter of course. But on a date, many women still appreciate it when a man uses these traditional courtesies.

"After You . . ."

Today whoever gets there first opens and holds the door for the next person. If a man isn't sure whether he will offend a woman or be appreciated, he can simply offer her a choice: "May I get the door for you?" She can reply either "Thanks!" or "No thanks, I've got it."

It's polite to open and hold the door for someone who is elderly, disabled, carrying a package, or managing small children. Most important, don't ever let a door close on the person behind you.

What about revolving doors? The person who arrives at the door first enters and pushes, or gives the option, saying, "May I start this for you?" Once through the door, either keep moving or step aside, usually to the right, out of the line of entering and exiting traffic, to wait for companions.

In an Elevator

- Entering

    - Allow those in the elevator to exit before you enter.

    - Do not enter a crowded elevator; instead wait for the next car and say, "I'll catch the next one, thanks!"

    - If you see someone rushing to catch the elevator and there is room in the car, hold the door and wait for them.

- In the elevator
  - When entering the elevator, push your desired floor and then move to the back.
  - If you cannot reach the button panel, ask another passenger to press your floor for you. "Ten, please."
  - End calls before entering an elevator and do not answer calls while in the elevator.
  - Avoid listening to music/watching videos without headphones. If you do use headphones be sure to pay attention and be aware of the people around you.
  - Do not use the mirrors in an elevator to assist with personal grooming. (They are there to make the space seem larger.)
  - Avoid lengthy, or in-depth conversations where other passengers are forced to listen. A quick, "Hello" if you see someone you know, or some brief comments with a companion are fine. But anything longer should wait until you're out of the car.
- Exiting the elevator
  - Let those closest to the door leave first.
  - Make room for those near the back to get out. Step out of the elevator and hold the door open if necessary.
  - Move away from the elevator entrance so as not to impede others entering or exiting.

In the Car

It's a real courtesy for both men and women to open a car door for a person who is elderly or who has a disability and if needed, give them a hand. Probably every male teen learned on prom night that a sure way to impress his date was to go around and open the car door for her. That was probably the first—and last—time, as most young women aren't inclined to sit and wait while their date scurries around to get the door. The wise man will ask, "May I get the door?" and the polite woman will respond, "Yes, thank you," or "No, but thanks. I can manage it."

Be aware that limousine and car service drivers are trained to open doors for their customers, so let them do their job and enjoy the extra service.

In a Taxi

Taxis present their own problems starting with the fact that, for safety's sake, passengers should exit and enter only on the curb side. So, should a man hold the door and let a woman enter first? Now the woman has to slide across the seat, which could be awkward, especially if she's wearing a skirt or dress. Alternatively, the man slides in and lets the woman get in last and deal with the door, both on entering and exiting. It's always a good idea to ask, "Would you like to get in first, or shall I?"

HOLDING CHAIRS

Tradition says that a man holds the chair of the woman on his right to assist seating her at the table. Today, women seat themselves, if they wish. At a business meal, men and women seat themselves. However, it's wise to ask an older female client, whose standards may be of a previous era, if she would like her chair held. It's never wrong to ask any woman, "May I hold your chair?"

Stairs, Escalators, and Moving Walkways

In general, keep right and pass left just as you do when driving. If you're the one who needs to pass, signal with a polite "Excuse me."

◆ When it's crowded, try to leave some space between you and the person in front of you.

◆ Be careful with luggage, backpacks, briefcases, and handbags so that they don't knock anyone around you.

◆ When you exit, keep moving or step out of the traffic so that you don't cause a logjam or an accident.

On the Sidewalk

In bustling cities, sidewalk etiquette is all about bobbing and weaving as expertly as possible—which means maneuvering past others without jostling or interrupting their path. It helps to keep your eyes looking ahead to find the clearest path. Here are some other ways to go with the flow:

echoes of tradition

The old rules for the ways men and women walk together and go through doors may have changed, but there are still plenty of people who prefer the traditional way of doing things, particularly on social occasions. Gentlemen, here's a rundown:

◆ On the street, a man traditionally walks on the curb side of a woman—shielding her from the hazards posed by passing horse and buggies, now cars, splashing through puddles.

◆ A woman precedes a man through a door, on an escalator (unless she needs help getting on or off), or in a narrow outdoor passageway.

◆ A man precedes a woman into a revolving door, a dark street or building, down a steep ramp or a slippery slope, on rough ground, and through crowds, taking her hand or arm as necessary.

◆ In times gone by, a man regularly offered his arm to a woman. Today, that's usually the case only if he's an usher at a wedding, or he's walking with an elderly woman or someone who needs assistance.

◆ If you're with a large group, break up into twos or walk single file.

◆ Leave some space between you and the person in front of you.

◆ Allow about three steps' worth of space before you cut in front of another pedestrian.

◆ Use caution going around the corners of buildings to avoid a collision with someone coming around the other way.

- Keep your elbows in and make sure umbrellas, briefcases, or backpacks don't bump others, especially when you turn.

- Be aware that you need more space when pushing a stroller or pulling luggage.

- Don't make sudden stops—move to the side, out of the flow if you need to stop, slow down, or have a conversation with someone you've just bumped into.

- If you accidentally brush or bump someone, be sure to say "Excuse me."

- As for jaywalking, use common sense. Even if it's not illegal where you are, it's still dangerous.

Joggers, Rollerbladers, Skateboarders, and Bikers

The general rule? Anyone who is moving slower than you has the right of way. Jogging or rollerblading on a suburban neighborhood sidewalk is fine so long as the sidewalk is relatively empty. Crowded city streets are another story; either go for your run in the early morning or find a recreation path.

Skateboards aren't just for sport; some people use them, or Razor scooters, as a speedy way to get around. Most riders are looking for the shortest distance between two points, which is usually a combination of the street and sidewalk, but they should keep clear of pedestrians. That doesn't mean passing with an inch to spare—give them a wide berth and take care not to startle them. The same concept applies to Segways, motorized scooters, and chairs: The pedestrian has the right of way.

Bicycles are meant for streets, not sidewalks. Stay on the road or bike path so you don't endanger pedestrians. On a bike path, keep right, except to pass, calling out, "On your left," as you overtake a biker or walker. On the street, you're subject to the same rules as automobiles. And "sharing the road" means riding single file to let cars pass. (See also Chapter 11, "Sports and Recreation," page 136.)

Walking the Dog

Whether for exercise or "relief," you have extra responsibilities when Fido is with you. The number one rule is that your dog should always be under your control. People who walk their dogs on sidewalks should always use a leash and make sure the dog doesn't block traffic or trip someone. For better control, use a short leash in areas where you're likely to encounter skaters, joggers, or cyclists.

Rule number two: Scoop the poop. It's the law in most urban municipalities, but law or no law, pick up after your dog on the sidewalk, recreation path, dog park, or neighbor's lawn.

ON PUBLIC TRANSPORTATION

Whether you live in a large city with a crowded rapid transit system or a small town where you're sure to find a seat anytime, you can help keep things running smoothly by being aware of what's going on around you.

- If the bus or train car starts filling up, move your bag or backpack from the seat next to you and stow it.

- Offer your seat to anyone who seems to need it—a person with a disability, a pregnant woman, a parent with a baby or young children, an elderly passenger, a passenger loaded down with packages, or someone who appears frail.

- When standing, move toward the middle or back of the bus or train car to make room for those boarding at the next stop. Say "Excuse me" to those in your way as you exit.

- Unstrap your backpack and carry it in front of you or stow it.

- Keep any conversation short and quiet. It's easy to disturb others by shouting over the noise of the train, using foul language, or having conversations of a personal nature.

- Text or email, but don't subject your fellow passengers to long or private cell phone calls. Also, turn off your phone's ringer.

- Put a wet umbrella under your seat or flat on the floor at your feet.

- If eating is allowed, bar-type food is okay, but avoid foods with strong, potentially offensive odors, such as raw onions or fried fish.

Riding the Bus

- When more than three people are waiting to board a bus, form a line.

- Have your change or fare card ready.

- Greet your driver pleasantly and say "Thanks" if you pass him when you exit.

On Subway and Commuter Trains

On a subway or other city train, if you're standing by the doors either move aside or step outside the train car to give others plenty of room to exit and enter. Inside the train, move to the center of the car if you can.

On a commuter train, most passengers are looking for a quiet ride. Be mindful of your fellow passengers, and keep cell phone calls brief and conversation quiet and to a minimum. Some trains have designated quiet cars where cell phone use isn't allowed.

Resist the temptation to put your feet on the empty seat opposite you or spread your belongings out over the seat next to you. Take any coffee cups or other disposables with you. It's respectful of the next person who uses the seat, as well as the transit authority cleaners.

IN TAXIS AND LIMOUSINES

When hailing a taxi on the street, be sure not to jump in front of anyone who was there ahead of you. At a taxi stand, go to the end of the line and wait your turn.

Once you're in the taxi, give the driver clear directions and let him know if you prefer a certain route. Many cabs take credit cards. Still, it's smart to have

small bills in your wallet in case the driver isn't able to make change. Tip according to quality of service. (See also Chapter 13, "Tipping," page 165.)

Car Services

If you hire a limousine or car service to take you to the airport or elsewhere, don't act as if you're a pampered rock star. You're not expected to become best buddies, but occasional small talk is thoughtful and might improve the service as well.

When your destination is a remote location with no services and your driver has to wait for two or three hours, see that he has something to eat and drink. If you're hiring the car yourself, ask if a gratuity is included in your bill. Some limo services don't allow their drivers to accept tips. If the car's been hired for you, it's harder to know, but you can always ask the driver what the arrangement is. No matter the arrangement, if the driver has been with you all day, you might consider giving him something extra. (See also Chapter 13, "Tipping," page 165.)

COURTESIES FOR PEOPLE WITH DISABILITIES

People with disabilities account for approximately 15 percent of the population of the United States. These 41 million individuals share the same human traits you do. Acknowledging this makes it easier to put aside any anxiety you might feel when you interact with people with disabilities and to just be yourself.

Some courtesies that apply across the board regardless of the person's disability:

- ◆ Never stare at or make jokes or cruel comments about someone with a disability.

- ◆ Respect the person's independence. A disability does not make someone helpless.

- ◆ If you want to offer assistance, *ask first,* since people who've mastered getting about in wheelchairs, on a crutch or a brace, or without the benefit of vision or hearing may not need it.

- ◆ Never ask personal questions of someone with an obvious disability. If the person wants to talk about the condition, he or she will broach the subject.

- ◆ Speak directly with the person, not through an attendant or companion as if the person with the disability isn't there.

- ◆ Some people with disabilities may have difficulty making eye contact, but that doesn't mean they aren't listening to you.

- ◆ Never take the seats designated for people with disabilities.

- ◆ Never park in a space marked "handicapped" unless you have a permit to do so.

Sensitivity in Language

Sensitivity starts with your language. Put people first by speaking of a "person with a disability" rather than a "disabled person," an "invalid," or a "victim." Also refer to a "person with cerebral palsy" or a "person with epilepsy" (not a "paralytic" or an "epileptic"). The words *deaf* and *blind* are fine to use, but *handicapped*—and especially *crippled*—should be avoided. A person in a wheelchair is a "person who uses a wheelchair" not one who's "wheelchair bound" or "confined to a wheelchair," both of which contradict the liberation that a wheelchair can provide. Also, many people who communicate via sign language prefer the word *deaf* over *hearing impaired*.

Watching your language doesn't mean banishing certain words and phrases. It's fine to ask a blind person, "Did you see the president's speech last night?" (the blind use the word *see* as much as anyone else), and to invite someone in a wheelchair to "go for a walk."

People Who Are Hard of Hearing or Deaf

There are degrees of deafness, from partial loss of hearing in one ear to a complete lack of hearing. When you're with someone who is partially deaf, it may only be necessary to speak a little more distinctly or to repeat a remark. If you know that the hearing loss is in one ear, sit on the side of the good ear at movies, a meal, or any other place where you may not be face-to-face.

If someone is completely deaf, you'll have more to consider:

♦ If the person isn't facing you and you need to attract his attention, a gentle tap on the arm or shoulder—rather than a shout—is appropriate.

---

magic words— another take

"I know you've got this, but I'm here if you need me." Or "I'm sure you do this all the time, but I'm here if you need a hand." These are magic words to Owen, who has been a quadriplegic now for several years. He teaches them to aspiring rehab therapists. He likes it when people add, "I'm in no rush." Memorize and practice these lines. With them you show that

♦ You respect the individual's independence.

♦ You're available to help *if needed*.

♦ You aren't pressuring the individual to hurry up and get out of your way. Given enough time, for example, Owen says he can open any door. He'll be direct and ask for help—when he wants it.

♦ Find out what the preferred method of communication is: lip-reading, signing, or writing.

♦ Speak slowly and clearly. Also be ready to repeat your statement in words of fewer syllables.

♦ Speak in a normal tone unless you're asked to change the pitch or rate.

♦ Maintain eye contact and keep your head up so that your lips are easily seen.

♦ Use meaningful facial expressions and gestures.

♦ Don't exaggerate your lip movements; distorted lip motions can confuse even the best lip-reader.

♦ If speech alone isn't getting a message across, it's perfectly acceptable to gesture or write notes.

♦ Never walk between two people who are signing; you'd be interrupting them.

If you're speaking with a person who has an interpreter, direct your attention to the person, not the interpreter. There's no reason to fear you're excluding her, since she understands her role and doesn't expect to participate in the conversation. Likewise, if conversing with a person over a TTY or TDD (text telephone), address him directly, as if the mediator weren't present. Don't say, "Tell him that..." or "Ask him to..." (For more on TTY/TDD phones, see "Text Telephones," page 227.)

People Who Are Blind or Have Low Vision

While people who are blind or have visual impairments usually know how to get around—especially if they use a cane, echolocation, or a guide dog—there will be times when they may need assistance. For instance, if you see a dangerous situation, alert them: "There's a hole in the sidewalk ahead. May I guide you?"

Instead of taking the person's arm, let him take your arm (press the back of your hand on his and he will take hold of your arm just above the elbow) and then walk one step ahead, pausing before any turn or obstacle and telling him what's there. If the person uses a guide dog or a cane, walk on his opposite side.

Indoors, warn of anything protruding at head level (hanging lamps or plants) or any pulled-out drawers or open cabinet doors. If you work with a person who's blind or you engage in group activities with her, always identify yourself when in her presence. Just as important, always introduce her to a group so she knows who's there.

If you're eating with her, do the following:

---

service dogs

Not all service dogs are guide dogs. Dogs also devote their lives to aiding people who are deaf or physically or mentally disabled.

While the person will welcome your comments on the good behavior and handsomeness of his dog, never pet, feed, or talk to the animal without asking the owner's permission. *Do* hold the door for the person and his dog if he's right behind you and do keep children from petting or playing with the dog. Attempting to gain the attention of the dog in any way will distract her from her important work.

- In a restaurant, offer to read the menu aloud.
- Indicate where the condiments are on the table.
- Using clock terms, let the person know where everything is on the plate: "Your pasta's at your six o'clock"; "Your spinach is at your twelve o'clock."
- Only if she asks should you cut her food for her.

When a person who's blind visits your home, lead him to a chair and then place your guiding hand on the seat. He can then run his hand down your arm to find the seat and sit down. If he's staying with you for any length of time, indicate where the various pieces of furniture are (then don't move them) and keep doors completely opened or closed—never halfway open.

Here are some more tips from the American Foundation for the Blind (www.afb.org):

- Use a natural tone of voice. Don't speak loudly or slowly unless the person has a hearing impairment.

- Feel free to use words, expressions, or adjectives that refer to vision. It's fine to say, "Watch out for that step!" or "The ocean is a really deep blue today."

- When ending a conversation or leaving a room, make a point of saying good-bye so that the person knows you've left.

- Never touch a person's cane or service dog.

People in Wheelchairs

When you meet someone in a wheelchair, offer a handshake just as you would for anyone else, except when the person doesn't have the use of her right hand. In that case, shaking her left hand is fine, as is gently touching her arm or shoulder as a welcoming gesture.

It's impolite to lean over someone in a wheelchair to shake a third person's hand. And don't treat the chair as you would furniture (leaning on the wheelchair, for example). A wheelchair is part of a person's personal space, so treat it as such. When conversing, either pull up a chair and sit at her level or stand far enough away so that she won't have to strain her neck to make eye contact.

If a person gives you permission to push her chair, ask for instructions; otherwise, you could accidentally detach one of the parts by lifting the chair improperly. When pushing, watch the ground in front of you so that you can steer around potholes, animal dung, broken concrete, large cables, or other hindrances.

People with Speech Impairments

Speech problems range from stuttering to stroke-induced difficulties. If you listen patiently and carefully to someone with a speech problem, your understanding of his speech (or of any device he uses) will improve as he talks and your ear adjusts. Remain attentive to the conversation even if there are delays, and don't complete sentences unless the person asks for help. If you don't understand what he's saying, ask a question that will help him clarify the part you missed.

Some other tips for conversing with someone who has a speech impairment:

- Don't assume a person with a speech disability also has a cognitive disability.

- Don't pretend to understand if you don't. Either ask her to repeat or repeat back what you think you heard for verification.

- Give the person your complete attention.

- If after repeated attempts you still don't understand, try written communication.

People Who Have a Mental Disability

While people with physical disabilities find it difficult to maneuver through space, those with mental disabilities more often have trouble with basic social and communication skills—listening, comprehending, giving appropriate responses both verbal and nonverbal, and reading social cues accurately. As a result, they find themselves being treated as "different," something to which they can be very sensitive.

People with mental disabilities feel things just as deeply as anyone else. When interacting with someone who has a mental disability, try the following:

- **Get past the communication barrier.** Give him time to express himself.

- **Interact at an appropriate level.** A person with a developmental disability may be more childlike, so interact with him at his developmental, rather than chronological, age. This doesn't mean using baby talk but using simpler sentences.

- **Be understanding.** A person with a mental disability may have struggled his entire life; it's accepting of you to try to understand what he's feeling or trying to accomplish socially.

- **Don't ignore.** If you're in a group, make a point to include him in the conversation, then let it be his decision whether to participate.

the art of conversation

4

Mastering the art of everyday conversation means remembering that it's a two-way street, with thoughts and ideas shared in both directions. Expressing interest in another person and clearly conveying one's own thoughts and feelings is the primary goal of ordinary conversation among friends and acquaintances. Like a good tennis volley, your goal is to keep the conversational ball in play.

We also "chat" all the time using digital devices. However, the electronic brick wall has given people a false permission to make rude comments that they would never say face-to-face. Unfortunately, the tendency to rude comments is finding its way into conversations. Be careful. (See "Beware the Electronic Brick Wall," p. 238.)

Must you be witty and eloquent? Not really. Few of us can continually pepper our conversation with engaging stories and words of wisdom. The good conversationalist keeps it simple and direct, uses tact, and is attentive to what other people have to say—skills that can be learned and mastered. The good conversationalist also knows that *what* we say and *how* we say it can make the difference between clarifying a point or confusing it, giving comfort or offense.

⟦ THE FUNDAMENTALS ⟧

Being a good conversationalist requires two things: "Think before you speak" and "Listen." It sounds simple, but it can be tricky to put into practice.

Thinking. Thinking—or more precisely, being thoughtful—applies across the board, from the conversation topic to the listener's reactions. Would a parent brag endlessly about his child's awards to someone

who doesn't have children? Ask yourself if it's likely that someone will be interested in the topic before you bring it up.

Listening. It's only natural to be thinking of what you're about to say next in a conversation. Will you respond? Agree with the point just made or take issue with it? Relate a similar story? Or will you change the subject? For many people, that's the normal flow of a conversation.

Instead of worrying about what to say next, focus on what's being said to you. Here are some tips for sharpening your listening skills:

◆ Empty other thoughts from your mind and concentrate on what the person is saying.

◆ Make eye contact, nod occasionally, and intermittently say, "I see" or "Really?" to indicate that you not only heard but understood what was said.

◆ Ask a question.

◆ Once you've picked up the rhythm of the other person's speech, you'll be able to inject longer confirmations without seeming to interrupt: "Oh, so Kevin's catch saved the day."

◆ If you *don't* understand something, ask for an explanation, a habit that comes naturally to a good listener: "Did you say the sun revolves around the earth?"

Personal space. A comfortable conversation involves more than just words; it has to take place in a comfortable space. Generally, stand no closer than about 18 inches apart, although cultural and personal preferences should be taken into account. (See Chap-

ter 10, "Traveling Near and Far," page 119.) Personal space is less of an issue when you're seated, but you still may have to lean in a bit to catch the words of a soft-spoken person, then back away when it's your turn to speak.

Also be conscious of height differences. Stand far enough away so that the other person won't have to look up or down at you, which can quickly grow uncomfortable. Be considerate of people with physical disabilities—such as a person in a wheelchair or with a hearing impairment—and don't expect anyone on crutches, in casts, or with bad knees to stand and chat for any length of time. (See also "Courtesies for People with Disabilities," page 30.)

Interrupting. There's a fine line between the occasional interruption made to confirm a point and one that's made because you're bursting to throw in your two cents' worth. The only time it's okay to interrupt in the middle of a sentence is when you need to communicate something that honestly can't wait. Even then, precede what you say with "I'm sorry to interrupt" or a variation.

When you're the one being interrupted, listen politely for a few seconds before trying to finish your thought. Raising your hand in a "please wait" gesture can politely deflect an interruption. Tempting as it seems, a blunt "Stop interrupting!" only answers one rudeness with another.

BODY LANGUAGE

While words and tone express the meaning of what's being said, a person's posture, facial expressions, and gestures send messages as well. Some of these messages are open to interpretation, but others come through loud and clear.

- **Posture when standing or sitting.** What a parent or teacher really meant when she told you "Sit [stand] up straight!" was that slumping or slouching while speaking to someone conveys laziness, disinterest, and disrespect.

- **Facial expressions.** A smile denotes warmth, openness, and friendliness, but don't overdo it. False smiles and never-ending smiles make you look insincere. Conversely, a frown or a furrowed brow suggests anger or worry, even though your words may be positive. Be aware of what your natural facial expression might convey.

- **Eye contact.** Looking into the other person's eyes shows your interest in the conversation. Staring, however, can be threatening, even strange, so shift your focus to other parts of the face from time to time.

- **Gesturing and fidgeting.** Go easy on the gestures. Using your hands to emphasize a point is fine, but gesturing nonstop is distracting. Also, avoid playing with your hair, tie, or jewelry; drumming your fingers; clicking a ballpoint pen; and jiggling the change or keys in your pocket.

- **Nodding.** Nodding doesn't necessarily mean you agree; it can indicate that you understand. But too much positive head nodding can make you appear overly eager to please, especially in a business environment.

- **Pointing.** Because American culture historically regards pointing at others as negative or hostile, the gesture can be misconstrued. Are you merely pointing someone out or are you making some comment about him? Pointing also attracts attention to a person who probably doesn't want to be the object of curious glances and stares.

VOICE AND VOCABULARY

Voice volume, tone, and rate of speech all contribute to the quality of a conversation. Speaking too loudly can be unnerving or threatening. Speaking too softly puts listeners in the awkward position of having to ask you to repeat yourself. Inflections enliven your speech but a monotone dulls it. Talking too fast makes you harder to understand, while talking too slowly may try the listener's patience.

Enunciation and accent come into play, too. Having good enunciation simply means pronouncing words clearly. Mumbling is both slurring words together and speaking so softly that you can neither be heard nor understood. At the other extreme, enunciating *too* perfectly sounds affected and prissy.

You shouldn't be embarrassed by your accent, whether it's a regional drawl or an echo of the country where you were born. Be patient with people who have difficulty understanding you. You may have to repeat yourself or speak more slowly when you have a strong accent, until your listener's ear becomes accustomed to it. When you notice another person's accent, don't dwell on it or make fun of it. Politely ask the person to repeat himself if necessary: "I'm sorry, I didn't quite understand. Would you mind repeating that a little more slowly? Thanks."

The Words You Use

Having a good vocabulary doesn't mean using big words in place of small ones; it means using the right word to convey your meaning. Develop a vocabulary that's wide-ranging, yet simple and direct. Also, the way we use words can sabotage our speech without our realizing it. Head off these habits in particular:

◆ Peppering your speech with "fillers"—*y'know, like, um, er* (or all of them strung together!)—and similar meaningless interjections.

Q: *When I speak with someone and he keeps looking over my shoulder or to the side, I feel he's not hearing a word. I want to say so, but how?*

A: The wandering eye will spoil a conversation virtually every time, and it's okay to do something about it. Stop talking in midsentence, then turn to look at what he finds so fascinating, and say, "Is something going on over there?" Hopefully, he'll bring his attention back to you and your conversation can continue.

◆ Overusing words like *absolutely, totally, actually, interesting, nice, great, super,* and *awesome.*

◆ Misusing grammar—e.g., *I* when you should use *me.*

◆ Referring to someone present in the third person.

◆ Choosing words or phrases that sound pretentious or pompous—*retire* for *go to bed* or *comestibles* for *food.*

◆ Using the wrong word—"I'm well" describes your health; "I'm good" describes your behavior.

MORE THINGS TO REMEMBER

There's an art to being a good conversationalist. The following tips will help you gain skill and finesse on your way to being well-spoken:

Know when to stop talking. People who talk too much give the impression of being wrapped up in themselves; those who talk too little can seem aloof. In conversation, the middle road is best: Hold up your end, but give the others a chance to contribute. There are seldom regrets for what you've left unsaid.

Don't horn in. Let people tell their own story. Don't break in to what someone else is saying—for example, a description of a movie plot—and press your own "improved" version on listeners. Likewise, finishing someone else's sentences is an annoying habit.

Avoid repetitions. The twice-told tale quickly becomes boring. If you think you might be repeating yourself, ask, "Did I already tell you about our week in Sicily?" If you're on the receiving end of a repeated story, politely let the speaker know: "Oh, yes, it sounds like you had such a good time!"

Don't whisper. When your conversation is whispered, it's exclusionary; others may think that they're the subject or that an especially juicy bit of gossip is being kept secret.

Watch inflection. Your voice should rise at the end of a question, not a statement: "Yesterday, I went to the gym? And I ran four miles? I felt great?"

Watch your slang. Slang is a part of everyday speech, but let your use of it depend on the situation and the person you're speaking with. "Later" or "See ya" is fine when saying good-bye to your friends, but not so fine when addressing your boss or a client.

Use foreign phrases judiciously. Sprinkling your conversation with words and phrases from another language can seem pretentious. But there are exceptions: 1) when the word or phrase is from your native tongue; 2) when it's widely used and understood, like *smorgasbord, hors d'oeuvre*, and *blitz.*

Avoid playing teacher. A thoughtful person corrects someone's grammar or pronunciation only when that person is her spouse, child, or extremely close friend or relative—and then only in private, never in front of other people.

THE ART OF SMALL TALK

Weather. Sports. Family. Work. News. Books. Movies. Music. There's lots to talk about! Some conversations flow naturally as one topic leads to another. Others

bounce from one topic to another with no rhyme or reason. Here are some tips to help you jump-start the conversation:

- **Learn what's happening.** Make an effort to know what's going on in your community, your state, the world, and current sports and entertainment. Take a little time to think about the topics you've come across in newspapers, magazines, podcasts, or on the radio or television, and you'll be surprised how naturally you can get a conversation going.

- **Know your audience.** Consider their interests, hobbies, jobs, and accomplishments. "So, how did you get involved in geocaching?" They'll appreciate your interest.

- **Ask people's opinions.** Asking questions is the easiest way to start a conversation and/or to keep one going. People love to be asked for their opinion, so instead of simply giving your own take on the latest celebrity doings or football game, bring the topic up and then ask for others' thoughts on the subject.

- **Be a good listener.** We can't stress it enough. Focus on the person you're talking to and maintain that focus.

- **Practice, practice, practice.** If you're shy, get used to talking to strangers in safe environments—such as people waiting in line with you in the supermar-

the three tiers

Knowing what is appropriate to talk about and when can be tricky. Use these three tiers to quickly determine if a topic of conversation is safe.

- **TIER 1–SMALL TALK.** Sports, the weather, food, music, movies, and pop culture are all usually safe territory. You can talk about these topics anywhere, with just about anybody. In fact it is a good idea to cultivate an interest in a few of these topics so that you have conversation fodder ready and at your fingertips.

- **TIER 2–CONTROVERSIAL TOPICS.** Politics, religion, and sex are all potentially controversial topics. People have strong and, often, differing opinions about them so they are best approached carefully, if at all. Don't assume someone holds the same views as you do, even if you share other things in common. If you express your opinion too strongly you risk alienating someone or, worse, causing offense.

- **TIER 3–PERSONAL INFORMATION.** Family, personal health, and financial matters are the most personal things that people talk about and you show discretion and tact by treating them as such. In most situations, don't ask probing questions of others or offer too much information about your own circumstances. These topics are best reserved for private discussion with those whom you trust to respect your personal information.

ket, store clerks, taxi drivers, or someone sitting next to you on a plane, bus, or train. A short (the operative word here is *short*) exchange can help you become more comfortable.

] CONVERSATIONAL PITFALLS [

Whatever course a discussion takes, the good conversationalist knows that certain subjects should be handled with care.

When It's All About You

One topic to be wary of is *yourself*. Good conversationalists don't let two very small pronouns—*I* and *me*—become the largest words in their vocabulary. This isn't to say that your opinions or your vacation plans aren't legitimate conversational subjects. But when every sentence begins with *I*, it's time to change the subject.

Too Much Information

How far to venture into your personal life—whether sharing information about your health or your latest romance—is up to you, but anyone except your closest friends is likely to be put off by stories that reveal more than they need or want to hear, so be respectful of their limits.

Your family. The state of your relationship with your spouse and your children is generally a topic for close friends only. If your wife got a promotion or your son won first place at the science fair, it's fine to let people know. How long you dwell on the subject should be determined by questions asked by the listener. On the other hand, serious family problems—an impending divorce or a teenager caught shoplifting—should be discussed only with your closest friends, usually when you're seeking advice or a friend has clearly offered a shoulder to cry on.

Your finances. For years, discussing money with anyone outside your family has generally been considered to be in poor taste. But there are some exceptions. The rent you pay in an area where rates have gone through the roof, taxes, and college tuition tend to be regular topics of conversation. Just avoid personalizing any discussion of finances; your salary or the cost of your jewelry and other personal possessions are off-limits.

Your love life. Discussing the details of your latest romance, your lovers' spats, and even your sexual preferences can be perceived as far too personal, especially by people you don't know very well. When you find a sympathetic ear in the form of a very close friend, don't bend it to the breaking point.

Your background. In general, family background should be a topic of conversation only when it naturally fits with the subject at hand or someone has asked you about it.

Your health. Almost every conversation starts with "How are you?" and most of the time the response is "Fine, thank you." It's a conversational opener and not meant to be taken literally. But when you're not fine, spare everyone the details. "I've been under the weather" or "I'm doing PT after knee surgery" tells the

---

conversational outs

Sometimes it's hard to extract yourself from a conversation. Here are some suggested ways to style your exit line.

- **A GENERAL OUT.** "This has been lovely, but please excuse me, I'm going to mingle for a bit."
- **WHEN THERE'S TOO MUCH MEDICAL DETAIL.** "And this is where I'm going to excuse myself. It sounds fascinating, but I'm a bit squeamish."
- **WHEN THERE'S TOO MUCH DETAIL ABOUT BUSINESS.** "Pete, I'm thinking we should get in touch next week and discuss these details. For now, let's enjoy the event."
- **ENDING A DATE OR CONVERSATION WITH SOMEONE WHO WAS HITTING ON YOU.** "It's been so nice to get to know you. Thank you and have a good night." Then walk away.

---

news without boring—or distressing—your listener. Save a discussion of a more serious illness for close friends and have it in private, not when you run into them at the grocery store.

Agreeing to Disagree

Even though the classic advice is "never discuss politics or religion," our present society loves to talk about both. These subjects can stimulate lively conversation and debate; they can also stir deep-seated convictions with passionate proponents on opposing sides. Religion and politics top the conversational taboo list, with sex and money following right behind. Today's advice? Avoid these topics when you are at a social engagement. Your host has gone to some trouble to have a party or dinner and your potential argument can be like a wet blanket on the affair. Keeping a disagreement from escalating into a war of words is essential to civil conversation. The trick is knowing when to "agree to disagree." If you do find yourself in a discussion about a topic and it's getting heated, you can always say, "Well, we obviously don't agree on this one, and we may not change each other's minds. Maybe we should move on to something else." And then change the subject.

Sometimes it's best just to drop the discussion altogether. When the sparks start to fly—voices are raised, you start talking over each other, or genuine anger erupts on either side—it's absolutely time to switch to another subject. Be willing to cede the last word to bring an argument to a halt.

Criticism and Gossip

Other people are often the subject of conversation. We all like to know what's going on with our friends, neighbors, and relatives, but when the conversation turns to criticism or gossip, it's time to call it quits. Spreading rumors, breaking confidences, or dishing dirt is both hurtful and cowardly.

When you find yourself in just such a conversation, change the subject or decline to join in: "Kira, Ally is a friend, and I really don't want to hear this." Then change the subject. "When are you and Joe going on vacation?" If you hear something you know

to be false, set the record straight if you can: "That 'guy' you saw Becca having lunch with last week is her brother." Even when someone makes unkind remarks about a person you don't particularly care for, find something positive to say. It should go without saying, but the only way to keep gossip from spreading is never to repeat it.

More objectionable than the garden-variety criticizer or gossip is the bigot—someone who makes joking or derogatory remarks about a religious, ethnic, or cultural group. Again, call a halt by saying, "Let's get off that subject," then introduce another. If that doesn't work, tell the person frankly that you find his remarks objectionable and would rather not listen. If he continues, say good-bye and walk away. (See also Chapter 7, "Living with Neighbors," page 79, and Chapter 34, "Workplace Relationships," page 428.)

〚 FUNNY OR NOT? 〛

The ability to make others smile and laugh is a gift, but even the wittiest conversationalist should use humor with care. When you inject a joke into a conversation, make sure it is at no one's expense, and that it's appropriate for your audience. Ethnic, racial, religious, or gender-based humor risks hurting someone else's feelings and makes you appear insensitive, or worse, a bigot. Some people may not get your humor, especially "inside" jokes that are only relevant to a particular group, and sarcasm is easily misunderstood. Until you know people very well, you're wise to leave jokes out of your conversations.

Humor and jokes are not the same thing. Some of our greatest humorists made their mark through their wry observations on the human condition, understanding that—unlike hurtful jokes—humor works best when it's natural, healthy, and positive.

⟩ WHAT TO SAY WHEN ⟨

Hearing news of one kind or another about someone's personal life is inevitable. In some cases you'll want to congratulate, in others, commiserate. If the person is a close friend, you'll probably have no trouble coming up with something to say; for those you know less well, a simple acknowledgment will usually do. Before venturing any comments, consider the following whenever . . .

Someone becomes engaged or marries. Genuinely wish the person well, with "What great news!" "I'm so happy for you," or "I know you're going to be so happy together." "Congratulations" and "Best wishes" are also traditional responses.

Someone is pregnant. "What great news!" "You must be so pleased." Be happy for your friend or acquaintance, but don't pry. Avoid giving advice that may conflict with current medical opinion; future parents need to have confidence in their physician, and it's unfair to undermine that relationship. And don't share terrible labor and childbirth stories.

Someone miscarries. A reply of "Oh, I'm so sorry" is enough. Never offer up phrases like "It was for the best" or "It was God's will," and never imply that the miscarriage may have resulted from something the person did or didn't do.

the art of the compliment

If an opportunity to compliment another person comes up, deliver it—but only if it's both deserved and sincere. "You look terrific," "Great job on the PTA benefit," "Those ribs were the best!"

Many people find it difficult to respond graciously to compliments, as if accepting the compliment is somehow "showing off." Saying, "Oh, it was nothing," tells the giver that you don't value what you did and that he was wrong to give you praise. The simple and gracious response is a sincere "Thank you!" perhaps followed by "I'm so glad you think so" or "Aren't you nice to say so?" After you've received a compliment, you might respond in kind if you can do so sincerely: "Thank you. I think the ribs came out so well because I followed your advice about parboiling them first."

Someone divorces. Because your response is dictated by individual circumstances and you can't always read someone's feelings (some may be happy, others sad), there is no all-purpose response. But "Thanks for telling me" or "I wish you the best" are safe ways to show your concern. (See also Chapter 41, "Separation and Divorce," page 511.)

Someone is ill. You can always say, "I'm so sorry to hear that." And if you can, offer to help out. If a friend or friend's relative is seriously or terminally ill, your actions will speak louder than words. Show sympathy by offering to help in any way you can—shopping for groceries, perhaps, or babysitting. (See also Chapter 43, "Illness," page 531.)

Someone dies. When a friend or acquaintance loses a loved one, simply give your condolences. You needn't worry about being eloquent. A simple "I'm so sorry" or "I'm thinking of you" will do. Never make comments such as "It was really a blessing" or "Be thankful his suffering is over." Offer practical assistance where you can. (See also Chapter 44, "Loss, Grieving, and Condolences," page 539.)

Someone is fired or laid off. A simple, sincere "I'm so sorry you've been laid off" is a good start. "It must be a difficult time for you." If you can give practical assistance, do—a recommendation, help with a resumé update, information on other job openings. Even if you don't have specific leads, you can be a sounding board for a good friend and offer encouragement.

Someone is depressed or addicted. What you say to a friend or acquaintance who has told you that she's depressed or addicted (most often to drugs, pain-killers, or alcohol) depends on your relationship and the

dealing with nosy questions

Some people, often total strangers, have no qualms about asking personal questions: "Why aren't you married?" "How much did you pay for that?" "Is this a planned pregnancy?" You can't politely answer, "None of your business," but you *can* use a little humor, change the subject, or say, "I'd rather not talk about that."

The temptation is to respond with a clever zinger of your own, but a rude response to a rude question is just being doubly rude.

seriousness of the problem. Give her the opportunity to confide in you: "Please know that I'm here for you if you want to talk." Then never repeat what was said in confidence. But be careful not to pry, especially if you're not close friends. If the person is in counseling, let her raise the subject. If a close friend seems seriously upset, volunteer to help her find professional help.

ten conversation stoppers

Remember to be sensitive to others' feelings when you speak; you wouldn't talk to your grandmother about how you dread getting old or go on about your raise to someone who was just laid off. Consider the person you're talking to and the circumstances. Here are some guaranteed blunders, if not downright conversation killers:

- "When are you getting married/having kids?"
- "Why aren't you getting married/having kids?"
- "Are you tired? You look it." "You look awful—are you okay?"
- "When are you due?"
- "I just heard! Are you and that awful Chris really getting a divorce?"
- "You look great—have you lost weight/had an eye lift/been doing Botox?"
- "How much does someone in your line of work make?"
- "Should you be eating that?"
- "Isn't your baby a little small for his age?"
- "You live *there?*"

5
image and attire

Whenever you ask, "How do I look?" of course you hope the answer is, "Fantastic!" We ask this question because we care about how other people see us. Caring is one of the keys to developing a good personal image. This image—what we wear, how we look—not only represents how *we* choose to present ourselves, but also reflects the importance we attach to the occasion and the people we're with.

Styles change. There's no question that casual, comfortable, and stylish describe how today's American prefers to dress. Jeans, for example, are now a fashion must-have and are worn almost everywhere. Would Emily Post approve? Most likely, yes. She was all for style with a dose of practicality. But when "casual" lapses into sloppy or inappropriate, she'd be the first to object. Whether casual or formal, the principles of respect and consideration for others, plus a strong measure of common sense, should guide your decisions.

The etiquette of dressing and grooming today involves few rules but a great deal of emphasis on doing what helps people feel comfortable in their interactions. Individuality and personal expression have their place, but a considerate person doesn't dress in a way that will make others feel embarrassed or uncomfortable.

WHAT'S APPROPRIATE?

When you're wearing the right clothes, you feel confident and as if you belong. Knowing what to wear in every situation can be challenging. It's one thing to stand out because you look great; it's another because you look out of place.

Sometimes there are dress codes, such as at work, a golf course, or a formal event. But more often there are no rules, so you'll have to let common sense and an awareness of the setting or occasion guide you. For example, you won't go wrong wearing jeans to the movies or dressing up to go to the theater. But what do you wear to dinner at a friend's or to a charity luncheon?

Whenever in doubt, your best bet is to call and ask the friend who invited you to dinner or the organization hosting the event.

Dressing appropriately and with consideration is also rooted in respect for cultural, religious, and regional customs. What about wearing jeans to a religious service? It's okay in *some* houses of worship. But in other congregations, wearing anything except your very best is considered disrespectful. In unfamiliar situations, it's usually wise to find out about any dress codes.

Be prepared to adjust what you wear to the situation. If you're selling a concept to the board of directors, you might choose a suit. If you meet with a client at a media company where jeans and T-shirts are the norm, dressing too conservatively could signal that you're out of touch with the culture there.

Traditional-versus-casual dress questions come up in social situations as well. Anything more casual than a sports jacket or fairly dressy dress may be inappropriate for a cocktail party, while shorts and flip-flops might be fine for a backyard cookout. Tradition does hold its own most firmly with formal wear.

GOOD GROOMING

The way you take care of your body and anything you put on it is an important part of your image. As with choosing what to wear, paying attention to grooming demonstrates respect for yourself and for others. The operative words are *neat* and *clean*. The people you're with can be turned off if you become lax about the condition of your clothes or personal hygiene.

Q: *Whenever we get together with family, our fifteen-year-old insists on wearing grungy jeans and a T-shirt. I've told him that dressing presentably is a sign of respect for us and others, but he says it's his style and I should leave him alone.*

A: Your son is old enough to understand that his grungy clothes are out of place in certain settings, but he's at an age when dress style is one of the ways that teens assert their independence. You probably don't want to make too much of an issue just before seeing your relatives, when he's likely to be most obstinate. Talk with him at a calmer time, before the event. Let him know that you appreciate that he attends family gatherings. But remind him that while you generally don't interfere with his clothing choices, there are occasions when he needs to dress up a bit and pay attention to his grooming. Listen to his ideas and work together to find a compromise: perhaps jeans, but without holes in the knees, and a collared shirt. He may be more inclined to dress appropriately for family occasions when he sees that you respect his independence and want to explore solutions with him.

Taking Care of Your Person

When you attend to personal grooming, do it at home or in a restroom, not in public. Consider your

Hair. Clean, shiny, well-cut hair looks great and never goes out of style. Comb it often to keep it neat.

Nails. The basics of nail care for women and men include neatly trimmed nails and cuticles, both of which can be done at home. If you wear polish, maintain it regularly. If you're a nail biter, keep your nails short and filed to prevent them from looking ragged.

And don't forget your feet! Open-toed shoes, sandals, or flip-flops call for well-trimmed nails and clean feet, whether you're a man or a woman.

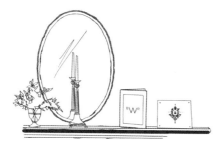

Breath. To keep breath fresh, try to brush your teeth after lunch as well as in the morning and at night. Regular flossing and brushing your tongue helps control odor. Breath mints can help, and it's a good idea to keep some handy. Not only is it a serious turn-off to others, but bad breath can also be a sign of ill health. If brushing, flossing, and mouthwash don't take care of it, pay a visit to your dentist or doctor.

Body odor. A daily bath or shower and use of a combination deodorant/antiperspirant is the best defense against body odor. So is showering before returning to work after a lunchtime workout. However,

how do you know if you have body odor or bad breath?

It's very hard to recognize if you have these problems. The only sure way to find out is to ask someone. It's best if that someone is a good friend or your spouse, a person you can trust. Try it. If he tells you that you don't have a problem, great. But if you do, you can now work on resolving it.

certain medications and health conditions can exacerbate body odor, so discuss any ongoing problems with your doctor.

Perfume and cologne. Apply perfume or cologne sparingly. If your scent lingers in the room after you leave, you're wearing too much. Unfortunately, the perfume you love may offend someone else or even cause an allergic reaction. Mixing scents—scented deodorant, hair and bath products, and cologne or perfume—can also be disagreeable. Some workplaces have "no scent" policies, so check yours out. The gym is another place to refrain from using perfume as exercise can intensify the scent. When choosing a scent, opt for something light for daytime or office, and save the heavier or more "romantic" scents for the evening.

Perfume is heavier and generally richer in fragrance than eau de toilette and cologne is the lightest mix. Because bodies react differently to scents, try a sample and wear it for a day or two before buying. Ask a few friends if it's pleasant or overpowering.

Taking Care of Your Wardrobe

No matter how expensive or stylish your clothing, if it's messy or ill-fitting, then style and cost mean little. Clothes send a message about how you want others to see you. Especially at work, clothes should be spotless at the start of each day; soiled or sloppy work clothing reflects on both you and your employer. Clothes should be

Clean. Don't be tempted to wear anything with spots or stains, or that's just plain dirty. Sometimes even clean clothes may not be as fresh as they appear, so apply the sniff test. Clothing picks up environmental odors such as tobacco smoke, perfume, and last night's stir-fry and may need to be cleaned or aired out before you wear it again.

Neat. Clothes should be free of wrinkles, lint, holes, and missing buttons. Hems should be intact. A good dry cleaner can make sure your clothing is in perfect condition—for a price. Investing in a few clothing-care tools and learning how to use them is also a good idea. Some of the basics are

- **Iron and ironing board:** Learn how to iron a blouse or dress shirt, trousers, and skirt.

- **Clothes brush or lint roller:** Hang one on the back of your closet door and keep one at work or in your car, and use it to remove loose dirt, dandruff, pet hair, and lint. Even if your clothes are clean, lint and pet hair will detract from your appearance.

- **Basic sewing kit:** Learn how to sew on a button and repair a basic hem.

Q: *My friend has body odor so intense that people joke about him behind his back. I'd like to help him. Is there a tactful way to broach the subject?*

A: Understandably, many people are reluctant to take on this difficult conversation. "Couldn't I just send an anonymous note or leave a hint like a stick of deodorant?" While easy on you, it would be humiliating and hurtful to your friend and now is the time to be a good friend. Before approaching him, have these goals in mind:

- Have the conversation in private.

- Focus on your friendship and your concern for his success, not the problem.

- Listen to what he has to say, and offer suggestions if you can.

- Assure him that the conversation will remain completely confidential.

You might say, "Tom, I'd like to talk to you about a difficult issue. I hope if the situation were reversed that as my friend, you would talk with me. Are you aware that you have body odor?"

Now that you've done the hard part and broached the subject, be sympathetic and supportive. If he reacts angrily, assure him of your friendship. Often when this happens, the person will come back and thank his friend once he's thought it over.

- **Shoe shine kit:** Regular care of your shoes—and other leather goods—makes them look great and protects your investment.

ACCESSORIES IN GENERAL

A great tie, the perfect earrings, or the right purse can really dress up an outfit. They can also dress it down. Just as with clothing, be aware of the event or context when you choose your accessories.

Hats

Hats aren't the essential they once were, but are still worn by both sexes for fashion and for function. Knowing when to remove a hat is actually a matter of respect. (For a chart on when and where to take off your hat, see "Hats On or Off?," page 23.) Head coverings worn for religious and cultural reasons generally aren't removed indoors. If you are attending a religious service in a tradition outside your own, check with someone of that faith about appropriate head wear for visitors.

Jewelry

Whether costume or the real thing, jewelry should complement, not overpower, your total look. In general, consider the occasion and the sensitivities of others. For instance, a courteous person won't wear conspicuous religious jewelry when attending services of another faith. In business settings, keep your jewelry industry appropriate: What works in the fashion world is a far cry from what's acceptable in banking. When in doubt, keep your choices simple and understated.

Be careful not to wear noisy jewelry where it could disturb others. Jingling bracelets are a distraction at work, the theater, or a religious service, and in both social and public settings, shut off watches that beep or chime.

It's fine to admire someone's jewelry, but don't ask how much it cost. If you happen to be on the receiving end of that question, say something like, "I have no idea, but to me it's priceless."

Piercings and Tattoos

Whereas one person's ideas of body art can be alarming to someone else, for many of today's millennial generation a tattoo is seen as a rite of passage. Those who are familiar and comfortable with tattoos and piercings should remember that not everyone accepts them as they do. For older generations tattoos and piercings have very specific connotations, and many of these are negative.

Many employers regard the display of tattoos and piercings as unprofessional. Career counselors still advise job applicants to avoid displaying piercings anywhere but ears and to cover visible tattoos, if possible, for job interviews. Fair or unfair, the choice to get visible tattoos or to wear stretching jewelry such as plugs or tunnels could be regarded as saying something about one's discretion and long-term decision-making. It is important to remember this reality when choosing to make a permanent alteration to one's body.

Those who are less comfortable with tattoos and piercings should remind themselves that these are much more common, particularly in some regions of the country and in some job fields. Remember, too, that while fashions change, the substance of some-one's character is what matters most in any situation. No matter how someone looks, they deserve not to be judged and to be treated respectfully.

Eyewear

Keep your lenses clean and your glasses in good repair. In a pinch, you may have to fasten a broken frame with a safety pin, but don't let it become permanent.

When you meet people, take off your sunglasses to say hello so that you can make eye contact. Eye contact is an important part of any greeting, and leaving your sunglasses on can come across as unfriendly. Unless you have a medical reason to wear them, take them off indoors, too. At the office, this means removing them completely: Wearing them on your head sends the message you'll be out the door shortly.

Handbags, Laptop Cases, and Briefcases

Purses and handbags should be appropriate to the occasion. An oversized leather purse would look out of place with a silk cocktail dress, for example. Bags and shoes don't have to match, and you don't need a purse for every outfit. Choose one as roomy as you need, but take care that an oversized bag doesn't inconvenience

Q: *My boyfriend and I were out for dinner last night with another couple. When my contact lenses started hurting while we waited for dessert, I changed them at the table. Later, my boyfriend said I should have done it in the ladies' room. Is he right?*

A: Yes, he is. What is a simple process for the contact lens wearer can be quite unpleasant for other people to watch. All personal care should be taken care of in a restroom. Even if your fellow diners are close friends, they deserve the same lens-changing courtesy you'd extend to someone you've just met. (If you have an emergency it's okay to remove your lens immediately, then excuse yourself to the restroom.)

others in crowded places or endanger the heads of small children. Keep your briefcase or laptop case in good condition.

MEN'S CLOTHING AND GROOMING

Men's clothing styles are much less formal than they used to be. However, while today's wardrobe leans toward the more casual, it doesn't mean it's okay to abandon what's appropriate. You won't compromise self-expression when you show respect by wearing a tie or removing your baseball cap, and a hint of formality can be an opportunity to set yourself apart.

No matter what your style, be sure you follow the basic tenets of good grooming. If you're in the dark about what to wear for a situation, be observant. What are well-dressed men wearing to work? To indoor concerts? To religious services? When you aren't sure, ask someone who knows. If you're going to a party, call the host. If visiting a business, call the receptionist or human resources department and ask what the men usually wear.

What About the Suit?

The suit remains an essential—if not always for the office anymore, then for weddings, parties, and funerals. It shows respect for the occasion, and it makes almost any man look his best. But the pluses are wiped out if the suit hangs sloppily or is rumpled or dirty. When you buy a suit, think less of making the latest fashion statement than of finding something that fits well and feels comfortable. A tailor is your best friend. He can adjust an off-the-rack suit to fit you perfectly.

Men's Accessories

These finishing touches to a man's wardrobe should complement his overall look:

Ties, scarves, and handkerchiefs. Neckties and scarves allow for personal expression. Bright colors and flashy designs may be fine at times, but your choice should be in keeping with the occasion. And any tie with a spot should head to the dry cleaner's.

A dress or chest-pocket handkerchief is for show only, not for use. The dress handkerchief is appropriate with a suit jacket, casual blazer, or sports jacket, and it can be worn even if you aren't wearing a tie. Pointed or straight folds are both fine, though, in business, the pointed fold is the more showy or "power-move" of the two.

Jewelry. Two words sum up the well-dressed man's use of jewelry: *minimal* and *subtle*. A wedding band and a watch aren't quite the limit, but they're close. Tie clips go in and out of fashion, but are perfectly appropriate. Keep anything else on the hands or wrists to a simple ring and cuff links and/or a simple bracelet, and wear a necklace inside your shirt. This is a safe look for the conservative business world. Unless it's the norm where you work, save chains or multiple rings and bracelets for your social image. Studs and cuff links can be rented or purchased for wearing with formal wear.

Wallets. A wallet should be thin enough not to cause an obvious bulge in your back pocket. You might opt for a very thin wallet for a few credit cards, ID, and a money clip for bills.

Hats. A hat can express your individuality—a radical shift from the conformity of times past. The choice of hat makes a statement (the fedora says retro, the panama, resort), but every man should know when to take off his hat. (See "Hats On or Off?," page 23.) Any hat should come off at work (unless it's normally worn on the job), whenever the national anthem is played, at the dinner table, and in restaurants. And, when you do take it off, don't put your hat on the table; check it, hang it on a hook, put it on an empty chair, or leave it in your lap.

The baseball-style cap has become entrenched in

the wardrobes of millions of men. The billed cap covers the head and shades the eyes from sun and glare. Avoid wearing it at work or on formal occasions.

Formal Wear for Men

There's some room for variation when dressing for a formal event (See "Dressing for the Occasion," page 683), but in most cases, personal expression is best saved for other occasions. Events are formal so that a certain tone will prevail. The following checklist will help you avoid mistakes when going formal:

At formal occasions, avoid wearing . . .

- Boots, loafers, sandals, or flip-flops. (An exception might be a black-tie affair with a western theme or a beach wedding.)
- Cuffed pants.
- A cummerbund upside down. (The rule is *pleats up*—handy to catch crumbs or store ticket stubs or matches.)
- A vest and a cummerbund—choose one or the other.
- White dinner jackets in cold climates.
- Puffy, frilly, or tieless shirts (banded collar or turtleneck), unless the invitation says "Creative Black Tie."
- A pocket handkerchief and a boutonniere—choose one or the other.

The Well-Groomed Man

Hair. No matter your style, well-groomed hair is clean, well cut, styled, and odor-free.

Facial hair. Neatness counts, so keep beards and moustaches trimmed. Long or straggly beards or moustaches and extreme styles such as handlebars need extra care and panache to be worn successfully.

Five o'clock stubble. This can be a problem if you have very dark hair or heavy stubble. An electric shaver will spiff you up for a late afternoon meeting or early evening out, so keep one handy if you need it, but only use it in the men's room (and clean up any stubble in the sink).

Then again, the "unshaved" look is a style, and there are even razors that will maintain that "three-days' growth" look. If it's your style, be sure it's appropriate for the occasion or situation.

Eyebrows, nose and ear hair. Check regularly to see if your eyebrows need trimming, your nose hairs need clipping, or your ears tweezing. A barber can take care of the eyebrows and ear hair; otherwise, tweeze at home, not in the restroom—or your cubicle—at work.

DRESSING AND GROOMING FOR WOMEN

Today's world of women's fashion is incredibly diverse. Norms and expectations can vary widely: by age groups, regions, industries, cultures—even neighborhoods and office departments. Women have more freedom of expression than at any other time in history, but with options can come confusion about what's appropriate. Always dress for the situation; it shows respect for others and the setting you're in. This doesn't mean sacrificing personal style; it means accommodating both. Dress and grooming choices should begin with a few questions:

- What is the occasion—a casual get-together, a business event, a fancy party?
- What are the general expectations about the dress code for the event?
- What will make *you* feel good about your appearance?

When Too Much Is Too Much

If people focus on the clothes you are wearing rather than on you, then you're wearing the wrong clothes. Consider where you'll be and whom you'll be with, then make sure your clothes aren't

- Too tight
- Too short
- Too low-cut
- Too loud
- Too sheer

(And gentlemen, take note: These guidelines are for you, too!)

Women's Accessories

Accessories can be a woman's best friend, but too much accessorizing can defeat the purpose by overwhelming

---

when to wear white

White can be worn 365 days a year. Today the real issue is the *weight* of fabrics—not the color. Lightweight fabrics (cotton, linen, voile, and the like) in white and pastels are worn in the warm and hot months, and heavier fabrics (woolens, heavy cottons and corduroys, suede, satin, and so forth) in a creamier "winter white" are worn in the cool and cold months. When going abroad, check local customs and weather forecasts before packing—in some countries, white is the color of mourning.

---

both the clothes and the woman wearing them. (See also "Accessories in General," page 50.)

Hats. Fashion hats have made a comeback in recent years. When a hat is part of a woman's outfit, it can be worn indoors, except in an office or when it blocks others' view, as in a theater. (See "Hats On or Off?" page 23.)

Gloves. Like hats, gloves may be part of a fashion look or worn strictly as outerwear. Winter gloves and mittens are removed and tucked away in a pocket or purse as soon as they're no longer needed.

Gloves are often worn for formal and semiformal parties. The length of gloves is generally a matter of personal taste and tradition, though mid-length and full-length fashion gloves are usually reserved for formal affairs. Jewelry, such as watches and rings, is worn underneath gloves. Gloves are kept on when going through or standing in a receiving line.

Gloves can be worn until any food or beverages

are served, but are removed completely for eating and drinking. At a seated dinner, lay your gloves on your lap (under your napkin) and then put them on again after the meal, if you wish.

The Well-Groomed Woman

Hair. No matter your style, well-groomed hair is clean, well cut, styled, and odor-free.

Nails. Whether they're polished or not, keep nails trimmed and shaped. Toes, too. Nicely manicured bare toenails are preferable to polished ones that are outgrown or chipped.

Makeup. Types and degree of facial makeup are matters of personal taste, but the most attractive makeup choices are based on circumstances. Sparing use of cosmetics for a clean, natural look is usually preferable for work and daytime activities, with a bolder look for nighttime social events.

DRESSING BY REQUEST

Invitations that include dress instructions, such as "Black tie," "Semiformal," or "Casual," are intended to be helpful by indicating the nature or type of attire that is expected for the event. When a social invitation doesn't mention dress, the event is usually one that you'll know what to wear. When in doubt, check with the host or another invitee. Be attentive to other dress information on invitations: If you're invited to a "masked ball," wear a mask; if the invitation says "festive," make an effort to reflect the holiday or theme.

primping in public?

Flossing on the bus? Applying nail polish on the commuter train? Cutting toenails at your desk? Why is it that some people feel it's okay to perform some of the most private grooming chores in public? We may feel anonymous but we certainly aren't invisible! Excuse yourself to a restroom or other private place to apply powder, blusher, mascara, or scent; brush or comb hair; floss, tweeze, or clip. Putting on makeup while driving is just plain dangerous!

And what about applying lipstick in public? It's okay if you can do so without being obvious. But it's hard to be discreet when eating dinner at a nice restaurant or sitting next to your boss in a business meeting. In these instances, excuse yourself and apply your lipstick in the restroom. Among friends at a casual occasion, it's fine to do a *quick* application of lipstick or gloss right after a meal.

Invitations to business-related functions often don't include dress notations, especially when guests come directly from work and aren't expected to change from their normal daytime attire.

dress codes

For a complete listing of formal, business, and casual dress codes and corresponding attire, see "Dressing for the Occasion," page 683.

table manners

emily Post summed it up perfectly: "All the rules of table manners are made to avoid ugliness." Essentially, eating is a gross activity: We put food in our mouths, mash it to a pulp, and swallow. Not so bad if you're by yourself, but eating is also a social activity.

Rituals and manners surrounding the preparation, eating, and sharing of food have been with us for eons. While particular manners may vary from culture to culture, their primary purpose is to make eating a pleasant activity for everyone. Like all manners, table manners have evolved over time: We no longer recline at the table like the Romans or eat from our knives like the Colonials. Our modern table manners marry the practical with the pleasant and considerate.

The world's not going to end because you don't know which fork to use. However, the more adept you are at using utensils and knowing basic table manners, the more confident you'll be. With experience and practice you'll instinctively choose the right implement for the job and common sense will tell you not to choose a dinner fork to eat an oyster or a teaspoon to eat soup. If you're truly in doubt, you can always take a moment to watch the host to see what he does.

Good table manners are unobtrusive and natural. Do something unexpected or gauche, such as reaching across the table for the salt, spitting pits onto your plate, slurping, shoveling your food, diving in before everyone is served, or taking food from someone else's plate, and you call unnecessary—and unflattering—attention to yourself. You break the flow.

Good table manners are always expected, but at times they become vitally important. Job applicants have been rejected because they chewed with their mouths open or held the fork like a shovel. Have no illusions: A potential employer is taking you to lunch not out of the kindness of his heart, but to gauge your overall finesse.

That's why it's a good idea to practice your manners on a daily basis at the family dinner table or even when eating alone. If you have any doubts about how you appear to others while you are eating, eat a meal in front of a mirror. When used routinely, table manners become second nature, lessening the chances of any missteps wherever you're dining.

THE TABLE

A good place to start is the table setting. You'll want all the items necessary for each place: napkin, dishes, glassware, and utensils. Which utensils and the way they are laid out also give clues as to which course will be served when. A fork, knife, and spoon are used for the average family meal consisting of a main course and dessert. A three-course meal—soup, salad, or starter; main course; and dessert—calls for another utensil or two. A meal of four or more courses requires yet more utensils.

Flatware is sold in sets, also called place settings. The modern place setting usually consists of five pieces, some of which are multipurpose: a large knife and fork for the main course; a large spoon for soup or dessert; a smaller fork for a first course, salad, or dessert; and a smaller spoon for coffee or tea or dessert, if the large spoon was already used for soup. Some sets also include a smaller knife, useful for a first course or salad, but the basic five are sufficient for most meals. Specialty implements, such as butter knives or oyster forks, can be added as desired.

There are a few general table setting guidelines:

◆ Only set utensils that will be used during the meal.

◆ Utensils are *placed in the order of use* from the outside in.

◆ The word *FOrKS* can help you remember the order of the basic table setting: **F**ork, **O** for the plate, **K**nife, and **S**poon.

◆ The knife blade always faces the plate.

The Informal Place Setting

The typical place setting for an informal, three-course dinner includes these utensils and dishes:

Dinner plate. It may be set in place on the table or plated in the kitchen and brought to the table when dinner is served.

Two forks. The forks are placed to the left of plate. The dinner fork (the larger of the two) is used for the main course, the smaller fork for a salad or appetizer. When an appetizer or salad is served *before* the main course, the smaller fork is placed on the *outside* of the dinner fork. If the salad is served *after* the main course, place it to the *inside* of the dinner fork, next to the dinner plate. This follows the "outside-in" rule.

Napkin. The napkin is folded or put in a napkin ring and placed either left of the forks or in the center of the dinner plate. It can also be folded and placed under the forks.

Knife. The dinner knife is set immediately to the right of the plate, cutting edge facing toward the plate. The dinner knife can also be used for a first-course dish. However, unless you provide a second knife at the place setting, be prepared to replace the used knives with clean ones for the next course. Use a steak knife in place of a dinner knife when needed for steak, and provide an additional knife for the first course, if necessary.

Spoons. Spoons go to the right of the knife. The soupspoon goes farthest to the right. If needed, the dessertspoon goes between the soupspoon and knife. When coffee or tea is served at the end of the meal, add a teaspoon between the dessertspoon and the knife.

Glasses. Drinking glasses of any kind—wine, water, juice, iced tea—are placed at the top right of the dinner plate, at about a 45-degree angle, above the knife and spoon.

Other dishes and utensils are optional, depending on what is being served:

Salad plate. If salad is served as a separate course, either before or after the entrée, a salad plate is necessary. When the salad will be eaten with the meal you can serve it directly on the dinner plate. However, if the entrée contains gravy or other runny ingredients, a separate plate for the salad will keep things neater. Place the salad plate to the left of the forks.

Bread or butter plate with butter knife. If used, the bread plate goes above the forks, with the butter knife resting on the top edge, handle pointing to the right and blade facing in.

Dessertspoon and fork. These can either be placed horizontally above the dinner plate (the spoon at the top with its handle pointing to the right; the fork below with its handle pointing to the left) or beside the

A SIMPLE PLACE SETTING FOR AN INFORMAL, TWO-COURSE MEAL: *main course and dessert; plus a beverage such as water, milk, iced tea, or juice.*

INFORMAL THREE-COURSE MEAL: *salad, main course, and dessert, with the additions of bread served on a bread plate, water, and wine.*

plate with the other utensils. If placed beside the plate, the fork goes on the left-hand side, closest to the plate; the spoon goes on the right-hand side of the plate, just to the right of the dinner knife.

Coffee/tea cup and saucer. When coffee or tea is served during the meal, the cup and saucer go slightly to the right of the knife and spoons, but below any glasses. If it's served after dinner, the cups and saucers are brought to the table with or after the dessert course and placed in the same spot.

Salt and pepper. It's a good idea to include a salt and a pepper shaker on your table. One set will do for a family, but for a more formal table or a really large family, consider putting a set at each end, or one set for every four people. Remove the salts and peppers when you clear the main course, before serving dessert. (See also "Guide to Food and Drink," page 686.)

Condiments. At the table, transfer bottled condiments, such as ketchup or mustard, to small dishes. Include a small underplate (for drips) and a serving utensil.

Butter or olive oil. Butter may be served in pats on individual bread plates. Alternatively, the stick or pats are placed on a plate with a small knife or fork to be passed around the table. Whipped butter is spooned into a small dish accompanied by a little knife

A FORMAL PLACE SETTING FOR A FIVE-COURSE MEAL: *seafood appetizer, soup, main course, salad, and dessert. The three glasses (right to left) are for: white wine, which will be served first; red wine, which follows; and water, which is served throughout the meal. A bread plate and a butter knife are on the left-hand side. In this example, the dessert fork and spoon are put at the top of the place setting. The other options are: 1) The dessert fork can be set to the right of the salad fork and the dessertspoon to the left of the soupspoon; 2) The dessert fork and spoon are brought to the place setting when dessert is served.*

or spreader. Olive oil, a popular alternative to butter, is served in a cruet with an underplate to catch drips or in a bowl with an underplate and a spoon. (See also "Guide to Food and Drink," page 686.)

Dressing It Up

There's also an art to setting the table, even for a family meal. While a bare table may promote a minimalist look, a place mat or tablecloth will protect the table's finish and helps define the diner's space. Candles make any

dinner more relaxing, and a simple centerpiece adds an artistic touch.

The Formal Place Setting

The formal place setting is used at home for a meal of more than three courses, such as a dinner party or a holiday meal. It's simply the informal setting taken to the next level, adding glassware and utensils for the foods and beverages served with the additional courses. It's also used at high-end restaurants that serve multiple courses. In addition to the general guidelines, apply the "no more than three" rule. In Victorian times, formal tables were set for nine, ten, or twelve courses. We can thank Emily Post, who decreed there should be no more than three of each utensil on the table at any one time, thus shaping the structure of the modern dinner party meal of four or five courses.

Everything on your table should be crisp and sparkling. White linens are still considered the most formal, but colored or patterned tablecloths, napkins, and place mats can be just as elegant. Other possible elements are candles, a centerpiece or multiple arrangements, and place cards. Place mats are centered in front of each chair, about 1 to 2 inches from the edge. A tablecloth is spread to hang evenly on each end and on the sides. The average drop is 12 to 18 inches, but don't worry if it's a little long or short—you just don't want it hanging too low, or it will end up in the diners' laps.

The *most* formal table is strictly symmetrical: centerpiece in the exact center, an even number of candlesticks, place settings spaced evenly around the table, silverware lined up and at the same distance from the edge of the table. However, feel free to vary flower arrangements and decorations as you like, creating a balanced and pleasing tablescape. The space not taken up by place settings is your available real estate. Being careful not to overcrowd the table, arrange your decorations so that diners sitting opposite can see each other.

Additional elements, silverware, and glassware required for a formal setting of more than three courses include the following:

Service plate. This large plate, also called a charger, serves as an underplate for the plate holding the first course, usually an appetizer, which is either in place before guests arrive at the table or served once they are seated. When the first course is cleared, the service plate remains in place for any other courses, such as a soup course, until the plate holding the entrée is served, at which point the service plate is removed. Service plates are not a required element of a formal table, but decorative ones have made a comeback and are a popular addition to both formal and less formal table settings.

Additional pieces: As you design your menu, think about what dishes you will need to serve each course. Soup cups or bowls, finger bowls, and footed bowls or coupes, such as those used for shrimp salad or ice cream, need underplates to catch drips and for resting utensils. You may need one or more various small plates for courses before or after the main course or for underplates; soup cups or bowls; bread, salad, or dessert plates; or cups and saucers for coffee or tea.

The order of the forks: Forks go on the left of the dinner plate in the order they will be used, following the "outside-in" rule. For example, if the menu consists of a fish course, followed by the entrée, and then salad, place, *left to right*, a **fish fork**, a meat or **dinner fork**, and then a **salad fork**. If you don't have fish or salad forks, then any small or medium-sized fork will do.

Oyster fork: If you're serving shellfish as a first course, then set out an **oyster fork**. This special, small fork goes to the right of the spoons. It's the only fork ever placed on the right and the only implement that can break the "no more than three" of any one utensil rule.

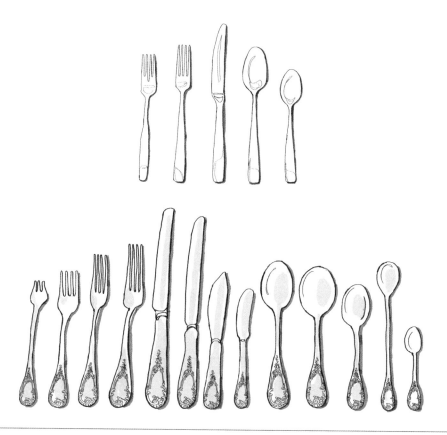

TOP ROW: THE MODERN, FIVE-PIECE PLACE SETTING: *a small fork for appetizer, salad, or dessert; a large fork for the main course; a knife for the main course; a large spoon for soup or dessert; a teaspoon for tea or coffee, or dessert.* BOTTOM ROW: TRADITIONAL FLATWARE (LEFT TO RIGHT): *oyster fork; fish, dessert, or salad fork; luncheon fork; dinner fork; dinner knife; luncheon knife; fish knife; butter knife; dessertspoon; soupspoon; teaspoon; iced-tea spoon; demitasse spoon.*

The order of the knives: All knives, except the **butter knife**, which is placed on the bread plate, go to the immediate right of the dinner plate. Using the "fish, meat, salad" menu, place, *right to left*, the **fish knife**; meat, steak, or **dinner knife**; then the **salad knife**, next to the plate.

Since knives are also weapons, they come with a few extra "rules" to indicate a nonthreatening purpose.

Most table knives, except for the steak knife, have rounded instead of pointed tips. Knives are always placed on the table with the blade facing either the plate or the diner, not anyone else at the table. It is impolite to point your knife at anyone at the table. As with the forks, if you don't have a particular knife, use the large knife for the entrée and smaller knives for the other courses.

The order of the spoons: Spoons are set to the right of all the knives. The most common spoons are the round **soupspoon**, the large, oval-bowled fruit or **dessertspoon** (which can double as a soupspoon), and the smaller **teaspoon**. If the menu calls for soup, ice cream, and coffee or tea, set the spoons, *right to left*, soupspoon, dessertspoon, teaspoon. An **iced-tea spoon** is placed in the glass of iced tea. It's left in the glass, or if a saucer is provided, it can be removed and placed on the saucer.

When your menu is elaborate and more than three courses are served before dessert, the utensils for the fourth course are brought in with the food; likewise, the salad fork and knife may be brought in when salad is served. Dessertspoons and forks are brought in on the dessert plate. If it won't break the "no more than three" rule, you can place the dessertspoon and/or fork horizontally above the plate, as in the informal setting. You also have the option of putting the teaspoon on the edge of the saucer when serving coffee or tea after dinner.

Glasses. The glasses indicate the beverages that will be served with the meal. Usually, no more than four glasses are set; any more and the place setting becomes crowded, not to mention increasing the chance for spills. The water goblet, which will be used throughout the meal, is placed directly above the knives. Fill water glasses before guests come to the table. Follow the "outside-in" rule when placing the other glasses to the right of the water glass. If you're serving white wine with the first course and red wine with the second, the red wineglass goes to the right of the water goblet and the white wineglass to the right of it. If you're serving champagne

with your appetizer, place the champagne glass to the far right. If you're serving champagne with dessert, place the glass immediately to the right of the water goblet, or, if your table is crowded, bring the glasses in just before dessert is served. As you clear each course, remove wineglasses as guests are finished with them.

AT THE TABLE

Before You Come to the Table

A meal is a social occasion. Creating a pleasant mealtime experience for all is everyone's responsibility, not just the person cooking the meal or setting the table. So, before coming to the table:

* Wash your hands (and face) and comb your hair.

* Wear a shirt and shoes.

* Change into clean clothes, if necessary.

* Take off your cap or hat. (Ladies may wear a hat if it's part of their outfit, as at a wedding.)

"Please Be Seated"

Unless you're invited to take a seat, it's considerate to wait until everyone has gathered at the table before sitting down. In a more formal setting, a man may offer to hold the chair for the lady on his right: Pull the chair away from the table so that she can sit easily, then hold on to the back while she adjusts the chair closer to the table. This is more symbolic than actual assistance, unless the person you are helping is elderly or frail. At home, as a sign of respect let your mother, the hostess, and any guest of honor sit first.

Saying a Blessing

In some families and at some events it's customary to say a blessing or prayer before the meal begins. If that's not your custom and you're a guest, just sit quietly until the blessing is finished. If asked, do join hands around the table—doing so will complete the circle.

Using Your Napkin

Whether it's cloth or paper, put your napkin in your lap as soon as you sit down or right after the blessing is said. Partially unfold the napkin instead of snapping it open. The custom of waiting until the hostess puts her napkin in her lap is observed only at more formal meals. Don't tuck a napkin into your collar, between the buttons of your shirt or blouse, or in your belt. (An exception can be made for the elderly or infirm.) For truly messy meals such as lobster or ribs, you'll be provided with a bib to protect your clothes.

Use your napkin frequently during the meal to blot or pat—not wipe—your lips, especially before taking a drink of your beverage to avoid leaving messy smears on the glass. However, your napkin isn't a surrogate washcloth. You should eat neatly so that the food goes in your mouth and doesn't wind up all over your face.

Whenever you excuse yourself from the table, put your napkin to the left side of your plate. Just leave it in loose folds, keeping any soiled parts out of sight. Don't leave it on your chair. At some very high-end restaurants, the waiter may replace your napkin with a fresh one; at others, they may fold it and hang it on the back of the chair. At the end of the meal, leave your loosely folded

napkin to the left or, if your plate has been removed, put your napkin in the center of the place setting.

The Particulars of Serving

How a meal is served depends on its style. A very formal dinner is **served**, meaning a waitperson serves each person each course individually. Starting with the person on the host's right, the server presents the dish on the diner's left. The diner either serves himself or says, "No, thank you." The server continues to the right, around the table, ending with the host. Alternatively, each course can be **plated** in the kitchen and then served to each diner. (For more on serving a meal, see Chapter 24, "Entertaining at Home," page 292, or Chapter 25, "Formal Dinners and Parties," page 314.)

A less formal dinner party may involve **buffet** service, where guests serve themselves from a buffet table and then proceed to the dining table. At a more casual meal, the food may be served **family style**. Platters are set before the host, who prepares each plate and then passes it, or the platters are passed around the table and the guests help themselves.

Here are a few guidelines to keep in mind when food and condiments are passed around the table:

- Pass to the right (counterclockwise). But, honestly, what's most important is that dishes move in only one direction so they don't cause a traffic jam.

- If you're starting a dish, hold it for the person on your right, who serves himself, then holds the platter for the person on his right, and so on. You'll be the last one served when the dish goes full circle.
- Position the utensils so that the person receiving the dish can serve himself easily.
- Dishes with handles should be passed with the handle toward the person receiving them.
- Any heavy or awkward dishes are put down on the table between each pass.
- Salt and pepper are usually passed together.
- Put butter on your bread plate and then pass it to the next person before buttering your bread.

Serving Yourself

Your first concern when serving yourself is to pay attention to what you're doing and avoid spills. Keep the following in mind:

- If the platter comes with a serving fork and spoon, use the fork under foods like sliced meat or asparagus, and use the spoon on top to steady the items during transfer to your plate. Use the spoon under foods such as peas or a whole baked potato, and use the fork on top to do the steadying.
- Gravy should be spooned directly from the gravy boat onto the meat, potatoes, or rice on your plate.
- Condiments, pickles, and jelly are put alongside the foods they're meant to accompany. Olives, nuts, radishes, or celery are put on the bread plate. If there is no bread plate, put these items on the edge of your dinner plate.
- If a dish is beyond your reach, ask someone to pass it to you instead of reaching for it.

- Don't request any condiments that aren't already on the table, unless it's something obvious like salt or pepper. Asking for anything else implies that the food is missing something.

"No, Thank You"

When you're among friends, it's fine to refuse a dish you don't care for with a polite "No, thank you." At a dinner party where the host has gone to a great deal of trouble, it's good manners to take at least a little of every dish being offered. Teach the concept of the "no thank you helping" to children, even for family meals.

If you're allergic to a particular food or on a restricted diet and your host urges you to help yourself to food you shouldn't eat, gently decline: "Sarah, shellfish is off-limits for me, but I'm enjoying everything else."

"Please Begin"

When can you start eating your meal? Wait until everyone is seated, served, and the hostess lifts her fork. That's the signal that everyone may begin. When there are many around the table and a risk of the food growing cold before the last person is served, the kind host will invite those served first to begin. Once the last person is served, the host may request a pause to offer a blessing, a welcome, or a toast. If so, put down your knife and fork and give him your full attention.

At a self-serve buffet, you may begin once you're seated. At a restaurant or an event such as a wedding when you're seated at a large table of eight or more, begin eating once at least three of you have been served. At a small table of only two to four people, it's better to wait until everyone has been served. At a formal dinner or business meal, regardless of how many people are at your table, either wait until everyone is served or begin when your host invites you to.

Which Fork?

Start with utensils on the outside first and work your way in. If you're confused, watch the others at the table and follow suit. Keep in mind the smaller knives and forks are used for salad, appetizers, or a fish course, and the larger ones for your main course. If you have good utensil skills, chances are no one will notice if you use the "wrong" one.

How to Hold?

To use your fork or spoon, hold it like a pencil, not a shovel: Rest it on the middle finger of your hand, and then let your forefinger and thumb grip the handle. Use either utensil to scoop the food, taking only enough for one, comfortable bite. Taking a heaping amount risks a spill or getting food on your face.

When cutting your food, gripping the handles of your knife and fork in your fists like daggers actually makes the job more difficult. Holding the knife and fork correctly provides you with the most control—and the least chance of sending a piece of meat flying. Here's how to do it:

- Take the knife in your dominant hand, blade down, and cup the handle in your palm, resting your pointer finger on the top of the blade, right where it attaches to the handle.

- Take the fork in your other hand, with the tines facing down. Cup the handle in the palm of your hand and place your pointer finger on top of the back of the handle, pointing toward the tines.

- Use your dominant hand when cutting with your knife or when you use your fork with the tines up.

- Pierce the meat with your fork to steady it, pressing the base of the handle with your index finger. Then use a sawing motion with your knife to cut off a bite-sized piece. As you cut, keep your elbows just slightly above table level and close to your sides so you don't bump your neighbor.

There are two different ways to use your utensils to get the food to your mouth: the American style and the Continental (or European) style. Both are equally correct. You can choose one style or the other, or switch between the two during the meal, whichever way is more comfortable or fits the type of food you are eating. The method for cutting food is the same for both techniques.

American (or zigzag) style. After the food is cut, place the knife along the upper edge of the plate, then switch the fork to your dominant hand before raising it, tines up, to your mouth.

Continental style. Your utensils don't change hands. Once the food is cut, lower your knife hand toward the plate and raise the food to your mouth with your fork, tines down.

Whichever method you choose, cut and eat one piece of meat at a time. It's also fine to use your knife as a "pusher" to help corral tricky foods like peas or rice,

HOLDING UTENSILS: *American style*

HOLDING UTENSILS: *Continental style*

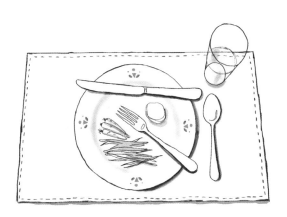

RESTING UTENSILS: *American style*

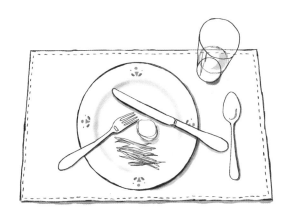

RESTING UTENSILS: *Continental style*

or push the meat more firmly onto your fork. However, if you use your fork "tines up," place your knife on the plate in the resting position (see page 67) while you take your bite.

Resting Utensils

Knowing where to rest utensils during and after the meal is important. First, never place a knife, fork, or spoon you've been using directly on the table. American style, when you pause to take a sip of your beverage or to speak with someone, place your knife along the upper edge of your plate, and put the fork below, at about the three o'clock position. Continental style, place your knife and fork on your plate near the center, slightly angled in a V and with the tips of the knife and fork pointing toward each other. (Tines may be up or down.) This resting position signals your host or your server that you're not finished yet.

At most restaurants, used utensils are replaced with clean ones for the next course. If a waiter asks you to keep your dirty utensils for the next course it's fine to request clean ones. Otherwise, rest them on an available plate.

At the end of the course, lay your knife and fork side by side diagonally on your plate. If your plate were a clock face, the handles would lie at the four and the blade or tines toward the ten. The knife blade faces inward but the fork tines can be either up or down, signaling your host or the server that you're finished. It also makes it easy for the person clearing the table: Standing on your right side to clear, the server can grip your plate with his right hand, easily putting his thumb

over your utensils, ensuring that they won't fall to the floor—or on you.

When soup or dessert is served in a cup, a deep bowl, or a stemmed bowl set on another plate, place your utensil on the underplate when you finish. If the bowl is shallow and wide, more like a plate, then leave the spoon in the bowl, not on the underplate.

DURING THE MEAL

A meal isn't just a refueling stop; if it was we'd just get the food in our mouths as quickly and efficiently as possible and then move on. More than just fueling, meals are social events, and the focus should be both on good food and good conversation. To help maintain that focus, everything you do at the table should be unobtrusive, so don't eat noisily, smack, wave your fork in the air while talking, lean across the table, or snap open a napkin.

---

a word on beverages

Beverages have a set of manners all their own. Remember to

- Use your napkin to blot your lips before taking a drink.
- Take a drink only when you have no food in your mouth.
- Sip instead of gulping.
- Take only one or two swallows at a time.
- Use a straw quietly—no slurping or blowing bubbles.

WHEN FINISHED, *place utensils at the 4:20 clock position to indicate the course is finished.*

WHEN FINISHED, *leave the spoon in a shallow bowl.*

WHEN FINISHED, *place the spoon on the underplate when the bowl is deep or footed.*

fingers or fork?

What foods can you eat with your fingers and how do you know when it's okay? Picnics, barbecues, and fast-food restaurants are all prime candidates for finger foods, while more upscale restaurants or a dinner at someone's home is not. Another clue is the messiness factor. If the food is sauced, has gravy, or is loaded with toppings, choose your fork.

ASPARAGUS	**Fingers** when served on a separate side plate with a dipping sauce. **Fork** when it's served on a dinner plate and already sauced.
BACON	**Fingers** when it's crispy and would break into little pieces if you tried to cut it. **Fork** when it's limp, thick, greasy, or already in pieces.
CHICKEN	**Fingers or fork** when it's fried. In the South, fingers are the norm. **Fork** when it's broiled, baked, roasted, or covered with sauce or gravy.
FRENCH FRIES	**Fingers** when served with a sandwich or other finger food. **Fork** when served as part of a main meal that's eaten with a fork. **Fork** when the fries are covered with gravy or ketchup.
PIZZA	**Fingers** when the pizza can be picked up without too much mess. **Fork** when it's gooey or has lots of toppings. In either case, use your fork to eat any of the toppings that fall to your plate.
SHRIMP	**Fingers** when served in a bowl or platter with a dip, or tail-on in shrimp cocktail. **Fork** when served tail-less in a shrimp cocktail or as a main course.
TACOS	**Fingers** when the taco is crispy. **Fork** when the taco is soft, unless it has little sauce and can be eaten neatly. As with pizza, use your fork to eat any filling that falls to the plate.

Most people won't notice a mechanical error, like using the wrong fork; they will remember the gross violations such as chewing with your mouth open or belching. Here are a few tips to refine your presence at the table.

Elbows?

A nice upright posture signals that you are attentive, engaged, and ready to participate. You don't need to sit ramrod straight at the dinner table, but hunching over your plate or slouching back in your chair sends a negative message.

As for keeping your elbows off the table, this drummed-into-us taboo applies only when you're actually eating. Between courses or when you're finished, it's fine to lightly rest your elbows on the table. In fact, putting your elbows on the table while leaning forward a bit during a conversation shows that you're listening intently. However, resting your head in your hands shows you're too tired—or bored—to participate.

Refrain from fidgeting—drumming your fingers, fiddling with utensils, jiggling your knee—and always keep your hands away from your face and hair. Tipping your chair onto the back legs is not only dangerous but you risk breaking the chair.

When something on the table is within easy reach of your arm, you can lean forward slightly to get it but don't lean past the person sitting next to you or lunge across the table. Remember to say "Please" and "Thank you" when someone passes you something.

Seasoning, Cutting, and Chewing

Always taste your food before seasoning it. Hastily covering a dish with salt or drowning it in ketchup risks offending the cook. Assuming that the dish is well seasoned to begin with is an implicit compliment to whoever prepared it.

Cut your food into one or two bite-sized pieces at a time because cut food cools and dries out more quickly. The exception to the rule is when you help a young child

assorted table tips

- When using your napkin, try to avoid leaving stains (especially lipstick) on a monogram or other embroidery—they're hard to remove.
- Use a piece of bread or your knife as a pusher, not your fingers.
- It's okay to sop up gravy; just be neat about it. At home, you can hold a piece of bread in your fingers to sop—just don't get your fingers wet. At a restaurant or someone else's house, use a fork: Put a bite-sized piece of bread into the gravy, spear it with your fork, sop, and eat.
- What about picking up bones, like chop or chicken bones? Always wait until your host or hostess picks them up or invites you to do so, and use the bone as a handle.
- If you need to leave the table, say, "Please excuse me," or for children, "May I be excused, please."
- When you've finished eating, put your utensils in the 4:20 position and offer your thanks for the meal.
- Use a straw quietly—no slurping or blowing bubbles.

cut his food or prepare a plate for an elderly person or someone with a disability.

Once you start eating, take a manageable bite, chew well, and swallow before taking another. Smacking, slurping, and collecting food in a ball in one cheek are major faux pas. But the number-one offense, a deal breaker for most people, is chewing with your mouth open or talking with your mouth full. If you have more than a few words to say, rest your fork on your plate and speak before you resume eating. Along the same lines, avoid taking a drink when you have food in your mouth. Swallow your food, pat your lips with your napkin, then take a drink.

CONVERSATION— AN ESSENTIAL INGREDIENT

Conversation is the other essential ingredient to every meal. If everyone kept his eyes on his plate and ate in silence, the meal wouldn't be very pleasurable, no matter how good the food. At the table, there are some conversational mechanics to keep in mind:

- Don't try to talk and eat at the same time.
- Look at the person you are speaking to.
- Talk to people on either side of you or across the table.
- Don't shout down the table.
- Show an interest in what others are saying; make comments and answer questions.
- Be a good listener.
- Be careful not to interrupt.
- Stay clear of offensive language and gross or sensitive topics.
- Only make positive comments about the meal and thank the cook and hostess.

For the most part, avoid controversial topics such as money, politics, and religion. That's not to say you can't discuss the news of the day, but be careful if you are with people who are staunchly on the opposite end of any spectrum. Also, stay clear of unpleasant topics. Talking about the details of your poor health or an operation can spoil the appetite of others. Repeating gossip ranges from mean to unethical. And at a family meal, use the time positively to regroup and enjoy one another's company, not as a time to discipline or criticize.

Safe Topics

You can always count on pop culture—sports, sports personalities, TV, music, and films. Local arts events, special school programs, or seasonal events are other good options, as are travel, vacations, and that old standby, the weather. But if the conversation does stray onto controversial ground, here are a few tips for defusing it:

- Stick to the issues and facts that you know.
- Talk about the subject without offending or making it personal.
- If you think the conversation is becoming personal or offensive, curb your inclination to respond.
- Don't argue—it's tough to argue when the other person refuses to participate.

- Whenever you want to move off a controversial topic, say so and then have another safe conversation piece ready: "I think we may never agree on this, but I know we both want the Saints to win this year. Did you see their last game?"

ENDING THE MEAL

Just as there are conventions to begin the meal, there are certain customs to end it. On a busy weeknight, the meal may be over as soon as everyone has finished dessert. At a dinner party or lazy Sunday brunch, everyone may linger for coffee or conversation. So how do you know when the meal is over? Just as your host invited you to begin, it's up to him to signal the end of the meal by getting up or perhaps offering coffee in the living room.

At the end of the meal, place your utensils at the 4:20 position (see illustration, page 69) to signal that you're finished. Then wait for the "head of the table" to rise. Fold your napkin loosely and place it to the left of your place setting, then rise and push your chair back under the table. At a dinner party or formal event, a gentleman may again assist the lady on his right with her chair. Be sure to thank your host or hostess and the cook. At home or with good friends, offer to help clear the table.

WHEN THINGS GO WRONG

Dealing with unexpected difficulties at the dinner table can be challenging. Most can be managed gracefully just by staying calm and keeping your sense of humor.

Spills. If you spill food on the table, neatly pick up as much as you can with a clean spoon or the blade of your knife; then wet a corner of your napkin in the water glass and dab the spot. If you knock over a drink, quickly set the glass upright and apologize to your tablemates. Use your napkin, or get a cloth or sponge and mop up the liquid right away. In someone's home, alert your

finger bowls: retro chic

Finger bowls are little glass bowls filled with cool or lukewarm water, sometimes garnished with a slice of lemon or a floating flower, and placed on top of an empty dessert plate. They're usually presented after a main course that involves messy finger foods such as lobster or ribs, so you can clean your hands for dessert. Dip your fingers—one hand at a time—in the water, swirl or swish gently, lightly shake off the excess, and dry them with your napkin. Then move the finger bowl (and accompanying doily, if there is one) to the upper left of your place setting, leaving the plate for the dessert.

At picnics and barbecues, you can offer disposable towelettes. Or pass a tray of wet rolled-up cotton napkins with a pair of tongs. Pass the tray around again to collect the used cloths.

host and help with the cleanup. In a restaurant, discreetly signal the server, who will put a napkin over any stains. (See also Chapter 9, "Dining Out," page 100.)

Food that's too hot or spoiled. If a bite of food is too hot, quickly take a swallow of water or any cold drink. If that's impossible or doesn't help, discreetly spit the food onto your fork or spoon (preferably not into your fingers and definitely not into your napkin), and put it on the edge of the plate. (If it's scalding, get it out of your mouth any way you can—safety trumps manners every time.) The same goes for a bad oyster, clam, or any other food that tastes spoiled. Remove it from your mouth quickly and unobtrusively.

Gristle, bones, or pits. There are two ways to remove something inedible from your mouth. One: Use your fingers to remove the item quickly and discreetly and place it on the side of your plate. Cup your hand in front of your mouth or raise your napkin to shield the removal. It's better not to put the food into your napkin—it's unpleasant for your server or it could fall into your lap. Two: Lift your fork back up to your lips or into your mouth and, using your tongue, gently push the unwanted item back onto your fork. Then place the item on the side of your plate. This second maneuver definitely requires some practice, and many people prefer to use fingers in all cases. Overriding the mechanics is the idea that however you remove food from your mouth, do it discreetly. If necessary, excuse yourself to the restroom and deal with it there.

Wayward food. If you notice a bit of food caught on your teeth, try to discreetly rub it off with your tongue. If the food stays put, excuse yourself from the table and

Q: *I was a guest at a small dinner party last week, and I found a hair in a helping of risotto. I didn't want to embarrass the hostess, but I couldn't bring myself to eat even a bite of it. No one said anything, but the hostess must surely have noticed my untouched serving. Should I have told her the reason once we were in private?*

A: You get a gold star for not bringing it up, since finding a hair, that proverbial fly in the soup, or any other foreign object should remain unmentioned. At the table, you don't want to call the hostess's or anyone else's attention to the problem. You did your best in an awkward situation, and in the process saved the hostess any embarrassment.

You can leave the incident unmentioned entirely, but if she asks you about it, tell her in private. At a restaurant, on the other hand, you can ask the waiter to bring you a fresh portion—just don't make a fuss.

If a foreign object isn't detected until you have it in your mouth, remove it discreetly with your fingers or your fork or spoon and put it on the side of your plate. It's then up to you whether to continue eating the food or leave it be.

remove it in the restroom. Using toothpicks and floss isn't appropriate at the table.

If you notice food stuck in a fellow diner's teeth or on her face or clothes, you're doing her a favor by telling her. If only the two of you are at the table, just say, "Marcy, you seem to have a little something on your chin"; if you're in a group, it's better to silently signal her by catching her eye and lightly tapping your chin with your forefinger.

Coughing and sneezing. When you feel a sneeze or a cough coming on, cover your mouth and nose with a handkerchief or tissue—or your napkin, if that's the only thing within reach. (In an emergency, your hand is better than nothing at all. Then excuse yourself to the restroom to wash up.) If a coughing or sneezing bout is prolonged, excuse yourself until it passes.

Coughing and sneezing often lead to nose blowing. Never blow your nose at the table. If you need to, excuse yourself and go to the restroom, where you can blow your nose and wash your hands afterward.

PART II
out and about

CHAPTER 7 Living with Neighbors 79

CHAPTER 8 Around Town 91

CHAPTER 9 Dining Out 100

CHAPTER 10 Traveling Near and Far 119

CHAPTER 11 Sports and Recreation 136

CHAPTER 12 Attending Performances 155

CHAPTER 13 Tipping 165

CHAPTER 14 Volunteering 175

CHAPTER 15 Official Life 179

living 7 with neighbors

Paul Simon put it well: "One man's ceiling is another man's floor." So did Robert Frost when he wrote, "Good fences make good neighbors." Whether they live in an apartment building or a suburban community, good neighbors respect boundaries and are aware that their everyday behavior affects the people who live around them. They're willing to exercise self-restraint and sometimes give up what they want in order not to inconvenience or impose on others. Without compromising their principles, they live up to their responsibility to promote peaceful, friendly relationships among neighbors.

[MEETING NEW NEIGHBORS]

Being hospitable to newcomers is a time-honored American tradition.

Calling on new neighbors is one of those rare instances when dropping by unannounced *is* good manners. Initial meetings are usually casual and brief. If you see your new neighbor in his yard, go over and say "hello" or knock on his door and introduce yourself. You might be invited in, or not if they're not ready for "company," but either way keep the visit short. The goal is simple: to welcome them and exchange names and perhaps telephone numbers. If the house is full of movers, just extend your welcome and promise to come back at a less hectic time. There's no statute of limitation on meeting neighbors. If you become aware of newcomers weeks or even months after they move in, you can still knock on the door and introduce yourself.

Welcome Gifts and Offers to Help

A welcome-to-the-neighborhood gift will brighten the newcomer's day and ease the hassle of settling in. Typically, gifts are homey and inexpensive: a plate of cookies, a bouquet of garden flowers, a stack of local take-out menus, or an extra phone book. If they're not at home when you stop by, you might leave your gift and a note in a safe place. (Don't forget to include your address so they know which neighbor you are.)

Offers of assistance require sensitivity to a new neighbor's actual needs. In most cases, you're a stranger to your new neighbors, and some may not feel comfortable accepting your well-intentioned offer, say, to babysit or use your pool, until they know you better. If you make an offer, say when you'll be available and what you can do. "If you'd like help getting the garden started, I'm available on Saturday afternoon until 5 o'clock." Only volunteer for things you are truly willing and able to help with.

Let new neighbors know you're happy to answer questions and give directions. Information about schools, places of worship, town services, online community forums, restaurants, grocery stores, good places to shop, and reliable service providers is always useful.

It isn't helpful to impose on your new neighbor's time, gossip about other neighbors, or in any way bad-mouth the neighborhood. Only an inconsiderate neighbor would use a first meeting to campaign for their religion, political party, or favorite local cause.

WHEN YOU'RE THE NEW NEIGHBOR

Who makes the first contact when someone moves into a neighborhood? It really doesn't matter who takes the first step. When you see a neighbor fetching the mail or recognize a person from the neighborhood when you're out, take a few moments to smile and introduce or identify yourself: "Hi. I'm Lynn Kovak, and we just moved to Hilltop Road. I believe we're neighbors." In multiunit dwellings, communal areas—elevator, laundry, exercise room—offer opportunities to say "hi" to a neighbor you haven't met and initiate a little pleasant conversation. Regardless of who makes the first move, meeting and greeting is a fundamental of good manners.

Thanks!

As the newcomer, you're likely to be on the receiving end of gifts, advice, and helping hands. It's certainly okay to decline help politely if you don't need it right then or postpone visits until you're a little more settled. But do be sure to show your appreciation to your new neighbors for their thoughtfulness. Verbal thanks are the simplest, but an offer of a cold drink to someone who helped you unload boxes or a simple note of thanks when you return the plate the cookies came on shows your appreciation and friendliness.

Welcome to Our New Home

A housewarming is one of the few parties you can throw for yourself. While it can be any type of party, a casual affair such as a backyard barbecue is an excellent opportunity to introduce neighbors to your family and old friends. You're not expected to invite the entire neighborhood, but be sure to include next-door neighbors and anyone you see regularly. (For more on housewarming parties see "Housewarmings," page 313.)

Establishing Your Boundaries

When you move into a new neighborhood, you may wish to establish your willingness or unwillingness to participate in neighborhood activities. Not everyone wants to join the homeowners' association or sign up for Neighborhood Watch. When asked, it's fine to state what you will or won't do: "Between my job and getting the kids settled, I really don't have time to join right now. But do call me if you need a cake or pie for an event." (For more on saying "no" politely, see "The Courteous 'No,'" page 9.)

On the other hand, it's smart to show support for your community and to participate when you can. You can maintain your privacy without being seen as standoffish. A donation to a local organization is a perfectly legitimate way to show community support. By attending the occasional block party or association get-together, you'll meet people and your neighbors will appreciate your presence. You can also look for everyday opportunities to show interest, such as buying lemonade from the children who set up a stand on the corner.

NEIGHBORLY BASICS

Good neighbors don't impose. But what exactly is an imposition? Some people enjoy casual, over-the-fence or hallway contact while others want their neighborhood relationships more structured. As you get to know neighbors and by paying attention to individual lifestyles, customs, and social cues, you'll learn their preferences. While not written in stone, here are some basics to keep things neighborly:

Greet neighbors whenever you see them. A smile, a wave, and a pleasant "hello" are probably the easiest ways to show neighbors that they matter to you. If you don't know a neighbor's name, ask.

Have an occasional chat. There's a lot you can learn through casual conversations: Discover a shared interest or catch up on news.

Call ahead before visiting. Some neighbors happily pop in and out of each other's homes without warning, but not all neighbors do. Call and ask if it's convenient for you to stop by.

Limit visits to a reasonable amount of time. Be attuned to what your neighbors are doing, and leave at the first hint that they're ready for the visit to end.

Be considerate of neighbors' schedules. Don't waylay neighbors in the hall or on the street for a long chat. Say "hello" and then call to make a date to get together.

Don't take advantage of a neighbor's expertise or talent. Living on the same street as a doctor, lawyer, mechanic, or anyone with special skills doesn't entitle neighbors to ask for free consultations or services.

Say thanks for any favors. Make sure you always say "Thank you," and be willing to return the favor.

Be respectful of privacy. Living in close quarters makes it all too easy to overhear conversations in hallways, on elevators, or around the pool. It can take some effort *not* to eavesdrop. And never repeat what you accidentally overhear.

Be respectful of property. Always ask for permission before entering anyone else's property. In apartment houses and condominium neighborhoods, do your part to keep common areas clean and report any damage to maintenance.

Tips for Apartment and Condominium Dwellers

You live in close quarters with people whom you may or may not know. While you each have your own private space, you share walls, ceilings, and common areas as well. Keep the following in mind to promote a pleasant living experience for all:

- **Common areas.** It may be the responsibility of a professional maintenance staff to clean and maintain hallways, elevators, laundry rooms, common living rooms, recreation areas, lawns, and shrubbery, but help take responsibility for keeping these areas neat and litter-free and report any damage to maintenance.

- **Trash disposal.** Use designated containers for trash and recycling. If the bin is overflowing, leave your trash bagged neatly and immediately report the problem to maintenance.

Q: *We have a neighbor who drops by and never calls first. I like her, but she shows up so often that I've started pretending that I'm not at home. There must be a better way to handle the problem.*

A: It sounds as if you haven't discussed this with your neighbor, so she probably thinks that you enjoy her unannounced visits. Using tact and patience, let her know that you prefer to be called first. The next time she shows up, you can say something like, "I'm glad to see you, Kathy, but I'm really busy right now. I'll call you later and let's set a time to get together." Follow up by calling and making a date for a specified day and time. Do this a few times, and she should get the message.

A more direct approach is to bring up the subject of visits. You could say, "Kathy, I enjoy our get-togethers so much, but it will work much better for me if we each call first to make sure the timing is good." By expressing enthusiasm about your visits with your neighbor, you can keep your friendship going, but in a more manageable way.

- **Noise.** Ceilings, floors, walls—at least one of them will connect you with a neighbor. Apartment and condo dwellers accept a certain amount of noise as a fact of life: phones ringing, babies crying, music playing. Establish quiet times in the morning and evenings. Common sense says that vacuuming at 10:00 PM is discourteous. It doesn't take long to figure out when your neighbors are home and when they're out. If there's a chance that your aerobics workout may disturb the guy below, be proactive and ask him. The same holds true for your daughter's trumpet practice. It's easier to come to an agreement ahead of time than be the subject of someone's complaint.

Tips for Homeowners

Your home may be your castle, but as a good neighbor it's important to keep your property looking neat, and to follow any local ordinances regarding lawn care, trash disposal, and yard sales.

- **Neat exterior.** There's no question that standards in property care vary person to person. Tastes can be varied, too, but so long as neighbors maintain their property, there's no call to criticize their fondness for garden gnomes.

- **Trash.** Bag garbage and stash it in tightly lidded containers (to discourage animal interest) and secure recycling so it doesn't scatter in the wind. Taking the trash to the curb isn't usually a problem, but bringing back the containers can be. Retrieve them as soon as you can.

- **Lighting.** When you install outdoor lighting, including holiday lights, consider your neighbors' point of view: Does the light shine right in their window? Is it on all night?

- **Power tool noise.** You may love the smell of freshly cut grass in the morning, but the roar of a lawn mower at 6:00 AM is unlikely to thrill anyone else. Limit the use of lawn mowers, leaf blowers, power tools, and the like to reasonable times or when permitted by town ordinances.

- **Leaf blowing and snow blowing.** When using leaf blowers or snowblowers, be careful not to blow leaves or snow onto the sidewalk or your neighbors' property.

- **Fall leaves.** Falling leaves respect no property lines, and the ones that fall in your yard, even from a neighbor's tree, are all yours.

Children at Play

When lessons in consideration start early, most children will have a fairly good understanding of what's off-limits by the time they reach school age. Still, it's up to parents to keep a watchful eye: Youngsters can

> ## lend a helping hand
>
> When something unavoidable (an illness or injury, a military deployment, a death in the family) prevents a neighbor from doing chores, it's kind to pitch in to mow, water, rake, or shovel until the person can make permanent arrangements. Offering to run an errand or delivering a meal is also thoughtful. Consider offering such help to an elderly or disabled neighbor on occasion as well.

pools, trampolines, hoops, and courts

If you wish to share your pool, trampoline, basketball hoop, or tennis or volleyball court with your neighbors, prevent potential conflict or bad feelings by carefully setting and clearly communicating your usage rules. Avoid the blanket over-enthusiastic invitation: "Come on over and use the pool anytime!" Instead, decide on times that work for you, ask neighbors to call first, or arrange a signal with your neighbors (some owners put out a flag when the pool or court is available). Because of liability issues, it's not a good idea to let others use your property when you're not present.

Pets

Dogs can be wonderful companions but terrible neighbors if their owners are irresponsible. As the owner, you are required to keep your dog under control at all times, and you are liable for any damage to person or property. In addition to obeying local collar, leash, registration, and pooper-scooper laws, dog owners should watch out for:

- **Incessant barking.** This will drive even the most tolerant neighbors up the wall. If it's your dog who's the culprit, talk with your vet about possible solutions. But what if the barking dog is your neighbor's and it never ceases while he's away at work? Since he doesn't know that Maxx is barking nonstop, politely let him know.

- **Going AWOL.** Leaving your property and digging in neighbors' gardens, pooping on their lawns, or pawing through garbage will put Rover on the most-wanted list. Keep dogs fenced or leashed and immediately offer to make amends if they make mischief.

- **Aggressive behavior toward passersby.** While your pet may be naturally defending his home, it can be frightening to others. If this is the case, keep Spike inside or in the backyard.

The independent feline is not governable like a dog, and there's no question that they think of birds as tasty treats, to the dismay of your bird-loving neighbor. While

easily forget their manners and the rules of safety when they're curious or caught up in play.

- **Teach children where they can and can't go.** Children shouldn't cross a neighbor's property, play on driveways and in yards without the owner's permission, enter closed gates, or play with pets unless the owners are present. Teach kids that fences mean "stay out."

- **Be aware of noise.** It's important for kids to respect "quiet times," too. Parents should be conscious of other annoyances like a basketball or tennis ball bouncing off a garage, or loud music. Teach children to walk softly on communal stairs, in halls, and on floors above neighbors.

you may not be able to keep Sylvester confined to your yard, a bell on his collar might give the birds a fighting chance.

Yard Sales

Tag sales, yard sales, moving sales, garage sales—they're an American institution. If you're planning to turn your "stuff" into someone else's treasure, take a moment to consider your neighbors. Yard sales have an impact on parking and the increased foot and car traffic can be an inconvenience as well. Begin by letting your near neighbors know your plan and be sure to follow your town ordinances. Most neighbors won't mind the signs and the hubbub for a weekend, but they won't appreciate a sale that turns into a permanent flea market. At the end, take down any signs and then put away the unsold items or arrange for their disposal or donation to a charity.

Borrowing and Lending

It's neighborly to be generous, but frequent borrowers can become neighborhood pests. While it's preferable not to borrow from neighbors, follow these etiquette principles if you do:

Ask for the item but don't persist. If your neighbor says "no" or seems at all reluctant, drop the matter with a polite, "I understand."

Give a time when you will return the item and be punctual. If the lender says she needs the item back by a certain time, don't abuse her trust.

Return the item in at least as good condition as when you borrowed it. Refill the tank before you take

---

bad gossip/good gossip

Everyone knows what bad gossip is: spreading false or unsubstantiated rumors, revealing information that should be kept private, breaking confidences, and generally dishing the dirt on people who aren't around to defend themselves. But all gossip isn't inherently evil. Tapping into the neighborhood grapevine can be a good way to learn important news—the arrival of a new family, an upcoming vacation, a neighbor's illness. Good gossip is informative, bad gossip is hurtful, and common sense will signal the difference.

---

the mower back. When "borrowing" a carton of milk or a can of motor oil, replace it exactly—same brand and size.

Repair, replace, or pay for anything that's damaged, broken, or lost. Don't just tell your neighbor what happened (or worse, ignore the whole thing) and expect him to let the matter slide. So don't borrow anything you could not afford to replace. If you're not a lender, then it's fine to say so: "I'm sorry, it's my policy not to lend things."

Soliciting Neighbors

Many neighbors will try to help out when another neighbor, especially a child, asks them to make a cash donation or purchase an item such as wrapping paper or cookies for a fund-raising event. But no one should be subjected to endless solicitations, no matter how worthy the cause. Be considerate of your neighbors' patience and budgets; limit solicitations and never use high-pressure tactics.

Outside solicitors—salespeople, people seeking employment, religious groups, charitable and political canvassers, and census takers—generally have legitimate motives, but it's wise to be cautious. Even if you've checked a solicitor's credentials and are certain that he or she is legitimate, don't offer referrals or give out any information about your neighbors. It's okay to turn away these solicitors politely. A simple, "Thank you for your time, but we don't accept solicitations" or "I'm not able to donate this year," is all you need to say.

It's Party Time!

It's all a matter of perspective: Your fabulous party with the awesome soundtrack could be your neighbors' nightmare. Many buildings, towns, and cities have noise restrictions or ordinances that address not just times but decibel levels as well. On occasion, it's nice to invite your neighbors to your party. But if that's not the case this time, it's a good idea to give them a heads-up before the event, as well as your phone number so they can call if they're disturbed. (Better you than the police!) During your party, step outside once in a while to check the noise level. If your neighbor does complain, immediately take steps to turn down the volume.

When planning your party, consider how it will affect parking. If communal parking is limited, make sure your guests don't take over your neighbors' spaces. You could

- Recommend carpooling or public transportation.
- Hire parking attendants for large gatherings.

Q: *I don't mind lending, but my neighbor, Jim, never brings anything back on time. How can I get my stuff back without being rude?*

A: While you don't need to embarrass him, you don't have to apologize for asking either. Approach your neighbor in a friendly way: "I'm working in the garden, and I just realized you still have my trimmer. While I'm here, I'd like to pick up Jen's bike pump, too?" If he can't comply at the moment, give him a specific time when you'll come back for the items.

Occasional forgetfulness may be excusable, but since your neighbor makes it a habit, how will you respond to his requests in the future? Keeping your goal of good neighborly relationships in mind, try a little humor: "I'll trade you my paint sprayer for my trimmer." But if it really bothers you, you'll have to be direct: "Jim, I'm reluctant to lend my sprayer to you because you still have my mower." If he still doesn't follow through after you've spoken with him, then you can turn down his requests in the future.

- Arrange off-site parking and shuttle service if necessary.
- Reserve parking in a convenient commercial parking center.

RESOLVING NEIGHBOR-TO-NEIGHBOR ISSUES

Your neighbors' dog buries anything that isn't nailed down. The kids use your yard as a shortcut to school. Next door's recycling blows into your yard. Small annoyances such as these can, over time, grow into resentment and outright feuds. What can you do? Begin by understanding that your neighbor can't control a situation of which he or she isn't aware. A one-on-one conversation is the ideal place to start. Most people are grateful to learn of the problem and will take care of it quickly so their neighbors won't be upset.

HOMEOWNERS' ASSOCIATIONS

Every buyer of a home in a community governed by a homeowners' association automatically becomes a

how to raise a concern politely

Maintaining a good relationship with your neighbors also requires clear, honest communication. If you have a legitimate concern or complaint, let your neighbor know. Your goal is to maintain your good relationship, so don't complain when you're angry. *Wait until you can address the issue with your neighbor calmly.* Be prepared to listen and be open to compromise.

Have a polite word with your neighbor. Take a calm, tactful, nonconfrontational approach: "Karen, I've noticed that after you go to work, the kids are cutting through our yard to get to school." "Sam, for the last couple of weeks, your recycling has blown around the neighborhood. Bungee cords solved that problem for me."

Write a courteous note if you can't catch your neighbor in person. Avoid any language that could be construed as insulting or threatening. Neighborhood petitions may seem like a good idea but are very intimidating, especially if your neighbor isn't aware of the problem.

Ask for help from building owners/managers or homeowners' associations. If your one-on-one conversation didn't do the trick, a letter from a higher authority will remind a negligent owner of the rules he or she is expected to follow. This can also be a reasonable approach if you don't know the owner or if she has a history of disregarding individual complaints.

As a last resort, take the problem to public officials. For serious violations, like a yard full of trash, or a persistent problem, such as an incessantly barking dog, it may help if several neighbors band together to talk with local authorities. An official letter of warning may be necessary. Realize that while this approach may be necessary and it may solve an immediate problem, it can cause resentment and do little to improve overall neighbor relations.

member of the association, subject to its rules. The goal of a homeowners' association is to oversee the community in a way that enhances the value of the houses and ensures a pleasant and attractive community living environment. Each association establishes, communicates, and administers specific common limitations on how homeowners may use their properties, both for the benefit of the individual homeowners and the neighborhood as a whole. Some common association limitations can include:

◆ the color of exterior paint on the house;

◆ yard landscaping (trees, hedges, lawns, plantings);

◆ outdoor lighting and ornaments;

◆ fences;

◆ mailboxes;

◆ pets;

◆ swimming pools, basketball hoops, and swing sets;

◆ laundry lines;

◆ and hours when power equipment may be used.

Before You Buy

It's important to make sure that the association's rules are compatible with your home ownership goals and lifestyle. *Before* buying a house that requires membership in a homeowners' association, familiarize yourself with its particular covenants, conditions, and restrictions (CC&Rs). Even if the house seller or the agent isn't forthcoming with the information, make sure to obtain a copy before purchasing (it's the right of the home buyer

to be aware of the association's CC&Rs and rules— *before* purchase).

Friendly Neighbors, Shared Responsibilities

What does all of this have to do with etiquette? Problems among neighbors or between a homeowner and the homeowners' association board can easily crop up if careful thought isn't applied to basic association living. These problems can be resolved—and often avoided altogether—when homeowners do the following:

◆ **Learn the membership requirements and regulations of your homeowners' association.** Ignorance isn't an excuse. Knowing and abiding by the rules is every homeowner's responsibility.

◆ **Communicate clearly and often.** Go directly to your association board to ask about what you don't understand, voice any concerns, and make suggestions.

◆ **Resolve any concerns and problems factually and calmly.** Homeowners' associations provide sounding boards for resolving problems. Use them judiciously.

◆ **Participate.** Keep current with key happenings, items that are up for vote, and changes in your association's CC&Rs. Attend the association's general homeowners' meetings and be sure to vote. You might even become a member of the association's board.

- **Attend some of your neighborhood social events.** Getting to know your neighbors can greatly enhance your daily living experience. Occasionally inviting your near neighbors to your house is one way to help foster a friendly relationship.

THE AWARE NEIGHBOR

There's a big difference between being nosy and being observant. Good neighbors watch out for one another and do what's appropriate if they see something that seems amiss—newspapers piling up on a doorstep, strange people at a neighbor's home when the neighbor is known to be away, children playing in an unsafe area. No one should be offended if a neighbor inquires about a worrisome situation. Assume you're being asked out of genuine concern. There may be a logical explanation—you canceled the paper and didn't realize it was still being delivered—or you may need to take action.

Watching out for neighbors also involves informing them of any activity that may cause inconvenience. Home renovations create noise and dirt problems that can go on for weeks. A large party may bring parking and noise issues. Neighbors usually understand if you tell them about your plans *in advance* and ask for their tolerance.

HANDLING DIFFICULT NEIGHBORHOOD SITUATIONS

The house down the street has been empty and overgrown for a year, and it's attracting vermin. You suspect that a neighbor's children are neglected or that teens in the neighborhood are forming a gang. Some problems require more than neighborly tolerance; they call for outside professional help. When directly involving yourself could put you in physical danger, 911 is the right call.

For serious property violations, start with your homeowners' or apartment association or co-op board if you have one. If the property is owned by a management company or landlord, talk with other neighbors and perhaps form an ad hoc group to approach them. If you don't get results or there's no neighborhood association, take your complaint to your zoning board or other appropriate public officials. In cases of suspected violence or abuse, you should report the situation to the police or family/children's services as quickly as possible.

YOUR NEIGHBORHOOD AT LARGE

Neighborhoods today are far more likely to be culturally, racially, and ethnically diverse than in the past. Creating a true neighborhood means finding commonality while respecting differences.

Avoid making judgments based on stereotypes. Categorizing individuals by their group is rude at best and can be dangerous. Good neighbors *work* at being open-minded. They don't form opinions until they've gotten to know someone well enough to have an opinion.

Use "people first" language. A person doesn't have to be politically correct to know that labels can cause pain. It's impolite to automatically describe or single out people by their race, national origin, religion, political affiliation, sexual orientation, or physical or mental condition. A person is a "neighbor," not "the foreigner across the hall" or "the lady with the handicapped child." (See "Sensitivity in Language," page 31, for more on people-first language.)

Be interested and ask polite questions. There's no better way to dispel myths and stereotypes than by asking people about lifestyle differences. No one is obligated to explain or defend himself, but when the situation is comfortable and questions are posed out of genuine interest, people often enjoy talking about the way they live and the history of their traditions. "So how do you celebrate Diwali?"

Show respect. Showing respect means accepting different lifestyles and customs. For example, it's respectful not to call an Orthodox Jewish neighbor on Saturday. It's considerate not to host a loud party if your next-door neighbor is ill.

BEING A PEACEMAKER

When neighborhood conflicts arise from ethnic, cultural, or lifestyle differences, some people choose not to get involved. But reticence can often be mistaken for agreement when people are intent on ganging up on someone perceived as different.

Your attitude can be influential, so be sure that neighbors understand your perspective. If neighbors engage in hateful conversation, don't give any appearance of taking part. If you do discuss differences, be certain you know what you're talking about. Keep conversations generalized and don't allow talk to degenerate into personal attacks. Make an effort to meet your neighbors and offer to introduce them to others. Prejudices often melt away when people get together in low-pressure situations. You can't change die-hard bigots, but by your example, you may be able to facilitate tolerance and encourage neighborly relations.

around town

imagine this: You're on your way to a parent inter-view at a potential preschool. Another driver cuts you off and you lean on your horn and make a rude ges-ture. Later, you walk into your meeting and you and the interviewer recognize each other. Not the first impres-sion you want to make. That afternoon you're waiting in the checkout line at the market and you hear someone chewing out the cashier. It's the new neighbor you were just about to ask over for dinner. How do you feel about him now?

Oops! So many people say they really don't *mean* to appear rude when they're out and about, but they're always in a rush. Let's face it: We live in a fast-paced world. It's easy to get wrapped up in our to-do list, obliv-ious of those around us: Snag a parking space, run a "pink" light, grab the groceries, demand service—now! Even unintentional rudeness adds to stress and cre-ates tension. A little kindness (letting the other driver merge into your lane) and civility (saying "thank you" to the store clerk) do make a difference. Try it. Your polite

actions will be an example and a reminder for others. Aren't you more inclined to be nice when someone was just nice to you? You and those around you will have a more pleasant day while "around town."

IN YOUR CAR

Driving the kids to practice, commuting to work, run-ning errands—many people spend a good part of their day in their cars. In today's world, rudeness compro-mises safety in more ways than one, and while we don't want to sound like your high school driver ed teacher, many of the courtesy "rules of the road" are grounded in safety. The two go hand in hand. Most of us can admit to being less than courteous behind the wheel at times. Developing patience and practicing defensive driving will make you a safer and more courteous driver.

Good Manners = Safety

Let's start this discussion with three reminders: 1) Always wear your seat belt and insist that your passengers do. 2) Never drink and drive. 3) Don't text and drive. While they're not really manners per se, these safeguards are the most thoughtful acts of all as they can save lives. Here are four other safety basics:

◆ **Driving a car requires your full attention.**
Distractions, such as putting on makeup, snacking, changing your music, or chatting on a cell phone (which in some places is illegal), or reading (yes, reading!), interfere with your ability to respond physically and mentally. If you must eat, groom, text, or finish your novel, pull off the road to a safe spot.

◆ **Signal your intentions.** Not everyone is a psychic. Using your turn signals before turning or switching lanes is another must.

◆ **Drive at the speed limit.** Believe it or not, driving too slowly can also cause accidents.

◆ **Keep some distance between you and the car ahead of you.** Tailgating is both aggressive and a sure way to rear-end someone who stops suddenly. Most likely you will be at fault if this happens.

◆ **Merge courteously.** Take turns and don't crowd.

road rage

Confrontations over perceived on-the-road slights can escalate to violence and sometimes even injury and death. While aggressive driving is dangerous and discourteous, road rage crosses the line to the criminal. Deliberately belligerent behavior—making a rude gesture, leaning on your horn as hard as you can, or intentionally tailgating someone or cutting them off—is potentially dangerous. You haven't the slightest idea who is behind the wheel of another car; if he or she is prone to anger and reciprocates, you'd be running a serious personal risk by indulging in this sort of provocative behavior. Call 911 to report anyone driving erratically or too aggressively and include the license plate number and a description of the car, if possible.

Driving Don'ts

There's no question that when drivers display a "me first" attitude, it annoys—if not downright angers—other drivers. Individual drivers have their own particular pet peeves, but the following behaviors by either aggressive or clueless drivers can aggravate even patient drivers:

◆ Blocking the passing lane for more than a reasonable amount of time. Even if you are "just going the speed limit" you can trigger frustration in drivers who wish to pass, setting up a dangerous situation. Switch to a nonpassing lane at the first opportunity.

◆ Speeding up when you're being passed.

◆ Driving in the breakdown lane to pass a long line of stopped traffic. (Generally, it's illegal, and don't be surprised if drivers are reluctant to let you back in line.)

- Using high beams to express your anger with another driver.

- Daydreaming at a stoplight after it turns green.

- Making left turns from the right lane, or vice versa.

- Not using turn signals.

- Creeping along while talking on a cell phone.

- "Blocking the box," or becoming stuck in the middle of an intersection. Advancing into it before it's clear leads to gridlock when your light turns red.

Don't Take It Personally

No matter how badly your day has gone, how many traffic jams you've suffered, and how many cars have almost clipped yours as they abruptly changed lanes, keep reminding yourself not to take traffic problems personally. Never focus your generalized anger on a single incident, which could become the flash point for a dangerous confrontation.

"Beep Beep"

Your horn has a voice. The secret is to use it in the right way:

- A succession of short, light beeps: "Hi!"

- A quick little beep: "Heads up—I'm here!"

- A slightly louder, slightly longer beep: "Hey, the light's been green for ten seconds" or "Watch it!"

Not in the wrong way:

- A longer blast, repeated several times: "Come on, let's go—I'm in a real hurry." (Watch it—your impatience level is rising.)

- A long, nonstop blast: "I'm really angry and I've lost control."

When you start taking your frustration out by using your horn, it's a sign you've crossed the line. To cure horn-itis, make a conscious effort to exercise a little patience and use your horn the right way—to let someone know what's happening on the road.

Be Considerate of Your Passengers

Not everyone can handle being driven around by a Danica Patrick. It can be nerve-racking to be a passenger in a car that's being driven too fast: You're not the one at the wheel, and essentially you have no control over your safety. When you're the driver, be aware of your passengers' comfort levels. Slow the speed down a little, take the turns a bit easier, and generally be more considerate in everything you do. Your passengers will feel safe and confident in your driving skills.

As the driver, you set the tone in the car. Yelling "Be quiet" at your passengers sort of defeats your goal. Speak pleasantly and calmly when making requests.

Handling a Backseat Driver

You know the type, they question your every move and offer unsolicited advice: "If we were in the other lane we'd be there by now," "You could have passed him easily," "Why did you turn on your blinker so early?" It's distracting and annoying, and there's no perfect retort that will silence your critic. Ignoring it or using humor is your best bet, but if it's more than you can handle, pull over (that will get his attention) and say, "Tim, please stop. It's hard for me to focus with all these suggestions."

Keeping Your Cool at Intersections

Traffic lights are there to be obeyed, not outfoxed—so don't try to race through a yellow light. It's hard to imagine what the second or third driver through a red light is thinking. "I've waited long enough and it's my turn now"? "One more won't matter"? Not only is it a setup for an accident, but it also contributes to further congestion and frustration as the cross traffic must wait for the intersection to clear.

If you have a green light and the block ahead is congested with traffic, don't cross the intersection until you know there's no chance of blocking everyone once the light turns red. This may mean waiting through a light cycle.

"Right on red" doesn't mean you have the right of way over cars that have the green light. At rush hour or at a congested intersection, it's better to wait for the green light instead of turning in front of drivers waiting for the intersection to clear so they can proceed. Turning right on red will overburden the traffic pattern and contribute to congestion.

Curiosity, Respect, or Emergency?

Rubbernecking—slowing to a crawl to check out an accident—is disrespectful to the victims, a hindrance to those trying to help, and a sure way to cause a traffic backup. Besides, you may see more than you bargained for. Yes, you should slow down so you don't endanger anyone, but keep moving.

Of course, let emergency vehicles pass by pulling over and coming to a complete stop. Keep the volume down inside the car so that you can hear any approaching sirens.

Parking Etiquette

Center your car in a marked space. It's rude to take up two spaces or to cram an SUV or other large vehicle into a space reserved for compacts. If someone is waiting to turn into a parking space, don't steal it. Nor should your passenger stand in an empty space to save it. If you encounter a stealer or a saver, just ignore them and move on. Cruise the lot or block until you find a spot, put your blinker on, and wait for the other car to vacate the space—that's the right way to indicate you want the space. Leave enough room on both sides for passengers to get out without bumping the adjacent car. When you're on a date or the weather's bad, it's kind to drop your passengers off at the entrance, then go and find a parking spot.

Taking Responsibility

Accidents do happen, and when they do, do the right thing. If no one's around and you bump the car next to you or accidentally take off someone's side mirror, leave a note with your name and number to handle insurance with the owner. It's also important to be a responsible borrower. When asking to use another's vehicle, say what you'll be using it for and for how long and ask for the appropriate paperwork, such as registration and insurance card, just in case. Then return the vehicle in *exactly* the same condition it was borrowed, plus a full tank of gas.

WHEN YOU'RE THE PASSENGER

One of the most annoying people in a car—to driver and other passengers alike—is the backseat driver, the person who can't keep his mouth closed, spouting off driving "tips." While most adults won't need a refresher on passenger courtesy, here's a good list to use with kids of all ages. The courteous passenger

- Does exactly as the driver instructs. Think of the driver as the captain of a ship or plane: She's the boss. She controls the seating arrangements and the knobs on the dashboard. She also sets the rules about food, beverages, smoking, and the radio.

- Buckles up and stays in his seat. Always!

- Asks if it's okay to open a window and keeps head and hands inside the vehicle.

- Keeps the volume down. Yelling, arguing, and playing loud music can distract the driver. So can constant cell calls.

- Keeps the car clean.

- Offers to share expenses, such as gas and tolls. (A good tip for teens.)

- Thanks the driver.

THE INS AND OUTS OF CAR POOLING

It's greener—and usually cheaper—to carpool. You might even save time by taking advantage of HOV (High Occupancy Vehicle) lanes to zip into town. Since you don't have to do all the driving, it can also lessen the stress of being behind the wheel every day. Many employers, states, and municipalities offer bulletin boards or services to help put car pools together.

Making It Work

The key to a smooth-running car pool is having everyone agree on the rules ahead of time.

- Share expenses equally. If drivers rotate, then there's no need to reimburse anyone.

- Set the car "rules." Radio on or off, types of music or news, windows up or down, how much talking, cell phones on or off, and if smoking, eating, or drinking is allowed. It's easier to keep the rules the same for all the cars in the pool so you won't have to remember, "Oh, it's okay to snack in Jeb's car but not in Joelle's."

- Decide in advance how you'll proceed when a driver is ill or his car has mechanical problems. It's a good idea for members to have one another's home, work, and cell phone numbers to make a backup plan.

- So that everyone gets to work on time, decide on the maximum time you'll wait for passengers. Five minutes is standard in most car pools.

- No matter how friendly you are with your fellow carpoolers, don't request a stop along the way. Picking

> **Q:** *Another mom and I carpool our daughters to day camp, but she often shows up a few minutes late—just enough that I miss my train to work. I've explained the problem, but she always has an excuse. What can I do?*
>
> **A:** One solution: When it's her turn to drive, offer to drop your daughter at her house on your way to the station. If that's not possible, simply end the car pool. Say, "I'm sorry, but our schedule isn't getting me to work on time, so I need to make other plans." Perhaps you can arrange something with another mom. If you do, be sure to make your morning timeline very clear to her right up front.

up a quart of milk or your dry cleaning is something you do on your own time.

⎡ RUNNING ERRANDS ⎤

The grocery store, the mall, the home improvement center—many of our daily or weekend encounters are with store clerks and salespeople. While it's to any business's benefit to train their staff to give excellent, courteous service, courtesy is a two-way street. It's essential to treat salespeople with respect. Say "hello," "please," and "thank you" and your errands will run all the more smoothly. The more courteous customers are, the

more likely salespeople are to respond in kind—and vice versa.

Don't hold salespeople responsible for things beyond their control. It's not their fault that the shirt you want is out of stock, the price seems too high, or you have to make an exchange instead of getting a refund. If you want to complain, either ask to speak to a manager or write a letter of complaint to the store. (See also Chapter 16, "Notes and Letters," page 197.)

Smart Shopping

Shopping can be a pleasure or a chore. Here are ways to make the experience a pleasant one for sales staff and customers, as well as for yourself.

- At the cash register, have your money, checkbook, or credit card ready.

- *Never* talk on a cell phone when you're paying for your purchases at the cash register. It's disrespectful to the cashier and the delay you cause is disrespectful to other customers.

- When you're shopping with a friend, it's nice to stop your conversation when you get to the register instead of ignoring or talking over the clerk.

- It's a good idea to shop with children when they're not too hungry or tired. If your child has a habit of disrupting things when you shop, make arrangements to leave him at home whenever possible.

Shopping "à la Cart"

How do you rate yourself on these other shopping dos and don'ts?

Do return an unwanted item to its proper place instead of stashing it on the nearest shelf.

Do tell an employee if you drop an item that breaks instead of just hurrying away from the mess.

Don't use a cell phone for long phone chats while in the aisles and the checkout line. A quick call to see if you forgot something is okay.

Don't block the aisles with your cart, especially oversized carts.

Do follow the express lane rules.

Do let those ahead of you in line go first when a new checkout line opens up.

Do make your items as accessible to the cashier as possible.

Do place the divider on the conveyor belt once you've unloaded all of your items.

Don't keep everyone else waiting in the checkout line while you go get something you forgot. It's better to finish checking out and go through the line again.

Do treat the cashier respectfully.

Do pitch in and bag your own items if the store is busy and there's no one bagging at your counter.

Do leave your cart in the spot designated for carts, not in a parking space in the lot.

---

sticky salesperson situations

WHAT CAN YOU DO WHEN...

... A SALESPERSON IS NOWHERE TO BE FOUND IN A DEPARTMENT STORE? Go to the nearest available register and ask where you might find one. If the cashier doesn't know, politely ask to speak to the manager.

... A SALESPERSON LATCHES ON TO YOU AND HOVERS WHEN YOU'RE BROWSING? So he won't worry that he'll lose his sale's commission, just say, "Thanks, but I'd rather just look on my own right now. If you'll tell me your name, I'll ask for you when I check out."

... A SALESPERSON TELLS YOU IT "LOOKS FABULOUS" ON YOU AND YOU'RE NOT SURE YOU AGREE? Thank her for her help and go your way: "Thanks so much! I'll let you know if I decide to go with it."

... A SALESPERSON IS RUDE TO YOU, KEEPS YOU WAITING, OR DOESN'T SAY "THANKS." Overwhelmed or underpaid, anyone can have a bad day. Even if your encounter was less then ideal, a *friendly* "thanks" from you is still in order as you end the transaction. If it was a serious breach, let the management know that someone on their staff is forgetting basic courtesies.

At the Bank

Banks probably have the fairest line system: Customers wait in a line until called to the next available teller. Customers expect privacy, so keep your eyes and ears to yourself while you're waiting, and lower your voice when speaking to the teller to keep your information private as well.

At the ATM, stand back and don't try to get a peek at whatever transactions the person ahead of you is making. Be patient, and don't complain if someone is taking more time than you think necessary.

Clothing Stores

Make an effort to get in and out of dressing rooms as quickly as possible during busy times. When you're finished in the dressing room, turn clothes right side out and put them back on the hangers or loosely fold them instead of leaving them in a heap on a bench or the floor. Then, depending on store policy, either leave the clothes inside or return them to a sales attendant.

Pharmacies

Just as at the bank, wait your turn to approach the counter to protect customer privacy. If your prescription medicine is expensive, your co-payment has increased, or there's some other issue with your insurance coverage, taking out your frustration on the person serving you isn't fair. All of these decisions are made by the drug and insurance companies, not by the pharmacist or the salesclerk. Unless you're prepared to wait, call in or drop off a prescription in advance. Pharmacists also have to deal with incoming calls from doctors and other

customers while giving prescription filling the attention it deserves, and that takes time.

Beauty Salons and Barbershops

Being late can slow things down for other customers for the rest of the day, so do all you can to arrive on time. If

---

cutting ties with your hairstylist

If you're not happy with your cut or color, let your stylist or the salon know as quickly as possible, since it could possibly be fixed the next day. (There is no need to tip for these fixes.) A thornier problem comes when you're thinking about switching stylists (especially from one you've had for a long time), whether at the same salon or elsewhere. First, give fair warning: Let her know what style or color you're looking for and give her a chance to achieve it. Bring pictures when possible so there is something concrete to compare the results against. If it still doesn't work, then it's time to move on.

While it's fine to simply stop going, most stylists say they want to know why a client leaves. Though you may feel awkward, they value the feedback; after all, they can't fix what they don't know is wrong. The key is to be both honest and polite. "I was hoping that we could work toward a new style, but honestly, I think I need a new perspective." Sometimes, it's your circumstances that have changed, and it's fair to let her know: "I've loved having you cut my hair, but I'm afraid my budget needs trimming, too." Thank her for her past service, and consider referring friends to her if it was a question of budget.

---

you need to cancel, do so in advance—ideally at least the day before. Calling to cancel ten minutes before an appointment may well cost your hairdresser or barber money, since your slot can't be filled on such short notice. Some salons will charge for a missed appointment.

Spa Day

By nature a spa is a place to relax and let time slip away, but do be on time for your appointments. Since quiet and relaxation are essential to the experience, spas should remain cell phone– and child-free. In the common areas, dozing, reading, or quiet conversation is the norm. It's fine to talk quietly while having a massage or other treatment but it's equally okay to remain silent. Do, however, give the therapist feedback on your comfort and any problem areas she should know about.

9
dining
out

ow wonderful it is to have someone else cook, serve, and clean up. Whether it's a special occasion at an upscale restaurant, lunch with a potential client, dinner with friends at the local bistro, or pizza with the kids at a chain restaurant, most everyone enjoys eating out. As long as we use our everyday table manners, that's all there is to it. Right?

Not exactly. The more formal the restaurant, the more likely it is that you'll want to watch your p's and q's. But good dining-out behavior applies as much at a coffee shop as it does at a white-tablecloth-and-candles four-star restaurant.

Besides table manners, which can be reviewed in Chapter 6, "Table Manners," page 56, it's good to know when and how to make a reservation and interact with the staff, what to expect in terms of table setting and service, how to order, how to handle any mishaps, how to pay, and how to tip (see Chapter 13, Tipping, p. 165). In addition, there are guidelines for hosting or being a guest at a restaurant meal. This chapter will help you consider the various aspects of dining out so that you can relax and enjoy the experience.

[RESERVATIONS OR NOT?]

Making a reservation is generally a good idea, but it's a must when you're the host. When you call, it's also your opportunity to ask questions and make special requests, such as a table in a quiet corner or on the patio. If you're unfamiliar with the restaurant, here are some things you might want to know:

- Do they accept reservations, and if not, how do they handle seating?
- What's the parking situation?
- Is there a dress code?
- Do they accept credit cards?
- Is there a service charge for large groups?
- Is there a cancellation policy?

Some restaurants will call you or ask that you call back to reconfirm your reservation a day or two ahead—and with good reason, given the number of people who don't cancel when their plans change. Many restaurants now ask for a credit card number when you reserve. If you don't call to cancel, don't be surprised to find a penalty charge on your next statement.

ON ARRIVING

Your first restaurant "etiquette encounters" are with the staff who get you from the parking lot to your table. Thank the **valet parking attendant** as he takes charge of your car. (Coming full circle, you'll reward the parking attendant with your thanks and a tip when your car is returned.)

On entering the restaurant, turn off your cell phone or any other communication device. If you're on call or have children at home with a sitter, put it on silent or vibrate. Then find the person greeting patrons or standing behind the podium in the entryway: the **maître d',** host, or hostess. If it's busy, step out of the way as you patiently wait your turn. Greet the maître d' with a smile and say "Hello." If you've reserved a table, say, "We have a reservation in the name of Mullins"; if not, then make your request: "We'd like a table for four, please." (Note:

Maître d' is the term more often heard in upscale restaurants. It's short for *maître d'hôtel*, a French term meaning "master of the hotel," and refers to the person in charge of the seating and running of the restaurant or dining room. While the terms *host* and *hostess* are similar, in this chapter we'll use *maître d'* to avoid confusion with a restaurant patron who hosts guests.)

If the restaurant has a **coat-check** room, it's your choice whether to check your coat or not, often dependent upon the amount of extra space at the table. Packages, briefcases, umbrellas, and other items are usually checked; exceptions are a notebook, folder, or other items that might be needed at a business meal. Rather than check their handbags, women take them to the table, where they're kept in the lap or at the feet—not on the tabletop. Putting your bag on the back of your chair isn't a good idea; it could be knocked off or easily stolen.

What if your fellow diners arrive at different times?

- If the meal is hosted, always wait for your host to arrive. As the host, make it a point to arrive early to greet your guests.
- In a group of friends, the first person to arrive can wait for the second or ask to be seated to hold the table. Alert the hostess or maître d' to the others in your party.

Being Seated at Your Table

The maître d' or hostess will show you to your table.

If you're ushered to a table in a disappointing location—a heavily trafficked area, under an air conditioner vent, or close by the kitchen, restrooms, or door—it's perfectly okay to ask for a different one. Be calm and polite: "Could we be seated a little farther from the door, please?" or "We'd prefer a table with a little more light, if one is free." You might not be accommodated, especially if the restaurant is a popular one. If that's the case, just grin and bear it. Arguing with the maître d' is unlikely to change the situation.

Who Sits Where?

In some restaurants the maître d' will choose the "best" chair and hold it for the first woman to arrive, but in most places you'll just be shown to your table. It's a nice tradition for the men in the group to then hold chairs for the other women, especially in social, as opposed to business, situations. If you're the host, you'll need to direct your guests to their seats (meaning you should have a seating plan in mind). A group of friends usually alternate men-women and try to split couples to give everyone a chance to chat. Otherwise, here are a few seating tips:

- The better seats are those that look out on the restaurant or a window onto scenery, not at a wall—something to keep in mind when you're hosting a meal or simply wish to give a fellow diner the better view.

- At a table with a banquette or cushy bench, women sit on the bench and men on the chairs opposite them.

- If the host doesn't give directions, guests should ask him where they should sit.

- The host and hostess usually sit opposite each other.

- A male guest of honor—say, a relative whose birthday is being celebrated—is traditionally seated at the hostess's right; a female guest of honor to the host's right.

AT THE TABLE

At most of the more formal restaurants, your place setting will be preset with some items. Others are brought to the table only as they are needed for the courses you've chosen. To begin, you may find

- A service plate in the center of your place setting and a bread plate on your upper left. Any courses— and there could be more than one—ordered before the entrée will be placed on the service plate. The service plate will be replaced by your dinner plate when the waiter brings the main courses.

- A first-course plate in the center of your place setting. This may be the case when no service plate is used. A salad plate may be placed either in the center of your place setting if salad will be served first or to your left if it will follow the first course.

- One or two knives and forks. Even the most formal restaurants rarely set tables with every utensil under the sun. Flatware is usually kept to a minimum, with additional utensils brought out whenever ordered dishes require them. (The exception is a banquet meal, when it saves time to set everything, including coffee cups, on the table.) In either case, the place setting will follow the "outside-in rule," meaning you'll start with the outermost utensils and work your way toward the plate. (For more on table settings, see Chapter 6, "Table Manners," page 56.)

- A water goblet and a wineglass. At more formal restaurants, two wineglasses—the larger one for red wine, the smaller for white. There may also be a champagne flute.
- A napkin, either centered on the service plate or to the left of the fork(s).

Napkins

The first thing you do after being seated and settled is put your napkin in your lap. At some restaurants, the waiter or maître d' will do this for you so go ahead and let him. You might be given a black napkin instead of the usual white one, a growing trend among upscale and thoughtful restaurateurs. The black one is offered to diners who are wearing dark fabric to eliminate the possibility of white lint rubbing off on their clothes.

[**WAITERS ARE PEOPLE, TOO**]

Much of the success and enjoyment of your meal hinges on your interaction with your waiter or waitress. Servers are quick to introduce themselves today—but even if they don't, a polite diner will treat them with respect. Respect doesn't mean thanking a waiter or waitress for every little task performed, but the occasional expression of gratitude is definitely in order. Treating a server as a robot or servant is unforgivably rude, and an imperious or condescending manner shows you not as superior but as a jerk. The following will start you off on the right foot:

> ## "oh, waiter?"
>
> Call your server by catching his eye, or, if he's some distance away, you can raise your hand to about head level, index finger pointing up. If he's looking elsewhere and isn't taking orders at another table, you can also *softly* call out, "Waiter?" or "Sir?" Snapping your fingers or waving your hand furiously is both annoying and disrespectful.

- Respond with a "hello" when your server first greets you.
- Add "please" to your requests, and speak in a friendly tone.
- Look at her as she recites the specials, and don't grimace if she describes something you don't like.

[**THE FINER POINTS OF ORDERING**]

Lots of thought goes into ordering, from choosing the predinner cocktails, to the course selections and the wines served during the meal. Some menus are so extensive that it could take you all night to choose! Still, it's important to make up your mind by the time the others at the table agree that they're ready for the server to take the orders. Here are four things to consider:

- Before you order, make sure everyone else at the table is ready to order as well.

- If you or your table aren't ready, simply tell your server that you need more time. Holding him there as you keep changing your mind keeps him from providing good service to his other tables.

- You don't need to rush your decision about what to order, but don't continually dismiss your server while your group chats away. Taking an excessively long time to place your order can create a lengthy delay before you're served.

- A *closed menu* is the signal that you're ready to order. If you keep browsing the menu after you've decided what you want, the server won't know you're ready.

- If your group wants separate checks, let your server know right at the start, even before you order a drink or appetizer. Asking for individual checks at the end of the meal slows down service and may not even be possible—you'll have to do the math yourselves. And if the restaurant doesn't allow separate checks, better to know it at the start, than the end, of the meal.

- If you do have separate checks, those paying together should order together.

Ordering Predinner Drinks

If there is a host, he (or she) can take charge and ask the guests what they would like. It's fine to order beverages the first time the waiter asks, even if every guest at your table hasn't been seated; latecomers can order when the server returns with the first round.

Ordering Meals

When your server recites a list of daily specials, it's smart to ask the cost of any that interest you, as some can be on the expensive side. This is also a good time to ask about market prices, sometimes noted as M.P. If you're the guest at a meal, however, it's best to let the host ask about any prices. (For menus without prices, see "Tips for Restaurant Hosts and Guests," page 111.)

Once you've narrowed your choices, it's fine to ask your server which dish she recommends. Many restaurants make sure that their staff has an opportunity to sample the menu just so they can give a recommendation. She should also be able to tell you about the ingredients in the dish and how it's prepared.

Is it necessary to order the same number of courses everyone else does? No, and it's certainly not a problem when you're getting separate checks. If you're the only one who orders an appetizer, think about when you'd like it served. It's fine to ask for it before the main course—your companions have drinks, the bread basket, and conversation to occupy them. But if your appetizer is your meal, then ask the server to bring it with the other main courses.

Tell the server if you'd like to share an appetizer or dessert—and possibly even a main course if you know the servings to be huge. Some restaurants charge an extra fee for splits; others let you order a half portion.

This is also the time to request small changes. "I'd like the dressing on the side, please," "Please hold the onions," or "Could I substitute the spinach for the broccoli?" are easy for the kitchen to handle. Making a wholesale change to a dish or asking for multiple substitutions isn't.

If you aim to have a leisurely conversation during the meal, order foods that can be eaten easily. Lobster or crab in the shell or unboned fish could make more demands on your time and concentration than you'd like.

Ordering Wine

Dinner wine should complement the food, so it's best ordered after the menu choices have been made. The person ordering can choose a wine that goes best with the greater number of dishes, ask tablemates about any preferences, or ask the advice of the server—or the wine steward (also called the *sommelier* or, if a woman, *sommelière*). The old rule "red with meat and white with seafood and white meat" is out of date. Nowadays, the focus is people's personal preferences for red or white wine.

For large groups the host should order one each of red and white wine. For smaller groups, ask people's preferences and order by the bottle or glass accordingly.

When the server brings the unopened bottle to the table, he shows it to the orderer. If this is you, nod to confirm that it's the wine you ordered because once the wine is opened, it will be on your bill. If the '01 was on the wine list and the server brings you the '02, or if he brings any wine other than what you ordered, he should tell you so up front and also tell you why. If the wine you ordered is unavailable, a similar wine should be offered *in the same price range*. If the substitute wine offered is unfamiliar to you, it's fine to ask about it and about the price. If the substitute wine is more expensive and a discount hasn't been offered, ask to see the list again and start over.

Your server then uncorks the bottle at your table and pours a small amount of wine into your glass. Briefly swirl the wine in the glass to release its aroma, then sniff before taking a sip. A simple "That's fine" will let him know that the wine neither smells nor tastes off—musty or sour and vinegary. If the waiter hands you the cork, put it directly on the service plate or on the table—there's no need to sniff or squeeze it.

Next, the server pours the wine, serving the host or orderer last. A diner who doesn't care to drink wine should either momentarily place his fingers over the glass when his turn comes or simply say, "No thanks." Turning the glass upside down is *not* the signal to use. From that point on, it's up to the orderer to refill the guests' glasses if the waiter doesn't return to pour. Fill glasses to the widest point of the bowl, both to allow the largest possible surface area for the wine to "breathe" and to leave enough room for the wine to be swirled without spilling.

While you do tip on the wine, there is no charge for the services of a wine steward. (See also Chapter 13, "Tipping," page 165.)

Being Served

The norm is for your waiter to serve your meal and any condiments or sauces on your left and pour beverages on your right. He'll remove dishes and glasses from your right.

Your main course may be served several ways:

- Most often, your plate is prepared in the kitchen and served to you, complete.

- Your server may prepare your entrée tableside, then plate and serve it to you. Typically this is the case with flambéed (flamed) main course or dessert dishes, where the drama of the cooking is part of the experience, or when a whole fish is boned and served tableside.

- Your waiter may serve family style, as at a Chinese restaurant, and set all the entrée platters in the center of the table. Diners pass the platters and serve themselves.

START-TO-FINISH GUIDELINES

For a complete discussion of table manners, refer to Chapter 6, "Table Manners," page 56. Here are a few quick reminders about manners that apply at restaurants, too.

Using Your Napkin

- Put your napkin in your lap shortly after you sit down.

- A waiter may place your napkin in your lap for you.

- At the end of the meal or if you leave the table during the meal, loosely fold your napkin (hiding any soiled spots) and place it to the left of your place setting.

- At some restaurants, when you return to the table you may find your napkin folded on the back of your chair or replaced with a fresh one.

Bread and Butter

Bread and butter may be on the table as you arrive or brought soon after you're seated.

- If the bread basket is close to your place setting, start it around the table before serving yourself. Offer others the last piece before taking it yourself. At a larger table, offer left, then serve yourself, then pass to the right.

- Bread, butter, jams, and finger foods, such as crudités, all go on your bread plate.

- As with all communal food, once you've touched it, it's yours: Don't tear off a piece of bread and then put the rest back in the basket.

- Break off a small piece of your bread, then butter that piece and eat it.

- When an uncut loaf (with cutting board and knife) is placed on the table, the host—or whoever is closest—cuts three or four slices, leaving them on the board. Make sure to use a clean napkin to hold the loaf when cutting it.

First Courses

- Appetizers are eaten with the outermost small fork to the left of the dinner fork. If you're having shellfish, use the oyster fork to the far right of the knives and spoons.

- If you're having soup, the server will probably bring the soupspoon with the soup; if it is already part of the place setting, it's to the right of the knife or knives.

- Pass any shared plates, such as antipasti, around the table, holding each so the next person can serve himself, using the serving utensils. If no appetizer plate has been provided, use your bread plate.

Resting Utensils

How you leave your utensils signals either "I'm finished" or "I'm still eating" to the server. (See illustrations, Chapter 6, pages 67 and 69.)

- If you're still eating, leave your fork and knife diagonally across the top edge of the plate or in an inverted V, with the handles at about four and eight o'clock.

- When you're finished, place the knife and fork together, diagonally across the center of the plate, with the handles at the 4:20 clock position.

- Whenever possible, avoid placing a used fork, knife, or spoon directly on the table. If the server asks you to "hold on to your fork and knife" for the next course (unfortunately, a messy reality in some restaurants today), it's fine to politely say, "I'd rather have fresh ones, thank you." But if your request is declined, then place your used utensils on your butter plate or on whatever you can find for resting them as neatly as possible at your place setting.

Main Courses

While eating the main course is fairly straightforward, here are a few situations you might encounter and how to handle them:

The food arrives at different times. If significant time elapses between the arrival of diners' hot dishes, the host (or if there is none, the other diners) should urge those who have been served to go ahead and eat. If everyone is having cold dishes, follow the rule of waiting until everyone is served.

You want to send food back. As a rule, send a dish back only if it isn't what you ordered; it isn't cooked to order (a rare filet arrives well done, for instance); it tastes spoiled; or you discover a hair or a pest. Just speak calmly and quietly to the server when making the request.

Your side dishes come separately. When vegetables are served in individual small dishes, you may eat them directly from the dish or transfer the food to your dinner plate, using a fork or spoon. You could also ask your server to transfer the side dish to your plate when he brings it and to remove the empty dishes so the table isn't overcrowded.

You want to taste one another's food. It's fine to offer or trade bites as long as it's handled unobtrusively. Pass your bread plate to your tablemate so he's able to serve you a bite or two. Just don't hold a forkful of food to another diner's mouth, and don't even think of spearing something off anyone else's plate. Don't share food at a business meal unless all the diners know one another well.

You'd like to share plates. When the whole idea of

the meal is to share plates—say, when you check out a new restaurant—serve others from your plate onto their dinner plate or bread plate before you begin eating.

You'd like to take home your leftovers. It's usually acceptable to ask for a "to go" bag. (Note: Citing health concerns, many restaurants now ask customers to "box their own.") When not to request one? At a business meal. It's okay to ask for one if you're dining with an associate who's a close friend and you're going "dutch"—but if she's the host, leave leftovers behind. Don't request one at a wedding reception or any other hosted function.

Condiments

◆ In a restaurant, salt, pepper, and butter are usually on the table. All other sauces and condiments will either be brought to the table or served to each diner.

◆ Never dip into communal condiments. Always spoon them onto your plate. (For more, see Resources, "Condiments," page 689.)

◆ Cream and sugar may be passed by the server or placed on the table to be passed by diners.

Finger Bowls, Hot Towels, and Towelettes

In some upscale restaurants, finger bowls are brought to diners after the main course. Gently dip your fingers, one hand at a time, in the water, then wipe your fingers on your napkin. The waiter will remove the finger bowl before serving your final courses.

Sometimes a steamed hot towel is presented at the end of the meal or after the main course. Use the towel to wipe your hands and, if necessary, the area around your mouth. Don't use it for a full washup. Usually, the waiter will take the towel away as soon as you've finished. If not, leave it at the left of your plate.

In some family-style restaurants you might be given an individually wrapped towelette—especially if you've ordered ribs or lobster. When you're finished eating, open the package, wipe your fingers on the towelette, and put it and its wrapper on your plate.

Fruit and Cheese Courses

It's possible that a fruit course may be served at some point during the meal—either with the salad, after the main course, or as dessert. The days of peeling your own fruit are largely past, but if you're given a whole fruit it should be quartered, cut into smaller pieces, and eaten with a knife and fork.

The cheese course is served before the dessert course. The server (a *fromager*, or *fromagère* if female) will either bring a tray of cheeses or wheel out a cart and suggest the most suitable choices. Cheese can be eaten on bread or crackers. Use a knife and fork for soft cheeses; hard cheeses may be eaten using fingers. Start with the milder cheeses and progress to the strongest.

Dessert

At many restaurants, once the main course has been cleared, the waiter will distribute dessert menus. Almost everyone loves reading the menu, and a few calorie-fearless indulge. It's also fine to ask to share, and your waiter will be happy to bring extra plates and utensils.

Some place settings already have a dessert spoon and fork set horizontally above the dinner plate. Otherwise, dessert utensils will be brought with the dessert course. Choose whichever utensil seems to fit the job at hand. You can always use the other utensil as a pusher. (See also Chapter 6, "Table Manners," page 56.)

Coffee and Tea

Coffee or tea is usually served individually, but if a waiter places a pot of coffee or tea on the table and doesn't pour, the person nearest the pot should offer to do the honors, filling her own cup last. Other than in a coffee shop, there's no dunking.

As with wineglasses don't flip your cup upside down if you don't want tea or coffee. Instead, simply say or gesture "No thank you" to your waiter. (For more on coffee and tea, see Chapter 6, "Table Manners," page 56, and Resources, "Guide to Food and Drink," page 686.)

Dinner Conversation

As long as the conversation is lively and engaging, any meal will be a success, even if the food or service isn't up to par. But a superb meal and stellar service with desultory or depressing conversation can't end soon enough. The same principles you use for dinner conversation at home or at a friend's house apply to a restaurant meal.

---

no elbows?

THE ANSWER: Sometimes. The no-elbows-on-the-table rule applies only when you're actually eating, not conversing. Whenever your utensils aren't in hand, it's okay to put your elbows on the table and lean forward slightly. It shows you're engaged in the conversation and makes it easier to hear in a noisy restaurant. "No elbows" applies only while you're eating or drinking, or to support your posture. If you're slouching so much that you need to prop yourself on your elbows, you appear disinterested in your tablemates.

Talk to the person on your left, on your right, and across from you. Be attentive, listen, and choose your subject with care. Watch your volume as well. The other diners at the restaurant have their own conversations to attend to. (See also Chapter 6, "Table Manners," page 56.)

Excusing Yourself

When you need to use the restroom, it isn't necessary to say where you're going—a simple "Excuse me, please" is sufficient. At other times, a brief explanation is fine: "Please excuse me while I check with the sitter." Leaving the table without a word is rude. Remember to fold your napkin loosely and leave it on the table, to the left of your plate.

Grooming at the Table

Personal grooming and hygiene issues should be taken care of in the restroom, not at the table. The one exception is that it's acceptable for a woman to apply a quick dab of lipstick or gloss (sans mirror) at the table at an informal restaurant and among friends, but not at a business meal or formal restaurant. What you *should* avoid is a primping routine—so, no compact, no powder, no mascara.

Whether you're a man or a woman, don't use a comb, or rearrange or touch your hair wherever food is served. Using dental floss at the table is a major never ever. At the table, the same is true of a toothpick.

When You Run into Friends

If you happen to cross paths with friends at a restaurant, is it necessary to introduce them to your dining companions? If a friend or acquaintance drops by the table, it's nice to introduce her if there are one or two others at your table. When it's a bigger group, the answer is generally no. But if your intuition tells you that introductions are expected—the whole table stops talking and is looking at the two of you, for instance—by all means make them. If you want to chat briefly with the person, it's better to step away from the table to do so.

It's still considered polite for men (and women if it's a business meal) to rise when someone is being introduced or has stopped by the table to talk. An exception is when you're sitting in a booth or on a bench, where rising would be difficult. When it's a large group, however, only those closest to the visitor rise.

If you run into friends on your way to being seated, it's okay to tell your tablemates that you'll "be there in a minute"—and then keep your word. The same is true

if you leave the table to visit. Don't conduct a lengthy conversation, leaving your party to peruse the menus or feel deserted.

"WHAT DO I DO WHEN . . ."

. . . I've dropped something? Don't pick up a dropped utensil and put it back on the table. Tell your server, who will retrieve it and bring a replacement. The exception is when you drop a utensil that might be stepped on or cause an accident; in this case, act fast and pick it up yourself.

It's fine to retrieve your wayward napkin if you can do it easily and not fumble around at your feet, or simply ask your waiter for a replacement if you prefer. Do inform the waiter if you've dropped food so it can be cleaned up, if not immediately then before the next diners are seated.

. . . my fork or glass is unclean? The next time a server stops by, discreetly ask for a replacement. Don't use your napkin to try to rub smudges off a utensil or glass. Also, don't announce the problem to everyone at the table—especially your host.

. . . I spot a hair or bug? If there's the proverbial fly in your soup (or anything else that doesn't belong), try your best to avoid any fuss. Simply catch the attention of the waiter and quietly alert him to the problem. He'll bring you a replacement or something else if you choose—usually pretty speedily. While it's probably impossible to keep the rest of the table from knowing something's wrong, insist that your tablemates continue eating, especially if you have to wait a bit for a fresh serving.

. . . someone at the table has food on his face? You'd want to know, wouldn't you? So do your friend a favor and subtly call his attention to it: "Oops, there's something on your cheek" or signal silently by using your index finger to lightly tap your chin. Dabbing your chin and upper lip with your napkin occasionally is the best preventative medicine.

. . . I knock over my drink? This happens to everyone at one time, so don't worry. Immediately set the glass upright and apologize: "Oh, I'm so sorry!" Offer your napkin to dam the flood. Summon your server, who will take care of the rest and provide dry napkins or utensils if necessary. If the spill stained a fellow diner's clothing, offer or arrange to pay for the dry cleaning.

. . . the waiter tries to whisk my plate away? If a server tries to take your plate before you've finished, don't hesitate to say, "Oh, I'm not finished yet," even if he's already on his way to the kitchen. If you *have* fin-

---

assorted no-nos

Slouching ✦ Fidgeting ✦ Smacking ✦ Crunching ✦ Touching your face or hair ✦ Blowing your nose ✦ Chewing with your mouth open ✦ Talking with your mouth full ✦ Pushing away your plate when finished ✦ Picking or flossing your teeth

---

ished but don't want those who haven't to feel rushed, you may still say you'd rather wait to have your plate cleared: "Thanks, but I'll wait till the others are finished."

TIPS FOR RESTAURANT HOSTS AND GUESTS

In our more relaxed world, people often dine together as a group with no one being the host or the guest. It's made clear from the initial arrangement that each person or couple is paying individually, as in "Let's get together at Bistro Sauce this Saturday." There are also times, particularly at a business meal, when there clearly is a host who extends the invitation, makes the reservations, oversees the guests, and pays the bill. "Please be my guest for dinner at seven on Saturday the eighth at Bistro Sauce."

When You're the Host . . .

Your primary job is to see to your guests' comfort and enjoyment. You guide your guests and set the tone. Since you are doing the inviting, you will be doing the paying, so make sure your invitation is clear. If you're inviting one or more people as your guests, do a little homework before deciding where to reserve. When you extend the invitation, it's okay to ask if a guest especially likes or dislikes certain cuisines or is a vegetarian. Alternatively, you could give the guest a choice of two or three restaurants. If you're hosting a group, pick a restaurant with a wide range of foods so that everyone will find something to his taste. It's also wise to choose a restaurant you know. Will the hot new bistro offer the quality food, good service, and kind of atmosphere you want your guests to enjoy? Better to save it until after you've given it a test run. And finally, consider your budget. You should be prepared to cover the cost of a meal at the mid to high range, plus any drinks or wine, plus tip and tax.

The following will help you to be a considerate and successful host at a restaurant:

- Reserve a table in advance. It doesn't make a good impression on your guests if they have to wait for a table or worse, be turned away.

- Have a seating plan in mind. (See "Who Sits Where?" page 102.)

- Arrive a few minutes before your guests, so you can:

  - Take care of payment arrangements and (optionally) arrange to collect stubs and pay for valet parking and/or coat checks. (See "Paying the Bill," page 113.)

  - Greet your guests as they arrive, either in the foyer or at your table. If you wait at the table, give the maître d' the names of the guests and ask him to direct them to you.

- If some guests are running late, go ahead and be seated, asking the maître d' to show tardy guests to the table.

- As the host, you walk behind your guests if the maître d' leads the way to the table. If he doesn't, you lead your guests.

- If a latecomer arrives after you're seated, stand as you extend your welcome.

- Whether you order a premeal drink or not, make it clear that your guests may order any type of beverage, alcoholic or not.

- The host chooses and orders the wine for the meal and offers the first toast, if it's a toasting occasion. This privilege shouldn't be passed to a guest.

- When ordering food, invite guests to feel free to order anything on the menu, including appetizers. "The crab cakes here are outstanding" or "I think I'll have the mussels first" gives guests the go-ahead for ordering firsts. As to entrées, either recommend a dish at the middle or high end of the price range or tell them what you're having. Choosing the least expensive items on the menu will make your guests feel as if they're imposing if they order anything pricier. At dessert time, again, encourage your guests to indulge.

- If meals arrive at different times, urge those who've already been served to go ahead and start eating, especially if their food is hot.

- If a mistake occurs—the wrong dish is brought to a guest, for example—tell the guest that you'll inform the waiter, then do so politely.

- When paying the check, don't display or disclose the total. Even a joking "Well, it's a good thing we enjoyed our food" could make guests feel they had ordered too extravagantly.

When You're a Guest . . .

It's a nice thing to be treated to a meal out, and your host certainly wants you to enjoy yourself. Still, it's important not to presume on your host's hospitality or take advantage of his generosity.

- Respond to the invitation right away.

- Be on time.

- If you've arrived before the host and have been asked to take a seat at the reserved table, it's best not to order anything other than water. When waiting for a close friend or family member, you might feel comfortable ordering a drink—but that's all.

- Never criticize the choice of table to the maître d', no matter how much you dislike the location. The host alone should request a switch.

- When ordering a drink, try to stay somewhat in line with what everyone else orders. In a free-spirited group, tequila shots may not raise an eyebrow. But such choices are a bad idea if everyone else is having iced tea, fruit juice, and club soda.

- As a general rule, don't choose the most expensive dishes on the menu, even if your host says, "Please don't hesitate to order anything you want." But don't feel you have to order the cheapest items on the menu, either. Try to order in the same general price range as your host or any other guests.

- If there are no prices on the menu, keep from going overboard by remembering that pork, chicken, pasta, and rice-based dishes are generally less expensive than beef, lamb, fish, shellfish, caviar, and anything with truffles.

- If you need to send food back, do it only if there is really something wrong with it, not because you've decided you don't like it or would prefer something different.

- Never complain about the food or service—that's the host's responsibility and he'll decide if and when.

- Since you're the guest, don't try to take the check or pressure the host to let you pay.

---

consider the other patrons

Less than desirable behavior is magnified in a restaurant because the other patrons are a captive audience. Restaurant staff also work hard to create and maintain a particular atmosphere. The following range from the annoying to the downright rude:

USING YOUR CELL PHONE. Turn your phone off when you arrive.

GETTING TOO ROWDY. Few things irritate restaurant patrons more than the tipsy table that continually erupts in a roar.

TAKING OVER. Groups celebrating a special occasion can sometimes forget that other patrons aren't part of the party. If you're planning on lots of toasts and special decorations, arrange for a private room.

LETTING KIDS RUN AROUND. It's both inconsiderate and dangerous.

- Thank your host twice: once at the end of the meal and again, ideally, with a handwritten note the next day. At the very least, a phone call or an emailed thank-you is in order.

PAYING THE BILL

If you're hosting a meal, it's a good idea to let the maître d' or waiter know in advance that the check should be given to you, in case an eager guest tries to chip in or pay it himself. Also, remember to make it clear to your guests that you're hosting: "Thanks, Alex, but dinner's my treat tonight." (Note to guests: Don't take the edge off the host's hospitality by trying to grab the check.) The reality, even these days, is that many servers still automatically present the check to the man. If you're a woman hosting a meal, make clear to the maître d' on your arrival that the check is to be presented to you and you alone. Here are some other ways to discreetly handle the check:

- Make advance arrangements for receiving the check (and sometimes for paying the bill).

- If it is a restaurant you know well and trust, you can leave your credit card imprint with the maître d' with instructions to add a 20-percent tip so all you need to do is check the bill and sign the slip.

- On the way to the restroom ask the maître d' to prepare your bill and hold it at the podium. On your return, take care of payment. The beauty of this method is that the bill never reaches the table.

When the check arrives, keep it out of view as you look it over. It's not a guest's business to know the cost of the meal—nor your obligation to disclose it. When you're ready to pay, signal the waiter by putting the check holder at the edge of the table with the bills or the credit card peeking out.

Splitting the Bill

When there is no host, splitting the bill can be approached in two ways. First, you each pay only for what you ordered; second, you split the bill in equal shares even though the cost of the food may not be even-steven. Many people, especially good friends, prefer the second method, mainly because it's simpler and friends don't usually mind if some pay a little less than their share.

There may be times, however, when you feel as if you're subsidizing the others: They shared two bottles of wine and you had none; they had filet mignon and you had an appetizer and a salad. Your dining companions might thoughtfully offer to split the bill accordingly: "Julie, your meal came to about $20. We'll take care of the rest." But if they don't make the offer, it's fine to speak up: "Here's $20 plus tip to cover my appetizer and salad." If this happens on a regular basis or you know your order will be out of line with the rest of the

dutch treat

While in the United States we use the term "dutch treat" to indicate that someone will pay for him or herself, almost every country has its twist. In Egypt it's to "pay English style," in Italy, "Roman style," and in parts of South America, it's to "pay American style." In the Philippines the acronym KKB—*Kanya, Kanyang Bayad*, means "pay for your own self."

However you say it, paying one's own way works well both with good friends who dine together often and for a group of people who don't know each other that well. Couples also may go "dutch" to keep the relationship on a "friends" basis. However, if it's a real date or any type of business meal, the person doing the inviting does the paying.

group, before the waiter comes to take your order say, "I'm only having an appetizer and salad. Would you all mind if we get separate checks tonight?"

CASUAL DINING

Eating out isn't limited to full-service restaurants. In fact we're more likely to find ourselves at a coffee shop, deli, or fast-food place. While these places may not be fancy, good manners still count.

Buffet Restaurants

The attraction of a buffet restaurant is that you can sample as many foods as you like. While a maître d' or hostess will seat you at your own table, you serve yourself. Servers usually just take care of beverages and clearing plates.

Because you can make as many trips to the buffet as you wish, there's no need to overload your plate. When you go back for seconds, leave your first plate and utensils on the table for the waiter or busboy to remove. Used utensils and plates could spread germs to a serving area and clean plates look more appealing. Because you serve yourself, you don't need to leave the customary 15- to 20-percent tip; 10 to 15 percent is appropriate for the waiter or busboy. (For more on tipping, see Chapter 13, page 165.)

line manners

- Don't switch from line to line. If you wind up behind someone ordering for a big group, you may move over to another line, but don't keep switching.

- If you're meeting someone for lunch, either wait until they arrive to get in line or go ahead and order your food and have them join you at your table when they get through. Don't invite them to join you—essentially cutting into the line.

- Be ready to order when you get to the counter. Make good use of your line time to decide what you want.

- If you have to wait for something you've ordered, stand to one side so the next person in line can get his order in.

- If you order for several people, ask one of them to help you carry things to the table.

Cafeterias

When a cafeteria is crowded and there are no empty tables, it's fine to join a table with an empty seat, but ask first: "Is this seat taken?" or "Do you mind if I sit here?" Diners who join a stranger are under no obligation to talk, but it's all right to start a casual conversation if the other person seems receptive. A tip isn't called for if you clear your own table; otherwise, leave a dollar or two for the busboy.

Diners, Coffee Shops, and Delicatessens

Depending on the individual place, these eateries either have booths and tables served by waitstaff or tables but no table service. If you have table service, all the guidelines for restaurant dining apply. When there's no table service, customers usually place their order and then either pick it up or wait until a counter person delivers it. The customer clears his table and disposes of paper plates and plastic utensils on leaving. No tips are expected in this case. If you're a regular patron, occasionally leaving a tip at the counter shows your appreciation for those who take your order and prepare your food.

Sitting at a diner counter is a quintessentially American experience. Seating is definitely first come, first served, although it's a nice gesture to try to accommodate two people who'd like to sit together. Some counter patrons are chatty, others aren't, but banter between customers and waitstaff is the norm. It's also typical for counter staff to be on familiar terms with customers—addressing those they know by name and those they don't by "Hon" or "Dear." Don't take offense—it's all part of the experience. Service is brisk, so take a quick glance at the menu and then give it up to the person wielding the order pad and pencil. While the service may seem unpolished compared to an upscale restaurant, your waitress's efficiency, the speed with which the food is served, and the attention to your coffee cup should all be rewarded with a tip—a dollar for a cup of coffee and a slice of pie, and at least 15 to 20 percent for anything more.

Fast-food Establishments

The etiquette you observe in these very casual restaurants boils down to this: treating those who serve you with respect, not disturbing other patrons, and throwing out your trash upon leaving. Give your full attention to the person taking your order, so don't talk on your cell or chat with your companions at the same time. Hand your bills and change to the person serving you instead of putting the money on the counter. And a "please" and "thank you" are essential, even at the drive-thru.

TAKING THE KIDS

Of course there are exceptions, but the simple truth is that very few children younger than eight or nine are ready for fancy restaurant dining. Young children just haven't developed the ability to sit through an entire

Q: *There seem to be so many things to dispose of during a meal—the paper for sweeteners (or for straws in more casual places) and the little containers for butter and jelly. Where do I put them?*

A: Place the containers for butter and jelly on the edge of the bread plate, and crumple any paper tightly and either put it under the rim or on the edge of your bread plate or coffee saucer. The aim is to keep the table looking litter-free.

meal of several courses without becoming bored or fidgety, not to mention table manners that can be relied on in public. That doesn't mean they shouldn't go to restaurants, just that you should choose ones that are child friendly. Restaurants that cater to children have become part of the American landscape, complete with birthday parties and children's entertainment. It's best to keep those first restaurant experiences short—and hopefully sweet.

Even in the most kid-friendly places, you'll need to coach your child to speak quietly, stay seated, and be on her best behavior when eating out. With some clear reminders and careful attention, eating out can be a good learning experience for children of all ages. (For specifics on table manners at different ages, see Chapter 38, "Children and Teens," page 478.) Some tips for eating out with children include:

◆ Before going, remind your child of what's ahead. She'll be given a menu, the waiter will take her order, and everyone will stay seated at the table until the meal ends. (This isn't the time for a crash course in all the table manners.)

◆ Bring a drawing pad or coloring book and crayons (or other quiet playthings) in case she gets restless. Just be sure to put them away when the food arrives.

◆ Place your order as soon as possible. Try to order something that could be brought for your child right away. For efficiency's sake, order for any child who's five or under. Be positive she knows what she wants before the waiter comes so he's not standing there while she repeatedly changes her mind.

◆ Keep children seated in their chairs. If they run near servers who are carrying heavy, scalding hot dishes, they risk harming themselves and others.

◆ If your child begins to misbehave or disturb others, take her out of the dining area immediately. A short walk and quiet conversation may do the trick and then you can both return to the table. If it's a real meltdown, you'll need to leave. Just understand that your child simply wasn't ready.

◆ If your child starts irritating other diners—say, by kicking the back of a booth—don't wait to put a stop to the behavior. If the diner says something before you do, apologize and say that it won't happen again. Then make sure it doesn't.

◆ Plan to leave the restaurant as soon as the meal ends. Others in your party will understand your early departure and appreciate your mindfulness.

COMPLAINTS AND APPRECIATION

Restaurateurs can tell you that keeping diners happy is one big job. They also point out that people are much more likely to voice their complaints than their appreciation. That's not to say that you shouldn't let it be known when there's a problem. A restaurant depends on its customers' approval for its livelihood, and its faults can't be corrected unless they're brought to the management's attention.

Make a complaint quietly, without attracting the attention of other diners. Speak first to whomever committed the error. If he makes no effort to correct the situation, take your complaint to the manager or captain.

It's not always your server's fault when service is slow. The restaurant could be short staffed or overbooked, or the problem could lie in the kitchen. If this appears to be the case, address your complaint to the management, but be careful not to put the blame on the server, who's probably no happier about the situation than you are.

Many restaurants address complaints with an apology and a reduction in the bill. If a dish wasn't prepared correctly (it's way oversalted, for example) the server will say, "I'm so sorry. I'll let the chef know and I'll take it off the bill. May I bring you something else?" If after making a legitimate complaint you receive no satisfaction at all, you have a couple of choices. If the problem is due to your server, reduce your tip, but not below 10 percent. If the service is slow but your server wasn't the problem or if the food wasn't up to par, your options are either to give the restaurant another try or to avoid it in the future. It's your call, made clearer by how the manager responds to your concerns.

On the other side of the coin, appreciative comments and a generous tip are more than welcome when you're pleased with the service. While tips are expected, comments like "The food couldn't have been better" or "The service was especially good" mean a great deal to someone who is trying to do her best. Since you may not have the opportunity yourself, it's also a nice gesture to ask the server to give your compliments to the chef if you really enjoyed your meal. The management will also appreciate hearing from a customer who is satisfied and doesn't hesitate to say so. Praise is important and always appropriate to give. (See also, Chapter 13, Tipping, page 165.)

10 traveling near and far

the joys of travel are countless. The question is this: Will your trip live up to expectations? With good planning, most likely it will—and your chances are all the better when you handle any problems that crop up with courtesy and flexibility. Although you have no real control over some glitches such as delayed or canceled flights, you *can* control your reaction. Getting to the resort hotel only to find that the "sweeping view" from your room is of the parking lot *is* disappointing; how well you handle your complaint could result in a better room. Travel etiquette boils down to three key courtesies, whether your trip is for business or pleasure, in the United States or abroad:

- **Put respect in the forefront.** Treat the people with whom you're traveling, those you meet, and those who serve you with respect and courtesy.

- **Keep your requests reasonable.** Asking to switch hotel rooms is fine. Making a scene when all the rooms with an ocean view are booked is not.

- **Don't "leave your mark."** Wherever your travel destination, remember that you are a guest. Avoid leaving anything unpleasant behind, from litter in a public park to the impression that you think things are "better back home."

This chapter charts the traveler's territory: preparing for a trip; traveling in groups or with children; traveling by plane, train, and automobile; hotel etiquette; cruise ship etiquette; and traveling overseas. (For beach, boating, and camping etiquette, see Chapter 11, "Sports and Recreation," page 136; for tipping while traveling, see Chapter 13, "Tipping," page 165.)

BEFORE YOU LEAVE HOME

Before traveling, it's sensible to *prevent* trouble. How to start? Make sure you have valid photo ID, in most cases a driver's license, but for international travel you'll need

a passport. Visit the TSA website for the latest information on security procedures. It's thoughtful to make a copy of your itinerary, including the names and phone numbers of hotels, and leave the list with your family and anyone else who might need it.

To get the most out of your travels learn as much as possible about customs and manners in the places you plan to visit; try your local library or the Internet (see "Traveling Overseas," page 131). Plan early and carefully, and keep records and confirmation numbers of reservations and agreements.

Be courteous when you deal with reservation and travel agents. Whether discussing your plans over the phone or in person, gather all the necessary details beforehand so you won't waste time. If you're having trouble getting the air fare, lodging, or service you need, calmly ask for alternatives. "Could you keep looking, please?" is more likely to get results than an "I can't believe there aren't any hotels in that price range!"

TRAVELING WITH FRIENDS

Traveling with friends can be a true test of friendship. Being cooped up together in a car, plane, or hotel room can easily lead to friction. To help stave off tensions, make sure you and your traveling companions have three things in common:

Similar tastes. If you prefer picnics in the country and simple country inns, don't travel with friends whose idea of heaven is a five-star city hotel and going to nightclubs.

Similar budgets. Having an overall idea of what you're each planning to spend on travel, meals, and lodging means everyone can enjoy the trip without worrying about finances.

Synchronized body clocks. If you like to be up and on the sightseeing bus by 8:00 AM, don't travel with people who prefer to sleep until noon.

When you plan your trip, make sure you agree on the general itinerary, and give each person the opportunity to include their "must dos" or "must sees." You and your companion don't have to do everything together. If you spend an afternoon at a museum while your friend explores the city, you'll be able to share each other's experiences over dinner that night.

However you handle the costs, work out your plan before you head off on your journey. A few options to consider:

- **Pay your own way:** With credit cards as widely accepted as they are, it's easy for individuals to pay for their own admission tickets and to split shared meals.

- **Settle up at the end:** Hold on to receipts when one person pays for the group, and do an accounting as you go along or at the end of the trip.

- **Use a "kitty":** For miscellaneous shared cash expenses, have each traveler (or couple) put the same amount of money into a kitty, which is replenished as needed. Any left over is divided evenly.

] ROAD TRIPS [

The "great American road trip" isn't a thing of the past. Legions of families and friends still cruise the highways

---

the pre-trip meeting

Whenever you're traveling with others or even sharing a vacation rental, have a pre-trip planning session, a fun way to get excited about the trip. It's smart to establish responsibilities and how things such as expenses will be handled. You can also prevent confusion down the line. ("I thought *you* were bringing the GPS.") Here are some things to discuss ahead of time:

- Travel information: flights, arrival and departure times, contact info, and where and when you'll meet up if you're not traveling together.

- The general itinerary: You don't need to plan every detail, but establish an outline of your trip.

- A list of each person's "must sees" or "must dos."

- How to handle shared expenses and who will be the trip's accountant.

- Meals and menus: How many nights you want to eat out or cook in? Do you need to supply your own breakfast? Do you need to outline your menus?

- Make a list of any trip provisions: gear, supplies, or food, and who will bring it.

---

and back roads of the fifty states for an up-close look at our national treasures. But being in a car together for hours on end can quickly take its toll—so it's imperative for everyone to make an effort to keep the peace and help everything run smoothly.

Whether you're the driver or a passenger, think about the other riders' comfort. Be flexible when it comes to setting the air temperature, opening (or closing) windows, and choosing music. If someone wants to nap, the others should tone it down. Request rest stops before you're desperate.

When You're the Driver

Keep in mind that you set the tone in the car. Complaining about things beyond your control such as slow traffic can put a damper on your passengers' enjoyment of the trip. Schedule regular rest stops.

If you're taking your time and sightseeing, practice give-and-take with other drivers on two-lane roads. If a car behind you wants to pass, slow down a little or pull to the side, and then signal for the driver to pass when you're sure that the road ahead is clear.

When You're the Passenger

Passengers should be careful not to distract the driver, particularly when in heavy traffic or when driving conditions are difficult. Assigning a navigator who reads the maps or handles the navigation device can be a great help.

Traveling with children can be challenging, starting with keeping them buckled up. With little ones, plan on making frequent stops for feedings and diaper changes, and during any crying spells. As children mature, you'll be teaching them to talk quietly in the car and not distract the driver by yelling, arguing, or throwing things. Set the rules and expectations before the trip and stick to them. You'll want to make the trip fun, too, so provide quiet games and activities, sing songs to change the mood, or play "I spy" games to make the miles go by. While older children may retreat to their earbuds and music players or handheld video games, long trips are a great opportunity for conversations, too.

LIFE AT 34,000 FEET

Air travelers have to face the reality of rigorous security procedures on top of flight delays and cancelations, anxiety about flying, and reduced or no meal service. How to cope? Patience, courtesy, flexibility, and a sense of humor will serve you well. It's futile to get upset about things over which you have no control. How well you work with airline or security personnel can affect how quickly you get to your destination.

Before You Leave

The courteous traveler is prepared for both airline check-in and security screening. Ask the airline about size and weight limits for carry-on and checked luggage and the number of pieces currently allowed. Have your photo ID and travel documents readily available and all your luggage tagged with your name, address, and phone number. Print your boarding pass or download your boarding pass to your smartphone before you leave.

Be prepared for going through security, too. Dress and pack with security in mind. Remember, you'll have to take off scarves, coats, jackets, and shoes. Consider wearing shoes that are easy to slip on and off. Be prepared to remove metal items that can set off the detector. It may be simpler to pack your belt and jewelry in your carry-on and put them on after you go through security. Know, too, that regulations change and be prepared to comply. If you have change and other items in your pocket, consider placing them all in a small plastic bag. They'll be easier to retrieve after being scanned.

At the Airport

Check-in. Because of security procedures, the general recommendation is to arrive at the airport 1 to 2½ hours ahead of your flight time, depending on the airport, the time of day, and your destination. Airlines are trying to make the check-in process more efficient. If you do need to check in at the counter, do your part and have your ticket and ID ready to hand over. Try to keep calm and be pleasant; the counter agent isn't responsible for the bad weather that caused a delay or the plane's mechanical problems.

Security. Have your photo ID and boarding pass ready. If a screener gives you a thorough wanding or goes through personal items in your bag, be patient.

At the gate. In the waiting area, don't take up more space than you really need. Place luggage on the chairs next to you only if there are plenty of seats to spare. There's usually no need to check in again at the gate, unless you're flying standby. If you need to use your cell phone, move to a more private location so your conversation doesn't disturb others. If it's crowded and you're using an electrical outlet to charge your computer or phone, unplug as soon as you have a full charge so someone else can use it.

Boarding the plane. Board the plane only when your row or group number is called—the more closely passengers follow instructions, the more quickly everyone will be settled in their seats. Pushing ahead or jumping the line is rude. As you walk through the Jetway to the plane, keep your place and be particularly patient with elderly or infirm passengers.

Switching seats. Must you comply when a passenger asks you to swap seats? You don't have to agree, though switching is a kind thing to do when it seems warranted, as when a parent and child make the request so they can sit together. If you decline, do so politely: "I'm sorry, but I'd like to stay where I am." The length of the flight may enter into your decision. A married couple who won't be able to sit together on the fourteen-hour flight from Los Angeles to Sydney has more reason to request a swap than a couple taking the shuttle from New York to Boston.

If you want to switch your seat, wait until the plane doors are shut and you're certain that the available

etiquette for carry-ons and overhead bins

There really is such a thing as "carry-on etiquette." Start by holding your carry-on or shoulder bag in front of you, not at your side, as you walk down the aisle of the plane. Backpacks and suitcases-on-wheels require careful navigation as well.

When you reach your seat, quickly put one bag into the overhead bin above your seat or one nearby, taking care not to squash other people's belongings. If you're next to a passenger who's having trouble lifting a suitcase, offer to help if possible—a good deed that also helps speed things up for those still waiting in the aisle.

With overhead bins, it's first come, first stowed— so if you can't find space, either put your bag under your seat (if it's small enough) or ask a flight attendant for help. If need be, accept that your bag must be consigned to the cargo hold.

seats aren't assigned. Or check with a flight attendant who may know of a seat you can move to.

In the Air

Once you're aloft, the real test of your civility begins. Airlines have reduced legroom and services to save costs, leaving passengers feeling just as pinched. It can be an effort to maintain a positive attitude.

As for minor incivilities, you have little choice but to grin and bear them. Anything truly unacceptable or behavior that causes you concern should be reported to a flight attendant.

Airplane Etiquette 101

Here are some basic plane manners that apply under most circumstances:

- If you have an aisle seat, keep your elbow or foot from protruding into the aisle.

- If the person in the aisle seat is sleeping and you need to get out of your row, softly say, "Excuse me," and, if necessary, tap him lightly on the arm. It's perfectly okay to wake someone as long as you do it gently.

- Be understanding if a passenger in your row repeatedly asks you to let her out—there could be a medical reason. You might offer to switch seats for her comfort and yours.

- Keep any work materials you're using from overflowing into your seatmate's space.

- Don't surreptitiously read the worksheets or laptop screen of the person beside you.

- Keep noise to a minimum, whether talking with a passenger or reading a book to a child. If you or your child play a video game or watch a movie on a laptop, use the headset or your earbuds. Your neighbor shouldn't be able to hear it.

- Don't stay too long in the lavatory; the full makeover can wait until you've landed. Leave the space neat and clean.

- Try not to block the view of those who are watching the movie or other entertainment. If you must stand to retrieve something from the overhead bin, be as quick as possible.

To chat or not? You're not in the mood to talk, but the passenger in the seat next to you is warming up for a marathon conversation. To nip things in the bud without offending, smile and answer any questions with a simple yes or no. If that doesn't work, be direct but polite: "It's been nice chatting with you. I'm going to use this time to read/work/sleep. Thanks for understanding." Then bury yourself in a book, magazine, or your work, or close your eyes for a snooze.

Another effective way to discourage conversation is to put on earphones as soon as you're seated, whether listening to music or not. Whatever tack you take, be gracious to your fellow traveler. Chatting is usually just a friendly gesture.

Seat etiquette. Your seat is about the only thing you have any control over in an airplane. At the same time, it can spell trouble, starting with the recline feature.

The battle rages on: Is reclining rude or is it your right? While it's nice to consider the personal space of the passenger behind you, it is your seat to recline if you wish. It's considerate to recline your seat only partway or to turn around and ask the passenger behind you whether he minds if you recline all the way. Always recline slowly to avoid banging the knees or tray table of the passenger behind you. If you're the one being squeezed, calmly ask the person in front if she could move her seat back up a little. "Would you mind waiting a little to recline? I'm still having my meal, but I'll let you know when I'm done. Thanks."

Then there's the shared armrest. Ideally, your and your seatmates' elbows will alternately occupy the armrest without causing trouble. But if your seatmate has other ideas, you could propose a compromise: "Why don't you take the front half of the armrest, and I'll take the back half?" Middle seat occupants face double trouble over armrest use. In the spirit of fairness, polite passengers in the aisle and window seats will cede the center armrests to the one in the middle.

Whenever you have to get out of your seat, it's natural to steady yourself by grabbing the back of the seat in front of you—but for the person sitting (or sleeping) there, it's a rude surprise. Whenever possible use your armrests or the back of your own seat to help you rise. If you must use the seat in front of you for assistance, do so gently. Another jostle alert: When you unlatch or secure the meal tray on the seat back in front of you, try not to push too hard.

Middle seat etiquette. Everyone gets stuck in the middle from time to time. It's okay to ask to switch seats with someone if you feel you need to, but be prepared for them to say no, which is within their right. If you've been assigned to a middle seat, ask the gate agent if there are window or aisle seats available. You might just get lucky.

Keep in mind that people on either side of you can see your laptop screen—even though they shouldn't be looking. Be aware of the content you have on-screen: banking, an R-rated film, personal email, or confidential work matters. Use of a privacy screen is considerate to those around you, but don't presume it guarantees privacy.

Babies and children. Kids are definitely part of the air travel package. Nevertheless, parents need to do what they can to keep children from disturbing others.

◆ **When you're the parent.** Try these pre-trip strategies to help make your trip more successful. When possible, fly during nap times or at off-peak, less crowded times. Check with your pediatrician for ways to prevent or lessen ear pain from changes in air pressure. On the plane, nursing or offering a bottle can soothe a baby and the physical act of swallowing can relieve the pressure that causes ear pain. Often, other passengers don't resent the crying as much when they see parents doing all they can to relieve it.

Let toddlers work off energy before boarding by walking them through the corridors or playing in the airport's children's area, if there is one. Just before boarding, take them to the restroom so they won't need to go again before the seat belt light goes off. Pack a small carry-on with snacks, comfort items, games, books, and small toys. Add a few surprises—stickers, finger puppets, a new book, or other items that may keep them occupied.

If your child does act up or disturbs another passenger, say, by kicking the seat, apologize and deal with the behavior immediately.

◆ **When you're the inconvenienced passenger.** If a noisy infant or restless youngster disturbs you, ask if a vacant seat is available. If you know crying babies bother you, stash earplugs in your carry-on bag. If a child behind you is kicking your seat, politely speak to the child's parent (or the child directly, if he's older): "Excuse me, you might not realize it but your child is kicking my seat." Most likely, the parent or child will apologize and put a stop to the behavior.

Disembarking

After the plane touches down and the seat belt lights go off, it really doesn't do any good to jump up and crowd the aisles. If you need to get off quickly because you have to make a tight connection, tell a flight attendant before the plane makes its final descent; he or she might be able to seat you closer to the front or make an announcement asking other passengers to wait. If not, inform the people around you of your situation and ask if they mind letting you go first. Be sure to thank those who help you out. Be considerate of others when they are in the same predicament.

When it is time to go, don't push yourself past people in the aisle. And if someone elbows past you from behind, try to let him pass. If you get separated from a traveling companion, stand aside in the Jetway to wait for her; otherwise, reconnect in the terminal.

TRAIN AND BUS TRAVEL

The same standards of courteous airplane travel apply equally to travel on a train or bus.

Seats and Seatmates

Except on certain trains and buses, seats aren't reserved. Still, your seat stays yours for the trip once it's chosen. It is a good idea to place a magazine on the seat when you use the restroom, or on a bus when you get off at rest stops, to show that it's taken.

Hogging space is a major breach of etiquette. Don't put a suitcase on the seat next to you to keep another passenger from sitting there; use the overhead racks for your luggage. You may be sitting for hours with a seatmate so it's nice to exchange a few pleasantries, but don't spend the trip chatting unless the person is clearly interested. (See also "To chat or not?" page 124.)

Electronic Devices

Passengers on trains and buses are usually permitted to use mobile phones. Some train services have introduced "quiet cars" where mobile phones and other electronic devices are prohibited.

As in all public places or where there's a captive audience, keep calls brief and speak quietly. No one minds calls advising others of delays and changes in schedules. Even then, try to move to the rear of the train car or wait for a rest stop when traveling by bus.

More Dos and Don'ts for Train and Bus Travel

♦ If you sit at one of the tables in the club car of a train, don't monopolize it. Eat your meal, then return to your seat.

♦ If you prepack a meal or snack, be considerate of your fellow passengers and don't choose things that have a strong smell or are likely to spill. And do clean up after yourself.

♦ Other than a quick swipe of lipstick or pass with a comb, take care of personal grooming in a restroom.

- When walking down the aisles, keep to the right if others are walking toward you. When you can, step into a vacant row when someone else is trying to pass.
- Watch your children. Don't let them run about or bother other passengers.

AT HOTELS AND OTHER ACCOMMODATIONS

No matter how weary you feel, be gracious as you check in to your hotel or motel. If, for example, there's something about your room you don't like, call the front desk and calmly ask for a change, giving the reason. Most hotels will try to accommodate your requests, depending on availability.

Hotel Staff

Large hotels have full-service staffs to assist their guests. Typically, this includes a doorman, valet parking attendants, bellmen, reception personnel, and housekeeping.

Large hotels have a concierge desk to provide information and services—giving directions, ordering theater tickets, suggesting restaurants and making the reservations, and even ordering flowers to send for you. Whatever the size of the hotel, treat the staff with respect—and don't forget to tip. (For tipping hotel staff, see "At Hotels," page 171.)

taking your pet?

Some pets may be better off left with friends, relatives, or in a kennel when you travel. While many places prohibit pets, there are pet-friendly hotels, motels, and inns. Doing some research before you leave home and double checking with the hotel before you book will ensure that there are no surprises when you arrive.

Even if your dog is perfectly well behaved, keep him on a leash at all times. Some hotels have designated pet walks; if not, walk your dog off the property. Take a pooper-scooper or plastic bag and *use* it. (See "Walking the Dog," page 28.)

In hotels, don't leave your dog behind when you leave your room, even if the management allows. In an unfamiliar environment the best-trained dog can damage furniture and carpeting, and the barking of a lonely dog can bother nearby hotel patrons.

When you're in the room with your dog, put the *Do Not Disturb* sign on the door so that housekeepers who might be wary of dogs won't face an uncomfortable—even frightening—situation.

Room Service

If there is no room service menu in your room, ask about prices before you order; they can be sky-high. It's okay to be wearing a bathrobe when you open the door. Servers are used to seeing guests in something other than street clothes. After the waiter has brought your order, sign the check. A gratuity is usually included, but if it's not noted on your bill, add it. When you've finished eating, call the room service staff to let them know your tray is ready to be picked up, then leave it outside your door.

At B&Bs and Inns

Bed-and-breakfasts, or B&Bs, are generally large private houses with rooms provided for a few guests. Guests share a family-style breakfast with other guests and the owner, who often serves as cook, housekeeper, and tour guide. Unless previously arranged, other meals usually aren't provided. Country inns, on the other hand, often have more rooms and guests, but the manners observed in an inn or B&B are much the same.

Make every effort to be both thoughtful and neat. Remember that noise can carry easily in old houses, so keep your voice down. If you plan to stay out late, ask the owner for a key so you can let yourself in and won't have to wake anyone.

In communal rooms, pick up after yourself; straighten magazines, put away books, and don't leave your personal items lying around. In some B&Bs and inns, guests share a bathroom. Be careful not to monopolize it, and leave it clean and tidy for the next person. Generally the owner of a B&B isn't tipped, but

airbnb and home shares

Airbnb-style home sharing is a great way to enjoy a new city or town. Be sure to do your homework up front. Most "hosts" will have explicit instructions, guidelines, and rules for their property. It's important to understand that if you book with this host, you are agreeing to their terms. If it's not already spelled out, ask your host about expectations for linens, use of any products or items found in the rental, expectations for replacement of food or products used, and any potential cleaning fees. Unlike a hotel that has cleaning staff, home shares often hire private cleaning services. The cost is either covered by the hosts or included in the rental rate. No tip is necessary. A good basic rule is to leave the place in the same condition—if not better—than when you found it. It's also important to make sure you have contact information for either the host or a caretaker should anything go wrong during your stay.

Most of these properties find success through positive ratings by guests. Be honest with your reviews of properties and your experience with your host.

tip staff, such as housekeepers, as you would hotel staff. (For tipping hotel staff, see "At Hotels," page 171.)

 ON CRUISES

In many ways, a cruise ship is a world apart, with an etiquette all its own. Companies that organize cruises do a great job of describing onboard customs and etiquette in pre-cruise booklets or on their websites. Be sure to read about your cruise customs, attire, and tipping before you leave.

Cruise manners start at the dock. The boarding process is well organized by the staff, so follow their directions. Your baggage will be tagged for delivery to your cabin; your ticket will be verified and your photo ID or passport checked; and you'll go through security. Common sense and courtesy will make the process go smoothly. As you wait to board, chat with a few of your fellow passengers; it's never too early to start meeting people.

Cruise Dress

Cruise ships have dress codes, which are usually outlined on their websites, in the pre-cruise printed material, and in the onboard daily program. Depending on the ship and the type of cruise, attire can range from very casual to black tie. Most cruise lines offer at least one formal evening and generally the requested attire is a tuxedo or formal suit for men and a cocktail or evening dress for women. Consider what you'll wear for shore excursions, so that you're dressed appropriately for the activity and culture where you're visiting. Unless the information has been provided, ask at the excursion desk about appropriate dress.

Meeting Others

Much of the fun of a cruise is meeting other people, and the friendly, fun atmosphere fostered by the crew makes it easy. You'll have many opportunities to meet new people. Don't be shy about introducing yourself and saying where you're from and what you do. That's expected on a ship. There will be lots to talk about but remember to steer clear of the conversational no-nos: politics, money, religion, and your personal health issues.

Recreational Activities

Most cruise ships offer a wide variety of activities. As you sample the works, consider this:

◆ Deck chairs are available for sunning and reading, but that doesn't mean they're your personal real estate. Don't leave your belongings on a deck chair to save it for later use, since they are usually in much demand.

◆ Most activities have sign-up sheets. Arrive on time for your scheduled activity. If you can't make it, call to cancel so that another passenger has the opportunity to join in.

◆ Limit your time on exercise bikes, treadmills, and other equipment to twenty to thirty minutes when others are waiting. Always wipe down any equipment you've used; it's not only polite but a health necessity.

◆ If you're a jogger, run only during the allowed times. Passenger cabins often lie beneath the jogging deck, and off-hour jogging might keep someone from sleeping.

◆ Limit hot tub time to fifteen or twenty minutes unless no one else is waiting.

◆ Use hand sanitizer frequently.

Meals and Entertainment

On many cruises you're assigned a table and dine regularly with the same passengers. If you are traveling with a group of friends and would like to sit together, make the request when you book the cruise. Soon after boarding, pay a visit to the dining room and speak with the maître d' either to confirm premade arrangements or to request special seating.

If you are seated at a table with people you don't know, make an effort to learn their names and a little bit about them. Restaurant manners apply. (See Chapter 9, "Dining Out," page 100.) At your first dinner together, decide how you and your tablemates will pay for wine: whether you take turns buying the wine or agree to split the bill each time. Of course, nondrinkers shouldn't be expected to chip in. If you're completely miserable with your tablemates, speak discreetly with the maître d' about a change.

Cruise ships are famous for their high-quality evening entertainment—shows, musicals, revues—and your talented crew are the stars as well. Seats are usually at a premium: It's first come, first seated. Be fair to other passengers and don't hold seats for anyone but your traveling companion. If you're with a large group, make plans to meet up after the show.

The Captain's Table

It's the custom on many ships for the captain and other officers to host a table. The criteria for invitations vary ship to ship, but generally dignitaries, celebrities, and passengers in the stateroom equivalent of a penthouse are invited. This perk may be extended to passengers who are frequent sailors and is sometimes arranged through a travel agent. If you receive an invitation you may be asked to wear formal attire. Remember to thank your host at the end of the meal and again with a short handwritten note.

Quiet, Please!

A cruise is a time to get away from it all, and some peace and quiet comes with the package. Noise carries on a ship: Talk quietly in corridors, don't let doors slam, and turn down TVs and radios. If you need to complain about noise, dial security so that you won't have to confront the offender yourself.

Interacting with the Crew

All crewmembers are trained to be friendly and helpful, and to do whatever they can to make your cruise as enjoyable as possible. Don't take advantage of this friendliness to monopolize their time or socialize with them beyond their official duties. Treat crewmembers respectfully and always say "please" and "thank you."

Tipping

The staff on most cruise lines is tipped, although some smaller lines have a no-tipping policy, including gratuities in the ticket price. When there is tipping, most cruise lines have simplified the process by charging a daily fee, ranging from approximately $10 to $15 per day, which covers restaurant and room personnel and is shared among the staff. You may wish to tip your cabin attendant or waiter more, which is fine. Put your extra tip in an envelope with the employee's name and hand it to him personally on the last day. Also, a 15-percent gratuity is generally automatically added to any beverages purchased, and 18 percent is added to spa services.

GROUP TOURS

When you sign up for a specialty tour, you're likely to spend concentrated time with the others in your group. These tips will help you get the most out of the group experience:

- Introduce yourself at the start of the tour and exchange a few friendly words. In later conversations, don't focus on yourself but rather what you're experiencing together.

- Be on time for all activities, whether it's the daily departure, a meal, a scheduled tour, or a lecture.

- Don't complain. Whining dampens everyone's enthusiasm and tries their patience. Also don't criticize what you're seeing; leaders of the group are often locals who could find your remarks hurtful or offensive.

- Pay attention to the tour leader's descriptions and explanations. Talking over the leader or conversing with someone else is rude.

thanking the tour guide

Whether you're on a group tour at an historical site or a private tour of a museum, it's thoughtful and customary to give your guide a tip if you've been pleased with your tour. Give the guide around $5 per person (per day if you have the same guide for several days). Or you could invite a private guide to join you for coffee or a meal if you've become friendly. Think about your tour support team as well: Consider a tip of a few dollars per day for your bus driver and for the gang that takes care of your bikes or gear.

- Make an effort to include single or elderly tour group members, inviting them to join you in conversation or for some meals.

- Thank the tour organizers at the end of the trip, and tip as generously as you see fit.

TRAVELING OVERSEAS

Never has it been more important to behave with friendliness and humility than when going abroad. Being critical or disrespectful of the customs, landmarks, language, foods, or government of a foreign country—especially in front of its people—marks you as a poor representative of your own country. There's no need to gush, but you should always behave with courtesy and respect.

Before you go, do some research. A short, self-taught history lesson, whether online or from a well-researched, current guidebook, will enhance your understanding

of the country's culture and its citizens. Depending on where you're going, it might be wise to check out the State Department's website (www.state.gov/travel/), which provides useful information including entry regulations, warnings of political unrest, and driving conditions, as well as cultural and historical information.

At the very least, know the following:

- A little something about the nation's history.
- Whether there's a national religion and, if so, what it is.
- The form of government (e.g., constitutional democracy, monarchy, theocracy) and what it means (whether political leaders are elected, for example).
- The significance of any national holiday that falls during your visit.
- A few words and phrases in the native language (at right).
- The currency and the exchange rate.

Language

What Americans see as directness can sound demanding to others. The American who walks up to a stranger and blurts out "Do you speak English?" without so much as a "Hello" projects arrogance. Tone is everything.

A small phrase book will smooth your path in any foreign land. Carry it along to consult as necessary; it's also smart to memorize a few words and phrases (or prepare a handy one-sheet) for these basics:

"Hello"

"Good-bye"

"Good morning"

"Good evening"

"Good night"

"Please"

"Thank you"

"Yes"

"No"

"Excuse me"

"I don't speak [language]."

"I don't understand."

"How much does it cost?"

"Where is . . . ?"

"How do I get to . . . ?"

"Left"

"Right"

"Ladies' room"

"Men's room"

"More, please."

"No more, thank you."

"The check [or bill], please."

Numbers 1 through 10

"Beautiful," "wonderful," "nice," "kind," and other complimentary words that will show your admiration or appreciation.

When attempting to communicate in English, do all you can to be understood. Speak slowly (though not as if you were speaking to a child) and enunciate with care. Watch the expression of the listener to gauge whether he's grasping what you say, and don't be afraid to repeat your words as often as necessary. Maintain a normal speaking volume—while people may not understand your words, it doesn't mean they're deaf.

Body Language

Body language is another important consideration, since certain facial expressions, gestures, and stances can be easily misunderstood by others. An example: In the United States, looking directly at the speaker's face is expected and shows you're paying attention; in Asia, Africa, and Latin America, making direct eye contact can be considered impolite or aggressive.

Gestures, too, can be misinterpreted. Beckoning with a curled index finger is considered offensive in many countries. Three gestures in particular—thumbs-up, the OK sign (thumb and forefinger held together in an O), and V for victory—should be avoided unless you're certain they have the same meaning in the host country. In some countries, raising your arm and waving your hand in greeting or to get someone's attention means "no."

The distance you stand from others matters as well. In the United States, we're comfortable standing about 2 to 3 feet apart. Northern Europeans and Asians expect more space in between, while southern Europeans, Latinos, and people from Middle Eastern countries prefer standing closer, less than 18 inches apart.

In Asia and the Middle East, the firm American handshake can be interpreted as aggressive, while in many Latin countries (South America, Spain, Italy) it may be accompanied by a touch on the elbow or forearm. In some Islamic countries, women do not shake hands; since this prohibition varies from country to country and region to region, wait for a woman to extend her hand first. In Japan and some other Asian nations, the bow is the equivalent of the handshake. In Thailand, the *wai*—placing the hands together at the chest, prayerlike, and bowing—is a traditional form of greeting, although the handshake is now more prevalent.

What about touching? Latin Americans and southern Europeans engage in casual touching more than North Americans do, so if someone touches your arm in conversation, don't take offense. The same is true in Africa, the Middle East, and India.

BASIC INTERNATIONAL COURTESIES

Cultural sensitivity to local customs is a must for overseas travelers. Whenever tourists behave politely, show respect, and express interest in a country and its people, they show themselves and their native country in the best light. Besides familiarizing yourself with the history, government, religion, and language of any country you visit, the following basic courtesies will smooth your way when you travel internationally:

- Greet others according to local custom. Be prepared to shake hands frequently in Europe and to bow or *wai* when in Asia.

- Allow for greater formality. Titles are often used, and you shouldn't immediately call a person by his or her first name unless they specifically request it.

- Pay close attention to your grooming and the standards of dress in the country. In general, neat, clean, and conservative is better.

- Be open-minded. Don't criticize customs in the host country, and never express frustration that things aren't done "the American way."

- Become familiar with gift-giving customs and protocol, which vary greatly from country to country. Consider who is receiving the gift, their status, what types of gifts are acceptable, and how and when it should be presented.

- Be respectful but careful about praising or admiring your host's possessions. In some cultures the host will be obliged to give the admired object to you as a gift, whether he can afford to or not.

- Respect the dietary customs of the country. If someone is hosting you, don't request food or drink that may be contrary to your host's practices.

- Refrain from being loud in speech and attention getting in your actions and dress.

- Stand to show your respect when the national anthem of your host country is played.

regional sensitivities

In order to show respect and avoid giving offense, certain customs must be observed in particular regions. For example, the following are guidelines for regions that have large Muslim populations, such as the Gulf States, Turkey, Egypt, Indonesia, Malaysia, India, Pakistan, and many African nations. In addition, please consult an up-to-date, reputable travel guide before you go.

- Avoid using the left hand when eating or handling a business or calling card.

- When seated in a chair, keep both feet on the floor and never show the soles of your feet.

- Don't touch anyone on the head, which is considered sacred.

- Do not ask a Muslim man about his wife or daughters.

- Wear only long pants or skirts.

- In public places, don't kiss or hold hands with your traveling companion.

- When visiting a mosque, remove your shoes before entering and leave them outside. Do not cross in front of someone who is in prayer, and never enter the mosque's main hall.

- If you want to present someone with a gift, avoid giving pictures of people or animals; Islam disapproves of realistic images of living creatures. Don't give a present of alcohol or anything made from pigskin.

ADVENTURE TRAVEL

Whether you're nineteen and exploring sub-Saharan Africa on a gap year or sixty-one and putting an early retirement to the test in the Argentine back country, here are a few travel tips that can help you get the most from your experience:

- Be considerate of people. As with travel anywhere, make an effort to know something about local/regional traditions, customs, and beliefs. Become a student of attitudes and styles, and practice moderating your behavior to conform and fit in as best as possible.

- Research available food and make a plan if you have dietary restrictions or food allergies that are nonnegotiable. Don't place an undue burden on your potential hosts.

- Consider packing your own toilet paper. People have figured out some ingenious as well as some obvious ways to handle the most basic bodily functions.

- Remember that patience is a virtue, even when it's tested. Fortunately there are still many places in this world that don't move at the speed of jet planes and cell phones.

- Smile. It works when things are going well. It also works when things don't go as planned (and that's definitely something you can plan on!).

11

sports
and recreation

fun and pleasure should be the goal of any sports or recreational activity, and for most of us, that's true. Boating and camping let us get away from it all and soak in the beauty of nature. Golf, tennis, a pickup basketball game—all provide us with a little friendly competition and a chance to hone our athletic skills or burn a few calories. And sitting in a stadium and cheering on a team is a national pastime. So why is the world of sports getting a bad reputation?

There's no question that the media focuses attention on unsportsmanlike or outrageous behavior by professional athletes; in minutes, videos of out-of-line conduct are uploaded to YouTube for worldwide distribution. It's no wonder that the idea of sportsmanship

seems tarnished and competing can too often mean winning at all costs. Fans, too, need to shoulder some of the blame, from fans who riot after their team wins the World Series to parents who berate coaches and refs at Little League games.

Yet sports and sportsmanship remain metaphors for life: competing, winning, losing. We compete for college admission and scholarships or jobs and promotions. The qualities of good sportsmanship are the same as the qualities of good leadership.

SPECTATOR ETIQUETTE

There was a time when a disruption at the ballpark was rare. But in recent years fan behavior has taken a turn for the worse. Televised games capture not just the play on the field, but the scene in the stands, and some fans purposefully push the envelope to try to gain attention. Disorderly behavior can be intensified when fueled by alcohol. Anonymity—being one of hundreds or thousands—can increase the rudeness factor as well. Unfortunately, the actions of a minority can make it seem as if fans in general are a boorish bunch. Stadiums have cracked down on fans who cross the line, even revoking season tickets.

Most fans behave well. The point is to have fun, yell and cheer, and experience the thrill of victory and the agony of defeat. It's also important to remember the kids in the stands. These are the fans of tomorrow and what they see, they will do. Here are a few pointers:

- Walk slowly with the crowd, not through it, when entering and leaving the stadium, taking care not to bump or shove others.

- Wait for a break in the action. Say "Excuse me" or "Pardon me" generously as you pass people on your way to your seat. As at the theater, pass with your back to those already seated.

- Raise your arm to signal a vendor (they're quick to spot a customer) or call, "Over here."

- If you're in the middle of a row and have to ask others to pass your money and food, be sure to thank those who did the passing.

- When a large group of spectators rises and blocks your view, go with the flow and stand. Sometimes someone gets wrapped up in the game and forgets to sit down. A *friendly* "Down in front!" works at a stadium, while "Excuse me, would you mind sitting so we can see? Thanks!" works for the individual in front of you.

- Watch your language. Obscenities in public are by nature offensive, no matter how free-spirited the atmosphere. Sporting events are for kids, too.

tailgating

Tailgating is the traditional pregame picnic off the back of your car in the parking lot. The atmosphere is upbeat, and there's a great feeling of camaraderie and generosity—after all, your team hasn't lost yet! If you get friendly with the tailgaters next to you, it's customary to share food. But if you're just wandering through to the stands, freeloading isn't okay; head to the concession tents.

- Cheer your heart out after a play that goes your team's way, but don't cross the line into obnoxious boasting.

- Yes, occasional booing occurs—but leave it there. Angry, derisive, or obscene shouting is over the line.

- At events where quiet is expected—a golf tournament, a tennis match, a game of billiards, or even a game of chess—stay still and silent when the players are trying to concentrate.

A WORD TO PARENTS

Poor fan behavior on the part of some parents is hard to ignore and can make it seem as if all parents are guilty. When taunts rain down on the referee of a Little League game, a mother stalks onto the field to protest a move by the coach, or two fathers come to blows over perceived slights in a soccer or hockey match, it puts a damper on the game for the rest of the spectators, the kids, and the refs.

Ask any kid over the age of six and he'll tell you that such behavior is out of line and embarrassing. Ask any kid over the age of six, too, whom he learns his manners from and he'll say, "My parents." **As a parent, be the spectator you want your child to be.** Here's how:

◆ **Leave coaching to the coach.** Shouting negative comments and instructions at the adult in charge will confuse a young child: Which adult is she supposed to listen to—you or the coach? Aggressive sideline coaching sets a bad example for all children, undermines their confidence, and can harm performance.

◆ **Don't criticize referees and judges.** If you disagree with a referee's call, keep the criticism to yourself. Even if you think he was completely off base, don't convey your hostile feelings to your child. You can discuss a decision with your child, but stick to the action itself: "I don't think the ref saw Josh touch home plate," and don't indulge in personal insults.

◆ **Compliment the opposition.** If the other team is playing particularly well, remark on their skills. Showing your appreciation for the other side isn't a betrayal of your own child but simply an essential part of sportsmanship and good manners.

◆ **Steer clear of tantrum-throwing parents.** You can't reason with a furious parent, but if you know the person, you may want to speak with him about his behavior at a calmer time. If a parent is throwing things or seems physically threatening, get the authorities immediately instead of taking on an out-of-control spectator yourself.

◆ **Talk with your child.** If your child has witnessed poor parental behavior, take some time on the way home to talk about it: "Mr. Archer sure gave the ref a hard time. What do you think about that?"

◆ **Point out good role models.** Whenever you watch televised events or attend live competitions with your child, point out the positive role models: those who follow the rules, even when it penalizes their team or score; those who win and lose graciously. Tell your child exactly why this or that player is a good sport: "So-and-so didn't win today, but I really like how he complimented the winner and what he said about his own play."

THE GOOD SPORT

Little did Emily Post know when she wrote in the 1945 edition of *Etiquette* just how apt her words would be today: "The quality which perhaps more than any other distinguishes true sportsmanship is absence of temper . . . not temper brought along and held in check, but temper securely locked and left at home." When you take to the course, court, or field, be an example of good sportsmanship.

---

respect the ref

Referees have a tough job. A baseball umpire, for example, makes around 150 calls each game. If he makes 3 that are questionable, he gets ripped apart by the fans, even though 3 out of 150 is a 98-percent success rate. Let's let them do their jobs.

---

the graceful winner
and loser

Things might get heated in the midst of
competition, but in the end, it's just a game,
right? The good sport downplays his or her
victories—"Good match! For a while there
I thought you had me"—and is generous in
defeat: "Nice win! Your serve was awesome
today."

- Let your performance speak for itself—nobody likes a braggart.

- Don't gripe about lapses in your own performance (and, naturally, *never* your opponent's).

- Watch your language.

- Be a good loser. It is just as important as being a gracious winner.

- Treat a sports ground of any kind as you would your own backyard. Pick up litter, stretch the tennis net tight after your game, repair any marks you left on the green, and return equipment to the locker room as necessary.

- Win or lose, shake hands at the end of the game.

Regular League or Team Games

When playing in a regular group—a weekly volleyball game or on an organized team—you have the advantage of knowing the other players. Even among close friends, however, a couple of key etiquette points are worth remembering:

- **Make sure that you understand the rules and expectations.** Are there dues/fees? Who is the point person if you have questions? What are the rules the group operates by? Knowing the answers will help you participate in a positive way and know where to turn if things go wrong or you have questions.

- **Always be on time.** Often, tennis courts, tee times, and field reservations are difficult to come by, and athletic facilities usually run on tight schedules. Being late is disrespectful to everyone involved in the game. Furthermore, coaches and teammates don't want players who ignore the team's starting time, either—they simply can't function if players don't respect start and end times.

- **Never take your fellow players for granted.** A good experience depends on the support of the entire group, not just the best players. Cheer everyone's efforts. Remember, you're *all* there to play the game and have a good time.

Pickup Games

During pickup games you don't always know either your opponents or your teammates. To make the games go more smoothly

- **Introduce yourself.** At the start of the game, shake hands with the other players and tell them your name. It's not just polite, it's easier to say, "Hey, Brad, I'm open!" than to yell, "Hey, you!" to a court full of players.

- **Tread lightly.** Now is not necessarily the time to take on the role of captain, as it could come across as overstepping or being arrogant. Leadership will be more welcome once you've established credibility with your teammates.

- **Avoid arguing over calls.** Since there usually aren't refs, arguing over fouls and penalties can cause friction—more so with people you may not know. Aggressive challenges among strangers can turn into full-scale confrontations.

Whenever You Play

Whether you play on a team, in a regular group, or in pickup games, these points of sportsmanship apply:

- **Don't let winning become worthless.** It's okay to want to win, but winning at all costs devalues the victory. Cheating on your golf score, calling an "out" shot "in" for your tennis partner, and sneaking in a cheap move to score a goal are unsportsmanlike ploys that make a win worthless.

- **Leave the game on the field.** Be a gracious winner and a gracious loser. Don't carry anger over a loss into the parking lot or down to the local bar.

GOLF ETIQUETTE

Etiquette is an integral part of the game of golf, so much so that Section I of the USGA's *Rules of Golf* is titled "Etiquette; Behavior on the Course." With the increasing popularity of golf and courses now crowded with beginners, knowing and practicing good golf etiquette is more important than ever. (For the complete rules of golf, visit www.usga.org.)

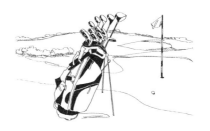

Club Rules

While the rules of golf are always in play wherever you play, clubs and courses can have local rules. Whether you're a member, a guest, or a paying player at a public course, it's imperative that you become familiar with and follow the club rules. Clubs aren't shy about asking offenders to follow the rules or leave. Two issues to ask about before your arrival: the club's policies about attire and cell phone usage.

- **Attire:** Shorts? Cargo pants? Jeans? Collarless shirts? Different clubs—public and private—have different dress codes, so it's a good idea to call the pro shop ahead of time so you arrive appropriately dressed. At a private club, you may have to forgo your round or buy some clothing at the pro shop if you're not dressed up to code. Typical golf attire is a collared (polo-type) sport shirt with shorts or long pants for men, and dress shorts or golf skirt for women. Almost all clubs require soft-spike shoes, and many do not allow denim or cargo shorts.

- **Mobile Phones:** Many clubs have rules about cell phones on the course and in the clubhouse dining areas; some go as far as limiting them to the parking lot only. Violators might be fined or asked to leave. Best advice? Leave your mobile phone in your car and enjoy your game. Even if you're just texting or tweeting, its use is both a distraction to others and takes your focus away from the game. Before using a phone for yardage and/or course apps, check with the pro shop, starter, or your host to be sure it's permissible.

Golf Is a Friendly Game

Golf is as much a social game as it is a sport. It's a long-honored tradition for the starter to create foursomes out of singles, twosomes, and threesomes. Good golf manners start with greeting your fellow players courteously, making introductions, and shaking hands. Around the course, players look out for each other by watching each other's shots, helping to look for a lost ball, picking up a club another group left behind, or picking up each other's clubs as they leave the green. They compliment each other's shots and thank each other for the compliments.

Basic Golf Manners

If you're a newcomer to the game, you might feel overwhelmed by all the rules and manners associated with golf. Observe the following and you'll be welcome in any foursome:

- Be on time for your tee time. Arrive early if you need to change or go to the practice tee. If you're late, your group may go off without you or forfeit their time, depending on club rules.
- Watch your ball. It's your job to have an idea where your ball landed so you don't hold things up looking for it.

- Follow the correct rotation for teeing off: The person with the lowest score on the previous hole has "honors" and goes first. Some groups, however, play "ready golf," meaning whoever is ready hits next. Just make sure you know what your group prefers.
- Avoid making noise when others are playing. Because concentration is key, never speak, rattle your clubs, or move when another player is making a shot. Even if your fellow players don't seem to mind noise, keep your voice down.
- Mark your ball on the green and be ready to putt when it's your turn.
- When on the green, don't walk on another player's line—between the player's ball and the hole.
- Respect the course. Repair any divots after your shot. When leaving a putting green, put the flagstick back in the hole and repair any marks made by your ball where it hit the green or any scuff marks made by your shoes. After playing a shot out of a bunker, rake the sand to erase your footprints and the hole made by your club strike.
- Don't litter. Keep any wrappers, tissues, or other trash with you until you can toss it into a trash can.
- Give and accept compliments graciously. Constant boasting about your great shots or putts is obnoxious, as is blaming everything but your lack of skill for poor ones.
- Keep your temper in check. What if your every drive is a hook into the rough? Frustrating, yes, but throwing clubs, stomping, and swearing won't be appreciated by anyone. Take a deep breath instead, calmly finish your round, and make a date for the practice range.

- Let smaller or faster groups through if there's an empty hole ahead of you.

- At the end of the round, move off the green, remove your hat, shake hands, and thank the other players.

Safety First

Safety is critical. Accidentally hitting another player with a ball or club can be deadly, and it's the last thing a golfer wants to do. Here are three ways to prevent it:

- When taking practice swings, stand a safe distance from others. Make sure there's no risk of hitting anyone with your club or anything propelled by your club (stones, sticks, or turf).

- Wait to tee off until those in the group ahead of you have hit their second shots and are outside of your range.

- When making a blind shot, send a caddie or ask another player to scout the area where your ball is expected to land. If other golfers are within your range, the lookout can signal for you to wait until the landing area is clear.

Speed of Play

So that the game will move right along, plan your shot before it's your turn. Then take only one practice swing (if any) before hitting the ball. Keep up with the group ahead of you. Make sure you don't leave an entire hole open ahead of you. If you do, you've fallen too far behind. Slow play is one of golfing's cardinal sins.

Normally, the golfer farthest from the hole hits first. However, one way to speed things up is for the group

to agree to play "ready golf." This allows a player who's ready to go ahead and hit, even if he's playing out of turn.

⌐ TENNIS ETIQUETTE ⌐

Sometimes tennis etiquette has as much to do with sharing a public or private court as it does with interacting with your opponent and your partner during the match.

- Arrive at your court on time.

- If you've reserved a court and arrive at your appointed time to find a match still in progress, tell the players you don't mind waiting until they finish the game in progress. Then wait patiently without pacing, bouncing balls, or appearing miffed.

- If you and your opponent are the players occupying the court and your allotted time is up, finish the game you're playing and then leave the court—even if you're near the end of the set.

- If players who have overrun their time limit refuse to leave until they finish the set, it's wiser to ask a tennis center staff member to intervene than handle the matter yourself.

- Public courts usually have a first-come, first-served policy. When there's a break in the action it's perfectly fine to ask those ahead of you for an estimate of how long they expect to play.

- When playing on an unreserved court, don't play on endlessly. Instead, tell new arrivals how long you plan to play and then try to finish your set within an hour. (Note: Generally, assigned public court time is 1 hour for singles, 1½ hours for doubles.)

- If your court is beyond someone else's and you have to cross behind, wait until they finish the point before heading to your court unless they motion you on.

- Return any runaway balls to their owners.

The Match

Etiquette starts with knowing the rules of the game and following them. It's advisable to purchase and read the U.S. Tennis Association book of rules or to go to the organization's website (www.usta.com/rules/).

Even if you're not playing well, act as if you're having fun. The game will be better for you, your partner (if you're playing doubles), and your opponent if you think positively—and you'll probably improve your play while you're at it.

No matter the quality of your play, avoid complaining about your bad shots; losing your temper or angrily slamming a ball (or worse, your racket onto the court); sulking when losing; and using foul language.

If you're playing in a tournament, never question the ruling of the linesman or referee. Even if you think your ball has landed *in* by a foot but the official says it's *out,* you should accept the official's decision as final.

Some other important points to remember:

- The server, not the receiver, calls out the score before serving.

- The receiver should refrain from returning a served ball called "out."

- When there's doubt whether a ball was in or out, the receiver makes the call. Unless the receiver clearly sees it out, the ball should be called good.

- Change sides every other game, on the odd game—starting after the first, then continuing after the third, fifth, and so on. It's a requirement in tournament play and a courtesy in a friendly match.

- If your ball bounces into a neighboring court, wait until the players have finished their point before asking them for their help in retrieving it.

- White used to be the required color of tennis clothes practically everywhere, but this is no longer always the case. When invited to play at a private club, ask your host if "tennis whites" are required; if you're the host, be sure to let your guest know the dress code.

- At the end of a match, it's a courteous tradition to shake hands with your opponent(s), congratulate him on his win, or thank him for a good match if he lost.

AT THE FITNESS CENTER OR STUDIO

Exercising on your own is one thing, but at a health or fitness club, sharing space and equipment with a lot of sweaty people calls for consideration.

- Rule #1: Always use the provided disinfectant to wipe sweat off mats and machines.

- No cutting! If someone else is next in line, the machine is theirs.

- Don't hog the weight machines. When others want to use them, agree to rotate your sets.

- Reset the weight machines and rerack the free weights. Wipe down and put away props.

- If all the treadmills or other cardio machines are full, limit your time to give those who may be waiting a chance. If your gym sets a time limit when people are waiting, respect it.

- A quick and friendly "hello" is one thing, but chatting to a fellow gymgoer who's working out could interrupt his routine.

- Save flirting for elsewhere. The time to try to strike up a conversation is when you're on your way out of the gym.

- Comply with the fitness center's rules, such as wearing correct workout shoes (black soles can be a problem), turning off cell phones, eating only in designated areas, and signing in at the front desk.

- Lay off the perfume and cologne (the aromas get stronger as you work up a sweat).

- Be on time for personal training sessions and group fitness classes.

- Keep your towels, water bottles, and fitness logs with you and out of the way of others.

- Pitch in for a tidy locker room: Keep your clothes and other personal items stored in lockers. Clean up after yourself when using showers and sinks, and throw towels in the laundry bin.

Yoga and Pilates Classes

Yoga and Pilates classes have their own codes of conduct and expected etiquette. Follow your teacher's lead to fit in well and make the most of any class experience.

- Show up early enough to get comfortably set up before class begins. This will mean leaving extra time while you are still learning a new routine.

- Don't just leave your phone behind; remember to shut it off completely. Challenge yourself to not turn it back on the second that class is over. Allow a bit of time for both you and your classmates to transition out of class.

- Wear appropriate clothes. You will need something that is clean and allows you to move freely in many directions but that is not too loose and revealing. This is why many people prefer to wear something elastic and formfitting that both permits free movement and keeps you covered up.

- Bring your own props or learn to take care of the props that are provided. Wipe down mats. Return blocks, belts, and mats to the place that you found them and pay attention to how they are folded, stacked, and cared for.

- Be an active participant and do your best to follow the class structure. Asking too many questions can be a distraction as can someone who insists on "doing their own thing" for the entire class. Make sure that while you take care of yourself and modify a class to fit your needs, you don't become an annoyance to everyone else.

- Keep the focus on the work you are there to do. Don't stare at or ogle classmates. While a class environment can be social and fun it is important to keep your primary focus on the purpose of the class.

- Offer to help someone who is new figure out how to follow any unwritten rules you have discovered along the way.

Working with a Personal Trainer

Your relationship with a personal trainer is likely to be improved by the same good etiquette that is part of every professional relationship.

- Be clear in all your communications, but especially in regards to fees. Know what services are provided and what the cost is before you sign on.

- Pay what you owe on time.

- Show up on time. Contact your trainer as early as possible if you need to cancel or change an appointment. Be prepared to pay for time that goes unused if you don't give adequate notice.

- Stay off of your mobile phone during a session. If you have to take a call, let your trainer know ahead of time and step away or go somewhere private to take the call.

- Know and respect the limits of the relationship. You are not visiting a counselor so keep the focus on training, not your personal problems.

- Consider offering an annual tip equivalent to the cost of one session if you have been working with someone for a year or more.

⟦ SHARING THE ROAD OR THE REC PATH ⟧

Recreation paths and even public roads are shared by cyclists, inline skaters, skateboarders, joggers, and

spitting and snot rockets

It's a gross part of sports, but when we exert ourselves, most of us find the need to spit or blow our noses, which isn't always possible midgame or midrun when we haven't tucked some tissues into our pocket. Spitting and blowing snot rockets is not considered good etiquette, but, realistically, they happen, and if you're going to need to do one or the other (or both) it's best to give a little thought and care into how you go about it.

Try to spit off the playing field and away from others and definitely aim for grassy areas, where the spit is less noticeable, rather than concrete or asphalt paths where others may be walking or running. If you can go straight for a trash can, all the better. Don't forget the wind factor: Spit downwind of others so that any potential spray doesn't get on them. If you do happen to have tissues—and you should—they are preferable to use, and make sure to dispose of them in a trash can. Littering is never appropriate.

walkers. As always, safety and courtesy go hand in hand. Those on foot have the right of way over those on wheels. Rec paths may separate bikers and joggers, so be sure to use the correct lane. If you're moving more slowly than others sharing the path, stay to the right. On a public road, walkers and runners should face oncoming traffic, while bikers and others on wheels move with traffic. Anyone out for some road-based exercise after dark should dress in brightly colored or

when you're in the race

It's important to rehydrate and refuel during a race, especially when running or biking long distances or in extreme heat. Drinking and eating on the run is made easier by race organizers and volunteers handing out water or flavored sports drinks and quick carbs along the course. Some racers drink the water while others cool down by pouring it over their heads. If you opt for the shower, try not to splash other racers.

Wondering what to do with the paper cup (or bottle, banana peel, or wrapper) once you've finished? Pitch your trash into one of the bins provided along the course, but if there aren't any, don't feel bad about tossing it to the side of the road for the volunteers to pick up. As you go along, shout out a general "Thanks!" to the volunteers for keeping you in the race and picking up after you.

reflective clothing or use a clip-on flashing light. It's also smart to carry ID (name, phone number, and contact person) when exercising by yourself just in case there's an accident.

Running

Whether you run in your neighborhood, on a recreation path, or on a track, go the extra mile by using a little consideration.

- In neighborhoods, try to jog where both foot traffic and auto traffic are light. Choose sidewalks that are sparsely traveled; then run or walk in the street only when you have to dodge an obstruction.

- If you are a street jogger, run against the traffic, watch for cars, and move out of the way of large trucks.

- On the rec path keep right instead of running down the middle, and don't hog the path by running two or three abreast.

- If you're running on a circular track with several lanes, leave the inside lanes for faster runners who might be doing timed sessions.

Cycling

The basics for cyclists? It's both good manners and safe practice to

- Wear a helmet.

- Follow all traffic rules, and obey stop signs and traffic signals. Racing through red lights and stop signs could end in disaster—for both you and an unwary driver or pedestrian.

- Ride single file on public roads to allow automobiles to pass. Remember, "Share the road" applies to bikers, too.

- Signal your intention to turn or stop.

- Warn before overtaking. Using a bell or a friendly "On your left" gives another cyclist a heads-up and a chance to move to the right.

⌈ ON THE TRAIL ⌉

Responsible hikers, horseback riders, mountain bikers, and cross-country skiers know not to disturb the flora and fauna of the wilderness and have respect for the trail and those sharing it. "Leave no trace: Take only pictures, leave only footprints" and "Pack it in, pack it out" are good principles to follow. Whatever your form of trail recreation, employ these courtesies:

- Observe and follow all posted signs.
- Take care not to damage any trees or shrubs, and leave the wildflowers (no picking).
- Stick to the trail, since taking a shortcut around hillsides or obstacles could contribute to an increase in erosion or, in alpine areas, destroy lichens.
- Be considerate of everyone else using or living along the trails, greeting them with a friendly "hello."
- Leave gates as you found them and don't climb fences.
- For safety's sake, don't smoke on the trail.
- Leave nothing behind. Pack it in and pack it out—and it's considerate to pick up the odd can or bottle along the way.

Hiking

Whether you're a day hiker or a backpacker, a group should move only as fast as its slowest member. Don't take a dog on the trail unless it's allowed and you can keep it under control. Use a leash if required and dispose of animal waste as you would on a city street.

---

the rule of the trail

Stay to the right, pass on the left, and yield the right of way to uphill traffic unless you're a downhill or cross-country skier (in which case traffic above you should yield to you).

Horseback Riding

Make sure the trail you plan to ride allows horses. Walking is the preferred gait on shared, multiuser trails. Most important is that you know your horse and its temperament; you, the rider, are responsible for your horse's behavior.

By nature, horses are flight animals, and their instinct is to run when spooked—dangerous for both horse and rider. To pass another rider, let him and his horse know by saying, "Trail, please"; the rider then should move his horse as far right on the trail as possible or simply stop his horse in its tracks. Thank the other rider as you pass. When greeting hikers or entering a camp, dismount and lead your horse. Also ask anyone you're greeting to approach your horse from the front.

Mountain Biking

Because of their speed, mountain bikers need to announce their approach to hikers and anyone else on the trail with a friendly shout. Thank anyone who yields the right of way to you, including other bikers. In addition, other bikers have the right of way when they have

---

happy campers

When you're at a public or private campground, you're essentially renting the space. So it stands to reason that you leave your campsite clean for the campers who follow. Here are a few essentials for campers:

Do abide by all campground rules, especially those regarding pets, trash and cigarette disposal, speed limits, and quiet hours.

Do leave the trees alone. Don't drive nails into the trunks or branches when hanging lanterns or hammocks. Even dead trees are home to many critters.

Do bring your own firewood. Don't forage wood to use as firewood. If the campground doesn't sell it, you'll more than likely find bundled firewood at gas stations or supermarkets in the area.

Do dispose of all trash appropriately, whether it's carrying it out with you or placing your garbage bags and recycled items in marked receptacles.

Don't put metal, glass, or plastic in the firepit; wood, paper, and cigarette butts are the only things that belong there.

Don't cut through other campers' campsites on the way to the showers, toilets, trails, or anywhere else. Their space may not have walls, but it's still their space.

Do observe quiet hours. Even when it's not defined quiet time, keep the noise level down. Loud music or laughter robs neighboring campers of the very thing they came for—peace and quiet. Excessive noise could get you evicted from the campground.

Do leave the campsite better than you found it.

---

children along, are traveling in a group, or are going uphill. If you want to pass, say, "On your left" or "On your right" once you're within speaking distance. (The usual phrase for racers is "Track, please!") Then follow with a "thanks" as you pass.

Many horses are easily spooked by bicycles. If you encounter a horseback rider going in either direction on the trail, slow down, announce your presence, and ask if it's all right to pass. Once the rider says it's safe, thank him as you proceed slowly and quietly. In some cases, it may be necessary to dismount, lift your visor (so as not to frighten the horse), and step off the trail to let horse and rider pass.

ON THE WATER

As carefree as a day on the water can be, boaters are subject to long-standing customs and traditions. Whether taking to the water in a canoe, a powerboat, or a 60-foot yacht, the boater's first concern is safety.

Know the rules, especially those regarding right of way. The rules and regulations can be found, among other sources, on the U.S. Coast Guard's website (www.uscgboating.org). The USCG provides information and navigational maps on coastal waterways, tides, and the placement of depth markers and other buoys, whereas state and local boating commissions are the authority for rivers and most lakes.

Besides operating their vessels safely, there's another general courtesy for boaters to observe: the effect their wake has on other vessels. When passing a slower vessel or a vessel at anchor, avoid rocking it by slowing your speed and giving it as wide a berth as possible. Keep clear of sailing regattas, and respect those living along the shoreline, being careful not to swamp their property with your wake.

At the Marina

The marina is a place where you literally don't want to make waves, so approach your anchorage or mooring at slow speed. Also be careful not to anchor your boat in close proximity to others, since a sudden change in the wind can cause boats to bang against one another and anchor lines to tangle.

If you plan any nighttime activities, anchor well downwind from your neighbors. Many boaters plan early departures and go to bed early. Voices, music, and the sounds of children's play—all of which carry exceptionally well over water—can keep others from getting a good night's sleep. The smoke from a barbecue can also be unpleasant for neighbors anchored downwind of your boat.

Following are some other considerations for the courteous boater:

- Don't warm up engines more loudly (or for longer) than necessary when leaving the dock early in the morning or late at night.

- When rowing around the anchorage, be friendly but not intrusive. If you decide you'd like to say "hello" to strangers on deck, approach their craft on the starboard (right) side and stay about 6 to 10 feet away.

- When you stop for fuel, don't jump the line. When you're finished fueling, pay and leave, or move your boat to another location. Don't leave your boat tied to the fuel dock to run errands onshore.

- If you see another boater docking or undocking and no dockmaster or other helper is around, offer to assist with their lines.

- Keep the dock area just outside your boat clear. Roll up and stow hoses and power cords so as not to trip passersby, and don't leave tackle, buckets, mops, and other items strewn around the dock.

- After using communal equipment such as carts, return them so they're accessible to others.

At the Boat Launch

Good launch ramp etiquette means being efficient and taking turns. Whether going in or out, it's first come, first served, so don't jump the line. When there are a number of boats waiting to get both in and out, alternate one in, one out. Don't hold up other boaters waiting at the dock when you launch. Get organized and take care of any maintenance in advance so when you launch, you can move your boat away from the ramp and your vehicle and trailer to the parking lot as quickly as possible, leaving the ramp available for the next boater. The same is true when you haul your boat: Complete any stowing or cleaning in the parking lot, not at the dock or ramp. While you're waiting to launch, it's courteous to lend a friendly hand to others to help speed things along.

On the Radio

Courteous use of open channel radio frequencies is a must. Channel 16 is for emergencies and Channel 22 for the coast guard. Channel 9 is for *short* vessel-to-vessel communications; it's not an open chat line. If you need to have a longer conversation, switch to a different frequency.

Hosting Guests Onboard

When extending an invitation, a good host will let guests know if they need to bring any special gear or clothing, and mention that if seasickness might be an issue, to take any motion sickness medicine well ahead of sailing. Whether guests are joining you onboard for the day, a weekend, or much longer, "show them the ropes" before you cast off, especially if they're inexperienced.

boating traditions: flag etiquette

Flags have a long history in marine tradition. Before modern radio or flash signals, flying flags told other vessels who you were and if you needed assistance. Whether you're flying your country's ensign or yacht club burgee, here are some flag etiquette tips:

- The **ensign**, the representation of the U.S. flag, should only be flown between sunrise and sunset. It's usually flown from the stern of a vessel.

- If you belong to a yacht club, you may fly its **burgee**, a small flag with the club's unique symbol, not unlike a logo. Your club may specify the burgee's location, but usually it's flown from the bow of a powerboat or the mast of a sailboat.

- There are forty distinct **International Code flags** that are used for signaling, and still useful if your radio's out. The flags can also convey a short message. For example, the flag for the letter O also means "man overboard," F means "disabled," and AN means "I need a doctor."

- In case of emergency, do carry a **distress signal** flag.

If you need them to handle lines or perform any other duties onboard, teach them how, if necessary.

Once guests are onboard, take a few minutes to demonstrate how things work, from the head (toilet) to the galley (kitchen) sink. Boats do have a special vocabulary, so it's a good idea to clue them in to the meaning of basic terminology such as port (left), starboard (right), fore (front), and aft (back). Also inform them

the good onboard guest

Spending time aboard a boat requires more than just showing up and hoping for a good tan. The special circumstances of being a boat guest require some special considerations, starting with what to bring.

- Take the minimum amount of clothing you'll need onboard and onshore and pack it in a canvas bag—not a hard suitcase, which is almost impossible to stow. (Most captains keep foul-weather gear onboard, but ask beforehand whether you should bring your own.)

- Wear rubber-soled, nonskid, nonscuff shoes, which will keep you from slipping and sliding on deck and won't mar the deck surface.

- Have your gear stowed and be ready to leave ahead of the departure time set by your host.

- On a boat, the captain's word is the law, so be sure to obey all instructions without question.

- Abide by your host's hours, rising and retiring as he does.

- Ask your host if you can bring a cooler of beverages or anything else to contribute toward a meal onboard.

- When sailing for several days, offer to chip in for expenses—paying for gas when refueling, treating for a meal onshore, or replenishing beverages or other staples.

- A thank-you gift for your host is appropriate. Unless it's either something small or for use on the boat, present it before or after the cruise so there's one less thing to stow on the boat.

of safety and emergency procedures and any rules of behavior that must be observed onboard. Remind them of the most basic safety rule: Always keep one hand for yourself and one hand for the boat.

If you're on an extended sail and visiting foreign ports, let your guests know in advance which documents they should bring, and if there are any local customs they should be aware of. (See also "The Pre-Trip Meeting," page 121.)

Once the trip is under way, be the first to rise every day. You're the one in charge, and your guests will be more comfortable if you make it clear that you are.

Water Skiing and Personal Watercraft

Operators of boats towing water-skiers should be constantly on the lookout, making sure the area is clear before starting and then making sure they don't cut in front of other boats. It's also a good idea to review and agree on hand signals—faster, slower, okay, cut—with the skier. If the skier drops a ski, the spotter should throw a spare life jacket or colored buoy to mark the ski, both so it can be retrieved and so it's not a hazard to other boats or skiers.

Jet Skis, or personal watercraft, while a lot of fun to ride, are controversial because of their noisiness, rolling wakes, potential for accidents, and ability to travel in shallow water, which can disturb wildlife habitats. Observing safe boating rules and local regulations, as well as practicing some basic etiquette, keeps it fun and complaints to a minimum:

- Share the water and watch out for others: boaters, fishermen, swimmers, and other skiers. Sailboats, commercial boats, and fishing vessels have the right of way.

- Respect the environment, the wildlife, and shallow water habitats.

- Respect those living along the shoreline. Operate after 7:00 AM and away from the shoreline.

- Keep noise to a minimum. Warm up your engine in the water, not onshore, and flush the engine at home.

- Use launch ramps efficiently. Do your preps and checks ahead of time.

Angler's Etiquette

Think of fishing and most of us picture the solitary angler in his boat, on the shore, or in a stream. When that's not the case, time-honored courtesies make sure that everyone has a chance of a fair catch. When fishing from a powerboat, don't anchor right next to other fishers who are catching; it's unfair to take advantage of their good luck.

Anglers who fish the surf from the beach should cast their lines far away from swimmers, or fish at dawn or dusk when the beach is apt to be clear of bathers. Beginner surfcasters should stand apart from others so lines don't cross on a wild cast. The angler with a fish on his line has right of way, so to speak; other anglers should lift their rods and lines so he can cross under as he walks down the beach, reeling in his fish. Anyone who fishes from a dock should always reel in his line when a boat approaches. Boat anglers also reel in when someone else has a fish on their line.

Make your approach to a fishing spot downstream of other anglers and enter the water quietly, so you don't spook the fish. When casting from the shore of a stream, a river, or a lake, give others as much space as possible so you don't risk (literally) hooking another angler or tangling lines with your cast.

] AT THE BEACH [

Whether you're lucky enough to have access to a private beach or you frequent a public one, go for the peace and quiet or extreme beach volleyball, "beach manners" ensure that everyone enjoys the day.

- Keep the beach clean and leave it better than you found it. Take all your gear and your trash home, plus a few extra pieces of beach litter.

- If you want to enjoy loud music or a game of Frisbee, move away from groups trying to chat, read, or rest.

- Watch where you lay your mat or towel. A good indicator: You're too close if you cast a shadow on other sunbathers or your movements kick sand on them. Also try not to block their view of the water.

- Shake towels gently and downwind so sand doesn't blow on others.

- Follow the dress code—naked is for the nude beach only, and think twice about wearing a thong bikini at a family beach.

- So they don't kick up sand, teach kids to walk—not run—around people on towels.

- Fill in the holes made by your sand castle project— a potential hazard to walkers and joggers.

- Smoke downwind of those around you.

Surfing

Surfers have their own code and etiquette, which can vary place to place, but the following are fairly common board courtesies:

- Respect the local community (don't speed through town), the local people (be friendly and courteous), private property (stay off it), and the beach (keep it clean).

- Learn the surfing right-of-way rules and follow them. (They're explained in detail on various websites found by searching "surfing etiquette.")

- Keep control of your board.

- Don't cut in line.

- Paddle back out of the way of active surfing— ideally so you can get back in line again.

- Share the waves. Kayakers, longboarders, and stand-up paddlers have an easier time catching waves. Make sure shortboarders and bodyboarders get a chance at good rides, too.

ON THE SLOPES

Most of the etiquette guidelines for skiers have grown from the need for safety. The same goes for snowboarding, which has brought more and more people to the slopes. Specific rules are based on common sense and should always be obeyed.

When waiting in the lift line, be careful not to step on others' skis with your own. Don't invite others to cut into the line with you. Be willing to ride up with a stranger, particularly if the line is long and you're riding the lift alone. Remember to thank the lift attendants for their help.

to tip or not?

Tips aren't mandatory for instructors or guides but they're certainly appreciated, and most people tip if they are pleased with the lesson or outing. The amounts vary. A tip is given either as a flat amount (say, $10 or $20 for a one- or two-hour lesson) or as a percentage of the cost. If a half-day lesson or guide costs $200, for example, tip 15 to 20 percent ($30 to $40) or more. Some clients treat their instructors or guides to a meal in addition to—or in lieu of—a tip. Customs vary from region to region, or resort to resort, so it's a good idea to inquire at the resort or guide service when booking.

Ski in control. It's your responsibility to avoid objects and other people. Skiers downhill (ahead) of you have the right of way, and you should yield to others when entering a trail or starting downhill. When stopping, make sure that those above can see you and that you don't obstruct the trail. If you need to wait for someone, step to the side of the trail.

Snowboarding. Many ski areas now also have trails and pipes just for snowboarders where they can ride and practice maneuvers. On shared slopes, remember that people downhill from you have the right of way and give others plenty of room. Jumps and quick turns obviously need to be carried out with safety in mind, and that means being aware of other skiers and riders at all times. Looking before leaping and staying in control are the smart, safe, and considerate ways to ride. When you want to rest, stop in a place that's out of the way of riders and skiers, but very visible—not below a bump or around a corner.

Cross-country skiing. When other skiers approach, keep to the right and yield to anyone coming downhill. If skiing on a snowmobile trail, stay as far right as possible when a vehicle approaches. Whenever you stop for any reason, be sure not to block the trail. If you fall, take a moment to repair damage to the trail. All of these guidelines apply to snowshoers as well.

Dealing with Falls

Whether you're snowboarding or downhill or cross-country skiing, the chances are high that you'll experience a fall or two. After a fall, quickly move to the side of the slope or trail, if you can, to prevent collisions and to allow other skiers and riders to pass. If you're unable to exit the slope or trail, you or someone else should plant your skis or poles in a vertical, crossed position—the signal that alerts other skiers that someone is down on the slope. If the injured person is in a blind spot on the slope, plant skis, poles, or other markers far enough ahead to warn oncoming traffic. Snowboarders should plant their boards above the injured person as a warning.

If for any reason you accidentally knock down another skier or rider, stop, apologize, and make sure they aren't injured before you continue down the hill. Never try to move an injured person. If the skier is unable to get up or is in pain, stay with him until another skier arrives. One of you should then immediately seek the help of the nearest ski patrol while the other stays with the injured skier.

Most skiers and riders are quick to lend a helping hand to anyone in trouble. If you see that someone has fallen, ask if they need assistance—then either seek the help of the nearest ski patrol or ask someone else to do so. In case of emergency, it's a smart idea to program the ski patrol phone number into your cell phone's speed dial.

Don't be the kind of skier or rider who blithely zooms by someone who has fallen without so much as a glance.

12
attending performances

Whether it's a Broadway spectacular, a rock festival in an open field, or the high school choir in concert at the school auditorium, truly enjoyable performances depend to a degree on the behavior of the audience. Courtesy to others in the audience and to the performers promotes attentiveness, and allows the people on both sides of the stage to fully appreciate the magic of words, music, and movement that transcend everyday experience. But the spell is broken when the woman in the next seat pokes you repeatedly with her oversized bag, a phone rings in the row behind you, or thoughtless parents don't take their crying child outside.

Some of the most common problems associated with public performances can be prevented with advance planning and awareness of the policies of the event location. Start by knowing when the performance will begin.

Be on Time

It's a good idea to plan to be in your seat at least five minutes before the performance begins. That means allowing enough time to park or navigate the crowds, buy or pick up tickets, meet friends, purchase refreshments, and get to your seat and settle in.

Tickets, Please!

Courteous people use line manners. It's not okay to let friends or latecomers jump the line and join you. If your group is purchasing separate tickets, either everyone should wait in line or you should delegate one person to buy all the tickets. If you must save a place, tell the person behind you that someone else is coming.

Taking a Seat

When there are ushers, it's best to allow them to guide you unless you know exactly where your seat is located. Ushers know how seats are numbered and, when seating isn't assigned, where seating is available. They're also prepared to help people with special needs such as aisle seating or wheelchair spaces.

Entering a row full of people is always inconvenient, but you can minimize the hassle.

if you're late

An accident delayed traffic for a half hour. The boss asked you to handle a last-minute task. Whatever the reason, you arrive after the performance or show has started. Some venues will let you proceed to your seat, but most allow only back-of-the-theater sitting or standing until a scene change, a break between musical numbers, or intermission. These rules benefit performers and patrons alike. Before trekking down the aisle, take a few moments to adjust to the low light; then scan for a convenient seat so you don't stumble over other patrons. If there's an usher, allow him or her to seat you.

- Begin by saying "excuse me" to the person on the aisle and then down the line and "thank you" to anyone who moves or stands to let you pass.

- Face the front or the stage. This means showing your back to the people in your row, but should you trip or stumble, it's easier to regain your balance (and maintain your dignity) by falling forward against a seat rather than into someone's lap.

- Proceed as quickly as you can—a sort of sideways semishuffle enables you to move along without stepping on feet.

- Be sure to hold purses, cases, backpacks, and coats high above the people around you. Be especially careful with umbrellas and canes.

When you're the one being passed in a row, it's often possible to clear space by remaining seated and turning your knees in the direction the person is moving. Standing may be easier if seats fold up, but once the performance is under way it's better to move knees than to stand, thereby blocking the view of those seated behind.

If you must leave a row during a performance, repeat the process but whisper your thanks and apologies. If returning to your seat will inconvenience people yet another time, it's better to sit or stand at the back of the hall until intermission. Anyone who may be summoned away during a performance should try to get a seat on or near an aisle, as should parents with young children.

Box Seating

Box subscribers to an opera, symphony, dance, or theater season alternate seats for different performances so that everyone gets a chance at the best views of the stage.

When box seating is for a single performance and seats aren't numbered, it's first come, first served. Still, gracious patrons will adjust, if seats can be moved, so that everyone has as clear a view as possible.

Open Seating

At some events, there are no assigned or ticketed seats so you're free to sit where you wish. While aisle seating may be preferred, try not to choose aisle seats on an empty row or the rest of the row will have to climb over you to get to a seat. It's also okay to save seats for friends, guests, or family members. Laying coats, hats, or programs on empty seats usually indicates that they're saved. If anyone asks "Is this seat taken?" simply say, "Yes, I'm saving it for my husband/friend/guest." If the rest of your party hasn't arrived once the program is about to begin, make the seats available.

When the House Lights Go Up

Intermissions are opportunities to stretch, visit the restroom, and perhaps enjoy something to eat or drink and chat with friends. When the performance is over, leaving should be a steady, measured departure. Neither intermission nor departing should be a stampede to the doors.

Intermission. Twenty minutes is the normal length of intermissions, but check your program to be sure. A good strategy is to head back to your seat five minutes before it ends. This lets you avoid the general rush when the warning lights or bells signal patrons to return

row d, seat 7

When seating is assigned by row and seat number, there's no room for debate. If someone's in your seat, don't make a scene. Check your ticket and say, "Excuse me, but I think you're in my seat." If the problem isn't solved with a check of seat numbers, then get an usher or manager and let him take over. Mistakes do happen, so be courteous.

to their seats. If you linger in the lobby or restroom after the intermission, you'll be inconveniencing others when you climb over them to reclaim your seat. If you want to stay in your seat during intermission, be courteous and leave your seat to let others exit your row.

Exiting. When the show ends, go with the flow. Don't block the aisle by stopping to chat with anyone and wait until you're outside to use your phone. It's discourteous to performers and patrons to leave a few minutes before the end of any entertainment to get a head start.

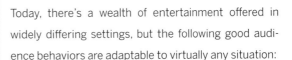

AUDIENCE ETIQUETTE

Today, there's a wealth of entertainment offered in widely differing settings, but the following good audience behaviors are adaptable to virtually any situation:

No talking, unless audience participation is requested by the performers. If something must be said, whisper it quickly. Excessively shushing of a talkative neighbor can be just as disturbing, so if the talk

doesn't stop after the first friendly "shush," calmly say, "Excuse me—I can't hear the music/dialogue." Or wait for an usher to intervene.

Use good posture. Sit up straight and keep your feet on the floor. Auditorium seating is often arranged so that the person in the seat behind can see between the two seats in front, so slumping sideways or lounging on a partner's shoulder blocks the view. Feet or knees shouldn't touch the seat in front. And share the armrests.

Remove hats. Ladies, if your hat is part of your outfit, you can keep it on as long as it doesn't block anyone's view.

Noises off. Turn off phones, beepers, audible watches, and any other sound-making gadgets before any performance. If you absolutely need to stay in touch with the outside world, put your device on vibrate or silent ring. If you must use your phone, wait until intermission; then find a secluded place. If it's an emergency, exit quietly and take the call in the lobby.

Lights out. Don't forget, the screen on your mobile device can be a distraction, too. (That means no texting, either!)

Snap, crackle, pop. No rattling of candy boxes or ice in cups, shaking popcorn containers, or slurping drinks. It's thoughtful to remove and dispose of any cellophane wrappers *before* the performance begins.

Normally, food and drinks are prohibited at a classical music, ballet, theater, or opera performance.

Control coughing. Muffle coughs and sneezes with a handkerchief. Cough drops and mints may be helpful, but leave if you can't stop the attack. If you have a cold or allergy and are inclined to cough, try to get an aisle seat near an exit so you can make a hasty retreat if needed.

Avoid other sounds that can disturb the people around you and the performers. Munching noisily, smacking or cracking gum, rattling the pages of pro-

Q: *My husband and I recently spent our vacation in England, our first overseas trip. We attended several plays and movies, and at the start, the audiences stood and sang "God Save the Queen." As Americans, we weren't sure what to do.*

A: Just as when "The Star-Spangled Banner" opens an event in the United States, when you're a guest in another country it's respectful to stand when the anthem of that country is performed. Men remove their hats and women their sports caps. Normally you wouldn't sing, place your hand over heart, or salute. If a statement of national loyalty similar to the Pledge of Allegiance is offered, stand respectfully, but don't say the words.

grams, tapping feet or drumming fingers, humming or singing along, rummaging in purses—these are just a few of the things that can annoy those around you.

Smoke only in designated areas. When the environment is totally smoke-free—as most indoor and many outdoor performance venues now are—leave and find a place outside if you want a smoke.

Don't take flash photos or shoot video during live performances. It's often illegal at professional performances, so check the policy of the performance venue. Even if it's not illegal, it's often requested that audiences refrain from taking photos or videos (including with phones). The point is to do nothing that will distract the performers or disturb others in the audience. A clicking, flashing camera or camcorder will do both.

Dispose of trash, including chewed gum, in waste containers. Tell an usher or attendant if anything was spilled, as a courtesy to the next person who has your seat.

What to Wear?

This subject can spur heated debate, especially when audiences show up to traditionally formal performances in everything from tuxes and evening gowns to jeans and T-shirts. Some believe that dressing more formally is a sign of respect for performers and the special nature of the occasion. Others say that as long as the audience is polite, the price of admission entitles ticket holders to wear whatever they like. As a general rule, the formality of dress is determined primarily by the nature of the event.

When you aren't sure what to wear, call the venue or ask someone who will also be attending or has attended similar performances. If you're someone's guest, talk with your hosts and be guided by their preference. If you can't get reliable advice, for most indoor music or theater performances you'll probably be fine in business attire—suit and tie; skirt and jacket or dress. There are, however, a few basics that apply regardless of fashion:

- ◆ Be conscious of personal hygiene, and use scents sparingly or not at all.
- ◆ Don't wear jewelry or accessories that clank or jingle.
- ◆ Space is small, so limit the items you take to your seat. If the venue has a coatroom, check any items you don't need during the performance.

Expressing Yourself

Every performer wants approval for good work, and hand clapping is the convention in the United States. Sometimes the audience is asked to hold their applause, so do comply. How long and how hard to clap is determined both by how much you've enjoyed what you've seen and heard and by the general audience reaction. Standing ovations and cheering are usually reserved for the end of the performance. (See "Performance Specifics," page 161, for more on the etiquette of applause.)

little patrons

There are excellent family-oriented entertainments available today—from G-rated movies to children's concerts and outdoor festivals. With so much to choose from, parents can introduce their children to a variety of cultural experiences in an environment that is child-friendly. This is a great opportunity to teach your child good audience manners so that by the time he is seven or eight, he is ready for a more adult concert or theater experience.

Thankfully, we've come a long way since the time when audiences expressed dissatisfaction by pelting performers with rotten vegetables and storming the stage. Polite but unenthusiastic clapping can register an audience's disapproval with deadly effectiveness. Most people who feel that a performance wasn't up to par will simply not clap and remain seated. Leaving early is also an option, but do so only between acts or at intermission when you won't inconvenience others.

Addressing performers in any way while they are performing is not acceptable, and heckling is tacky. Voicing complaints loudly to the people seated around you is just as bad. Don't spoil someone else's enjoyment because the performance failed to meet your standards. Practice the "Three Block Rule": Hold any verbal criticism until you are well clear of the venue.

Outdoor Etiquette

Many outdoor performances and open-air film presentations have a relaxed, laissez-faire atmosphere, but a little consideration will make the experience enjoyable for all.

Keep it down, please. Drowning out the performance with shrieking catcalls and ear-popping whistles is obnoxious and disrespectful. Unless the performers encourage you to, don't sing along or repeat dialogue.

Keep charge of children and pets (if they're allowed). Know where they are at all times. Sit near the edge of the crowd in case you need to take your daughter or your dog for a walk. Immediately clean up after your pet.

Preserve the view. Blankets, folding campstools, and low lawn chairs are fine at many outdoor events. Seating and accessories that can block others' view or cause congestion should be placed as far from the center of the crowd as possible. Kids on shoulders can be view-blockers, too.

Be careful with food and drink. Generally, it's close quarters, so be careful not to spill or slosh a drink on your neighbor. Wipe up spills, especially on surfaces where others may sit or eat.

Smoke away from the crowd. If you smoke and it's permitted, head for the fringes where the smoke is less bothersome and you're unlikely to bump a lighted cigarette into someone.

Clean up. Obviously, it's disrespectful to leave a mess. Plus municipalities and private event organizers often spend thousands of dollars for trash disposal after outdoor events, and eventually the money comes out of your pocket (either in higher taxes or ticket prices).

PERFORMANCE SPECIFICS

Different types of presentations have evolved their own etiquette. The event-specific courtesies included here reflect both tradition and common courtesy. (See also "The General Courtesies," page 155.)

At the Theater, Opera, and Ballet

At the ballet, opera, and sometimes musical theater, the orchestra conductor is applauded when he or she enters, before the curtain goes up. Enthusiastic audiences often applaud stars at their first entrance or exit from the stage. Operagoers applaud after a well-sung aria and the same is true at a musical, where applause follows the songs. At a play, however, it's good manners to hold clapping until the end of each act. At the final curtain, you can clap and cheer as enthusiastically as you like, but when the performers have taken their final bow, it's time to leave.

Going backstage to congratulate performers is a matter of being invited. Autograph seekers should wait at the stage door exit and have ready a pen and the article they wish signed.

At Classical Music Performances

People who are classical music novices often worry about when to clap. The appropriate times for applause are as follows:

bravo!

It's a tradition to applaud musical performers with the Italian cheer *bravo*, meaning, "Well done!" Shout *bravo* for a male performer and *brava* for a female.

When the conductor, concertmaster, and guest artists walk onstage. Once the conductor steps on the platform and raises his or her baton, all clapping ceases and the audience becomes silent. At performances by ensembles and soloists, watch the performers carefully; they will signal by eye contact and nods when they are ready to begin.

At the end of each entire piece. It's sometimes hard to know a piece has ended because there's usually a pause between movements, or sections, and you may think the piece is over. (Hint: Count the number of movements listed in the program and applaud after the last one is completed.) At the end of the piece the conductor may turn immediately to the audience, but some don't, so if you aren't sure the piece is completed, follow the audience's lead. They may not always be right, but at least you won't be clapping by yourself.

At the end of the concert. The conductor will turn to the audience and bow and may point out members of the orchestra for recognition. Guest artists and occasionally composers will come onto the stage for more applause. Don't rush for the exit at intermission or the end of the performance; remain seated until the clapping begins to die down and the people around you start to move. (See "Exiting," page 157.)

Although the mood and manners are less formal at pops concerts and audience participation is often part of the program, the concert manners above still apply.

At the Movies

Movie theater etiquette tends to be a bit more relaxed than that for live performances. While soft whispering, coughing, and opening candy wrappers won't disturb on-screen performers, it can bother other patrons. Considerate moviegoers adhere to the basics of performance etiquette—and instruct any children with them to be quiet during the movie.

As in any other theater, phones and other devices should be off or on vibrate, and any necessary calls taken in a quiet corner of the lobby. Texting during a movie is also annoying and taboo, as the screen light is distracting.

What do you do about someone who insists on talking during the movie? If they're near you and a friendly "shush" or "quiet, please" doesn't do the trick, speak to an usher or the management and ask them to handle the situation.

Coffeehouses and Clubs, Arenas, and Outdoor Festivals

Stepping into a coffeehouse to see a small local band is a different experience than road-tripping to a summer music festival with 70,000 other fans, but there are a few principles that apply to both situations—as well as to clubs, arenas, and everything in between. The two

most important points to keep in mind when attending a concert of any kind are to make sure your enjoyment of the performance doesn't have a negative impact on those around you and to make sure you're respectful of the performers.

In a small, intimate venue, whether you're seeing a folk singer in a coffeehouse or an a cappella group in a church, your voice will carry very easily. In the case of the church, it is best to not talk during the performance, as doing so will surely distract those around you, who came to see the group. As the venue gets bigger and the volumes get louder, there's a matter of degree to consider. If you're at a small club and the band is at eardrum-shredding volume, no one's going to mind if you talk—or yell—to get across to your date that you're having a great time. The same is true when you're at an indoor arena or outdoor festival. But if the performance is quiet, your best bet is to be quiet, too.

Small, intimate, or seated performances follow the same late arrival etiquette as at any other theater: If you arrive late, you won't be seated until the group is between pieces. This is also a respectful—and classy—way to leave small performances. Let's say you can only stay for a few songs or you've decided after paying the $5 cover at a club that the band isn't doing it for you. You are ready to go. Your departure will not only be easy to see and perhaps distract from the performance, but it could send a subtle message to the artists that you're not interested in their work. Wait until the band has played their song or piece of music, and leave once they're between performances.

At Parades, Street Fairs, and Street Performances

From the smallest rural town to the largest cities, people gather in and along their streets for entertainment and celebrations. For more popular parades, people line the route ahead of time. Just because a parade is a casual and free form of entertainment, it doesn't mean you leave your manners at home. While it's easy enough to walk out onto the street and stand in front of others, that's a breach of etiquette. Saying "excuse me" when you're trying to get to the street to cross it; using reasonable, calm, and considerate behavior; not saving places for a large group coming later; and keeping kids under control are all good parade watching manners.

Usually, street fairs have no entry fees, and many are publicly funded. Virtually anyone is welcome to watch performances or shop at food and craft stalls. While police and security personnel are often present, maintaining order essentially depends on the good natures and manners of the people who attend. In addition to the guidelines for outdoor performances (page 160), pay attention to direction signs, respect barriers, and observe the general pattern of foot traffic. Be sure to hold young children's hands or keep them in strollers, and don't allow older children to wander.

When stopping to enjoy a street or subway entertainer, be especially aware of the people around you.

Q: *I met a friend at a coffeehouse for a chance to catch up with each other. As we were chatting, a band started setting up and, when we were deep in our conversation, began to play. We didn't know if we should stay and talk or leave. I've run into similar situations when there's a live band at a restaurant. Is it impolite to keep talking and ignore the band?*

A: If the band is loud, you can probably keep up your conversation—if you can hear yourselves talk! But if they're playing quiet music, your conversation may be heard over the music. Though you were "there first," it may be the best choice to call it a night, or move to another, more conversation-friendly location.

As for meeting up at a restaurant and finding a jazz ensemble playing dinner music, don't worry: You're there to have dinner, and unless the event has been widely promoted or involves an artist of extraordinary prestige, you should be able to carry on your dinner conversation as you usually would. If the music's too loud, ask the host to move you. And if you're not sure if you should talk while the group is playing, also ask the host, a manager, or your server: They will be able to give you a tip on how to enjoy your evening with both dinner conversation and great musical accompaniment.

dancing, drinking, and smoking

A club, an arena, a field—if the music calls for dancing, people will dance. Go ahead and dance if there's enough space, and while you dance, enjoy the space available to you. If you start knocking into people, reconsider what you're doing and reel it in a bit.

When you're twenty-one, you're free to drink at performances with a bar or a beer garden. It's easy to go from buzzed to obnoxious to belligerent. Think about keeping things in moderation so you don't become that guy who's screaming, "Freebird!" during every song break.

Though smoking indoors is illegal in many states, some allow it, and it's still legal outdoors in most places. Be careful with lighters and cigarettes. You want the *band* to be on fire, not your entire section. Though smokers have every right to smoke where it's allowed, cigarette smoke can be very irritating to those around you. Consider how tight the seating or standing area is; the most considerate thing to do would be to smoke away from a dense crowd, then rejoin the party.

You'll probably want to drop a tip (your spare change to one or two dollars) in the hat or instrument case, and move on quickly if the attraction is blocking sidewalks, doorways, or access to turnstiles and train platforms.

13

tipping

tipping is one of the most difficult and confusing aspects of etiquette today. One of the reasons it's so confusing is that who we tip and how much changes, and can even vary by state and region. In this chapter you'll find the basics for determining tips. For up-to-date specifics refer to the tipping chart at emily post.com/advice/general-tipping-guide.

First and foremost, a tip isn't a substitute for thanking a person for service received. The tip and the thank-you go hand in hand. Certainly, tipping is a significant way to show appreciation for a job well done; however, treating the person who's served you with respect is every bit as important. No amount of tip money makes up for treating someone dismissively. Furthermore, praising the person himself—and, when you can, commending him to his supervisor—goes a long way toward letting him know what constitutes good service.

[JUST HOW MUCH?]

Recommending precise amounts for everyday tips is easier said than done. Three basic guidelines will cover you in most circumstances:

- 15–20 percent of the cost of a service.
- $2 for the first effort and a dollar for each additional.
- For holiday tipping, 15 percent or the value of one instance of service.

Tipping should also take the overall situation into account as well. For instance, your tip may vary according to the difficulty of the service you've received. Consider the mover who hauls your armoire up three flights of stairs as opposed to placing it in the living room on the first floor.

Some additional guidelines for tipping are straightforward and may help you decide:

- When in doubt about tipping, ask in advance. If a store is scheduled to deliver your new sofa, call and ask whether tipping is customary; in a hair salon, ask the receptionist.

- Tip on the pretax amount of the bill, not on the total.

- Tip discreetly. It's a private matter, so don't play the "big spender" flashing bills.

- Money is the tip of choice in most cases, but sometimes a small gift, usually given during the holidays, can be substituted. A gift is also a good way to "top off" the tips you've given over the year—to your hairdresser or barber, for example. (See also "Holiday Tips and Gifts," page 174.)

RESTAURANTS

Today, tipping in restaurants is expected and, in fact, mandatory. Think of it as part of the contract you agree to when you choose to eat in a restaurant. That contract says you'll get served a meal, charged a price, and then pay 15 to 20 percent of the bill to help pay the waitstaffs' wages. As the diner you have some discretion. Generally, 15 percent indicates good service; 20 percent is the standard for great service; and 25 percent is reserved for outstanding service. Many people tip 20 percent because it's easier to figure. Whatever amount you choose to tip, it's reasonable not to tip on the tax.

the counter tip jar

While you're under no obligation to put money in a tip jar, you might choose to because your server or barista provides a little something extra or you're a frequent customer and tip occasionally. Unlike waiters and waitresses for whom tips augment their hourly wage, which may be less than minimum wage, workers at counter service businesses receive at least minimum wage salaries. Still, minimum wage doesn't go very far, so do consider a tip.

when to tip less

A multitude of things can go wrong: The rare steak you ordered is served well done, or you wait so long for the dessert menu that you wonder if the pastry chef went home early. Regardless of the infraction, leave a tip—at least 15 percent. Many restaurants pool tips and split them among all the staff. To begin with, the person serving you may not have caused the problem and others who did their jobs well—the busboy or the sous chef or the dishwasher—will be penalized unfairly. Leaving no tip (a drastic step, in most people's eyes) may not make your point. Rather than realizing his service was poor, your server may think you forgot or that you're just a cheapskate.

The best solution: Talk to a manager, explain the situation, and let her know your future patronage is in question. This way, there is a reasonable chance that the problem might be corrected.

the problem with
restaurant tipping
in America

Currently, restaurant waitstaff are paid less than minimum wage. They depend on tips to bring their pay up to par. Several states have enacted legislation to require that waitstaff be paid at least a minimum wage. However, a diner may not know if the state he's in has such a law or not. Consequently, he pays the 15 to 20 percent he customarily pays regardless of the wage law.

Restaurant tipping is meant to be a reflection of quality of service. If the goal of a tip is to incentivize the server to do a better job, mandatory tipping does nothing to make that happen. In addition, if you're never going to go to the restaurant again, then paying a tip at the end of the meal doesn't result in better service, either.

There are two particular problems with the current system:

- Restaurant owners are passing the responsibility for fair compensation to patrons.
- When tipping is an expectation, it's not a true demonstration of appreciation for good service.

Etiquette does change over time. Currently there is a debate about restaurant wages and tipping, and what is fair for employee and patron alike. Even though change is coming slowly, it is coming; perhaps we will soon return to a system of tipping that more accurately reflects appreciation for quality service.

When the restaurant is self-service. At a buffet restaurant, 10 percent of the bill is customary, since the waiter isn't serving your meal. Your tip is a thank-you for providing beverages, clearing the table, and answering any questions.

When the waiter has been especially accommodating. If a waiter was particularly helpful you might want to tip at the 20-percent end of the spectrum.

When a gratuity has already been added to the bill. Check the bill for a built-in gratuity or service charge—usually 18 percent. It's often added when a table has been booked for groups of six people or more. While a built-in gratuity is common overseas, it's a growing trend in America, so check the menu carefully to see if a gratuity will be automatically added. If one is added to your bill, you can leave an additional tip when you think it's well deserved.

When your stay at a crowded restaurant is lengthy. Most restaurants depend on turning the tables fairly regularly every night. If you've lingered over your meal for an especially long time, it can mean lower nightly receipts for the owner and less money for waiters. Tacking on an extra 10 to 15 percent over your regular tip is a way to say "thanks."

When you use a coupon ("Buy one entrée and get the other at half price"). Thoughtful diners will leave a tip commensurate with the full price of both meals.

Hosts, Hostesses, and Maître d's

Tipping the host, hostess, or maître d' who greets and seats you is not the norm. Usually such tipping is a concern only for regular patrons, who offer the host $10 to $20 every once in a while for extra service—remembering their favorite wine or seeing that they're seated at a favorite table.

When you're not acquainted with the maître d', a tip is in order only if he's gone out of his way to find a table for you on a busy night when you've arrived without a reservation (offer him $10 to $15 *after* he's shown you to the table). If your dining party is large, double or triple the tip, depending on the number of people.

Offering a maître d' you've never seen before a "$20 handshake" to get a table on a busy night may be seen as an insult. And charging to the front of the line and flashing a large bill only compounds the problem.

Bartenders

How much you tip a bartender depends in part on whether you're waiting at the bar for a table in the adjoining restaurant or you're at a bar for its own sake.

◆ When you're waiting for a table, if you pay for the drinks or run a tab, add a 15- to 20-percent tip when you pay for the drinks. If the drinks are transferred to your dinner bill, include them when you calculate your tip.

◆ If you're at a bar simply to have a drink, tip between 15 and 20 percent of the total; tip at the higher end if the bartender has run a tab for you.

Wine Stewards

When you receive service from a wine steward, tip him directly at 15 to 20 percent of the value of the wine. Yes, that means if you order a $400 bottle of wine the tip is $60 to $80. And if you order another bottle, that's another $60 to $80. You can add a line item on your credit card receipt specifying his tip, give it to him in cash when he pours the last of the wine for you, or at the end of the meal. When tipping a wine steward, tip your waiter only for the food portion of the bill.

musicians: play it again, sam

When you tip musicians, keep these tips in mind:

◆ It's thoughtful to tip $2 to $5 on leaving, even if you've made no request; receptacles for tips are usually in clear view. Expressing appreciation to the pianist as you leave the tip is considerate. If you *have* made requests, add an extra dollar or more for each tune.

◆ For strolling musicians who serenade you at the table, the basic tip is $1 per musician, while a total of $5 is usually sufficient for a group. If you make a special request, add an extra dollar to each musician's tip. You needn't stop eating when musicians perform tableside. Just smile and say "thank you" as you tip when the musicians finish.

Checkroom

Tip the coatroom attendant when you pick up your coat: $2 for the first coat and $1 for each additional coat is standard.

Washroom Attendants

Tip washroom attendants at least fifty cents for keeping the facility in good order and handing you a paper towel. If they brush off your jacket or whip out a needle and thread to mend your hem, give $2 or $3. If a small dish of coins is on display, place your tip there instead of handing it to the attendant. If washroom attendants do nothing but stand there, no tip is necessary.

Valet Parkers

Tip the parking attendant $2 in smaller cities and up to $5 in large cities. Give the tip when the car is brought to you, not when you arrive.

Busboys

Busboys aren't tipped, with two exceptions: If you spill a drink and the busboy cleans it up, you might tip him $1 or $2 when you leave. When the busboy in a cafeteria carries your tray to a table, $1 to $2 is in order.

] IN TRANSIT [

Except for commuting to and from work, travel generally requires keeping a pocketful of dollar bills handy. From curbside check-ins at the airport to taxi or limousine rides, you'll be giving tips for any number of services.

At Airports

Airline workers who staff the counters at the terminal, the gate, and the information booths at baggage claims aren't tipped, even if they do you a favor. Unlike airline workers, these airport personnel are given tips for their services:

Curbside baggage checker, skycap, or airline porter. The standard is $2 for the first bag and $1 for each additional bag—a little more if the bag is very heavy.

Wheelchair attendant. A $2 to $5 tip is standard. If the attendant goes the extra mile, such as pushing the wheelchair from one end of a large airport to the other, tip on the higher end (or even more).

Courtesy and hotel shuttle bus driver. When a driver helps you with your luggage, tip $2 for the first bag and $1 for each additional bag.

On Trains

On an extended train trip, you're expected to tip a number of railroad employees. The amounts below are standard, but tip a bit more if the service is special.

Dining or club car waiter or waiter delivering to sleeping car. Tip 15 to 20 percent of the bill and not less than $1.

Redcap or train porter. $2 for the first bag and $1 for each additional bag.

Sleeping car porter. $2 per person per night.

In Taxis, Private Cars, or Limousines

A tip to a taxi driver is generally about 15 to 20 percent of the fare, with a minimum of $1; round up any small amounts of change. A slightly larger tip is always in order, if it's not included in the fare, for a driver who helps with your luggage or packages. In general, add $2 for the first bag and $1 for each additional bag. Be prepared by having smaller bills available if you plan to pay by cash.

---

digital tipping

From taxis to restaurants, service providers are doing all they can to encourage tipping by making it as simple as pushing a button. Swipe your card in a taxi, pick your pre-loaded tipping percentage, have the receipt emailed to you, and the payment and expense receipt part of your ride is done in seconds.

Customer beware: Preloaded tipping options can start at 15 percent and can go as high as 30 percent, far outside the recommended norms. Unless you are a math whiz, it's not obvious if the restaurant tip is figured with the tax included or not. (There's no need to tip on the tax.) While it's possible to input your own tip, the process can be deliberately cumbersome.

While definitely convenient, these programs are designed to increase the amount we tip service providers. Tipping used to be at the discretion of the customer, to express appreciation for good or excellent service. There's something a little impersonal and "demanding" when the service provider is suggesting the amount the customer tips, and skewing the options on the high side.

If you give a taxi driver your card to pay for the ride, calculate the tip, add it to the fare, and ask him to charge that amount on the card: "I see that's $45 dollars, please add $9 for your tip and make the total charge $54." Alternatively you can give the driver the tip in cash and have him charge just the amount of the fare on your credit card.

For car and limousine services, the easiest way to tip is to tell the service to add the gratuity to your bill; do it when you request service. In larger cities, the standard tip is about 20 percent; in smaller cities, 15 percent. If a gratuity is included in the fee, there's no need to tip more. (For a car arranged for you, see "In Taxis and Limousines," page 29.)

Charter Buses and Bus Tours

Tour bus drivers are tipped 10 to 20 percent of the cost of the trip. Alternatively tips can be calculated per person per day: $2 to $5. The daily amount varies depending on the level of service the operator performs. Similarly, if you have a tour guide, tip $2 to $5 per person per day.

ON CRUISES

Most cruise ship operators anticipate passengers' confusion about tipping, and either provide guidelines and envelopes for tips or add a substantial service charge to the fare, in which case only extra-special service calls for a tip.

To be sure you know what's expected, you can find tipping policies on your cruise line's website, or discuss tipping amounts and procedures with your travel agent or cruise line agent who books your trip. Tipping customs can differ depending on the nature of your trip, but in general tips will add 10 to 20 percent to the cost of your cruise.

⌠ AT HOTELS ⌡

Like restaurant workers, hotel staff depend on tips to augment their salaries, so have some dollar bills available before you check in.

Doorman. A doorman isn't tipped for opening the door for you (a smile and a "thanks" will do), but is given a small tip for other tasks. Tip him $2 for the first bag and $1 for each additional bag when he takes your bags and hands them to a bellman or when he takes your luggage from the bellman and loads it into a vehicle. Tip $1 to $2 for hailing a cab for you.

Bellman. Tip a bellman who brings your luggage to your room $2 for the first bag and $1 for each additional bag. A bellman who takes your bags and points out facilities in the lobby and your room should receive a dollar or two more. In some luxury hotels, someone from the manager's office may show you to your room; he isn't tipped, but do tip the bellman who follows behind with your luggage.

Each time a bellman does something special, such as bringing an item you've requested to your room, tip $2 to $3.

Concierge. Concierges aren't customarily tipped for basic services such as providing directions or general information about the area; giving you a map, brochure, or newspaper; or recommending restaurants.

A concierge is generally tipped $5 to $10 for each special service he performs—for instance, making dinner reservations. Extra-special service, including making multiple reservations and obtaining hard-to-get tickets for any event, calls for $15. Another way to tip for tickets: Give 10 to 20 percent of the cost of each one. (That's $10 to $20 for a $100 ticket.) Tip a concierge when he performs the service; if you wait to tip until the end of your stay, he may not be on duty.

If the concierge fails to get what you want but you know that he made a real effort, tipping shows appreciation for his hard work. Tip 5 to 10 percent of what those tickets *would* have cost.

Room service waitstaff. The room service bill will almost always include a gratuity (usually 18 percent) and a room service delivery fee of about $3. While there is a room service fee, providing a $2 tip directly to the person bringing the order ensures she receives a tip. If a gratuity isn't included in the bill, add it as you would if you were in the dining room, and give the person who brought the order a $2 tip directly.

Housekeeping staff. It is customary to tip the housekeeper who cleans your room $2 to $3 per night. You might want to tip more if you're in a suite or the service is exceptional. Tipping daily rather than when you check out ensures that the tip goes to the housekeeper who actually cleans your room that day. You can tip in person if you see your housekeeper, adding your personal "thank you." Otherwise, leave your tip with a piece of notepaper or in an envelope marked "Housekeeper" and add a written "thank you." While some guests leave their gratuities for the housekeeping staff in their rooms at the end of their stay, it doesn't guarantee that the housekeepers who did the cleaning will actually get the tip.

Valets. If you're in your room when clothing is delivered, tip $1 for the delivery for one or two items, $2 or $3 for several items.

Other hotel staff. Barbers, hairstylists, manicurists, massage therapists, and other personal service providers are tipped as they would be outside the hotel. Pool, beach, or sauna helpers; fitness club assistants; and other special service attendants receive tips only if they perform a special service. For example, if an attendant sets up beach chairs and umbrellas for a large group, tip him $1 per person.

AT A PRIVATE CLUB

Some clubs have strict "no tipping" policies, so when you're a guest, ask your host or at the club's office about tipping norms for club personnel. At most clubs, a gratuity is automatically added to restaurant and bar bills but other staff—such as caddies and locker-room attendants—may be tipped individually.

If tips are permitted, tip $2 to $5 per service. Members may choose to tip in a lump sum at the end of the season, $25 to $100.

BEAUTY SALONS, BARBERSHOPS, AND SPAS

When you're attended to by several beauticians, use the totals for each service on the bill as the base for tips. Or simply give 15 to 20 percent of the total bill to the receptionist when you pay and ask that it be split among the people who provided you with service that day.

Salon owners may or may not accept tips—it varies widely, salon to salon. When in doubt about tipping an owner, ask the salon receptionist.

A barber's standard tip is 15 to 20 percent of the bill (but not less than $1), even if other people performed additional services. Shampooers and shavers are tipped $1 to $2, manicurists $2 to $3.

At a spa, the customary tip is 15 to 20 percent. If it hasn't already been added, include the gratuity when you pay for your service and ask that it be split among the people who provided you with service. If the gratuity is included, then you don't need to add it, but if you received exceptional service from someone you can add a tip in person or ask that it be given to them.

TAKE-OUT FOOD DELIVERIES

For take-out food delivered to your door, tip 10 percent of the bill. For especially quick or courteous service, or if the deliverer walks up more than one flight of stairs, tip 15 percent. (For a pizza, $2 is adequate if the bill

tipping your doctor?

In general, doctors, lawyers, nurses, and teachers aren't tipped, but you might want to give a gift as a token of appreciation. Many businesses, schools, and agencies have policies regarding gifts or extra compensation for employees. Always check before offering a gift, monetary or otherwise.

is between $10 and $15. A tip for a larger order may be between $3 and $5, depending on the number of pizzas.)

Options for tipping for grocery delivery range from $1 per bag, or $5–$7 per delivery. Tip more if the weather was really bad or if there are several flights of stairs involved. For online orders you can opt to add a tip to the order, or choose "no tip" and give it in person in cash.

A delivery charge on your bill usually goes to the owner to help cover delivery costs, so a 10 percent tip assures that the deliverer is thanked.

HOME HELP

Part-time domestic workers. Rather than being tipped each time they work for you, a regular cleaning person (who usually comes weekly or every other week) is typically tipped at holiday time with an extra one-job payment. For babysitters, a small tip (say, $5) is appropriate for each sitting in some communities, but you may also tip her a larger amount at holiday time and include a small gift chosen by your child.

Salaried domestic workers. Household employees on a salary don't receive a tip. Rather, consider an end-of-year bonus, one month's pay or more, and a holiday gift. A nanny is also given a small gift chosen by the children in her care.

RESIDENTIAL BUILDING PERSONNEL

Residential building personnel are customarily tipped during the end-of-year holiday season. How much to tip depends on the custom in your town or city, the type of building, the size of the staff, and the amount of time they spent helping you over the year. Employee seniority and any special services performed at a resident's request are also taken into account. If you tipped employees throughout the year—each time the doorman hailed a cab for you or received your dry cleaning, for example—then your holiday tip can be smaller. Some buildings create a holiday fund that residents can contribute to, with the proceeds apportioned according to job and seniority.

tips for party hires

When you hire help and possibly even entertainment for a party, tips will likely be in order. Some caterers include gratuities in their total price; others send a bill indicating that you may add a tip. The important thing is to establish the method of payment and tipping at the time the help is hired so you can head off any embarrassment or unpleasantness later.

If you're not being billed later, pay help hired through an employment agency or by you personally at the agreed rate before they leave, adding a 15- to 20-percent tip if the gratuity isn't included in your bill. Catering company employees are usually tipped $10 each, but if there's only one server, the tip is doubled.

Entertainers hired for a party, whether musicians or magicians, are generally tipped 15 to 20 percent of their fee. Check the contract to see if a gratuity is built in.

HOLIDAY TIPS AND GIFTS

When the holiday season arrives, it's customary to thank those who have regularly served you throughout the year: your dog walker, sitter, hairstylist, cleaning person, letter carrier, doorman, building supervisor, or trash collector, to name a few. Whether and how much to tip varies widely, depending on the quality and frequency of the service, where you live (amounts are usually higher in large cities), and your budget. If you ordinarily tip throughout the year at the time of service you can consider giving a smaller tip or a gift. Try to include your child in deciding on any gifts for teachers, daycare providers, nannies, and babysitters. (Visit emily post.com/advice/holiday-tipping-guide for the latest tipping guidelines.)

14

volunteering

V olunteers make a big difference in their communities and local governments, as well as to nonprofit institutions both large and small by sharing their time, talents, or money. Volunteering and manners couldn't be more intertwined. By volunteering you are showing consideration for your community and others, some who may be less fortunate than you. The gift of your skills is invaluable to those who need them: the student struggling with algebra, the prisoner with no family, the elder who counts on the delivery of nutritious meals.

Some people volunteer to lend a hand, to teach a skill to others, to feel needed and valued, or to express gratitude for help received in the past. Others want to meet new people, explore an interest, learn a skill, and build self-confidence. Volunteering can be a way to learn how to organize an event, run a meeting, recruit or supervise a team, or learn new software or a skill. For example, building a house for Habitat for Humanity may make you a great handyman around your own house.

For business reasons, volunteering can lead to important networking contacts, enhance a resumé or college application, provide the means to gain work experience, or learn about career opportunities. Whatever one's motive, being an effective volunteer means finding an opportunity that suits your personality and schedule. It also means treating your volunteer commitments as seriously as you would a paid job. Once you've said, "Yes, I can," you're expected to fulfill your promise.

FINDING A GOOD MATCH

There's a seemingly limitless need for volunteers, but before you raise your hand, take some time to do a little research. Organizations want their volunteers to be enthusiastic and feel positive about their role. After all, feeling good about what you do goes a long way to compensate for not being paid. Here are some things to consider when choosing a volunteer opportunity:

What's important to you? One way to narrow the field is to define the causes and issues that are of interest to you, then see which organizations in your community serve those interests. You can be selective so that the experience benefits you as much as those you are helping. You will be more effective working within an organization that is close to your heart—something you really care about and want to see improved in your community.

Assess your skills and your personality. Think about how you are most effective and what you'd like to get out of the experience. If you're tired of office meetings, doing something one-on-one, such as mentoring or sharing a hobby with a young person or chaperoning a ski trip for a youth group, could be a refreshing change. On the other hand, if you love what you do, sharing it may be your best route: for example, the accountant who helps elders prepare their tax returns. Preparing a resumé will help you define your experience, skills, and strengths. Even if you don't need to use it to apply, it will help you articulate why you're a good match for the organization or the volunteer position.

How much time do you have? Be realistic about your time. If you're a busy mom, one or two hours a month may be all that's realistically available to you. Better to start small and possibly offer more time as you have it than to bite off more than you can chew and have to renege.

SIGNING UP

When you've narrowed down your choices, visit the organization, both online and in person. Make sure you agree with the organization's mission, its ethics and its values, and that you truly have an interest in doing the work: reading to the blind, planting a garden, fundraising, doing bookkeeping, or making meals.

If it looks right for you, fill out an application or make an appointment with the volunteer coordinator for an interview. Treat this as seriously as you would an interview for a paying job: Dress appropriately, be on time, and thank the interviewer. Be honest about your goals and intentions.

ON THE JOB

Whether you've committed to take a shift at a soup kitchen, be the class parent for your daughter's first grade, be a volunteer guide at a local museum, or work on the financial advisory committee for a local nonprofit, all volunteers share the following responsibilities:

- Show up on time. Better a few minutes early than late.

- Call your supervisor if you're going to be absent or unduly late. Not showing up at all reflects poorly on you and may ruin a planned activity. Staff can't always fill in on short notice. (If they had enough staff, they wouldn't need volunteers.)

- Dress appropriately for the task at hand: taking the kids to the theater, painting the recreation room, escorting someone to a chemo appointment, pulling invasive species from a lake shore.

◆ Take part in any orientation or training programs. Remember, they too are trying to make this a meaningful experience for you so that you will continue to be involved.

◆ Follow all organizational rules, such as signing in and out, attending volunteer meetings, dress codes, and smoking policies.

◆ Be dependable. Carry out assignments promptly and reliably, and make sure you complete any tasks you agreed to at the last meeting or activity.

◆ Act professionally and respect confidences. What you learn about a patient's treatment, a child's disability, or an elder's family should never be discussed outside your volunteer role.

WORKING WITH A SUPERVISOR

In most volunteer jobs, you'll work with a paid staff member—your child's teacher, a volunteer coordinator, or an intern supervisor, to name a few. It's important to establish a good rapport and maintain a positive relationship with your supervisor or support person. As a volunteer, you are expected to follow their lead and direction. While volunteer managers will ideally provide feedback and show appreciation, they probably have another role in the organization as well. Be respectful of their time. Give succinct reports and be prepared with any questions. The less direct supervision you need, the more valuable a volunteer you will be.

If you have ideas for improving things, speak up.

Your input will probably be quite valuable. Just be sure not to push your suggestions too hard, and don't be hurt if nothing comes of your effort. Often, new volunteers, full of enthusiasm and ideals, want to solve all the organization's problems at once. "If you change the schedule, we'll be able to take more kids in the after-school program." You'll be more effective if you have a practical solution to offer and take your concern to the appropriate staff member. There may be a good reason why something is done the way it is. Often the organization is doing the best it can with limited resources.

internships

Being an intern, paid or unpaid, is a wonderful way to gain career experience while still in college. Treat your internship opportunity as you would any other job: Dress appropriately for the interview and write a thank-you note to the interviewer. After you're hired, arrive on time, observe the organization's dress code, and follow all company rules. Your intern supervisor may have already outlined your tasks, some of which may be quite basic. However, you are there to get a feel for the particular industry or field, so don't be shy about speaking up if a project interests you. "I'd like to learn more about book production schedules. Would it be all right if I sit in on your upcoming editorial call?" At the end of your internship, be sure to write a thank-you note to your supervisor. (For more information on applying for jobs and office etiquette, see Part V, Getting the Job, page 393, and Part VI, On the Job, page 409.)

SERVING ON A VOLUNTEER BOARD

Hospitals, foundations, private schools, colleges, and universities are all organizations that are run by a board of directors, usually composed of employees of the organization and outsiders. While you don't ask to join a board (usually you are asked), you may want to mention your interest in serving on the board to a current board member or employee. That person can submit your name to the appropriate person. Boards have vetting processes and nominating committees whose job it is to recruit, screen, and recommend potential new members. Most boards look for evidence of a serious commitment from its organization's members. This may include chairing a committee, such as a hospital fund-raiser or school annual fund; career expertise in a needed area, such as insurance, law, or accounting; or being able to make a substantial gift to the organization. Many boards require varying degrees of financial support from their members; other, smaller boards may only want a member's skills—though they'll never turn away money.

Being a good board member involves both business and volunteer etiquette. It is a prestigious leadership position, and you are expected to be both a supporter and an ambassador for the organization. Failure to take the honor and the responsibility seriously can be damaging to one's reputation both socially and in business. While similar to some of the points made earlier about volunteering in general, it is especially important for board members to observe the following:

- Always attend meetings. They should be a "must go" event on your calendar, not to be canceled lightly. If you cannot attend, make sure you ask for and read the minutes so you're up to speed.

- Be on time.

- Dress appropriately. If you're a first-time member, ask about the dress code for board meetings, then dress one notch up.

- Be an active participant, but don't interrupt or dismiss another member's opinion. On some boards, you raise your hand to be recognized by the chair.

- Complete any assignments in advance of the meeting. Take good notes so you can follow up on any commitments or specific responsibilities.

- Be observant of the organization's resources and needs. For example, is the boardroom equipped to assist members who are hard of hearing? Could the facility benefit from a high-speed Internet connection? Is the exterior of the facility attractive and in good repair?

- Be an ambassador for the organization. Never speak about it critically.

- Support the organization's extracurricular or fund-raising activities. This can mean anything from manning a youth center's car washing event to organizing a table at a major fund-raising benefit.

15
official
life

In its official sense, protocol is a system of universally accepted etiquette used when the representatives of different nations deal with one another. It also applies to official dealings on the national, state, and local levels. The word is derived from the Greek *proto kollen,* or "first glue." It's the "glue" that holds official life together—the diplomatic rules of etiquette regarding precedence and rank, and the proper forms of address, when participating in meetings and ceremonies, and when entertaining dignitaries.

Some of these "official" manners are observed by ordinary citizens on occasion. Protocol comes into play when you write a letter to a member of Congress or are introduced to a member of the clergy or the military. There is also protocol for displaying and handling the American flag and for behavior during the national anthem. (See "The Flag of the United States," page 186; "The Pledge of Allegiance and National Anthem," page 190.)

to learn more . . .

Representatives at the Department of State's Office of Protocol (202-647-1735) are available to answer protocol questions over the telephone—such as where to seat a state governor, a U.S. senator, and the town mayor at a dinner honoring a philanthropist. They also provide information about the American flag, the national anthem, and the respective ranks of U.S. government officials.

Address state government protocol questions to the governor's office in your state capitol. Questions on local government protocol can be answered by the mayor's office in your city or town. For answers to questions about military protocol, call a branch of the military in your city or state.

PRECEDENCE AND RANK

The Table of Precedence, used for ceremonies of state, is a list of the titles of U.S. government officials. It is unofficial, in that every new administration has the right to establish its own order of precedence. Below is an abridged list in the traditional order, with different administrations assigning executive appointments to the list.

TABLE OF PRECEDENCE

The President of the United States

Foreign head of state or reigning monarchs

The Vice President of the United States

Governor (when the event is in his state)

Mayor (when the event is in his city/town)

The Speaker of the House of Representatives

The Chief Justice of the United States

Former presidents of the United States, in order of term

Ambassadors of the United States (at post)

The Secretary of State

The Secretary General of the United Nations

Ambassadors of foreign powers accredited to the United States, in order of presentation of credentials

Widows and widowers of former presidents of the United States

Ministers of foreign powers accredited to the United States

Associate Justices of the Supreme Court, in order of appointment

Retired Chief Justices of the United States

Retired Associate Justices of the Supreme Court (by appointment)

Members of the Cabinet, in order of the creation of their department

President Pro Tempore of the Senate

Members of the Senate, by seniority

Governors of states (when outside their home states), by order of their state's admission to the Union

Former Vice Presidents of the United States, in order of term

Members of the House of Representatives, by seniority

State and Town Governments

The following is a typical order of precedence for . . .

STATE GOVERNMENTS

Governor

County commissioner, in own county

Mayor, in own city

Lieutenant Governor

Comptroller

Attorney General

U.S. Senators, in home state, by seniority

U.S. Representatives, in home district

Chief Justice of the Court of Appeals

State Senators, based on seniority

State Representatives, based on seniority

CITY, MUNICIPAL, AND TOWN GOVERNMENTS

Mayor

President of the city council

Public Advocate

City Comptroller

State Senators, in order of seniority

State Assemblymen/Representatives, in order of seniority

District Attorney

Members of the city council, in order of seniority

Deputy mayor

Chief of staff

SEATING AT AN OFFICIAL LUNCHEON OR DINNER

At official luncheons and dinners the host or hostess seats the guests according to rank, so as not to slight any of the guests.

Traditionally, the host and hostess sit at the head and foot of the table. When they are friends with a number of the guests, they may choose instead to sit opposite each other at the middle of the table, where it will be easier for them to converse with more people.

When the event is attended by both men and women, seating is as follows:

- The highest-ranked male guest sits to the right of the hostess.
- The man next in rank sits to the left of the hostess.
- The highest-ranked woman, or the wife of the man of highest rank, sits to the right of the host (if the man is unmarried, the woman of highest rank takes this seat).
- Spouses in attendance who don't hold an official position are seated according to the rank of their husbands or wives.
- Men and women should be alternated at the table insofar as possible.

What to do if the guest of honor is outranked by one or more people in attendance and therefore isn't "officially" entitled to the place of honor? One solution is to make sure the guest of honor *is* the highest-ranking guest; otherwise the honoree will need to sit farther down the table. Alternatively, well ahead of time the host could ask the highest-ranking guest to either act as a cohost or to decline the seat in favor of the guest of honor. Another practical solution is to divide the seating between two or more tables and appoint a cohost and cohostess for each one.

Guests who have no protocol ranking (as specified by the Table of Precedence) are seated as the host assigns them, basing his decision on age, social prominence, personal accomplishment, and mutual interests shared by seatmates. Proficiency in a foreign language also comes into play when foreigners are among the guests.

Other considerations when creating a seating plan include:

- When the guest of honor and second-ranking guest have been placed, nonranking guests may be seated between those of official rank.
- At meals hosted by U.S. government personnel overseas, foreign guests have preference in seating over Americans of equal rank—except for the American ambassador of the country.

Titles on Place Cards

At official functions, there's a simple way to determine whether just the title or the title and surname are written on a place card. When only one person can occupy the office, such as the president of the United States, the cards carry only the title of the office, without names:

The President

The Vice President

The Archbishop of . . .

The Ambassador of . . .

The Mayor of . . .

In cases when more than one person can hold the title, the surname is added: Senator Holmes, Governor Billings, Ambassador Martinez, Father Brusco.

Surnames may also be added at less formal affairs, except in the case of the president and vice president. The names of guests without official titles appear as "Mr. Robineaux" and "Mrs./Ms. Stockwell." Remember that the object of a place card is twofold: to show every-

one where to sit and to give others at the table the correct form for addressing them.

OFFICIAL TITLES IN CONVERSATION AND INTRODUCTIONS

In official circles, specific forms of address are used. The president and various other officials, including cabinet members, are addressed by titles alone: "Mr. President," "Madam Secretary." Surnames are added when a position—associate justice of the Supreme Court, for example—is held by more than one person: "Justice Kagan."

The following general rules apply whenever you introduce or speak with certain officials at a public function. (See also Resources, "Official Forms of Address," page 678.)

The President of the United States

The correct introduction of a man or a woman to the president is, "Mr./Madam President, I have the honor to present Mr./Mrs./Ms. Michaelson," adding, "of Denver, Colorado," if further identification is necessary. Both men and women respond in the same way, saying: "How do you do, Mr. President," but let the president initiate a handshake. The vice president is addressed and introduced in the same way as the president.

Once out of office, the president and vice president become "Mr./Mrs./Ms. Greene," although they're introduced or referred to—but not addressed directly—as "the Honorable" followed by their full name: "The

Honorable George Herbert Walker Bush, former president of the United States." (For more on the correct use of "the Honorable," see page 184.)

U.S. Senators and Representatives

A senator is always "Senator Boxer," even when she is no longer in office. A member of the House of Representatives, on the other hand, is addressed as "Mr./Mrs./Ms. Carson" not "Representative Carson," except when being introduced; nor are the terms "Congressman" or "Congresswoman" used in conversation with—or in the introduction of—a member of the House.

Governors

Present and former governors are introduced and announced (but not addressed) as "the Honorable." On ceremonial occasions, one would present "the Honorable Jim Douglas, the governor of the state of Vermont." After leaving office, former governors retain the title "the Honorable."

It is improper to call a governor "Mr./Mrs./Ms." In public, he or she is "the governor"; in conversation, "Governor Douglas." Less formally, simply using "governor" is fine.

Cabinet Members

Members of the cabinet are usually addressed as "Mr. Secretary" or "Madam Secretary." However, when several are present and confusion could result, they are addressed as "Madam Secretary of State" and "Mr. Secretary of Commerce."

Justices of the United States

All associate justices are addressed with "Justice" and their surname: "Justice Stevens," not "Mr. Justice Stevens." The same rule applies to the chief justice: "Chief Justice Roberts" or "Chief Justice." Present and former justices are both introduced as "the Honorable" and keep this title after retiring.

The Diplomatic Corps

In Washington, D.C., and other international capitals, all the accredited representatives of various foreign states and their staffs are collectively known as the diplomatic corps.

An ambassador is a diplomatic agent who is the personal representative of the head of state of his country. Officially, ambassadors are called "Mr. or Madam Ambassador" rather than "Ambassador Wainwright."

Religious Officials

The titles of Protestant clergy vary according to the denomination, although most are called "Pastor" or "Reverend," with or without the surname. If a Protestant member of the clergy holds the title of doctor, dean, or canon, his or her surname is always added to the proper title: "Dean Cavanaugh."

A Catholic priest is addressed as "Father" (with or without the surname), whatever his other titles may be.

When introductions are made to church dignitaries, the layperson is always the one presented. To a cardinal, say, "Your Eminence, may I present Mrs. Trent?" A non-Catholic bows his head slightly, but a Catholic drops on

correct use of "the honorable"

The title "the Honorable" can cause confusion. Federal custom in the United States bestows the title "the Honorable" first when the person assumes office, and then by courtesy for life on the following dignitaries:

President and vice president

U.S. senators, congressmen, and congresswomen

Cabinet members

All federal judges

Ministers plenipotentiary and ambassadors

State governors

State senators and mayors are also referred to as "the Honorable," but only during their term in office; when they retire, so does the title.

The use of "the Honorable" is limited to introductions and to the announcement of the arrival of the person at a large public function: "I am proud to introduce the Honorable Joseph Graham Davis, former governor of the state of California." The title isn't used to address the official directly, nor does the official use it when introducing himself. Likewise, the title isn't printed on the official's letterhead and business cards, nor does he use it when signing his name.

the right knee, places the right hand (palm down) under the cardinal's extended hand, and kisses his ring.

When introduced to an archbishop, Mrs. Trent would correctly say, "How do you do, Your Excellency?" to a monsignor, "How do you do, Monsignor Walton?"

Rabbis are called "Rabbi," with or without their last name: "Rabbi" or "Rabbi Rosen." (For other clerical titles, see pages 679–680.)

Rank. In the Roman Catholic church, following the pope in rank are cardinal, archbishop, bishop, monsignor, priest, and brother and nun. Some Protestant denominations have bishops, who rank above clergy. In the Jewish religion, rabbis rank above cantors.

Professional and Academic Titles

Physicians and judges are always introduced and addressed by their titles: "Doctor Morales" and "Judge Stone." When addressing a judge officially, as in court, use "Your Honor."

A person who has earned a doctorate degree uses the title "Dr." professionally, and may choose to use it socially as well. The use of the title also depends on what's customary within the field. For example, though attorneys have doctorates they don't use the title "Dr."—but they may choose to use the initials "J.D." (juris doctor) after their names.

If you're unsure how to address someone with a doctorate, follow this general rule: It's better to "Dr." a person who would rather be referred to as "Mr." ("Mrs." or "Ms.") than to do the reverse.

Military Titles

In the armed forces, the various grades of colonels, generals, and admirals are spoken to simply as "Colonel," "General," or "Admiral"; their surnames can be added, but during a prolonged conversation the title alone is the simpler option. However, they are introduced with their full titles: "Rear Admiral Gates." Noncommissioned officers and lower ranks are similarly addressed; for example, "Sergeant" serves as the form of address for the many types of sergeants—staff sergeant, sergeant

Q: *I was invited to a government reception and was introduced to a person who was obviously a VIP, possibly even a cabinet member. Because the person who introduced us didn't use the person's title, I was at a loss for how to address him. What should I have done?*

A: When the introducer leaves you high and dry, it's safe simply to say to the person to whom you've been introduced, "How do you do?" If the conversation continues and the title remains unknown to you, you're on safe ground by addressing the person as either "Sir" or "Ma'am." In fact, when titles are used during a conversation, it's preferable to use these courtesy titles occasionally, since the constant repetition of "General Barcroft" can begin to sound a bit stilted.

first class. As with officers, introduce all uniformed personnel by rank and last name.

- In the army and air force, noncommissioned officers are also addressed officially by their titles, although they may also use "Mr." socially. In the army, warrant officers are called "Mr." or "Ms.," both officially and socially.

- Chaplains in any branch of the service are called by their rank—"Colonel Smart"—although informally they are addressed as "Chaplain," "Father," or "Rabbi."

- Doctors in the service are generally called by their rank, "Major Hollingsworth," although they may be called "Dr." socially when they are junior officers.

- Members of the regular armed services may retain their titles in retirement, per their individual service regulations. However, reserve officers who served for only a short time—or those who held temporary commissions during a war—shouldn't continue calling themselves "Captain" or "Colonel" in retirement. They do, however, use the titles if they resume an active status in a reserve unit or the National Guard. In this case, the initials of their service always follow the name: "Colonel Victor Bacovich, U.S.A.R." Reserve officers who remain in the service and retire with pay after twenty or more years are, like a member of the regular service, entitled to use their military titles.

Representatives of Other Nations

Because customs vary greatly from country to country, no rules of official protocol apply across the board in the nations of the world, which number close to 200.

military academy students

The social titles of students attending any of the five U.S. military academies are "Mr." or "Ms.," since they're not permitted to be married. But the official title for both male and female students varies by branch of service. All students at the United States Military Academy (West Point), the United States Air Force Academy, and the United States Coast Guard Academy are officially called "Cadet [surname]." Those at the United States Naval Academy and the United States Merchant Marine Academy are officially called "Midshipman [surname]."

However, help is at hand before you travel abroad. The three main sources of information are the Washington, D.C., embassy for your country of destination; the consulate in the major city nearest you; and the mission to the United Nations in New York. All are able and willing to provide information to facilitate your communication and dealings with people in their homelands.

Here are a few guidelines for American social or business travelers who have been invited to an official reception or ceremony and for hosts or hostesses who will be entertaining dignitaries overseas:

- Professionals from other countries are often given titles that, out of courtesy, should be used. In Italy, for example, a man who has completed university and earned a degree is called "Dottore" (Doctor) and a woman "Dottoressa"; a male German corporate president is called "Herr Direktor." It is only polite to respect the customary titles in other countries—certainly, at least, until bonds of friendship are formed and you're invited to use more personal forms of address. (See also Chapter 10, "Traveling Near and Far," page 119.)

- European heads of state, ambassadors, cabinet officers—and in some countries, high-ranking members of the clergy—may be referred to as "His [Her] Excellency"; they may be called "Your Excellency" in conversation. In correspondence, they would be addressed as "His Excellency, Ichiro Kawamura, Ambassador of Japan."

- The king or queen of most Western European countries is addressed as "Your Majesty" and is referred to as "His [Her] Majesty."

- A prince or princess or other royalty, such as a prince consort, is called "Your Royal Highness," "Sir," or "Madam" in conversation.

- Countries that were formerly monarchies still refer to their royalty with the titles that were once held.

- A duke and duchess are called either "Duke" and "Duchess" or "Your Grace" in conversation—not, for example, "Duke Charles" or "Duchess of Kent."

THE FLAG OF THE UNITED STATES

The premier symbol of our patriotism, the American flag, proclaims our country's commitment to freedom. Our flag is considered a living entity and never dips to any person or thing. The flag should always be handled respectfully. The rules and customs governing the flag's care and display are something that all citizens of the United States can easily learn.

Care of the Flag

The American flag should be carefully protected in storage and in use so that it won't be damaged. Every precaution should be taken to prevent it from becoming soiled, tattered, or torn. It should also not be permitted to touch the ground, water, or a floor.

- When handling the flag, don't let it brush against other objects.

- If the flag gets wet, it should be smoothed and hung until dry—never rolled or folded while still damp.

- Keep the flag clean by dry cleaning it, and keep it in good repair. It's fine to trim and repair ragged edges or resew stripes that have separated in the wind.

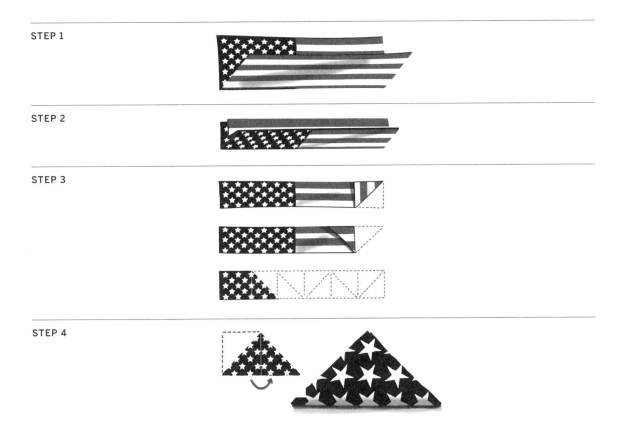

STEP 1

STEP 2

STEP 3

STEP 4

FOLDING THE U.S. FLAG: *Following the diagrams in steps 1–3, keep the folds crisp and tight. The final folds in step 4 ensure that only the Union is showing; open edges are folded in.*

Raising and Lowering the Flag

The flag should be unfolded or unfurled and raised briskly, and lowered slowly and solemnly. When flown at half-staff, the flag is hoisted to the peak for a moment and then lowered to the half-staff position; the flag is again raised to the peak before being lowered for the day.

Saluting the Flag

Whenever the flag passes by, as in a parade, men and women pay it their respects.

◆ All citizens stand quietly and place their right hands over their hearts.

◆ Men remove their hats and hold them in their right hands over their hearts. This rule also applies to women wearing sports caps.

◆ Men and women in the armed forces give the military salute as the flag passes.

Displaying the Flag

American flags are out in force on patriotic holidays—especially the Fourth of July, Flag Day (June 14), Veterans' Day (November 11), and Memorial Day—but it's perfectly fine to fly the flag every day of the year.

Always display the flag with the blue union up, aloft and free. Flying the flag upside down is a distress signal. The traditional time for flying the flag is between sunrise and sunset, but it may also be flown at night as part of a patriotic display as long as it is illuminated. The flag is not customarily flown in inclement weather, but it is proper to continue flying it if the flag is made of all-weather material.

According to The United States Flag Code, Title 4, Chapter 1, "The flag, when it is in such a condition that it is no longer a fitting emblem of display, should be retired and destroyed in a dignified way, preferably by burning." Many American Legion posts provide this service.

Following are some basic rules for displaying the flag:

On Memorial Day. The flag is displayed at half-staff until noon and then raised to full staff thereafter until sunset.

On an angled staff. When the flag is displayed from a staff projecting horizontally or at an angle from a windowsill, balcony, or the front of a building, the blue union should go all the way to the peak of the staff. The exception to this rule is when the flag is flown at half-staff.

Over a street. When displayed over the middle of a street, the flag is suspended vertically; with the union to the north in an east-west street, to the east in a north-south street.

Over a sidewalk. When the flag is suspended over a sidewalk from a rope extending from a house to a pole at the edge of the sidewalk, the flag is hoisted union first.

In a house of worship. When the flag is used on the chancel or platform in a house of worship, it should be placed on a staff on the clergyman's right (any other flags are on his left). When displayed in the seating area in the place of worship, the flag should be on the congregation's right as they face the front.

other names for our flag

When the flag is flown from ships and boats it is an *ensign*.

When the flag is carried by a tank, car, or truck or by a person on horseback it is the *standard*.

When the flag is carried by dismounted military units it is the *colors*.

On caskets. When used to cover a casket, the flag is placed so that the union is at the head and over the left shoulder. The flag should not be lowered into the grave or allowed to touch the ground.

On cars and boats. On a car, the flag is flown on a small staff affixed to the right front bumper, in line with the fender and with the union toward the front. The staff should be tall enough so that the flag clears the car hood.

♦ On a powerboat, the flag is flown from 8:00 AM until sunset. It flies from a staff at the stern when the boat is anchored. If the boat has a gaff, the flag may be flown from the gaff when the boat is under way.

♦ On a sailboat, the flag is flown from the stern in the harbor or under power. It's permissible for the flag to be flown while the boat is under sail.

Note: *A flag that has become soiled or tattered should be promptly removed and cleaned or retired and replaced.*

When mounted. When the flag is displayed but not flown from a staff, it should be hung flat against a wall (not tucked or draped), whether indoors or out. The union should be uppermost and to the flag's own right, meaning that it is on the observer's left.

As a lapel pin. Wear the pin on the left side, close to the heart.

In Displays with Other Flags

The American flag is often grouped with other flags in various ways, and rules apply in these cases as well.

Crossed staffs. When displayed with another flag from crossed staffs, the American flag should be on the flag's own right, and its staff should be in front of the staff of the other flag.

On a flagpole with other flags. When the flag of the United States is flown on the same flagpole with

staff or mast?

On land, a flag is flown from a staff (pole); at sea a flag is flown from a ship's mast. So, correctly, a flag is at "half-mast" at sea and "half-staff" on land.

flags of other states or cities, or with pennants of societies the U.S. flag is always at the peak.

Next to other staffs. When flown on a staff adjacent to staffs flying other flags, the national flag should be hoisted first and lowered last.

In a large grouping. When a number of flags of states or cities are grouped and displayed from staffs, the American flag should be at the center or at the highest point of the group.

If the flags of two or more nations are displayed, they should be flown from separate staffs of the same height, and the flags should be of approximately equal size. International usage forbids the display of the flag of one nation above that of another nation in time of peace.

In a procession. When carried in a procession or parade with another flag or flags, the American flag should either be on the marching right, or when there is a line of other flags, in front of the center of that line.

For more information on U.S. flag customs and etiquette, visit the website of the National Flag Foundation at www.americanflags.org.

THE PLEDGE OF ALLEGIANCE AND NATIONAL ANTHEM

In 2007, Congress addressed etiquette for the Pledge of Allegiance and the national anthem in 36 USC 301. When saying the Pledge of Allegiance, citizens of all ages should stand at attention, face the flag, and salute by placing the right hand over the heart. Men should remove their hats, and women any sports caps. When in uniform, military personnel, firefighters, and law enforcement officers should give a military salute.

Everyone, even very young children, should rise, stand at attention, and salute by placing the right hand over the heart during the entire playing of "The Star-Spangled Banner"—first note to last. The anthem isn't easy to sing, and you needn't do so if you don't have the necessary range. But you must stand quietly until "O'er the land of the free, and the home of the brave" has rung out and the music ends.

If you're on the way to your seat at a sports event or any other public place and the first strains of the anthem are heard, stop where you are and stand at attention until the end. Do not talk, chew gum, eat, or smoke during the singing of the anthem.

At a large private party if the orchestra plays the anthem at the start of the dancing, the guests all rise and show their respect. The anthem is never played as dance music, and should be performed so that citizens who wish to sing along may do so.

When the anthem of another country is played along with our national anthem, the guest anthem is played first, out of courtesy. Americans should stand respectfully, but not salute.

guidelines for people of other nationalities

When certain patriotic customs are observed in the United States, people who aren't citizens should join in to an extent.

- When "The Star-Spangled Banner" is played, foreigners, as well as American citizens, stand. It is then up to the individual whether to sing or not.

- When the Pledge of Allegiance to the flag is said, foreigners stand, but they do not repeat the words.

- When the anthem of a foreign country is played officially—as, for instance, in honor of a visiting team of athletes—everyone present rises and stands at attention. Men remove their hats (and women their sports caps), but Americans do not salute.

- Foreigners residing in the United States may display the flag of their own country on its national holidays. Out of courtesy, they should display the American flag, too.

- On U.S. national holidays, a foreigner should display the American flag or none—not his own.

- When a foreigner attends a parade or other patriotic event, he stands respectfully while the flag passes by, but he need not salute in any way or recite the Pledge of Allegiance.

WHITE HOUSE ETIQUETTE

Although customs vary somewhat during different administrations, the following represents the conventional pattern from which each administration adapts its own procedures.

A Formal Invitation to the White House

An invitation to lunch or dinner at the White House is a great honor. It automatically cancels almost any other engagement that isn't of the utmost importance and a response should be given within twenty-four hours. Respond in the same way the invitation was given, or according to any added instructions. Sometimes invitations are issued by phone, and then a p.m. card (*pour memoire*, "to remind") is mailed. Unless you're ill, have a death or wedding in the family, official duty, or an impossible-to-break business appointment, you should accept.

An engraved invitation to an evening at the White House should be taken to mean black-tie attire unless white tie is specified on the card. Women wear conservative evening dresses, not pants; to a white-tie dinner, they also wear long gloves. If the invitation says "Informal," then men wear a suit and women wear cocktail or semiformal attire.

All the names of guests expected at the White House are posted with the guards at the gate. You give your name to the guard, present your invitation or admittance card, and wait a few moments until you are recognized and escorted to the appropriate room. Men remove their hats when entering the White House.

After the guests arrive, the president and the first lady enter and speak to each guest and shake hands. Guests, of course, remain standing.

At a formal dinner the president goes into the dining room first with the highest-ranking woman guest. The first lady follows with the highest-ranking man.

An Informal Invitation to the White House

Informal invitations to dinner or luncheon at the White House are now issued more frequently than formal invitations. They are sent by letter or may be extended by telephone by the president's or first lady's secretary. The replies should be made, in the same form, to whoever issued the invitations. Again, the most important thing is to reply promptly.

Meeting the President and First Lady

When you're invited to the White House, your invitation will tell you what to wear and when to arrive. If you have any other questions, it's fine to ask when you RSVP. Make sure you're not late. It is an unpardonable breach of etiquette not to be present when the president makes his entry.

The president, followed by the first lady, enters at the set hour. If the group present is small, the president and first lady make a tour of the room, shaking hands with each guest. If the occasion is a large reception, they stand in one place; the guests then form a line and pass by in turn to be greeted. Men precede their wives unless she is the more prominent or invited one; an aide serves as announcer. Guests are greeted first by the president and then by the first lady.

If a woman is wearing gloves, she removes the right one before shaking hands with the president. If the president speaks with you, you address him as "Mr. President." In a long conversation, it's proper to occasionally alternate "Mr. President" with "Sir." Call the wife of the president "Mrs. [surname]" and exchange pleasantries with her as you would with any formal hostess: "Thank you for your kind invitation." Don't linger in conversation unless the president or first lady initiates it. After you have left the line, remain standing while either the president or the first lady remains in line.

Gifts

Not only should you avoid taking a present to the president unless your doing so has been cleared with an aide, but you shouldn't send anything to the White House without receiving permission from his secretary or one of his aides, either. For security reasons, the gift must be cleared with the proper authority; otherwise, the intended recipient will never have the opportunity to enjoy it. Instead of a gift, the Obama-Biden administration prefers that citizens make a charitable donation in their communities instead, a gesture that is both meaningful, useful, and always appropriate.

[AN AUDIENCE WITH THE POPE]

An American tourist visiting Rome can indeed be granted a group audience with the pope. General audiences are usually held on Wednesday mornings when the pope is in Rome, either in St. Peter's Square in good weather or in an indoor auditorium with more limited seating. It's essential to arrange for tickets ahead of time, and the farther ahead the better. This can be done through your hotel concierge, or by writing or faxing the Prefecture of the Papal Household, 00120 Vatican City State; Fax: +39 06 6988 5863. The Vatican City website (http://www.vatican.va) has a calendar and download-able application form. Tickets are free.

When he is in Rome, the pope also makes an appearance from his library window Sunday noon and blesses the crowd in St. Peter's Square. This is free and open to the public.

Requests by Americans to attend papal masses and events, as well as the general audience, can be facilitated by The Pontifical North American College in Rome. Their website (www.pnac.org) has complete information on current requirements, and they can be contacted at visitorsoffice@pnac.org or by phone at +39 06 6900 1821. Since they must liaise with the Vatican, requests for specific events should be made at least two weeks ahead. While many applications and recommendations are made by pastors and bishops, individuals may write for themselves.

The General Audience

General audiences are held at 11:00 AM on Wednesdays at St. Peter's. During the summer months, they take place at 10:00 AM and in the winter at 9:00 AM. People without reserved seats should arrive very early if they want a location with a good view. Choice places are often filled early in the morning.

Everyone rises as the pope appears; when he sits down the people may then be seated. He delivers a short address, and then everyone kneels as he gives his benediction to all those present as well as any articles they have brought to be blessed.

The group rises, and if the pope has time, he greets each person in the special area. The audience is over when he mounts his portable throne and is carried out.

Dress Code

For general audiences, dress in good taste: no shorts; skirts should be below the knee, and shoulders should be covered and necklines modest. Head coverings are no longer required for women. At a Mass or other papal event, consider more formal dress: coat and tie or suit for men, conservative dress or suit for women.

Non-Catholics at Audiences

At a general audience, every person present—including non-Catholics—kneels, rises, and sits at the prescribed times. Non-Catholics need not make the sign of the cross.

PART III
communication

CHAPTER 16 Notes and Letters 197

CHAPTER 17 Social Names and Titles 215

CHAPTER 18 Telephone Manners 221

CHAPTER 19 Personal Communication Devices 230

CHAPTER 20 Online Communication 237

16
notes
and letters

Once limited to ink on paper, envelopes, and postage stamps, written communication is an integral part of our virtual world in the form of email, texts, and IMs, not to mention blogs and forums. It's great to have options; the trick is choosing the right medium to deliver your message.

Let your style of communication match the occasion. There's no question that a text or an email is more practical than a letter for short, informational exchanges or for informal or last-minute invitations. The more serious or formal ones—an invitation to a formal party, a thank-you for a wedding gift, or a condolence note—lend themselves to ink on paper.

Notes and cards have other subtle advantages that emails can't match: They're warm, tangible, and representative of the time and care taken to choose the card, write the note, and address and mail it. If you're in doubt about which way to write, remember this: People delete emails; they save notes, letters, and invitations.

YOUR STATIONERY WARDROBE

The once-prim stationery drawer, housing white, cream, or gray sheets, has blossomed into a wardrobe stocked with gorgeous new possibilities, including brightly colored papers and inks as well as chic designs. And if you can't find what you're looking for, you can design your own on your laptop. High-quality stationery is widely available for laser and ink-jet printers. What was once considered "proper" stationery is now but one of many choices, giving way to papers that reflect the writer's personality. Stationery with fanciful designs happily coexists with the calling card, which also has gotten a modern makeover. (See "Social Cards," page 209.)

Notepapers

Notepapers are available as **fold-over note cards, correspondence cards** (one-sheet cards of stiffer paper), and **informals** and can be used for thank-you notes, acceptances and regrets, invitations, and other short correspondence. Because they come in countless styles, it's easy to find ones that suit your taste. After choosing the color and style you prefer, you can decide whether to add your initials or your name or to leave the paper blank.

Fold-over note cards and **correspondence cards** are on the more casual side, and you may choose any color paper, border, design, and font color. If you decide to have your name printed or engraved on either, it's fine to substitute a nickname for your full name. On fold-over notes, the name is printed in the center of the first page; on correspondence cards, it is centered at the top: *Katherine Bellavista*. Titles (Mr., Mrs., Ms., Dr.) aren't used.

Despite their name, **informals** are actually the most formal and traditional note card. They come only in white or ecru paper, sometimes with a plain raised frame, and any printing or engraving is in black only. Traditionally, women use informals for writing more formal short notes, for issuing invitations, as printed acknowledgments for condolences, and as gift enclosures. A woman uses her full social name, including "Mrs." or "Ms.": *Ms. Cynthia Ramos*. Men generally use informals

> ## it's a matter of size
>
> Correspondence cards (usually 4¼ by 6½ inches) are the largest of the three types of notepaper. The smaller fold-over notes and informals vary slightly in size but are at least 3½ by 5 inches, the minimum allowed by the U.S. Postal Service.

only when part of a couple who jointly issue invitations: *Mr. and Mrs. Sanford St. John*. While informals for thank-you notes are offered as part of a bride's wedding stationery suite, most brides opt for fold-over note cards that complement the design of their invitation.

Stationery for Men

The **monarch sheet,** measuring 7¼ by 10½ inches, was traditionally the standard paper for a man's personal stationery, but today the most popular choice for handwritten notes is the **correspondence card**. Monarch sheets are more versatile as they can be used for all correspondence, printed, typed, or handwritten. White, cream, taupe, and gray are popular colors. If desired, a device or icon, such as a fleur de lys or family crest, or the man's name can appear at the top center: *Mark Javits*. For personal stationery no title (Mr. or Dr.) is used. Optionally, the full address can be added beneath the name, as well as telephone/cell/fax number and email address. Monarch sheets fold in thirds to fit into the envelope.

CORRESPONDENCE CARD

SUSIE SMITH

FOLD-OVER NOTE CARD

SSB

Stationery for Women

Besides the various note card options, a woman's personal letter stationery is generally smaller—approximately 6 by 8 inches. A **correspondence or letter sheet** is one page that is folded once, top to bottom, and placed in its envelope. The most formal stationery for women is a double sheet that is folded along the left side and opens like a book. (It, too, is folded in half to fit its envelope.) Conservative paper colors for very formal correspondence are white, cream, light blue, or light gray; but for personal letters, the sky's the limit—any combination of colors for paper, ink, and borders is appropriate.

Stationery for Kids and Teens

Whether it comes from a stationer or is designed on the home computer, one of the easiest ways to get kids to write thank-you notes is to give them their own personal stationery. Fun fonts and designs—even lines for beginners—make note writing kid-friendly.

Stationery for the Family

House stationery, printed or engraved with a device, such as a pineapple, the name of the house, or the address (on two lines), can be used by all members of the family and even by guests: *Shady Oaks or 57 Oak Lane / Montclair, NJ 07042*. Some families mark or emboss their stationery with a family crest. Technically, one should be used only by those who are directly descended from an ancestor who had the right to use a coat of arms as a personal, family, or clan mark.

WHERE DOES THE WRITING GO?

There's no fixed rule about where the writing should go on a fold-over note that's longer than one section. When using a blank fold-over write on the first, second, third, and fourth pages consecutively. If an initial, design, or name is printed on the top of the front page or along the left side of a fold-over note, the writing can start on the front page. If the printing appears in the center of the first page of a fold-over, start writing on the open center pages.

On single-sheet stationery, it's fine to write on both sides, unless the paper is thin and the writing shows through, making the letter hard to read.

Linings

Linings aren't necessary, but they can be gorgeous. Some are so lovely that customers design their stationery around them. Linings ensure that the contents of the letter can't be seen through the envelope, but they can be costly and the extra weight could require additional postage as well.

Writing on four sides of a fold-over note card.

Writing on two sides (or one side) of a fold-over note card.

a printing primer

At one time, almost all printed invitations, announcements, letterheads, and social cards were engraved. But modern technology offers a number of options. The following brief descriptions can help you choose the look that's right for your style and budget.

ENGRAVING. The most costly method, engraving is done from a metal plate, usually copper. The lettering can be felt as slightly raised on the top of the sheet, with an indentation, or "bruise," on the back of the paper. Most engraved stationery must be ordered through a stationer.

LETTERPRESS. Letterpress uses raised type or designs on wooden or plastic blocks to press ink into the surface of the paper, leaving an indentation. Although an old-fashioned printing method (it's the same movable type invented by Gutenberg), it's had a fashionable comeback. Letterpress can be as expensive as engraving.

THERMOGRAPHY. Less expensive than engraving or letterpress, thermography uses heat to affix ink to the page. The lettering is raised above the paper and often has a shinier appearance than engraving. When well done, thermography can be similar in look to engraving.

LITHOGRAPHY. Also called flat printing, lithography applies ink directly and flatly to the paper. It's what most print shops use today, and has a crisp, professional look. Normally, it's less expensive than thermography.

LASER. Whether done on a home printer or by a print shop, good laser printing looks similar to lithography. It's the least expensive option, best suited for informal or casual invitations or stationery.

EMBOSSING. Often used for monograms and symbols, embossing uses a plate into which the image is cut. When pressed onto paper, the image is raised above the surface, creating a three-dimensional look. In blind embossing, no ink is applied; in debossing, the image is depressed below the paper surface.

The quality of any printing is directly related to the quality of the paper, so it's smart to work with an experienced printer or stationer when you need printed materials.

Addressing

Is there a correct way to address an envelope? Yes.

- Rule #1: Make sure the writing is perfectly legible, even if it means using block letters.
- Rule #2: Double-check the address—it can take weeks for a misaddressed letter to be returned.

You probably remember the rest of the rules from Ms. Grundy's sixth grade English class, or you can visit the U.S. Postal Service (USPS) website at www.usps.com for a refresher.

The return address. Because the USPS uses high-speed scanning machinery to "read" and route mail, it prefers the return address on the front of the envelope in the upper left-hand corner, whether it's a printed label or written by hand. Printed envelopes for personal stationery usually have the return address printed on the back flap, which is fine, too.

The recipient's address. As Ms. Grundy instructed, the recipient's address may be written in block form, as for a business letter, or with each subsequent line indented, as for a friendly letter.

The USPS prefers that all addresses be written or printed in all uppercase letters, but legible handwriting just plain looks more personal. State names may be written out (Arizona), or use the USPS's designated abbreviation (AZ). In the United States, the five-digit zip code or zip plus four follows the state: AZ 85001.

Block, or business form:

> Mr. and Mrs. Milton Reid
> 7100 La Mesa Boulevard
> Phoenix, AZ 85001

Indented, or friendly form:

> Mr. and Mrs. Milton Reid
>   7100 La Mesa Boulevard
>   Phoenix, AZ 85001

Double-check addresses for international destinations, as their formats differ. For example, in some European countries, the street number may follow the street name and the zip code may precede the city:

> Sr. Antonio Crispini
> via del Leone, 24
> 00186, Rome
> Italy

---

correct forms of address

Depending on the style of the correspondence, letters are addressed formally using titles and informally without. The most respectful way to address someone is by the name and title they prefer. For a complete discussion see Chapter 17, "Social Names and Titles," page 215. For a handy reference, consult "Official Forms of Address" in Resources, page 678.

"Personal" and Other Notations

Add the notation "Personal" to a social letter only if it is being mailed to the recipient's business address. On a letter to his home it would imply that you suspect another family member might open it.

For the most part, use "Confidential" only for business letters. Keep in mind that letters bearing this notation are sometimes opened by executive secretaries. If you want only the recipient to open it, it's better to mark a confidential business letter as "Personal."

If a letter addressed to someone else is delivered to you by mistake, just write "Please Forward" and then leave the letter in your mailbox for the letter carrier. At times, you may accidentally open a letter addressed to someone else, especially a letter that's put in your box by mistake. Write "Opened by Mistake" and your initials on the face of the envelope, seal it with a piece of tape, and leave it in your box for the letter carrier.

Seals

Envelope seals are of two types:

1) Stamps that feature a charity or other nonprofit organization and help to raise money for the organizations that distribute them.

2) Decorative wax or adhesive seals embossed with an initial or a design.

Organizational stamps or seals, which are affixed to the back of the envelope so that they overlap the flap, show your support for a worthy cause and encourage others to contribute. While these seals may be used on personal or business letters, they shouldn't be used on notes of condolence or on formal invitations and replies.

Decorative seals add a nice finishing touch to an envelope, particularly for special events such as charity balls and weddings.

SO MANY NOTES

The handwritten note—brief and informal—is the most popular form of personal communication. While mainly used for thank-you notes, here are other reasons to send these little warm messages:

- Thank-you for a gift
- Thank-you for a dinner party or overnight stay
- Thank-you for a favor or when you return something you borrowed
- To congratulate someone on the birth of a baby, a graduation, a promotion or appointment, or a special achievement
- To acknowledge a celebration: birthday, wedding, anniversary
- As invitations

folding letters

Which edge of a letter is inserted first into the envelope? It doesn't really matter, but those who stand by tradition insert the open, or unfolded, edge first. This way, when the recipient takes it from the envelope and opens it, the writing is right side up. The paper should be folded evenly and neatly—once for an envelope half as deep as the paper, twice if one-third as deep.

- To stay in touch
- To thank your host(s) when you've been the guest of honor
- To send condolences on the loss of a loved one
- To apologize for a mix-up or mishap

THANK-YOU NOTES

The two most important things to strive for when writing thank-you notes are sincerity and promptness. A note arriving more than a week after an event loses its fizz. When writing the note, use expressions that come naturally, as though you were actually having a conversation with the recipient.

While many people choose to use their personal stationery, commercial cards, including those with the words *Thank You* printed on the front, are perfectly fine, as are any other type of blank card. Cards that include a message written by the greeting card company *always* require the addition of a personal note of your own.

A thank-you note need not be long, but it should be personal and heartfelt. If this were a conversation, what would you say? Be sure to say actually say "thank you," mention the occasion or reason for the note, and express your appreciation for the giver.

Whom to Address

When you've received a gift that comes from more than one person—a birthday present with a card signed "the Hansons," for example—to whom do you write the thank-you? It's unwieldy to list every last member of

sample notes

You can find the following sample notes in other chapters:

Thank-you notes for wedding gifts (page 630)

Thank-you notes for gifts in general (pages 362–365)

Invitations and announcements (page 272)

Congratulatory notes (page 206)

Notes and letters of sympathy (page 553)

the family in the envelope address, so just use "Mr. and Mrs. Arthur Hanson." In the note itself, the salutation could read "Dear Art and Leslie," and the children could then be included in the text: "Please thank Diana and Sandy for me, and tell them how much I enjoyed the chocolate truffles."

When you've been hosted by a group of people, as when several friends host a party for you, thank each of your hosts individually, sending a note to each couple or individual host. If the hosting group is very large, it's fine to write to the organizer, thanking her and the group, and asking that your note be shared.

For Dinner or Overnight Visits

While close friends may give each other a call or send an email after spending an evening together, a note is the way to go when someone has entertained you for the first time. Whether they're new friends you met at the gym or through your child's school, or people who included you when you were visiting friends or relatives

in another city—a note will not only thank them but reaffirm your pleasure in the meeting.

Dear Chandra and Tony,

It was such a pleasure to meet you, and so kind of you to invite Richard and me to your home. The meal was one to remember (paella worthy of a Spanish chef!), and the conversation was just as enjoyable.

The evening was one of the high points of our trip to Seattle, and I hope we can return the favor if you're ever in Phoenix. In the meantime, thank you for your generous hospitality. Richard joins me in sending regards to you both.

Very sincerely yours,

Barbara Beckett

Dear Jessica and Malik,

Jamie and I had such a lovely time last night and it was so thoughtful of you to include us. Jessica, the grilled salmon was delicious—the essence of summer—and what a treat to be able to dine under the stars. Truly an enchanted evening—thank you!

Sincerely,

Alysha

However, when you've stayed overnight or longer at someone's house, you *must* write a note of thanks to your hosts, and promptly. Two exceptions are when the hosts are relatives who frequently spend the night at each other's homes or friends who are so close that you consider yourselves "family." Even so, do send a note if you don't expect to see your hosts for some time.

Following are a couple of examples—the first is for very close friends, the second for people you know less well:

Dear Roseanne,

You and Chas are such wonderful hosts. Once again, Frannie and I can tell you that there's no other house where we have such a good time and hate to leave so much. We especially enjoyed the party Saturday evening. Thank you so much for including us!

Yours truly,

Brian

Dear Mrs. Silverman,

Last weekend was the high point of my summer. Everything you planned was terrific, especially the hike up Mt. Philo on Saturday. What a view!

I truly enjoyed every minute with your family, and I thank you again for inviting me.

Very sincerely,

Chelsea

When You've Been the Guest of Honor

Whether you've been welcomed to the neighborhood with a coffee get-together or a close friend has thrown your birthday party, a gift for the host(s)—a thank-you arrangement of flowers or other token of your appreciation—is a good way to say thanks. It can be sent either the day before the party or the day after. While you could follow up with a phone call, a note is more in keeping with the time and effort made on your behalf. If there was more than one host, send a note to each.

Dear Phoebe,

You and Julia are such dear friends to make my birthday so special. I must admit, I was a little apprehensive about turning thirty, but surrounded by my best pals I didn't give it another thought! Thank you for making it a day to remember.

Love,

Wendy

] CONGRATULATIONS! [

A note or a card is a great way to celebrate life's successes. Your niece has just graduated from high school or a close friend calls to say he got the promotion he's been waiting for or perhaps a friend has a new baby. It's likely that you'll fire off an email as soon as you hear the news, but following up with a note expressing your happiness or delivering a compliment reinforces the importance you place on their accomplishment.

It's customary, but by no means obligatory, to share

---

your natural voice

The best notes and letters are conversational, reflecting both your personality and speech. A few simple steps will make the recipient feel as if the two of you were chatting:

- Use phrases typical of your speech rather than more formal language. Someone who would say, "The buzz at work is . . ." sounds stilted and self-conscious when he writes "The topic engendering the most gossip . . ."

- Use contractions. Since you almost certainly say "I don't know" rather than "I do not know," go with the same words when writing.

- Occasionally insert the person's name to add a touch of familiarity and affection. "And, Beth, guess what we're going to do this summer?" makes Beth feel as though you're there with her.

- Use punctuation to enliven your writing. Underlining a word or using an exclamation point after a phrase or sentence gives emphasis where you want it. (Just don't overdo it.) Setting off phrases with a dash—"We went to a dance last night—what a party!"—has more pizzazz than "We went to a dance last night, and it was great."

- Keep it short.

---

important social news with a printed announcement. Births, adoptions, marriages, and graduations are typical occasions for announcements. An announcement comes with no obligation to send a gift, but acknowledging the news with a note or card is always thoughtful. If you learn about the good news in the paper, it's nice to include the clipping with your note or card.

When you receive a congratulatory note or card containing a personal note, show your appreciation by thanking the sender in person, or with a call or a return note.

Dear Sam,

Uncle Jim and I are delighted to have another University of Michigan grad in the family. We wish we could have been there for commencement, but your Mom emailed us some great pictures. A double major and top honors—congratulations! We're all very proud of you.

Love,

Aunt Marsha

Dear Aunt Marsha and Uncle Jim,

Thanks for your kind words. Your support—and your insider knowledge—meant a lot to me over these past four years. I'm looking forward to starting work at an environmental engineering firm in San Diego next month, but hope I'll be able to make it home and join you in the bleachers for the Ohio State game.

Love,

Sam

Notes of Apology

A note of apology may be called for when you've been responsible for something that adversely affects someone else. In most cases a phone call is all that's needed (and often can seem more sincere and contrite), but at other times you may want to follow a call with a note.

Dear Janeen,

I do apologize for having to cancel Monday night. As I said on the phone, I accepted your invitation forgetting that Monday was a holiday—which meant that our houseguests from Rochester were actually staying till Tuesday.

Again, let me tell you how disappointed we were, and hope it won't be too long before we can see you and Rolf again.

Affectionately,

Monica

Occasionally, an unfortunate accident occurs. Although what happened may have been beyond your control, your note should offer to make amends:

Dear Mrs. Lee,

Your son has just informed me that our dog dug up your flower bed and ruined your beautiful zinnias. I feel just terrible. My husband will repair the fence this evening so that Rover won't be able to escape again.

I will also replace the zinnias, although I'm afraid that new ones can't compensate for those you lost. If you would kindly call me and let me know the varieties, I will place an order with the nursery. In the meantime, please accept my apologies.

Sincerely yours,

Joy Caswell

GREETING CARDS

Commercial greeting cards expressing good wishes for holidays, birthdays, anniversaries, and other occasions will mean much more if you add a short message of your own. No matter how delightful, a printed message can't beat a personal one. Many people prefer to use cards that are blank inside so they can write sentiments that are theirs and theirs alone.

Signatures on Greeting Cards

When the signature is handwritten, either name can come first: "Lisa and Charles" or "Charles and Lisa" are equally correct. Last names aren't used on cards sent to close friends, and it's fine to use nicknames: Lisa and Charlie.

When signatures are printed, the last name is always used, but, again, the order is your choice: "Lisa and Charles Bell" or "Charles and Lisa Bell." No social or professional titles are used for greeting card signatures.

When children's names are included, the father's name always comes first: "Charles and Lisa Bell and Charles, Jr." Cards sent by a large family have more signature options:

- "The Johnstons"
- "The Robert Johnstons"
- "The Johnstons—Bob, Jean, Bobby, Zoe, and Jen" (listed in order of birth)
- "The Johnstons—All Five"

In blended families with more than one surname in the mix, the simplest solution is to write "Chris and Peg Morita and all the family" or ". . . and all the children." If you do wish to include the children's names, use their last names, too:

"James Morita, and Lilly and Sam Nolan."

Holiday Newsletters

Holiday cards are often used to share family news or pictures with a wider circle of friends, and it's fine to include brief notes or special thoughts to people you haven't seen for a long time. Then there's the printed history of the past year—the holiday newsletter.

Holiday newsletters are fine in themselves, but stick to the highlights—most people will be happy to know that you survived knee surgery and are back on the court, but they won't want to know the details of your grueling rehab. An Emily Post Institute survey showed

"IT'S BEEN A GREAT YEAR . . ."

WHEN WRITING YOUR HOLIDAY LETTER,

SAY . . .	NOT . . .
Scott was accepted at LSU.	Scott scored 2350 on his SATs.
Melissa loves competing on her horse, Star.	Melissa got blue ribbons at 16 out of 17 horse shows.
Buddy was promoted to senior vice president.	Buddy got a 75K raise and a new Tesla.

that people have mixed feelings about these newsletters: 53 percent liked them and 47 percent did not. With that in mind, enclose newsletters *only* in cards to those you think will be interested. Here are some tips to keep your news reader-friendly:

- Share only news that's positive and not too personal.

- Keep your letter to one page or less.

- A handwritten salutation—"Dear Karen and Phil"—is warmer than the printed "Dear friends," and signing each letter individually personalizes it more.

- Write a one- or two-sentence personal message in the card that accompanies the letter.

- Don't turn your letter into a brag sheet.

SOCIAL CARDS

They're back in style and it's a good thing. A social card—also called a calling card, personal card, or visiting card—is like a business card except it's for your personal use and speaks to your out-of-the-office life. They're a great way to round out the introduction process and for letting friends—especially new friends—get in touch with you. Much more polished than scrawling your home phone number on a business card or matchbook, they're also useful for leaving a short note, such as when you pay a visit to someone and she's not at home, or as a gift enclosure.

Q: *I'd like to send electronic greetings this year, but is doing so appropriate?*

A: Emailing personal greetings or a holiday card downloaded from the Internet is perfectly fine, but be sure you only send them to people you email regularly. Here are a few tips for success:

- Do write your message as you would on a traditional card.

- Don't overuse shortcuts such as acronyms, abbreviations, and lowercase letters: The easier it is to read, the better the message.

- Use the BCC feature when sending your holiday greeting to multiple people. It's your responsibility not to share email addresses between people who may not know each other.

The Basics

You can design your card to reflect your personality and have virtually anything printed on it so long as it's in good taste. Before you rush to the printer, think about what contact information you'd like to share. Typically, social cards include your name plus phone number (home and/or cell) or email address, or all three. Most people don't include their home address on their social card, mainly for security reasons. You can always jot it

Q: *Is it okay to send email thank-yous for holiday gifts?*

A: It may be all right if you and the giver email each other frequently, but it's still no substitute for a handwritten note. Thanking the giver the old-fashioned way will emphasize how much the gift means to you.

on the back of the card for someone who needs to mail you something.

What About Titles?

Using your title on your card is a matter of choice. A courtesy title—Mr., Mrs., Ms., or Miss—may seem unnecessary and a little fussy to some people, while others prefer this slightly more formal touch. Unless you use it socially, a professional title, including "Doctor," is optional. (For more on titles, see Chapter 17, "Social Names and Titles," page 215.)

PERSONAL LETTERS

It used to be that the only way to communicate quickly, cheaply, and reliably was the handwritten letter. With the advent of inexpensive telephone service and even cheaper email service, the golden age of handwritten letters may be past. Still, receiving a long, newsy letter is a treat, and there are times when nothing but a mailed letter will do. Somehow, a folder of emailed love letters doesn't evoke the same romance as handwritten letters, tied in a ribbon and tucked away in a drawer.

Whether handwritten, printed, or typed, the standard letter format hasn't changed, and simple logic dictates where the various elements of a letter are placed on the page.

Your Home Address and the Date

If your stationery or its electronic version doesn't include your printed address, it's a good idea to add it for your correspondent's convenience, usually in the upper right-hand corner of the first page. (Placing it just below your signature is reserved for business correspondence.) The date follows one or two lines below the address.

If your address is already printed on your stationery, the date is placed in the upper right-hand corner of the first page.

The Body of the Letter

The best letters will share news and information, mix good with bad news, respond to the questions asked or news shared in a previous letter, and ask about the recipient. You should include only information you would be happy for others to see. This means no idle gossip, no defamatory or unattractive remarks about others, and nothing so personal that it would prove embarrassing to you or anyone else. There's a better chance that mailed personal letters will remain private; emailed ones can too easily be forwarded, either inadvertently or intentionally.

Letters Best Left Unwritten

The words you speak won't live forever, but those you put down on paper just might. Think twice about writing anything that could come back to haunt you.

The woe-is-me letter. A letter full of misfortune and unhappiness won't give your reader pleasure and will probably leave her worried or depressed.

The tell-all letter. Remember that people change— and "people" includes you. There's nothing wrong with pouring your heart out in a letter, but providing too many intimate details of a love affair could eventually lead to embarrassment.

The gossip letter. It's wrong to tell everything you know about someone's trials and tribulations (especially if you've been sworn to secrecy)—so check your impulse to gossip.

The angry letter. Bitter spoken words fade away in time, but written words stay on the page forever. Put a letter written in the heat of anger aside for twenty-four hours, then read it cold; you'll probably soften the tone or leave the letter unsent.

Ending a Letter

End a letter on a positive note. If you can, wind up the letter with something your correspondent can relate to. If you've reported on a trip, for example, "The mountains were so beautiful" is a simple statement, while adding "They reminded me of when we were in Colorado together" establishes a connection.

Signatures

There are a few practical guidelines for adding your signature to your letter. The first is to let the recipient know who is writing. Just signing "Jack" on a letter to a virtual stranger won't do much good.

◆ Sign with your first and last name if you're writing to someone you've never met face-to-face: Georgia Delaney.

◆ Put your last name in parentheses if you've only spoken with the person on the phone—on a business call, for example: Georgia (Delaney).

◆ Use your first name or nickname on letters to friends or business associates who know you: Gia.

When you write for yourself and your spouse (or sister, brother, or anyone else), sign your own name only. It's not a faux pas to sign "Joyce and Paul," but since Paul isn't writing the letter it's better brought up in the text: "Paul and I had such a terrific time last weekend." Or "Paul joins me in sending thanks and love to everyone." On holiday cards and other greeting cards, however, joint signatures are fine.

the complimentary close

In earlier days, the complimentary close of a letter—the word or phrase that precedes your signature—was long and flowery, but it has gradually been pruned. "Sincerely yours," "Best wishes," and "Yours truly" are often shortened to "Sincerely," "Best," and "Yours." The standard complimentary closes for modern times depend on the type of note or letter:

- The preferred ending to formal social or business correspondence is "Sincerely," "Sincerely yours," "Very sincerely," or "Very sincerely yours."

- "Kind regards," "Kindest regards," "Warm regards," and "Warmest regards" fill a nice gap between formal and more intimate closings.

- In friendly notes, the most frequently used closings (from the least intimate to the most) are "Cordially," "Affectionately," "Fondly," and "Love."

- "Gratefully" is used only when a benefit has been received, as when a friend has done you a favor.

- "As always" or "As ever" is useful in closing a letter to someone with whom you may not be close or haven't seen for some time.

- "Faithfully" and "Faithfully yours" are rarely used today but are appropriate on very formal social correspondence: letters to a high member of the clergy, a member of the cabinet, an ambassador, or anyone holding an equally important post. The same applies to "I have the honor to remain . . ." followed by "Respectfully yours."

Other signatures. There are some occasions when the issue of signing comes up.

- Husbands and wives sign a guest register, such as at a private club, with their married name, "Mr. and Mrs. Matthew Harrison," or "Ms. Judy Allen and Mr. Matthew Harrison."

- When asked to sign a guest book, such as at a wedding or funeral, it's helpful to sign "Judy and Matt Harrison" so that the wife's first name is on record.

- Be sure to write legibly—otherwise it's hard for the hosts to know whom to thank for attending.

- On lists of patrons or sponsors of a fund-raising party or other function, names are listed with titles (Mr., Ms., Mrs., Dr., and so on).

- On professional or business listings, the name is used without the title—"Richard Peterson" or "Amanda Grayson," which is also the correct signature when the person signs reports, certificates, and the like.

BUSINESS LETTERS

Business correspondence in our private lives consists of everything from letters of reference to letters of complaint. These letters are always printed or typewritten and are best addressed to an individual, not "To Whom It May Concern." A call to the company or a visit to their website can give you the information you need. (For job application letters, see Chapter 31, "The Job Search," page 395; for business thank-you notes and letters, see Chapter 36, "The Social Side of Business," page 442.)

Letters of Reference and Recommendation

When you're asked to write a recommendation or reference letter, assess your own feelings. Do you know this person well or only casually? Are you enthusiastic about his capabilities, or only lukewarm? Because your letter must be honest, it's kinder to politely refuse than to write a letter that, despite your best efforts, will likely betray your true feelings.

If you do write, you'll want to include key information such as:

- Your relationship to the person you're recommending.
- The length of your acquaintance.
- Your evaluation of the person's qualifications.
- For a job applicant, you should cite examples of his workplace experience.

Don't hesitate to be enthusiastic—but only if you're certain the person can live up to your glowing review. Indicate that you're available to answer any questions, and include a telephone number and times when you can be reached.

The same guidelines apply to social letters of reference, such as a letter recommending someone for club membership or a co-op building:

I am pleased to have the opportunity to write to you on behalf of Neil and Tanya Heilman. I am quite sure that you will find them to be great neighbors and a real asset to your building.

I've known Neil and Tanya for several years, both socially and as coinvestors in a local health club. Neil serves on the board and Tanya on the marketing committee. It is with confidence that I can recommend them to you, and I'm sure you will be pleased to have them as a part of your community.

Letters of Commendation

It's sad but true that people are usually quick to complain and slow to commend. Often others perform acts of kindness or professionalism beyond anyone's expectation, and a letter commending the person(s) is important—especially when sent to his or her supervisor. Just be sure to include specifics.

Letters of Complaint

The difference between getting satisfaction or going nowhere often boils down to attitude. If the overall tone of your letter is angry or sarcastic, the chances of having the matter corrected may be reduced. The person who receives the letter may very well be both innocent and ignorant of the problem. So write with a positive tone and avoid accusations, threats, and snide or derogatory comments. Here are some tips to improve your chance of success:

- Address your complaint to the highest person up the chain of command, making sure to use the correct name and title.
- It's more professional to send a printed or typewritten letter using standard business letter format. Use business letter format for an email also.

- If you have something positive to say, it's a good way to start the letter: "I've always enjoyed shopping at your store and received good customer service. However, I recently experienced some difficulty . . ."

- State your complaint clearly in the opening paragraph; then give all the particulars necessary. If, for example, the difficulty is with an order or invoice, give the identification number.

- Include all information that supports your complaint while avoiding negative or demeaning remarks. "The hotel desk clerk was unable to find any record of my reservation, credit card information, or confirmation . . ." is clear.

- Propose a solution and make it reasonable. For example, when an order has gone astray, it's reasonable to ask for a repeat order to be sent express, with the shipper covering the cost of the mailing.

- Close on a positive note. Thank the reader for their attention and sign off.

- Keep a copy for your records.

emailing or e-chatting customer support

Nowadays, your first contact with customer service may be with customersupport@xyzsuperstore.com. If that's the case, "To Whom It May Concern" is the polite way to start your communication. Even though you're using email, structure your communication as you would any business letter, and include your full contact information: name, physical address, phone number, and email address.

An e-chat is another great way to get real-time customer support. Even though you are conversing by writing back and forth, don't forget the common courtesies of "please" and "thank you." At the end of your chat be sure to thank the support person for their time and effort.

17

social names and titles

the most respectful way to address someone is by the name and title he or she prefers. But that can be tricky, especially since women have a number of options: married, but kept her maiden name; married, prefers Ms. It's a good idea to make some sort of notation in your address book if your friends have preferences. The following are the basics of how to use social and professional titles. (See Resources, pages 676–682.)

[BASIC SOCIAL TITLES]

The default social titles are "Mr." for a man and "Ms." for a woman. Formally, boys are "Master" until about age six or seven, then have no title until age sixteen to eighteen, when they assume "Mr." Girls are "Miss" until about sixteen to eighteen, when they use "Ms."

Suffixes

Junior, senior, II, III—suffixes are used to differentiate family members who have the same name. They are mostly used by men, but women may use them as well. For example, a man with the same name as his father, John Parker Davis, is John Parker Davis, Jr. The father may add "Sr." (senior) following his name, if he wishes. After the father dies, the son may drop the "Jr." or keep it, especially if it's useful to distinguish his wife, Mrs. John Parker Davis, Jr., and his widowed mother, Mrs. John Parker Davis.

In writing, a comma is used to separate the last name and the suffixes Jr. and Sr. When spelled out, *junior* and *senior* are written with a lowercase *j* and *s*, respectively, and the comma is used.

Numerical suffixes are a little trickier:

- II or 2nd (spoken, "the second") is used for a man named after his grandfather, uncle, or cousin.
- III or 3rd (the third) is used for a man named after his father, who is a junior.
- IV or 4th (the fourth) is used for a man named after his father, who is a third.

When a man marries, his wife also uses his suffix when using his name: Mrs. John Parker Davis, Jr.; but if she uses her first name she's Mrs. (Ms.) Deirdre Allen Parker.

In some families, names are carried through the generations: Sr., Jr., III, IV, and V. So what happens when John, Sr., dies? Does everyone "move up"? The only "rule" in this regard is to use common sense. Changing suffixes is bound to cause confusion, not to mention the expense of updating stationery, bank accounts, and anything else linked to the name. While keeping a name through the generations reflects a proud family history, practicality says to limit it to three generations, giving the fourth-generation child a different first or middle name.

Women's Names and Titles

Today, a married woman has numerous options for her name and social title—a decision based on her personal preference and one that should be respected. She can choose Ms. or Mrs., use her married name, her husband's name, or her maiden name. Generally, address social correspondence to a married woman using her first name, Mrs. (Ms.) Cheryl Esteban, or her husband's name, Mrs. David Esteban. At one time, only a divorcée used her first name, but today both forms of address are appropriate. For informal correspondence, it's fine to leave out the social title: Cheryl Esteban.

When a married woman uses her maiden name, she is addressed Ms. (not Mrs.) Cheryl Williams.

A married woman who is widowed, divorced, or separated will need to decide how to adapt her name to fit her situation. Here are options for these special situations:

Separation. During a separation a woman can continue to use her husband's name, Mrs. Thomas Wells, or her married name, Mrs. (Ms.) Courtney Wells. Since she's not divorced, she wouldn't change her name at this point.

Divorce. After a divorce, a woman does not continue using her husband's name, Mrs. Thomas Wells; rather she is simply Mrs. (Ms.) Courtney Wells, which is practical and less confusing. Most divorcées use Ms. and drop Mrs.

Multiple divorces. When a woman has been divorced and remarried more than once, she drops her previous husband's last name and uses her first name, middle or maiden name, and her current husband's surname. For example:

- First marriage: Beverly Griffen marries Douglas Turner: Beverly Griffen Turner.
- Second marriage: She marries Thomas Reese: Beverly Griffen Reese.

Or she can also choose to dispense with her husbands' surnames altogether and take back her maiden name.

Divorcées with children. After a divorce, children generally keep their father's last name. If their mother chooses to take back her maiden name, it can cause confusion, especially among those who don't know the family well.

Widows. Traditionally, a widow retains her husband's name until she remarries: Mrs. Thomas Wells. Today, Mrs. (Ms.) Courtney Wells is equally correct. If you don't know how to introduce or address a widow, it's preferable to side with tradition and use her husband's first name. Better yet, ask and make a note of her preference.

When a widow remarries, she has the choice of using her previous husband's last name as her middle name, Mrs. (Ms.) Courtney Wells DuPree. Many women who were married for years or who have children from their prior marriage prefer this option. Otherwise, she can use her own middle or maiden name, Mrs. (Ms.) Courtney Jenson DuPree, or her husband's name, Mrs. Alfred Lang DuPree.

An unmarried mother. Children of single mothers usually are given the mother's surname.

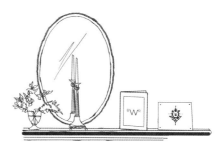

Addressing Couples

Formal social correspondence to a married couple is addressed to Mr. and Mrs. David Esteban. For informal notes, Cheryl and David Esteban is fine. When a married woman keeps her maiden name, correspondence to both is addressed Ms. (not Mrs.) Cheryl Williams and Mr. David Esteban, on the same line. When first names are used, either name may come first, so, David and Cheryl Esteban or Mr. David Esteban and Ms. Cheryl Williams is just as correct. When the name is too long to fit on one line, use two lines, with the second line indented:

Ms. Cheryl Williams
    and Mr. David Esteban

Correspondence to established couples who live together but aren't married is also addressed on one line:

Ms. Mira Patel and Mr. James DeFranco

These same guidelines apply when addressing married or unmarried gay and lesbian couples.

Individuals at the Same Address

If you're addressing a letter to housemates, or perhaps two sisters or brothers living at the same address, write each individual name on a separate line without using "and":

Mr. Allen Briody

Ms. Penelope Davis

] PROFESSIONAL TITLES [

Most professional titles or designations, such as "Esq." or "CPA," are just used in business. Medical doctors, dentists, clergy, and other professionals are addressed by, and introduced with, their titles socially as well as professionally. Here are some of the finer points of addressing people with professional titles.

Doctor

It's more common for women to use the title "Doctor" socially as well as professionally than in the past. People who have earned a Ph.D. or any other academic, non-medical doctoral degree have the choice of whether to use "Dr." both professionally and socially. If, when meeting people with doctorates, you're unsure how to address them, "Dr." is always correct. If they'd rather the title be dropped, they'll let you know.

honorary degrees

Honorary degrees bestowed by a university are truly prestigious awards. Does that mean that the recipient should now be addressed as "Doctor"? That depends. The recipient is addressed as "Doctor" while on the campus of the institution that awarded the degree, and all correspondence to him from the institution uses "Dr." However, off campus or at another university, the title shouldn't be used. It's also not used on business cards or in personal or business correspondence. A recipient may list his honorary degree following his name, Paul Sousa, D.Ed., but on a resumé or in a biographical sketch, he should write Paul Sousa, Doctor of Education, *honoris causa*, to indicate that the degree wasn't earned.

When a married woman uses the title "Dr." (either medical or academic) socially, addressing social correspondence to the couple is a little trickier. If her husband is *not* a "doctor," address letters to Dr. Sonia and Mr. Robert Harris. Her name comes first because her professional title "outranks" his social title. If her husband is also a doctor, the address is either The Drs. (Doctors) Harris or Drs. Sonia and Robert Harris (the order of the names doesn't matter).

The Reverend

In introductions and in correspondence, many Protestant clergy are referred to as "The Reverend." While business correspondence is addressed to The Reverend James Norris, (D.D., if held), social correspondence is slightly different: The Reverend (Mr./Dr.) and Mrs. James Norris. In conversation, a clergyman or clergywoman is addressed as Dr./Mr./Mrs./Ms./Pastor/Rector/Reverend Norris.

Addressing a husband and wife who are both "Reverends" follows the same format as a husband and wife who are both doctors: The Reverends Norris or The Reverend Mrs./Ms. Patricia Norris and the Reverend Mr. James Norris. If either of the couple also has a doctorate degree, that person's name would go first: The Reverend Dr. James Norris and The Reverend Mrs./Ms. Patricia Norris.

Esquire

Today "Esquire" is largely confined to business correspondence between attorneys and justices of the peace. An alternative is to write:

Mr. David Bowman

Attorney at Law

using two lines, no indent, and including the titles Mr. or Ms.

When "Esq." or "Esquire" is used, the name is never preceded by Mr., Ms., Mrs., or other titles such as Dr., and is written David Bowman, Esq. "Esquire" isn't used in introductions: "I'd like to introduce attorney David Bowman/Mr. David Bowman/David Bowman." It also isn't used for social correspondence, as when writing to a lawyer and his or her spouse or addressing a social invitation. Mr. and Mrs. David Bowman is the correct form.

Professional Designations

Professional designations such as CPA (Certified Public Accountant) or CLU (Certified Life Underwriter) are only used on business cards or business correspondence. They follow a person's name, and Mr. or Ms. isn't used: Martha Dawes, CPA; Phillip Olner, CLU. If a person has more than one designation, they're listed in the order received: Phillip Olner, CLU, CFP. Socially, use Mr., Ms., or Mrs. without the professional designation: Ms. Martha Dawes.

Other Titles

Every day we run into people who have an official title. The police officer at the desk is Sergeant Flynn; the head of the fire department is Chief Elmore; the club chef is Chef Rossi; the pilot on your plane is Captain Howe; and so forth. When on the job, such people are always addressed by their titles, just as they are when the matter at hand is related to their work. Socially, many don't use their titles, though they may. Sometimes a title sticks: A local judge, for example, who's been called by his title for a number of years, is usually addressed as "Judge" even after his retirement. (See also Chapter 15, "Official Life," page 179.)

LEGAL NAME CHANGES

Anyone who changes the name by which he or she has been known should notify social and business associates to avoid confusion and embarrassing situations. Today, the quickest and easiest way of informing others is by email or postcard:

Greetings, friends,

Just want to let you know that Leah, Joe, Ellen, and Robbie Nichtersdorf have changed their last name to Nichter. Please make a note in your address books.

Many thanks!

The Nichters

"sir" and "madam"

"Sir" and "Madam" (usually shortened to "Ma'am") are titles of respect and show deference on the part of the speaker. For this reason, they're never used between people of equal age and status. No matter how charming a gentleman may be, a woman of the same age doesn't address him as "Sir," nor does a man address a female contemporary as "Madam" or "Ma'am."

On rare occasions, an older man may say "Sir" to a male contemporary, especially if he doesn't know the other's name. "Sir" and "Ma'am" are also used to address distinguished people, to avoid too many repetitions of a formal name and title. "Sir" and "Ma'am" are widely used in the military to address both service people of higher rank and civilians. (See also Chapter 15, "Official Life," page 179.)

It's perfectly fine (and polite!) for a salesperson to call a customer "Sir" or "Ma'am." In some parts of the United States, children are taught to address teachers and other adults using these titles. In short, the terms are used when addressing someone elder or when one person is serving another in some way.

telephone manners
18

today's telephone, in its many guises, is a multifaceted communication device. Depending on the type of phone and service plan, you can make and receive calls, identify who's calling, be alerted and switch to another incoming call, leave a voice message, send a text message, have a video chat, take and send pictures, as well as connect to email and the entire world of the Internet.

With such a rapid evolution in technology, have telephone manners changed as well? Telephone etiquette basics still apply, no matter which device you use. However, the phone's added capabilities—conference calls, speakerphones, texting, hands-free headsets, and picture-taking capability—cause us to examine what are the best, most considerate, and respectful ways to use them.

Where do today's phone manners start? Begin by thinking about **who** is with you and **where** you are. The person or people you are with, face-to-face, deserve your full attention, a way to show them your respect.

Your interaction or conversation shouldn't be interrupted. Saying, "I'll just answer this," when your phone rings, looking at email, or writing a text message is just plain rude. No matter which type of phone it is, use it only when it won't bother or interrupt others, as might be the case on a bus, in a checkout line, or at the movies.

When you're on the phone, speak **clearly** and **distinctly**, especially if you have an accent. Watch your **volume**. Keep your voice low whenever you're in the presence of others. Whether you're making calls in an open-office environment or on your cell phone, you want to be considerate and avoid disturbing those around you. Finally, be careful of your **tone**. Unless you're on a phone with video capability, there's no way for the person you're speaking with to interpret your facial expressions. If your tone isn't a match for your words, your message may be misinterpreted.

PHONE MANNERS IN GENERAL

No matter what type of voice device you use, there are certain guidelines for phone usage that apply across the board, from answering or placing calls to using special features such as call-waiting, caller ID, and voice mail.

Answering the Phone

Except for business calls, a straightforward "Hello" remains the greeting of choice—particularly today, when you never know when a stranger is calling. An equally polite but less personal greeting is "Hello, this is the Marshalls (Marshall residence)," which is also used when you're answering the phone at another person's home.

It's just as important to know what *not* to do when answering the phone. Some things to avoid include

◆ Brusquely asking "Who is this?" when the caller is unknown or the call is for someone else. If the caller hasn't stated her name, you can ask "May I ask who's calling?" or "May I tell her who's calling?" (See "Placing Calls," page 224.)

◆ Saying, "Wait a minute," and keeping the caller waiting while you vanish on an errand of your own. If the call comes at an inconvenient moment, it's okay to say, "I'll call you back in a few minutes," as long as you follow through.

◆ Letting a very young child answer. It can be difficult for a child under six to understand a message and relay it to the right person. (See also Chapter 38, "Children and Teens," page 478.)

When It's for Someone Else

When an incoming call is for another person in the household, respond with, "Please wait a moment; I'll get her." Immediately find the person and deliver the message. Try to avoid shouting, "Annie, it's for *yoo*-ou!" If you do have to call out to the person, be sure to cover the mouthpiece first.

If the person isn't available, offer to take a message, then *write it down* and leave it in a place the person will see it. Keeping a pad and pen within reach of the phone ensures that you're not wasting a caller's time while you search for something to write on. Be sure you get the name and number right by repeating them back to the caller. It's also helpful to note the day and hour of the call.

Wrong Numbers

When you're on the receiving end of a wrong number, "I'm sorry, you have the wrong number" is the direct and polite response. If the caller asks "Who is this?" you can reply, "What number are you calling?" or "Who are you trying to reach?" Only give out your number if you feel comfortable doing so. If the caller wants to argue (unlikely, but it happens), you might say, "Please understand: There is no Jason here," before hanging up. (See also "Dialing a Wrong Number," page 224.)

Caller ID

Caller ID is handy both for screening calls and as a record of missed calls if the caller didn't leave a message. On the positive side, caller ID allows you to decide whether it's worth interrupting what you're doing to take a call. However, answering your phone by saying, "Hi, Jim," can throw the caller off guard unless he's a close friend or make you look foolish if it's actually Jim's wife calling.

Offensive Calls

The most unwelcome call of all is the obscene call. If your "Hello" is answered with heavy breathing or worse, hang up at once; responding will only give the caller the satisfaction of hearing you become upset. If the call is repeated immediately, leave the receiver off the hook for a while.

Prank calls are innocent by comparison, but a nuisance nonetheless. Like more upsetting callers, a kid looking for a laugh will soon give up when he gets nothing but a busy signal. If obscene or prank calls keep coming, notify your telephone service provider or local law enforcement authorities.

---

it's 1-800-buy-this calling

Directing your anger at telephone solicitors is about as constructive as throwing the phone across the room. It's the organization that hires the solicitor that's to blame, not the individual who's trying to make a living. Common sense says that taking your frustration out on the solicitor isn't going to stop the calls.

You can, however, take steps to stop telephone solicitations. First, ask that your name be removed from the calling list, which the solicitor is bound to do by law. You're more likely to succeed if you're polite about it: "I know you're just doing your job, but I have a policy of not accepting telephone solicitations. Also, could you please see to it that I'm taken off your organization's list? Thanks." Another preventive measure is to sign up for the national Do Not Call registry at 1-888-382-1222 or online at https:www.donotcall.gov/. This will block most, but not all, unsolicited calls.

Even if you're on the national Do Not Call registry, calls from political organizations and charities are exempt, as are calls asking you to take a survey. Again, it's fine to say a polite "No, I don't accept phone solicitations," and request to be removed from their list, if you wish.

If a solicitor won't take no for an answer, be firm: "I'm sorry, but I'm not interested, and I have to hang up now." Then do so. Just don't slam down the phone.

PLACING CALLS

When you place a call, good manners start even before the other person answers—with the number of rings. Let the phone ring five or six times to give the person you're calling a chance to reach the phone. Then hang up and call again later, or leave a message if voice mail picked up. (See "Voice Mail," page 228.)

Five other considerations to remember when calling:

Make the call in a quiet place. Background noise, such as a noisy bar or traffic and wind noise in a car, can make it difficult for the person you're call-ing to understand you. If you're having trouble under-standing someone, it's fine to suggest a call back. "I'm sorry, but it's difficult for me to hear with the noise in the background. Could you please call me back? Thanks."

Minimize dropped calls. Don't place a call when you know you're in a poor service area or are about to enter a tunnel. Wait and call when you know you can complete your conversation.

Identify yourself. When the call is answered, state your name. It's polite, even when you're talking with a family member or close friend who knows your voice. If someone other than the person you're calling answers the phone, keep your conversation brief: "Hi, this is Louise Silva. May I please speak with Joan?"

Ask if it's a good time to talk. If you expect your call to last more than a minute or two, saying, "Is this a good time to talk?" or "Are you in the middle of some-thing? I can call back," shows that you're considerate of the other person's time.

Keep any messages brief. If the person you want isn't there and you want to leave a message, keep it short. Unless it's urgent, it's thoughtless to expect whoever answers to write down a lengthy or compli-cated message.

Dialing a Wrong Number

It's a good idea to double-check phone numbers before dialing, but when you *do* dial a wrong number, simply

---

invitations by phone

When calling to extend an invitation to a friend, be direct from the start: "Hi, Marianne. We're having a few people over on Saturday night to play bridge. Can you and Hank come?" This approach leaves the person free to accept or to say, "Oh, I'm so sorry but we're busy Saturday," if she'd rather not. Don't start out saying, "Hi, Marianne. Are you and Hank busy Saturday night?" It gives her no options.

When responding to a telephone invitation, don't say, "I'll let you know," unless you explain immediately: "I'll have to ask Hank if he's already made plans" or "We have tickets for the high-school play for that night, but I might be able to exchange them for two on Thursday." Otherwise, "I'll let you know" sounds as though you're waiting for a better invitation. In any case, respond to the invitation within a day or possibly two, calling back with an answer when you said you would.

say so and apologize. Don't demand, "What number is this?" Better to say, "I'm so sorry. I must have dialed the wrong number. I was trying to reach 749-555-5903," which will keep you from sounding abrupt. Never just hang up without a word when you reach a wrong number; it's considerate to offer a simple apology for inconveniencing someone.

Timing Calls

As a general rule, place your calls between 9:00 AM and 9:00 PM unless you're certain a friend or relative doesn't mind being called earlier or later. Even those who don't go to bed at nine o'clock may consider their day "closed" after that hour. Check with friends who have babies or young children so you don't disturb nap or bedtimes. Also, be aware of time zone differences when placing your call.

If people you call frequently say or imply that they'd rather not be called at certain times of day, then comply. It's easy to tell yourself, "I know Scott corrects papers after dinner, but I doubt if he'll mind if I call to invite him to my party." But resist the temptation; a call at the wrong time is no less disruptive because it comes from a friend.

When Calling on Someone Else's Phone

If you need to use someone else's landline or cell phone, always ask permission first and keep the call short. Since many phones have caller ID, identify yourself: "Hi. This is Liz Chou calling from Dan Baker's phone."

⟨ CALLS IN PROGRESS ⟩

The guidelines for effective conversation apply as much to a phone call as a face-to-face talk. (See Chapter 4, "The Art of Conversation," page 35.) Speak clearly and be careful not to shout (many people unconsciously raise their voice while on the phone). Avoid focusing entirely on yourself; rather, ask the person you're talking to what he's been doing or inquire about friends or relatives—anything that expresses interest in him. As you listen, let him *know* you're listening. Since you can't show attention with a nod or a smile, use verbal responses instead: "Yes, I understand"; "Of course"; "I see."

In the past, phone calls were short because they were expensive. While calls may be more affordable today, it's still courteous to be respectful of other people's time.

Call-Waiting

Call-waiting service is a double-edged sword. It's useful for people such as children or elderly parents who must get through to you in an emergency or when you use it for business calls at home. It also has the potential to cause offense. If you feel insulted when asked, "Do you mind if I see who this is?" you're not alone. Your impulse might be to answer, "Yes, I do mind!" But it's better to say, "Go ahead," then wait. But if more than ninety seconds pass, it's fine to hang up. When you're eventually reconnected, try not to betray your annoyance. Politely say that you were unable to hold and leave it at that, even though the person should have returned to you more quickly.

When your own call-waiting signals, *your responsibility is to the person you are speaking with on the original call*. If you decide you need to answer, apologize and say you'll return immediately; put her on hold and quickly explain to the second caller that you'll have to call back. The first caller should never be left on hold for more than twenty seconds (thirty at the most).

There are exceptions to the rule. If you're expecting an important or long-distance call (especially from overseas), say so at the outset of the call: "I'm waiting to hear from my brother in the military/my doctor/my plumber. If she/he calls, I'll have to take it and get back to you." When the call comes in, arrange a time to call back—then do so. If you alert someone at the beginning of the call, it will keep her from feeling brushed off when you need to take the call-waiting.

Other Interruptions

You're on the phone and the doorbell rings. Because you don't know who awaits you on the other side of the door or what they might want, it's probably best to end your call: "There's someone at the door. May I call you back in a little while?" Then be sure to return the call as soon as you can. If you're not expecting anyone and you're concerned, you might ask your caller to stay on the line while you answer the door.

Mechanical Glitches and Dropped Calls

When a phone call in progress is disconnected—often the case if you're on the edge of cell service—it's the caller's responsibility to call back. If you initiated the call, immediately redial the person you were talking with and apologize, even though the equipment was at fault: "I'm sorry; we somehow got disconnected. I think we left off with your dinner with Ann and Gary." Redial even if your conversation was nearing an end; not calling back is like walking off in the middle of a face-to-face chat. When it's a cell call, wait until you're in a location with good service before calling back.

If you're the one who was called and the call was dropped, stay off the line; then phone the person if he hasn't called back in a few minutes. Saying something like, "I'm not sure why the phone went dead, but I just wanted to make sure we didn't have anything else to discuss," draws the call to a proper close.

If a bad connection or static on the line makes it difficult to hear, you can ask the other person to hang up so you can try again. A second call often solves the problem.

six phone call faux pas

The following are common telephone errors. In personal calls, they qualify as minor missteps; in business calls, they can make you look unprofessional.

TALKING TO SOMEONE ELSE. When you're speaking with someone on the phone, talking to someone else in the room is permissible only when the third party's participation is necessary or you say something like, "I hope you don't mind if I quickly ask John what he thinks about this."

BUSYING YOURSELF WITH OTHER THINGS. Typing, washing dishes, or shuffling papers while on the phone signals that your attention is elsewhere.

EATING. Eating while on the phone is not only impolite but is viewed by many as crude. Avoid the temptation to make a call using a hands-free phone while you eat lunch.

CHEWING GUM. Hearing the smacks of a gum chewer can be annoying. To be on the safe side, save the gum for later.

SNEEZING OR COUGHING INTO THE RECEIVER. If you have to sneeze, cough, or blow your nose, either turn your head away or excuse yourself for a moment and put down the phone.

DON'T MAKE THE CALL FROM THE STALL. Sure it's a private spot, but subjecting the person on the receiving end to the accompanying noises is gross. Subjecting others in a restroom to your conversation is inconsiderate.

ENDING CALLS

Traditional telephone etiquette says that the person who originates the call is the one who terminates it. If you're the one who placed the call, say something like, "Barbara, I'm glad I reached you, and we'll be looking forward to seeing you on the seventh. Bye."

If you're having difficulty ending a long-winded call, you may have to be firm. At the first pause in the conversation, say, "I'm sorry, but I really have to go now. Let's pick this up again soon." Take this route whether you placed the call or received it, and only when really necessary.

TEXT TELEPHONES

The text telephone is a technological benefit for the deaf or hard of hearing. Also called teletypes (TTYs) or telecommunication devices for the deaf (TDDs), these devices, which look like small typewriters, permit two people to communicate by typing back and forth in a conversational manner over a phone line, similar to texting on a cell phone or instant messaging. It's also possible for someone with a conventional phone to speak with someone using a TTY/TDD by using a relay service provided by the telephone company. The hearing caller speaks to a mediator, sometimes called a CA, or communications advisor, who translates spoken words into typed messages that the person who is deaf or hard of hearing can read. Likewise, the CA can translate the typed message from a TTY/TDD caller into speech for a hearing recipient. It's important for the hearing party to speak slowly and clearly to facilitate accurate translation. While some people may feel uncomfortable discussing certain subjects with a third party involved, having a CA is both routine and confidential, and shouldn't limit what needs to be discussed even if it's personal or unpleasant.

⌐ VOICE MAIL ⌐

Whether you use an answering machine or are connected to a voice mail system, on a landline or cell phone, certain considerations should come into play.

Recording a Greeting

In a word, keep your greeting *short*. A musical overture, a long intro of how pleased you are someone has called, or a child's cute chatter keeps the caller waiting unnecessarily. There's no need to say, "We can't come to the phone right now," which is obvious, as you didn't answer. The simpler your message, the better. Basically, you want your caller to know two things: who he has reached and that he should leave a message. "This is Julio Hernandez. Please leave a message and I'll call you back." It's also handy to give an alternate way to reach you, but don't give more than one option: "This is Julio Hernandez, please leave me a message or try my cell—802-555-2020." If you prefer not to give your name, try, "You've reached 719-555-4526. Please leave your name, number, and message and I'll get back to you." Some people opt not to make a commitment to call back. "Hello, thanks for calling. Please leave me a message." At the end of any message you can add, ". . . or give us a call back later."

Think, too, about setting the number of rings so that you have enough time to get to the phone before voice mail picks up, but not long enough to frustrate your caller. Four to six rings before the phone goes to voice mail is usually adequate; a person who is elderly or who has a physical disability may require more rings.

Leaving a Message

A cardinal rule when leaving a message on someone's answering machine or voice mail is to state your name and number *first*, and say them *slowly*. Many people ramble on until they're about to be cut off, then give their number so quickly that it's unintelligible. When you leave your name and number at the end of the message, the recipient may have to listen to the whole ramble again (and again) if he couldn't catch the number.

Keep your message brief, suggest a time when the recipient can reach you, and close by repeating your number—a sign-off that gives the listener another chance to jot it down without having to replay the message. If he does have to replay your message, your name and number are available at the beginning.

If you tend to get tongue-tied or ramble on when

it's time to leave a message, try writing down your key points before you make your call. Sometimes it's possible to rerecord a message, a helpful option on many cell phone voice mail systems.

RETURNING CALLS

The golden rule for returning calls left on your machine or voice mail is to do it within twenty-four hours, if possible. When you're out of town, most phone answering systems allow you to check your messages via a remote message retrieval system.

If you reach voice mail on your return call, you can lessen the potential for telephone tag by stating where you can be reached and when.

19
personal communication devices

It's fair to say that cell phones are ubiquitous. Their use has spread around the globe and it's hard to think of someone who doesn't own one. For many young people or people without traditional landline service, the cell phone has become their connection to the world. They're an obvious advantage to communication, giving us the security of knowing we're able to be in touch anytime, and can be a lifesaver in an emergency.

Once just limited to voice calls, phones are now equipped with digital cameras, the capability to send text messages, and the ability to access or receive messages via the Internet. Using a smartphone you can fully access the Web, communicate via email, store documents, connect to your social network, employ hundreds of useful applications (apps), play games, listen to music, read books, watch movies, and more.

Society's irritation with the cell phone isn't with the device; it's with the thoughtless ways it's used. And society reacted. Little signs (*etiquettes* in French) began to appear in theaters, waiting rooms, and restaurants: "No cell phones." It wasn't long before people came to a consensus about where, when, and how we should use them. More to the point, whether it's a basic cell phone or a fully loaded smartphone, considerate use involves taking personal responsibility and being in command of your device, instead of being at its mercy. And that starts with using the convenient "Off" button.

SMARTPHONES

While it's likely that our personal communication devices will continue to advance technologically, adding features and capabilities we may not even be able to imagine, the etiquette guidelines for their polite use remain the same: Be respectful and considerate of who you're with and those around you. All the manners for cell phone calls and texting apply to mobile device users, too. Because of their email and Internet capabilities, as well as the ability to store documents, users should be particularly wary of keeping confidential or work-related information on a mobile device. Lost, stolen, or hacked into, that information could easily become public. While some workplaces encourage the use of smartphones and tablets during a meeting, others do not. Know what's appropriate at your company or in your department. If you're not sure, ask before the meeting starts if you can use your device. Even if its use is legitimate—to ask for information germane to the meeting—the perception is that it's being used for personal communications. In either case, your attention isn't on the people you're with, it's on the device. Let the meeting leader decide if PDAs will be useful or a distraction. If they are allowed, turn off the ringer and let voice mail pick up your calls.

- Without exception, turn your device off in a house of worship, restaurant, or theater; during a meeting or presentation; or *anytime its use is likely to disturb others*.

- If you must be alerted to a call, put your device on silent ring or vibrate, and check your caller ID or voice mail later. (Put it in your pocket; a vibrating phone, skittering across a tabletop, is just as disruptive as a ring.)

- Wherever you are, if you must make or take a call, move to a private space and speak as quietly as you can.

- Keep calls as short as possible; the longer the call, the greater the irritation to those who have no choice but to listen.

- Don't discuss confidential information anyplace it might be overheard.

Take-Care Zones

The where of a cell-phone conversation is an important consideration. Special care should be taken when having a chat on the street, in stores, in restaurants, in your car, and on public transportation and airplanes.

On the street. Don't shout into your phone while walking outdoors. Talking loudly is both intrusive and inconsiderate. Watch out for others when you're on a crowded sidewalk; don't get so involved in your call that you bump into passersby. For safety's sake, pay special attention when crossing streets.

In stores. No one should be slowed down in a checkout line because you're having second thoughts about the blouse you've chosen and need to phone a friend for advice. Also, it's disrespectful to the cashier, who is trying to serve you. She deserves your full attention.

In restaurants. Most restaurants require that cell phones be turned off. If cell phones aren't off-limits, turn yours off anyway and don't make calls at the table. If you must call, excuse yourself and go to the lobby or outside.

when it *is* okay to use your phone in public

Most people don't mind short, quiet calls: in the grocery aisle to double-check your list, in the theater lobby to let someone know you've just scored tickets, when you've made it through security and are waiting to board, or if your plane has landed and you'll be waiting outside baggage claim B. The key words here are *short* and *quiet*.

four mobile phone don'ts

Talking too loudly into a mobile phone ranks first on the annoyance scale, but four other habits aren't far behind:

Leaving the ringer on in quiet places. You're at the movies, George Clooney is moving in for the big kiss, and . . . someone's phone rings. A ringing phone can cause an even greater disturbance in a concert hall or house of worship. Turn it off or switch to vibrate.

Ignoring those you're with. Don't make or take calls when you're in the middle of a face-to-face conversation. By doing so, you're making whoever you're with feel second best, or that your phone matters more than they do.

Making repeated calls. Keep calls to a minimum on public transportation, in line at the bank or movies, or in busy areas like airports. Placing one call after another (especially just to pass the time) eventually exasperates even the most understanding captive listener.

Using offensive language. Oblivious to those around them, some cell phone users feel free to pepper their conversation with obscenities. The people nearby may try not to listen, but it's hard to ignore.

In the car. Recent studies have shown that people who are talking, texting, or otherwise using a cell phone while driving are significantly slower to react to a red light and are at least four times more likely to be involved in an accident. Many states have outlawed cell phone use while driving. Hands-free phones may lessen the risk somewhat, but the smartest choice is to pull into a parking area and stop before making a call.

Traffic noise may cause you to talk more loudly when making cell phone calls from your car. This can be annoying to the person on the other end of the call. Also, let the person you call know if there are other passengers who will hear the conversation.

On airplanes. It's a courtesy to everyone on board to wrap up your call quickly when the flight crew instructs passengers to turn off all electronic devices before takeoff. When phone use is permitted after landing, keep your calls short, limiting them to information about your arrival: "Hi, we just landed at 7:30. I'll meet you outside baggage claim in about a half hour." Save any longer calls for a private spot in the terminal.

On buses and trains. The most common problems on buses and trains are volume and intruding on the other passengers, so keep conversations short and *soft*. Try to limit your calls to those that are really necessary. While it might seem like a good use of your time to call and confirm the guest list for your dinner party, the people who are within earshot will be irritated listening to the same call repeated numerous times. Some commuter trains have quiet cars where cell phone use is prohibited.

Ring Tones

Think about what your ring tone says about you. Is your frat boy hip-hop tone the right ring for your new job as a trainee at an accounting firm? How about repeated rings: Does your family cringe when they hear "Dancing Queen" for the umpteenth million time?

FaceTime or Video Calls

Video calls via your computer or phone are a fantastic way to keep in touch and communicate. Here are five tips for success.

- Take care with your appearance and surroundings. Chatting to your sister while wearing PJs may be okay; not so when talking to office mates.

- Try to plan the call ahead of time. Since a video call involves more connection (audio and visual) it's more likely that the recipient will need to be in the right place and without distraction to be able to receive your call.

- Be aware of who is around you. Let the person you are calling know if others are in the room but just off screen or if they could be passing through the background from time to time.

- Stay focused on the person you are talking to. Looking away or walking off screen during a call without giving a reason would make you appear distracted or even rude.

- At a family gathering, it's fine to pass the phone around so everyone gets the chance to say "hi."

Cameras

Photos, video, video chat—your mobile device can do it all. A fun snap of you and the kids on vacation or a picture of the drain trap you need to replace at the hardware store are great ways to use your phone's camera. However, taking photos or videos that would embarrass someone and then transmitting or posting them is a breach of manners and ethics. Don't use a cell phone in a restroom or locker room. Not only is it rude to sub-

Q: *Do I have to respond to every text? Both my mother and my future mother-in-law expect that every text message be answered and even seem offended if a message is not responded to quickly. Is this a generational difference or is it improper etiquette to leave some messages unanswered?*

A: Think of your texting as a conversation: If you would respond in the conversation, then respond in the text. Texts are such short little informational bursts that it can seem ungainly to have an endless back and forth of "thanks" and "byes." A short "TY" to acknowledge that the message was received is a simple way to end the conversation, and, in your case, avoid annoying the moms.

ject others to your call, but even the possibility that you could use the phone as a camera or video is enough to warrant not using it at all.

Text Messaging

Short messaging service (SMS), also known as text messaging or texting, involves typing messages on a cell phone or smartphone and zapping them to the recipient in an instant. Billions of text messages are sent each year: They're fast and relatively inexpensive, depending on the provider plan. Even better, you can get a message to someone without having their phone ring at an inopportune time.

Text messaging is a strictly casual communication. You shouldn't use text messaging when informing someone of sad news, business matters, or urgent meetings, unless it's to set up a phone call on the subject. Also, don't communicate only via text: Respond to voice mails with a phone call, unless the call warrants a short, simple response.

Most important, be aware of where you are. The backlight will disturb others if you text in a theater or house of worship. Even though texts are silent, when you text, your attention is elsewhere, not on the people you're with.

Other guidelines include the following:

- Be aware—not everyone has unlimited texting as part of their service plan.

- Keep your message brief. If it's going to be more than a couple of lines, make a call and have a conversation.

- Don't be a pest. Bombarding someone with texts is annoying and assumes they have nothing better to do than read your messages. Would you call them that often?

- Be very careful when choosing a recipient from your phone book; a slip of the thumb could send a text intended for a friend to your boss.

- When you text someone who doesn't have your number in his directory, start by stating who you are, and clarify if you have a common name: "Hi, it's Kate (yoga class). Chiropractor's # is 802-555-2020. Good luck!"

Q: *When I was at the movies recently, a phone rang and the owner proceeded to have a conversation as if he were in his own living room. Two people yelled, "Shut up!" which I thought was just as rude. How do I politely let it be known I'm upset?*

A: What seems like the simplest, most reasonable solution—quietly asking the person to end the call or move to the lobby—may backfire by being just as disruptive or leading to a confrontation. Instead, find an usher or the manager and ask him to deal with the culprit. In this day of constant reminders about curbing phone usage, it's highly unlikely the offender isn't aware that his behavior is wrong—all the more reason to let someone official request that he put his phone away or move to the lobby.

- Whenever you have a chance, respond to text messages, either by texting back or with a phone call.

- If you receive a text message by mistake, just return it to the sender with a short "Sorry wrong number" message.

- Don't text at the movies, a play, or a concert—the screen light will disturb others.

- Don't text anything confidential, private, or potentially embarrassing. You never know when your message might get sent to the wrong person or forwarded. Not to mention if someone finds your lost phone.

◆ As with email, you can't know for sure when the recipient is going to read his or her messages. Don't be upset if your text doesn't get an immediate response.

Text Speak

Before the advent of qwerty keyboards on phones, it was cumbersome to text using an alphanumeric keypad. "Text speak" uses many abbreviations for short, commonly used phrases for speed and to avoid thumb fatigue. Again, keep your recipient in mind, but here are some widely used abbreviations:

IMHO in my humble opinion

TTYL talk to you later

IDK I don't know

BTW by the way

LOL laugh out loud

CYA see ya

BRB be right back

J/K just kidding

OIC oh I see

THX/TY thanks, thank you

L8R later

BFF best friends forever

ILY I love you

B/C because

---

voice mail vs. missed calls

The cell phone generation is less likely to spend time leaving a voice mail. People are more likely to just redial a missed call than they are to listen to a voice mail and then call back. If you do need to get your message across right away, send a text.

Conference Calls

All participants should introduce themselves so that everyone else can link voices to names. To reinforce the link, participants should identify themselves the first few times they speak: "This is Cindy. I'm wondering . . ." If you aren't sure who's speaking, ask.

Make sure everyone has a chance to talk. Because there are no facial cues, it can be difficult to know when to jump into the conversation.

Speakerphones

Speakerphones are useful when you have several people in one place who would like to be in on a call, such as when you and your children call your parents, or when you need your hands to take notes. Start your call with the handset and ask if it's okay to use the speakerphone. Begin by introducing everyone else on

> Q: *During a lull in a staff meeting, I used my smartphone to enter some appointments and check over my grocery list. A coworker later told me I'd been rude. Was she right?*
>
> A: Unless that "lull" was an official break, you shouldn't have flipped open your phone. Taking care of *personal* business during a meeting is unprofessional. Keep your focus on the business at hand, and check your messages or schedule after the meeting or during a break.

the call. "Hi, Mom, it's Jeff. May I put you on speakerphone? I'm here with Liza, Jack, and Megan."

While convenient, talking on a speakerphone for one-on-one conversations can give the impression that you're doing something else at the same time. That may be okay if you're chatting with a close friend, but others may think that you're not paying attention. In addition, it's not always easy to hear someone on the other end, and being on a speakerphone can seem less personal. If the person with whom you're talking is using a speakerphone and it bothers you, politely ask, "Are you using speakerphone?" If she doesn't offer to switch to a handheld phone, you could say something like, "I can't hear you well. Would you mind switching to the receiver?" If she still doesn't switch, then ask if you can talk later when she's able to use a regular phone.

Earbuds

Wireless earpieces are a great help to people whose job requires them to constantly be on the phone—event planners, brokers, salespeople setting up appointments. However, when you're with other people in a social setting or participating in a face-to-face conversation, remove your earpiece and focus your attention on the people with you. Often, people are on calls while they're on the go—walking down the street, on a bus, at the market. As far as making calls in public, the same rules apply as for mobile phones. (See page 230–32.)

Music

We really can have music wherever we go . . . on the plane, on the treadmill, on a boat in the middle of nowhere. So what are the top manners for listening to music on a phone or portable music device?

- Keep the volume down. If other people can hear your music through your earbuds, it's too loud. People also shouldn't have to shout to get your attention. When you're jogging or biking, for safety reasons you need to be able to hear traffic noises or sirens.

- Take the earbuds off when talking to others. Don't have them hanging around your neck, or even worse, leave one in when having a conversation.

- Before using one at work, check if your company permits it.

20 online communication

The etiquette of electronic communications is constantly evolving, as new portals, capabilities, and ways of interacting and forming communities online are launched. (See Chapter 30, "Life Online," page 383.) The quest for an etiquette for Internet users reminds us that the more things change, the more they stay the same.

Whether you're sending an email, commenting on a forum, or writing on a friend's Facebook page, three key considerations will help you communicate politely and effectively:

Human contact still matters. Don't communicate electronically at the expense of personal interaction. There's a reason people need to discuss things face-to-face, and there are times when no substitute will do—for example, when you're breaking up with your boyfriend or asking your boss for a raise.

Watch what you say—and how you say it. While electronic devices can bring people together, their impersonal nature can lead people to write things they wouldn't think of saying in person.

Be careful when clicking "Send." Whatever you say or post in cyberspace *cannot be taken back*. You have no control over where your message goes once you've hit "Send"; it can be saved and forwarded by any recipient who chooses to do so, and words have come back to hurt people, destroy friendships, and ruin careers. Similarly, once something is on the Web, it tends to live forever.

[EXEMPLARY EMAILING]

A 2015 study by the Radicati Group reported that an estimated 205 billion emails were sent every day (with about 90 percent being spam or containing viruses). That's more than 2.4 million emails sent every second. Whether using email for personal correspondence or business matters, misusing email can have serious consequences; understanding the nature of email can help you use it effectively and responsibly. Keep the following points in mind:

- **Email isn't private.** Emails are public documents. If you can't post it on a public bulletin board, don't write and send it in an email. Never send confidential or sensitive information electronically, as messages can be sent to the wrong person or forwarded to others without your consent.

- **Email isn't always reliable.** The more serious the message, the less appropriate email becomes as the medium. Spam filters and misaddressed mail can prevent your message from being delivered. Some news—the death of a family member, your job resignation—should be delivered in person, if possible, otherwise by phone.

- **Your boss owns your email.** Any electronic communications produced or received on equipment provided by your company—PC, laptop, smartphone—belongs to the company. Use your own phone or computer for personal communications.

Reminding yourself of the nature of email can help you decide if it's the right way to deliver your mes-

---

beware the electronic brick wall

The electronic brick wall is diabolical. Electronic communications such as texts, emails, tweets, and IMs occur without the benefit of any of the visual and auditory cues that help a recipient judge the tone of the message: Is it meant to be joking or sarcastic, or is it rude or disrespectful? That same electronic brick wall also leads to intentional rudeness in communications. Because the recipient is not right there in front of us, we become emboldened to say or write things we simply would not communicate when face-to-face.

The electronic brick wall is detrimental to communications in three ways:

1. Anonymity. We email, IM, post, tweet, and respond to blogs or comments in the mistaken belief that we are anonymous. We are not.
2. Rudeness. The fact that we feel safe because we cannot see the recipient emboldens us to say or write things we wouldn't if face-to-face.
3. Lax social skills. We learn how to interact with others by being with them. When, instead, communication is solely by electronic means, the opportunity to develop social skills is diminished. Then, when confronted by a difficult in-person situation, resolution may be compromised because we don't know what to do.

Tear down your electronic brick wall by meeting with people, by spending time with others, by getting out of your chair and talking with the person to whom you were thinking of just sending an IM or text.

sage. When you do send email, here are a few points to keep in mind—from the moment you start writing to clicking "Send":

Address with care. Good manners are called for even as you fill in the address line. When sending an email to a long list of recipients, don't put all the addresses in the "To" and "Copy" headers. Most people don't want their email addresses (often with full names included) displayed for all to see. It's better to send messages individually or create a group (Joe's Family). Recipients see the group name, but not the individual members and their addresses. Another option is to use the blind copy (Bcc) feature, which allows you to show only one address in the "To" line. (For more on when to use Bcc, see page 241.) Also, be careful when selecting names from a list: The first Peter may be your boss; the second your friend. Some people fill in the address line *after* they compose their message. If there's an accidental "send," the message will fail if the "To" line is still empty.

Send delay. If your email program has a "send delay" feature, use it. Instead of sending immediately when you push the "Send" button, your email will wait in the outbox for a specified period of time before launching. Even a few minutes' delay can make a difference.

What's your subject? Take the time to fill in the subject line, even in personal emails. Keep it short and direct: "Confirming dinner on July 26," "Acme order #12345." A subject line gives the recipient a clue about the nature or urgency of your message, especially if he doesn't recognize your email address. A blank subject line in an email to someone you haven't corresponded with before will probably be deleted, unread. Spam filters can block messages with blank subject lines, as well as subject lines that suggest the email is spam.

Keep it short and sweet. One of the benefits of email is the ability it gives us to communicate concisely and quickly, so keep messages brief.

No yelling, please. Avoid typing your entire message in capital letters because CAPS ARE THE EQUIVALENT OF SHOUTING. So use upper- and lowercase unless you have something to shout about: I'M ENGAGED! All-caps messages are also much harder to read.

Watch those emoticons. Emoticons or emoji are symbols used to indicate your emotional state. If used, emoticons (some examples are shown below) are better suited for casual messages between friends than business emails.

:)	*smile, happy, laugh*
:(	*frown, sad, unhappy*
:O	*angry, yelling, shocked*
;)	*wink, kidding*

Texting has made the use of abbreviations widespread. Again, while fine for messages with friends and family, they're not appropriate for business communications. (See "Text Messaging," page 233.)

Check it over. Although email tends to be informal in style, be sure messages are clearly organized and grammatically correct. Write in complete sentences and *always* check spelling and punctuation—especially in business emails. Even when sending a casual note, give it a good once-over. And watch out for autofill or autocorrect—they're famous for unintended bloopers.

> **Q:** *I wrote a friend an email that included some pretty catty comments about a mutual friend named Diane. But for reasons I won't go into, I ended up accidentally sending the message to Diane at the same time. How do I make amends for this major goof?*
>
> **A:** You've just learned an emailing lesson the hard way: It's all too easy for messages to fall into the wrong hands. As difficult as it may be, you must apologize. Contact Diane immediately, meeting with her in person if possible. Admit your insensitivity and tell her how terrible you feel about hurting her (if this is how you truly feel). Ask for forgiveness, but don't expect the friendship to be patched up overnight; it might take months before she trusts you again. In the meantime, remind yourself of one of the edicts of email culture: You can never be too careful.

Cutting the Spam

Given the amount of clutter in email inboxes these days, it's not surprising how many people regard forwards as just more spam. Deciding what to send or forward to friends, relatives, and business associates deserves thought, so use common sense to judge whether a forward is going to be seen as just one more irritation.

Some people enjoy receiving jokes and chain letters while others would rather be spared. If you're inclined to forward such material, be sure your recipients are receptive. Check with them (via email, naturally!) *before* putting them on your list.

Be particularly wary of chain letters and virus warnings. Chain letters, which promise everything from easy money to petitions that implore you to "have your voice heard," are usually little more than time wasters. Virus warnings are legitimate about a tenth of the time, so check the validity of the warning first. An Internet search for "virus hoaxes" will lead to sites that instruct you how to distinguish a real warning from a hoax. The Internet can be a hotbed of misinformation. Unsubstantiated (and often irresponsible) rumors spread like wildfire on the Net, so don't propagate them with forwards.

To stem the flow of forwards from friends and relatives, send an email asking them to take you off their forwarding list: "I enjoy hearing from you, so please don't hesitate to write, but I'd appreciate it if you would take my name off your forwarding list."

Email Extras

Email systems have a number of extra features, and they too have their dos and don'ts. Here's a sampling:

Automatic signatures. Many email programs can be set up to automatically sign your message with your name, address, email address, and phone number—a letterhead of sorts. If your program doesn't have this feature, add the information yourself for anyone who might want to know other ways to reach you.

Avoid a default complimentary close, such as "Thank you," because it may not always be appropriate. Beware, too, of using a company logo that appears as an attachment on the recipient's end; the message may be ignored or flagged to be opened later. Finally, check the automatic message that comes on your phone's email program. "Sent from my iPhone/Galaxy" lets the recipient know you're on the go, but do add your own signature line. And skip the phrase "Sent from my _____; please excuse any typos." With all the spell and grammar check capabilities of email and messaging programs, it makes you look lazy.

Attachments. When you're on the receiving end, never open an attachment when you don't know who sent it or why. Once an attachment containing a virus is opened it could send itself to everyone in your address book or crash your whole system.

Cc and Bcc. The Cc (carbon copy) function allows the sender to send a copy of the email to someone other than the primary recipients in the "To" field. When you use this function, the primary recipients can see that another person was sent a copy of the email. Bcc (blind carbon copy) allows the sender to send a copy to someone without the primary and carbon copy recipients knowing. It's a function that can appear deceptive, so take care how you use it. One appropriate use is when you are sending out a mass email and you don't wish each recipient to be able to view the members of the entire list. By using Bcc this way, you protect recipients' email addresses from being shared.

A more transparent way to achieve the same result is to create a group—Condo Owners—which tells recipients that several people will be receiving the email without revealing group members' email addresses. When in doubt, use the Cc function and let the primary recipient(s) know why: "Jen, I'd like to have the materials ready to go by Friday. As you can see, I've Cc'd my assistant, Katherine, so she's aware of our proposed deadline and can be ready to ship the materials."

Reply all. Be *very* careful using this feature, as your response will go to all primary and Cc'd recipients. Ask yourself: "Who needs my input?" If it's the entire group, then by all means, hit "Reply all" and compose your message. If only the primary recipient needs to know, choose "Reply."

Return receipts. These are the equivalent of certified snail mail—a notification that the recipient has opened your email. Senders see it as a way of confirming that an email is received, and a kind of proof that they did their part in sending the message. Recipients can consider it insulting, suggesting that the recipient can't be bothered to read his email. The bottom line? Use the feature for a good reason and be careful not to imply that the recipient isn't reliable. If receiving "read receipts" annoys you, there's usually a setting in your email preferences that turns off the display of the return receipt message.

Responding to Emails

Junk mail and forwards meant for entertainment can be ignored, but you should always respond to a real message, whether it's an invitation, a meeting notice, or a hello from a friend. If you receive a lot of emails, your life will be easier if you set aside a few times during the day to read your messages and respond in an orderly way.

How fast should you respond? Within one to two days for personal messages and within twenty-four hours for business email, depending on how pressing the matter is. Even if you can't take the time for a full response, let the sender know that his message was received and when you'll get back to him.

If you'll be away from your computer for a few days or longer, use the "out of office" or auto reply feature, a return message that tells the sender the email was received but you're unable to reply until a designated date and whom to contact, if that's appropriate. When you return, don't forget to turn off the auto responder, then deal with your inbox as promptly as you can.

BUSINESS EMAILS

In the workplace, your employer's email system is meant for business messages—not office gossip, the latest jokes, or personal rants. Likewise, the Internet is a powerful research and communication tool for businesses, not a toy to amuse you at work. Save your Net surfing, game playing, and social networking for your own time.

Beyond that bedrock advice, here are several guidelines to keep in mind when sending business emails:

Brevity. Like memos on paper, business emails should be purposeful and to the point—so keep them brief.

Timeliness. Email is the way the business world communicates, but staying on top of it can be challenging. If you're in PR, you might be checking your email constantly; in HR, several times a day may be sufficient. Your goal is to keep your responses timely while allowing time to get your work done. Turning off the audible signal indicating you have email can help you concentrate on your work.

Purpose. Don't send unnecessary messages or include people who don't need to know. It's the voice equivalent of interrupting. Take special care before sending a "Reply all."

Caution. Once sent, email can't be reliably retrieved. Horror stories abound: the intern who criticized the way the company was run, the man who trashed the new boss, and worse. The "recall" option does you no good if the message was already received and opened.

Privacy. All electronic communications should be considered public documents. If you wouldn't write something in a memo and pin it to the bulletin board, don't email it. Your company has the right to read email originating from or received on their office equipment.

Confidentiality. Use snail mail or other traditional forms of communication for private or sensitive materials—contracts, business plans, salary, and sales information. Unless your system has an encryption program, email isn't private, and messages can be accidentally or intentionally intercepted.

Appropriateness. The more serious the message, the less appropriate email becomes. Don't issue serious complaints or criticisms by email, and never email a letter of resignation.

Discretion. Be careful about the messages you forward. If a former employee sends you an acerbic rant about his boss or gossip about a colleague, keep it to yourself. Broadcasting such emails to friends can backfire if they eventually reach management or human resources.

Professionalism. Even though email messages tend to be informal and familiar in tone, keep your emotions in check. Save "I'm so upset I could die!" for personal, not business communications. Avoid using informal texting abbreviations and always double-check spelling and grammar. Take as much care with your emails as you would with a printed business letter.

Urgency. Flag messages as "high priority" or "urgent" only when they really are. Recipients who rush to read a message only to find it routine will be rightfully irritated.

Pornography. In many businesses, transferring pornography via email is grounds for dismissal. If a subject heading or address suggests porn spam, ask a member of the tech support team to deal with it and block future emails from the source. That way, the company knows you didn't request it.

The end? If you're leaving your job, be sure your email account is closed and incoming messages are forwarded to the appropriate person. Then update your contacts with your new email address.

INSTANT MESSAGING

Instant messaging (IMing) is the Internet version of texting. It allows those connected by the Internet or an intranet to send real-time, typed messages to others using the same IM service. When the IM program is activated, there's a feature that shows all the members of the network who are "available" to IM. Instead of calling one another with questions or information—along with the attendant ringing and talking—IMers communicate not only immediately but silently. Add a webcam, and you can have a real-time virtual face-to-face meeting. Because speed is the name of the game, IMers use the same abbreviations for standard phrases as in texting or emailing.

At work, instant messaging is the fastest way to receive and convey information. For example, during a phone call with a client you can IM another department to get the answer to a question. Such speed is one of the reasons IM has become an invaluable tool for businesspeople who regularly hold conference calls or do Web-based presentations. Be careful, though, not to fall into a trap of multitasking. When on the phone, it's not acceptable to send instant messages that have nothing to do with the call. Your focus should stay on the person you're talking to and the subject being discussed.

Instant messages have their drawbacks. They can come so thick and fast that they're intrusive. When you don't wish to be interrupted, turn on your "do not disturb" feature, or send a message that you'll be back later.

IMs are ultracasual but don't use words that are off-color: You never know who might see your IM at work and at home. There's no guarantee that your IM is for the recipient's eyes only. Here are some other ways to keep IMs on track:

- Be as cautious with IMing as you are with email. If you IM a stranger, be sure to introduce yourself. Aliases and screen names can make it difficult to know who you're talking to.

- Never offer any personal or private information via IM. As with all other forms of electronic communications, IMs can become public quickly.

- Choose your screen name wisely.

- Just because someone's IM service shows them as being "available," it doesn't necessarily mean that they are. If you IM and get no response, wait and try again later. They could be busy with something else or away from their computer, so don't take it personally.

- Respect "Do not disturb" status or "Be right back" messages.

- At work, keep messages on task. Remember, each time you IM, you are interrupting someone.

- Keep track of your conversations. Because IMing happens in real time, the thread of a conversation can get disjointed, and responses get separated from the original point. It's a good idea, when a conversation really gets tangled, to copy and paste what you're responding to into your IM.

- Don't IM from a friend's computer unless you're both in on the conversation.

- Sign off clearly. A simple, "Well . . . I have to run" or "B4N" (bye for now) lets others know you're exiting the conversation.

[VIDEO CALLS]

Services that offer VoIP (Voice-over-Internet Protocol) allow subscribers to use their computer as a telephone. With the addition of a small camera attached to the computer, simultaneous video is possible as well. This modern miracle has been a great benefit to families who have one or more members in far parts of the globe, such as servicemen and -women on active duty. Not only can kids talk to Daddy, they can see him as well, making phone visits all the more personal. What the camera sees is what the receiver (and anyone else in the room) will see, so take care with your appearance—or what's going on in the background—before you switch it on.

[YOUR TABLET AND COMPUTER]

It's hard to imagine life without them. Computers are the interface for many facets of our lives: email communications, social networking, entertainment, news, research, and work. While computer etiquette mostly concerns the ways we interact and communicate with each other, there are a few situations that call for thoughtful use of the computer itself. One is when we share a computer or tablet with others, either at home, in a dorm, or at work. The other is when we use a laptop, smartphone, or mobile device in public.

Manners for Shared Devices

When you share a computer or tablet with family members, roommates, or coworkers, there are some basic courtesies that everyone should observe:

- Let other users know when you need to use the device. Think about priorities; your game can wait if someone else has real work to do. Parents need to help children negotiate screen time, especially when the device is required for schoolwork, and to monitor its use carefully.

- If you're working on a long project, like a research paper, be considerate when someone needs to do, say, a quick Internet search, and let the person have access.

- Never open another person's documents or files without permission; this is tantamount to reading someone else's mail. When deleting files, be careful not to dump something that isn't yours. If you need to close someone else's document, save it first.

- Don't look at email that hasn't been sent or received by you; don't use anyone else's accounts, screen names, or passwords.

- If you have a shared home page, don't change the contents without the agreement of everyone included in the page.

- Keep the computer area picked up. Clear the work area before you leave it. If the mouse is sticky, clean it; if the printer cartridge needs replacing, do it. Tell the person who buys supplies when the paper is low, and report any problems to the person who maintains the computer, if that's not you.

- When computers are shared in the workplace, users are often on different shifts and may not see one another. If there's any problem with the computer or supplies, leave a note clearly explaining the difficulty in a place where the next person will find it easily.

Using Your Device in Public

Whether you're on your laptop, tablet, smartphone, or mobile device, or you're using a public computer in a cybercafe, privacy and security are concerns.

- **What's on your screen?** There's a very good chance that what you're viewing, others can see, too, even if they shouldn't be looking. Be aware of what kind of content you're viewing. Is it banking? An R-rated film? Personal email? A privacy screen

---

social networking

For information on social networking and using social networking sites and services, see Chapter 30, "Life Online," page 383.

---

is a good investment if you need to work while traveling or commuting.

- **To Wi-Fi or not?** From cafes and wine bars to airport terminals and commuter ferries, the ability to sign on and connect to the Internet is becoming easier and more widespread and, in some places, free. While convenient, unsecured networks are risky: Your computer can be hacked or infected with a virus. Don't even consider signing on unless you have adequate virus protection.

- **Do you have a name tag?** Take a couple of minutes to tape your business card or attach a label with your phone number to your computer (and your cell phone or mobile device). If it's lost, you have a better chance of having it returned to you.

PART IV
social life

CHAPTER 21 Hosts and Guests 249

CHAPTER 22 Houseguests 261

CHAPTER 23 Invitations and Announcements 271

CHAPTER 24 Entertaining at Home 292

CHAPTER 25 Formal Dinners and Parties 314

CHAPTER 26 Celebrations Through Life 320

CHAPTER 27 Ceremonies and Religious Services 334

CHAPTER 28 Giving and Receiving Gifts 349

CHAPTER 29 Dating. 370

CHAPTER 30 Life Online. 383

21
hosts and guests

*e*ven for an occasion as simple as "Drop by for coffee," we automatically assume the roles of host and guest, each with its own expectations and responsibilities, grounded in making someone feel welcome in our own home and how to behave at someone else's.

BEING A GOOD HOST

There's an art to being a good host. It combines qualities like cordiality, hospitality, warmth, charm, and graciousness with down-to-earth practicalities such as planning, creating a compatible guest list, sending invitations, providing and serving food and drink, setting a table, greeting and making introductions, keeping conversations going, seeing to your guests' comfort, and perhaps even giving a toast. Before you throw up your hands and say, "There's no way I can do all that!" think about what you already know how to do. Really, you're just pulling together a combination of skills and qualities you already have.

Being a good host isn't difficult, but it does take forethought, practice, and a little talent for multitasking. The most important thing is to make your guests feel comfortable and welcome.

- **Plan a guest list of congenial, compatible people:** Emily Post knew this was at the heart of hosting. A great group of people will make any gathering a success, even if it rains on the picnic or the food is a flop.

- **Invite clearly:** Make sure your invitation lets your guests know what to expect. For small groups or casual events, you might choose a phone call or email; for larger groups or fancier parties, printed invitations lend importance to the occasion. Whether you invite by phone, email, or written invitation, let your guests know who, what, when, where, and why. Add when and how to respond, plus any special info your guests should know, such as what they should wear or what they should bring. (See Chapter 23, "Invitations and Announcements," page 271.)

- **Be ready ahead of time:** Prepare as much as you can *before* everyone arrives. Have your meal ready, your table set, and be dressed at least fifteen minutes before party hour. (For how to set a table, see Chapter 6, "Table Manners," page 56.) Even for informal visits, tidy yourself and the rooms you'll be using and have refreshments ready.

- **Be consistent:** Don't tell guests the dress is casual and then open the door draped in a sequined evening dress.

- **Be prepared:** Check each room that guests might use. For example, in the guest bathroom, make a quick check that toilet paper is in good supply, there's a small can of air freshener, and fresh soap and clean hand towels.

- **Remain calm:** Your mood sets the tone. Take a few minutes to relax before your guests arrive. And no matter what happens—red wine on a tablecloth, a broken glass—never let your guests think you're stressed out. It will make them feel anxious and uncomfortable, too.

- **Be welcoming:** Making your guests feel at home and seeing to their comfort are what being a host is all about. Greet them enthusiastically, even if it means excusing yourself from a conversation with another guest. (**Note:** If you're hosting with a partner, only one of you needs to greet guests at the door.)

- **Be the spark:** Circulate among all your guests. Introduce newcomers and stay with them long enough to get a conversation going. If one of your guests doesn't know any of the others, enlist a friend to make introductions and see that he isn't left on his own. (See Chapter 2, "Essential Manners," page 8, for more on greetings and introductions, and Chapter 4, "The Art of Conversation," page 35.)

- **Be mindful:** Keep an eye on guests' refreshments and offer refills before they have to ask.

- **Be the leader:** It's your job to end the cocktail hour, to call guests in to dinner, and to raise your fork so they can begin eating. If you plan to serve yourself last, say, "Please begin," once three or four guests have been served, so their meal doesn't get cold. (Emily Post herself always did this.) It's also up to you to get up from the table to indicate the meal is over.

- **Make a toast:** To many people, making a toast seems like a daunting prospect. But it's really as simple as welcoming your guests, thanking the chef (if it wasn't you), or wishing health and happiness to the guest of honor or your friends around your table. A thoughtful toast transforms any gathering into an occasion, and it is a special way to extend a warm welcome to all. (See "Toasts and Toasting," page 258.)

- **Be appreciative:** Let your friends know how much you enjoy spending time with them. Thank them not just for coming, but also for any gifts or contributions to the meal. See also Chapter 24, "Entertaining at Home," page 292.

Greetings and Introductions

As the host, it's your job to greet your guests and introduce new and old friends. Before the party, take a little time to think about each guest. Does everyone know each other? Is there someone new who needs to meet everyone? Think about your guests' interests and general background information—who likes music, films, wine, sports, or finance. Offering a point of common reference between two people is an easy way to get a conversation going when strangers meet. "Matt, have you met Jamie? I understand you're both big Bruins fans." (See "Greetings," page 10.)

Promoting Lively Conversation

In the same way that you keep an eye on your guests' glasses, keep an ear tuned to the conversation. As the host, you'll need to fill in the gaps or redirect a discussion that's gone astray. Small talk is a characteristic of the cocktail party, where conversations tend to be short exchanges of information or light give-and-takes about what's going on.

Dinner parties lend themselves to more in-depth discussions. As the host, see that the discussion remains friendly and respectful. In some circles, a really heated debate is a sign of a great evening. That's fine, if everyone's in on it and understands the (often unspoken) ground rules. If that's not the case, then you'll need to change the subject if the sparks start flying. Stepping in with "How 'bout those Red Sox?" (or some other completely off-topic comment) is a clear way of saying "we've hit the uncomfortable zone" to

guests. At the same time, it injects some humor and lets another discussion begin. Then, again, if you're in Yankees territory, that quip might set off an explosion, so be aware of your context.

Accidents Will Happen

Sometimes being the host means coping with accidents, mishaps, or even bad behavior. It's inevitable that at some point red wine will be spilled or something will break. For starters, if you're worried about having your heart broken over an accidental mishap, *think twice* about using glasses or dishes that are beloved heirlooms or vases so valuable that a guest couldn't possibly afford to replace one if he breaks it.

The truly good host is gracious and unflappable, no matter *what* happens. This is where a sense of humor and an awareness that "stuff happens" come in handy. So does a supply of cleaning products and paper towels. Stay relaxed and look for creative solutions if an accident occurs. The more you take things in stride and handle them gracefully, the better your guests will feel.

Staying Flexible

It's not easy to keep calm when you've been thrown for a loop, but by maintaining your cool you can turn even the most socially awkward situation into a success. Imagine that you've planned a dinner party for six, but when you greet one of the couples at your front door, they've taken the liberty of bringing along their friend Jane, who's visiting.

As awkward as this is and as much as you might

want to say, "What were you *thinking*!" you graciously greet the couple and their friend. Make sure your facial expression, tone, and body language match your gracious words or the whole effect will be lost.

Yes, you'll have to rearrange a few place settings and fiddle with portions, but your gracious welcome has smoothed over what could have been a very uncomfortable moment. In fact, the other guests may not even notice that Jane wasn't on the original guest list! (It's okay to call the couple the next day and let them know how much you enjoyed having Jane at the party, but that if this kind of situation comes up again, you'd really appreciate a call ahead of time.)

When a Guest Has Had Too Much to Drink

The one thing you can't ignore is a guest who's over the limit. First, stop serving him or her alcohol, and second, take away the car keys. Offer a bed or a couch for the night or take on the responsibility of seeing Mr. or Ms. Tipsy home and safely inside—but whatever you do, *never* let him or her drive. Calling a cab or asking a friend to take the drunk person home only makes him someone else's responsibility. That would be unreasonable and inconsiderate on your part.

CONTINGENCY PLANS

SOME GUESTS ARE LATE.	Wait 15 minutes, then start without them.
A GUEST BREAKS OR SPILLS SOMETHING.	Smooth over the incident and clean up the spill quickly. The guest should apologize and offer to pay for damages—but if he doesn't, chalk it up to the cost of entertaining a less-than-considerate guest.
A GUEST MAKES AN ETHNIC SLUR OR AN OFFENSIVE JOKE.	Interrupt and change the subject, or ask for his help in another room, where you can tell him that his off-color jokes or remarks are making others uncomfortable. Be sure to apologize privately to anyone who might have been offended.
UNEXPECTED GUESTS SHOW UP AT YOUR DOOR.	Greet them graciously and do your best to include them. Set extra places at the table if possible (even if your place settings aren't an exact match). If all else fails, eat on laps in the living room.
A GUEST HAS HAD TOO MUCH TO DRINK.	Cut off the alcohol and take away the car keys. Offer him a place to sleep for the night or drive him home yourself.
THERE'S NOT ENOUGH FOOD.	Plate the food, using smaller portions of what's short and larger ones of what's in good supply. Augment the salad, and add bread if possible. Signal "FHB" (Family Hold Back) to family members.
DINNER IS OVERCOOKED, UNDERCOOKED, OR AN OTHERWISE COMPLETE DISASTER.	Laugh and order pizza!

Time to Say Good-bye

All good times come to an end, whether it's afternoon tea with a friend or a full-scale dinner party. When you're the host, it's your job to signal that it's time to wrap things up. The hardest time to do this is when it's late in the evening and your guests show no sign of leaving. If you need to call it a night you can, in the following order:

- Close down the bar.
- Turn off the music.
- Start cleaning up.
- Yawn—repeatedly.
- Be direct: Stand up and say, "Wow—look at the time! I've got yoga (a meeting, a class) first thing tomorrow. Let's call it a night."
- Start turning out the lights.
- Go to bed.

Tips on Cohosting

Cohosting with friends is a great way to throw a big party or dinner that may be too expensive or too much work for an individual or a couple. Communication is the key to successful cohosting. As soon as possible after you say, "Let's do it!" sit down together to discuss dates, guest list, budget, and who's doing what. Divide the duties as evenly as possible, taking advantage of each person's skills and interests. When you entertain as a couple, consider yourselves cohosts, equally responsible for hosting duties. At the end of the party, thank and compliment each other on a job well done.

BEING A GOOD GUEST

As important as it is to be a good host, it's equally important to shine as a guest. Good guest manners begin the minute you receive an invitation. Whatever its form, once you receive an invitation your first obligation is to send a prompt response, preferably within a day or two. It's a basic courtesy, and will be truly appreciated by your hosts. Waiting until the last minute or until your host calls for your answer implies that you don't think much of the host or that you're waiting for a better invitation to come along. If you don't know right away if you can attend, contact your host anyway and let him know when you can give him a definitive answer.

RSVP

RSVP is the abbreviated form of the French *Répondez S'il Vous Plaît* or, in English, "Please reply." These four little letters are the signal that your hosts want to know whether or not you can make their event. Most invitations have some sort of a reply mechanism—an enclosed response card, or a phone number, email address, or mailing address that guests can use to RSVP. Reply promptly in the manner your host requests. (See Chapter 23, "Invitations and Announcements," page 271, for more on responding to various types of invitations.)

Can You Change Your Mind?

Check your calendar carefully before you reply, because once you've sent your response you're committed. Changing a "yes" to a "no" is only acceptable if there's a very good reason: an illness or injury, a death in the family, an unavoidable professional or business conflict. In such a case, call your hosts as soon as you can and explain and apologize. Canceling because you have a "better" offer is a surefire way to get dropped from *everyone's* guest lists, while being a no-show is just plain unacceptable.

Changing a "no" to a "yes" is a slightly different matter. It's okay *only* if it's unlikely to upset the hosts' arrangements. For example, if it's a flexible kind of party—cocktails or a buffet—hosted by someone you know really well, then call right away and explain the change; you're sure to be welcomed. Otherwise, if it's an occasion such as a sit-down dinner party it's better to stick with your "no" and hope you'll be able to make it next time.

"May I Bring . . . ?"

Invitations are extended to the people the hosts want to invite—and no one else. The biggest offenders seem to be parents who think their children are automatically included in grown-up invitations. Consider these points before asking to bring . . .

. . . **a date?** Only when your invitation says "and guest" may you bring a guest or date. When you reply, it's thoughtful to give your guest's name, preparing your hosts for introductions or place cards.

. . . **my children?** If they were invited, the invitation would have said so. If you can't get a sitter, it's best to decline the invitation. This is true not just for formal parties like weddings, but for informal get-togethers as well when your hosts may prefer a grown-ups only eve-

---

leave it to your host

Whatever the circumstances, never assume an invitation comes with an automatic plus one, or automatically includes your kids. It is ALWAYS up to the host to decide on extra guests.

ning. It's up to the host to decide whether your circumstances can be accommodated or not.

. . . **my houseguest?** If you're hosting a houseguest and get invited to a party, it's best to turn the invitation down but explain the reason. This gives your host the *option* to extend the invitation to include your guest. If the event is casual and flexible, that's probably what will happen. If it's a more formal event, extras might not be feasible.

Of course there are exceptions to every rule. If you receive an invitation addressed to you alone and you've recently become engaged or are in a serious relationship, let your host know. Again, it's best to decline the invitation and explain why, putting the ball in your host's court to offer to include your significant other or not.

Guest Manners 101

As a guest, it's your job to put all your positive qualities on display: enthusiasm, congeniality, consideration, and thoughtfulness. You won't go wrong as long as you practice the following party manners basics:

Arrive on time. Anywhere between five and fifteen minutes after the designated start time is okay—but *never* show up early. If you're going to be more than fifteen minutes late, call your hosts with an estimated arrival time so they can decide if they should start without you.

Turn off your ringer. While you're at a party or even just visiting, ignore incoming calls. If you're expecting a call or must be reachable, put your phone on vibrate and excuse yourself to another room to take the call.

Be considerate. Wipe your feet before entering. Don't put your feet on furniture. Use a coaster for drinks. Leave the bathroom neat for the next person. If you smoke go outside to smoke. If you have a cold or other spreadable illness, call with your regrets and stay home.

Be complimentary. About the food, the decor, the garden, the company. You don't have to gush—just be gracious and sincere.

Respect your host's trust. Don't snoop in medicine cabinets, closets, or desks. Take care with your host's belongings. If you break something, let your host know immediately—and offer to pay for the repair or replacement.

Be a willing participant. Take part in—or at least try—whatever your host offers, whether it's charades, mushroom soufflé, or the opportunity to chat with new people. If you're served food you don't care for or that's new to you, try a "no thank you" (i.e., small) helping. At a seated dinner, be an active—but not dominant—participant in the conversation, and be sure to spend time chatting with the people on both your left and your right.

All things in moderation. Try not to overindulge, whether it's the hors d'oeuvres or the pinot noir.

Offer to help when you can. This depends on the circumstances of the party, but where assistance is welcome there are lots of things guests can do to help out: pass hors d'oeuvres, light candles, help serve dessert. If your offer is turned down, don't insist—just enjoy yourself, knowing you did your best to pitch in.

Unless invited in, keep clear of the kitchen. Some people love to cook with an audience; others really can't concentrate. If your host says "no thanks," go enjoy yourself at the party.

Don't switch place cards. Your host has gone to the trouble to come up with a seating plan. Your spot was chosen especially for you, so enjoy it!

Leave with the group. Don't settle in as others are saying farewell, unless you've been invited to stay. In general, dinner guests are expected to stay for about an hour after dinner. If you need to leave early, let your host know before the party or when you arrive so they aren't surprised (or worse, insulted) at your early departure.

Thank your hosts on the way out. As you're leaving, make sure to say "good-bye" and "thank you" to each of your hosts. If they're not by the door, seek them out and thank them personally before you go. If they're in a conversation wait for a pause, say, "Excuse me," and then extend your thanks and good-byes.

┌───┐

tips for hosts and guests on allergies and special diets

Guests

- Do let your host know if you have a life-threatening allergy or a medical or religious dietary restriction.
- The good guest doesn't make his or her allergy or diet the center of attention.
- Don't impose your latest diet on your host. A host always wants to please, but a guest must understand he is not going to a restaurant.
- Do offer to bring a dish that meets your needs.

Hosts

- Keep notes on guests' allergies, restrictions, or preferences.
- Try to master one or two gluten-free vegan side dishes. You can always substitute tofu for grilled or broiled fish or meat, often using the same marinade or rub.
- Do your best to accommodate your guest's needs, and make an extra effort for a houseguest. Ask what staples would be useful to have on hand.
- People with serious allergies are vigilant and may ask about ingredients, then just avoid the foods they can't eat.

Thoughtful Afterthoughts

The really thoughtful guest thanks her host twice: once as she's leaving the party and again the next day. The written thank-you note is always, always appreciated, but is only *expected* after a formal dinner party or an overnight visit. If you don't send a note, call or send an email expressing your thanks within a day or two of the party. If someone hosted a party in your honor, you were a houseguest, or you had an especially enjoyable time, now's the time to send flowers or a thank-you gift (if you didn't arrive with a gift in hand).

Allergies and Other Special Conditions

If you're invited to a cocktail party, large dinner party, buffet, or reception, it's probably not necessary to inform your host that you're a vegetarian, mildly allergic to milk, or diabetic, because there's bound to be a variety of foods to choose from. At the party, it's fine to ask about the ingredients in a particular dish. If it's a small dinner party, however, or if you're severely allergic to certain foods or pets, it's a good idea to let your host know up front when you respond to the invitation and give him a chance to adjust his menu if necessary. If you have serious food allergies, let your host know when you first respond. More than the disappointment of serving a guest something he can't eat, it really is a question of your safety. Shellfish and nuts, for example, can cause severe, even deadly reactions.

If you're allergic to dogs and your allergy can't be controlled by medication, you might have to forgo an invitation to a house that has cats or dogs—there's only so much cleaning your host can do. Even if you can tolerate them, your host will want to know so that the animal can be kept in another room and extra care is taken when cleaning before the party.

When your dietary restrictions are based on religious tenets, it may not be practical to accept some invitations. If the invitation is for a small gathering, you can explain to your hostess that you'd love to accept, but that you'll have to bring a dish that you've prepared according to your dietary rules—provided that's acceptable to her. As a large part of entertaining is about being social, many hosts will encourage you to attend and bring your special dish.

If you don't drink alcohol, it's fine to ask for water, juice, or a soft drink instead. You don't have to give a reason unless you wish to. Never feel you have to drink alcohol, even if pressed by a host or another guest. The rudeness is theirs, not yours.

How exactly do you let your host know this sort of thing? Simply say, "I'd love to come, but I should tell you that I am completely allergic to shellfish"; "I'd love to come to the barbecue, but I should tell you that I'm a vegetarian. I could bring a tabbouleh salad if that's all right with you." Always give your host the option to accommodate you or not. In some cases it may not be possible, so don't take offense.

Should I Bring a Hostess Gift?

A gift for your host or hostess is a lovely way to thank them for their hospitality and is always appreciated. It doesn't have to be elaborate or expensive; simply consider the nature of the occasion and local custom when making your choice. In some parts of the country, a hostess gift is considered obligatory, while in other places a gift is brought only on special occasions. If it's the first time you're visiting someone's home, then it's a very nice gesture to bring a small gift. If you have a few extra minutes to wrap it, even if you only use tissue or a decorative bag, it adds to the gesture.

Wine, flowers, specialty food items, and small items for the house all make good hostess gifts. Bring flowers in a simple vase or glass jar. You could also offer to put them in water yourself when you arrive so your host doesn't have to arrange them. If you bring wine or food, don't expect your host to serve it that evening. Gifts aren't usually taken to large, formal dinners, especially if you don't know the hosts well. Here are a few tips on what to bring when:

Casual or informal dinner party. Dinner party guests usually bring a hostess gift unless they are close friends who dine together frequently.

When there's a guest of honor. If it's a birthday, anniversary, or graduation, bring a card or gift for the honoree, unless the invitation specified "no gifts."

When you're the guest of honor. Bring a gift for your host or hostess, or send flowers before the party. After the party, send a thank-you note.

Housewarming. It's customary to bring a gift to a housewarming. It doesn't have to be expensive, but it should be something for the house, pantry, or garden.

Weekend visit. Either bring or send a gift. Your gift choice will depend on the length of your stay and how elaborately you're entertained. Your gift should be

Q: *We've been invited to attend several holiday parties this year. Is it okay to "double-book"?*

A: This is one of those times when it's fine to double-book and go from one holiday party to another. The casual, drop-in nature of most holiday parties makes this okay. Just be sure you do each event justice—a lightning quick drop-by simply doesn't cut it. And don't double book when you've been invited to a dinner party or a small gathering with a set time to arrive and a limited number of guests.

sincere, thoughtful, personal, and fit your budget. (For gift ideas, see "Twelve House Gift Ideas," page 268.)

Reciprocating Hospitality

Some invitations—to weddings, balls, official functions, and events you pay to attend—don't carry any reciprocal obligation. But invitations to social events in someone's home or a private party hosted at a restaurant or club do call for some sort of reciprocation. This isn't a quid pro quo. The goal isn't to replicate the event you were invited to, but simply to return the hospitality you've enjoyed and spend some social time with your hosts. So, a dinner invitation may be returned with an invitation to lunch. If your hosts put on a lavish gourmet feast and you're not an accomplished cook, treat them to an evening out at a favorite restaurant or the theater.

Whatever you decide on, try to arrange to get together within a few months of the original party. If your hosts can't accept your first invitation, give it at least one and preferably two more tries. If you're still not successful, put the return engagement on hold for a later date.

Lastly, if you decline an invitation to a party or dinner, are you still obligated to return the favor? In this case your obligation isn't as strong—but since the intent was to include you, you should still try to send a return invitation in the not-too-distant future.

TOASTS AND TOASTING

Toasts can range from the most routine—"To us!" (spoken while clinking glasses)—to the most touching—an homage from the father of the bride that can make grown men cry. In one form or another, toasting to love, friendship, health, wealth, and happiness has been practiced by almost every culture from the beginning of recorded history. The following is a guide to toasting basics:

◆ It is okay to toast with a non-alcoholic beverage or even with water. It is also okay to take the tiniest of sips of an alcoholic beverage if there are a number of toasts being offered.

◆ At a dinner party, it's the host or hostess's prerogative to give the first toast.

◆ If a host doesn't offer a toast, a guest may propose a toast saluting the hosts.

your little black book

It's a good idea to keep some form of social diary, either as a part of your calendar, on your phone, or in a separate notebook. You can keep track of invitations you've accepted, the name(s) of your host(s), the date, and what type of event it was. When you've returned the favor, you can check off those names. You can also keep track of your guests' preferences, allergies, and even what you served.

- The "host toasts first" mandate *does* still apply at formal dinners, receptions, and other large functions (though the best man usually leads the toasting at a wedding reception).

- Typically, toasts are proposed as soon as the wine, champagne, or other beverage is served—usually at the beginning of the meal or just before dessert.

- The person proposing the toast stands, or raises a glass and asks for everyone's attention (not by clinking the glass with his spoon) before launching into the toast itself. When there's a noisy crowd it's more courteous to repeat, "May I have your attention," as often as necessary.

- Direct attention to the honoree(s) and maintain eye contact during the toast.

- At the conclusion of the toast, everyone except the honoree(s) raises their glasses and drinks.

- Stand and raise your glass at a formal occasion or when asked by the toaster; otherwise, you may stay seated.

- The honoree doesn't rise or drink the toast, but she should acknowledge the gesture with a smile or nod.

- After the toast is finished, the honoree drinks to her toasters in return with a "Thank you" or her own toast. She may rise or not.

- No need for everyone to drain their glasses during a toast—a sip will do just fine.

Prepared Toasts

If you're going to deliver more than the simplest toast, it's a good idea to prepare it beforehand and mentally rehearse it so you don't fumble the words. Keep whatever you say short, positive, and to the point—you want the spotlight to be on the toastee, not you. While a touch of humor is rarely out of place, keep it clean. Stories that might embarrass the honoree are off-limits.

If, however, your toast has been designated as the principal one of the event, think of it as a small speech that should be prepared and rehearsed. When you deliver the toast, a glance at your notes is acceptable, but you still want to seem fairly spontaneous.

Spur-of-the-Moment Toasts

You don't need a special occasion to make a toast. If the mood is right, it's lovely to give an informal toast to good friends around the table. The best toasts are short and come from the heart. Should you draw a blank when you're suddenly asked to offer a toast, just remind yourself that a few sincere and complimentary words are all you need: "To Gloria and Jimmy, there's no better place to be than in your company." Another trick is to tie the toast to the occasion. In a pinch, try toasts along the lines of these:

"To Suzanne—a terrific hostess and a fabulous cook."

"To Anya: May each birthday find you among good friends."

"To Phil—a great boss who will be an even better VP. Congratulations."

"To the class of '17—the smartest and best-looking by far!"

22 houseguests

aving friends or relatives stay in your home overnight or for the weekend is a chance to have a more personal visit. You can share your morning coffee, enjoy relaxed dinners or a night out, or spend an afternoon catching up on each other's lives or trading memories of the good old days. But hosts and guests have a delicate balancing act to perform. While the host's most important duty is making his guests feel at home, the guest's is to adapt to the host's home and schedule. Whether you invite one person for one night, or a group for a long weekend house party, successful visits hinge on communicating expectations. Clear communication between host and guest makes the visit a success, while ambiguity can cause tension and awkward moments.

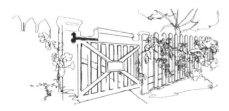

[SETTING A DATE]

As the host, set the dates for the visit and then ask your houseguest for an arrival and departure time. Otherwise, saying, "Stay as long as you like!" may be taken literally. It's not rude to set boundaries; it's practical. "Of course you can come for the weekend! I'm booked for Friday, so plan to arrive on Saturday morning. Will you need to be home Sunday night for work on Monday?" This direct approach lets both guest and host know what to expect. Conversely, if you're a guest and your host doesn't set a date or time, be sure to ask. Regardless of who sets the date, avoid extending your stay beyond what's been planned.

Once you've agreed on dates and times, the host should follow up with an email, text, or note to prevent any confusion. This is the time to let guests know what, if anything, you have planned for their stay. That way they can pack appropriately for a day of hiking or dinner at a nice restaurant.

If your guests are coming by car, give them clear directions in advance, send a link to a map program, or your address for a car GPS unit. If guests are arriving by train or plane, discuss the options for getting to your house—you can pick them up, send a car service, or suggest a taxi or public transportation.

WELCOMING HOUSEGUESTS

Once your guests arrive, show them to their room or sleeping area and the bath they'll use. If they're unfamiliar with your home, conduct a quick tour whenever they're ready: the bathroom, cabinets for towels and other items, and light switches. Show them how to adjust the air-conditioning or heating and how to log on to your Wi-Fi. Then give them a chance to tidy up and unpack. Invite them to help themselves to snacks or beverages from the fridge during their stay, noting any foods that are off-limits: "Please help yourself to anything you see except the blueberries—they're for the pancakes tomorrow morning."

THE GUEST ROOM

The best way to know how comfortable and well equipped your guest room is is to spend a night there as a guest yourself. There's nothing like firsthand knowledge to tell you the blind is broken, the mattress is sagging, or the closet door is squeaking. Here's a list of basics that every guest room should have, as well as a few extras that will add a nice touch:

In the guest room or sleeping area . . .

- A bed, sofa bed, futon, or air bed made up with clean sheets and pillowcases
- Extra blanket at the foot of the bed
- A good reading light at each bed
- Reading matter (magazines, short books)
- An alarm clock
- Good curtains or blinds on the windows
- Water carafe and glass on the night table
- Box of tissues
- An empty wastebasket
- Dress hangers and hangers with clips or bars
- Luggage rack, if you own one

In the bathroom . . .

- Fresh bath towels, face towels, washcloth, bath mat
- Fresh soap
- Glasses for drinking water and brushing teeth
- New roll of toilet paper in the dispenser and an unopened one in the cabinet
- Box of tissues
- Shampoo and hand lotion on the washstand
- A new toothbrush (just in case) and toothpaste
- Headache and stomachache medications; extra feminine supplies

No Guest Room?

If you live in a one-bedroom apartment or a house with no guest room, don't think you can't play host.

A sofa bed, futon, or air bed can be set up in the living room or den, or children could be doubled up to free up a room if the visit isn't lengthy. (In the latter case, arrange the toys neatly, remove some clothes from the closet, clear enough drawer space for the guest's needs, and make sure the room is sparkling clean.) Don't move out of your own room so you can give it to your guests, though—it could make them feel they're imposing.

The important thing is to give your guests advance warning that they won't have a separate room or will have to share. Some guests may be perfectly fine sleeping on a sofa or air bed in the den, while others may decide to stay at an inn or hotel instead.

SCHEDULES AND ROUTINES

Share your routines with the guests: "Sunday is our morning to sleep in—if you get up first, the English muffins are in the bread drawer and the coffeemaker will be all ready to go—just push the start button." Also give them a heads-up on any absences you foresee: "I have to go to a meeting Monday morning, so I'm leaving you on your own. I should be back around eleven o'clock."

If your guests are visiting during weekdays, it's important that you share your normal schedule with them so they can plan their time accordingly: "Mom and Dad, the girls leave for school at 7:30, so we're up and running at about 6:45. I wanted to warn you because that's when they take over the bathroom." This is a gentle

Q: *My son and his girlfriend are students at a nearby college, and we've invited them to spend their Thanksgiving break with us. They've been living together for six months but we'd prefer that they don't share the same room at our house. How should we handle the situation?*

A: Parents have a right to insist that their standards be observed in their own home, and you should make that clear to your son. If he says, "Well, then we won't be able to come," you have to decide whether your relationship and continued communication with him is more important than upholding your standards. (This is an individual matter of conscience, not one of etiquette.) Still, you can stand your ground. If you and your son understand each other and have a good relationship to begin with, he's more likely to accept the rules you establish than to put you in a difficult position. Just be sure to let your feelings be known from the very beginning—not when he and his girlfriend are carrying their bags up the stairs.

way to familiarize your visitors with the way things are done in your household and help them fit right in.

This doesn't mean expecting your visitors to do everything your way; they're your guests, and their happiness and comfort are as important as yours. Yes, your routine will be disrupted, but the more forthcoming you can be about what happens when—and why—the more pleasurable the visit will be for everyone.

As the host, you're the inside source on what activities and attractions are available in your area. The best agenda is a mix of things that both you and your guests enjoy. Have some ideas in mind before your guests arrive, rather than just saying, "What do you want to do?" when they show up. Local points of interest, parks and beaches, hikes and bike rides are all things that you can enjoy together or your guest can do separately. By suggesting options, you and your guest can create a schedule that includes "together time" as well as time for them to be on their own. Plan for some downtime too; guests will need it—and so will you!

Besides activities, plan your meals and make any restaurant reservations ahead of time. If you intend to cook, prepare as much food ahead of time as you can. This way, you'll be able to enjoy your guests rather than worry about what's for dinner.

Because one of the joys of a weekend away from home is being able to sleep late, ask your guests if they would prefer a wake-up call or to sleep in. Unless you've told your guests to help themselves to breakfast, make coffee and prepare or put out breakfast foods before they rise. It's okay to go ahead and eat—but if you do, be there to greet and serve guests as they arrive.

When good friends are visiting, don't be afraid to ask them to pitch in: "Belinda, would you mind reading

Q: *Is the host responsible for providing all of the meals for houseguests?*

A: Normally that's the standard, but you also need to take the length of stay into consideration. With an overnight or weekend guest, the host pays for the groceries. If houseguests are staying longer than that, they should offer to contribute to or split the grocery bill and come to an arrangement with their host. It's fine for a guest to treat the host to a restaurant meal as a thank-you for the visit. Otherwise, decide how to handle any restaurant bills ahead of time. The host should make it clear that he's treating, if that's what he'd like to do, or it should be clear that the bill will be split. If a restaurant is proposed that seems to be out of a guest's budget, he should let his host know: "I'm sorry, it looks great, but I think Chez Antoine seems a little out of my reach. Is there someplace else we could go?"

the children a bedtime story while I get dinner ready?" Or "Tom, would you watch the grill for a few minutes?" Do accept their offers. Most guests sincerely want to help out and might feel uncomfortable if they're consistently rebuffed.

WHEN GUESTS DEPART

A polite host not only tells his guests how much he enjoyed their stay, but also sees his guests to the door and stays until they're out of sight, waving the occasional good-bye. A hasty retreat could leave the impression you're eager to get back to your routine. (You may be, but in the spirit of good manners, don't let it show.)

Even if your guests must get up at 4:00 AM to catch

an early plane and you choose to stay in bed, you can help with their departure plans ahead of time—perhaps by arranging for a taxi to get them to the airport.

when kids come too

The children of houseguests might be invited, particularly when they're roughly the same age as the host's children. Most of the time, the kids can be left to play together. It's a good idea to plan kid-friendly activities during the visit. Even if the host has no children, she might arrange a playdate for her visitors and other kids in her neighborhood. Just be sure to check with your guest first to make sure she and her children will be okay with your plans.

Parents obviously shouldn't shirk their duties, no matter how much they're looking forward to a relaxing visit. It's their responsibility—and theirs alone—to keep their children in line, clean up after them, and get them to bed at their regular hour.

Guest Books

Keeping a guest book is a lovely tradition. Before leaving, guests sign, often adding a comment on their stay. Good stationery stores sell books for the purpose, so you can find one that fits your style, from ultracasual to formal.

GUIDELINES FOR GUESTS

Just as a host should be clear when issuing an invitation, houseguests should be prompt with their reply and precise about their arrival and departure times. Promptness is all the more important if the invitation is for a longer visit or you're one of several guests.

Replying to Invitations

Handwritten, phone, or email replies should be made right away, regardless of the nature of your visit. Include the day and time of your arrival and departure and your means of transportation. If you can't give a definite answer or promise one within a day or two, it's better to decline so that the host can fill your place with someone else, if he wishes.

the guest who stays too long

Most of us know the proverb that equates houseguests with fish: Both "start to stink in three days." But a Portuguese proverb says it more subtly: "Visits always give pleasure—if not the coming, then the going."

If the guest has to stay longer because of airline cancellations or other unavoidable problems, be as helpful as you can. The situation is probably as difficult for him as it is for you.

But what about a guest who just stays and stays? Here's some sample language for starting the conversation. Remember that tone is key: keeping it light but honest is important.

"Tom, Karen and I wanted to give you the heads-up that while we have enjoyed your stay, as of Monday, you're going to need to find other accommodations. We're happy to suggest a few hotels in the area."

If Tom has been a good guest but just stayed too long, it's fine to tell him you look forward to a future visit (when you will of course set start and end dates for the stay). Making sure that Tom knows you still view him favorably will help ease any embarrassment he may have about overstaying his welcome.

THE GOLDEN RULES FOR HOUSEGUESTS

There's more to being a good houseguest than just being nice and doing your part to help out. And family members, take note: Guest manners are called for, even when you stay with relatives. Here are some important things to consider when you plan to stay over at someone's home:

Definitely Do . . .

- make your visit short and sweet. Generally keep your visit to no more than three nights.
- bring your own toiletries.
- clean up after yourself. Make your bed. Keep your bathroom clean: Wipe up any ring in the tub, shaving cream residue in the basin, or hair on any surface.
- offer to help out, especially in the kitchen (unless your host objects).
- be adaptable. Be ready for anything—or for nothing.
- show that you're enjoying yourself.
- offer to pitch in for groceries if you're staying more than two or three nights.
- double-check to make sure you have all your belongings before you leave.
- bring or send a gift, or treat your host to a night out.

- send a handwritten thank-you note following your visit.

Definitely Don't . . .

- ask to bring your pet. If you must travel with your pet, inquire about a good kennel in the area or offer to stay in a hotel. This also gives your host an opening to invite your pet if she wishes.

- accept an invitation from someone else during your visit without first checking with your host.

- use your host's phone, computer, or any other equipment without asking.

- use more than your share of hot water.

- snoop.

How to Leave the Bed

On your last day, ask your hostess what she would like you to do with your bed linen, then follow her wishes. Standard practice is to remove the sheets, fold them, place them at the foot of the bed, and pull the blanket and spread up neatly so that the bed will look "made."

If you're close friends and you visit frequently, go ahead and ask for fresh sheets. It's a nice gesture and saves your host from having to do it later.

Saying "Thank You"

Overnight visits require handwritten thank-you notes—with the emphasis on "handwritten"—within a day or two of your return home. (The only exception is when your hosts are relatives or close friends who often visit you in return. Even then, a call the next day is appreci-

Q: *When I'm visiting someone for the weekend, how can I gracefully excuse myself for a while to give us both some space?*

A: As long as you don't do it in the middle of dinner preparations or a planned activity, your hostess will appreciate some time out so she can regroup, take a nap, or simply have a break from entertaining for a while. Just say, "Jenna, all this sea air has wiped me out—would it be all right with you if I took a nap?" or "If you don't need me for an hour or two, I think I'll drag out my laptop and check my email," or "That hammock looks so inviting—if nobody else has claimed it for the next hour or so, I'd love to climb in with my book."

ated.) Emailing your thanks to anyone but your relatives and closest friends is inappropriate because it reduces the host's considerable effort on your behalf to the level of a casual lunch or a lift to work.

twelve house gift ideas

Houseguests are expected to give a gift to their host(s). For an overnight stay, something on the order of a bottle of good wine is sufficient. A longer stay requires something a little more substantial. If the hosts have young children, it's also nice if the gift is something they can partake of, too, such as a box of chocolates or a family game.

You can take a gift with you and present it as soon as you arrive or you could buy one during your stay (you might get a good idea of what the host wants or needs after a day or two). A third option is to send a gift as soon as possible after you leave.

House gift ideas include

- New best-selling book
- Consumables, such as a gift basket of gourmet treats, fruit, or chocolates
- Hand towels or beach towels
- Place mats, napkins, and napkin rings
- Bottle of liqueur or cognac you know your host is fond of
- Sturdy canvas tote bag (monogram optional)
- Two or three unusual kitchen utensils, or a set of nice nesting bowls
- For a golfer, a dozen golf balls
- Set of nicely packaged herbs and spices
- Picture frame, with a picture taken during your visit sent later
- Candles and informal candlesticks
- Houseplant in a decorative pot

⎰ EXTENDED VISITS ⎱

Extended visits are almost entirely restricted to family members who come to stay for a week or more. But it might also be a friend who's in town to do some job searching and could use a place to stay. Here are a few guidelines for dealing with problems that may crop up over the course of a longish stay:

Tips for Hosts

- When you're invited somewhere, should you ask if you may bring your guest? In general, don't. For an invitation to dinner or any other occasion that requires the host to have an exact guest head count, you can say, "I'm afraid we can't come— Mom is staying with us." This leaves it up to the host whether to suggest that you bring your mother.

- If you have tickets for an event during a house-guest's stay, either try to get another ticket for your guest or give yours away. If your guest is a close relative who's visiting for more than a few days, you might agree that it's fine for you to go alone. Just be sure he has something to do while you're away.

- Plan together how you and your guest will handle your routines (work, school, shopping, and so forth) and any special activities—together or separately?

- Be up front about the availability of your car, so, if necessary, he can rent one or make other plans for his transportation needs.

- Consider whether or not to offer your guest the use of your computer for email and Internet access.

- Offer your guests the use of your washer and dryer.

Tips for Guests

- Thoughtful guests make a point of immediately saying that no one needs to entertain them—then proving the point by having things to do.

- It's disruptive when the guest follows the host from room to room or chats nonstop with a child who is trying to complete his homework.

- A thoughtful guest doesn't sit in on every conversation, but rather goes on a walk or to another room in the house so that the host and hostess can have a minute to finish a conversation in private.

- A guest who has to stay longer than expected for business reasons, interviews, or other scheduled events should share his schedule with the host.

- Helping with routine activities (shopping, preparing a meal, or assisting the children with homework) helps keep the host's daily life from being unduly disrupted by the guest's extended stay.

When It's Family

Just because you're related, doesn't mean it's okay to drop in for the weekend without notice, or to assume that your relatives can accommodate your pets and children. All the host/guest rules apply. While invitations are usually casual, you still need one. It's fine to ask, "We're going to be in Cleveland on the 16th and 17th, is there any chance we can stay with you?" but respect your host's answer; it really may not be convenient for you to stay at that time. Be mindful of your host's accommodations and opt for a nearby hotel or B&B if you and your traveling companions won't fit.

Using a Family Member's Home

A member of your family offers her vacation home for your next holiday. Or she suggests you stay at her house or apartment while she's away. Whatever the situation, living temporarily in a family member's home is a responsibility. You should take as good care of a family member's home as anyone else's. Family shouldn't be expected to be more tolerant of messes or damage than strangers. If you request to use a family member's home for any length of time, offer to pay rent. If your family member asks you to house-sit, be sure you both understand the terms of the agreement. Treat a relative's home with care; leave behind a clean house, a warm note of appreciation, and perhaps a house gift.

23
invitations and announcements

An invitation reveals the style and purpose of an occasion. Is it for a laid-back barbecue? Or will it be an elegant dinner party? As the host, you'll want to match the style of your invitation—and the way you deliver it—to your event. You'll also need to know how far in advance of your event to issue them, and what to include on the invitation itself—the important who, what, when, where, and why that tells your guest what to expect.

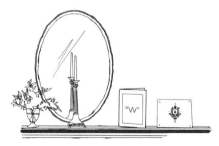

Receiving an invitation is a compliment. It says that you're important to the hosts and they want you to be part of their special event. As a guest, you'll need to know how to respond to various types of invitations.

Whenever you receive an invitation you have a social obligation to respond. Even when you can't attend, thank your hosts for inviting you.

THE BASIC ELEMENTS OF INVITATIONS

From a phone call inviting friends over for a bridge night to the most formal invitation to a gala ball, all invitations should include the following:

- **Who:** For almost all invitations, use the hosts' first and last names: Anisha and Raja Peshara. Formal printed or engraved invitations call for full names and social titles: Dr. Anisha and Mr. Raja Peshara.
- **What:** The nature of the occasion—cocktails, dinner, Super Bowl party.
- **When:** State the day and time you wish guests to arrive: 7 o'clock, Saturday, January 12. (Usually, adding the year isn't necessary, but it is customary on wedding invitations.)

- **Where:** The location of the event: your house, a club or restaurant, the beach.

- **Why:** Let guests know if there is a reason for the party and the name of any honoree—Gary's 30th birthday, Lauren's graduation, a baby shower for Lynn and Alex.

- **How to respond:** Do you want responses by phone, mail, or email, and by when?

- **Any special instructions:** Things a guest may need to know ahead of time, such as directions and a map to the location, a notation about what to wear, or requests such as what to bring or not bring: "It's a surprise!" "No gifts, please," "Bring a bathing suit," "Casual."

Choosing the Type of Invitation

In Emily Post's day, mail was delivered once or twice a day, so mailed invitations were fast, convenient, inexpensive, and reliable. Telephoning was considered too informal—on a party line anyone could be listening in—and besides, it was expensive. Today, we have numerous ways to extend an invitation that reflect varying degrees of formality.

Mailed invitations are still the preferred mode for formal celebrations such as weddings or black-tie affairs, or for special parties at your home. Phoned, emailed, and texted invitations are now part of the invitation establishment, although they're mostly used for more casual get-togethers. Think about your guests and how you regularly communicate with them. There's no sense in emailing an invitation to someone who doesn't check email frequently. Each delivery method does have its drawbacks: Mail can go astray, email can be diverted to a spam folder or accidentally deleted, and phone or text messages lost in voice mail or overlooked.

No matter how you issue your invitation, *all your guests should receive their invitation the same way*. If you send written invitations, send them to everyone, even guests you have spoken with already. The point is to avoid having a guest think that she wasn't on your original list and is a last-minute fill-in, or not worthy of the full guest treatment. If you asked someone very far in advance, sending an invitation (or calling when you call other invitees) serves as a polite reminder.

By Phone

Inviting by phone is perfect for those occasions when you want to ask close friends to an informal gathering such as brunch, a small, casual dinner, a birthday party, barbecue, or cocktails or dessert. You'll know right away who can come and who can't, plus you'll be able to settle any "What can I bring?" or "What should I wear?" issues on the spot.

Start with the facts: "Hi, Chloe, it's Trish. We're having a few people over for dinner next Saturday night. We'd love it if you and Sam could join us. It's casual, starting at seven. How about if you check with Sam and call me later?" This is a much better way of inviting someone than ambushing Chloe with "What are you doing Saturday night?"

Notice that this invitation includes all the information the guest needs—nature of the event, day and time, location, and even a request for a reply. The person can accept on the spot or take a little time to consider. In either case, you've been a considerate host by leaving the decision to her.

What if no one's at home? It's fine to leave a voice mail message, but try to call again and issue the invitation "in person" in case the message doesn't get delivered.

Email, E-vites, or Texts

Email works well for casual invitations, such as "Let's get together for lunch on Friday." For a more serious invitation, such as when you're having a dinner party or hosting a celebration, you'll want to weigh some pros and cons. Using email or online invitation services, which organize and customize the invitation process for you, can save time (you don't have to go to the store) and money (they're free), and build some excitement at the same time (there are designs and choices for every occasion). They're also a greener alternative to paper invitations.

On the other hand, e-vites aren't as personal as a phoned or written invitation, and might not provide enough fanfare for a formal event or be special enough for an intimate gathering. They can end up in a spam folder or undelivered as a result of a computer glitch. Even though they make it easy to RSVP, you still may have to follow up with people who don't respond.

Watch out for the option that allows invitees to see the guest list and who has responded, "Yes," "No," or "Maybe." Let guests respond to your invitation, not because of who is or isn't on the guest list.

By Mail

If you're hosting a more formal event—honoring a special guest or celebrating a milestone, for example—a mailed invitation is the better choice. You can mail invitations for informal dinners and parties, too—even the simplest get-together is elevated to party status by an invitation in the mail.

More formal events call for more formal invitations (see "Formal Invitations," page 280). For less formal parties, choose a fill-in invitation that suits the occasion from a stationery shop. Many stationers carry computer-friendly invitations: Supply the wording, select a font, and either have them printed out for you at the shop or do it yourself on your home computer.

The most personal invitation? A note handwritten on your own stationery. These are only really practical for parties with a small guest list or to extend a houseguest invitation. Handwritten invitations are few and far between these days, but when they receive one, your guests will know they're cherished friends.

Invitation Extras

Some invitations require some extra information:

◆ **If more than one person is hosting,** be sure to list all the hosts on the invitation: "Please Join Marcia and Bob Heiddecker and Linda and Ian Williams for . . ." The name of the person at whose home the

facebook invitations

Using social media sites such as Facebook to send out invitations for events and gatherings can be a great way to connect with groups both large and small. There are a few things to keep in mind when using Facebook to send invitations.

- **Facebook invites are informal by nature.** Because they are sent out as mass messages, these invitations are considered casual ones. For impromptu gatherings and informal events, Facebook invites may be appropriate. For formal events like galas, special celebrations, formal dinners, and weddings, it's important to use invitations that will reflect the formal or special nature of the event.

- **Be sure that those on your guest list are active Facebook users.** While friends and acquaintances may have accounts, recipients could easily miss your invitation if they are not very active users, and/or don't set up notifications from the site. It's considerate to give friends who you know aren't Facebook frequenters a heads-up that you've posted an event or sent out invitations via Facebook. It's always okay to follow up with a text or call to see if a guest has seen your invite.

- **Be clear with the details.** Your invitation should clearly state: **what** the event or gathering is; **who** is invited; **where** and **when** it is being held; and **who** is hosting. Additional information—like what guests are expected to bring, special instructions on parking or accessing the location—should be included.

- **Be aware of the guest list.** You have the option of making your guest list private. The focus of your responses should be on whether or not your guests would like to attend the event, not whether or not certain people will or won't be there. Look at your options when setting up your invitation and decide what is best for your type of event.

- **Follow up on RSVPs.** Depending on your timetable, it's okay to follow up with guests who have not RSVP'd a few days to two weeks before your event. Send a quick message, text, or give a call and ask if they are able to provide their response.

- **Say "Thank you."** After the event be sure to post a thank-you message to all those who attended. It's a nice way to cap the entire experience and it lets your guests know how much you appreciated their participation.

event will be held is listed first. Aside from that, the order for multiple hosts' names is up to you. Alphabetical listing is easy. If the hosts are from the same family or represent several generations, the list might go from eldest to youngest. Sometimes names are listed in the most visually appealing style on a printed invitation—alternating shorter and longer names, for example.

- **If your party is in someone's honor,** list the honoree on the invitation as well: "Please join us for cocktails to celebrate Antoine's birthday . . ."

- **Dress instructions,** such as "Black tie," "Semiformal," or "Business casual," can be added if the formality or informality of the occasion might not be clear to guests. On written or printed

tips for e-vite success

- Make sure that the email addresses you use are correct, and that all of your invited guests check their email regularly.

- Be familiar with all the options. For example, you may want to turn off the feature that lets guests see who else is invited. This is especially important for people who don't know each other well. Doing so hides email addresses and respects their privacy.

- Include all the important info: who's hosting, what kind of party it is, why the party is being thrown (if there's a reason), when and where it is (including links to maps if necessary), and RSVP details.

- Fill in all the details the site asks for and remember to include a personal message.

- Proofread before you hit "Send." Invitations are the first hint of what a party will be like, so make a good impression.

- Be prepared to follow up by phone if you don't receive an RSVP in a timely fashion, just in case your message wasn't delivered or is lingering unopened in an inbox. (Note: One of the advantages of using a service, compared with using your own email account, is that it lets you know if the recipient has viewed the invitation yet.)

- Follow up with a reminder to the group a day or two in advance.

invitations, dress instructions, such as "BLACK TIE," "CASUAL," or "COSTUMES" are printed in the lower right-hand corner. (See Resources, "Dressing for the Occasion," page 683, for a chart defining attire notations.)

- **End times** aren't generally included on an invitation, with a few exceptions. Children's parties list an end time so that parents know when to pick up their kids. Invitations to cocktail parties or parties that precede another scheduled event (theater, sporting event) have a start and end time so that guests can go on to dinner or to the next event. End times are also given for open houses and other events where guests are free to come and go during the specified time.

You may need to include other information for your guests with, but not on, the invitation. This is done by using enclosures. Simply place enclosures in front of the invitation, which is inserted with the written side facing the flap side of the envelope. This way, the recipient sees the writing on the invitation and the enclosures as the invitation is removed from the envelope. Some typical enclosures are

- **Maps and directions.** Be sure to add a contact number—just in case!

- **Schedule of events.** Useful for weddings or reunion weekends.

- **Tickets.** For graduations, or if you're inviting friends to a concert or game.

- **Raffle tickets.** For charity events, for example.

- **Registry information.** For bridal or baby showers. (Note: Registry information is *not* included with a wedding invitation.)
- **Response card.** Make sure the envelope or postcard is addressed and stamped.

Requesting a Reply

RSVP is the abbreviation of the French phrase *répondez, s'il vous plaît*, which means, "please respond." (R.S.V.P., Rsvp, rsvp, and r.s.v.p. are correct as well.) It's also fine to write "Please respond by (date)." Most invitations include some sort of RSVP; it lets the host or hostess know how many guests will be attending—crucial if you're having a sit-down dinner, for example, or a catered party that demands a head count. The initials *RSVP* go on the lower left of a formal or printed invitation. (See examples, pages 281 and 282.) Add a physical address, a phone number, or an email address on mailed invitations, and if calling, include your number if you leave a voice mail message.

A guest is obligated to reply to an RSVP, so if you haven't heard back from someone within a reasonable amount of time, it's perfectly okay to call and ask (politely of course!) for a yes or no. It could be that the invitation went astray. Include a "Could you let me know by Thursday?" for anyone who still seems to be on the fence. Remember, the hope is to have that person there.

Instructions. If you want only written replies, the RSVP is sufficient, and guests will send them to the return address on the envelope. No other instructions are needed unless you wish responses to be sent by a certain date or mailed to an alternate address (add the address for replies below the RSVP). If there are multiple hosts, the name and address of the person who is to receive the replies is included below the RSVP. The names and numbers of two or three hosts might be provided when you want phoned replies, making it easier for invitees to get in touch. Hours to call ("between 5 PM and 8 PM") can be included with a phone number when a host is difficult to reach at other times. In the same fashion, if you prefer emailed replies, include the address below RSVP.

Regrets only. For a large party, you might be tempted to add "Regrets only" to save yourself from being inundated by phone calls. It's not your best option, especially if you need an accurate head count. Many guests find it confusing and either call anyway or simply forget to call and then fail to show up. When you do need to provide a head count for a caterer, including a "Reply by" date, usually a week or more before the event, is practical.

Reply cards. For weddings, large events such as balls or benefits, and business events, reply cards make it easy for guests to make a menu choice or send payments or donations. (See "Reply Cards and Enclosures," page 288.)

Addressing Written and Printed Invitations

There is a basic, commonsense rule for addressing invitations: Include all the names of the people you're inviting. Generally, send a separate invitation to each single adult or couple who live in the same household. Teenag-

ers usually receive separate invitations, as does a child who doesn't live with his parent when you are inviting them both.

Young children are included on their parents' invitation, which could be addressed to "Mr. and Mrs. Lawrence Rickman and Family." It means just the Rickmans at that particular address, but is sometimes misinterpreted as inviting other extended family members living elsewhere. The following address makes it clear:

Mr. and Mrs. Lawrence Rickman

Michael Rickman

Gloria Rickman

[*or* Michael and Gloria Rickman]

A single invitation is sent to married couples and to unmarried couples who live together in established relationships. Their names are listed on one line, joined by "and." You can send separate invitations to housemates or siblings who live at the same address, or send one invitation and address the individual names on separate lines. For informal invitations, it's fine to use first and last names and nicknames. For formal invitations, be sure to use titles and full names. (For more on forms of address, see Resources, page 676.)

If you're inviting guests to bring a date or guest,

potluck, byob, and byof

BYOB on an invitation means "bring your own beverage"; guests bring their beverages and the hosts supply glasses, mixers, appetizers, or a meal. BYOF stands for "bring your own food" and indicates the guests should provide whatever they want to eat, say, for a picnic. When it's a "potluck" party, guests bring a dish that all the other guests can share. Each guest takes home any leftovers of their contribution or offers to share it out. Those who brought their own liquor aren't expected to leave the bottle for the organizer, but do check local liquor laws before transporting an opened container.

Technically, events at which the guests bring food or drinks are *organized*, not hosted, and are casual, often last-minute entertaining. They're a fun and easy way for family and friends to share time together without one person bearing the brunt of the work and expense. (For more on potluck parties, see Chapter 24, "Entertaining at Home," page 292.)

this is noted on the invitation itself but *not* in the mailing address on the envelope. A casual or informal invitation might include a handwritten line such as "Jeff, please bring a date [*or* a guest]." (For information about addressing formal invitations, see page 280.)

When Do the Invitations Go Out?

Whether you mail, email, or phone your invitations, timing is important. Nowadays, sooner rather than later is the rule to best accommodate guests' busy work and social schedules. How soon? Give your invitees enough time to respond—and give yourself enough time to organize the party. If you're hosting a holiday party or if guests have to travel to get there, invitations might go out as early as six weeks ahead. Here are some general guidelines on timing your invitations, but feel free to adapt them to fit your particular circumstances:

FORMAL DINNER	3 to 6 weeks
INFORMAL DINNER	A few days to 3 weeks
COCKTAIL PARTY	1 to 4 weeks
LUNCH OR TEA	A few days to 2 weeks
CASUAL GET-TOGETHER	Same day to 2 weeks
BIRTHDAY, SHOWER, OR ANNIVERSARY	3 to 6 weeks
GRADUATION	4 weeks
CHRISTENING	2–4 weeks
BAR/BAT MITZVAH	4 to 6 weeks
HOUSEWARMING	A few days to 3 weeks
HOLIDAY PARTY	4 to 6 weeks
THANKSGIVING (OR OTHER HOLIDAY) DINNER	2 weeks to 2 months
WEDDING	4 weeks to 2 months

Casual Invitations

A picnic and ball game in the park, a backyard barbecue, an easygoing brunch with close friends—casual get-togethers are events where the mood is relaxed and most of the frills of formal entertaining are set aside (except good manners, of course!). "Casual" also describes most children's and teen parties. Invitations are issued in person, by phone or email, or perhaps by mailing a fill-in card. Most casual invitations request a phoned or emailed response, often giving both options.

Informal Invitations

When the style of occasions such as luncheons, teas, dinner parties, cocktail parties and buffets, and events honoring special guests falls between casual and very formal, they call for informal invitations. These invitations can be designed and printed for the occasion, or you might prefer printed, fill-in cards. You could send a handwritten note if your guest list is small; otherwise it's impractical. It's also fine to issue informal invitations by phone, possibly following up with a reminder card.

Some of the characteristics of informal invitations include the following:

- Informal printed invitations aren't engraved. Today, they're most likely to be laser printed, which is cost effective, or printed using lithography or thermography, which is more expensive. Colorful papers, borders in complementary colors, and predesigned papers that can be printed at a stationer's or at home are all possible options. You can also choose any typeface that complements your design.

- Reply cards can be included and may be accompanied by a stamped, preaddressed envelope (or a stamped, preaddressed postcard), but adding an RSVP, "Please reply," or "Regrets only" is more typical.

- The wording of a printed invitation doesn't need to be in the third-person voice that's traditionally used in formal invitations. Hosts and guests can be referred to by first names, "Diana and Craig

DeRossi," or by courtesy titles, "Mr. and Mrs. Craig DeRossi."

◆ Abbreviations for months, states, and street addresses can be used. Numbers can be written numerically. Times are indicated as "7 o'clock." Use AM or PM if there might be any doubt about time of day.

Please join us
for our annual
New Year's Eve Bonfire
December 31st
10:30 PM to 1:00 AM
The Landers'
1706 South Road
Charlotte
RSVP 802-555-4321
Kids and houseguests welcome

This sample informal invitation is for an event hosted in someone's honor:

Let's celebrate Anna's 30th!
Friday, June 19th
at 7:00
Leah and Katie Gray
145 High Meadow Lane
Guilford

RSVP by June 15th   casual
555-8765 or
leah@mymail.com

Here is a sample of a fill-in invitation:

YOU ARE INVITED FOR DINNER

ON *Sat., March 1*   AT *7:30 p.m.*

AT *42 Piedmont St., Apt. 1-A*

BY *Amita and Kamal Gupta*

RSVP *555-4398*

Using Your Informals for Invitations

You can use your own informal fold-over stationery. This type of invitation is a little more personal, but also a little more formal and works if you're inviting a small number of guests. If your notes are printed with your name(s), the invitation is written:

Brunch
MR. AND MRS. HOWARD WANAMAKER
Saturday, September 18
12 noon
1444 Post Road

RSVP
555-6655

When notes are plain or monogrammed, the invitation takes the form of a handwritten personal note. In the following example, the hostess signs her first and last names, and includes her address, indicating the location of the event:

September 1

Dear Keisha,

A.J. and I hope that you, Alex, and the children can join us for brunch on Saturday, September 18, at noon. Please let me know by calling 555-6655.

Alisa Malca

1444 Post Road

FORMAL INVITATIONS

Despite the informality of American entertaining these days, there are still plenty of occasions that call for formal invitations. Formal weddings come first to mind, but there are also presentation and charity balls, and inaugural balls following many federal, state, and even local elections. Official receptions and dinners are common in Washington, D.C. Private affairs—dinners, dinner dances, teas, luncheons, cocktail receptions—offer other opportunities for formal entertaining, and even in our casual times, people often look forward to a change of pace and the fun of dressing up.

The first notice that an event is formal is the invitation itself; both its look and wording immediately distinguish it from casual and informal invitations, starting with a heavy, cream-colored, hand-addressed (sometimes by a calligrapher) envelope. The following list includes key points on the style and language of formal invitations:

- Formal invitations are printed or engraved on cards of good-quality paper stock. The paper is traditionally white or cream, but pastels are now options for all but the most formal events and official occasions. The standard proportions are three by four (three units high by four wide or vice versa); postal regulations require that all first-class mailing envelopes be at least 3½ inches high by 5 inches wide.

- Papers may have a raised border or be edged in a color, such as silver for a twenty-fifth anniversary party. Black borders traditionally have been reserved for death announcements, but today some black-and-white-themed parties or weddings use black-bordered invitations. This is fine as long as the invitation doesn't look funereal.

- Type style is a matter of choice, but plainer, serif faces—classics such as Times Roman or Palatino—are easier to read. Work with your stationer or printer to select a single typeface; they can show you samples of appropriate styles. (For an explanation of different printing methods, see "A Printing Primer," page 201.)

- Full names—not initials or nicknames—and courtesy titles are used on invitations and for envelope addresses. If someone doesn't want to include his first or middle name, it can be left off the invitation: "Mr. and Mrs. Thomas Arthur Giordano," "Mr. and Mrs. Thomas Giordano," or "Mr. and Mrs. Giordano."

- Courtesy titles (Mrs., Ms., Mr., Mx.) are abbreviated, as are "Dr.," "Sr.," or "Jr.," but religious, professional, and elected/appointed titles are written in full. Military ranks of commissioned officers are never abbreviated. (For more on the correct use of titles, see Chapter 17, "Social Names and Titles," page 215.)

- The invitation is phrased in the third person. "Request the pleasure of your company . . ." is the standard wording for formal social invitations. "Request the honour [or honor] of your presence . . ." is used for occasions held in a place of worship. As a bow to tradition, the British *ou* spelling is preferred.

- Punctuation is used only for words on the same line that require separation ("Saturday, the twenty-fourth of January") and for abbreviations ("Mr. and Mrs.").

- Numbers for dates and times are written out. Months and state names are written in full, as are addresses: "September," "Wisconsin," "Highland Crescent." When addressing envelopes, the two-letter postal abbreviations for states can be used: "Lansing MI" with no comma between city and state.

- Street numbers are written numerically—"1042 Belgrave Boulevard"—unless the street number is a single number: "Three Santa Fe Circle."

- Times are written as "seven o'clock." Half hours are written as "half after seven o'clock."

- If the year is included—and this is optional—it appears below the date and is written out: "two thousand twenty."

- Reply requests may be written as RSVP, R.S.V.P., R.S.V.P., R.s.v.p., "Please reply," or "The favour [or favor] of a reply is requested." Use "Please reply by" when a date is included. Be consistent if using the British *ou* spelling in the wording of the invitation.

- The notations "Black tie" and "White tie" are traditionally excluded from invitations to weddings and private parties. But these days hosts may include dress instructions to be clear that an event is formal. "Black tie" or "White tie" is conventionally printed in the lower right corner of invitations to proms, charity balls, formal dinners or dances, and any event, such as a wedding, for which clarification of dress standards may be necessary.

The following example illustrates the language and style of traditional, printed formal invitations:

Dr. and Mrs. Joseph Edward Cooke
request the pleasure of your company
for dinner and dancing
on Friday, the thirteenth of August
at half-past seven o'clock
Rivercrest Club

RSVP   Black tie
250 Garden Court
Louisville, Kentucky 40207

Although rare these days, formal invitations written by hand follow the same form as an engraved or printed invitation.

How to Add "and Guest" to a Formal Invitation

When a guest is invited to bring a date or companion, there are several ways to extend the invitation. What you don't do is write "Ms. Halley and Guest" on the outer envelope. If there's an inner envelope, such as for wedding invitations, it's addressed to "Ms. Halley and Guest," but the outer envelope is addressed only to "Ms. Susan Halley." If the invitee's name is written on the invitation itself, write "Ms. Susan Halley and Guest." Otherwise, either issue the invitation to bring a guest personally, or enclose a short, handwritten note.

Fill-in Formal Invitations

Printed or engraved fill-in cards are a convenience for anyone who frequently entertains formally. Guest names and information specific to the event are written in by hand, as in this example:

Mr. David Dulac and Mr. Kyle Walker

request the pleasure of

(Mr. and Mrs. James Walker-Martin's)

company at

(dinner)

(on Saturday, the fourth of December)

(at half after seven o'clock)

1020 Old Towne Road

Palo Alto, California

RSVP

If there is a guest(s) of honor, a line is handwritten above the host's or hosts' names: "To meet Senator Gayden Lang and Mrs. Lang." If the invitee may bring a companion, then the guest's name line is written as "Mr. Harry Evans and Guest."

Formal Invitations Sent by Groups

Today, very large, formal events are more likely to be hosted by groups and organizations than by individuals. The invitation format is similar to those for other formal occasions, although there is normally a reply card with return envelope and possibly other enclosures. When additional information, such as a list of patrons or underwriters, is printed on the invitation, a single- or double-folded sheet of paper is used rather than a card. They're addressed as any other formal invitation. (See "Formal Invitations," page 280.)

To a private benefit. When an event is held to benefit a charity or the sale of tickets is expected to cover the costs of the event, a card including the amount of the subscription is enclosed with the invitation, as are a reply card and envelope. Lists of patrons, committee members, and debutantes (if the event includes a formal presentation) may be printed inside the invitation. The guest list is limited, usually to members or subscribers. Invitations are mailed four to six weeks prior to the event. Returning the subscription card and a check constitutes acceptance; regrets aren't necessary.

The Board of Directors of the
Cleveland Women's Club
invites you to subscribe to
The Thirtieth Annual Diamond Ball
to be held at the Peacock Hotel
on the evening of Saturday,
the eighteenth of September
two thousand twenty
at half after six o'clock

Black tie

To a public occasion. Formal dances and banquets are often hosted by a charitable group, a club, or some other association. Invitations are sent to a large list of people who might be interested in attending. Guests pay set ticket prices. The prices are included on the invitation, and response cards (normally including a "Please reply by" date) and envelopes are enclosed. A list of patrons, committee members, and underwriters may also be enclosed. Invitations are usually sent four to six weeks before the event.

Returning the reply card and a check (or your credit card information) constitutes an acceptance; there's no need to send regrets unless requested on the reply card. Some cards give the option of regretting but also making a contribution to the charity or cause.

The Directors of the Cancer Patient
Support Program
request the pleasure of your company
at its Winter Ball
for the benefit of
The Breast Cancer Center
Saturday, the thirty-first of January
two thousand twenty
at seven o'clock
Hampton Convention Center

Single Ticket $75.00   *Black tie*
Couple $150.00
Table of ten $700.00

Presentation balls. Today, balls at which young women are formally presented are hosted by private organizations and cotillion clubs. These are usually large, elegant affairs, with invitations limited to members of the organization, the families and friends of the honorees, and special guests. Proceeds from ticket sales often benefit the sponsoring group.

The invitation might be printed or embossed with the logo or symbol of the organization. Lists of committee members, sponsors, and the young people to be presented can be printed on the invitation or a separate sheet. Reply cards and envelopes and sometimes a separate card listing ticket prices are enclosed. Invitations are usually sent six weeks before the event—earlier if the ball is held during a busy social season.

The South Carolina Alumnae Association
of the Delta Theta Delta Chapter
requests the pleasure of your company
at the Wisteria Cotillion
to benefit the
Delta Theta Delta Children's Medical
Research Foundation
on Saturday, the fifteenth of May
two thousand twenty
at eight o'clock
Silverpoint Country Club
Columbia

Please reply   *Black tie*
by the first of May

Note: When proceeds for an event are donated to charity or when a large number of invitations are sent for a public event, the enclosed reply envelopes usually aren't stamped because the cost of stamps can be a considerable expense for the organizers.

⎡ HOW DO I RESPOND? ⎤

General Guidelines

Rule #1: Always reply to all invitations, no matter how informally extended. No one is obligated to accept an invitation or to explain the reasons for not accepting. However, *every invitee is obligated to respond promptly when an invitation requests a reply*. An RSVP asks you to notify the sender whether or not you will attend. It may also be written as "Please reply" or "The favor of a reply is requested."

The notation "Regrets only" means that you're expected to reply *only* if you can't attend. Replies are made according to the following guidelines (see also Chapter 53, "A Guide for Wedding Guests," page 662):

Respond in a timely fashion. Ideally, do it right away before you forget. If the RSVP or an enclosed card includes a request that you reply by a certain date, mail written replies so they will arrive no later than that date.

For in-person or phoned invitations, you can accept or regret when asked, but unless it is a last-minute invitation, it's acceptable to delay your response until you've checked your schedule. Always consult your spouse, live-in partner, or anyone else included in the invitation before replying to an invitation to you both. Just tell the host that you'll call as soon as possible, and follow up within a day or two.

Reply in the manner indicated on the invitation. If the RSVP appears on an invitation with no other notation and no reply card is included, then you're expected to send a handwritten response to the host at the return address on the envelope. When there are several hosts, the name and address of the person who is to receive replies will be written below the RSVP.

If telephone replies are preferred, the phone number (and sometimes calling hours) will be included with the RSVP. It's best to talk to the host in person. If you leave a voice mail message, try to follow up with another call as messages sometimes get missed. When an email address is given reply with an emailed note.

Keep replies brief. Whether you write or phone, get to the point. You have no social obligation to offer excuses when you decline. You may want to explain, but there's no reason to go into great detail. The following two examples, which work for a handwritten or emailed note, illustrate first a polite written acceptance and then an equally polite note of regret with a brief explanation:

Dear Denisa,

Neil and I are delighted to accept your invitation for lunch on Saturday, April 10.

Yours truly,

Claire

Dear Mrs. Duvall,

I am so sorry that Nora and I must decline your invitation for March 21. We will be accompanying our daughter to the high school debate finals in Springfield that weekend.

Sincerely,

Alicia Barnes

If you're replying by phone, these notes contain the gist of your message.

Reply even if you have a potential conflict. There are times when you want to accept, but there's a possible conflict with another commitment, such as a tentative business trip or an ongoing family matter. When the event is informal or casual, go ahead and contact the host or hostess to explain: "I'd really love to come to the picnic, but there's a chance I may have to go to Portland for a client meeting. Can I let you know in a day or two?"

If the event is formal or on short notice, and your delay in replying might inconvenience the host, it's usually best to decline the invitation.

When some people can accept and others must regret. Everyone on the invitation could contact the host, but it's often easier for one of the invitees to accept and regret for everyone. For example, an informal reply to an invitation sent to a couple and a live-in parent might be worded like this:

Dear Barbara,

Peter and I are really looking forward to attending your garden party on May 22. My mother will be visiting a cousin in San Diego, and she is very sorry that she must regret your kind invitation.

Kindest regards,

Tania

When replies aren't requested. You aren't expected to reply to an invitation that has no RSVP or "Regrets only" notation. However, it's always polite to notify the host when you can't attend; a phone call will usually suffice, though you might send a personal note or an email.

When you receive an invitation too late. If you receive an invitation after the event—say, you've been out of town—it's courteous to call the hosts, tell them what happened, and express your thanks for being invited.

HERE'S HOW TO RESPOND TO DIFFERENT KINDS OF INVITATIONS:

MAILED INVITATION WITH A PHONE NUMBER	Call and make sure to give your response in person (even if you left a message on a machine), as answering machines can be unreliable.
EMAILED INVITATION	Write a short response and hit the "Reply" button.
E-VITE	Follow the directions to reply. Most let you reply with a "Maybe" if you aren't sure—even that's a help to your host—but be sure to give a final answer within a day or two. (See "Email, E-vites, or Texts," page 273.)
PHONED INVITATION	You can respond right away or, if you prefer not to be put on the spot, say, "Let me check my calendar and get right back to you." Just be sure you do exactly that! Before replying, always check with your spouse, live-in partner, or anyone else included in the invitation before replying for you both.
MAILED INVITATION WITH A RESPONSE CARD	Fill in the card and return it in the enclosed envelope. Mail it in time to be received by the date indicated.
MAILED INVITATION WITH RSVP AND NO RESPONSE CARD	Send a prompt handwritten reply to the host at the address on the envelope, or respond by phone or email if requested.
REGRETS ONLY	You only need to reply if you *can't* go. It's always polite to notify the host when you can't attend with a phone call, personal note, or an email. If your host doesn't hear from you, he's expecting you to be there!
AN INVITATION IS RECEIVED TOO LATE	Give your hosts a call with an explanation—you were out of town when the invitation arrived.

Replying to a Formal Invitation

Unless a formal invitation includes a telephone number, email address, or reply card, handwritten responses are expected to RSVP and "Regrets only" requests. Replies are sent to the host(s) at the return address on the envelope or the address that appears with the RSVP. If there are several hosts, one name and address is usually included with the RSVP; you send your response to that person, though the names of all the hosts are included in a formal written reply.

There are two ways to reply to a formal invitation: a formal note that follows the wording and style of the invitation or a personal note. Personal notes might be sent when the invitee knows the hosts well and wishes to explain briefly why she or he must regret.

The formal note is much easier to write than people think, because the wording reflects the wording of the invitation itself. Replies like the following are handwritten on plain or monogrammed notepaper, and lines are centered just as in the invitation. No punctuation is used except for social titles and to separate words on the same line.

Notice that the time is included in the acceptance, but not in the note of regret. This is to assure hosts that the guest has the correct time for the event.

Two versions of a formal acceptance:

> Mr. and Mrs. Nicholas Stamos
> accept with pleasure
> the kind invitation of
> Mr. and Mrs. George Fletcher
> for dinner
> on Friday, the ninth of July
> at half past eight o'clock

[or]

> Mr. and Mrs. Nicholas Stamos
> accept with pleasure
> Mr. and Mrs. George Fletcher's
> kind invitation for dinner
> on Friday, the ninth of July
> at half past eight o'clock

Two versions of a formal regret:

> Dr. and Mrs. Vincent Alvarado
> regret that they are unable to accept
> the kind invitation of
> Ms. Ann Alt and Mr. Keith Ambrose
> for Friday, the sixth of August

[or]

> Dr. and Mrs. Vincent Alvarado
> regret that they are unable to accept
> Ms. Ann Alt and Mr. Keith Ambrose's
> kind invitation
> for Friday, the sixth of August

When only some of the invitees can attend, write the following:

> Mr. and Mrs. Peter Carlson
> accept with pleasure
> Mr. and Mrs. Bollinger's
> kind invitation for
> Saturday, May twenty-second
> at seven o'clock
> but regret that
> Ms. Tina Carlson
> will be unable to attend

Replying to multiple hosts. When there is more than one host, all the names appear on the reply, though the envelope is addressed to the host listed with the RSVP or whose name appears with the return address on the invitation envelope. If there's no name indicated to receive replies, address your envelope to the first person or couple listed on the invitation and the address on the envelope. In your reply, list the hosts in the order they appear on the invitation:

> Ms. Juliana Varden
> accepts with pleasure
> [or regrets that she is unable to accept]
> the kind invitation of
> Mrs. Chambers and
> Ms. Underwood and

Mrs. Knight
for Wednesday, the thirteenth of October
at half past twelve o'clock
[The time isn't included in a regret.]

Replying to a committee. When an invitation issued by a committee includes a long or complicated list of names, you can reply as follows:

Mr. and Mrs. Ken Ichida
accept with pleasure
[or regret that they are unable to accept]
your kind invitation . . .

Replying to an organization. RSVP requests from an organization normally include a reply card or a name and address and/or phone number. It would be unusual, but if you did need to send a note of reply, it includes only the name of the organization:

Mx. Casey Wyatt
accepts with pleasure
[or regrets]
the kind invitation of
the University Club . . .

⟮ REPLY CARDS AND ENCLOSURES ⟯

Nowadays, reply cards are the best guarantee that hosts will receive responses to their invitations. Whatever the reasons, people are more likely to respond

getting the name right

You might receive an invitation on which your name is spelled incorrectly or the title is wrong: Your name is Jon, but the invitation says "John," or the invitation is addressed to "Mr. and Mrs." and you prefer "Ms." This is especially the case for invitations to a charity event where the administrative office may not have that information on file. Just reply as requested, but use or include the right spelling or title: add it to a reply card, note it in an email, or mention it in a phone message: "This is Sandra Gates. John Burns and I will be attending the gala on the 25th. Also, when you next update your mailing list, please note that we are Mr. John Burns and Ms. Sandra Gates, not Mr. and Mrs. Burns. Thank you."

On the other hand, if the mistake could indicate that the invitation was sent to the wrong person, you should contact the host or organization to clarify before you accept, regret, or just ignore it.

promptly on their own when a reply card is enclosed; it's hard to avoid replying when the host has supplied a simple card and an envelope that's already addressed and stamped.

A reply card is usually smaller than the invitation but printed in the same style. The card is placed, face up, on top of the invitation. When a reply envelope is provided, the card is placed under the envelope flap and again, placed on top of the invitation so that the front of the card is visible.

M r. and Mrs. Vernon Henry
☑ accept(s)
☐ regret(s)
Friday, January second
Columbus Country Club

M r. and Mrs. Vernon Henry
will _not_ attend
Friday, January second
Please reply by December fifteenth

The recipient need only fill in his name and those of anyone else included in the invitation and indicate whether they will or won't attend. These two examples above illustrate just how easy a reply card is to complete:

The card on the right includes a printed *M*, which is completed as *Mrs.*, *Mr.*, etc. If you have another title, strike through the *M* and write in what's appropriate for you (*Dr.*, *Rev.*). To save space, titles can be abbreviated on formal reply cards. If you're replying for several people, write their names under yours, but never add extra people, such as a date or children, who weren't named on the invitation. People sometimes add a brief personal sentiment to a reply card ("Can't wait to see you!" or "I'm so sorry I can't be there"), but this isn't necessary or expected.

RECALLING INVITATIONS

When an event is canceled or delayed, it's essential to contact all invited guests as soon as possible. Calling is best, but emailing and texting are other good options. When there's enough time to do so, formal invitations are recalled with a printed (not engraved) card, like the example given below. However, telephoning or emailing may be the most expedient method. In the case of a death or serious emergency in the family, friends can take over the responsibility for notifying guests.

A printed card canceling a formal social event:

*Owing to an illness in the family
Mr. and Mrs. Carlo Marchetti
are obliged to recall their invitation
for Thursday, the ninth of December*

When something like an unavoidable business trip is the cause for canceling, the host may be able to reschedule and give guests a new date for the event. This could be done by phoning, mailing, or emailing a personal note.

ANNOUNCEMENTS

Social announcements are sent to family members and friends to let them know about major events and achievements. Births, adoptions, graduations, and weddings are the most common announcements, followed by change of address or a legal name change. Traditional formal announcements are either printed or engraved cards, worded in the traditional third-person style. But today, announcements are often less formal in both language and design. As with invitations, instead of formal cream or white cards with a raised border and engraved with black ink, your announcement may be a colored or designed paper that fits the occasion, have a font and ink that complements the style, and be printed through a stationer or at home. Nowadays, it's also common for people to include the news in a letter or email, or post it on their social network page.

A key point of etiquette for both senders and recipients: *An announcement does not obligate the recipient to send a gift*. No response is required, but it's nice to acknowledge an announcement with a note or card of congratulations when appropriate. Whether to send a gift is entirely your choice.

Business Announcements

In business, announcements may be sent to colleagues, clients, and friends when a person joins a new firm; completes criteria that entitles her to use a professional designation, such as CPA; or receives a promotion to a position of prominence in a company. Companies also send announcements to notify clients, vendors, and other interested parties when they change the company name, move to a new location, or merge with another firm.

Newspaper Announcements

There's a good deal of misunderstanding about how announcements, such as those for engagements, wed-

dings, or company news, are placed in newspapers. There are two basic types of published announcements:

- Information submitted to the newspaper and published without charge, at the paper's discretion
- A notice published in space purchased by the person who supplies the information (as one purchases space for classified ads)

For announcements published at the paper's discretion, the information is usually given to the paper by filling out a standard form, which is often available on the paper's website. Newspaper staff then write the version that appears in print, including the headline. Information sent in a press release will likely be rewritten and perhaps shortened in accord with the publication's style and available space. Or it may not be published at all. You can't dictate the contents of an unpaid announcement or the date when it will appear. Publication is a service of the newspaper, not an obligation.

A paid notice appears as you wrote it and usually on the date requested. However, newspapers may check the information for accuracy and suggest wording, and they can reject notices that include questionable language and facts. You pay for the space and placement in the appropriate section. For example, marriage, birth, and adoption notices might be printed in a paper's social or lifestyles section, obituaries in the obituary column.

Whether you want a paid or unpaid announcement, contact the newspaper as far in advance as possible. Ask about deadlines, submission forms, and pricing for paid notices—usually a per-line rate with a minimum charge. Always ask because some newspapers now charge to print announcements that were once considered a public service. Sometimes announcements in the paper's online version are free.

For announcements in newsletters and bulletins, contact the publication's editor and ask what information is needed and when submissions are required. Publications of social and service groups, internal employee newsletters, the bulletins of religious congregations, and so forth don't charge but will usually write and edit announcements to their style specifications.

entertaining at home

24

From impromptu backyard barbecues to dinner parties, Americans love to entertain at home. The style is casual, and the focus is on gathering friends and family for a meal or celebration. While formal dining is still a staple for certain business and ceremonial events, the at-home dinner party is less so. The traditional "Sunday dinner" is making a comeback—even if it's not on Sunday. Friends and family share the cooking and gather round the table for a long, leisurely meal. Rigid rules have been replaced by flexibility. Today's successful hosts are more concerned with the needs of their guests than the perfection of their table settings. Whether a seated dinner with candlelight and professional servers or a grab-a-plate-and-serve-yourself cookout, a great party is always grounded in enthusiasm and friendliness.

Whatever your entertaining style, you can't throw a party on good intentions alone. Even the most casual get-together requires careful organization, thoughtful execution, and courteous manners.

THE FIRST STEPS TO A SUCCESSFUL PARTY

Fun as it may be to dream up a scrumptious menu and think about whom you'll invite, practical things must be decided first—when will you hold the party, how many guests you can accommodate, and how much money and time you're prepared to spend. These businesslike basics underscore all other decisions.

Date and Time

The time of your party is up to you, but be conscious of local customs and work schedules. Check with a guest of honor before setting a date, or with a family member

if the party will be a surprise. If you plan to hire help, keep in mind that caterers, waitstaff, and bartenders are usually booked well in advance for holidays as well as graduation and wedding seasons.

The Guest List

All sorts of things might go wrong during the evening, but your party can still be a rousing success with the right guest list. Your goal is to invite guests who are likely to be interesting to one another, even if they don't know each other, and whom you can count on to be sensitive, thoughtful, and entertaining.

Sometimes the occasion itself drives your guest list, such as a business dinner for work associates or a lunch for members of a club. If the event is in someone's honor—a birthday, anniversary, shower, or graduation—the honoree usually helps provide the guest list.

How Many Guests?

Most people can manage cozy dinners for four to six people; entertaining larger numbers depends on your entertaining space. How many people can fit comfortably in your dining room? Is your outdoor space available this time of year? If you have a small apartment and no dining room, can you rearrange furniture to accommodate your guests? You can always start by inviting only a few guests, which will give you an idea if you can accommodate more people at your next party. Your goal is to make sure that your guests can move about easily and that everyone has a comfortable place to sit.

Expandable tables, folding tables, tabletops (placed on top of smaller tables and covered with a tablecloth), and folding chairs can turn dinner for four into dinner for six or eight. There's no rule that says dinner needs to be at a dining room table. Smaller tables placed around a living room can work just as well. At the most casual parties, guests can eat on their laps.

Take stock of your party supplies. Do you have enough plates, glasses, utensils, and table linens for the number of people you want to invite, or are you prepared to purchase, borrow, or rent the necessary items?

Experienced hosts take everything into account, including the weather. Twenty people may be optimal for a buffet in the warm months, when guests can overflow onto a porch or yard. But the same number may be too many to confine inside in the dead of winter.

Budgeting Money and Time

Budgeting is another early planning step, so decide up front how much you can spend on the evening and account for everything. For most party givers, food and beverages are the key ingredients, so be sure your budget gives them priority. It's better to trim your decorations than to skimp on food and drinks. If you're planning a large party, your budget will also determine if you can afford to hire help or rent supplies.

Wise hosts budget their time as carefully as their money. One person, or a couple, can manage a small casual dinner, but extra help may be needed for a larger group. Do you have family members or friends who can help with cooking and service? Would it be a good idea to hire one or several servers, kitchen assistants, or bartenders for the evening? Or is professional soup-to-nuts catering the best way to go? (See "The Catered Party," page 306.)

Cooking and serving are only part of a host's responsibilities. If you're stuck in the kitchen or preoccupied with getting the meal on the table, who will greet your guests, make introductions, and keep conversation going? Hosting a dinner party is a good example of

---

alternatives to dining at home

Hosting at a restaurant or club is often the only way that very busy people can entertain. It enables them to give parties in distant locations, making arrangements by phone and email, or to entertain on a larger scale than is possible in small apartments and condos. It's also a great way to reciprocate those who have hosted you when you don't have the capacity for at-home dinner parties. Considering all the expenses of an at-home party, plus your time, your actual expenditure for dining out may be the same or even less.

The first steps of planning are the same as for a party at home: Decide on the date, the guest list, and how much you want to spend. Then scout for a place if you don't have one in mind; consult with proprietors; settle on the menu, seating arrangements (you may want to book a private room or terrace seating), and type of food service (seated or buffet, with or without bar service); and organize the method of payment, including gratuities. Unless you're familiar with a restaurant or club, ask to sample the cuisine before making a final commitment.

---

multitasking, so decide which tasks you can handle and which require help.

PLANNING A DINNER PARTY

With the day, time, guest list, and budget decided, you're ready to plan exactly how to organize the evening. For many hosts, this is their favorite part of preparation—calling for equal parts of creativity and common sense.

The Predinner or Cocktail Hour

The predinner hour serves as time for your guests to enjoy themselves while you put the finishing touches on dinner: prepping plates or setting up the buffet or family-style dishes. But be sure to spend time greeting and mingling with your guests. Set aside about an hour before you plan to serve dinner to allow your guests ample time to arrive, mingle, get to know each other, or catch up a bit before sitting down together. Typically, this is when to serve cocktails, wine, beer, or other refreshments, as well as hors d'oeuvres. Here are some things to think about when planning your cocktail or predinner hour:

- **Timing:** Have a general idea of how long you'd like your cocktail hour to last based on when you would like to serve dinner and the punctuality of your guests.

  TIP: Create a cocktail hour playlist; you'll know that by XYZ song, you should start clearing away hors d'oeuvres and inviting guests into dinner.

- **Timeline:** Your timeline might look like this:
  - 20 minutes greeting guests
  - 20–30 minutes mingling
  - 10–20 minutes plating dinner or setting up the buffet/family-style dishes

- **What to Eat:** Consider your dinner menu when planning the hors d'oeuvres. For a heavy dinner you may want to go light—mixed nuts, olives, some fruit and cheese with crackers. For a light dinner, heavier hors d'oeuvres may help balance out the menu: chicken skewers, shrimp cocktail, vegetable dumplings, raw vegetables with heavier dips.

- **What to Drink:** It's nice to take your guests' preferences into consideration. Popular options are: a full open bar, a pitcher of a mixed cocktail, beer, wine, or champagne or sparkling wine. Remember to include nonalcoholic options as well: sodas, seltzers, and juices.

  TIP: The more that your cocktail hour can be self-service, the more you'll leave yourself available to greet guests, deal with coats, and make introductions, and to enjoy the cocktail hour yourself.

The Dining Format

There are two basic formats for dinner parties—the seated meal and the buffet—but each allows for a good deal of variation.

Seated dinner with food served at the table. When guests are seated at the table there are three ways to serve the meal:

- **Served.** Servers bring the food on serving dishes or platters and serve each guest each course individually. This is the most formal style, but it isn't practical if you're on your own—you'll need to hire servers or enlist the help of a friend or partner. (See "The Formal Dinner Party," page 314.)

- **Plated.** Food is arranged on plates in the kitchen and then served to each guest, women first. This is an attractive way to present a dinner and suitable for a small number of guests. For a larger group, enlist help so that the food doesn't cool off too quickly.

- **Family style.** This is the least formal style. The host passes platters at the table and each guest serves herself, or the host prepares each plate from platters set on the table, and then the plates are passed to each guest. After service, the food platters are returned to a warming tray on a sideboard or to the kitchen.

Semibuffet, or seated dinner with buffet service. Food and plates are put out on a separate buffet table or tables. Guests serve themselves and then proceed to the table. Drinks, dessert, and sometimes the salad course may be served to the guests at their tables. Semibuffets adapt beautifully for large groups or outdoor parties with seating at patio or picnic tables.

Buffet with casual seating. This is the classic buffet. Everything necessary for the meal—plates, napkins, silverware, food, condiments, and beverages—is set out on a buffet table or tables. Guests serve themselves at the buffet and then sit where they please in the party area. A buffet requires adequate seating and tabletop space so diners will have a place for glasses and cups and saucers. Casual buffets include barbecues, pool parties, and brunches.

Inviting Your Guests

Casual dinners may be arranged at the last minute, but invitations to a dinner party are normally issued a week or two before—three to six weeks if the occasion is formal or the social calendar is crowded. In general, the more formal a dinner, the earlier the invitations are extended. The formality of the event usually dictates the nature of the invitation:

Very formal dinners and cocktail receptions: printed, engraved, or handwritten invitations

Less formal dinners: printed cards, preprinted fill-ins, handwritten notes, emails, phone calls, or in person

Potlucks and BYOB: mailed, emailed, texted, or phoned, but do expect to follow up with a conversation to discuss or confirm your guests' contributions. (See also Chapter 23, "Invitations and Announcements," page 271.)

Determining the Menu

Your menu also depends on the formality or informality of your party, whether food is served at the table or buffet, who will be cooking, the limitations of your kitchen, your guests' tastes, and your budget.

If you're the chef, ask yourself what you do well. A basic rule when cooking for a group is to avoid experimenting. You'll feel more confident preparing foods that you're familiar with, and it's usually easier to adapt recipes you know than to try something totally new. If you're not into cooking at all, you can still create a great meal by buying delicious prepared foods, ordering takeout from a local restaurant or specialty food store, or hiring a caterer.

An at-home dinner party menu might include a starter course, entrée, and dessert, with coffee after. Salad can be served as a starter or accompany or follow the entrée.

A buffet dinner menu may eliminate the starter course but usually features more than one entrée and a variety of side dishes. Buffet-style dessert might be set at a separate table featuring several desserts, including fruit, or a single, spectacular creation such as a tiered cake. Dessert plates, forks, and spoons are put on the dessert table.

A cocktail buffet menu may be just hors d'oeuvres or a hearty spread of foods that can be eaten while guests stand.

Choosing and Serving Wines

Trust your taste buds. If you think a wine tastes good with a certain food, your guests will probably agree. Very good wines need not be expensive or rare. A wine shop with a knowledgeable staff can make recommendations

dietary considerations

Some precautions a host or cook can take without even consulting guests are to avoid cooking with peanuts, peanut oil, and additives like MSG that commonly cause allergic reactions. Another is to steer clear of very hot or heavily spiced dishes unless you know your guests enjoy them. You're not expected to tailor your meal to each guest's preferences, but given the prevalence and range of dietary restrictions, it's a good idea to add a gluten-free or vegan dish to your repertoire.

A conscientious host will ask first-time guests if they have any particular allergies or dietary restrictions. If the host doesn't ask, it's especially important for the guest to inform him of any allergies, medical conditions, or religious prohibitions. (See Chapter 21, "Hosts and Guests," page 249.)

how to uncork champagne

Hold the bottle at a 45-degree angle, pointing it away from yourself and others. Remove the foil and untwist the "pigtail" to remove the metal bail, exposing the cork. Cover the cork with a towel. Hold the cork and twist the bottle. The cork should release with a gentle "pfft," not a "pop."

based on your menu and your budget. Food and wine publications also offer useful suggestions, but try to sample a wine you don't know ahead of time and with the food you plan to serve. Keep a record of wines and brands you particularly like for future reference.

You don't have to serve a different wine with every course, and one wine can be served throughout the meal. The following fundamentals can help with wine selection and service—and eliminate some misconceptions:

Red and white. Generally, white wines are served before red wines, and dry ("sec") wines before sweet.

Traditionally, red wines were served with red meat and white wines with fish or chicken. Today, most people simply go with what they like and what pairs well with the menu.

Uncorking. In the kitchen, uncork the wine about a half hour before serving in order to let it aerate, or "breathe." Taste the wine, checking for "off" smells or a vinegary taste. Champagne is poured as soon as the cork is popped.

Temperature. Generally, white and rosé wines are chilled before serving; red wines are not. But the custom of serving reds at room temperature began back when room temperatures tended to be colder than in modern housing, so a red wine may benefit from slight chilling. Any wine that's too cold or too warm loses its distinctive flavor. Your wine dealer can provide temperature guides, but again, trust your instincts and your taste.

Between pourings, a chilled wine is returned to the fridge or kept in an ice bucket on a side table. For serving, the bottle is usually wrapped in a large dinner napkin or white towel to hold in the chill and prevent drips from condensation.

Decanting. Aged red wines and port develop sediments, so they're decanted—poured into a glass container or carafe—to separate the clear wine from the sediment. To properly decant, store the bottle upright for twenty-four hours; then carefully pour the wine into the decanter until the sediment reaches the neck of the wine bottle. Either stop pouring at this point or pour the rest into the decanter through cheesecloth. Other wines can be poured into carafes to aid aeration or simply because it's an attractive way to serve.

Pouring. At the table, pour the wine before each food course if there's a new wine for that course. This gives the diner a chance to smell and taste the wine on its own. The host pours for women and older guests first, then for men, and fills his or her glass last. At a buffet, however, wine is offered when a guest is seated or set out on the drinks table for guests to serve themselves.

- Wineglasses are filled to the widest point of the glass, approximately halfway. Sparkling wines are poured to the two-thirds level so the drinker can enjoy the bubbles. Filling a wineglass near the rim makes it difficult to savor the aroma, and a full glass is easier to spill.

- Still wines are poured into the center of the glass, but sparkling wines are poured against the inside of the glass (tilt the glass slightly) to preserve the natural carbonation.

- To prevent drips, give the bottle a **slight** twist to end pouring.

Holding the glass. Since white wines are normally chilled, hold a white wine or champagne glass by the stem to prevent the transfer of heat from the hand. The larger, heavier red wineglass can be held by cupping the bowl, but the modern practice is to hold it by the stem to prevent the wine from being warmed further. Another advantage of holding by the stem is that it prevents unattractive finger smudges on the glass. The bowl of a cognac glass is cupped in the hand because cognac benefits from warming.

The shapes of standard wine and liqueur glasses have evolved in order to enhance enjoyment of the aroma, or "bouquet," and to maintain the correct temperature. Whether plain or crystal, transparent glasses give a clear view of the color and body of the contents.

Stemless glassware. Stemless wineglasses are very popular and are now a standard alternative to their stemmed predecessors. They are available in the same shapes as the stemmed version for red, white, and sparkling wines. On the plus side, they are less likely to tip over and they can fit into the dishwasher. On the negative side, they must be cupped in the hand, which will warm a white or sparkling wine, and fingerprints are a given.

CHARDONNAY

RIESLING,
SAUVIGNON BLANC,
PINOT GRIGIO

BORDEAUX,
CABERNET

BURGUNDY,
PINOT NOIR

CHAMPAGNE
(COUPE)

CHAMPAGNE
(FLUTE)

SHERRY,
PORT

CORDIAL

BRANDY

STANDARD GLASSWARE *for white wine, red wine, champagne, sherry or port, cordials, and brandy*

⟦ SETTING THE SCENE ⟧

Another key ingredient for a successful dinner party is ambience—the mood set by the surroundings. As you prepare, think about how you can best organize your home to make your guests comfortable. As host and perhaps chef and server, you have a lot to do, and your physical surroundings should facilitate your every movement.

Your House

A clean and tidy home is the obvious place to start. Even though the party is at night, the exterior should be neat and well lighted. If you live in an apartment, check your hallway for clutter. Inside, have a place for guests' coats, umbrellas, and boots.

Adequate seating is a must. At very casual dinners, some guests may sit on the floor, but not everyone is comfortable that way, so provide as much seating,

Q: *I have a number of friends who rarely or never drink alcohol (several are recovering alcoholics) and others who, like me, enjoy a cocktail or wine with dinner. I always worry about how to make everyone happy when I entertain.*

A: First, be sure to stock your bar with a variety of nonalcoholic beverages: soft drinks, still and sparkling waters, flavored waters, tonic, fruit juices, and iced tea. Offer alternatives with meals. If you serve champagne, you can also chill a bottle of nonalcoholic bubbles: ginger ale, sparkling water, or fruit juice for spritzers.

The goal is not to call special attention to guests who don't drink alcohol. Also be attentive to seating arrangements. A friend in recovery shouldn't have to spend the evening next to a wine aficionado extolling the virtues of every wine served.

◆ Put out plenty of drink coasters and ashtrays if smoking is allowed.

◆ Set drink and buffet tables apart from main gathering points and doorways.

◆ Avoid using strong-scented flowers, aromatic candles, pungent potpourri, or room fresheners.

◆ Adjust room temperatures—slightly lower-than-normal heat settings and higher settings for air-conditioned spaces.

◆ Adjust lighting—bright enough for people to see, but not glaring.

◆ Adjust the music—just loud enough to be distinct.

The Dinner Table

Table setting is discussed in detail in Chapter 6, "Table Manners," page 56. The following ideas apply particularly to a dinner party:

Table linens. Keep tablecloths and place mats uncomplicated. Very frilly or lacy mats, napkins, and table runners, and crocheted tablecloths can snag utensils, glass bases, even guests' watchbands, causing spills. Plastic tablecloths and mats are fine for casual outdoor dining, but they can detract from the overall appearance of a more formal table.

Cloths for dining tables should fall about 12 to 18 inches below the edge of the table. You don't want them so long that they hang in guests' laps or so short that they look skimpy. Cloths for buffet, bar, and serving tables may touch the floor—a good way to keep bottles, ice chests, and other supplies out of sight.

including floor pillows, as you can. If you don't have enough chairs either borrow or rent some or use items like sturdy trunks, low stools, and ottomans that can do double duty as seating and tray tables.

A few more suggestions for setting the scene include the following:

◆ Rearrange furniture and other items if necessary to facilitate conversation and freedom of movement.

Table decorations. Place flowers and other decorations in the center of the table and in low containers, so they don't block guests' views of each other. For the same reason, candelabra are placed with their broad sides facing the ends of the table, and clusters of candlesticks are avoided if they'll interfere with guests' line of sight. Candles should be new, unscented, dripless, and burn higher or lower than the eye level of seated diners. Light candles before guests enter the dining area.

Everything else on the table should serve the cause of dining, so don't clutter place settings with decorative extras. Guests shouldn't have to forage through table favors and other knickknacks to find their plates and utensils.

Buffet tables. Think about traffic flow when you choose the location of a buffet table—you want your guests to move easily through the line to the table or seating area. Protect surfaces such as wood with a tablecloth or use trivets or hot trays under hot dishes.

The placement of dinner plates indicates the starting point of a buffet table, followed by platters, serving dishes, and utensils for each item being served. It's a good idea to label the dishes with what will go in them, either to jog your memory or to aid any helpers.

When serving buffet style, lay out the salad first,

followed by vegetables, starch, and side dishes, and then the main event—the meat, fish, or other protein dish. Put condiments and gravies next to their accompaniments—chutney next to the chicken curry, herb butter next to the rolls—so it's clear what they're intended for. Breads and rolls are placed at the end of the line; otherwise they can become soggy with sauces, meat juices, and dressings.

Offering the salad and side dishes first allows guests

Q: *I'm having a buffet supper for twenty, and some of my guests have never been to my condo. My sister says I should be prepared to show it off, but I'd like to confine the party to my downstairs and backyard.*

A: Except for a housewarming, hosts have no obligation to give house tours, though they may if they wish. A host should make it obvious where guests are and are not to go. Before anyone arrives, you can shut doors to upstairs rooms and turn off your upstairs hall lights. Courteous guests know not to open closed doors or enter unlighted areas. If asked for a tour, you (or perhaps your sister) might take a guest on a quick walk through your downstairs. If you see someone wandering into an area where he isn't wanted, divert his attention with some polite chat and gently usher him back to the party area.

to "compose" a balanced plate. It also avoids the "my eyes are bigger than my stomach syndrome" in which people load their plates with more of the fish or meat dish than they can possibly eat, and thus ensures that the salmon or steak won't go to waste and that there will be enough for all.

Putting utensils at the end of the buffet frees guests from carrying too many items as they serve themselves. You can also provide dinner trays—set with utensils and napkins—at the end of the serving table. For a seated semibuffet, dining tables are set with everything except plates.

Flowers are pretty on buffet tables, if there's room. Arranging buffet food at different heights, while intended to showcase the food, can actually hamper self-service and sometimes put a dish literally beyond a guest's reach.

When serving drinks buffet style, it's usually more convenient to use a separate table. Guests can take their filled plates to wherever they are sitting and return to the drinks table. Expecting guests to juggle a full plate, utensils, and napkin while pouring a beverage is an open invitation to accidents.

Creating a Seating Plan

Be prepared to answer the question "Where should I sit?" *before* your party starts; otherwise, just when you're preparing to serve dinner, you'll have to stop and come up with a seating plan on the spot. Of course, place cards answer the problem completely, but even if you don't use them, have a plan in mind—and on paper if you're hosting a large group.

The goal of a good seating plan is to honor any special guests and pair up other guests so that the conversation will flow. Here's how to make that happen:

- Usually, the host and hostess sit at each end of the table.

- Seat any honored guests at the host's or hostess's right: the man on her right and the woman on his right. Alternatively, if there is only one host or hostess, the honored guest may be seated at the opposite end of the table.

- The spouses of honored guests (or other honored guests if there are no spouses) sit at the host's and hostess's left.

- Don't worry about boy-girl-boy-girl. If you have an uneven number of men and women, simply space them as evenly as possible.

- When there's more than one table, the host sits at one and the hostess (or guest of honor if there's no second host) at the other.

- In general, split up married couples and close friends—they tend just to chat with each other, and the point is to visit with people you might not see all the time. It's fine to seat couples together who are newly dating, engaged, or married.

- If they're not the honored guest, seat any newcomer near the host and hostess, and place someone with similar interests on his or her other side.

- Consider interests and temperament. Pair people who have similar interests. Pair shy types with outgoing types. If two of your guests are on the polar opposite end of any spectrum, try to seat them at opposite ends of the table. You want conversation, not a heated argument.

- Consider special needs. Seat a person who is left-handed on a corner so that his left elbow doesn't bump his dinner partner. A person who's hard of hearing may be more comfortable with her best ear to the conversation or seated next to someone who speaks clearly.

Place Cards

At a formal dinner, place cards are written on folded white or cream card stock. For a less formal party, it's fine to use cards—purchased or made—that complement your table decor or party theme.

When it's formal, use titles and last names: Mr. Smith, Ms. Wang, Judge Stevens. Use first names only if two people have the same last name: Mr. Tucker Smith, Mr. Adam Smith. Among friends, use first names and add a last initial if needed: Caroline P. and Caroline B.

LET THE PARTY BEGIN

The host or hosts should be ready a few minutes ahead of party time to relax and take a last look around. As guests arrive, greet them graciously, take coats, usher guests to the party area, make introductions as necessary, and then offer your guest a drink or direct him to the bar.

If separate groups of guests arrive at the same time, welcome everyone inside first, then make introductions. At a large party couples and cohosts can share greeting responsibilities, but it's practical for a single host to ask one or two good friends to help with introductions and beverages.

Q: *. What should I do with hostess gifts? Do I have to serve gifts of wine or chocolate? And what if a guest brings a bottle of chilled champagne?*

A: You can open a hostess gift on the spot and thank the giver, or set it aside to open at another time, in which case a call of thanks is in order. You do not have to serve wine or any gifts of food unless you wish to. As to the chilled champagne, serve it up to add a festive note; otherwise store it in the fridge until you wish to use it.

Once everyone has arrived, a host should mix and mingle while attending to these essentials:

- Encourage conversation.
- Pass hors d'oeuvres and offer to replenish drinks.
- Pick up empty, abandoned drink glasses.
- Check periodically on bar supplies and napkins.

At least once during the party, take a quick look in the guest bath and tidy or replenish supplies if needed.

Dinner Is Served

When the group is small, the host simply announces that dinner is served. With larger numbers, the host approaches conversation groups and invites them into the dining area. Try to spot a few good friends who will lead the way; most people will then follow.

the etiquette of drink glasses

If you're holding a partly consumed cocktail when dinner is announced, you can take it to the table. Or you can leave your glass on a side table atop a coaster. Just don't take an empty drink glass to the table. Do the same with a wineglass, as your host will have fresh glasses set on the table for dinner wines.

Specialty beers are increasingly popular as an aperitif and are usually served in a pint or pilsner glass. Sometimes a bottle and empty glass are provided, so the guest can pour for himself, but beer and soda are served in cans or bottles only at the most casual affairs.

At the dinner table, don't turn wineglasses upside down to indicate you don't want wine. Instead, simply say, "No, thank you," when wine is offered. Or put your hand over the glass (above, not on, the rim) to signal a server to pass you by. An experienced server will then remove the glass.

When to start eating. The signal for guests to begin is when the host lifts his fork. Some hosts give a welcome toast or say a blessing before the meal. But when you're serving or the group is large, you may want to tell your guests to begin eating before you, so their food won't go cold. It really is fine for guests to start eating before the host if he encourages them to do so.

At a buffet, guests normally begin eating when they sit down. Once everyone is served, it's nice for the host to gather everyone's attention with a few words of welcome, a toast, or a blessing to mark the "official" start of the meal. (See "Toasts and Toasting," page 258, and "Saying a Blessing," page 64.)

During dinner. Hosts keep an ear to the conversation, guiding it if necessary. Don't be panicked by natural lulls; people tend to stop talking when a course is served and they begin to eat. Then the chatter picks up. Be alert to uncomfortable situations, such as when one person is dominating the table talk, or a controversial subject is making some guests uncomfortable. It will be up to you to change the subject or include others in the conversation.

Hosts should also keep an eye on guests' plates and offer second helpings when most have finished the main course. Replenish water and wine glasses as needed, either by passing carafes and pitchers, or, more formally, pouring for your guests.

Ending the meal. It's up to the host to signal the end of the meal by rising and inviting his guests to join him: "Let's have coffee in the living room," or "Let's move our conversation to the living room, where it's cozier."

After Dessert

Coffee and cordials are served either at the table or in the living room. Though coffee traditionally follows a meal, it's fine to serve it with dessert. It isn't obligatory to offer after-dinner drinks, and today's hosts might pass up this finishing touch if guests are driving home.

When the meal is over, hosts aren't expected to

clearing the table

Places are cleared between courses, including the utensils used for that course and empty wineglasses if you'll be serving another wine. Make clearing as efficient as possible, because after you clear, you also need to prep and serve the next course. Designate a place in the kitchen where dirty plates and utensils can be placed, but save washing dishes or loading the dishwasher for later, after guests leave. It goes even faster if two people are clearing, so when you don't have servers, arrange in advance for a friend to help. Clearing isn't difficult, and even children can learn the finer points and help out at the family meal.

- Wait until everyone has finished the course.
- Remove two plates at a time, but don't stack them.
- Remove from the guest's right side. ("RR"— "Remove Right.")
- Remove both the plate and the used utensils for that course, as well as any condiments for the course.
- Before dessert is served, remove all salts, peppers, bread plates and knives, bread baskets, condiments, and any predessert utensils that weren't used. Basically, the decks should be cleared for dessert.
- At the end of the meal, clear the dessert plates and blow out the candles. Finish the rest of the table clearing after your guests leave.

continue providing food, but passing mints, nuts, chocolates, or small fruits with coffee is a nice touch. The after-dinner hour is your reward—a time to relax with your guests and enjoy the pleasant afterglow of your party.

Conversation is the most popular after-dinner activity, but guests may enjoy listening to music, dancing, or playing cards or trivia games or charades. It depends on the mood of the evening, so don't force guests into an activity.

Saying Farewell

All good things must end, and well-mannered guests will know when to depart—approximately forty-five minutes to an hour after dinner or when the host starts to wrap things up. When guests leave, show them to the door and tell them how much you enjoyed their company—a nicety that's a must.

Don't begin cleaning up or washing dishes until your guests have gone (unless someone has seriously overstayed his welcome and more subtle hints have failed).

leftovers, encore

As a guest, do not ask your host for a "to go" bag. It's one thing at a restaurant where you are paying for your meal, but it's tacky when you are being hosted in someone's home. If you contributed a dish to the meal, let the host make the call as to who keeps the leftovers.

friends don't let friends . . .

A host's last duty is to see that guests depart safely and soberly. Do not under any circumstances allow an inebriated guest to drive. If you haven't already, stop serving him alcohol and take away his car keys. Offer a bed or a couch for the night or take on the responsibility of seeing your guest home and safely inside. Calling a cab or asking a friend to take the tipsy person home only makes him someone else's responsibility.

In general, if a guest offers to help you clean up respond with a pleasantly firm, "Thanks, but this is your night out. We're not doing dishes now." The exception might be if guests are close friends or family members and it's customary that you all pitch in when dining at each other's homes.

If guests brought food, you may want to return their serving dishes washed and dried when they leave. If you borrowed items for the party, it's probably best to return them the next day or within a few days.

If you've hired servers or caterers, you must see that they're dismissed with your thanks (and payment and tip if that is the arrangement). Don't delay an employee's departure beyond an agreed-on time. If you want a worker or workers to stay throughout the party, be sure that's clear when you contract for services.

THE CATERED PARTY

Caterers can be lifesavers for busy hosts, and catered meals are often less expensive than people imagine. But finding and hiring just the right caterer requires a considerable investment of time. Firsthand knowledge is best, so if you go to a party where the catering is outstanding, get the caterer's card or make note of the name for future reference. Or ask family and friends for recommendations: Was the food delicious? Did the event go as planned? Was it on budget? Search carefully, meet personally with prospective caterers, and check every detail before signing a contract.

◆ Before calling caterers, establish your budget; the date, time, location, and format of the party; and the approximate number of guests.

◆ Think about what you want the caterer to do—full meal and bar preparation and serving, food preparation only, all the food or just part of the meal. Do you need other staff, such as a valet parker?

◆ Do you want the caterer to supply plates, dinnerware, and glasses? Some also offer furniture rental, table linens, and decorations and flowers.

◆ If you don't have a specific caterer in mind, meet with several and get more than one estimate.

◆ Sample the cuisine and ask to see photos of catered meals to get a sense of the caterer's presentation style.

◆ Discuss the menu in detail and inquire about your options.

- Caterers usually give average per-person estimates, but you can ask for an itemized list that breaks out food, serving personnel, supplies, and equipment costs. Does the estimate include tax and gratuities? How is payment to be made?

- Check references.

- Finally, you should have a comfortable professional relationship with the catering service you hire. The caterer and his or her helpers will be working in your home, and even if they handle everything, you should oversee the work so that it's done to your satisfaction.

LUNCH, BRUNCH, AND OTHER PARTIES AT HOME

While the evening dinner party is particularly suited to today's busy schedules, there are lots of other opportunities for at-home entertaining—lunch, brunch, barbecues, potlucks, cocktail parties, and the one party you can throw for yourself, the housewarming. Whatever the time of day and degree of informality, entertaining good company with good food is hospitality at its best.

Luncheons

The lunch hour can be the perfect time to join friends to catch up or meet colleagues and conduct a little busi-

ness. Luncheons are most often held at restaurants and clubs, but an at-home lunch is a very nice way to host a club or committee meeting, entertain business associates, and honor out-of-town visitors and special guests. Traditional lunch parties, including bridge and bridal luncheons, are usually scheduled on weekends to accommodate guests' work schedules.

Luncheon food is normally lighter than dinner fare: a starter or salad course and an entrée, a salad or soup and sandwich, or a generous luncheon salad plus dessert and coffee. Because many people prefer not to drink alcohol in the middle of the day, it's less common to offer true cocktails, but guests might enjoy a glass of champagne or a light wine before or during the meal. Water, hot or iced tea, fruit drinks, and coffee are the mainstays of luncheon beverages.

Whether a lunch is seated or served buffet style, the etiquette varies little from the basics of dinner parties, only that food and service are often streamlined. The meal begins soon after guests arrive and serving tends to be informal. Hosts have to be attentive to the time constraints of their guests, just as guests shouldn't be tempted to linger.

Breakfast

A breakfast party is a more elaborate version of the everyday morning meal, and often precedes an occasion like a graduation ceremony, a morning wedding, a noontime sporting event, or a business meeting.

The menu is based on the classic eggs-bacon-toast formula. Dishes such as eggs Benedict, omelets, ham and biscuits, French toast, Belgian waffles, and sweet pastries are typical, though providing alternatives such as fresh fruits, oatmeal, or granola for health-conscious guests is also standard. A variety of juices as well as coffee and tea are served; alcoholic drinks are not. Breakfast can be served buffet style in the dining room or kitchen if you have a large enough space.

Brunch

Brunch combines the virtues of a late breakfast and an early lunch. It seems made for leisurely weekend get-togethers. Brunches are a good choice for showers, or for entertaining out-of-town guests on the day after a wedding or graduation.

Typically, brunches begin around 11:00 AM or noon. Even relatively fancy brunches have a casual mood. They're often served buffet style so that guests can mingle. Menus blend traditional breakfast and lunch fare: quiches, creamed chicken on waffles, sausage or ham rolls, frittatas, fruit salads, green salads. Foods tend to be light and feature fresh fruits and vegetables in season.

Bloody Marys, with or without alcohol, and mimosas (champagne and orange juice) are popular, as are lighter wines. Alcohol-free fruit punches go well with brunch food, and be sure to have plenty of nonalcoholic beverages available such as juices, sparkling water, and coffee and tea, iced or hot.

Late Suppers

When people don't have the time or appetite for a meal before a night at the theater, a concert, or a sporting event, a late supper is a good way to draw the evening to its end. When you host a small group of friends, the atmosphere is relaxed and convivial. The supper menu is lighter and less extensive than a full dinner. Choose foods you can prepare in advance and assemble quickly or whip up at the last minute, like omelets. If you include dessert, serve something refreshing, like a sorbet. Quality chocolates and mints or cookies served with coffee can easily substitute for a dessert course. Depending on the lateness of the hour you could serve wine, but guests may prefer water, coffee, or another nonalcoholic beverage. Service tends to be informal—from a buffet or on dinner trays—no matter how simple or elegant the meal.

Picnics and Barbecues

Day or night, picnics and barbecues exemplify the American style of home entertaining. The informal nature of the typical backyard gathering makes it a popular last-minute activity.

Picnic and barbecue menus are virtually limitless. If others bring food, you'll want to coordinate so that you don't wind up with too much of the same thing. (See "Potluck Suppers," right.) Be very conscious of food safety and be careful to keep foods at the correct temperatures.

An etiquette note: Consider neighbors when grilling or barbecuing—especially if you live in close quarters. If outdoor cooking is permitted, check that the cooking area is well ventilated so smoke and odors don't collect in hallways or blow into a neighbor's windows.

a tidy ending for outside occasions

At picnics, tailgate parties, and other events away from home, cleanup is an absolute. Use waste containers available at the site or bring your own. Don't leave any food behind; your leftovers will attract animals. Pick up and dispose of litter, including cigarette butts, drink cans, bottles, and tops. If outdoor cooking is allowed, bring along a fire extinguisher. Be sure that all fires, including grills, are completely out before leaving the site: Douse coals with water and rake ashes for any smoldering embers. Someone must clean up the mess, and the ultimate responsibility falls on the host. Even if you miss the kickoff, do the right thing and leave the area clean and safe for the people who use it next.

Potluck Suppers

Potluck suppers are a fun way for family and friends to share a meal in a casual and inexpensive way. Basically, a potluck (or covered dish) supper is organized by one or more people, and everyone who comes contributes something to the meal.

Organization is important so that the potluck menu will be varied. Usually organizers let participants know how many people are expected and then offer a choice of salads, side dishes, breads, casseroles, and desserts. To assure a balanced spread, the organizers should know what participants plan to bring.

Sometimes the organizers provide an entrée, such as fried chicken or burgers and hot dogs, or a dessert

family gatherings

The following courtesies can help make family gatherings low-stress, fun occasions:

SPREAD THE RESPONSIBILITIES AROUND WHEN POSSIBLE. It's okay to ask family to help out. Better yet, when a guest, offer to help when a family member holds a get-together. Perhaps alternate locations for events or share child-watching duties.

FOLLOW THE HOSTS' LEAD AND ADAPT TO THEIR STYLE OF ENTERTAINING. Your sister may enjoy preparing every dish by herself, while Cousin Lily prefers a potluck and Uncle Lee insists on taking everyone to his favorite restaurant.

AVOID BRINGING FAMILY PROBLEMS TO THE GATHERING. This isn't the time to air grievances. Negative talk about anyone who isn't present will probably get back to them and cause hurt feelings.

ACCEPT ONE ANOTHER'S QUIRKS. Be open-minded about harmless idiosyncrasies—as long as your relative's actions and words aren't hurtful.

INDULGE THE FAMILY STORYTELLERS. Stories of past and present are often the means by which younger generations and new in-laws learn the family's history.

like homemade brownies or ice cream. Those who don't cook can bring packaged items such as buns and chips or paper plates and napkins, coolers and ice, or bags of charcoal. While the organizers may provide drinks, participants usually bring their own alcoholic beverages.

It's a good idea for contributors to label their containers with name and phone number so they can be returned. Share out the leftovers or let each guest take their contributions home. For wine and liquor, the contributor isn't obligated to leave an opened bottle, but do be aware of local open container laws.

][THE COCKTAIL PARTY][

The interest in cocktails (both classic and new) is only one reason cocktail parties have enjoyed a resurgence. Cocktail parties also require less preparation than a dinner party, can be less expensive, have set time limits, and make it possible to entertain a lot of people in a small setting. On the minus side, hosts and guests don't have time for long chats with each other.

Please Come for . . .

Cocktail parties can be large or small and as simple or elaborate as you wish. For a small or last-minute party, it's fine to invite by phone, text, or email. For a larger party, invitations on fill-in cards are the better choice.

A cocktail party invitation typically specifies a set time: "Cocktails from 5:00 to 7:00." If you're planning a cocktail buffet—a cross between a cocktail party and a buffet dinner—your invitation need only state the arrival time: "Cocktail buffet at 6:30."

"Cocktail buffet" tells guests that more than snacks will be provided. Although you needn't set out a soup-to-nuts buffet, guests should have enough food so they won't need to make dinner plans for later.

Should you include an RSVP? It's not an etiquette imperative. Some hosts choose to leave RSVP off the invitation, especially if the party is a big one. For one thing, they could be inundated with phone calls (the usual way to respond to parties of this kind); for another, cocktail buffets don't need the exact guest count normally needed for dinner parties. It's risky, though, and most hosts like to have a reasonably good idea of how many guests to expect. Whether to add an RSVP notation is your decision.

Advice for the Host

When hosting a cocktail party, stock your liquor cabinet with the basics: vodka, Scotch, bourbon, a blended whiskey, gin, rum, white and red wine, and beer. If you know several guests are partial to martinis or Bloody Marys, plan accordingly. Also make sure you have a variety of juices, soft drinks, bottled waters, plenty of ice, coasters, and napkins.

Hors d'oeuvres are the only food served unless you're hosting a cocktail buffet. Any finger food will do as long as it can be eaten with little fuss: crudités, canapés, olives, nuts, cheese, and crackers. At a small party, the hors d'oeuvres are served on a buffet table or passed by the host, but it's also a good idea to have bowls of snacks placed around the room—nuts, chips, olives, and the like.

If you and your spouse or partner are acting not

only as hosts but as bartenders and servers as well, follow your greeting to a guest with an offer to get him a drink. If the choice of beverages is limited, save embarrassment all around by asking, "Will you have a martini, wine, beer, or juice?"—not "What would you like?"

You can also invite your guests to refill their own glasses if they want another drink. Just be sure to have the beverages, a jigger, and bucket of ice in clear view. A self-serve bar will help free up your time to visit and perform other duties.

At a large cocktail party, guests expect to stand for long periods, but do provide enough chairs for those who need to rest. When the guest list is small (say, six to ten), people are more likely to gravitate to chairs and couches, so make sure there are enough seats for everyone present.

Need Hired Help?

If you're planning a cocktail party for more than twenty people, it's wise to hire a bartender. If the guest list is in the forty to fifty range, two bartenders will be needed, with their tables set up in two different places to prevent a crush at the bar.

Instruct the bartender how you want the drinks mixed and tell him to rely on a jigger or other measure. If you let him pour by eye, you may find your liquor supply running out long before you'd planned. (You might also have some unexpectedly boisterous guests on your hands!) Ask your bartender to wrap a napkin around each glass, whether a fresh drink or a refill. Napkins prevent drips and make holding an icy glass more comfortable.

The Art of Mingling

If as a guest you find yourself on the sidelines, don't be embarrassed to introduce yourself to someone. When the person is alone, the introduction is easy (see Chapter 2, "Essential Manners," page 8). More difficult is joining a group conversation. To smooth the way, walk past to see what is being discussed. (Not that you want to eavesdrop, but this is a party, where mixing is desirable.) If the subject is sports, movies, a current news story, or any other impersonal subject, you've found a conversation open to all. Smile and make eye contact with one or two people, and wait for someone to acknowledge your presence. Then listen patiently and wait for a lull before introducing yourself and joining in. If, on the other hand, the subject is personal or about people you don't know, move on.

Juggling Acts

How do you juggle your drink and your plate and shake hands at the same time? Only with great difficulty, so try to find a place to set one of the items down.

Standing close to a table could solve the problem. Some people are poised enough to joke about their dilemma, asking someone to hold their glass while they extend their hand. The important thing is to make the effort to greet another person in a pleasant way.

What to do with toothpicks after you've eaten an hors d'oeuvre? There's usually a small receptacle on or near the food platter for used ones. If not, don't place used items on the buffet table. Instead hold any items (including drink stirrers) in your napkin until you find a wastebasket.

cherries, olives, and swizzle sticks

Go right ahead and eat cocktail garnishes like olives, cherries, or onions—those on cocktail picks are easy to retrieve. Once you've finished your drink use fingers for garnishes in the bottom of a short glass and a spoon for those in a tall glass.

When you drink a cocktail, the only nonedible item you should leave in your glass is the straw; swizzle sticks and tiny paper umbrellas go onto the bar or your bread plate or, at a party, hold them until you find a wastebasket.

"Would You Please Leave Your Shoes at the Door?"

While removing your shoes when entering someone else's home isn't typically a part of American culture, as it is in Japan and elsewhere, politely asking family, friends, and party guests to do so is fine—especially in places with long seasons of inclement weather. Just make sure you have a stash of comfortable slippers, flip-flops, or nonskid slippers or socks for visitors to wear. That way, guests won't feel so uncomfortable about exposing their bare or stocking feet. Be careful, though. If you're throwing a more formal party or you don't know your guests all that well, asking them to remove their shoes would be awkward.

THE ULTRACASUAL PARTY

Some gatherings are so casual they hardly qualify as parties: the after-work get-together at a coworker's apartment or the impromptu invitation for a few neighbors to "drop by this evening." Many of these parties are potlucks, with each guest bringing a dish or dessert.

The invitation and dress may be casual, but it's still important to perform the usual hosting duties. Make sure the party area, kitchen, and bathroom are tidy, and close off any messy rooms. Unless the party is both a potluck and BYOB, make sure you have enough food and beverages for your guests, even if it's takeout pizza, salad, and wine and water. Paper napkins are the sensible choice for very casual parties, as are sturdy biodegradable plates, utensils, and disposable cups. They're not only in keeping with the spirit of the affair but also make cleanup easier. If you're using your own dinnerware and utensils, there's no need to match styles and patterns.

OPEN HOUSE PARTIES

Most open houses—parties where guests can arrive anytime between the hours specified in the invitation—are usually housewarmings or holiday parties. Depending on the degree of informality (open houses can be quite casual), you may send written or printed invitations or commercial fill-ins, or invite people by phone or email. It's a good idea to include an RSVP to get an approximate head count. If it's a large party and a few people haven't responded, there's probably no need to call them for an answer.

Refreshments range from the simple—dips and chips, sandwiches, bowls of nuts or olives, and punch—to elaborate buffets of country hams, hot biscuits, quiches, and bowls of shrimp. Guests generally stay no longer than an hour or hour and a half so that the crowd won't balloon to unmanageable proportions.

HOUSEWARMINGS

If you've recently moved to a new house or renovated your apartment, you might choose to host a house-warming, typically an afternoon open house, a cocktail party, or buffet, for friends and neighbors. Depending on the casualness of the party, you can send written invitations, call your friends, or email them, but it's a good idea to issue the invitation two to three weeks ahead. A housewarming is similar to an open house, and it's fine to add an end time on the invitation. Three to four hours is typical, with guests coming and going throughout. If you're just having a few people over, adding the end time isn't necessary.

Expect to spend a good deal of time giving tours unless you're comfortable letting guests explore on their own. Needless to say, everything—even closets—should be in tip-top shape. At a housewarming it's considered fair game for guests to look anywhere and everywhere, so for everyone's sake make sure personal items—bills, prescriptions, underwear—are stashed away. If you are the tour guide, designate a partner or friend to greet guests at the door.

It's traditional for guests to bring gifts to a house-warming party. If the group is small enough and every guest has brought a present, opening them can be a part of the festivities. If the party is more of an open house, with guests coming and going, either open each gift as it's given or wait until after the party—in which case a thank-you note is in order.

Typical gifts for housewarmings are guest towels, place mats, houseplants, drinking glasses, nice dish-cloths or napkins, garden bulbs and seeds (for the host who enjoys gardening), or a guest book intended as a keepsake of the party. Tickets to local movie theaters or a gift certificate to a local restaurant is also a thoughtful gift.

25
formal dinners and parties

t the highest end of the formality scale are official dinners and balls hosted by or for high-ranking public officials and diplomats. These events are governed by strict protocol, and guests are informed of (and often instructed in) the rules by protocol officers. Those opulent balls familiar to us from the movies—men in tails swirling elegantly gowned women around the floor to the strains of a Strauss waltz—may have gone the way of the dance card, but they are echoed in today's formal dances, whether they're club dances, school formals, corporate events, or charity or debutante balls.

[THE FORMAL DINNER PARTY]

People today tend to regard at-home formal dining as an opportunity to dress up, set a beautiful table, use their very best manners, and enjoy lively conversation over an excellent meal. True formal dining calls for meals served by staff. For most people, this would require hiring servers for the evening. In addition, there are some particular points regarding table setting, service, and seating that characterize the formal dinner. It's fine if you'd like to incorporate some of these elements in your own formal dinner parties. More to the point, this is what you are likely to encounter at a high-level government or diplomatic dinner.

◆ A housekeeper, butler, or other domestic employee opens the door to guests, takes their coats, and shows them to the party area, where they are immediately greeted by the hosts. The hosts greet, make necessary introductions, and mingle during the traditional predinner "cocktail hour," which may be shorter than an hour but rarely longer. The host then invites the guest in to dinner.

- At very formal dinners, a gentleman may be given a small envelope containing a card with the name of his female dinner partner. If that's the case, when it's time for dinner, he escorts his partner to her seat in the dining room.

- Typically, place cards are used for a formal dinner of more than four. Seating is, as far as possible, man-woman. Guests of honor sit to the right of the hostess and host; otherwise, hosts determine the seating order following the table of precedence if government officials or members of the military or diplomatic service are guests.

- If place cards are used, the hostess or host enters the dining room after all the guests. Otherwise the host or hostess leads the way and indicates where guests are to sit.

- Women sit as soon as they find their places; men stand at their places until the hostess is seated or the host signals them to be seated. In the traditional man-woman-man-woman order, each man customarily holds the chair of the woman on his right, his dinner partner, but women today may seat themselves if they wish.

- **The formal table** is laid with a *white* cloth of damask, linen, or lace, which falls about 18 inches

below the edge of the table—long enough to look sumptuous, but not so long as to fall in diners' laps. Damask and linen cloths are laid over a silence cloth—a felt pad or white blanket folded to fit the table; lace cloths are placed directly on the table surface. Matching white napkins are a generous size: approximately 24 inches square. To be truly formal, dining room candles are white.

- **The table setting** is precise and symmetrical—at Buckingham Palace they use rulers—otherwise, the table is set according to the number of courses to be served. (See Chapter 6, "Table Manners," page 56, for a full discussion of table setting.) Center-pieces are in the center, or evenly spaced down the middle of the table, as are candles. Often, chargers, or service plates, are used for the first courses. Salt and pepper are the only condiments placed on the table, preferably one set for each diner. Before guests enter the dining room, water glasses are filled, butter pats are put on individual butter plates, and candles are lit. Bread and condiments are passed by servers.

- **The meal** is either served plated or from platters presented to each guest by servers. Plates and platters are served from the diner's left side. When there is more than one server, one sets the plates with the main item—fish, meat—before each diner, and another server follows, offering vegetables, side dishes, bread, or condiments. When *all* diners have finished with the course, the plates are removed from the diner's right.

- **Wine is served** from the diner's right before each course, and is replenished as needed. The wine-glasses at each place indicate the number of differ-ent wines to be served. Water glasses are refilled throughout the evening. Coffee cups and saucers aren't included in the original place setting, but may be brought if a guest requests coffee or tea with his meal.

- **The salad course** generally follows the main course, but if salad accompanies the entrée, it's served on a separate plate, to the left of the place setting. The salad is usually dressed, either in the kitchen or at a side table, then plated and served.

- **Dessert forks and spoons** may be set on the table with the original place setting positioned horizontally above the plate or brought to the table with the dessert course. (See Chapter 6, "Table Manners," page 56.)

- **The server** may sweep the table between courses by brushing crumbs into a plate, either with a tightly folded napkin or a silent butler held just below the table edge. This is done unobtrusively so that conversation isn't interrupted. The server will add or replace knives, forks, and spoons as needed.

- **Finger bowls** may be brought before dessert. (See "Finger Bowls," page 73.)

- **Coffee and tea** may be served at the table or when the guests retire to another room. The hostess may pour, or the hot coffee can be brought to each guest from the kitchen or served from a serving table. Coffee spoons are placed on the saucer. Since tastes vary, a tray set with a sugar bowl, a bowl with various sugar substitutes, and a creamer is passed to guests. After-dinner cordials and fortified wines like port are served with the coffee course.

- **Leaving the table.** The host or hostess rises to signal the end of the meal.

FORMAL PARTIES

Unlike the grand private parties of old, today's large formal parties and galas are usually hosted by a committee, and many are organized as charity fundraisers. Invitations to private balls and parties call for a handwritten reply; those to public events usually include a response card and require payment. In either case, "elegant" is the watchword and formal attire and manners the centerpiece. Whatever the occasion, it's a chance to be Cinderella and Prince Charming, if only for an evening.

The Party Begins

Once you've arrived, you'll most likely begin the evening with predinner drinks and hors d'oeuvres served from a bar, buffet tables, trays carried by waiters who circulate through the room, or a combination thereof. A guest's concerns at this phase:

The bar. If there's no true bar on the premises, bartenders will serve from a table, mixing drinks or pouring wine or beer. Before ordering, be certain it's your turn; if in doubt, a gracious "You go first" will be well received.

Waiters may be passing through the room with trays serving wine or champagne. Don't make a beeline to a waiter; either wait patiently until the waiter comes your way or go stand in line at the drinks table or bar.

Take a cocktail napkin and keep it wrapped around the base of your glass, and remember to keep the drink in your left hand so that your right one is ready for handshakes. When your glass is empty, look for a sideboard or table where used glasses and plates are deposited; if you can't find one, ask a waiter or the bartender what to do with your glass.

Don't tip the bartender unless there's a cash bar, in which case you will pay for your drinks—an arrangement unlikely at a private party, but more usual at charity events. When there is no cash bar, the gratuities are built into the waitstaff's fees, so leaving money on the table or tray puts the bartenders and waiter in an awkward position.

Passed-tray service. This may be the only food service, or it might be combined with self-service at a buffet table. Try not to take the hors d'oeuvre directly from the tray to your mouth; instead, put it on a plate or napkin before eating it. Also remember not to eat, talk, and drink at the same time. (See "Juggling Acts," page 311.)

A buffet table. When hors d'oeuvres are set on a buffet table, guests pick up plates and help themselves to both finger foods and dishes that require a fork. Take small portions, and don't return for plateful after plateful; at this stage of the party the food should take a backseat to the people around you. For sanitary and aesthetic reasons, use a fresh plate when returning to the buffet for seconds. A waiter will clear your used plate.

Food stations. Food stations are smaller tables set in strategic locations around the room each holding a different kind of food—ethnic specialties, perhaps, or all vegetarian dishes. Try not to frequent only one; other guests may be just as fond of Thai food as you are.

"shall we dance?"

When there's dancing, it's so much more fun when everybody dances—even those who claim two left feet. These days, women don't have to be asked to dance but can take the initiative and do the asking. Tradition says that every man at a private ball should dance with the hostess and the women he sits between at dinner, but he dances the first dance of the evening with his partner or date.

- If the dance floor is crowded, dance in compact steps and keep your arms in.
- If you bump someone, say, "So sorry!"
- Don't correct or criticize your partner on the dance floor.
- Execute any drops, flips, lifts, or turns only when you have plenty of space.

When a man "cuts in" on a couple, he taps the dancing man's shoulder and then takes over as the woman's dance partner. The "double cut" is when gentlemen trade dancing partners. Today, it's not as common as it once was, but if someone wants to cut in, comply graciously.

Dress for a Ball

"Black tie" (tuxedo) is accepted at most balls, even if the invitation says "formal"; only if the invitation specifies "white tie" must a man wear white tie and tails.

For women, dresses are usually long. A ball is also the time to wear your finest jewelry. Pants on women are acceptable only if they are very full and styled to look like a ball gown. With sleeveless or strapless gowns, women may wear long gloves, which they leave on through the beginning of the ball but remove when they begin dancing or eating. (See also Chapter 5, "Image and Attire," page 46, or the chart on page 683.)

Receiving Lines

A receiving line includes the host and hostess at a private ball, the committee heads at a public ball, and honored guests and their escorts. At a large function, this may be the only time a guest is able to say hello to the hosts and thank them for the party.

It's fine for a guest to hold a drink while waiting in the line, but the glass and any food should be disposed of before he or she gets to the first person to be greeted. Women precede their escorts through the line. If there is no one announcing guests, then the guest introduces herself to the first person in the receiving line, shakes hands, and briefly exchanges a few pleasant words. She is then passed along with an introduction to the next person in the line, with whom she also shakes hands and says a few words, and so on down the line.

Midnight Supper or Breakfast

Since most balls begin well after the dinner hour, a late buffet supper (or "breakfast") is often served, beginning after midnight and continuing for an hour or more. Food might consist of a variety of sandwiches, platters of cold meats and assorted vegetables, or eggs with bacon or ham. There may be hot drinks or bowls of iced fruit punch, or champagne.

People may serve themselves whenever they feel like it, and small tables are provided. Guests can sit where they please—in any vacant chairs or with a group making up a table.

When you're ready to leave a formal ball (usually after the supper, though older people often leave before it), find the host and hostess and thank them, just as you would at a smaller party. If there's a guest of honor, you should say good-bye to him or her as well.

AT DEBUTANTE BALLS

The phrase "presenting a debutante to society" has seen its day, but in some parts of the country debutante balls are still popular. Customs vary regarding the age of the debutante, her dress, the number of her escorts, and the rituals of the ball or party.

The most elaborate party is a private ball. Somewhat less elaborate is a small dance; less elaborate still is a tea dance. Often, a dance is given for, or by, the families of several debutantes. Or the dance could be given by an organization that invites a group of girls to participate. Many balls or cotillions of this kind are benefits, handled by a committee representing the sponsoring charity. These balls serve a double purpose, since the parents of the girls invited to participate are sometimes expected to give a substantial donation to the charity in return for the privilege of having their daughters presented.

Whether the party is a ball or dance, the debutante's mother—or grandmother or whoever is giving the party and "presenting" the debutante—stands near the entrance. The debutantes stand next to them (each debutante paired with her mother or other presenter), and they are the only people who formally "receive." On entering, the guests approach the hostesses, who introduce the debutantes to those who don't know the young women being presented.

Each debutante receives guests for about an hour, after which she's free to enjoy the dancing. She usually dances the first dance with her father and the next with the man (or men) she's asked to be her escort(s) for the evening. The debutante goes to supper with her escort(s). She will have invited in advance those who will join her at the table reserved for her group.

The debutante's dress. The debutante traditionally wears a white gown, but the committee or organization will inform the girls about the type and color of dress that's expected, a decision that must be followed. While the young women normally wear the same color gown, they may choose their own style. Usually, long white gloves are worn during the presentation.

Parents' and guests' attire. The mothers of the debutantes wear evening dresses in any color except white or black, while other female guests wear evening dresses in any color other than white. Traditionally, long gloves are worn, unless a woman's dress is long-sleeved. Male guests' attire is black tie, but the escorts and the fathers of the debutantes usually wear white tie.

Flowers and gifts. It's customary for family members and very close friends to send flowers (whether bouquets or baskets) to the home of the debutante at the time of her debut party. The debutante's escort(s) may also send flowers or give her a corsage if one will be worn, but he should ask before doing so. Young women often don't wear flowers on their gowns, but instead pin them to a purse or wear them on the wrist.

Relatives and very close friends of the debutante or her family can also send gifts, though this isn't required. Members of the organizing committee and guests of the family can also send gifts if they wish. The debutante should acknowledge all gifts, including flowers, with a thank-you note. (See also "Debutante Parties and Balls," page 326.)

26
celebrations through life

marking the important steps along life's long and winding road is a meaningful and steadfast tradition. This chapter spans the incredible journey, starting at the very beginning with baby showers for the parents-to-be, birthdays, graduations, anniversaries along the way, and ending with retirement parties, which celebrate years of work and the start of yet another new phase of the journey.

Celebrating these milestones raises many questions—how to plan special events, ways to invite, what to wear. Then there are the perennial concerns about gift giving and thank-yous. This chapter offers the answers, plus some insights into dealing with changes in long-standing traditions. For specific information on invitations and announcements, see Chapter 23, "Invitations and Announcements," page 271, and "Sample Invitations and Announcements," page 685. For a discussion of gift etiquette, see Chapter 28, "Giving and Receiving Gifts," page 349.

[BABY SHOWERS]

It's hard not to make a fuss over a new baby, even before the little bundle of joy is born. That is why we "shower" parents-to-be with presents. Not only will these gifts make their lives easier and provide for the new member of the household, they also help family and friends to feel connected to the big event.

When and Where?

In an effort to beat the clock, showers are usually held four to six weeks before the baby's due date. Parents who receive gifts in advance of the birth also have the advantage of knowing what they'll need to buy or borrow. However, it's also reasonable to hold a shower within the first few weeks after the birth.

Showers may be held at the home of the hostess, a local restaurant, a club, or even at the home of one of the guests. Wherever it's held the location should have enough space to accommodate the guests and any meal or food service, and feel festive and celebratory for welcoming a new baby.

Honorees and Hosts

The mother is the traditional shower honoree, but fathers are often included. When the shower is held after the baby has arrived, the baby is an honoree, too, and the whole new family unit is celebrated.

Generally, close friends (including men), parents, grandparents, cousins, aunts, and sisters- and brothers-in-law of the parents-to-be host and attend showers. And who should *not* host? The parents-to-be shouldn't host a shower for themselves. While it used to be said that the honoree's close relatives also didn't host a shower, in our more mobile society there may not be a friend of the couple who could act as host. In this case a family member certainly may have a shower to welcome the new baby and help the parents with things they'll need as they grow their family.

Invitations

Baby shower invitations can be casual or informal and are often very creative. Invitations can be issued by phone, email, or in person but printed or fill-in invitations are the norm. Send invitations from three to six weeks before the shower.

Gift Information

Gifts are expected except from those who can't attend. While it's okay to include a line such as "It's a boy!" or "The nursery is yellow and apple green" to guide guests, the host shouldn't make specific gift suggestions on the

second or third time around?

Today it isn't unheard-of to give showers the second and even third time a couple has a baby. Because the parents may already have a good share of baby clothes and equipment, consider a theme shower designed to make the parents' lives easier, such as restocking basic items for the new baby, or treats for Mom and Dad.

invitation itself. However, if a guest inquires, it's fine for the host to give suggestions.

Registering for shower gifts at a store or online can be practical and time-saving for the mother-to-be and guests alike. Registry information may be enclosed on a separate piece of paper or card with the invitation or spread by word of mouth. It's not necessary for a guest to choose a gift from the registry. Remember: The choice of a gift is *always up to the giver*.

Thank-Yous

Thank-you notes should be written for shower gifts, even when thanks were expressed in person. It's the hostess's responsibility to provide the mother-to-be

a shower for an adopted child

When the shower is for the parent(s) of an adopted child, it's a good idea for the hostess to include the child's age (and perhaps clothing size) on the invitation to help guests choose appropriate gifts. If the shower is for an older child, choose invitations that don't feature a new baby theme.

birthday parties are not babysitting opportunities

An invitation to a child's birthday party is no different from an invitation to an adult party, and the same rules of courtesy apply. Reply promptly and do not drop off uninvited siblings. It's really rude.

with a list of the names and addresses of the guests. It's not acceptable for the hostess to hand out blank envelopes to shower guests so they can address their own thank-yous. While this is intended to be helpful, it suggests that the honoree sees thanking the givers as something of a chore.

HAPPY BIRTHDAY!

Birthday Parties for Children

Remember "party clothes" and "party manners"? Birthday parties are the "primary school" for learning to plan a party, be a good host and a good guest, give and receive gifts, and say thanks.

Involve your child in the planning. It may be as simple as asking her who she'd like to invite or what kind of cake she'd like to have. As she gets older, involve her in more of the details, such as planning the guest list, activities, and menu. By the time she's eleven or twelve, it's a sure bet she'll be well on her way to being a great hostess.

Who's Invited? The old guideline of inviting the child's age plus one is still a good one. Of course, consider your child's temperament—a shy six may only want to invite one or two friends.

As with any party, keep the basics in mind: the type of party you're planning, the space you have for entertaining, and your budget. Bottom line? Be reasonable and don't overwhelm the birthday boy or girl with too many guests.

Invitations. Though invitations are often issued by phone or in person, send written (fill-in) invitations when you can. Send invitations to the child's home. To avoid hurt feelings, don't distribute invitations at daycare or school, unless you're inviting everyone in your child's group or class. Birthday invitations to children's parties contain the usual invitation information plus start and end times (so parents know when to bring and pick up their children).

Also include your full name and phone number so

parents can contact you if they need to. An RSVP notation is helpful, especially when you need a guest count to plan games and other activities. Add any special information such as bringing bathing suits for a pool party. If the party location isn't familiar to everyone, include directions or a map and a phone number for a site other than your home. If you plan to take the guests to another location during the party, include this information, too. Invitations are addressed to the child and

Q: *My son Ronnie, who's nine, just told me that he "hates" a classmate we've invited to his birthday party. Ronnie says the boy picks fights and is mean to everybody. Now I'm afraid the party will be a disaster. Is there a way to rescind our invitation to this troublemaker?*

A: No. Once given, an invitation cannot be taken back, except when an event must be canceled. Whatever the reason for your son's animosity, you should meet the child before passing judgment. Good adult supervision at the party will head off any possible problems, though you don't want to embarrass your guest by hovering over him. Before the party, talk to your son about his duties as host and encourage him to give the boy a fair chance. Who knows? The "troublemaker" may be a charming party guest.

should always be clear about the nature of the party and who is invited, without any reference to gifts. Invitations for children's parties are sent two to three weeks ahead.

Inviting the Whole Class. Most birthday party guest lists are drawn from the groups your child is involved with: a few from school, the neighborhood, the soccer team, or scout troop. Kids need to be sensitive to others' feelings. Teach them not to make in-person invitations or talk about their party in front of people who aren't being invited. However, when the idea is to invite an entire group—the class, team, or troop—the most important thing is to invite EVERYONE. To exclude one or two—for whatever reason—is not an option. Your child needs to understand that EVERYONE includes children they may dislike, and that they'll need to greet their not-so-favorites as enthusiastically as their best friends.

Gifts. Gifts for children's birthdays should be selected on the basis of the child's age and interests. Young children enjoy receiving games and toys. Older children and teens may be just as excited by money or a gift certificate.

Think about the birthday boy or girl when you consider your gift: Does he like to draw, is she a reader, who's her favorite musician or group, does he or she play sports or have a favorite team? You can give almost anything at a birthday party. As with any gift consider two things in addition to your knowledge of the recipient:

1. **Your budget.** There's no need to buy something more expensive than your budget can handle.

2. **Your relationship to the birthday boy or girl.** How well do you know them? How close is your friendship or family relationship?

As soon as they are old enough to participate, include children in selecting the gift. Children need to see that choosing and giving a gift takes time, thought, and care.

You don't have to give a present if you miss the party. It's not expected. However, if the party is for a cousin or special friend, your child could still give a gift either before the party or at their next get-together. (See also Chapter 28, "Giving and Receiving Gifts," page 349.)

Thank You. Excepting one- or two-year-olds, all kids should be able to accept a gift and say "Thank you." You'll say it for your one- to two-year-old, you'll prompt your three- to six-year-old, if necessary, but a child seven and older should be able to say thanks automatically. And what if your child receives a gift they don't like? For the brutally honest three- to five-year-old, you'll have to be vigilant and nip any comments in the bud—stopping them at "thank you." Before the party, talk to your older children (from six through teens) about how to react to a gift they don't like: Think of one positive thing to say along with thank you! "Thanks for the sweatshirt. I really like this color blue."

Planning Pointers for Parents. Because constant supervision of small children is essential, it's often a good idea to include parents for toddler and pre-schooler parties. Even parties for older children can use an extra hand or two. If the party is off-site, remember that your helper is a guest, too, and you should pay for meals or tickets.

The watchwords for successful children's parties are *simple* and *short*. Simple food, simple decorations, inexpensive party favors, a short duration, and a short guest list will add up to a special experience.

Get some help.

Set reasonable times and time limits.

Avoid overplanning.

Choose age-appropriate entertainment.

Supervise present opening.

Party Favors—or Not? Favors aren't a must, but they are popular at any birthday party. They don't need to be expensive: A goody bag with treats and a prize or two, or something more lasting, like a water bottle, T-shirt, or hat. Most parents agree—extravagant favors are out. Favors can be put at each child's place at the table, or the birthday child can give them out when saying "thank you" and "good-bye" to each guest at the end of the party.

Birthday Parties for Adults

Birthday parties bring out the kid in us all, regardless of our age, and it's a rare party that doesn't include singing "Happy Birthday to You," blowing out the candles on the cake, and opening the presents. Still, beyond these three rituals a birthday party is conducted like any other celebratory gathering, whether it takes the form of a backyard barbecue or a dinner dance. (See Chapter 24, "Entertaining at Home," page 292.)

Invitations. Depending on the formality of the party, invitations may be printed, filled-in, by phone, or by email, and should be made or mailed three to six weeks before the party. The invitation reflects the formality or informality of the party and follows the form of all invitations with the addition of the honoree: "Let's Celebrate Anna's 30th!" or "In honor of Alex's birthday." A note of caution: Hosts should always check before mentioning age. Though people today tend to be less sensitive about their years, it's still a personal issue; good manners dictate asking permission before revealing anyone's age.

Gifts. Almost anything is suitable as a birthday present so long as it's not too personal or too expensive. Homemade gifts reflect the additional gift of your time and talent. Gag gifts have their place, but it's wise to give them only in conjunction with a "real" birthday present. That cheap aluminum walking cane for a friend having his fiftieth birthday won't be quite so funny if every other present he opens is genuinely thoughtful.

COMING-OF-AGE PARTIES

Coming-of-age parties are part of many cultures and are an exciting time for both the celebrant and their friends and families. Some coming-of-age parties reflect cultural traditions and may even have religious overtones, such as bar/bat mitzvahs and quinceañeras. Others like

---

the twelve birthstones

You can "personalize" a gift of jewelry by choosing items that feature the recipient's birthstones. These are the traditional stones for each month:

JANUARY:	Garnet
FEBRUARY:	Amethyst
MARCH:	Aquamarine, Bloodstone, or Jasper
APRIL:	Diamond
MAY:	Emerald
JUNE:	Pearl
JULY:	Ruby
AUGUST:	Sardonyx, Peridot, or Carnelian
SEPTEMBER:	Sapphire
OCTOBER:	Opal
NOVEMBER:	Topaz
DECEMBER:	Turquoise or Lapis Lazuli

---

a Sweet Sixteen may simply be a slightly more special birthday party that recognizes that the celebrant is no longer a child. Debutante balls, depending on the debutante society hosting them, are often about presenting the celebrant to society as an adult, usually around age 18. (For information on Bar and Bat Mitzvahs, see page 339.)

Quinceañera

A coming-of-age tradition that originated in Latin America, a quinceañera (or *quince*) commemorates a girl's

special occasion gifts

When a teen is invited to an event at which presents are customary, such as a birthday party, confirmation, bar or bat mitzvah, graduation, or quinceañera, he or she is expected to arrive with a gift. But when your invitation includes an "and Guest," does your date bring one as well? If your date received her own invitation, then both of you bring presents. You and your date might give a joint present, but since this generally indicates a close relationship between the gift givers, you may want to stick to separate gifts or join with several more friends to purchase a group gift.

However, if your date didn't receive a separate invitation, then he or she isn't expected to bring a gift. You are responsible for purchasing the gift. While the present is assumed to be from both guests, the gift card is signed by the person who received the invitation.

fifteenth birthday. Depending on the practices of the family the event may comprise a religious ceremony, usually a Catholic Mass, followed by a party or a party only. Although it can be an informal gathering of family members and friends, some quinceañera parties are formal dances (black or white tie) with the young honoree wearing an elaborate gown and participating in a variety of traditions.

Invitations. Invitations are issued by the honoree's parents or by the honoree and her parents. For an informal quinceañera a phone call, personal note, or informal card are good invitation choices. But for a formal event invitations may be printed or engraved and might include a "Black tie" or "White tie" notation.

A printed, formal invitation to the religious service would also include a reception card inviting guests to the quinceañera party afterward. Since the invitation itself is to a religious service, it does not include an RSVP, but the reception card does.

Gifts. It's customary to take gifts to a quinceañera party, but presents aren't opened at a formal ball. Religious items such as rosaries or crosses are appropriate and traditional; monetary gifts and personal items for teenage girls are also popular. The young honoree must send written thank-you notes to all friends and family who gave her a gift.

Debutante Parties and Balls

The purpose of debutante parties of old was to introduce wealthy or upper-class young women of marriageable age to suitable young men, with the aim of making a match. Thus a young woman made her debut, or first foray, into adult society. Balls and parties were arranged by the debutante's family, and, in large cities, the number of debutantes and balls and accompanying parties and teas created a debutante season.

Today's debutante balls are hosted by a debutante society or a committee, although an individual family or a group of families might throw a private ball. The customs vary from community to community. For some balls, a committee, usually composed of former debutantes and influential community members, issues invitations to young women who are recommended by them. Others are more open to anyone who would like to participate. In either case her parents pay an entrance fee or subscription, or sponsor a table, which, in some cases, can be a fairly hefty sum. Often the ball doubles as an event to raise money for a charity.

Participants in debutante or cotillion societies attend lessons to learn basic social and dancing skills, which culminate in an annual ball. The debutante ball is reserved for young men and women approximately eighteen years old.

Typically a young woman wears a long, white formal gown, white shoes, and elbow-length white satin or kid gloves. She is accompanied by her father and one or two male escorts, often a brother, cousin, or friend. Other friends and family members, such as grandparents, aunts, and uncles, may also be included in the debutante's party. The ball opens with the presentation of the debutantes. Each young woman is escorted to a stage or dais by her father and is presented to those in attendance when the master of ceremonies announces her name and the name of her parents or sponsor. She then is escorted by her date(s) for an evening of dinner and dancing.

Invitations. Formal invitations are issued by the sponsoring society or committee, often months in advance. Then, it is the responsibility of the young woman to invite her escorts, which can be done informally. Invitations to a private ball are also formal and sent two to three months in advance of the debut. Response cards are the norm, and the debutante (or her parents) enters the name(s) of her escorts and any others in her party.

Gifts. Traditionally, gifts are personal or something a young woman will keep for a lifetime. Her parents might give her a special piece of jewelry that she might wear the night of the ball, such as a necklace, bracelet, or earrings. While gifts for the debutante are not obligatory, invited friends and relatives might give gifts such as an evening purse, elegant shawl or scarf, silver picture frame, or decorative items for her room.

PROMS

Winter balls, homecoming, and junior and senior proms are often the first formal social events at which teens are the stars.

While each generation will party to its own themes, the guidelines that follow will almost guarantee an experience that will be remembered with pride and pleasure.

High School Proms

To be successful, prom nights require more planning and preparation than the usual social events a teen attends. The courteous promgoer:

Asks early. Give your date plenty of advance notice—often six weeks or more.

Thinks about the budget. Proms and the associated activities can be costly, even when dates share expenses. Be clear with each other about who will pay for what. Think creatively, and you and your date can cut corners but still have a special time. A corsage of fresh gardenias is lovely and less expensive than orchids. Dinner at a midrange restaurant can be as much fun as dining at an expensive one. An at-home gathering of

corsages and boutonnieres

The tradition of giving corsages and boutonnieres to prom dates is still alive and well at many schools. Before ordering a corsage, it's a good idea for a boy to check with his date about the color of her dress and ask if she prefers a corsage or wristlet, which is worn as a bracelet. With this information, a florist can recommend an attractive choice. When you present a corsage, your date will decide how to wear it and pin it on. The traditional corsage is attached at the shoulder (with the blooms facing upward) or to an evening purse.

A boutonniere is a single flower—usually a rose or carnation—given by a girl to her date. The boutonniere is pinned to the left lapel (so it doesn't get crushed when dancing) of his jacket where the buttonhole would be. The girl may pin it on or let her date do it.

chatting with parents. At the party, be sure to dance with your date, and don't abandon him while you go off with friends. Introduce your date to anyone he or she doesn't know.

Thanks everyone who helped with the prom. Creating a successful prom is no easy task, so express your appreciation to classmates, school officials, parents, chaperones, and others who made the evening memorable.

Plans after-party activities carefully. Although some schools plan after-prom events, teens often prefer to hold after-dance parties, especially all-nighters, at a classmate's home with parents and chaperones present. Prom night is not an excuse for alcohol or drug use, pranks, or vandalism—any behavior that can cause harm or damage reputations.

GRADUATION

Graduation marks the end of years of work, the meeting of goals, and a move to the next step along life's journey, and the celebration recognizes it all.

Invitations

Because seating at most graduations is limited, invitations are generally sent to the graduate's closest relatives, and even then families may have to choose who will be asked.

Printed invitations to high school and college graduations are usually provided by the school and are formal in appearance and wording. Since the invitation is issued in the name of the graduating class or the

classmates and their parents for snacks, supper, and photos is popular—and a money-saver.

Arranges for rental vehicles well in advance. Study the details of the rental agreement and make reservations early because limousines and vans may be in short supply around prom time. (Be respectful of the limo driver and the vehicle, and be prepared to tip at the end of the big evening. See Chapter 13, "Tipping," page 165.)

Respects his or her date. Courtesy means a lot on a big night, so arrive on time or be ready when your date is at the door. Plan to spend a few extra minutes school, each student may be provided with social cards printed with his or her name. The student may substitute his own printed cards or write his name on plain social cards (available from stationers, paper suppliers, and printers). A card is included with each invitation so guests know who is inviting them.

Families or friends may also want to host a party for the graduate after the official ceremony—either on the day or sometime later. These invitations can be casual, informal, or formal depending on the occasion, and should include the honoree's name.

Announcements

Given the limitations on invitations to high school and college graduations, families may want to send announcement cards informing relatives and friends of the new graduate's accomplishment. Announcements carry no obligation to send gifts, but some people may want to give one to the graduate. It's fine to have your own, more creative announcement printed through a stationer. Young graduates are sure to announce the news on their Web or social network page.

Some institutions provide printed formal-style announcements, and the graduate's name is written in by hand. If a college, university, or graduate school announcement doesn't specify the degree earned, note it following the graduate's name: "Deborah Cushman, M.D."; "Joshua Beane, Ph.D." Otherwise, social titles are used.

Printed announcements aren't usually sent for middle school or eighth-grade graduations, though you can write personal notes or an email to inform family and good friends.

Gifts

It's always nice to choose a gift that reflects the significance of the graduation. Parents traditionally give something of special value and personal meaning. Other relatives and friends might choose gifts that welcome the graduate to the adult or professional world, such as monogrammed stationery and address books, fine pen and pencil sets, leather-bound books, picture frames, framed art or photography, and luggage. Gift certificates and money gifts are also appropriate, especially if the giver isn't sure about the graduate's tastes and interests. Graduates should write personal thank-you notes for every gift and also send notes to anyone who entertains or does special favors for them.

Graduation Parties

Graduation represents the completion of many people's efforts, and proud parents, family, and friends often want to honor the graduate. Following morning or afternoon ceremonies, a brunch, luncheon, or supper party can be held at home or a local restaurant or club. While there's no explicit time limit on when parties can be given, it's sensible to entertain within a few weeks of the graduation. It's not appropriate to hold a graduation party before the guest of honor has actually graduated.

High School Graduation Night Parties

Teens naturally want to celebrate their new diplomas with their friends, but the dangers of graduation night are well known. A smart option is to hold a party at a parent's home, provide plenty of good food, soft drinks, and entertainment, and let the grads party safely but in their own way.

Planning a graduation night party requires that parents and teens work together so that everyone's expectations are crystal clear. Parents who host a party in their home should have other responsible adult chaperones in attendance. Since the noise may continue into the early morning, let neighbors know about the party. Inform local law enforcement, who are often out in force on graduation and prom nights, that there will be a party at your home. Host parents have a right to know who is invited, so they can be on the lookout for gate-crashers, and pay close attention to younger teens who may be brought as dates.

Don't serve alcohol (including beer), and watch for party guests who attempt to drink or use drugs. Never allow a teen who has been drinking or using drugs to drive. Some parents make the surrender of car keys a condition of attending an all-night graduation bash.

A number of local and national organizations, composed mostly of parents, now provide excellent ideas and advice for safe graduation night activities. Try an Internet search or check with your school's guidance or principal's office for suggestions.

ANNIVERSARY PARTIES

Parties are usually held only for milestone anniversaries: the first, tenth, fifteenth, twenty-fifth, fiftieth, and seventy-fifth. In other years, the couple might share a romantic dinner for two, a weekend "vacation" at a fine local hotel, or a small, informal party at home with friends and family. The planning of big anniversary parties is fairly straightforward: a cocktail party, buffet, dinner dance—almost any kind of party is appropriate. If the celebration will be large, get an early start on planning. For popular venues and when family members must travel, that may mean starting a year in advance.

Traditional Elements

Some elements can give an anniversary party a special touch:

Decor. Pictures of the couple, whether displayed in frames, blown up on posters, or as a slideshow, have become an almost essential addition to the decor, documenting the couple's life together and stirring memories for family and friends. Family photo albums can also be displayed.

Music. Background music, including songs from

the era when the couple was married, can be provided by a piano player, a DJ, or a family member who's put together a playlist.

Guest book. A guest register that allows space for comments makes a nice keepsake for the couple.

Invitations

The form of the invitation depends on the nature of the event, but most people mail fill-in or printed invitations. The wedding and anniversary years are sometimes included at the top of the invitation. Formal invitations to twenty-fifth anniversaries are often bordered in silver, or gold for fiftieth anniversaries. The celebrating couple is listed either as the hosts or as the honorees. "No Gifts, Please" may be added at the bottom of the invitation, if that's the couple's wish. (For more on "No Gifts, Please," see page 359.)

Anniversary Gifts

Today, emphasis is placed on gifts that are sourced ethically and sustainably, which is why ivory is no longer on the list. You can use the traditional gifts as a guide but make choices in keeping with your values. Animal- and sea-themed gifts, which replace ivory and coral, offer endless options. From a small carving of an elephant or tropical fish made from a sustainable material to a safari in Africa or a dive on the Great Barrier Reef, the only limit to the possibilities is your imagination.

Traditional and Modern Anniversary Gifts

1. Paper or plastics
2. Calico or cotton
3. Leather or faux leather
4. Silk or synthetic material
5. Wood
6. Iron
7. Copper or wool
8. Electrical appliances
9. Pottery
10. Tin or aluminum
11. Steel
12. Linen (table, bed, or the like)
13. Lace
14. Animal themed; gold jewelry
15. Crystal or glass
20. China
25. Silver
30. Pearls
35. Jade or sea-themed
40. Ruby
45. Sapphire
50. Gold
55. Emerald
60. Diamond
70. Diamond
75. Diamond

restaurant dinners: who pays?

Small parties celebrating a birthday, anniversary, or graduation are often held at a restaurant. Who pays the tab depends on whether the dinner is being 1) hosted by a member of the honoree's immediate family or 2) organized by a friend or group. The issue of who's paying should be clear up front and settled well before the event.

- **The person who does the inviting does the paying.** The hosts listed on an invitation—a wife hosting a birthday dinner for her husband or children hosting an anniversary dinner for their parents—pay for everyone invited, whether the event is at home, a club, or a restaurant. A host cannot ask a guest to pay for his or her meal.

- **A coordinator is not a host.** When a friend organizes a group lunch or dinner to treat a mutual friend, she lets it be known from the outset that everyone will pay their own way and chip in for the honoree. Invitations are usually phoned or emailed with the details: "Several of us are getting together at The Black Sheep to celebrate Jodie's birthday. Hope you can join us. Dinner is about $30 apiece, and we'll all treat Jodie."

- **When it's an event.** If coworkers organize a celebratory dinner for someone who's retiring and the tab isn't being picked up by the company, the organizers should state up front what the probable per-person cost will be. This gives invitees the option up front of participating or not.

Reaffirming Your Marriage Vows

Couples don't have to wait for a milestone anniversary to reaffirm their wedding vows—any time that is meaningful to the couple is the right time. Some couples might have gotten married on a shoestring and now want a grand celebration, or have had a civil ceremony and want to add a spiritual component to their vows.

The ceremonies are often personalized with vows written by the couple. The couple can host the ceremony themselves, or their children could play hosts. The guest list can be confined to close friends and family or include long-lost friends and new acquaintances. As with other anniversary parties, the couple may have "No Gifts, Please" printed on the invitations, if they choose.

Afterward, the reception can take any form, from a quiet family dinner to a gala affair with a re-creation of the couple's original wedding cake, a round of toasts, and dancing.

[CELEBRATING A RETIREMENT]

When a retirement party is thrown by a company, parties can range from a group lunch at a nice restaurant to a lavish affair complete with speeches, skits, or even a roast. The nature of the party has to do with the rank of the retiree and the style of the company. Always include the retiree's spouse or partner, and any adult children who can attend.

A retirement party may also be given by family and friends, instead of or in addition to a company party. It's generally a good idea to invite a few of the retiree's close work mates. Because they share a work history with the retiree, they'll be able to speak of specific accomplishments in any speeches and toasts. (See also Chapter 21, "Hosts and Guests," page 249.)

For someone whose work has spanned many years and different organizations, a large celebration complete with many of the retiree's current and former associates can be especially meaningful. Plans can be as grand as the organizers envision. In a typical scenario, a group of the retiree's colleagues determine the guest list, choose the site for the party, and arrange for catering if necessary. Guests who toast or speak about the honoree do so during a specified period, and at a company-sponsored party the employer presents the honoree with a gift. Individual gifts are rarely given, but guests bring cards, either singly or collectively.

27

ceremonies and religious services

As a child grows and matures, there are a few special occasions that commemorate his religious growth and maturity. Although parties aren't obligatory, some kind of celebration is customary and friends are usually invited. If the ceremony is conducted in a faith other than your own, you're not expected to do anything that is contrary to your own beliefs. At the same time, you'll want to follow along respectfully and participate in other aspects of the service, such as standing with the congregation.

[BIRTH CEREMONIES]

The earliest ceremonies provide an opportunity to welcome a new baby into the world and introduce her to the faith community. Invitations to any religious ceremonies for infants—including Christian christenings and baptisms, the Jewish Brit Milah or bris, the Hindu rice eating ceremony, and the Muslim *akikah*—are usually issued by phone, in person, or by personal note.

Christian Ceremonies for Infants and Young Children

Different Christian denominations have different ceremonies for baptisms and christenings. The words are used interchangeably here, but there is a difference. Both of these Christian sacraments use water in the ritual, but a baptism admits the individual into Christian life, whereas a christening is a baptism in which the person is named. While most churches simply sprinkle or pour a little water on the child's forehead, Baptist, Seventh-Day Adventist, and Eastern Orthodox churches practice total immersion.

Because of busy church schedules and, in some churches, the requirement of preparation classes, parents who wish their infant to be baptized need to make arrangements well before the expected birth date. Godparents will need to be selected and asked, a custom in many Christian denominations and a requirement in some. While there is no age requirement for baptism and many children are baptized when they are toddlers or young children, the christening, which is a naming ceremony, occurs when the baby is very young. (See "About Godparents," page 336.)

The child's clothes. Traditionally, infant christening or baptismal gowns are worn by both boys and girls, with white the usual color. The baby's gown is provided by the parents, not the godparents. In some families the dress is an heirloom, passed on to each new baby, or a dress handmade by the mother or other relative. However, it isn't necessary to go to the expense of buying a traditional christening dress if you don't have a family heirloom; any simple white dress will do.

Older children who are being baptized dress nicely, as for church, but don't have to wear white or other special clothing. The exception is when church custom calls for white robes, most often when the baptism is by total immersion.

The church ceremony. In most Protestant churches, baptisms are held during the regular church service or directly afterward. In many Catholic churches, a special baptismal ceremony is arranged, either for one baby or several. The minister or priest will explain to parents how the ceremony will be conducted.

No fee is ever required for baptism, which is a church sacrament. However, a donation commensurate with the elaborateness of the christening is given to the officiant after the ceremony (put the money or check in an envelope). When the officiant is a close friend of the family, a personal gift is often given as thanks—a desk set, an article of clothing, or other appropriate item.

The christening party. Receptions, which can range from the simple to the grand according to the family's tradition, are often held, but aren't required. An at-home gathering for close friends and family enables the parents to relax and enjoy their guests as the baby naps. Often, christening cake—an elaborately iced white cake—and champagne or punch is served. Eating the cake symbolizes partaking of the baby's hospitality, and toasts are made to her health and prosperity.

Gifts. If the christening follows within a few weeks of the child's birth, relatives and close friends who've already welcomed the baby with a gift aren't expected to bring a second gift to the party. When gifts *are* given, they often have religious overtones, although any age-appropriate gift is fine for an older child. Typical christening gifts include a keepsake Bible, a cross for a necklace or bracelet, or a picture frame, perhaps engraved with the date of the celebration.

Jewish Ceremonies for Newborns

Rituals for Jewish infants include the circumcision of boys, naming ceremonies (usually for girls), and, in traditional congregations, redemption of the firstborn.

Brit Milah

A healthy male child is initiated into the Jewish community on the eighth day after birth through the covenant of circumcision, known as Brit Milah (covenant of circumcision) in Hebrew and bris (covenant) in Yiddish. If the parents choose to have the bris performed before the child comes home from the hospital, they should check the hospital's facilities and policies regarding the use of a room for the bris, whether or not refreshments may be served, and the number of guests permitted.

about godparents

Godparents should be either family members or very close friends. Because the obligation of godparents is traditionally a spiritual one (at one time, their role was to see that the child was given religious training and confirmed at the proper time), godparents are usually of the same faith as the parents, and at least one godparent of a Catholic child must be Catholic. Although only one godparent is actually required, a female and male are usually chosen, though not necessarily a couple.

Beyond spiritual obligations, a godparent is expected to take a special interest in the child, much as a relative would. He remembers his godchild with a gift on birthdays and at Christmas until the child is grown. However, if the godparents have lost contact with the child and his or her parents, they need not continue to give presents. Nor are godparents obligated to adopt or give financial help to godchildren who lose their parent(s), contrary to what some people think.

A godparent always gives a christening gift to his godchild—as nice a present as he can afford. The typical gift is an engraved silver cup, mug, or bowl with an inscription: "Beau Burns/ March 29, 2018/from his godfather/Don Newberry." Other popular presents are a silver fork and spoon, a government bond, or the start of a small trust fund to which the godparent makes yearly payments until the child reaches age eighteen.

Relatives and close friends are invited to the bris by telephone since the time between birth and the ceremony is short. When the bris is held in a synagogue, family members and guests dress as they would for a service; tradition requires that all men wear yarmulkes or hats, but the specific rules of the synagogue, be it Orthodox, Conservative, or Reform, determine whether women should wear head coverings. Non-Jewish female guests might check with a member of the baby's family or telephone the synagogue to find out if head coverings are required. If the bris is held at home, men wear hats and sometimes women wear head coverings.

Gifts. In general, guests are expected to bring a gift for the baby. Either a gift of money or a lasting memento of the occasion (say, an engraved silver picture frame, a comb and brush, or a fork and spoon) is usually given.

Naming Ceremonies

Girls are named in the synagogue on the first Sabbath that falls closest to thirty days after birth, when the father is called up to the Torah. The naming ceremony is the *brit bat* (the covenant of the daughter) or the *brit hayyim* (the covenant of life). The mother may be present with the child. In some Reform congregations, boys are also named in the synagogue (in addition to being named at the bris); both parents are present, and a special blessing is pronounced by the rabbi. Friends and relatives may be invited to attend the religious service during which the baby is named. There may be a reception following the service.

Gifts. Invited guests usually give a small gift to the child—not necessarily with religious overtones, but simply any gift that's commemorative or appropriate for a baby.

Redemption of the Firstborn

The Orthodox and Conservative Jewish ceremony of redemption of the firstborn, the *pidyon haben*, takes place only if the firstborn is a boy and may be performed when the baby is thirty-one days old (unless that day is the Sabbath or a holiday). The occasion consists of a brief ceremony and a celebration, generally held in the home. Informal notes of invitation to a redemption ceremony are sent about ten days beforehand to close friends and relatives.

Gifts. Because the *pidyon haben* occurs so soon after the bris, an additional gift isn't necessary.

Islamic Birth Ceremony

Some Muslims practice an *akikah,* or birth ceremony. The form of the ceremony varies greatly but it is always a welcome to a newborn infant. Men and women usually sit in different parts of the room.

Clothes. While men generally dress in a shirt and slacks, women should wear a dress or a skirt and blouse and a head covering. Arms should be covered, and hems should reach below the knees. Neither visiting men nor women should wear visible crosses, Stars of David, or jewelry that depicts signs of the zodiac or the faces or heads of people or animals.

Gifts. Guests bring gifts to the ceremony, which is generally held in the home of the parents or in a general purpose room in the mosque. It's a good idea to ask family members for gift suggestions.

Other Birth Celebrations

Those who have friends from other cultures and other faiths should never hesitate to ask them about the best ways to celebrate their new baby. What's important is that friends participate in welcoming the child, whether they attend a religious service or not.

COMING-OF-AGE CEREMONIES

There are a number of big events that mark the passage from childhood to young adulthood. In order to enjoy and appreciate these special occasions, teens need to be prepared for what will happen and what will be expected of them.

First Communion

First Communion for a Catholic child takes place at around age seven. It is the first occasion on which he or she actually receives communion—an important event in the child's religious life. The child attends a course of instruction to learn both the meaning and the ritual of communion, and class members sometimes receive their first communion together. Although some families celebrate the occasion with elaborate festivities, most take into account the youth of the participants and restrict the party to relatives and perhaps a few close friends.

For Protestant children, their first communion takes place at an older age, usually between eleven and fourteen, depending on the denomination. In many Protestant churches, the children take part in communion along with their families without any ceremony or fanfare.

Clothes. At their first communion service, Catholic girls traditionally wear white dresses, and sometimes veils and headpieces. The boys wear dark suits, white shirts, and ties. In some parishes, children simply dress in their Sunday best.

Gifts. In Catholic congregations, immediate family members give meaningful gifts of a lasting nature—a personalized Bible, for example, or a religious medal. A guest invited to either a Catholic or Protestant communion reception or party brings a gift—either one that's commemorative or that has religious significance, such as a pendant with a cross.

Christian Confirmation

Confirmation—the moment when a young person confirms the vows that were made for him or her by parents and godparents at the time of baptism—is a religious occasion, not a social one. Because it is a thoughtful and serious event, it is celebrated with a measure of restraint.

Both Catholic and Protestant children are generally confirmed at adolescence, approximately between the ages of twelve and fifteen. Some Protestant confirmations may also include baptism and/or first communion. If no childhood confirmation occurs, a person can be confirmed at any age; there is also a special confirmation ceremony for those who change their faith.

Catholic candidates for confirmation choose an adult sponsor, a person they consider a spiritual mentor, or person who is strong in their faith. Sponsors should be asked well in advance of the ceremony date either in person, by phone, or by note.

Protestant confirmation is normally part of Sunday services. In the Catholic church, the confirmation ceremony is held separately from the regular Mass and attended by family and close friends. In both traditions, services may be followed by church receptions attended by family, sponsors, friends, and church officials and then luncheons at the home of the parents or relatives or at a restaurant. After-parties are usually restrained in tone.

Clothes. At the service, Catholic girls and boys often wear red robes to signify the fire of the Holy Spirit; the most common alternatives are white dresses for girls and jackets and ties for boys. Some Protestant ministers request that the girls wear white, but most only ask that they wear simple, modest clothes in quiet colors and that boys wear shirts and slacks (with or without a jacket and tie).

Invitations. First communion for Catholic children and confirmation services in the Catholic and Protestant traditions may be followed by gatherings to celebrate these major events in a young person's life. The guest list is usually limited to family members and close friends, so invitations are commonly issued by phone, in person, or by a personal note from a parent. A printed informal invitation is an option for larger gatherings.

Gifts. While gifts aren't expected, those that are given are usually of a religious nature—a Bible imprinted with the child's name, a prayer book, a gold or silver cross, a medal, or a charm of a religious nature. It is customary for a sponsor to give a gift to the child he or she sponsors.

Bar Mitzvah

The coming-of-age ceremony for male Jewish adolescents is the bar mitzvah ("son of the commandment"), which celebrates his acceptance as an adult member of his congregation. In the Orthodox and Conservative branches and some Reform congregations, it takes place on the first Sabbath (Saturday) after the boy becomes thirteen and has completed a period of religious instruction.

Bat Mitzvah

In some Conservative and Reform congregations the bat mitzvah, the corresponding ceremony to the bar mitzvah for girls of twelve or thirteen, is a tradition that began in the twentieth century. *Bat mitzvah* means "daughter of the commandment." The ceremony closely resembles the bar mitzvah ceremony for boys, with girls reading from the Torah, leading other parts of the service, and delivering a speech to the congregation on the importance of attaining religious adulthood. Like a bar mitzvah, a bat mitzvah is part of a larger service and is almost always on a Saturday.

The Celebration. The bar mitzvah or bat mitzvah is one of the most important events in a young Jewish person's life, and the family generally makes every effort to make it as wonderful an occasion as they can. The religious ceremony, which takes place on Saturday morning in the synagogue, may be followed immediately by a gathering in the synagogue's social rooms. This reception is open to any member of the congregation who wishes to offer congratulations.

The party—luncheon, dinner, or reception—that follows later in the day usually includes all the close friends of the parents as well as friends and classmates of the boy or girl. Only those who receive invitations may attend.

The reception itself is just like any other. Dinners and luncheons may be sit-down or buffet, and the party may be held at home or in a club, hotel, or restaurant. There may or may not be a band, but if many young people are invited, they will enjoy dancing after the meal is over.

Dress. For the ceremony, guests wear the clothes that they ordinarily choose for a religious service. And if the party is a luncheon, they go directly to it without changing. If the celebration is later in the day, guests may change into clothes more appropriate for an evening party. If the affair is formal or black tie, this should be specified on the invitation. Otherwise the women wear cocktail dresses or long skirts and the men wear dark suits.

Guests. Guests should follow the practice of the synagogue during the service, with men wearing a yarmulke on their heads for all but some Reform congregations. Yarmulkes are available outside the sanctuary. Some Conservative synagogues also require that women wear a hat or other form of head covering. When a *tallit*, or prayer shawl, is available at the entrance to the sanctuary, it is only for Jewish people. Non-Jewish

Q: *My son received dozens of presents for his recent bar mitzvah, but he's so busy with school that he can't get his thank-you notes written. Since his father and I gave the party, would it be all right for me to write some of the notes?*

A: You gave the party, but your son received the gifts. Writing thank-yous is his responsibility, and gift givers will rightly feel slighted to receive notes from anyone but him. If your son seems overwhelmed by the sheer number of notes, have him write just one or two every day, perhaps before he begins his homework. You might help by seeing that he has the necessary addresses, stationery, and stamps. Just don't let him fall back on thanking people by phone or email. Appeal to his conscience: How would he feel if he devoted time and money to choosing just the right gift for a special occasion and never got a thank-you in return?

people should neither pick up a *tallit*, nor wear conspicuous religious symbols of other faiths, out of courtesy for the members of the host congregation.

Invitations. Members of the young person's congregation may be invited to a reception at the site immediately after the service. The invitation for this reception is issued at the service by the rabbi.

Traditionally, a by-invitation social reception or party follows later in the day, with the guest list including family, friends, and often the classmates of the honoree. Invitations to these parties reflect the formality or informality of the occasion. Invitations by phone or personal note are fine for informal luncheons or dinners. Printed invitations are sent for a large or more formal occasion, and RSVPs or reply cards are recommended. Invitations may be sent as early as a month to six weeks before the party.

Gifts. Everyone invited to a bar mitzvah or a bat mitzvah is expected to send, or bring, a gift. Any of the following gifts are acceptable: prayer book, religious charm or pendant such as a Star of David or the *chai* symbol, a gift of money, jewelry, a fine book, or a pen and pencil set. Select your gift based on your closeness to the young person. From peers, gift certificates for music or clothing are popular. Thank-you notes are expected for all gifts.

Jewish Confirmation

Some Reform congregations have replaced the bar mitzvah with a confirmation service. Both boys and girls are confirmed, sometimes at an older age than the traditional thirteen. Confirmations are held as part of Saturday services, and the service may be followed by a reception at the synagogue, open to all members of the congregation. A luncheon, dinner, or reception for invited guests may be held later in the day. These invitation-only social events can be as simple or lavish as the family desires. Gifts, which may be religious or secular, are expected and can be sent or brought to the party.

ATTENDING RELIGIOUS SERVICES

People go to houses of worship for regular participation in the practices of their faith, to visit houses of worship other than their own, and to celebrate weddings, funerals, special holidays, or holy days.

Much has changed, from what one wears to the nature of services themselves. In some evangelical churches, for example, traditional services have given way to spirited participatory ones where hymns and organs have been replaced by rock music and electric guitars. And there's more to consider when you attend a service for a religion other than your own, as discussed on pages 342–47.

Your Own House of Worship

The most important thing to remember at a religious service is also the most obvious: Be quiet and still, especially during prayers and in respect of others who are worshipping or meditating. Remember to turn off phones, pagers, tablets, game devices, and watch alarms. Talking and fidgeting are simply annoying at a performance or movie, but in a house of worship they

intrude on the meditation of others. If you become ill or for any other reason have no choice but to leave, simply follow the rules of common courtesy and slip out at a time when your departure is least likely to be noticed.

Punctuality. If you arrive after the service has started, enter as unobtrusively as possible and wait for an appropriate moment to take a seat—preferably one near the rear. It's all right to enter a row during a prayer, but only if you don't have to move past anyone to take a seat. Otherwise, remain standing until the prayer is finished.

Seating. When seated at the end of a row, it's helpful to move toward the center when someone else wants to take a seat (*always* move in when the person is elderly, infirm, or a parent with young children in tow). At a wedding, however, people who arrived and were seated first aren't expected to move; instead, they rise and let others move past. If you ever expect to leave before the end of the service, choose a seat near the back so that your departure will be less noticeable.

Singing. The congregation acts as one during a service, but joining in the singing of a hymn is a matter of choice. If you are able, do stand with the congregation for the hymn. Don't worry about being able to carry a tune; you're singing a song of praise, not performing.

Photographs. Picture taking usually isn't allowed in a house of worship without permission from the officiating clergyman before the service begins. Some houses forbid taking pictures for religious reasons; even those that allow picture taking want to keep the service as free of distractions as possible.

> Q: *Whatever happened to dressing for church? I recently attended a service in a large city as the guest of a friend, and I was surprised by how many people in the congregation dressed casually. In my small-town church, people still wear their best.*
>
> A: The casualness that has swept through American life has reached even into houses of worship. It once was a given that men wore a jacket and tie, and women a dress or suit and a hat to services. But no more: In some congregations even shorts and jeans are acceptable.
>
> Today's advice is to follow the lead of the congregation you're visiting. In most places, that means your clothing should at least be presentable: clean, pressed, relatively subdued, and—for women—not too revealing. When in doubt, simply call the church office and ask how the church members typically dress.

Attending Services of Other Faiths

Visitors to houses of worship other than their own are usually attending weddings, funerals, or memorial services. But when you attend a regularly scheduled service—whether at the invitation of a friend or because you want to learn more about the faith—it's natural to feel a little nervous about unfamiliar rituals. Unless you're with a friend who prefers to sit in the front, you'll feel more comfortable if you take a seat farther back.

Your best bet is to watch and see what others do and then follow suit—rise when the congregation rises, sit when they sit. You don't need to kneel or participate in reciting a creed or doing anything else contrary to your own religious practices, nor are you expected to. Following are overviews of what to expect when attending services of the major religions.

Roman Catholic Churches

Roman Catholic masses are held on Sundays, Saturday evenings, and holy days; and in some parishes daily Mass may be celebrated. On entering the church, Catholics may dip the first two fingers of the right hand into the fonts of holy water (located at the church entrance) and make the sign of the cross. Often, they genuflect before entering a pew, a sign of respect for the presence of God.

The Catholic Mass involves extensive participation on the part of the congregation in reciting prayers and in song. An order of service and hymnals are available in the pews. A visitor is always welcome to participate, singing hymns or reciting prayers. He also follows the congregation's lead for standing and sitting. Kneeling isn't expected, and if he chooses not to he can remain seated.

At the most solemn part of the Mass, the preparation of Holy Communion during which the congregation kneels, the priest prays aloud and elevates the host and the chalice of wine, which at this point Catholics believe become the body and blood of Christ. In most churches only Catholics can receive communion. Those not receiving communion remain seated, but allow others to exit the pew.

Stands holding votive candles (nowadays often electric candles) are placed in side chapels or before statues of saints, with receptacles for contributions nearby. Catholics light a candle and offer a prayer and guests are welcome to do so as well.

For Catholics and visitors alike, no head covering is required—neither for men nor for women. Men wear jackets and ties or shirts and slacks. Women wear skirts, dresses, or slacks.

Protestant Churches

Protestant services, held on Sunday mornings with the exception of Seventh-Day Adventists who have services on Saturday, are somewhat similar to one another in form. Usually, a printed bulletin provides the order of service, guiding the congregation to specific pages in the worship book being used and making it easy to follow along. The services of some denominations involve kneeling; others do not.

Dress standards can vary among Protestant denominations. Mormons, for example, see shirts and slacks for men as fine but draw the line at jeans and shorts. Some Baptist or Pentecostal churches in or near beach communities even welcome members wearing T-shirts. Generally, coat and tie or shirt and slacks for men, and dresses, skirts, or slacks for women are the norm.

In most Protestant churches, every baptized Christian is welcome to receive Holy Communion. There are several different practices in the way communion is administered, including drinking from the common cup, electing to use individual cups, and intinction (dipping the bread or wafer into the wine). If a visitor doesn't wish to receive communion, she need only stay seated in the pew when others go forward or pass the communion tray along.

Orthodox Christian Churches

There are two branches of the family of Orthodox Christian Churches: Eastern Orthodox and Greek Orthodox. Individual churches use national titles—Russian Orthodox, Serbian Orthodox, Romanian Orthodox, and so on.

Visitors are welcome to attend Orthodox services and aren't expected to take part in any element of the liturgy. As the priest makes his processionals through the sanctuary, everyone stands and faces him as he circles through; while worshippers make the sign of the cross as he passes, visitors may merely bow their heads. Visitors do not take communion, nor do they follow the worshippers' lead and venerate (kiss) the prominently displayed holy icons.

Traditionally, Eastern Orthodox churches were not furnished with pews. Nowadays many have pews; others have chairs placed to the side of the sanctuary. Sit erect; looking too relaxed (and even crossing your legs) is considered disrespectful. Visitors should stand when the congregation stands, and may kneel when it kneels if they choose. When greeting the priest before or after the service, the congregants kiss his hand; visitors offer a standard handshake.

holy days

In an increasingly multicultural society, it is respectful to know what people of other religions are celebrating during holidays and whether there is a traditional holiday greeting. Saying to a workmate, "Hope you have a blast on your day off!" is hardly appropriate for either Good Friday or Yom Kippur, both days of serious reflection. In the list that follows, most holy days have no traditional greetings; those that do show the appropriate greeting.

Buddhist Holy Days

NIRVANA DAY. The commemoration of the death of the Buddha.

HANAMATSURI DAY. The commemoration of the birth of the Buddha.

BODHI DAY. The day on which Siddhartha Guatama said he would meditate under the Bodhi Tree until attaining enlightenment.

Christian Holy Days

CHRISTMAS. The celebration of the birth of Christ.

Greeting: Merry Christmas; Happy Christmas in the United Kingdom and British Commonwealth

ASH WEDNESDAY. First day of Lent, the season of preparation and penitence before Easter.

MAUNDY (OR HOLY) THURSDAY. The day commemorating the institution of the Eucharist; observed three days before Easter Sunday.

GOOD FRIDAY. The day commemorating the crucifixion, death, and burial of Jesus; observed two days before Easter Sunday.

EASTER. The celebration of the resurrection of Jesus.

Greeting: Happy Easter

PASCHA. The Eastern Orthodox celebration of the resurrection of Christ.

Greeting: Christ is risen

Response: Truly He is risen

Hindu Holy Days

DIWALI. The five day festival of lights, regarded as the most significant Hindu holiday.

DUHSERA/DURGA PUJA. The celebration of the triumph of good over evil.

HOLI. A joyous springtime celebration, often referred to as the festival of colors.

KRISHNA JANMASHTAMI. The celebration of the birthday of Krishna.

Islamic Holy Days

RAMADAN. A monthlong time for reflection and spiritual discipline, including fasting, between dawn and dusk.

Greeting: Ramadan Mubarak ("May God give you a blessed month")

LAYLAT AL-QADR. The last ten days of Ramadan, during which special prayers are offered.

'EID AL-FITR. The Feast of the Breaking of the Fast, celebrated at the end of Ramadan.

Greeting: Eid Mubarak ("May God make it a blessed feast")

'EID AL-ADHA. Commemorating Abraham's obedience to God.

Greeting: Eid Mubarak (see 'Eid al-Fitr, above)

ISAR AN MI'RAJ. A day commemorating the Night Journey and the Ascension, the night when the Prophet Muhammad is believed to have ultimately traveled to the heavens, where God commanded him to initiate prayers five times a day.

Jewish Holy Days

ROSH HASHANAH. The celebration of the religious New Year.

Greeting: Happy New Year (*Shana Tovah* in Hebrew)

YOM KIPPUR. The Day of Atonement, set aside for fasting and repentance.

Greeting: There's no traditional greeting, but "Have an easy fast" is appropriate.

SUKKOT. The Feast of Booths, a joyous, eight-day holiday celebrating both the harvest season and the end of the forty years the Israelites wandered in the desert.

Greeting: Happy holiday

CHANUKAH. An eight-day celebration, called the Festival of Lights, commemorating the rededication of the Temple.

Greeting: Happy Chanukah

PURIM. A celebration of deliverance from destruction.

Greeting: Happy holiday *or* Happy Purim

PASSOVER. The celebration of the Jewish people's freedom from slavery in Egypt.

Greeting: Happy Passover

Jewish Synagogues or Temples

Services in Reform, Reconstructionist, Conservative, and Orthodox synagogues or temples differ widely in practice. Services are usually held on Friday evenings (the beginning of the Sabbath) and Saturday mornings. The amount of Hebrew spoken during the service varies, with the least usually used in Reform services and the most in Orthodox services. During many Orthodox services, some portions of the service are read individually and out loud, which may sound confusing to the visitor who is unfamiliar with this practice. Visitors can use prayer books and read along with the congregation when the prayer is in English.

Guests may be seated where they wish, but they should respect the separation of men and women in Orthodox synagogues. Visitors are expected to stand with the congregation, but need not read prayers aloud or sing if this would be contrary to their own beliefs. Some congregants kneel in Orthodox services, but non-Jews do not.

Jackets and ties are appropriate for men, and women usually wear dresses or skirts; pant suits for women are not worn to Orthodox and most Conservative services. In Orthodox congregations, women should wear clothing that covers their arms, hems should be below the knees, and heads should be covered with a hat or veil. Women should not carry a handbag to an Orthodox service because this is a form of labor (carrying an object in public), which is prohibited on the Sabbath. Men wear a yarmulke, or skullcap, on their heads in most synagogues or temples. These are usually available for visitors outside the door of the main sanctuary.

Many times, a *tallit*, or prayer shawl, is worn by adult male congregants. Non-Jews do not touch or wear the tallit.

In many congregations, the rabbi or other leader will make announcements periodically about the service. In others, it is assumed that those present are familiar with the order of service and there are no announcements.

Islamic Mosques

Muslims are required to pray five times a day, either in a mosque or wherever the individual happens to be at prayer time. Prayer is preceded by washing with water (or even a symbolic washing with soil) to cleanse the body and spirit. Worshippers face Makkah (Mecca), prostrate themselves or bow, and recite fixed prayers.

Like the worshippers, non-Muslim guests remove their shoes when entering a mosque. Guests then have the freedom to sit on the floor or in a chair and also to come and go. In most mosques, non-Muslim visitors (including women) do not have to cover their heads as long as they are dressed conservatively—no bare shoulders, arms, chest, or knees. However, it is respectful to do so.

At a Muslim worship service, men form the prayer lines in the front, with children behind and women in the back. Some mosques have a separate worship area for women. In the first part of the service, an imam leads the prayers voiced by the Muslim congregants in unison; in the second part, the congregants pray individually as they wish, bowing or prostrating themselves as the imam delivers the sermon.

Buddhist Temples

Services, which can last one to two hours, take different forms. Some are services of silent meditation while others include a sermon by a priest. Usually there is chanting, silent meditation, and a sermon, with an incense offering by the priest or a monk. Some temples have seats, while others have meditation floor cushions instead.

Neither men nor women are required to wear a head covering. Clothing should be comfortable for worship in those temples where seating is on floor cushions.

Other Religions

From Hinduism to Shintoism, a number of other religions are practiced in the United States. If you're not attending a service with a friend who can guide you, the simplest way to get answers to any questions about behavior is to call the administrative office beforehand and ask. Most, if not all, will welcome you and see to it that you feel comfortable.

when you're a sightseer

The world's great cathedrals, temples, and mosques are not only houses of worship but tourist attractions as well. The point is that the place you are visiting is a house of worship first and a tourist attraction second. Millions of visitors a year are drawn to these international treasures—not only to worship but to soak up the history, architecture, and art. But what if a service is being held when you arrive?

Show respect. That means not walking around to take in the sights, even if you tiptoe and stay silent. Either stand still until the service is over, sit in a pew, or exit and come back later. When a private ceremony is being held at the main altar or in a side chapel, you may sightsee as long as you keep your distance and avoid intruding. Remember that even if no service is in progress, you are obliged to conduct yourself reverently and quietly. It is also customary for a sightseer to leave a donation in the offering box to support the upkeep of the building.

Showing respect also means being careful how you dress. At cathedrals, mosques, and temples, revealing clothing—which could include shorts, short skirts, and bare arms—can be considered disrespectful. Carrying a shawl can make most outfits acceptable.

GREETINGS FOR CLERGY

One of the most confusing aspects of greeting officiating clergy is knowing what to call them. Keep in mind that while there are correct titles, it's not uncommon for someone who is called by one title to refer to himself by another—for example, a pastor who introduces himself as Reverend Thompson. You might find that some clergy prefer to be called by their title and first name, such as Pastor John. A female Episcopal priest might ask to be called Reverend Weatherly or Mother Anne. Catholic priests are called Father and most nuns are addressed as Sister. A rabbi is addressed as Rabbi and an imam is addressed as Imam. Generally, a Buddhist priest is addressed as His Holiness or His Eminence, a male Hindu priest as Swami, and a female priest as Swamini.

Your best choice is to ask a congregant or the clergy directly about their individual preference and then use the desired greeting. (See also "Official Forms of Address," page 678.)

28
giving and receiving gifts

One of life's great pleasures is giving and receiving gifts. Almost every culture has gift-giving and receiving traditions and etiquette. Giving a gift is one way we can express generosity, appreciation, thanks, and love, and recognize special occasions and achievements. A gift isn't necessarily about the object itself but is a representation of the emotion and sentiment behind it.

People have so many questions about gift giving, and fret endlessly about choosing just the right one. From a candle to the Statue of Liberty, the spirit of the gift is more important than the gift itself. In this chapter we discuss how to choose, present, and acknowledge gifts gracefully.

[FIRST CONSIDERATIONS]

With so many choices, how do you find the right gift? First, think about the recipient, the occasion, and your budget: A bar of gorgeously scented hand soap makes a great hostess gift, but probably wouldn't be the right choice for your parents' twenty-fifth anniversary. You'll also want to consider whether your gift should be lasting or temporary in nature, and how personal it is. Finally, figure out how much you can afford to spend. From the giver's perspective, it's important to stick to your budget.

Temporary gifts. Falling into the temporary, perishable, or consumable category are flowers; candy and specialty foods; wine, champagne, or liquor; soaps and lotions; and paper goods, such as cocktail napkins or note cards. They're perfect for hostess gifts, a friend's birthday, or for the person who "has everything."

Holidays	Naming ceremony	Graduation
An overnight visit	First Communion	Anniversary
Dinner at your host's house	Confirmation	Retirement
A "thank you" for doing a favor	Bar or Bat Mitzvah	Engagement
Year end to a service provider	Get-well gift	Wedding
Baptism	Condolence gift or contribution	Wedding or baby shower
Bris	Ordination or Profession of Vows	Housewarming
	Birthday	

Also in the temporary category, but more lasting, are gifts that keep on giving, such as a magazine subscription, or a subscription for fruit or plants that arrive monthly and can be enjoyed all year long. Tickets to the theater or a sporting event give the pleasure not just of the event itself, but of the memories as well.

Enduring gifts. Gifts that last range from hardcover books and decorative items to kitchen appliances and cookware, sporting equipment, furniture, items for a collection, or jewelry, to name a few. An engraved silver bowl or picture frame can be a lasting commemoration of a special event or a milestone, such as an anniversary. The nature of the occasion will help you make your choice. A silver cup engraved with a baby's name and date of birth might be the perfect christening gift, while a retiree who's looking forward to weekdays on the golf course might enjoy a new putter or golf bag more than an engraved silver picture frame.

Personal gifts. Clothing, jewelry, and perfume or cologne are all personal gifts that are usually given to spouses and significant others or family members and very close friends. Think carefully about your relationship with the recipient and how your gift will be received. For instance, giving personal gifts isn't appropriate in the workplace. It may be fine to give your assistant a nice sweater or hand lotion, but because of their romantic overtones, lingerie or perfume wouldn't be.

Cost. Whenever you choose a gift, be respectful of your own budget. It's nice to be generous, but you'll get more pleasure in giving a gift you can afford. An extravagant gift can be overwhelming to the recipient, and, if completely out of proportion to the occasion, embarrassing. Some of the nicest gifts don't cost money. A gift of your time—a hospital visit, an afternoon of babysitting for a new mom, an offer to grocery shop for a neighbor who's ill—can sometimes be the most meaningful gift of all.

FOOD, WINE, AND FLOWERS

Food, wine, spirits, and flowers are almost always a hit, even though they may not be long lasting. Before you buy, though, check on food or plant allergies, and make sure that a gift of wine or spirits is appropriate. For religious, personal, or health reasons, many people do not allow alcoholic beverages in their homes.

Put some thought into the kind of flowers you send: While a mixed arrangement is always appropriate, long-stemmed roses imply romantic feelings and certain flowers may have particular connotations or symbolism. In Italy, for example, chrysanthemums are sent for funerals and memorials, not as a nice fall arrangement for a dinner party. An experienced florist should be able to guide you.

GIFT CERTIFICATES, MONEY, AND DONATIONS

Gift certificates or **gift cards** are everywhere—there's hardly a virtual or physical store that doesn't offer them. For some people, gift certificates lack the personal touch. For others, they offer the recipient the freedom to choose exactly what she wants and needs. A gift card can be the perfect solution for the person "who has everything," a teen who'd like the chance to browse for books or music, a teacher who enjoys a daily dose of coffee, or a hobbyist to purchase supplies or add to a collection. The recipient is guaranteed to find something they'd like or need. Check the details of any gift card you purchase: Some expire within a specified time period and others may deduct a "dormancy" fee. Also, gift cards won't be honored if a retailer goes out of business—a real downside.

Money, too, is a popular and appreciated gift. Teens especially enjoy having extra cash, and more frequently, money is the gift of choice for brides and grooms who are saving for the down payment on a house or for a special honeymoon. Whether to give money or not depends on the occasion and on how well you know the recipient. While gifts of money are usually given by relatives for holiday or birthday presents, in some traditions it's customary to give money as a wedding gift or a gift for a religious coming of age celebration, even if you aren't a close friend of the recipient.

Stocks, bonds, and certificates of deposit are often given to young people as coming-of-age gifts. Long-term bonds usually mature just when the recipient is launching his own life—a wise gift that's worth the wait. Or, a thoughtful godparent or relative could make annual gifts of financial instruments, starting a portfolio when a child is born.

Charitable donations, in lieu of gifts, are becoming increasingly popular as substitute wedding gifts, especially for encore weddings, as wedding favors, and as holiday or birthday gifts. If you're choosing a charity for someone else, be careful to pick something that matches his or her interests. A dog lover would appreciate a donation to an animal shelter, a reader a donation to a literacy program. Avoid choosing political or overly religious organizations unless you're certain the dona-

a gift of yourself

Gifts don't have to be tangible or cost even one cent. In fact, gifts of your time or your talents are sometimes the most appreciated. They can include the following:

- Grocery shopping or running errands for someone who's recuperating from an illness.
- Babysitting for a new mom so she can have some time to herself.
- A weekly visit with someone who's housebound.
- Shoveling the walk for an elderly neighbor.
- A regular outing with a grandchild.
- Sharing the bounty of your flower or vegetable garden.

tion would be received positively. If a charitable donation has been requested in place of gifts, it's completely up to you whether to participate or not: The choice of a gift is always up to the giver.

GROUP GIFTS

A group gift is appropriate on many occasions, for instance when

- friends invited to an anniversary party pool funds for one big present.
- coworkers pitch in for a gift to a workmate or boss.
- weekend guests band together to give their host something nicer than they could afford individually.

There are several ways to organize a group gift, but just remember to be respectful of each participant and his or her decision to join in or not, as well as with the amount they're able to contribute. Be sure to thank everyone who participated and include a card listing all the givers so the recipient will know whom to thank.

The following tips will help you get a group gift together while avoiding the pitfalls:

- Invite people to participate. Since the choice to give a gift is always up to the giver, no one should be pressured to contribute.
- Pick the gift ahead of time, either as a group or based on a suggestion from the organizer. People like to know what they're contributing to and how much it costs: "Tim and Suzanne love camping. For their tenth anniversary, we'd love to get them a two-person tent. The total cost is $295. If you'd like to participate, anything you contribute would be welcome."
- Include a "respond by" date, so there's time to purchase the gift. "If you're interested, please let me know by March 10th."
- Communicate how the gift will be presented: "If we collect enough, we'll purchase the tent. If we don't, we'll give them a gift certificate toward the tent. If we collect extra, we'll give them a check for the difference so they can pay park fees or purchase accessories."
- When individuals band together, keep the donation amounts anonymous. As the organizer, be respectful of all contributions, the large as well as the small. Include a card with the gift, listing all the givers but not the actual amounts they contributed. The recipient will want to know whom to thank.

a variation on a theme

Sometimes the *recipients* of a gift might be the "group." For example, rather than giving a holiday present to every child in a family, an aunt, uncle, grandparent, or friend could give a game or play equipment that all the children can enjoy. If you're a godparent, however, it's better to honor the special relationship with your godchild with a personal gift, rather than including siblings in a group gift.

Q: *I'm constantly being asked to contribute to gifts for officemates. Do I have to participate?*

A: No, you don't. It's fine to take a pass: "Thanks for asking me, but I just can't go in on joint gifts at this time." If the occasion is to celebrate a coworker, say, a birthday or a wedding shower, it's nice to give a card extending your good wishes if you're not joining in on the gift. Bottom line: Try to be a participant in a friendly but realistic way.

♦ An alternative is to collect contributions first and then choose and purchase a gift with the funds. This works well in office and school class gift situations, with large groups of people you may not know very well. Again, it's important to let donors know what was purchased and to keep the contributions anonymous. To avoid singling out nonparticipants, sign the card "From the office" or "From the class."

♦ With small groups of friends or family members, often the group sets a budget and then splits the cost of the gift evenly.

♦ Usually, the cost of a group gift for parents is shared by the siblings and doesn't include spouses when figuring the split.

GIFT REGISTRIES AND WISH LISTS

Years ago, gift registries were associated just with weddings, and brides "registered" their china, glass, and flatware patterns with a department or gift store. Guests could then give a dessertspoon or a dinner plate in hopes of helping the bride acquire a complete table setting. Today anyone can register for almost anything from tools to travel. General gift registries and individual "wish lists" are a natural outgrowth of the Internet's ability to make life a little easier in an increasingly hectic world, but be careful how you use them. There's a fine

Q: *I'm the class mother for my daughter's third grade and I'm in charge of organizing the holiday gift to her teacher. I realize not everyone can contribute money for the gift. How do I handle putting names on the card? I don't want to single anyone out.*

A: Here's a situation that calls for tact and discretion. In this case, you can have the card describe the group without listing the contributors: "To Mrs. Peach, from Your 3rd Graders." Or have each child sign the card. You wouldn't want a child to be hurt or embarrassed because their name wasn't on the card. And, remember, money isn't the only contribution someone can make. Perhaps they can help with the shopping or the wrapping, or help at the class party. As for the parents, be sure to thank everyone for their donation and be understanding of those who can't.

five tips to simplify gift giving

These tips will help keep gift giving simple and fun:

- **KEEP A RUNNING GIFT LIST THROUGHOUT THE YEAR.** Include hints from friends and relatives for birthday or holiday gifts, as well as your own ideas. Be on the lookout for the items when shopping, and when browsing catalogs and websites. You might keep catalog pages in a folder, keep notes on your phone, or make a gift folder in the bookmarks tab of your Web browser: Sam's Birthday Ideas.

- **TRUST YOUR JUDGMENT.** Lose the idea that the gift has to be perfect. If you think the recipient will like it, you're probably right.

- **STICK TO YOUR BUDGET.** Spending more than you should takes the fun out of gift giving.

- **BUY IT WHEN YOU SEE IT.** If you're shopping in July and see a sweater that your mother would love for Christmas, buy it. Chances are it won't be there when you look in December.

- **KEEP A FEW EMERGENCY GIFTS STASHED AWAY IN THE CLOSET.** Just make sure they're nice ones, and only give the gift when you think it's the right match for the recipient.

line between letting your family and closest friends know what you'd like and maintaining a standing "Buy me this" list. Think of a registry as a communication tool.

So how do you politely let people know about your registry? For wedding and baby showers, which are all about gifts, it's okay to include registry information *with* the invitation. However, brides and grooms, take note: No matter how tempting—and retailers will encourage you to do it—forget about including your registry information in your wedding invitations. Recipients see it as "Please buy us a gift, and by the way, here's your invitation to our wedding." Of course, if anyone asks, it's fine to tell them where you're registered, but be sure to let them know that you'd appreciate any gift they choose to give. (See Chapter 50, "Wedding Registries, Gifts, and Thank-yous," page 624.)

Individual "wish lists" or personal registries are handy if a close friend or family member wants to know what to get you for a birthday or holiday gift. But keep in mind, sharing this registry or list is appropriate *only* as an aid for people with whom you ordinarily exchange gifts. They don't have to make use of it, but when they're at a loss for what to give, your wish list can provide an answer. Steer children away from using online and in-store registries as it could teach them to focus on gifts more than their relationships with family and friends.

If anyone other than a close friend or family member asks what you'd like for a certain occasion, just say, "Since you asked, here are a few ideas." Referring to a personal registry puts the emphasis on "what's in it for me" instead of the friendship.

Including registry addresses on an invitation to a housewarming party (plus salting the list with big-ticket items) is over the top. A housewarming is a party that you throw for yourself. People do bring gifts to a house-warming, but drawing such pointed attention to gifts is likely to make guests suspect that the party is being held just so you can rake in the goodies. (See "House-warmings," page 313.)

PERSONALIZING GIFTS

A gift marked with a monogram or anything else specific to the recipient(s) is all the more special. Beyond the traditional engraved silver or monogrammed towels is a wealth of possibilities: an original poem or song lyrics to the person written in calligraphy and framed, a coffee mug bearing a picture of a child or family member, a T-shirt with the recipient's favorite saying or quotation.

Because a personalized gift can't be returned, make sure that it's something the recipient actually wants and that it's the right size. It's also possible for the recipient

gifts you can personalize

Flatware	Vases	Towels
Glassware	Trays	Robes
Barware (ice buckets, shakers, measures, decanters)	Tote bags	Sheets
	Luggage	Pillowcases
Tablecloths	Luggage tags	Throws
Napkins	Lunch boxes or bags	Christmas stockings
Napkin rings	Toiletry or cosmetic bags	Doormats
	Jewelry boxes or bags	

to have the gift marked later. If free engraving is offered with the purchase, ask the retailer to include a note to that effect so that it will be honored at a later time. If there's a charge, arrange with the retailer to bill you, or make it clear to the recipient that the bill should be sent to you, no matter how much time has passed since the gift was received.

Gifts of silver can be engraved to commemorate special occasions such as a twenty-fifth anniversary or a graduation. For anniversary or engagement parties, hosts sometimes mark paper goods such as match-boxes, napkins, and coasters with the date and/or the honorees' monogram. It's a nice touch for the party and serves as a memento as well.

ALL ABOUT MONOGRAMMING

A personal monogram consists of three initials (first, middle, last) or uses the last name initial only. The initial of a nickname is not normally included in a monogram. Traditionally, married couples use his and her first initials plus their last name initial, or just their last name initial. For their personal monograms, a husband's initials don't change unless the couple uses a hyphenated last name; and a wife generally uses her maiden name as her middle name. But today, with some couples using both last names and some wives keeping their maiden names, monograms can be a bit more complicated.

Tips for Monogramming

Wedding gifts. Be guided by the way the couple plans to write their name(s). If you aren't sure, check with the couple's parents or a bridal attendant, or give them the gift with the promise to have it monogrammed later.

Stationery. Any of the forms listed on the above chart are appropriate. When husbands and wives share stationery, the last/married name initial, hyphenated initial, or double last name initials (when the wife retains her maiden name) are used.

Linens. Many people prefer the single last name initial, or hyphenated initials for couples with a hyphenated last name. The other forms on the chart to the right are also appropriate.

Towels are marked at the center of one end. Top sheets are monogrammed so that when the sheet is folded down, the letters can be read by someone standing at the foot of the bed. Pillowcase monograms are centered and approximately 2 inches above the hem. Rectangular tablecloths are monogrammed at the

it's a woman's choice

A woman who remarries after a divorce generally does not use initials from her previous marriage or marriages in monograms. She follows the forms above, using her first name, maiden name, and new married name initials. A widow, however, may wish to retain her former husband's last name as her middle name.

CREATING A MONOGRAM

This chart will help you choose the right monogram. The order of initials depends on whether the letters are of the same size or the initial of the last name is larger, in which case it's centered.

	WHEN INITIALS ARE THE SAME SIZE	WHEN CENTER INITIAL IS LARGER	SINGLE INITIAL
FOR A COUPLE NAMED JANE ANNE BOWEN AND THOMAS RYAN NELSON:			
Single woman (used for personal items & stationery before marriage)	first, middle, last **JAB**	first, last, middle **JBA**	last **B**
Single man (used for personal items & stationery before & after marriage)	first, middle, last **TRN**	first, last, middle **TNR**	last **N**
Married couple		wife's first name, married/last name, husband's first name **JNT**	married/last name **N**
Married woman (for personal items & stationery)	first, maiden name, married/last name **JBN**	first, married/last name, maiden name **JNB**	married/last name **N**
Married couple with a hyphenated last name		wife's first name, hyphenated married name, husband's first name **JB-NT**	hyphenated last name **B-N**
Married woman or man with a hyphenated married/last name	first, middle, hyphenated last name **JAB-N** **TRB-N** (or) first, hyphenated last name **JB-N** **TB-N**	first, hyphenated last name, middle **JB-NA** **TB-NR**	hyphenated last name **B-N** **B-N**

	WHEN INITIALS ARE THE SAME SIZE	WHEN CENTER INITIAL IS LARGER	SINGLE INITIAL
Married couple when wife keeps her maiden name	wife's maiden name and husband's last name initials separated by a dot, diamond shape, or other design B * N		
	FOR LYNN CARTER-JAMES AND JOHN LEWIS-WIESNER:		
Married couple when wife keeps her maiden name and both wife and husband come with hyphenated last names	same as above, or C-J*L-W		
	FOR ANNA SMITH VON HAEGEL:	**FOR ANNA AND CARL VON HAEGEL:**	
Individual or married couple when the last name includes a capitalized article, making it two words: Von, Van, Du, etc.	ASVH	AVHC, or VH	
	FOR PETER JAMES O'NEIL:	**FOR LESLIE AND PETER O'NEIL:**	
Individual or married couple when the last name begins with Mc, Mac, or O', but is only one word	PJO	LOP, or O	

center of each long side, and square cloths at one corner. Dinner napkins are marked diagonally at one corner.

Flatware. The choice of monogram is usually determined by the shape of the flatware handle. The last initial or hyphenated last initials are often used. In some cases, a couple's initials are stacked in an inverted triangle shape, with the couple's first name initials on top and the last initial below:

J T
N

Clothing and other personal items. Choose the individual's personal monogram or the married/last name initial (single or hyphenated).

WHAT NOT TO GIVE

Whenever you give a gift, think about it from the recipient's point of view. Is this something he would truly want and enjoy? Be careful of giving gag gifts that can cause embarrassment or simply leave the recipient wondering what on earth you were thinking. Every year at holiday time we hear about truly thoughtless gifts: lingerie to a coworker, liquor to a nondrinker, a box of candy—with a few missing, clothing that had been worn, items that target a person's weight or complexion problem. The saddest is when a child is given a pet without the parent's consent. These gifts aren't gifts in any sense of the word. Not only do they trigger embarrassment or dismay when they're opened, they leave a lasting negative impression of the giver.

WRAPPING PRESENTS

Having spent the time to find just the right gift, take a few extra moments to think about presentation. A beautifully wrapped gift, complete with ribbon and card, is the time-honored classic. Gift bags are popular and practical, and, since they can be reused, they're more environmentally friendly. By the same token, brown paper bags and newspaper can be creatively recycled as wrapping paper and look smart when tied with raffia or embellished with a sprig of greenery. Thin colored tissue makes a great wrapping; just be sure to use enough layers to hide any printing on the gift's box. Tissue can also be used in decorative gift bags to hide their contents.

Any box will do for gifts, although it makes sense to use a box provided by the retailer. In this age of recycling, it's fine to reuse a box—just be sure the recipient knows that the box doesn't indicate the store where the gift was purchased in case an exchange needs to be made. Also, don't forget to remove or obliterate the price on the tag.

While it's not necessary to wrap a hostess gift, do take care in the presentation. Wine for the host of a dinner party requires nothing more than removing the price tag and giving a quick polish to the bottle, but a ribbon knotted around the neck adds a nice touch and a gift bag quickly kicks the presentation up a notch. Homemade cookies or other treats packed in a pretty container is a dual gift of sorts, since the container can be saved and reused. Don't forget to attach a little tag or card so your hostess will know whom to thank if she opens the gift after the party.

GIFT RECEIPTS

Even with all the care taken to choose just the right gift, things don't always work out. It may be the wrong size, color, or style, a duplicate, or damaged. Gift receipts are a clever and kind way to let the recipient know that she's free to exchange your gift for whatever reason. Basically, a gift receipt is a duplicate sales slip but without any pricing information. Most retailers offer them, but be sure to ask for one when you start the payment process, as it's not always a part of the salesperson's checkout repertoire.

"NO GIFTS, PLEASE"

Gifts are expected for birthday or anniversary parties, showers, and weddings, but when honorees really don't want presents, their wishes should be respected. It's a courtesy to inform guests when presents aren't expected. The etiquette is to write "No Gifts, Please"

> Q: *I've been exchanging Christmas presents for years with a few friends and relatives with whom I'm no longer especially close. I'm trying to simplify things around the holidays. Is there a graceful way to let them know I'd like to bow out?*
>
> A: Yes, and it's not as hard as you think. Be frank. Well before Christmas, write, call, email, or say to the person, "I know we always exchange gifts, but this year is tight. Would you be comfortable if we just held off or exchanged cards? Please write us with family news—that will be the best present of all." Or, "I know we normally exchange gifts, but could we have dinner (lunch, coffee) together this holiday season instead?"

at the bottom of all but wedding invitations. Why not on wedding invitations? While it's a well-established custom to give a wedding gift, any mention of gifts, registries, or even requesting no gifts distracts from the very personal and special nature of this invitation. If the couple really doesn't want wedding gifts, relatives and attendants can spread the word, the couple can make their wishes known if asked directly, or post their preference on the registry page of their wedding website.

When you receive an invitation with a "No gifts, please" request, take it seriously. Showing up with a present when asked not to would embarrass the hosts, the honoree, and other guests who correctly didn't bring one. If you want to give a special token of affection, do so at another time.

WHEN GIVING TO . . .

. . . coworkers and business associates. Generally, gifts aren't exchanged at the office unless it's a part of a holiday party. An exception is when a group pools resources for a shower or retirement gift for a coworker. Businesses often give gifts to clients or vendors at holiday time. Be sure that the recipient is allowed to accept a gift, as some companies have strict policies: Gifts may be allowed up to a certain dollar amount or prohibited altogether. Business gifts should not be of a personal nature. If you wish to exchange gifts with a colleague whom you see socially, do it outside the office to avoid offending others.

. . . doctors, lawyers, and other professionals. While professionals aren't given gifts for services rendered, a patient or client may wish to express special thanks for extraordinary consideration or to give a holiday gift. In such cases, any of the following gifts are appropriate: a fruit or specialty food basket; homemade cookies or a product made by the giver, such as a box of pastries from a baker or a glass ornament from a glassblower; or a gift certificate for two to a nice area restaurant.

. . . nurses. Gifts of money should never be offered to hospital nurses, but cookies, candy, fruit, or flowers that can be shared or enjoyed by everyone at the nurses' station are always welcome. Because hospitals usually have two or three shifts, it's a good idea to give two or three of the same gift item, clearly marked "first shift," "second shift," and "third shift." Leave the gifts, with a note to the effect that "This is for all of you who have been so caring," with the nurse on duty at the nursing station. If you wish to give a gift to a particular nurse, you should do so privately.

Private-duty nurses who work for an agency may also be prohibited from accepting gifts of money. Instead, choose specialty food items or, for someone who has served over a period of time, personal gifts, such as a sweater, scarf, gloves, or accessories. If the nurse or caregiver is an independent, then the choice of gift, including cash, is up to you.

. . . **teachers.** Christmas, Chanukah, and end-of-year gifts are probably the most common times for giving gifts to teachers. Always check the school's gift policy first, and involve your child in the choice or creation of the gift if you can. A box of your lemon squares and a card created by your child can be enjoyed every bit as much as store-bought gifts. Unless it's a first-year teacher, they probably have quite a mug collection already. While gift shops offer a wide selection of teacher-oriented items, you may want to consider a couple of other options. For example, you could give a donation to a worthy cause in the teacher's name, or a gift that the teacher can enjoy personally, such as a gift certificate to a nice local restaurant or bookstore, or tickets to the theater, a concert, or sporting event.

. . . **clergy.** It's appropriate to give a member of the clergy a gift at holiday time, for a birthday, for an ordination, or when he or she leaves for another post or retires. Depending on the occasion, any of the following would make suitable presents: books; a magazine subscription; tickets to the movies, theater, symphony, or sporting event; specialty or homemade food items; a gift certificate for two to a local restaurant; a gift certificate to a local department store; a wristwatch, leather diary or address book, wallet, or briefcase.

. . . **household help.** Holiday gifts are given to live-in housekeepers and other household help, usually as an accompaniment to any bonus or cash gift. Typical gifts include articles of clothing, such as sweaters, scarves, or outerwear; soaps or lotions; items related to a special interest; or (if they live in) something for their rooms. A nanny or au pair would receive a present from the children in addition to any gift or bonus from the parents.

. . . **service providers.** During the holiday season it's customary to thank the people, seen and unseen, who help your life run smoothly throughout the year. While you might choose to give cash to a doorman or newspaper deliveryperson, a gift may be more appropriate for someone with whom you have a more personal or long-term relationship, such as a hairstylist. Choose a gift that's personalized, but not too personal: Gloves or a scarf for your dog walker is an example. Including a note or card makes a cash gift more personal.

Giving annual gifts at holiday time can become overwhelming, so establish and stick to a budget. If you're strapped for cash, just be more conservative and give to the two or three people whose services you couldn't live without, and write a heartfelt note of appreciation to the others. (For more on holiday giving and tipping, see Chapter 13, "Tipping," page 165.)

RECEIVING AND ACKNOWLEDGING GIFTS

It's an honor to receive a gift. Someone has taken time to choose or create something they hope you'll enjoy. So the most important thing, especially when opening a gift in the presence of the giver, is to thank the person enthusiastically. It's so important to express your appreciation for their thoughtfulness sincerely. It *is* the thought (and the time and effort and creativity) that is so much more important than the actual gift. So if the present isn't quite right, sincerely thank the giver for his thoughtfulness: "It's so nice of you to think of me in this way!"

All gifts must be acknowledged either verbally or in writing, and thanks of any kind should be prompt—especially when a gift wasn't presented in person. Otherwise, the giver is left wondering if it even arrived.

Depending on the circumstances, you can express your appreciation in person, with a phone call, in an email, or with a handwritten note.

HANDWRITTEN, EMAIL, OR PHONE CALL?

It's always correct to send handwritten thank-yous, and people always appreciate receiving them. Handwritten notes are warmer and more personal than a phone call or an email, and only second best to thanking someone in person. The general rule is: If you open a gift in the presence of the giver, then your verbal thanks are sufficient. For example, if you receive a hostess gift, a birthday gift from a good friend, or a holiday present from a relative and you open the gift and express your sincere thanks personally, then a follow-up thank-you is optional. If the giver wasn't present, then a phone call is fine. Email is great when you just need to say a simple thanks quickly. Following up with a note may not always be necessary, depending on your relationship, but it is always appreciated.

There are some situations when a note is required. Even if thanks were given in person, the special nature of these occasions calls for extra effort on the part of the honorees. Here's a rundown of when a note is expected:

◆ **Wedding or baby shower gifts.** A note is still expected whether or not you've given thanks in person. After giving shower gifts, the majority of people consider it rude if they don't receive a written note of thanks. These notes should be written soon after the shower.

- **Wedding gifts.** A note is required. Each wedding gift should be acknowledged with a written note within three months of receipt of the gift, even when you've given thanks in person. It's best to write the notes as soon as possible after the gifts arrive.

- **Congratulatory gifts or cards.** Send a note to anyone who sends a present or a card with a personally written message to acknowledge an accomplishment, such as a graduation or promotion.

- **Gifts received when sick.** Notes should be written when the patient feels well enough, or a relative or close friend can write notes on his or her behalf. (It's fine to acknowledge get-well cards with a phone call or in person.)

- **Condolence notes or gifts.** Send a written thank-you to anyone who sent a personal note, flowers, or a donation. It's fine for a close friend or relative to write notes on the recipient's behalf.

(For examples of thank-you notes, see Chapter 50, page 632, for thank-you notes for wedding or shower gifts; Chapter 44, page 555, for acknowledgment of condolence gifts.)

DIFFERENT GIFTS, DIFFERENT THANK-YOU NOTES

Different kinds of gifts and occasions merit some tweaking to the standard thank-you note.

Gifts of money. In your note, let the giver know how you'll use a money gift—to furnish your apartment or add to your savings. Mentioning the amount is

---

tips on writing thank-you notes

Use these tips to make writing your thank-yous a pleasure:

- Just do it! The sooner you write, the easier it is.

- Write the note as if you were speaking with the person you're thanking. Draft the note, if that helps you to get started.

- Keep it short and sweet. Save the family news for another letter.

- Personalize the note, referencing the giver and the gift.

- Be enthusiastic and sincere.

- Focus on the positive and don't mention any dissatisfaction with the gift. (If you need to exchange it—wrong size, a duplicate—say it in a conversation with the giver.)

- Always remember the generosity and spirit of the giver.

- A thank-you note is always appreciated, even if you've given thanks in person. A note is the extra way of telling the person you truly value what has been done for you.

---

optional, but if you can be more specific about the use, do so: "Dear Aunt Trish: Wow! Your fifty-dollar check was just what I needed to be able to purchase my new guitar. Thank you for the perfect gift."

Holiday and birthday gifts. Write thank-you notes for holiday and birthday gifts as soon as possible, preferably within two or three days. A good standard is to acknowledge Christmas or Chanukah gifts before New

the perfect thank-you note

While there's no formula for the perfect note, the ones people remember are those that express your sincere feelings. Before you write the note, take a moment to think about the person you are thanking. How would the conversation go if you were thanking them in person? Look at the gift when you prepare to write; it can provide inspiration. Here are two examples of notes, both perfectly fine, but the second is more personal:

Dear Aunt Susan and Uncle Jeff,

Thank you for the lovely martini shaker you sent us for Christmas. I'm sorry you weren't able to be here this year, but we hope to see you when you come to Cape Cod next summer. Maybe we can get together then.

Thanks again and Happy New Year.

Love,

Courtney

Dear Aunt Susan and Uncle Jeff,

I'm looking right now at the lovely martini shaker you sent and imagining Sam wowing our next dinner party guests with his Lemon Drops. It is one of our favorite Christmas presents and we thank you.

We really missed you at Christmas this year, but I know you've been planning your New Zealand trip for ages. We'll just have to catch up next summer when you come to Cape Cod. You bring the photos and we'll provide the martinis!

Again, many thanks for the shaker and your sweet note. Happy New Year!

Love from both of us,

Courtney

Year's Day. Even though a warm "Thank you!" in person is technically all that's required, a handwritten note is always appreciated, especially by friends and family of an older generation—and a *must* when you haven't thanked someone directly.

When it comes to acknowledging children's gifts, a child who is old enough to write is old enough to handle his own thank-you notes. Even a preschooler can draw a picture and "sign" his name on a note you've written for him. It's never too early to begin teaching the habit.

Other gifts. Thank-you notes are not always necessary for presents that have been given in person at a housewarming, going-away party, or similar occasion. If a sincere thank-you was expressed in person when the gift was received, that's sufficient. However, a follow-up thank-you note or additional verbal thanks is always appreciated.

Thank-you gifts. Do thank-yous need to be written for thank-you gifts? In some cases, yes. Gifts sent as a "thank you for . . ." require a note of appreciation in return. These gifts, as with any others, mean that someone put effort in selecting something for you to enjoy. It's necessary to let the sender know that the present arrived and is appreciated. If the gift was received and opened in person and thanks expressed, then the note is optional.

Acknowledgment cards. Printed acknowledgment cards expressing appreciation can be used in three instances:

- After the death of a prominent person when scores of sympathy notes, gifts of flowers, or donations to charities are received.

- When a public official is elected and receives a landslide of congratulatory messages.

- When a bride has such a large wedding that she and the groom simply cannot write personal thank-you notes immediately. The printed acknowledgment states that a personal note will come later.

A newspaper "Card of Thanks." In some small towns and rural areas, it is not only permissible but expected that recipients of a large number of gifts or contributions—after a birthday, anniversary, retirement party, funeral, or even a political campaign—put a public "thanks" in the newspaper. It's also a way to acknowledge hospital staff and caregivers after someone has experienced a prolonged illness. The notice is typically headed "Card of Thanks" and is followed by a brief message such as: "We wish to express our thanks to all the wonderful people and organizations who sent cards and gifts on the occasion of our fiftieth wedding anniversary. Sincerely, Mr. and Mrs. Samuel Briggs."

When a card of thanks is published, personal notes have to be written only to people who went out of their way to give something very special, or who assisted or participated in the celebration.

WHEN IT'S JUST NOT RIGHT

Broken or Damaged Gifts

The crystal vase your friend mailed to you looks beautiful, but it's broken into three pieces. What to do? Any reputable store will replace merchandise on reasonable evidence that it was damaged in transit. Either take it, along with its packaging, to the shop where it was purchased or mail it back with a letter describing the problem. Most catalog and Internet stores include return information and labels with the gift, and many will arrange for a carrier to pick up the package for return. There's no need to mention the damage to the giver unless she mailed the package herself and insured it—in which case you have to inform her so that she can recover her costs and replace the gift. If a gift of fruit, flowers, or plants arrives spoiled, just call the company and ask for a replacement, which they'll most likely provide.

Truly Awful Gifts

How do you react when a gift is a real clunker? Sure, it's the thought that counts, but sometimes we have to secretly wonder what on *earth* the giver was thinking!

The key is "secretly." Think what you wish, but make sure you don't hurt the gift giver's feelings. Keep your response neutral as any hint of enthusiasm, in addition to being dishonest, could mean a whole collection of Waterfalls of the World plates is in your future. Vague comments on the order of "The bowl is so unique" or "You do have the most original ideas!" are also risky, since they're often recognized as code for the fact that you dislike the gift. Better to simply stress your appreciation and avoid describing the gift: "This is so thoughtful! Thank you!"

Duplicate Gifts

If it turns out that you've given someone a duplicate gift, be a friend and encourage them to exchange it. "Julie, please exchange the mixer for something else." If you receive a duplicate, go ahead and make an exchange and let the giver know. "I love those hand blenders so much I already own one! I exchanged it for the food mill I've always wanted for making my tomato sauce. Thanks for making my life in the kitchen easier."

Overly Expensive Gifts

Receiving an overly expensive gift from anyone other than a significant other or close family member puts the recipient in an awkward position. It becomes a lopsided relationship and the receiver can feel either owing or owned. If an overly generous friend gives you an over-the-top gift, say something like "Tara, this is stunning, but you really shouldn't have!" You've thanked her while gracefully dropping a hint. You aren't obligated to reciprocate in kind.

In some cases, when the gift is so far out of context with the relationship, you might just have to return it. Very expensive jewelry from someone you're dating or don't know that well is such a case: "John, this necklace is beautiful and I cannot tell you how much I appreciate the sentiment behind it. However, at this point in our young relationship, I really can't accept such a lavish gift."

If an overly expensive present comes from a business associate, it's inappropriate to accept it because it could be viewed as a bribe. Tell him that, as much as you appreciate his thoughtfulness, you (or your company) have a policy of only accepting small gifts from those with whom you do business. Some businesses issue written statements that are mailed to clients and other associates, stipulating that gifts over a certain monetary value can't be accepted. Including a copy of the statement in a "Thanks, but I must return your kind gift . . ." note could smooth out an awkward situation.

Inappropriate Gifts

Some gifts are just plain wrong, no matter the good intentions of the giver. If, for example, a relative gives your ten-year-old a violent computer game you'll have to return the gift. If your child opens the gift in front of the

Q: As I was leaving a recent baby shower, the honoree handed me a scroll tied with ribbon. When I unrolled it, I found a one-size-fits-all computer-generated thank-you letter. At another baby shower I was asked to address my own envelope, presumably for a thank-you note. Have these practices become acceptable?

A: In a word, no. While you might plead a case that the practice will encourage prompt thank-yous, any note is much more meaningful when it is personalized. You and the other shower guests surely felt slighted and saw the honorees as lazy. In the first case, the honoree should have mailed handwritten notes after thanking guests individually at the party. One of the keys to a sincere thank-you is a mention of the specific present ("I can't wait to see the baby in the new jumpsuit!"), which you can hardly do in a one-size-fits-all note.

Having guests address their own thank-you note is another "time-saver" that's essentially rude. Some hostesses use the envelopes in a drawing for a prize for a guest, killing two birds with one stone, so to speak. Surely, it's simple to put guests' names on a slip of paper, and the shower hostess can provide the invitation address list to the honoree, who should handwrite both the note and the envelope.

giver, let your child say "Thank you," and then take the gift and ask to speak to the giver aside, in private. "Jay, do you have a minute? Thank you, a video game is totally up Brendan's alley, but this one is going to be too violent for him. I have to ask that we exchange it for one that's good for his age." Now, Jay can either choose to make the switch or suggest that you do it. The important things to remember are that you still thank the giver, and you have the corrective conversation away from the group. If the giver isn't present, it's okay to let your son or daughter know right away that the game isn't appropriate. "Oops. Looks like Uncle Jay didn't realize that video game is for adults. We'll exchange it for one that's for kids." You can then call Uncle Jay to thank him, but let him know that you'll have to make the exchange.

"REGIFTING"

"Regifting" buzzed its way into our lexicon January 19, 1995, when it was the subject of the popular *Seinfeld* show episode, "The Label Maker." Jerry received a label maker from Dr. Tim, and suspected that it is the same one Elaine gave to Tim previously, making Tim a "regifter." The practice isn't entirely new—white elephant parties were a fad in the 1800s—but it was frowned upon as part of formal gift-giving practice. Today, those under age 45 are more likely to regift than their elders. December 18 is National Regifting Day. So, how did a once unacceptable practice—unless done in fun—become mainstream, and is it a good idea?

Regifting is a symptom of the surplus of "stuff" many people find themselves with, and their desire to be practical and give away things they know they'll never use. Sounds sensible, but every holiday season the media regales us with tales of regifting horror stories or tells us how to regift without hurting feelings or getting caught. That alone should be a warning that the practice is less than honest or considerate, which is why it's best avoided. Rather than presenting a wrapped gift under

when you want to exchange a gift

In most cases, you needn't feel guilty about exchanging a gift. The giver's aim was to please, not to give you a sweater that will forever hang in the back of your closet. If the gift is the wrong size, it's okay to make the exchange, but not really necessary to mention it in your thanks. If it's the wrong color, a duplicate, or something you just didn't care for or can't use, exercise some tact in your in-person thanks: "Susie, you were so kind to give me a salad spinner. My kitchen's so small that I just don't have any room to store it, so I hope you'll understand why I exchanged it for a set of lovely placemats." The time *not* to exchange is when you've received something so unique— like a piece of artwork or a decorative object— that the gift giver would undoubtedly be hurt if you opted for something else. You'll know when extra thought has gone into the gift selection.

Many stores make exchanges easier and less awkward by enclosing a gift receipt—listing the item but not the price—and it means the giver wants you to be able to make the exchange.

Q: *What do I do if someone gives me a holiday gift and I don't have one for them?*

A: Don't panic. Since this isn't a person with whom you normally exchange gifts, it's fine to respond with an enthusiastic thank-you—by phone, email, or in person—and follow up with a short note or card and leave it at that. You could give a gift in return, if you wish. This may trigger a gift-giving tradition, though, and you might not want to go that route. Another alternative is to have some nice gifts on standby for this type of situation—some pretty ornaments, small boxes of high-quality chocolates or nuts, or a batch of a home-made specialty. Just be sure to give something that you're fairly certain the recipient would like.

false pretenses, unwanted or duplicate items can be given to a charity, sold through an online auction service, or given away unwrapped: "Karen, I received two copies of this cookbook. Would you like one?" However, if you choose to regift, be sure the following criteria are met:

- You didn't use the words *hideous*, *ugly*, or similar adjectives to describe the original gift.

- You're certain that the gift is something the recipient would really like to have.

- The gift is brand-new (no used items or hand-me-downs allowed) and comes with its original box and instructions.

- The original gift tag (or wedding number code) and/or receipt is removed and the item rewrapped in fresh paper.

- The gift isn't homemade or one that the original giver took great care to select.

In short, *take care not to hurt feelings*—neither the original giver's nor the recipient's. Would the person who gave you the gift mind that you passed it along? Do he and the recipient of your gift know each other, and would it be awkward if they realized that you've recycled a gift from one to the other? Only you can

decide whether to pass along a gift, and if so how to do it appropriately. Think through each situation carefully and then, if in doubt, don't do it.

you've been regifted!

It is pretty obvious when you receive a gift that has someone else's monogram or a little numbered sticker from a wedding gift log that you've been regifted. What do you do? The best way to handle it is to laugh, and then make it your little secret. There is no polite way to call out the regifter. Who knows? You might have an occasion to gift it back—in good humor, of course.

 dating

Once upon a time, he asked her out and then paid for everything. She followed his agenda. Males were chivalrous; females were demure and coy. That was the ideal back in the 1950s, when dating was regarded as the first step in a natural progression toward marriage and family. Dating by the rules has given way to more casual encounters and relationships, and marriage is no longer the immediate objective for all single people.

On the other hand, lots of singles complain that it's harder than ever to meet potential partners. Others opt out entirely, saying that their busy careers don't leave time for the dating rat race. Many are looking for clear-cut standards and expectations—something between the strict dating rules of their grandparents' day and the modern dating scene.

[BEGIN WITH SOME SELF-APPRAISAL]

Whether you've been dating fairly routinely or you're returning to the dating scene, it's a good idea to take stock of your own attitudes and experiences. Ask yourself how you define a date. Your expectations may have changed over time. For example, the dating customs from high school or college may not be suitable for dating in your late twenties. And those getting back to dating after a number of years out of circulation often need to readjust their thinking.

Honestly appraising your own attitudes—and evaluating past experiences, good and bad—should enable you to be more sensitive to others. Here are some basic guidelines that can help make any date pleasant for both parties:

Treat people as individuals. Stereotypical thinking—"All men are afraid of commitment"; "All women are emotional"—is a barrier to successful dating.

Be realistic. There's no perfect man or woman, so don't place the bar so high that it's impossible for anyone to leap over it. If you expect every date to be Mr. or Ms. Right, you're sure to be disappointed.

Communicate. Participate in the conversation and be honest and straightforward. A date deserves to know whether you want to go out for the sheer fun of it or if your goal is a long-term commitment.

Show respect. Courteous manners speak volumes about your attitudes toward the people you go out with and your own self-respect. If halfway through your dinner you realize he's not someone you'll ever see again, that's okay. But it's no excuse to spend the rest of the evening ignoring him.

Be gracious. There's no reason to make another person feel uncomfortable or inadequate because a date doesn't go as you hoped. When a date turns into a disaster, the blame rarely lies with one person alone.

] MEETING PEOPLE [

Introductions through friends, family, and colleagues are still the favored way of meeting other singles. If you're thinking about setting up two friends, let them know beforehand so they know what to expect. Double-dating and matching single people at dinner parties are

"setting up" friends and acquaintances

A woman at work shares an interest with your good buddy and you think they'd enjoy meeting. How can you set up a meeting that doesn't sound like the dreaded "blind date"? First, ask yourself if the two are likely to be compatible; consider their total personalities, not just a single common interest. If you think they'll get along, try to arrange a meeting that involves more than just the two of them. Include them in a group get-together, or ask them both to lunch and see what happens. If you can't organize an introductory meeting, ask if they'd like to exchange phone numbers, but don't give out numbers until both agree. However you go about it, avoid overselling with exaggerated descriptions: "She's absolutely gorgeous." Your goal is to introduce two people you like, not to play marriage broker.

good ways to "set up" friends without the awkwardness many adults associate with blind dates. A great way to meet people outside your immediate social circle is to ask some of your guests to bring a non-mutual friend, someone new to you, to a casual social gathering, such as a holiday party or barbecue.

Work, school, special interest clubs, volunteer organizations, places of worship, cultural events, sporting venues, the health club, bars, and coffeehouses are some of the many places to meet. It's easy to get stuck in the home-job-home-again rut. To meet other people, you have to go where they are. Seek out places where people like you gather and participate in activities that interest you.

Internet dating services and apps have grown in popularity and acceptance, in part because they allow people to get to know each other behind a veil of anonymity. (See "Online Dating," page 380.) Religious and social groups now provide opportunities for singles to meet, and even matchmakers and speed dating may be worth a try. It's up to you to make the most of your opportunities.

Don't forget to introduce yourself—if only so that you don't lose an opportunity to get in touch. Be open-minded about the people you meet and don't dismiss someone right off the bat. A lot of chances to meet are thrown away simply because people fail to notice a nice smile or a pleasant comment.

ASKING AND ANSWERING

Surveys indicate that men still like to do the asking and women still enjoy being asked. But like so many dating customs today, the issue of who asks is largely situational, and a woman is certainly free to ask a man out. Whoever does the asking:

Ask directly and give the necessary information. "What are you doing after work on Wednesday?" is too general. Instead, say, "Would you like to go to dinner with me Wednesday night?" This invitation politely gets to the point and gives the person a clear idea of what the date will entail.

Discuss the arrangements. Where will you meet? If in a public location, agree on a definite spot. Will you be paying or are you each paying your way? (See "The 'Who Pays?' Dilemma," next page.) You might give some information about what to wear. Also, alert your date if you'll be meeting a group of friends.

Call back and confirm. A quick call, email, or text the day before or the day of the date to confirm the details shows consideration and prevents embarrassments like showing up at the wrong time or the wrong place.

Accept a "no" without argument. Chances are that a turndown isn't a personal rejection, but even if it is, there's no reason to quiz the other person about his or her motives or demand an explanation. If you sense the person would like another opportunity, try again later. If not, don't take it too personally.

Saying "Yes" or "No"

It's a compliment to be asked on a date, but it doesn't mean you're obligated to accept. Whether you accept or regret, your answer should be gracious and include a thank-you.

If you have a prior commitment, explain. It's fine to suggest a future get-together, signaling your interest: "I have to work on a project all weekend, but maybe we could get together next week." However, if changing or canceling your existing plans will inconvenience others (for example, backing out of a dinner party or leaving houseguests on their own), then you should definitely say no to the date. Again, it's fine to ask if you can reschedule.

What about someone who can't take no for an answer? Most people will get the message after a couple of rejections. But if they're persistent, you need to be firm and clear, but not cruel: "It's flattering but I'm not interested," or "No, but thank you for asking." When there's a specific, *truthful* reason, state it: "I've made it a rule never to date anyone I work with" or "I'm seeing someone exclusively."

Avoid any remark that might give the person false hope. "I'm so busy working on my thesis that I can't go out with anyone right now" may lead to more unwanted offers in the future. Whatever you say, don't make up excuses or tell a "white lie" that will come back to haunt you.

Rejecting a Date

When it comes to dating it's especially important to be thoughtful not just when we ask someone to go on a date but in the way we say no to dates we don't want to go on. Making up excuses doesn't serve anyone. You're almost sure to be caught in a white lie or invite further invitations if you aren't clear. Here's some sample language to help.

You are asked by someone with whom you'd rather just be friends:

"Becca, thank you for asking me. I would like to keep our relationship to the friendship that we have." Be sure to reach out to Becca soon and invite her to do something that you typically would do as friends so that she can see through your actions that you are sincere about remaining friends.

You are asked on a date by someone you don't know and have no desire to get to know:

"Thank you for asking me, but I'm going to have to say no. [or, I'm not interested.]"

You are asked on a date by someone you would like to go out with but it isn't good timing:

"Miles, thanks for asking me. I really would like to, but I admit that things are a bit busy for me. I know it could be a ways away, but could I reach out to you when I'm not juggling quite so much? I truly would like to go out."

THE "WHO PAYS?" DILEMMA

Women can pay for a date, but it's not a universal given. In some cultures and regions, the "man always pays" rule is still observed, especially on first dates and in the early stages of a relationship. Older men and women who grew up with the "man pays" rule might find it hard to conform to the new attitude.

Following are some helpful guidelines based on sensitivity and common sense. John and Alison are our couple du jour.

- For a first date it's very common to split the check and this decision can be made when the check is presented. Otherwise, the person who asks should pay unless both parties agree in advance to share expenses. By asking Alison out, John signals his intent to pay.

- If Alison (who isn't paying) suggests doing something in addition to or more costly than John's original plans—say, going to a club after a concert—

then it's courteous for Alison to offer to pay or split the extra costs.

- ◆ When a date "just happens" and wasn't an ask, it's reasonable to share the costs. This doesn't always mean splitting everything straight down the middle. John might pay for dinner, and Alison could get the concert tickets.

- ◆ Always be prepared by taking cash or credit cards. Alison can offer to cover her share, but shouldn't make an issue if John insists on paying. The same holds true for John if Alison is paying.

Paying for a date doesn't oblige the other person to anything. To expect or demand any kind of intimacy or future dates because you picked up the check is totally out of bounds.

BREAKING A DATE

As with all social invitations, once you've agreed to a date, don't break it. Of course there are times when you must, but do so only when there's no alternative. For parents, any emergency involving their child must take precedence. But changing one's mind, getting a "better" offer, or "just not feeling up to it" is no excuse. Standing someone up is inexcusable.

THE ETIQUETTE OF A DATE

The etiquette basics that you probably learned in high school still apply, but it never hurts to review these key points before starting out:

Be on time. Five minutes late may be okay, but if you're going to be any longer, call and give your date a reasonable idea of the length of the delay.

When your date is picking you up, be ready to go. Expecting a date to entertain himself for a half hour while you dress is like saying that your time is more valuable than his.

Go to the door. Don't park at the curb and honk or call on your cell phone to let her know you're waiting— unless that's what you and your date agreed on. If you're meeting at a workplace, let your date know that you've

a timeless courtesy

When you arrive at a date's home, be prepared to meet and greet anyone else in the household: parents, children, roommates. Be especially attentive to a date's children; they need to feel that their mother or father is going out with a nice person. Don't go overboard; just a few minutes of chat shows your interest. Teens should be sure to introduce their dates to their parents.

When someone is coming to your home, introduce your date to others. Even if you aren't quite ready to go, meet your date at the door, make introductions, and help get some conversation started.

arrived and then wait . . . patiently. If you're meeting in a public place, try to arrive a few minutes early.

Review your plans. On a first date, reviewing plans can be a conversation starter, and on any date, it's respectful to discuss any changes to the original plans. You'd said Italian but you'd rather have Thai—bring it up as an option. Your date may agree or not, or you both might be happy with Mexican. If you or your date is responsible to others—young children, elderly or ill relatives—be sure that they and/or their caregivers know where you're going and how to reach you.

On the Date

Good manners on both sides can make any date more enjoyable.

Transportation. The person who makes the date is normally responsible for transportation. If you're driving, be sure your car is clean, gassed, and in good running order. If you use public transportation, check schedules in advance and have the necessary change, tokens, or tickets.

---

opening doors and holding chairs

Whether a man should open doors and hold chairs for a woman depends largely on whether the woman will appreciate these gestures. On a date, the man's best bet is to ask. Like so many matters of modern etiquette, a little communication between the people involved removes awkwardness.

Conversation. People naturally worry about what to talk about on a first or second date. Keep it light until you get to know each other. Don't think you have to be a brilliant conversationalist or avoid obvious topics. There's nothing wrong with commenting on the weather or asking about her job or his hobbies to get a conversation going.

Having a lot to say about a lot of topics may be great, but the key to successful small talk is *listening*. Listen for clues to your date's interests and cues for new topics. Your comment about the rain might elicit the fact that he's canceled a couple of camping trips because of the weather. Now you know that he's a fan of the outdoors. (See also "The Art of Small Talk," page 39.)

There are some topics that are best to steer clear of in the earliest stages of a relationship.

- **Personal money matters.** Asking about a date's income is out of line. So is disclosing your own financial status, particularly in an effort to impress.
- **Previous romantic relationships.** Talking about the wonderful or awful qualities of your exes is both annoying and boring.
- **Gossip.** It's one thing to talk about the latest celebrity news, but quite another to tell tales on mutual acquaintances.
- **Politics and religion.** These subjects aren't off-limits but are better when eased in to. A first date is the last place to campaign, preach, or proselytize.

Dining. Most dates involve some kind of meal. Whether it's a leisurely dinner at a fine restaurant or a quick bite at the local deli, good table manners will make a good impression. (See Chapter 6, "Table Manners," page 56.)

People usually place their own orders in restaurants, but if your date is familiar with the menu or cuisine and you're not, ask for recommendations. When the place is pricey, thoughtful dates stick to the middle price range unless their dates do the ordering. When each person is paying his or her own way, order what you can afford. (See also Chapter 9, "Dining Out," page 100.)

Both people should speak up if they don't care for certain foods or cuisines. A vegetarian or a person with religious restrictions or food allergies should let their date know this when accepting a lunch or dinner invitation.

When you accept a date that includes a meal, order amounts you can comfortably eat and be sure it's food you like. Then eat most, if not all, of it. If you're on a diet or normally eat light meals, explain: "I'm really watching what I eat right now, so I'm just ordering two appetizers."

Bringing It to a Close

There are important courtesies for the end of every date:

- Whether the date has been a success or not, both people should express their thanks graciously.

- It's fine to say, "I had a really great time this evening, I'd like to see you again," if that's the case. Unless you really intend to get in touch again, don't make any promises you can't keep.

- Particularly when a man asks a woman out, it's his responsibility to see that she gets home safely: Escort her to the door, see her to her car, or wait with her until her transportation arrives. In some circumstances, it makes sense to call and check that she got home safely.

- Never allow a date who is intoxicated to drive or wander off on his or her own.

The Next Day

After a date, it's important to follow up with a call or email thanking your date for a nice evening. If you're not interested in more dates, just leave it at that. If you are, this is a great time to say, "Let's do this again."

While you might be excited to talk to friends about a great date, remember the adage "Don't kiss and tell."

[DATING AND THE WORKPLACE]

The workplace is an obvious place for people to meet and personal relationships to bloom. But before starting an office romance, workers should check their employers' policies. Some businesses have no problem with employees dating other employees, but other companies do. Difficulties can arise if the relationship interferes with work or causes conflicts with other employees. Ask your supervisor or human resources department for information, as in some cases there may be severe penalties for office romance, including transfer or dismissal.

the manners of safe sex

The emergence of HIV/AIDS and the increase in other sexually transmitted diseases (STDs) have transformed the issue of disclosing and discussing sexual histories with a potential intimate partner. What was once an extremely embarrassing discussion is now a matter of personal health.

Admittedly, it's not easy to raise the subject, but it is absolutely essential whenever a relationship is likely to include sex. There are ways to approach the subject. With someone you've only recently met, it's perfectly okay to say, "I'm sorry but until we know each other better and feel comfortable talking about sex, we just can't get involved sexually. There's too much at stake." If a person tries to pursue sexual intimacies without revealing his or her sexual history, he or she doesn't have your best interests at heart. Your life and health aren't worth the risk.

Honest discussion isn't a matter of prying; there's no reason to name names or give the intimate details of other relationships. The purpose is to disclose everything that can affect a partner's health and life. Both people should be willing to have blood tests and medical checkups and to exchange the results. People have been known to lie about test results, so a literal exchange of records is reasonable.

Men and women are both responsible for condom use, and each partner has the right to insist that condoms are worn. A woman should never hesitate to provide condoms if her partner is unprepared.

Depending on the circumstances, dating a person you work with can be problematic even if there's no official policy. Dating a superior can raise issues of favoritism and unfair promotion. The situation can be trickier for the superior, who may risk running afoul of sexual harassment and discrimination policies and laws.

In general, the etiquette of dating a coworker is to keep the relationship out of the workplace: Avoid displays that are distracting or offensive to others (including customers and clients) and that reflect poorly on the business and its management. Maintain a professional attitude toward each other during the workday or at work-related events. (See also Chapter 35, "The Social Side of Business," page 442.)

Sending Gifts to the Office

The date was great, and you want to send something that says "I had a wonderful time." Is it appropriate to send a bouquet of roses or balloons to his or her workplace? Maybe. A person with a private office or cubicle probably has space for a vase of flowers, but someone on a retail floor or in an assembly area may have no more than a locker or cubby.

A better option may be to have flowers and the like delivered to your date's home, or send something smaller. A nice card with a personal message can be just as impressive as a large bouquet. Each says that you enjoyed the date.

BREAKING UP

Ending a relationship is hard. Ending it well may seem impossible, but it can be done if both people stay true to the principles of respect, consideration, and honesty. When one person ends the relationship, he or she is responsible for giving the news in a manner that shows genuine concern for the other person. Putting it off, not answering phone calls, or avoiding or ignoring the person only leaves him or her in emotional limbo. No matter how uncomfortable the situation, there are certain decencies that must be observed.

Meet personally. Someone you've been close to is owed a face-to-face meeting. *Ghosting*, or simply ending all communication without offering explanation,

is hurtful and inappropriate. Don't use anyone else as an intermediary. Don't resort to a "Dear John" or "Dear Jane" letter, email, or text. Phoning may be necessary when time and distance are a problem, but don't leave a brush-off message by text or on voice mail. If ending the relationship is your choice, face up to it.

Meet privately. To deliberately stage a breakup in a place where other people are close by—hoping that the presence of others will keep things calm—is cowardly.

Get to the point. Don't try to ease the blow by taking the person out for a nice time, then dropping the bomb at the last minute. The person will probably feel that he or she has been made a fool of if you do.

Avoid blaming. Neither party will benefit from a rehash of their faults and failings. Blaming or hurling insults is childish and cruel, as are phony and superficial excuses. A person may say hurtful things, but you don't have to respond in kind.

See to the other person's well-being. Be sure that he or she is reasonably in control before leaving. A person who is extremely upset or angry isn't in the best shape to drive or go off on her own.

The details of a breakup should be kept private. What's past is over, and talking disrespectfully about a former partner only reflects poorly on the one who does the talking.

---

ghosting

When a relationship reaches a conclusion it is up to you to end it well. *Ghosting*, or simply ending all communication without offering explanation, is hurtful and inappropriate. Whether it is a friendship or a more romantic relationship, give people enough information before you break your usual communication patterns so they don't wonder what has happened to you. Sometimes it can feel like the easiest course of action is to stop communicating with someone entirely when a relationship has reached a conclusion, but this lack of contact will likely leave an ex feeling confused and abandoned. Take the time to end a relationship with the same effort and care that you put into it.

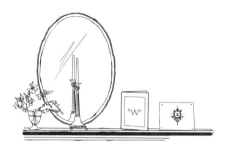

GETTING BACK TO DATING

For someone who has lost a spouse through divorce or death or experienced the breakup of a long-standing relationship, it can be very difficult to begin dating again, and many people put their social lives on hold. There are many reasons not to date for some time—to adjust to the single life and avoid a rebound relationship, to heal old wounds and rebuild trust after a failed relationship, to get established as chief wage earner and head of household. Widows and widowers need time to grieve the loss of a beloved spouse and may feel that dating someone else is a kind of betrayal.

But sooner or later, most people decide it's time to take a chance and reenter the dating pool. When that time comes, it can be helpful to consider the following:

- Give yourself permission to enjoy yourself and the companionship of other adults. Dating isn't a lifelong commitment. It's an opportunity to get to know someone else, do something that may not be routine for you, and have fun for a few hours.

- Understand that times have changed. Talk with some of your contemporaries who date to get a clearer picture of how things are done in your social group. Dating customs can vary considerably among regional, cultural, and age groups, and you'll feel more confident when you know what to expect.

- Don't be embarrassed to express your feelings and preferences and to ask questions of a date. If you're more comfortable sharing expenses, say so. Be willing to offer suggestions and alternatives when someone asks what you'd like to do or suggests an activity that you'd rather not do. If a date proposes seeing a movie that you've already seen, speak up.

- Tell dates about your family responsibilities, such as children, or a family member who relies on you for care. It's better to know at the outset whether someone is or isn't interested in a relationship that comes complete with a family.

Considering the Children

When a parent decides to begin dating again, children deserve to know. Young children may be satisfied just to hear that you're going to a party with a friend. Older children and teens may want more details about your dates and your plans. To a child, dating may signal that their other parent is being replaced, and those worries have to be treated seriously.

If your relationship becomes steady, your child may experience split loyalties between his or her other parent and your new partner. Another concern for children is that they'll be relegated to second place in their parent's affection. Children need a lot of reassurance, but they also need to understand that every parent has the right to some private grown-up time with grown-up friends.

Divorced parents should respect each other's right to a social life. Their children shouldn't be questioned about people their other parent is dating or subjected to negative criticism of their other parent and his or her new partners.

Be sure to introduce your date to your children, but be cautious about including him or her in family activities and routines early in the relationship. Think seriously, too, about having a date sleep over. A younger child may not understand the meaning of adult intimacy, but he may resent the intrusion of someone into his home and life. Or he may grow attached to a person who is frequently in his home and suffer genuine pain if the person is no longer around.

Adult children also need to know when a parent begins dating. Some may not react well at first, but most will understand their mother's or father's need for companionship. (See Chapter 42, "Elder Etiquette," page 520.)

⌐ ONLINE DATING ⌐

The same manners that apply to traditional dating apply to online dating. From the time you set up your profile to an in-person meeting, your conduct defines your image and can have a significant impact on your success. While some advice is specific to different stages of online dating, these tips apply across the board:

- ◆ Use a reputable online dating service. Check it out before you sign on.

- ◆ Don't give out personal information. Protect your privacy by using the email provided by the online service.

- ◆ Respect privacy. It's unethical to share names (real names or screen names) and personal information with anyone else.

- ◆ Just as you can casually date more than one person, it's okay to interact with more than one person while you're still playing the field.

- ◆ Tread carefully with controversial topics, including sex, politics, religion, personal finances, and obscene jokes. Don't assume you know the other person's feelings or beliefs. Don't gossip about friends or coworkers, or share proprietary information from work.

- ◆ If you set up a date, show up. It's a commitment that must be honored except under unavoidable circumstances.

Building Your Profile

Be honest and genuine from the beginning, in your profile and in all your communications. It's critical to building a relationship. Even small fabrications and embellishments can end up being a problem. When the truth comes out, you'll lose the trust you've been building with the person. From that person's perspective the question becomes "What else are you willing to stretch the truth about or outright lie about?" Once the trust is lost, your chances for advancing the relationship are lost with it.

Interacting Electronically

If you don't hear back from someone within a few days or a week, then try again. They may not have gotten your first email. If you don't hear after your second attempt, move on.

It's okay to be selective; you don't have to respond to everyone who contacts you. When you respond, do it politely, starting with a simple greeting. In your message, be sure to mention at least an item or two from the person's profile so it's obvious that you actually read it.

The email stage is a time to begin to find out about each other. It's fine to ask a few questions, but not a barrage. Think of it as a conversation: Ask a question, answer a question.

Good email etiquette applies to online dating as well. This is your chance to make a good first impression, so take care with your mechanics as well as your messages. Keep them short: You don't want to say everything you have to say in one email and then be left with nothing to say in the next. Pace yourself; it's a process. (For more on email etiquette, see Chapter 20, "Online Communication," page 237.)

The Next Level: Talking on the Phone

When you're ready for the next step, usually a phone call, it's easy to appear too forward. For instance, instead of saying, "By the way, here's my phone number in case you want to call me," you could ask, "Would it be all right if I sent you my phone number?" A mobile phone number is safer than a landline number.

The First Date

For most people, the whole point of online dating is eventually to meet and date in person. If you decide to meet, agree on a public place that's easy to get to, well lit, but quiet enough to have a conversation. Now, first date etiquette is in play:

◆ Be on time. Start out on the right foot before you even say "Hello."

◆ Dress appropriately. Even casual clothes should be clean and neat, and show you put some effort into your appearance.

◆ Put your phone on vibrate. Texting and talking to your friends while on a date could make it your last. Focus on the person you're with.

◆ When introducing yourself, stand up, smile, look the person in the eyes, say your name and repeat their name, and use a firm—not bone crusher or limp— handshake.

◆ Be a good conversationalist. Don't be a hog; let the other person speak, too. Use what you learned from their profile as a starting point for topics. Ask their opinion about something but avoid too many detailed personal questions. And as important as anything, listen, listen, listen.

◆ Keep it simple. On the first date, it's easier if each of you pays your own way.

- Follow up. After a date, it's a great gesture to call or send a thank-you email the next day. It can either be encouraging, saying you'd like to meet again, or it can be a "thanks but no thanks" message: "It was fun meeting you, but I don't think this will work for me. Thanks for the opportunity. I wish you the best." You can always thank someone for meeting you.

Building a Relationship

You may be ready to jump in, but he or she may not be, so take your time and respect the other person's need to move slowly. If the relationship does move forward, then it's time to take down your profile and focus on the person you've chosen to date.

safety first

For safety's sake, meet in a public place and make sure a friend you trust knows you're going out on a date made with someone from the dating service you use. Give your friend the person's profile information, the location of the date, and how long you expect it to last. Set up a check-in schedule with your friend and put a reminder on your phone. Tell your friend what you want him or her to do if you miss a check-in: call you, call your parents, call the police. Then when you get home, call to let your friend know that you're safe.

30 life online

facebook, LinkedIn, Twitter, Instagram, dating, interest groups, gaming—with more people connecting and communicating than ever before, online and social media manners have never been more important. The online world is the new frontier for etiquette. As people find each other online in greater and greater numbers, the social expectations that we have in these virtual spaces continue to grow. The good news is that while they sometimes look and feel different, new manners for the online world are based on the same principles of consideration, respect, and honesty that are the basis of all good etiquette.

⟦ VIRTUAL MANNERS ⟧

As with in-person interactions, online manners boil down to thinking about other people, making choices that respect others, and operating from a place of honesty and integrity. Treating others well is a golden rule of etiquette and it absolutely translates online. In fact, it might even be more important online. Cues that indicate humor, sincerity, frustration, or appreciation are often absent. Without the benefit of tone of voice, facial expressions, or other physical signals, it is hard to know the other person's intentions. The nature of communicating online means we have to take extra care with how we represent ourselves and how we choose to communicate with others.

"Whenever two people come together and their behavior affects one another, you have etiquette." That's what Emily Post said about etiquette, and it's just as true about the world of electronic communication. You may not see or hear the other person, but it's still an interaction between two people that calls for the same manners as though you were in a room with them.

Be Polite

The saying goes "You'll catch more flies with honey than vinegar." It certainly applies to online communications. People in the electronic community are no different than people you encounter face-to-face. If you want them to visit your space and read your content, then treat them positively and politely.

Remember, once you've put something out there on the Internet, it's out there—forever! You can't take it back or undo it. Post a picture of a friend in a compromising situation and you can't pull it back and pretend it never happened. Post a disparaging remark in the heat of the moment about somebody else within an online community and you can't get it back; you'll have to accept the responsibility of your post. Even if you can recall or delete your post, there's still a good chance that someone else will have seen it and forwarded it.

You're Not Anonymous

As easy as it is to think no one knows who you are, don't believe it for a minute. People think that just because they've created a clever username that their identity is protected. It's no guarantee that their comments, phrasing, or tone won't be recognizable to acquaintances.

Everything Online Is Public . . . and Permanent

One litmus test for deciding whether to make a comment or post is to ask yourself, "If I posted this on a bulletin board for anyone to read, would that be okay?" Twitter, Facebook, LinkedIn—these are all virtual bulletin boards that anyone can access and see. A college graduate should be aware that posts and pictures of vacations and parties on Facebook may well be seen by bosses and prospective employers and can affect getting and keeping a job. The same is true for employees whose tweets and blogs malign a company or individual. Assume that unflattering comments about friends, ex-friends, significant others, exes, or even public figures will be seen not only by the targets themselves, but also by their friends and families. Their opinions of the posts and of you will be affected. Remember: Nothing online is private, and the Internet has a perfect memory.

Intentionally making disparaging remarks has no place in personal communications, and it has no place online, either. It's not simply a matter of expressing your opinion, but crafting it to stay on topic and contributing constructively to the conversation.

It's Your Image

What You Communicate

In any online space that you engage in, you'll want to think about what you feel comfortable contributing. Opinions and thoughts? Images? Personal photos of friends and loved ones? Videos? To the best of your ability make intentional choices of what you post online.

Word choice. Take care that the words you use have the meaning you think they have. Try saying them aloud before you post them. Ask yourself if there is any other way these words could be interpreted.

Content choice. What type of content you decide to write about or share online is up to you. Maybe you only post political views on message boards and in forums with like-minded users. Maybe you use a site like Facebook to engage during election years. It's your choice what content you engage with and where you choose to present it.

Images. The images (photos, videos, illustrations, and memes) you choose to post will definitely have an effect on your image. So consider carefully who might see them and how they could be interpreted before you like, share, or post anything online.

How You Communicate

Not only does what you say matter; how you say it reflects on you as well. The rules of good writing apply just as much online as they do to traditional pen and paper.

Spelling and grammar. Proofread, proofread, proofread. You want the focus of your readers on your content, not your errors. If you're a notoriously poor speller, write your post using a word processing program and take advantage of spell-checking and grammar tools. Then cut and paste your message.

Sentence case. Use correct capitalization and punctuation so your writing is clear and comprehensible. Avoid using all capitals—online, this indicates shouting—unless it's something to shout about: "IT'S A GIRL!"

Punctuation. Proper punctuation helps a person know what you mean. The title of the book *Eats, Shoots and Leaves* by Lynn Truss (Gotham Books) is a perfect example of how important punctuation is. One comma significantly changes the sense of the title. Written as *Eats Shoots and Leaves*, the title implies a cookbook for vegetarians: punctuated *Eats, Shoots, and Leaves*, it could suggest a murder mystery. Punctuation matters. Period.

Text-speak abbreviations. Except when writing text messages, avoid using abbreviations. B4 may be simple to figure out, but 2GTBT (too good to be true) could be misinterpreted. If your reader doesn't understand it, then his focus shifts from getting your message to deciphering it. Twitter is the exception because of the 140-character limit.

⌈ SOCIAL NETWORKS ⌉

How social network platforms are used depends on the users, not necessarily the designers. When Facebook was just a college chat room for Harvard students, its creator probably didn't imagine a worldwide membership of hundreds of millions, nor the ways in which businesses and individuals would use the site to connect with one another.

Social network sites are dynamic, constantly changing environments and each community develops its own standards, rules, and best practices. Think of a social network as the main street in your town or city. Keep your interactions on it clean and civil. You wouldn't want to do anything in the social media world you wouldn't feel comfortable doing on the street of your hometown. The following may help you choose a social network community that's best for you:

Choosing a Site

- ◆ All social networks are not equal. Each one has its own rules. Pay attention to the norms and user patterns of a community before you jump in.

- ◆ Learn about the nature and reach of the social network before you set up an account and go live. This includes learning about the privacy settings for the site.

- ◆ Ask a more experienced user if there are things you should know or consider before joining.

Managing Your Space

- ◆ Learn how to use privacy settings to limit the content others can share on your site.

- ◆ Learn the features of your site, like tagging, hashtags, likes, endorsements, shares and the like. Understand how using them will affect the people you interact with on the site.

- ◆ Decide ahead of time, how you will present yourself in this space. (See "It's Your Image" page 384.)

- ◆ There is no etiquette imperative that says you must accept everyone who requests to be a friend, especially strangers. It's easy for someone who wants to take advantage of you to create a false online persona. Strangers in the virtual world can be as dangerous as in the real world.

- ◆ If you want to connect with someone you don't know, say, as a business contact, explain why you're contacting him. You'll have a better chance of having him accept your request.

it's your page

It's okay to . . .

. . . ignore a friend request.

. . . untag yourself from a photo or ask someone to remove a photo of you from their page.

. . . delete a friend's comment on your page.

. . . unfriend someone whose presence on your page makes you uncomfortable.

. . . ignore quizzes, groups, and widely marketed event requests.

. . . use privacy settings to restrict access to your page.

- ◆ Be careful not only with your own images, but also with the images of other people on your pages. Don't post comments, photos, videos, or links that could be embarrassing to others.

- ◆ Be careful about who you tag in your photos. You can and should remove your tag from anyone else's site if you are uncomfortable being identified in a photo. If you are uncomfortable or upset by the image, ask the person who posted it to take it down immediately.

- ◆ Ask permission before "scooping" someone's news or posting photos of their event before they do.

Unfriending, Unfollowing, and Ignoring

Part of participating in a social media network is about making connections. However, letting go of connections or not engaging in them in the first place also happens. On sites such as LinkedIn and Facebook, you may end up friending a person whom you later want to unfriend. Both in the real and virtual world, the concept of unfriending someone can be uncomfortable.

Many "friends" on a social network site are, in reality, casual acquaintances: your tent mate from camp, your project partner from a college business class, or someone who knows a friend of a friend who's also a photographer. After the initial excitement of finding each other wears off, you don't have to keep responding and you can let the contact dwindle. Ignoring a friend request blocks the person from being able to make the request again until you accept or decline the original request.

It is definitely okay to actively unfriend someone you no longer feel comfortable being connected with. Most sites don't send a person a message if you unfriend them—their friend count simply goes down by one—but check the FAQs first to be sure that your technology matches your intent.

When someone has unfriended you. Depending on your "in real life" connection to them, you may have to get creative with how you choose to acknowledge their online presence when interacting with mutual friends and family. For example: Exes may want to maintain a social network connection where they may find it useful to tag each other in photos of their kids so that those good times can be shared and seen by both parents.

Popular Sites

- **Facebook.** This is the social social network. Keep it light and personal—not too much business, although businesses do use Facebook to engage their customers regularly. There are lots of features, so learn how to build groups and use privacy settings to share what you want with whom you want to share it.

- **LinkedIn.** This is the social network for business. Keep it professional, especially with your profile pic-

Q: *My ex-boyfriend and I are connected on Facebook, not just to each other but to many mutual friends. Should we unfriend each other?*

A: Some couples will want to do this, while others will be fine with keeping the tie. The choice to unfriend an ex is a question of personal comfort with your experience on Facebook, and it does not have to be a mutual decision. One part of moving on after a relationship ends is severing ties. If your ex unfriends you, understand it's part of the process of breaking up and allow him his space. On the other hand, there's nothing wrong with people who have an amicable breakup remaining friends online. Be sure to change your relationship status within a reasonable amount of time to accurately reflect your new situation.

ture. Use it like an online business card or resumé. Keep it current and know that your profile is public.

- **Instagram.** This is the social network for pictures and images. Use it to share pictures with your friends and family and possibly other users. Remember that it is public unless you make your account private.

- **Twitter.** Brevity may very well be the soul of wit; it is also the heart of Twitter courtesy. This short message application limits characters to 140 and encourages the quick sharing of thoughts. Messages can be re-posted—"retweeted"—with such speed that even someone with just a few followers could soon see their message go viral. Be sure you really want to post what you wrote before submitting it to this platform. NOTE: Beware of linking Twitter to your Facebook page. Your frequent tweets work on Twitter, but may be annoying to people who get feeds from you through Facebook.

COMMENTING ONLINE

Whether it is the comment section on your local radio or newspaper, your Facebook home page, or a Reddit message board, commenting is a big part of online etiquette. This real-time communication platform has its own evolving etiquette:

- Hold yourself accountable. There is often no live person looking back at you to hold you emotionally accountable for what you post. We all know comment sections can be cesspools of troll comments and content. Don't add to the mess. It is like litter:

The world is a better place if there is less of it. You may feel anonymous, but your words can hurt others.

- Someone might be watching. However anonymous you think you are, be careful. Sometimes it is a certain perspective, piece of information, or turn of phrase that will reveal your identity as much as a recognizable username.

- Don't insult, attack, or impugn someone's character or even make fun of their typing skills. Keep the focus on the content of a discussion.

- Remember "sticks and stones . . ."? The good news is they are just words. But if you are reading and asking yourself "Why? Why?? Why???," take a break. If the tone upsets you, take a break. You don't have to interact, so if reading comments starts to affect your emotions too much, STOP.

GAMING

As online communities have grown, competitive and recreational gaming has moved online as well, expanding opportunities to compete anytime with like-minded players anywhere in the world. Gaming communities are very similar to other public competitive environments— youth athletic events, professional sports, or the chess club.

The rules of good conduct apply to the virtual arena as well.

- As always in a public space, watch that your conduct is in line with the norms of your community. If you're unsure, look up the site's rules and observe the way others use the space.

- *Rules of good sportsmanship apply.* Be a good winner and a good loser.

- Emotion can run high in competitive environments. Just because you're alone at your computer doesn't mean you're alone on the Web. Remember to keep your emotions in check and think before you post.

- A certain amount of bravado and fansmanship can be appropriate. Good-natured trash talking, cheering, and even some jeering can be okay if they're in line with good sportsmanship and the character of the site.

- Be a responsible teammate and player. Keep appointments, communicate clearly, and treat the group facilities (whatever they may be for your community) with respect and consideration.

LIFE IN THE
WORKPLACE

PART V
getting the job

CHAPTER 31 The Job Search 395

CHAPTER 32 The Job Interview 403

31
the job search

the job search is a process that goes beyond sending out resumés or responding to ads or online postings. Whether you are in school or already have a job, you can make the next search much easier by building and maintaining your network, a team of advisors and contacts who can assist you. To be most successful, do this both online and in-person.

[NETWORKING THAT WORKS]

Your network consists of people who might be able to facilitate your job search or advise you as you build your career in a particular field. Some of these you will seek out:

- Professors or advisors from your major who can suggest how to put your study into practice.

- Friends of your parents who have contacts in your field and might be willing to provide introductions.

- Former employers, such as a boss whom you admire for his honesty, the way he deals with people, or his ability to get the work done.

- A coworker whom you have sought out as a mentor or who has moved on to another job in your field of interest.

- A client with whom you have developed a strong relationship and who knows your capabilities from working with you.

- A friend who is successful and respected for her business skill.

Others you will meet by chance as you pursue leads. By far, the most common way to build a supportive job search or career network is through social media, with LinkedIn being the biggest facilitator.

Do stay in touch, but not so often that you become a nuisance. Some unobtrusive ways to remain in contact are to mail or forward an interesting or helpful article, call or email to report news (not gossip) about a mutual

your personal card

When conducting a job search, use a personal card, not your company business card, to share contact information with others. Your company card is only used for work-related purposes. What goes on a personal card? Your name and any other contact information you wish to share, such as a personal phone number and/or a personal email address. You can always write your physical address on the back of your card if you want someone to contact you by mail.

friend, or offer to treat your job-search advisor to coffee or lunch.

Networking Tips

Networking isn't a process you use only when actively searching for a job. Work on building and communicating with your network on an ongoing basis. Then, when you suddenly find yourself in the job market, your team will be ready to help. Be sure to contact all of them and let them know your situation. Because you've already laid the groundwork and built a relationship, you don't need to overwhelm them with emails and information.

If you receive an offer of help, listen closely so that you'll fully understand what is being offered. (There's a difference between discussing the various options within a certain field and having the person recommend you.) Once you know how the contact can help, you should

- Decide which materials give the best overall picture of your life experience and work history in relation to the offer of help and send that information to your contact.
- Determine how often you may call the contact to follow up.

Be sure not to overdo your networking. Avoid the following missteps:

- Being a fair-weather friend who gets in touch only when he needs something.
- Pestering your contacts with frequent calls or emails.
- Constantly bragging about your connections.
- Being without a personal card printed with your name and contact information. (Having to fumble for paper and pen looks unprofessional and wastes time.)
- Failing to get back to the person with periodic updates.
- Forgetting a follow-up and thank-you at the end of your search.

Handle your networking with care. The better you pace your communications and balance self-confidence with humility, the more likely you are to get results.

thank-you notes

As you look for a job, write or email thank-you notes to everyone who's offered help in any way. If, for example, you chat with someone at a friend's party who says he'll mention you to his boss, your note will show you are polite and help to jog his memory. Here's a sample:

Dear Russell,

    It was great to meet you at Sara Buchwald's party last Saturday. It's not often that I bump into anyone whose first love is statistics! I also appreciate your offer to give my name to your boss, since Garrett & Associates sounds like the kind of place I'd be interested in hearing more about. I'll get in touch with you next week to see whether I should send my resumé.

    Thanks again for your kind offer, which means a lot to me.

    Sincerely,

    Paul Tomassi

If you use stationery or a note card that has no preprinted address and phone number, write both under your signature. (Even if you exchanged cards with the recipient, he may have misplaced yours.)

Another thank-you note is in order if Russell's nice gesture leads to a job. This second note also gives you the chance to say, "Please call on me if I can ever help."

STARTING OUT COLD

Networking often leads to a referral, but there may be times when you have to write or phone a potential employer who's never heard of you. A well-composed mistake-free letter or email asking about job openings will give you an advantage. If you place a cold call to a company, you can increase your chances of being taken seriously by using good telephone manners (see Chapter 18, "Telephone Manners," page 221).

Call the company to find out the correct spelling and pronunciation of the name of the person who either does the interviewing or the hiring for the department you're interested in, as well as his or her title.

Polite persistence is often seen as a plus; just don't become a pest. A good standard? Call no more than three times over the course of a month. If an assistant answers, say that you realize the person must be very busy, then ask what time of day is most convenient for him to be reached. A friendly and upbeat attitude may charm the call screener, but be considerate of his time by getting to the point quickly.

If you're put through to the person, ask if this is a good time to talk. If it is, be succinct but not terse. In a friendly voice, introduce yourself and give a brief description of your relevant professional experience

and current job (if any). Say that you're interested in learning about potential openings in her department. If she seems receptive, ask if you may send a cover letter and resumé.

Before hanging up, thank her: "I really appreciate your talking with me." Then mail or email a thank-you note, whichever is more appropriate (see "Thank-you Notes," page 397). Not only is it the appropriate thing to do, but it also reminds her of your call and demonstrates your relationship-building skills.

⌐ SEARCHING ONLINE ⌐

The Internet has become the principal gateway and research tool for the job search. While searching for a job online is a great way to increase your chances of finding one, avoid the trap of assuming that because it is online you can be more informal. All the rules that apply to the in-person job search apply to the online search as well. Your virtual appearance needs to be professional. Your electronic communications don't have facial expressions, tone of voice, or body language to help create a positive impression of you. Don't write anything you wouldn't say in person. Take special care with the following in your cover letter and resumé:

- Use formal salutations such as Mr. or Ms.
- Write in complete sentences. Avoid abbreviations and textspeak.
- Use sentence case—a capital letter at the start of a sentence and for proper names.
- Keep it brief.

- Watch your tone. Best practice is to read your letter out loud and listen to how it sounds, or have a friend or relative read it and then be willing to listen to their critique.
- Finish with a closing that includes your name and contact information.
- Proofread, proofread, and proofread again. No spelling or grammar mistakes.

Beware that technological capabilities don't become liabilities. Keep the formatting simple. The gorgeously designed resumé and cover letter with the stylish font that works so well in print can backfire if the recipient doesn't have the capability to display it. Your goal is to keep your communication clear, concise, and complete.

The following tips can increase the success of your online job search:

- *Do* repost often, since most job sites list resumés chronologically, and yours will slip farther down the list every day.
- *Do* include keywords—industry words or phrases that highlight your professional and technical areas of expertise. Often, communications are screened electronically. You want to make sure that yours reaches the human level.
- *Do* use the job title or code in the subject line of an email. If you know neither, type your objective in three or four words: "Paralegal job opportunities sought."
- *Do* remember that when you post your resumé, anyone (including your current boss) can access it.

- **Do** check with a potential employer to find out how they want to receive electronic resumés: as an attachment or embedded in the email.

- **Do** carefully check and correct your resumé once you have cut and pasted it into email format (sometimes carefully designed formats are altered when embedded into an email). Make sure the line breaks and type styles are the way you want them.

- **Don't** give out your at-work email address for job search communications. Email is hardly private,

and your company could easily discover that you're job hunting. It's also unwise to job hunt using your company computer.

- **Do** be aware your online job search is in a public forum. Your boss may be monitoring your LinkedIn space.

- **Don't** try to attract a recruiter's attention by adding popular keywords that don't fit your experience. Misrepresenting yourself is dishonest and could also mean big trouble down the line.

Respond quickly to job postings by sending your online resumé and cover letter, then follow up with an email or phone call, safeguards in case your online submission was misplaced or didn't get through.

linkedin

LinkedIn is the social network for business and could be an important part of your next job search. Think of your LinkedIn profile as an online resumé or business card and give it at least as much attention as you give to your other printed materials. LinkedIn is searchable by Google so it is a good way to get a professional, first-page search result connected to your name. Follow these tips to build an effective profile.

- Use a current and professional-looking headshot.
- Complete your profile with accurate information. This includes a headline, a summary statement, and listing of experience and skills.
- Connect with people with whom you have worked or recognize. Remember that often it is the quality of your network that matters most, not the size.
- Ask colleagues and coworkers to endorse you.
- Participate with the larger LinkedIn community through groups.

EMPLOYMENT AGENCIES AND HEADHUNTERS

Job seekers could turn to employment agencies or to headhunters, who generally serve job seekers at the executive or managerial level. Be sure to show respect for the recruiter's expertise and time. Courteous behavior will reap benefits: Like an employer, a recruiter is looking for strong social skills as part of the package.

When you meet with a recruiter, dress as you would for a job interview, arrive on time, and bring a resumé and list of references. Be prepared to showcase your goals, accomplishments, and skills.

Also be ready to "come clean" by telling the person anything in your employment or personal history that could be construed as controversial. A recruiter answers to the employer, so she doesn't want to be hit with any surprises after giving a glowing recommendation.

YOUR RESUMÉ AND COVER LETTER

Sending a resumé without a cover letter is pointless. Consider the cover letter as your personal introduction and the resumé as a fact sheet of your qualifications and experience.

The care with which you prepare your job application can make the difference between a potential employer scheduling an appointment or simply tossing your resumé aside. "Care" in this case means being sure there are no grammatical and spelling errors; such sloppiness can make you look inattentive, lazy, or both. "Care" also means brevity. Paring down your resumé and cover letter makes the information easily accessible—a courtesy that saves time for the reader.

Getting other things right is equally important. Whether applying "cold," answering an online posting, an ad, or writing with a personal referral, call the company to make sure you have the correct full name and spelling, courtesy title, and business title of the recipient. If "M. A. Forbes, Human Resources Director" is Mary Ann and your salutation is "Dear Mr. Forbes," you're already off on the wrong foot. In addition, check to be sure you know how to pronounce the recipient's name.

Before sending your letter and resumé, check the prospective company's website or call the HR department to find out how the company wishes to receive your information: regular mail or email, and if email, what type of attachment, if any. When mailing your resumé, use the best quality personal stationery you can afford, printed with your relevant contact information: name, address, telephone number, and email address. If you print your own letterhead, don't skimp on the quality of the paper.

The Effective Cover Letter

While the resumé effectively telegraphs the essentials of who you are and what you want, the cover letter allows you to expand on how your background makes you a good fit for a specific company or job. While you can use an overall template for your letter, tailor it to the particular company or recipient. As with a resumé,

honesty is the best policy

Exposing false claims of past experience has become something of a media sport over the past few years. Famous writers, professors, and military officers have been caught claiming advanced degrees, military honors, high-level jobs, or wartime service that was real only in their imaginations. As an ordinary citizen, you won't have to worry about news coverage, but lying on your resumé about past accomplishments can be uncovered by a Google search and disastrous to your job prospects. The embarrassment alone isn't worth the risk. The truth may not always get you the job, but a lie uncovered will inevitably lose it.

less is more, so keep the letter to one page. If essential information—a list of your technical capabilities, for example—can't be squeezed in, list it on a separate sheet and cross-reference it in the letter.

If you're writing as the result of a personal referral or recommendation, say so in the first sentence. If you *don't* have a referral, make your opening paragraph dynamic. "I am applying for the position of sales representative . . ." may be informative, but it's hardly attention grabbing. A personal anecdote that can be related in a few words is one possibility: "I realized I wanted to go into public relations in college, upon discovering how much I enjoyed conducting summer tours for prospective students and their parents." A fresh lead-in can give you a leg up over letter writers whose openings are predictable.

In the body of the letter, make sure you

- State what you can do for the company, not what the company can do for you.
- Sell your abilities, skills, and experience, mainly as they relate to the employment needs of the company.

End the letter with a brief thanks. "Thank you for your time and consideration" or "Thank you for considering my application for the position" conveys your sentiments without sounding too effusive.

Should You Bring Up Salary?

In general, the only time when you should address the issue of salary in a cover letter is if the employer has asked for your salary requirements. If so, you may give the actual amount of your present salary or a range. But it's also acceptable to say that your current salary is "consistent with standards in the market" or that your needs are negotiable.

More Dos and Don'ts for the Job Seeker

- *Do* highlight your skills and abilities by relating your specific accomplishments. Merely listing jobs you have held will leave the reader wanting more.

- *Do* your homework even before you write your cover letter. Knowledge of the company will give you credibility and prepare you for interviewing. A well-thought-out letter can also be a big factor in getting you an interview.

- *Do* tailor each letter to the company and the job, individualizing each. Never send photocopies or a generic, one-size-fits-all letter.

- *Do* keep the resumé to one or two pages, and the cover letter to one.

- *Do* keep your cover letter and resumé direct and clear; don't try to be funny unless you're applying for a job as a comedy writer.

- *Don't* use your current job letterhead or business card. If you wish, have a personal card printed (or make your own on your computer) with your home address and phone number. Get a personal email address as well so you aren't using your work email.

- *Don't* simply repeat the facts from your resume in your cover letter. Use the letter to point out and expand on information that directly relates to the job you're seeking.

- *Don't* sell yourself with capabilities you don't have. Letters that make extravagant claims like "There's no task I can't accomplish" are both inflated and untrue.

- **_Don't_** include personal material unless it relates to the job. Your hobbies, world travels, creative jobs during school years might be relevant (if you do mention them only do so briefly), but other personal information (age, marital status, health history) should be omitted. Many times, something unusual from the personal part of your resumé gets you into the door. "Founded and ran a lawn-mowing business for four years" on a college graduate's resumé shows a lot of positive history to an interviewer.

ABOUT REFERENCES

Take care to be courteous as you recruit references. After you draw up your list of potential references, contact them and ask if they're willing to be named. If they are, ask whether they would rather have their home or office phone number, or email address given, and if they would prefer that you notify them before each potential inquiry.

Thanking References

Thank each reference twice. First, when he accepts the role, an email is appropriate—and a handwritten note is all the better. Second, write another note once you've been hired. Even if references weren't contacted by your employer, tell them where you've landed and thank them for offering their help. Whenever you can, mention your desire to return the favor in some way.

32 the job interview

the face-to-face, here-I-am meeting with a potential employer is without doubt the main event in the job search. If you do a better job of connecting with your interviewer than your competitor does, you significantly increase your chances of winning the job. Your people skills have to shine in an interview. They not only reflect your good manners but also show you as a strong candidate with a positive attitude.

INTERVIEW BEHAVIOR

Perspective matters, both in business in general and in interviews in particular. When you dress for the interview, it matters not only how you see yourself in the mirror, but also how the interviewer sees you. In everything you do before, during, and after the interview, ask yourself, "How will others see me?"

Your attitude, appearance, and how you handle yourself in the interview matter just as much as your expertise, experience, and ability to field questions. Fair

or not, legions of "perfect" job candidates have been scratched off the list for seemingly minor mishaps, proving that little things *do* mean a lot. For example, an otherwise qualified candidate may be dropped after a mealtime interview because he held the fork like a shovel, patronized the waitstaff, or ordered alcohol. Success can also hinge on the clothes you wear, your body language, and even the inopportune ringing of your cell phone.

Be on Time

Get to the building where the interview is being held at least ten to fifteen minutes early, since you might be delayed by slow traffic or other unanticipated problems. You can always hang out nearby and then "arrive" five minutes before the appointed time. Once you enter the offices, be cordial with the receptionist and anyone else you speak to, but not overly friendly. You want to look professional, and you never know how much influence is wielded by someone with whom you've chatted briefly.

Looks Do Count

Clothes are important to a first impression. They're a gauge of your grasp of larger issues, including appropriateness and respect.

Tailor your outfit to the expectations of the company. If your interview is at a bank, for instance, dress conservatively—suit and tie and dress shoes for a man, a skirt suit and pumps for a woman. At more casual companies, loosen up a bit. Men can wear slacks, an open-collar shirt, and a sports coat; women, a dress, pants or a skirt, and a blouse. At ultracasual companies, both men and women may actually lose points if they show up in classic business wear.

When in doubt, dress on the conservative side. Even though you think that boldly patterned tie looks perfect, you're better off wearing a more muted one instead of taking a chance that the tie may turn the interviewer off. Check the company's website for information on its dress code or call the company's human resources department to ask about dress standards: "I'm coming in for an interview next week. What is your company's dress code?" Also, dress up a notch when you're not sure. If you don't wear a tie or don't have one with you, you're out of luck if everyone else is wearing one.

Besides dressing to look as if you fit in, follow this advice:

Keep it understated. It is what you *say* that's important to the interviewer, so don't let your clothes detract from your words. If your clothes attract the wrong kind of attention, then they're the wrong clothes.

Be sparing with jewelry and scents. With both of these, less is more. Women should avoid big, jangling earrings or bracelets, and men should limit their jewelry as well. Keep earrings to a minimum—advice that applies as much to men as to women. Perfume and cologne should be used very sparingly, if at all.

Groom, groom, groom. Bathe or shower. Clean your fingernails, wash and comb your hair, and show up in clothes and footwear that are clean and presentable.

piercings, tattoos, and the job interviewer

While tattoos and piercings are a means of personal expression, the question of perspective matters. If you arrive with plugs, tunnels, multiple piercings, or showing multiple tattoos, what the interviewer thinks of them can affect your success. In addition, if the interviewer is distracted by your tattoos and body modifications, she's not focusing on building a relationship with you. It may be wiser to remove your jewelry and cover your body art.

Consider carefully how all facets of your appearance affect the interviewer. In the world of job searches, her opinion is the one that matters.

five easy steps to a successful job interview

While whole books have been written on successful interviewing, remembering and using all the advice can be daunting. We believe that implementing the following five actions will help you in your interviews:

Be on time. It's almost impossible to recover from the bad impression you make when you're late. Many employers say that an interview is "over before it starts" if the applicant doesn't arrive on time.

Dress appropriately. An interview isn't the time to make a fashion statement with your clothes. It's far better to be memorable because of who you are, not because of what you wear.

Be prepared. Practice your answers to such regularly asked questions as "What is your greatest strength?" and "What relevant experience have you had?" and "What are your weaknesses?" Preparation also means *asking* questions, so study up on the organization beforehand. (See also page 401.)

Be confident. It's a key trait of successful businesspeople. Smiling, looking people in the eyes, and a firm (not bone crusher or dead fish) handshake convey your confidence, not only to your interviewer but to everyone with whom you interact.

Show your appreciation. Expressing "Thank you" to interviewers is critical. In addition to your spoken "Thank you" when the interview is over, a thank-you note either written on quality paper or sent as an email is a must—preferably sent within twenty-four hours. (For more on email vs. handwritten notes, see "An Essential Thank-you," right.)

As you're dressing for the interview, conduct a spot check for stains on clothing, runs in stockings, scuffs on your shoes, chipped nail polish, and so forth. Just before the meeting, stop in the restroom to take care of wind-blown hair, lipstick on the teeth, or other problems.

Demonstrate Your People Skills

There's no need to self-consciously "strut your stuff," but you do want your actions and overall look to impress the interviewer—so make sure you do the following:

Greet warmly and politely. When you're introduced to the interviewer, stand, smile, look her in the eye, and extend your hand in greeting: "Hello, Ms. Bowman. Thanks so much for calling me in." Be composed, friendly, and relaxed.

Keep smiling. Not constantly, but enough to show that you're enjoying your time with the interviewer. You want to look confident, not worried, and the occasional smile (combined with eye contact) is one way to do so.

Show some restraint. Appear self-confident and answer questions clearly, but be careful not to come across as a know-it-all or someone who's prone to condescend. Avoid starting out with, "Everyone knows that . . ." or "It's clear that . . ." or "Surely you can see that my qualifications prove that . . ." If the interviewer gives you a compliment, accept it graciously—"Thank you" instead of the cocky "Oh, I always write well."

An Essential Thank-you

A post-interview thank-you note is imperative, reinforcing your interest in the job and showing good manners in the bargain. Send your note within a day or two of your interview.

Whether to handwrite and mail or email the note is the tougher question. The answer is this: Find out how the company wants you to communicate with them. For high-tech companies or those committed to a paperless workplace, a handwritten thank-you note might not be appropriate. For others, such as a conservative law firm, a handwritten note might be perfect.

Best practice: If you choose to send a handwritten note, precede it with an email thank-you and indicate a note will follow. An initial emailed thank-you assures that the interviewer receives your thank-you right away. A perfectly legible note on quality notepaper shows that you care enough to take the time to write and helps you stand out from the crowd.

When writing, mention the day of your meeting and the position you're seeking. Answer any questions that arose, and deliver on any promises, whether additional facts or something tangible. "I was very impressed by your design department, and my talk with Ms. Tunnicliffe was particularly helpful. I'm enclosing a copy of the marketing brochure we discussed." The note needn't be long; two or three brief paragraphs will do.

End on an upbeat note by thanking the interviewer and expressing your hope for a positive outcome:

interviewers should follow up, too

Just like the interview process, appreciation is a two-way street. Much is made of interviewees writing thank-you notes, but it's just as important for the interviewer to thank the candidate. Too often candidates leave the interview without ever hearing another word from the company. A follow-up communication indicating status—yes, no, maybe—shows both respect and appreciation to the candidate for making the effort to come in. It also demonstrates to the interviewee the kind of considerate and respectful workplace the interviewer represents.

"Thank you for your time and interest. I look forward to the possibility of joining your staff" or, more noncommittally, "Thank you again for meeting with me last Friday. I look forward to hearing your decision about the position."

More Interview Dos and Don'ts

Interviews can be intimidating, but if you prepare carefully and study what to do (and what *not* to do), it should go well.

♦ *Do* practice your answers to interview questions. Practice in a room where you can speak out loud so you become used to hearing your voice and your mouth becomes familiar with forming the words.

Q: *As a new father, and with times so tough out there, I've come to realize that salary is especially important to me. Can I bring up pay in an interview?*

A: You'll do better to let the interviewer broach the subject of salary. If *you* do so, the interviewer may not have had time to decide that you're a prime candidate for the job and therefore quote the lower end of the salary range. Also, if you focus too quickly on salary, it might seem that you care more about what's in it for you than the work itself.

If the interviewer asks you what salary you expect, respond with a question: "Could you give me an idea of the range?" When you finally say how much you're looking for, it's all right to mention an amount a little higher than the target salary based on your market value; this will give you some negotiating room. Just be careful not to throw out an unrealistically high figure that might put you out of the running.

- **Do** sit up straight and look the interviewer in the eyes. Having good posture and making eye contact shows that you're engaged with—and interested in—the person you're talking with.

- **Do** be enthusiastic whenever asking or answering questions—just don't confuse "enthusiastic" with "long-winded."

- **Do** ask questions. An interviewee who isn't curious enough to ask about various things will raise a red flag with the interviewer. Good questions include specifics about job responsibilities, the company's strengths, the job's biggest challenges, and what would be expected of you if you're hired.

- **Do** turn off your cell phone, smartphone, or mobile device. Having your cell phone ring during an interview is a major faux pas.

- **Don't** do anything distracting. That includes chewing gum, popping your knuckles, fidgeting, jiggling your knee, twirling a strand of your hair, or gesturing too broadly.

- **Don't** criticize your former employers or coworkers. Not only is it unprofessional but it could also make you look like a malcontent who'll be quick to criticize people in any other job.

Responding to Inappropriate Questions

A job interview isn't a one-way street: You're taking stock of the potential employer even as he's evaluating you. One consideration is how well your values mesh with the company's culture. An interviewer who asks inappropriate questions, including those that are unlawful (your age, national origins, marital status, sexual preference, and religion, among others), sounds the alarm that the company might not be a place where you want to work. The most direct way to respond to an inappropriate question is to say, "Sorry, but I'm uncomfortable with that question."

Waiting to Hear

No matter how important getting the position is to you, remember that you're only one of the hiring manager's concerns.

As the interview comes to an end, if no mention has been made of when you can expect to hear a decision, it's acceptable to ask. If you don't ask, you'll be in an awkward position of wondering when to make a follow-up call.

If the interviewer specified a time frame (say, a week) and it has passed without your hearing a word, call to ask whether a decision has been reached—and to reiterate your interest in the job. A more indirect route is to make a brief call saying that you're just checking in to see if there is anything else you should send. This may either spur the company to explain the delay or give you the news on the spot.

[RESPONDING TO AN OFFER]

If you have no doubt whatsoever that you want the job, accept it at once. However, it is perfectly okay to defer your answer by saying, "Thank you for the offer. I can get back to you by tomorrow morning with an answer if that's acceptable to you?" You'll probably be asked to reply within a few days, so be prepared to say when you'll decide.

Responding to a Rejection

If you are told you didn't get the job, don't just think, "Well, that's that." Be careful that your response doesn't burn any bridges. Be courteous and respectful in any comments you make. "Ms. Smith, I understand your decision, and I want to thank you for giving me the opportunity to be considered. If the situation changes, please don't hesitate to call me."

Sending a note thanking the company for considering you will show you as a person of substance and resilience. What's more, there's always a chance that you almost got the job and could be reconsidered for another one in the future.

---

the interview meal

Every moment you're with an interviewer, you're being assessed. Even the interview meal is a test, putting your skills at building relationships and making a positive impression on the line. The interviewer will be assessing

- How you handle small talk. (See Chapter 4, "The Art of Conversation," page 35.)
- Your table manners. (See Chapter 6, "Table Manners," page 56, and Chapter 9, "Dining Out," page 100.)
- Your ability to project a positive image—think body language. (See also Chapter 5, "Image and Attire," page 46.)
- Your skills as a good listener. (See also "The Importance of Active Listening," page 438.)
- Your compatibility with the company's culture.
- Your confidence.

PART VI
on the job

CHAPTER 33 At the Office. 411

CHAPTER 34 Workplace Relationships 428

CHAPTER 35 The Social Side of Business 442

33
at the office

Your professional demeanor inspires confidence in you and your business. To be successful in your workplace you do what you promise, solve problems instead of causing them, and understand the importance of common courtesies, from punctuality to treating everyone you encounter civilly and with respect.

Workplace problems will crop up—some you can do something about, and others you simply cannot. What you can *always* do is conduct yourself in such a way that shows you contribute to a harmonious positive workplace atmosphere, not a negative, difficult one. That means calling on your better qualities and putting manners into play right from your very first day at work.

THE FIRST DAY AT THE OFFICE

The first day at a new job is a time of excitement mixed with trepidation. In many cases you are meeting for the first time the people you will be with eight hours a day, five days a week, fifty weeks of the year. Getting off on the right foot with your colleagues will go a long way toward making your workplace experience positive, and your time there interesting and fulfilling.

Here are six tips to help you make the best impression on the first day and the days afterward:

- **Be on time.** It shows that you are both organized and respectful of your colleagues.

- **Dress appropriately.** Research what to wear ahead of time. Remember: It's not how you see yourself in the mirror, it's how others see you that matters. Will the focus be on your ability or on your clothes?

- **Know some names.** Before you arrive, make an effort to find out about the other members of your team and learn how to pronounce your manager's name. A little preparation will make those first moments much less stressful.

- **Defer to the formal.** If unsure, use titles and last names for bosses or administrative staff and wait until you are asked before using a first name.

- **Be a good listener.** Now's the time to pay attention to what you are asked to do and to do it efficiently; it isn't the time to criticize procedures or work tasks, or offer your opinion on how they could be done better.

- **Keep your after-work schedule clear.** If your colleagues plan to get together after work, try to be available to join them. You don't always have to go with them, but that first time is a great opportunity to get to know each other.

OPEN OFFICE COURTESIES

Workers in cubicles or common work spaces are so visible that they seem always to be available to one another and everyone else. Remind yourself that they're not. However compact or noisy the arrangement, workers in open-office areas deserve to have their time and space respected. A worker's cubicle is as much his territory as the CEO's corner office is hers.

Just as you wouldn't barge into anyone's office through a closed door, don't enter a cubicle without asking, "Is this a good time to talk?" Workers who interact for much of the day are exempted from this courtesy, but anyone else who arrives unexpectedly should ask permission in one way or another.

For the same reason, keep the practice of standing up or hanging over the wall to speak to the person in the neighboring cubicle to a minimum. If you want to show your disapproval, choose your words with care: "Mary, I know it's easier to talk over the wall, but would you mind coming around? Or I could come see you in a minute."

Such a request serves as a reminder to both you and your neighbors that there's no substitute for communicating face-to-face.

An unfortunate by-product of cubicle life is the ability of those around you to hear everything you say—and vice versa. It takes a strong-willed person to tune out the voices around him, and it's often impossible. Improve your lot (and your neighbors') by trying the following:

- Gently dissuade coworkers from loitering or socializing around your desk. A polite "Would you guys mind taking your conversation elsewhere? I'm working on something complicated, and I really have to concentrate" should get the message across.

- When hosting visitors, meet in a common area or a conference room so you won't disturb your neighbors.

- Be discreet—discuss confidential matters in a private space so it doesn't become office gossip.

- Whenever you don't want a phone call to be overheard, find an unused office or conference room, or make the call after hours.

- If you walk up to someone in a cubicle (or an office) and he's talking on the phone, don't hover and wait for him to hang up. Try again later.

Who Rises, and When?

Male or female, courteous people rise when someone enters their work space. You should stand for managers, clients, and prospects. It's even nice to stand to greet a workmate who hasn't dropped by your office or cubicle for a while. Rising isn't an empty gesture done for the sake of "rules"; rather, it's a quiet way of showing respect.

Assistants and other people who come and go with regularity don't expect you to pop up every time they walk in.

THE OFFICE

If you have an office with a door, real walls, and maybe even a window, remind yourself to be considerate when interacting with workmates who don't. Don't flaunt it.

The Welcoming Office

The way you arrange your office and the body language you exhibit when people come to visit advertise your attitude as welcoming or standoffish. If your office must be set up with visitors' chairs across the desk from you, then act to keep the desk from being a barrier. Stand up and move around your desk to greet a visitor. Instead of returning to your side of the desk, try sitting in a chair next to your visitor, facing her. No matter who the visitor is or what the situation, anytime you leave your desk and sit near someone, you set the stage for a more relaxed discussion.

the privacy problem

Privacy and confidentiality is a concern regardless of the nature of your workplace. A little discretion on your part is an excellent way to show respect for your colleagues.

COPYING. If you open the lid of a copier to find someone has left an original sheet, don't get curious if it has the look of something private. It's also considerate to return it to the person or put it in his inbox.

EAVESDROPPING. Try not to listen to your neighbor's phone conversations, especially when they are personal in nature. Consider taking a break to give your colleague some privacy. If, despite your efforts, something obviously private or intimate catches your ear, *keep it to yourself.* Many a rumor has started because of something overheard, or worse, misheard.

PRYING. Keep your eyes off screens and don't trade passwords. Even if a coworker broaches the subject of his or her love life, finances, divorce, problem teenager, or health, don't dig for more information.

Managing Your Door

Shut your door only when you must: when you need quiet to concentrate, when you're meeting with a visitor, or when you're discussing a confidential matter with a manager or coworker.

Beware of slamming your door. If you're bothered by a conversation going on outside your door, get up and shut the door as softly as possible.

REQUESTING AND OFFERING HELP

The best way to get help in the workplace is to give it. For instance, if you see an officemate working through lunch to collate a large client packet and you pitch in to help, your generosity will likely be returned in kind. Take a little time to welcome a new officemate or temp and answer their questions. Whenever you voluntarily help out around the workplace, your reward is a coworker's gratitude, not extra pay. The person who is genuinely willing to help is one who doesn't demand favors in return.

When you receive a helping hand, a thank-you is always in order, no matter how small the favor. If a coworker gives up his lunch hour to help you, you could thank him with a card, a little gift, or an invitation to lunch. When possible, compliment helpful coworkers directly and mention the good work to their supervisors.

OFFICE CONVERSATIONS AND SMALL TALK

Manners at work begin with greetings and small talk. Every workday will inevitably go better if workers show a modicum of respect and consideration for everyone they encounter, from front desk personnel to coworkers to supervisors.

Being courteous doesn't mean having to say hello every time you pass someone; a preoccupation with what you're doing is expected when you're busy and shouldn't be taken as an affront. You'll want to greet coworkers the first time you see them with "Good morning" or "How's it going?" but as the day goes on, a quick smile or nod will do. More important is what *not* to do when passing people in the workplace—staring straight down at the floor with a sour look on your face or grunting in response to a "hello."

Small talk with workmates is an inevitable part of the workday, but be careful what you say: Criticism of a coworker, a too-vivid account of a hot date, or remarks about the eccentricities of your boss are easily overheard in work environments, especially the kind without walls. Here are a few small talk guidelines (see also Chapter 14, "The Art of Conversation," page 35):

- When initiating small talk, be attuned to the other person's receptiveness. If he seems distracted or unresponsive, take the hint and back off.

- When the person is willing to chat, don't overstay your welcome. Visiting shouldn't get in the way of business.

- During a short hallway chat, *stand to one side* so you won't block traffic.

- If other people want to join in, make an effort to include them. In some cases, this might mean switching topics to something everyone can discuss.

- Be aware of the impact of small talk on those working around you. Keep your voice down; then read the body language of anyone nearby to judge whether to keep talking or to take your chat elsewhere.

the good boss

If you're a manager, remember that you have as many obligations to the people you manage as they have to you. Showing concern and respect for them will benefit you both.

YOU'RE A GOLD STAR BOSS IF YOU . . .

. . . MAKE YOURSELF AVAILABLE. Strike the right balance between paying attention to those you supervise and leaving them alone.

. . . COMMUNICATE CLEARLY. Make sure a worker understands the duties outlined in her job description and that any instructions for a specific task are crystal clear.

. . . REMEMBER THE SMALL COURTESIES. Saying "please" and "thank you" when you speak to anyone.

. . . PRAISE A JOB WELL DONE. Giving compliments shows that you understand the skill a task required and that the worker was up to the job.

. . . SEE THINGS COMING. Prevent conflicts between workers by making sure everyone clearly understands who is responsible for what. You can't keep a volatile situation from boiling over unless you know that it's brewing.

. . . ACCEPT RESPONSIBILITY FOR YOUR MISTAKES. Blaming another person, another department, or "circumstances beyond your control" not only marks you as a buck passer but could also raise questions about your integrity.

. . . DON'T DELAY DELIVERING BAD NEWS. It's preferable to deliver bad news right away rather than wait for the weekly or monthly staff meeting.

. . . FIRE GENTLY. Deliver the news quickly and straightforwardly. Don't hide behind a text message, email, or voice mail. Have the courtesy to meet face-to-face and in private with the person you're firing.

- Whispering suggests gossiping or secretiveness. Don't do it.

- End the conversation pleasantly with a remark like, "Well, I think it's time I got back to work" or "This was really interesting. We'll have to talk again."

- If a coworker who feels like chatting interrupts your work, suggest another time. "You've caught me at a bad moment. Can we touch base after I've finished these letters?"

- If *you* interrupt, be sensitive to the other person's reaction. If she says she can't stop, take "no" for an answer and don't feel rejected.

SHARING SPACE AND EQUIPMENT

Communal office equipment can be a lightning rod for the "it's not my job" attitude among workers. Even if machine maintenance isn't technically your responsibility, take care of things when you can. If a printer or copier needs toner or has a paper jam, either do the job yourself or call whoever is in charge of machine maintenance right away. This applies twice over in small businesses, where everyone—including the boss—should pitch in.

Copiers and Printers

When you pick up your print job, check the paper drawer and refill it as necessary. Either replace toner cartridges or notify the person in charge of the copier.

If a job hasn't been picked up, either place it face up where it can easily be seen or put it in a space designated for finished jobs. Of course, it would be thought-ful to drop off a job if it's obvious who printed it, but respect the other person's privacy and don't read the document.

The Kitchen

The kitchen can be the messiest room in an office, so be thoughtful and do your part to keep it clean.

- Don't leave your dirty dishes in the sink. Wash them right away.

- If you spill something, wipe it up.

- As necessary, wipe down appliances (including microwaves) after you use them.

- Refill an ice cube tray if you've emptied it.

- Refill a communal coffeemaker or water pitcher if you pour the last cup.

- Don't leave milk or leftovers in the refrigerator until they start to smell.

- Avoid foods that smell while cooking, such as cabbage and fish.

- Label your food containers with your name and the date.

annoying anonymous notes

You've seen them around the office: "Would whoever took my Mickey Mouse mug return it to the kitchen?" "Whoever you are, quit spraying perfume in the ladies room!" "The kitchen is a pigsty—be a grown-up and do your dishes!" Not only are these notes annoying, they're ineffective. No one ever admits to being the "someone" in the note.

Instead of posting a passive-aggressive note, ask your office manager if a little time can be reserved at the next staff meeting to deal with housekeeping topics such as changing the copier paper, the cleanliness of the kitchen, disappearing coffee pods, or refilling the filtered water pitcher. Some suggestions might even become office policy: no strong perfume, no smelly foods, no personal use of the copier. You'll have a better chance of effecting change than with an annoying note.

In the Restrooms

Tips for keeping a restroom presentable are simple.

- Dispose of paper hand towels and any personal hygiene products in the trash receptacle.

- Wipe the sink clean of any toothbrush suds, makeup spills, soap, shaving cream, or water.

- Don't have conversations from a stall.

- Don't linger.

- Don't use a phone. It's annoying to have to listen to another's conversation.

- If you're the hygiene-minded type who arranges toilet paper on the seat, be sure to flush it when you leave instead of leaving it to litter the floor.

- Be sure to flush completely.

- Report any malfunctions to maintenance immediately.

THE TROUBLE-FREE MEETING

Meetings can be the bane of an office worker's existence, yet they shouldn't be. As both an organizer and a participant, you can affect the outcome of the meeting by your preparation, involvement, and follow-up effort.

As the Organizer

It's your job to make sure the meeting is productive, runs on time, and achieves the goals you set for it.

Plan your meeting ahead of time. Set a time, date, and duration for the meeting. For an internal meeting, let the participants know ahead of time—try to give them at least twenty-four hours' notice, longer if possible. For a meeting with clients or prospects it may be necessary to plan several days or as much as a week or two ahead to assure that participants won't have a conflict. If a meeting is scheduled well in advance—say, more than a week out—it's a good idea to issue a brief reconfirmation of the date and time a day or two ahead.

Identify the purpose and the goal(s) for the meeting. In your invitation let the participants know why you called the meeting and what you expect to accomplish.

Invite only those people who really need to be there. Too often workers complain about having to attend meetings that only peripherally affect or involve them. Send them meeting notes instead if they just need an FYI.

Have an agenda and supporting documents. Prepare these and distribute them ahead of time. It's a waste of everyone's time to hand out a document at the meeting and then expect them to sit there and read it for the first ten or fifteen minutes.

Start on time. Too many meetings start late, an obvious disrespectful time waster for all who arrive on time.

Segment when possible. Try not to make people who need to be there for only part of a long meeting sit through the whole thing. Segment the meeting with breaks so that those who are no longer needed can make a graceful getaway.

Be in charge. It's your job to keep the discussion focused on the topic and not let it wander. Pay careful attention to how participants are interacting and be prepared to intervene if tempers flare or one participant treats another disrespectfully.

At the conclusion, sum up the decisions and the tasks that need to be accomplished. Then prepare minutes of the meeting that reflect the decisions and tasks and distribute them immediately.

As a Participant

As a participant, meetings are your chance to demonstrate your skills and knowledge and to show you know how to be a positive team player. You can accomplish this by being prepared, participating constructively, and then making sure you complete any assignments expeditiously.

Respond in a timely manner. When you receive notice of a meeting, respond as quickly as possible. If you're not sure you can attend, let the organizer know right away and give her an estimate of when she can expect your answer.

Be prepared to bring the materials and information assigned to you. Nothing is more frustrating than to arrive at a meeting ready to move a project forward and have a participant announce that he doesn't have his work prepared. Notify the organizer ahead of time if you can't meet the deadline or of any change in your plans as soon as possible. If meeting materials were sent to you ahead of time, be sure to read them before the meeting.

Be punctual. Showing up late simply tells the others that you are disorganized. It's also controlling and disrespectful behavior. If you are going to be late, let the meeting planner know ahead of time, as soon as you know. When you arrive, move quietly to your seat with as little disturbance of the conversation as possible. Don't disrupt by rattling papers, snapping a briefcase open and shut, getting coffee, or whispering to your neighbors.

Have business cards ready. If you're meeting someone new—a colleague, client, prospect, or supplier—be sure to have enough business cards to give to each person. (See "The Dos and Don'ts of Business Cards," page 440.)

Turn off your smartphone, cell phone, pager, or watch alarm. The meeting is a time to focus squarely on the people you are with. Answering your phone, looking at a text or page to see who's contacting you, or using your mobile device to keep up with emails or instant messages is disrespectful of the other participants. If you *must* take or make a call during the meeting, let the leader know in advance. Have your phone on the vibrate mode and step outside the room before talking on the phone.

Keep a positive demeanor. Body language can often reveal your true opinion, even if you don't say anything. Actions such as rolling your eyes, shaking your head, drumming your fingers, and slumping way down in your chair imply you are impatient or uninterested. Fidgeting, shaking your foot, or twirling your hair belies the confident demeanor you want to exhibit by indicating your nervousness. Looking participants in the eye shows you are engaged and listening to what they have to say. It also demonstrates your confidence.

Don't contradict each other. In a meeting with outsiders, don't contradict a colleague over an issue that's better discussed one-on-one and in-house. Maintaining a united front is vital. The only time to intervene is to correct a misstatement of fact that's critical to the discussion, and then do it calmly and without criticism.

Q: *A manager in my department holds meetings that almost always run at least twice as long as they should. For one thing, he often goes to great lengths to explain details that are already clearly laid out in his handouts. How can I let him know that we feel our time is being wasted but not offend him?*

A: Enlist one or two coworkers to go with you to meet him. This keeps the focus on the problem and not on you as a complainer. Direct your points to the *effect* of the long meetings rather than on his personal trait of rambling. Then couch your solution in positive terms: "Chris, we want to talk with you about the length of the meetings. We have an idea for shortening them we'd like to run by you. We think your handouts do such a good job of explaining the situation that we're wondering if there is really any need to elaborate before engaging in discussion. Would you be willing to try that next time? We could probably keep everyone's attention better and the meetings might end on time more often."

Be a good listener/participant. Avoid daydreaming, dozing, and looking bored. Wait patiently for your turn to talk, either at the next break in conversation, or as that topic is wrapping up.

Be clear about expectations and follow through.

At its conclusion, the meeting is summarized, decisions are made, and any to-dos handed out. Be prepared to follow through on your assignments quickly.

OFFICE APPOINTMENTS

Meetings in your work space are different from group meetings. Your goal is to make participants welcome and comfortable. When you have a guest from outside your company, hang up his coat and offer him a comfortable place to sit and something to drink until it's time for the meeting. If you don't have a receptionist, perform these courtesies yourself.

- Consider reserving a meeting room for your appointments if your work space isn't private.

- Be on time for your meeting. If there's an unavoidable delay, apologize—in person when you can. If you'll be delayed more than fifteen minutes, offer to reschedule.

- If your visitor arrives too late for you to see him, accept his apology and arrange another meeting.

Office Meeting Courtesies

The following courtesies will get your meeting off to a good start:

- Have all the necessary meeting materials at hand.

- If coworkers are participating, arrange for them to be present when your guest arrives, then make introductions all around.

- Activate the do-not-disturb feature on your phone.

- If the meeting runs overtime, politely end it: "I wish we had more time to discuss this, Alex, but I have another appointment. Shall we make plans to talk more later?"

- Be sure to walk your visitor back to the reception area, or, if you're unable to, arrange ahead of time to have someone else escort him.

THOSE EMBARRASSING MOMENTS

Spinach stuck in the front teeth, an open fly, or a bra strap that is showing—when they happen to you, all you can do is laugh and blame bad luck. When they happen to a coworker, step in and help. Tell the person discreetly (and privately if possible). If you're a woman and too shy to tell a male colleague that his zipper is undone, get another man to do it. When a coworker alerts you that there's a blob of mustard on your tie or something in your teeth, don't take offense. Be thankful that a friend has saved you from an embarrassing moment.

EXCHANGING GIFTS

When you're presenting a gift to either a coworker or a business associate from outside your company, your gift choice should depend on the occasion, your relationship to the recipient, and your position in the company. Moreover, *whether* to give or accept a gift from outside depends on the policy of the organization; some have hard-and-fast rules regarding gift giving. If a gift is permitted, don't let your choice cross the line into inappropriate. For example, jewelry, most clothing, and anything with romantic overtones such as perfume, roses, or lingerie are off-limits; books, music, tickets to an event, or outerwear are usually safe bets.

Acknowledging your workmates' birthdays, weddings, and other milestones shows you respect their lives outside of work. This doesn't mean showering them with presents, but some occasions call for at least a card. While chipping in for a group gift is fine, you might also want to send a separate card to someone with whom you're especially close.

Regardless of the occasion, the actual presenting of a one-on-one gift should be done outside the office or in private in order not to make colleagues uncomfortable. Here are some additional guidelines (see also Chapter 28, "Giving and Receiving Gifts," page 349, and "Office Collections," page 423).

Birthdays. There's no reason to give something to a colleague every time his birthday rolls around, but it's a good idea to recognize a significant one, like the 0s. Usually, a card is sufficient, but a close friend may want to give a gift privately.

Weddings. For the wedding of a coworker, send a gift if you've been invited. If you haven't been invited, the choice of whether you send a gift is yours, but a card is a nice acknowledgment. (For more about wedding gifts, see "Choosing and Sending Gifts," page 664.)

New babies. If you're close to the new parent(s), you'll probably want to give a gift. Sometimes coworkers chip in for a joint gift, in which your participation is optional. But if you *attend* a baby shower for the new mother (either at work or off the premises), then you're obligated to give a baby present or contribute to a group gift.

Illnesses. A get-well card is usually an appropriate gesture when a workmate or business associate is ill, injured, or in the hospital. If you have a close relationship with the person, consider a gift as well, such as a book, flowers, or a potted plant.

Retirement. While the company is responsible for any party or gift, a card or personal note to the retiree is a good way to express your sentiments and say good-bye.

Deaths. Whether to send a separate, rather than group, condolence note or memorial gift depends entirely on how close a friendship you've had with either the person who died or a member of his family. A handwritten condolence note or a note added to a store-bought card is preferable to just signing a pre-printed card.

Accepting and Declining Gifts

When receiving a gift at the office, it's fine to open it right away; usually, the giver will want to see your reaction and be thanked on the spot. However, if other coworkers aren't taking part in the gift exchange, it's polite to present and open gifts in private. At an office baby or wedding shower, opening the presents is part of the fun.

If you have to decline business gifts, it's usually because the gift either came from a business associate outside the company, the cost is over the limit your company allows, or it's too personal. In the first two cases, it's the company, not you, that's declining. A note, on company letterhead, clearly stating so is all that's needed, as long as you say that you appreciate the person's thoughtfulness:

Dear Jonathan,

I received your gift this morning. Unfortunately, my company's policies prohibit employees from receiving gifts, so I must return it. Thank you so much for the thoughtfulness. I hope you understand.

Sincerely,

Ethan

A gift with romantic overtones can also be a problem. The best course of action is to return the gift. You can explain either in person or through a note that while you know he meant well, sending such gifts is inappropriate in light of your business relationship:

Dear Sam,

Unfortunately, I must return the gift you sent to me. While beautiful, it is really too personal for me to accept. I hope you understand. I value our business relationship very much and want to see it continue to grow and be successful for both of us. Thank you for your thoughtfulness and your understanding.

Sincerely,

Joanna

If you receive a sexually provocative gift, such as lingerie, return it on the spot. Don't keep such a gift "just to be polite." Tell the giver you cannot accept the gift because it is inappropriate. It would also be wise to reiterate your objection in a brief note, making a copy for your file. (See also "When Professional Turns Personal," page 436.)

Dear Harry,

Unfortunately, I feel compelled to return the gift you sent me. I have always appreciated our business relationship and hope it can continue, but the gift itself is not appropriate, and I believe it is better to return it than to keep it.

Sincerely,

Serena

Where to Draw the Line?

Here's a quick guide to the appropriateness of exchanging gifts with the people with whom you work. In every

> Q: *I'd like to give a Christmas present to my boss, who went out of his way to look after me during my first year at work. Would that be inappropriate?*
>
> A: Giving a gift to your boss after working only one year is inappropriate. A handwritten note expressing your appreciation of his attention during your first year is a better alternative.
>
> One option, which is a nice gesture: Join with other employees to present a gift for a holiday, birthday, or anniversary. A group gift also has the advantage of not looking as if it were given to score points.

case, you should avoid gifts that are too expensive or too personal.

With coworkers. Exchange gifts privately with coworkers so that other workmates won't feel left out. Don't choose a gift with too-personal overtones, like perfume. Even if you're romantically involved with the recipient, save that type of gift for your out-of-the-office life.

With supervisors. Group gifts for the boss are always fine, as are small individual gifts but only when the two of you have had a long-standing business relationship. Even if you're certain it's fine to give the boss a gift on your own, an expensive one could look like an attempt to curry favor.

With business associates from outside. Com-pany policy usually dictates whether you can give or receive gifts from outside associates and, if gifts are permissible, sets cost limits (typically $25). If you plan to give a gift to a customer or client, check his company's policy first. Token gifts from business associates are generally within bounds, especially during the holidays; but if you receive a gift that violates company policy, it's essential that you return it—and without embarrassing the giver. (See also "Accepting and Declining Gifts," left.)

With your employees. While as a manager you can accept both group gifts and small gifts from employees with whom you've worked for a long time, you're better off giving a gift to your subordinates as a group, not just a select few. Gifts can range from a gift basket of fruits, chocolates, or nuts to fleece vests or jackets with company logos. One employer went all out in a good year by treating everyone on her staff to a relaxing half day at a spa. Another took her department out to lunch and personally picked up the tab.

With your support staff. Some companies provide annual holiday gifts for employees, but as a manager you may also want to reward your assistant(s) yourself. The gift choice depends on length of service, with long-term employees receiving more generous gifts (around $35 or $40) and anyone who's been there less than five years receiving something around $25.

OFFICE COLLECTIONS

Office collections for birthdays, showers, weddings, the birth of a baby, or charities are acceptable but can make workers feel they're being nickel-and-dimed to death. At the start of the year, decide what you'll give to and then use that plan to respond to requests. Before you ask for donations, consider how often employees have been solicited in recent months.

If office policy allows collections, they should be organized so they don't get out of hand. Some official guidelines are a good idea. In many workplaces, a "celebration kitty," to which each employee contributes a small amount ($5 or $10) once or twice a year, has dual benefits: It supplies enough funds while keeping the donors happy.

For organizers of such events as a coworker's bridal or baby shower, remember that if you have a party for one person in your office or department, you have to have one for any other workmate getting married or expecting a baby. Selectively organizing such events will cause hurt feelings. Also, don't single out those who can't contribute. Sign the card "From the office."

When You're Asked

If you can't chip in for one more birthday gift, don't feel guilty, no matter the reason. Simply say, "Oh, I'd love to, but I'm afraid it's impossible for me to contribute this time." As for charitable donations, if you've already contributed to one organization and a workmate asks you to contribute to another, explain that you can give only so much each year and that you hope she understands why you must decline.

If the frequency of collections still doesn't let up, don't refuse across the board, or you risk looking like a Scrooge. Instead, you could adopt a policy of giving only for certain events, like showers.

BRINGING CHILDREN TO WORK

When stopping by the office with a new baby or a young child, remember that a little goes a long way. Workmates' *oohs* and *aahs* shouldn't cause too much disruption to those not taking part as long as the visit is brief. Gatherings that last more than five minutes, however, should be taken to an empty conference room or any other room where the cooing can continue behind closed doors.

Children at Work

Sometimes the inevitable happens—a babysitter is suddenly sick, a school is closed—yet you don't want to miss work. If your company allows it, bringing your child to work may be an option. Always check ahead of time with your manager to be sure it's okay. It may be wiser to request to pick up work and take it home.

If you do bring your child, it's up to you to make sure he doesn't cause any disruption. Then plan ahead by bringing videos or books to occupy his time. Under no circumstances should you let a toddler or preschooler run free about the office. Your coworkers will no doubt greet your child if he happens to poke his head in their doors, but a disruption is a disruption, no matter how cute the offender.

Never bring a sick child to work. Exposing coworkers to illness won't be appreciated either by them or your boss.

Breast-feeding or Pumping at Work

In an ideal world your workplace has a daycare center and a private, quiet space where mothers can nurse babies or express milk if their babies are at home. That's rarely the reality. By law, a workplace must have a clean, private place for their employees to pump or breast-feed. Being relegated to the restroom—hardly a clean environment—is not an acceptable solution. If you are a nursing mother, work with your boss or HR manager to come up with a good situation that guarantees you can pump or breast-feed when needed and in private. (See "Breast-feeding on the Go," page 480.)

[THE HOME OFFICE]

Millions of Americans have bailed out of the traditional workday world to work at home. If you're one of these at-home workers, you'll have all sorts of advantages—the freedom to move your business in your own direction, control over your time and schedule, and the pleasures of informality. But you'll also hit new problems head-on, such as separating work from home life and maintaining relationships with colleagues at the main office. Your aptitude for etiquette can help smooth out the bumps along the way.

Tips for Home Office Workers

While many of the concerns of home-based workers are no different from those of workers in traditional offices, others are unique. Some of the most important are:

Watch out for work creep. Your balancing act requires knowing when to put your work aside for the sake of your family and friends. Work creep—when work impinges on nonwork time—is insidious for the home-based worker. It's easy to let your deadlines and projects spill into your personal life, but don't become so preoccupied with work that you ignore your nearest and dearest.

Get out of your home office regularly. Have lunch with customers and colleagues, discuss the latest innovations, and get a fresh perspective on trends.

Don't brag about the joy of being your own boss. Gloating may also annoy clients and colleagues by making you look a little too self-satisfied. Avoid the "I can't believe I get paid to do this!" comment. It makes it look like you're not really working while your office-bound colleagues are.

Don't let the home office be an excuse for not meeting people face-to-face. Even if it's a little more inconvenient to drive to a meeting from home than it was from your main office, make the effort to meet in person.

Take care with your attire. Some home-based workers find that dressing as they would for the office (business casual clothing) has a psychological effect that helps them get their work done. Others say they do their best work in their broken-in slippers and bathrobe. Meeting with people is an entirely different story because a professional has to look the part. You may no longer belong to the corporate world, but you have to adhere to its standards when you deal with clients—and that includes dress. (See Chapter 5, "Image and Attire," page 46.)

Beware the videophone. Skype and other online phone systems offer easy-to-use videophone capabilities. With the inclusion of a minicamera on many computers, your appearance matters more than ever. Taking a call at home while still in your bathrobe may have been possible previously; now you'll have to be dressed appropriately to answer that business call.

Explain your working rules to your neighbors. Be neither apologetic nor wishy-washy. To protect your time, privacy, and resources, be polite but firm. Be clear that, except for emergencies, you are not to be disturbed between certain hours; that your business line is for business calls only; that the fax machine and photocopier are not there for the neighbors' use; and so on.

Dealing with Clients

As a home-based worker, you'll have to cope with the full range of human foibles. Even good clients can be unpredictable, and at times you'll have to juggle patience and courtesy with firmness and self-interest. Imagine: A client calls you at all hours, including nighttime. If ill-timed phone calls are a problem, spell out your working hours to every client, get an answering service to take after-hours calls, or let voice mail or an answering machine solve the problem.

Some home-based workers have a policy of not hosting meetings at home, preferring to visit the client or, when groups are involved, setting up a conference call. If you do welcome clients to your home, you'll probably have to make some accommodations, starting with your "office" environment, and take steps to maintain privacy.

The furnishing and decor of the room where you receive clients, colleagues, or even your boss doesn't have to look corporate—just professional. Above all, your furnishings should be comfortable and serviceable, for you and your clients alike.

Trouble Zones

Visitors deserve your full attention, so do whatever you can beforehand to make sure your meetings are free of interruptions.

Children. Unless you can enlist a competent babysitter, either schedule meetings when the children are away at daycare or school or arrange a playdate at a friend's house.

Neighbors. Even if you've established a work hours policy with neighbors, if they have a habit of dropping by warn them in advance that you'll be unable to answer the door while your meeting is going on. Tell them specifically when you're going to be unavailable. An even safer bet is to hang a handwritten sign on the front door: "Meeting in Progress: Please Do Not Disturb."

Phone calls. Don't take phone calls during the meeting; let your answering system take calls and turn the sound control or phone ringer to silent. If you have a cell phone or pager, set it on silent or vibrate.

About those pets. Forewarning the visitor that you have pets will tell you whether it's necessary to schedule the meeting elsewhere. Vacuum up pet hair and put pets outside or in another room when visitors are expected.

Families and phones. Rare is the client who isn't charmed when a child replies with a polite "Yes, sir" and "Thank you, ma'am." Teach your children a simple response for answering the phone: "Hello, this is Ramone's Custom Cards. May I help you?" Older children can be taught to take careful messages, and they will usually be flattered to be trusted with this important job.

34
workplace relationships

eight hours a day, five days a week, fifty weeks of the year you spend time with work associates. The hard part is that these people aren't necessarily people you would choose to associate with or whom you even like. Yet you very well may spend more waking time with them than you do with your significant other or your family. Inevitably you will run into difficult situations involving work associates. The choices you make as you interact with them will go a long way to determining whether your work experience is pleasant or difficult.

So often in business it's not a question of "if" you're going to do something, it's a question of "how." Did your workmate include you when describing who was responsible for a report or did she take all the credit herself? How do you approach your cubemate who talks too loudly on the telephone? How do you tell your boss she has bad breath? How do you react to two coworkers who always are talking in another language, and you think they're gossiping about you?

Deciding how to react is couched in the principles of etiquette: being considerate, respectful, and honest (make that benevolently honest) in your dealings. At the same time, make an effort not to see the situation and your solution just from your perspective. Ask yourself, "How will other people see me or react to me?" In business, how other people see you—your boss, clients, coworkers, suppliers—is critical to your success. Did you really intend to appear brusque toward your supplier or were you simply trying to get three other things done when he called you with a production issue? Or perhaps you think the clothes you're wearing are appropriate, but others—especially clients or your boss—wonder "What was he thinking wearing that?" If that's the case, you're wearing the wrong clothes, and your reputation can suffer.

The workplace is full of opportunities to make choices. Be conscious of how others perceive your actions and consider carefully the ramifications of your choices.

RESPECTING RANK

Regardless of whether you like to think of it this way or not, rank is power, so be conscious of the position of the person with whom you're talking. Just because you're chatting with your boss about last night's baseball game doesn't mean you can be overly familiar. Maintain a respectful conversational distance (at least 18 inches) and avoid backslapping, nudging, hugging, elbowing, or other touching that implies a close friendship.

These days, many offices operate on a first-name basis—for employers and employees alike. If this isn't the case in your company or any you happen to visit, you should address your boss and other senior people as "Ms. Jackson" or "Mr. Wells" unless they ask you to use their first names.

COMMON OFFICE PROBLEMS

Squabbles, gossip and rumors, offensive comments—sooner or later, you're likely to find yourself at odds with a coworker or dragged into someone else's quarrel. Drawing on your social skills will help defuse these situations and demonstrate your strengths as a relationship builder.

Dealing with Conflicts

You're certain that an extra day per week should be built into a project schedule, but the project manager refuses. Or you find yourself having to defend a coworker whom another worker unjustly demeans. Conflicts such as these can happen in virtually any workplace. *The first rule for handling them is to do so in private.* Then follow these steps toward a resolution:

Stick to the subject. Don't allow a disagreement to wander onto nongermane issues. Avoid referring to old conflicts. Just because you were proved right in the last argument doesn't mean you're automatically right this time.

Keep it nonpersonal. Steer clear of criticizing. Something as simple as "I can't believe you think that" immediately shifts the conversation from the topic to an attack on the other person.

Be open to compromise. Although you may not get everything you want, some resolution is better than lasting hard feelings. Document the outcome of the disagreement; if it's business related, you should confirm the final resolution with a memo to your "opponent." Documentation and confirmation are important if it becomes necessary to take the matter to a higher-up.

Know when to postpone. There are times when disputes are integral to the work process—during a brainstorming session, for example, or a policy meeting. In such situations, state your case clearly and engage in debate if necessary, but don't be stubborn. Pay attention to the reaction of others. As soon as you sense resentment or annoyance, bring the conversation to a close; otherwise, it could degenerate into personal attacks. "Actually, I think it would be better if we talked about this later" is one way of defusing the situation. Or you could try "Let's take this up when we can get [the supervisor] to help us figure out the direction the company wants to go."

Don't gloat. Avoid the temptation to say "I told you so."

Lodging Complaints

Raising issues effectively is something of an art. You can avoid some common pitfalls by asking yourself the following questions:

Is your complaint worth your boss's time? Before going to the boss, calmly examine the problem in the light of common sense. Is the problem persistent and serious enough to warrant intervention? Also choose the right time; if the issue isn't urgent, wait until your boss isn't busy with other obligations. Even better, schedule a time to talk: "Could I see you for about fifteen minutes sometime today? It's not urgent."

Are you the right complainer? The best person to raise an issue is the one who's best positioned to make a solid case. For example, if you've been reprimanded for tardiness, you'll be on shaky ground complaining about a coworker who habitually takes long lunch hours. Let Ms. Punctuality handle the job.

Should you make your case in person? Bosses are usually either "listeners" or "readers"—the former preferring to talk it over in a private meeting, the latter wanting to learn of complaints and other matters in a well-prepared, confidential memo.

> ## the incessant complainer
>
> Does everything seem to frustrate you? Do you find yourself criticizing your coworkers and your boss all the time? Be wary of becoming the office griper, the person who complains constantly. You only have so much business capital to spend before people stop taking your complaining seriously. So before you complain about Tom who didn't put paper in the copier, ask yourself if his lapse is really worth making an issue over.

Have you documented the problem? It's important that you have support for your complaint, especially when your boss may have to take the issue to higher levels. Serious accusations, including office theft or sexual harassment, require proof (suspicions and gossip don't count). Keep a journal or diary of events, assemble paper evidence, and find others who can back up your claim.

Do you have solutions in mind? Be ready with suggestions for solving the problem. But let the boss take the initiative; you don't want to look as if you're usurping his leadership role.

Complaining About Conditions

Before lodging a gripe about workplace conditions, know whom to approach: the boss, the boss's assistant, the office manager, your coworker, or, if you're a union member, your steward. Then determine how best to present the problem. Minor problems like a malfunctioning copy machine or chair can be covered in a brief memo or email. More serious complaints (an unreasonable share of work, the repeated theft of lunches from the office refrigerator, or malicious gossip) call for a meeting. Report potentially dangerous problems (the presence of a stranger on the premises or a locked fire door) as quickly as possible and by the fastest means available.

Problems such as excessive overtime and short-staffing are trickier. Don't jump to the conclusion that the boss is at fault; she may already be working to fix things. If not, inform her in a polite, nonaccusatory manner. You may get the results you want if you frame the complaint in terms of productivity—for example, instead of saying you're overworked, tell the boss that the lack of staff is causing missed deadlines and errors.

If conditions don't improve, it may be time to rally the troops and meet as a group, which can be made up of department representatives or the whole department. The advantage of a group complaint is that numbers can impress even the most insensitive supervisor; most bosses want to avoid serious and widespread morale problems. If group complaining doesn't work, you may have to appeal to a higher authority (see "Going over the Boss's Head," page 433).

Complaining About Coworkers

Start by talking to your coworker. If that doesn't resolve the situation, the next step is to go to your boss. You and your colleagues can often work out difficulties among yourselves, but sometimes you'll want your boss to step in—especially if the problem is serious or has legal implications. Sexual harassment, racist remarks, theft, lying, fighting, threatening behavior—these are examples of serious problems that can affect the entire company, and your direct supervisor needs to know about them.

Be sure that any complaint is valid and not a mere personal issue. Arrange a private meeting with your boss instead of writing a memo (and never complain via email, which in effect makes your words public property). In your meeting, be calm and focus on the troubling behavior, not the person: "Henry leaves a half-hour early at least three days a week, and we're having a problem getting his time sheets" is far better than "Henry is irresponsible and deceitful." Be as objective as you can, and don't be tempted to express moral judgments.

Like it or not, sometimes you must simply tolerate difficult people whose value to the business outweighs their quirks. The conceited saleswoman who is always

---

taking responsibility

It's not a matter of *if* you are going to make a mistake, it's a matter of *when*. And when you do, how you deal with the situation will make a huge difference in how successfully you recover from your error. Most important, take responsibility and apologize, and then, if possible, have a solution so you don't turn your mistake into your boss's problem. "Ms. Sanchez, I need to talk to you. I'm very sorry, but I made an error in the report I sent you. I've corrected it. Here's a copy of the corrected report. I've emailed it to you as well."

---

five steps for dealing with difficult situations

The first step in dealing with a difficult situation involving a coworker is to try to talk directly with him. Before you engage the person, think carefully about what outcome you want from the conversation. Once you determine the outcome, you can develop a solution to achieve your goal. Then, with a solution in mind, take these five steps in seeking a resolution that's mutually agreeable:

1. **STAY CALM; AVOID ANGER IN YOUR ACTIONS OR WORDS.** If you need to, disengage and calm down before initiating a conversation. Your composure will help to calm the other person down as well.

2. **STICK TO THE FACTS.** As soon as you start using suppositions rather than facts, the other person will perceive the unfairness and the conversation degenerates into a defense of each person's position instead of advancing toward a solution. It also undermines the credibility of your position.

3. **ASK FOR THE OTHER PERSON'S PERSPECTIVE OR OPINION.** Not only is it important to ask for the other person's side of the story, it's important to listen carefully. He may have a valid point you hadn't considered previously.

4. **PROPOSE YOUR SOLUTION.** Be willing to negotiate to find a mutually agreeable solution.

5. **ASK FOR THE OTHER PERSON'S BUY-IN.** This is the most important step. Without the person's buy-in at the end of the conversation, nothing has changed. "Tom, are you okay with this approach?"

the top producer, the ill-tempered art director who wins the most coveted awards, the sharp-tongued assistant who can quickly master the most complex computer program—they may irritate your boss even more than they bother you. But bosses have the responsibility to balance any shortcoming of the individual against the general good.

Handling Offensive Comments

What do you do when a coworker makes blatantly sexist or racist remarks, calls you or someone you know to be trustworthy a liar or a cheat, or treats coworkers and subordinates with extreme disrespect?

You have an obligation to yourself and your company to confront or report offenders, just as you would a thief. If you just sit back and listen, in essence you're condoning the behavior. If you can talk with the offender in private, do so. Frame your statements as criticism of the remarks, not the person himself, and be specific: "You probably didn't realize it, but that comment you made about Leslie's short skirts really was sexist and could land you in big trouble." Because people who repeatedly offend or degrade others rarely take hints, they're more likely to cease and desist when they think their own reputation or job is at stake.

Some remarks require immediate and public response. Be direct, but remember to confront the remark rather than the speaker. Stay calm and take care not to sound patronizing. For example, if a coworker's subject is racial politics, try something on the order of "People are treated fairly here, Steve, and I know that Harold got his job because of his talent."

Gossip and Rumors

Gossip is inevitable in the workplace, but suspicion and speculation about who's trying to snow the boss, who's taking credit for someone else's work, or who's going to the movies on their telecommuting days can belittle a person in the eyes of coworkers and result in serious, job-threatening consequences.

If you become the focus of false gossip or rumors, uncover the source immediately. Begin by talking to the person who clued you in, explaining that the story is untrue and you want it stopped. If you promise confidentiality, there's a good chance you'll be told who originated the gossip.

Talk with the gossiper in private. Adopt an attitude of concern, not anger: "Jessica, I hear you told a couple of people that I'm looking for a new job, and that I've been meeting with a headhunter. The truth is that I had lunch last week with my old college roommate, and she happens to work for an employment agency. I'm *not* job hunting, and having people think I am could make things pretty awkward for me here."

To avoid becoming the subject of office gossip, keep information about yourself close to your chest. Seemingly innocuous questions can set you up for gossip and innuendo. You don't have to answer or discuss details about your personal life, no matter how hard anyone tries to pry. How do you handle a persistent coworker? Without showing any annoyance, simply say, "Carrie, I'd prefer not to talk about my personal life at work," and then change the subject: "Did you catch the latest episode of _____?"

Listening to gossip makes you an active participant,

---

going over the boss's head

You must inform your boss (preferably face-to-face) if you're going to meet with one of his superiors. Blindsiding a boss will only make matters worse between the two of you, regardless of the outcome of your dispute.

---

even if you don't spread the story. If you feel a colleague is trying to draw you into gossiping, be tactful but firm: "I wouldn't know," "I'm not going there," "It's not for me to say." Then politely refuse to listen: "Sorry, but I'd just rather not know." If he won't change the subject, excuse yourself and leave.

GIVING AND ACCEPTING COMPLIMENTS

Naturally, you and your workmates need occasional pats on the back. Saying "well done" or "good job" to someone not only raises her spirits but communicates that you're a thoughtful and observant person, capable of giving and sharing credit when it's deserved.

Receive compliments graciously. A momentary burst of genuine gratitude, plus a little immodesty—"Thanks so much! I'm really pleased"—is an excellent way to appreciate a compliment. Two little words can solve all compliment dilemmas: "Thank you."

Q: *I work in an office that has three employees from Italy. They all speak flawless English, but speak only Italian among themselves—sometimes even when the subject is work-related. Am I wrong in thinking this rude?*

A: It's an unfortunate reality that speaking in a language others don't understand has the same connotation as whispering. It's exclusionary and gives the impression of gossiping. Whenever possible, workers should speak in the common language of the workplace so they can be understood by all within earshot. If they wish to converse in a different language, they should try to do so in a private area. Despite the frustration you may feel, before lodging a complaint, ask yourself: How harmful is their conversation to the work atmosphere? If the habit is simply annoying but not detrimental to the work at hand, this may be a case where ignoring it is the best solution.

INTERACTING WITH COLLEAGUES: SMALL GESTURES MATTER

The numerous interactions, verbal or written, that occur every day determine whether the office atmosphere is clear and calm or stormy. In fact, the skill with which you interact and socialize with your workmates can make the difference between advancing or being left behind.

You don't have to be perpetually perky or wear a fixed smile and constantly utter hellos or give high fives; forced friendliness is tiresome. The best kinds of interactions are those that are both effortless and sincere, based on respect and thoughtfulness. Small gestures matter, like these:

- You're working late and the cleaner arrives in your office. You say "Hello" and exchange a few pleasantries, a simple act that lets the cleaner know he's not intruding and that you appreciate the work he does to keep your workplace tidy.

- You've witnessed a coworker defuse a tense situation between two other employees. Later, in private, you compliment him on the way he handled it.

- A coworker is the subject of a rumor you know to be false. You do your part to set the record straight and politely inform the source of the rumor (if you know who it is) that she was wrong.

- You unofficially take under your wing a newcomer, who is faced with names to remember, places to locate, policies to master, and hierarchies to understand.

- During a staff meeting, you sincerely praise a coworker's work on a project.

HOW NOT TO WIN FRIENDS AT WORK

Staying on good terms with your coworkers also depends on what you *don't* do during the workday. Petty annoyances come in all guises, some more serious than others. Three particularly problematic areas are noise, odors, and offensive language.

Sounds

◆ The number one office complaint? Coworkers who talk too loudly on the telephone. It raises the overall noise level as others talk even louder to be heard over the din. You don't need to talk any louder than your normal conversational voice. Keep that in mind even if it requires posting a reminder on your desk.

◆ Use a speakerphone only when necessary—ideally in a closed office and only when more than two people on your end need to be on the call.

◆ Pick up the handset when dialing: Using the speakerphone and subjecting those around you to the electronic tone of each number as it's dialed is annoying and unnecessary.

◆ Never shout a request or response to someone in a nearby office or work area. Walk over, pick up the phone, IM, or email instead.

◆ Use headphones or earbuds to listen to music. Keep the volume low enough to be sure you can respond to a call or visitor.

◆ If you're using earbuds and someone engages you in a conversation, take both buds out of your ears. Don't leave one in so you can listen to music while conversing.

◆ Don't repeatedly click a pen while talking on the phone.

◆ Chew gum quietly; a gum chewer who pops and cracks his gum can drive nearby workers up the wall.

Odors

◆ Always test a new scent before wearing it to work, since body chemistry can intensify the power of fragrances. Apply perfume or cologne lightly. If your company has a "No Scent" policy, be sure to follow it.

◆ Practice good personal hygiene so you won't offend others with body odor, bad breath, or smelly feet.

◆ When eaten at your desk, smelly foods like fish, onions, and vegetables in the cabbage family are pungent and tough on neighboring officemates.

---

which bad office manners get you fired?

In a theLadders.com survey, 69.7 percent of executives said they would fire an employee for bad personal manners. What *are* the top five bad office manners that would get a person fired?

◆ Bad language

◆ Excessive workplace gossip

◆ Drinking on the job

◆ Leaving the office without telling anyone

◆ Too many personal calls

- Keep breath mints handy for after lunch and before meetings.

Words

- Tolerance of foul language is waning in business. While the stance on profanity is grounded in company culture, more and more companies are instituting rules banning it.

- Bigoted and sacrilegious comments are intolerable, especially when aimed at individuals. It can be considered harassment and dealt with as such.

- Be careful what you post on your walls. Never put up materials that are offensive, obscene, or have sexist or racist undertones.

WHEN PROFESSIONAL TURNS PERSONAL

Flirting and romantic relationships are inevitable when workers spend a large part of every day together, but in many workplaces, they're a potential minefield and can have serious consequences. (See also Chapter 29, "Dating," page 370.) Questions of conflict of interest, favoritism, distraction from work, and the unpleasant ramifications of a fling's sour ending are but a few that arise.

- Learn the company policy about dating clients, colleagues, or others at the company and abide by it.

- If you ask a coworker out and she declines more than twice, stop asking—unless she seems genuinely disappointed that she can't accept. Persisting after repeated turndowns may get you reported to management.

- Public displays of affection are unprofessional and inappropriate in the workplace or at work-related events.

- Don't gossip about an office romance.

- Calling someone "sweetie" and "honey" sounds condescending or suggestive even when said out of affection. Such terms are out of line in a work environment.

the smartphone camera

Be respectful of your coworkers by not taking pictures or videos of them with your phone's camera. They may resent that you have captured them without their permission, or they may have a cultural aversion to having their picture taken at all.

About Sexual Harassment

As a legal matter, sexual harassment requires a showing of *unwelcome* sexual advances or other verbal or physical contact of a sexual nature when that conduct: becomes a term and condition of employment; or the basis for punishing someone who does not go along with the conduct; or creates a hostile work environment. Even if behavior does not meet this legal definition, it may violate your company's policies and could get you fired. Know your company's policies.

Sexual harassment comes in many forms, but you can identify it as such if the following occur.

- The behavior constitutes sexual advances or verbal or physical contact of a sexual nature.

- The behavior is unwanted.

- The offensive behavior is repeated, even after it is known or should be known to be unwanted.

- The behavior has the purpose or effect of creating a hostile work environment or interferes with your work.

Part of the criteria for classing behavior as harassment is that it is repeated and known to be unwelcome, so do your part by making it clear to the perpetrator that you won't tolerate it.

If the behavior continues, keep a record of your encounters with the person complete with

- What was said and done.

- Any witnesses.

- Specific times and dates.

- Copies of any offensive texts, emails, social media posts, or other documentation.

Then,

- Speak with your supervisor (or, if your supervisor is the offender, speak to his or her supervisor), Human Resources, and any other people designated by a posted notice or in your employee manual to whom the event should be reported.

- If asked to provide a written complaint, keep it short and to the point. Describe the offending behavior and your efforts to proactively resolve the issue. Have your documentation available.

- If you make a complaint of unlawful harassment, your employer has an obligation to investigate your claim promptly. If found true, the employer needs to make it stop. Remedies may mean anything from a verbal reprimand to firing.

- You also have the option to file a complaint with the federal Equal Employment Opportunity Commission (EEOC) (www.eeoc.gov) or a local state agency such as a Human Rights Commission or your state's Attorney General's office. This information should be posted in your workplace and your employee handbook, if there is one. You do not have to make an internal complaint before you take this step, but you may want to do so anyway.

THE IMPORTANCE OF BUILDING RELATIONSHIPS

A talent for your line of work and the mastery of the necessary skills aren't the only things that spell success on the job. Your ability to build strong relationships not only with colleagues but also with business associates outside your company will directly affect your success. From the tone of your emails and phone voice, to your ability to engage in small talk, to the care with which you choose your dress, everything you say and do will impact those relationships.

Best advice: Think before you act and then make the choice that's best for everyone involved, not just the choice that's good for you. For instance, if you find yourself having to shake hands with a client who has a cold, it's better for everyone—the client, the company, and ultimately you—if you choose to shake hands (and then go to a restroom to wash your hands) than if you refuse to shake the client's hand. Refusing to shake creates an awkward, embarrassing moment for you, the client, your manager, and your company. It could even lead the person to wonder about doing business with you. Shaking hands, which is clearly the accepted manner when a hand is offered to you, makes the interaction go smoothly and helps you to build the relationship.

DEALING WITH YOUR OTHER WORK ASSOCIATES

You and your fellow workers may be fully committed to great customer service, but satisfying customers is seldom completely under your control. Delivering a quality product or service to your customer and getting it to her on time often depends on the cooperation of other people, both within your company as well as those outside, such as contractors and vendors. Getting along well with your customers, vendors or suppliers, and contractors requires treating them with respect and courtesy, which starts with listening to and showing interest in what they have to say.

The Importance of Active Listening

Listening means more than just paying attention. Whether you talk business in a face-to-face meeting or over the phone, use active listening. Most importantly, keep your attention riveted on the person you are with. Listen to every word, every tone, every pause. Try your best to fully absorb what the speaker is saying and why he is saying it. Take notes if the situation permits. If you're not sure about the propriety of notes at certain times, simply ask, "Mind if I jot down a couple of your points?"

Show you are listening and hearing by nodding your head, interjecting a comment or recapping, or asking tactful, intelligent questions. Occasionally, reflect back what was said: "Don, just to be clear, if we supply the graphics by the 6th, you'll deliver the software on the 25th." A businessperson who listens actively and knows how to guide the conversation in a polite way builds trust and sets the stage for smoother business dealings down the line.

Showing Your Appreciation

You want to show your customers and clients how much you appreciate their business. But instead of merely saying "thanks," reinforce the ways they will benefit from their decision to do business with you. For example, you might call after closing a deal and ask, "Have any problems come up since we signed the contract? Can I do anything else for you now?" Then keep the lines of communication open. If your client has a concern, you'll be the first to know—and can promptly address it.

You could also take a favored customer, client, contractor, or vendor to a lunch, dinner, show, or ball game. Express your appreciation of the business relationship at some point during the event.

Complaints and Other Problems

When you're hit with a heated complaint about a defect in one of your products or services, it should be obvi-

five ways to keep business associates happy

Treating your contractors, suppliers, and vendors with care is the right thing to do and can reap big rewards, especially when you need their extra effort on a project. Here are five simple steps you can take to make your working relationship with them the best that it can be:

- Treat a contractor courteously at all times.
- Be reasonable with deadlines, and don't ask him to rush a job unless you honestly have to.
- If you must ask someone to go the extra mile, make sure he knows how much you appreciate it.
- Pay promptly at all times.
- If you ask for a favor, be ready to return a favor in the future.

ous that the caller or writer wants immediate action. When you respond, remember that what he wants to hear isn't a spiel about warranties or your company's excellent quality control procedures, but that you'll fix the problem.

If the complaint is made by phone and you can't promise an immediate solution, let the person know you appreciate the urgency of the matter by saying, "I'll look into it immediately . . ." or "I'll ask my supervisor the minute I hang up . . ." Express some sympathy: "I'm sorry to hear that you're unhappy"—which you truthfully should be.

Ask for a time when you can call back with an answer. Then call when you promised you would. It's especially effective—and good manners—to get back to an angry customer at the agreed-upon time for your call, even if you *don't* yet have the complete answer for him. Far from setting you up for more trouble, this kind of response shows your customer that you're reliable and his problem is being worked on. Ignoring him is *not* the way to effectively build your customer's trust.

DEALING WITH ANGRY CALLERS

Some people have short fuses and tend to blame whoever's on the other end of the line. In these situations, don't take any remarks personally, even if you're being attacked. Here are some tips for handling an irate caller:

- Let the caller complain for a minute or two, which usually vents his anger.
- Don't interrupt, even if he pauses or says something that sounds like it's leading to an apology: "I don't like to get this mad, but . . ."
- When he starts to calm down, say something that shows you've listened closely and understand how important the problem is to him: "I know what it's like to get lost in an instruction manual."
- If things get worse and the caller rants on or is abusive, ask for his name (if he hasn't given it) and number and either end the call or say you'll call back in an hour or two or at a specified time the next day. Then use the delay to collect your

keeping commitments

Whenever you promise something to a customer—whether he has given you an earful or simply asked for more information—it's essential to follow through.

- If you say you'll call back, do it.
- If you say you'll ask someone else about a problem, ask.
- If you explain why you can't do what the customer wants done, get your facts straight.

Keeping your word isn't just common courtesy, it's also good business.

thoughts, and talk to your supervisor or coworkers about how to proceed.

- Once you've decided how to resolve the problem, call back and tell the caller what actions you *will* take (even if they don't fully meet his demands), not the actions you can't take. Never promise anything you can't deliver.

- Sometimes it's best to have a supervisor make the callback. He or she may have the authority to offer more options.

At times, nothing you say will satisfy an angry caller; no matter how rational and calm you are, your company is going to lose a customer. But if you did all you could to be courteous, then take a deep breath, relax, and focus your energy on what's next on your plate.

THE DOS AND DON'TS OF BUSINESS CARDS

A business card serves as an introduction and a resource. At a glance, the card should convey the essentials: the name of your company, your position, and any relative contact information. Typically, a business card has

- The name, physical address, and Web address of the company
- Your name and company title, if you have one
- Your contact info: office number, cell phone number, fax number, work email.

Today's business card may also include a company logo or slogan. Both design and format have gone far beyond black type on cream or white cards. Color and two- or folded four-sided cards are common, but beware choosing an odd size or shape that won't easily fit into a wallet or case.

Names and Titles

A business card should carry the name by which the person is known in the business world. For instance, if a woman's full name is Katherine Powell Thompson but she uses her maiden name for business purposes, her card will read "Katherine Powell." People who use nicknames may either use their full names or their nicknames; a full name often sounds more professional, so it's fine to say, "Please call me Kathy, not Katherine," when handing out cards.

Titles, including Mr., Ms., and Dr., aren't used on business cards, although credentials may follow the name: "Katherine Powell, CLU." An exception is when the person has a name that could be either male or female (Dana or Alex, for example); in such a case, placing Ms. or Mr. in front of the name is useful. In a business setting, "Ms." is preferred to "Miss" or "Mrs." (For more on names and titles, see Chapter 17, "Socal Names and Titles," page 215.)

The Etiquette of Business Cards

Here are some dos and don'ts for handing out business cards:

- ◆ *Do* wait until a businessperson who outranks you gives you her card before giving a card to her. If,

after a while, that more senior person doesn't offer you her card, then you can present yours and ask for hers. With businesspeople of equal rank, don't hesitate to initiate the exchange.

- ◆ *Do* keep your cards in perfect condition. Carry them in a business card holder to prevent smudging and creasing.

- ◆ *Don't* put a business card you've just received away without a glance. Taking a moment to look at the card demonstrates your interest and respect.

- ◆ *Don't* shove a person's card into your pocket or pocketbook. Put it away carefully and treat it with respect. Think of it as an extension of the person.

- ◆ *Don't* use a business card for social purposes. As its name makes clear, it should be limited to business. (See also "Social Cards," page 209.)

- ◆ *Do* brush up on business card protocol before traveling abroad. Customs can vary widely from country to country.

the social side of business

usiness is more than just business. There's a social component that impacts directly on your chances for success. From office parties to water cooler talk to meals with colleagues or clients, you'll have numerous opportunities to interact with people inside and outside your workplace.

[LUNCHES AND OFFICE PARTIES]

Purely social get-togethers at work include lunches (whether in the company lunchroom or the deli down the street) and parties that range from holiday banquets to a send-off for a new retiree or a shower for a mother-to-be.

Communal Lunches

Having lunch together is a great time to get to know your coworkers. More important, lunch is a great time for them to get to know *you*. Avoid sensitive work topics, since people at other tables may overhear. Also bypass topics that are too personal—your love life, health issues, or trouble you're having with your child. Lunch is a time for relaxing and taking a break, not the place for conversation that would be better conducted after work, if at all.

Always eating at your desk may make you seem unsociable—even if you don't mean to be. If a coworker drops by and asks if you want to go get a bite, appreciate the gesture and try to join him sometimes.

Office Parties

Office parties provide employees with the chance to become better acquainted and even to forge the bonds of real friendship. To navigate the office party successfully, consider the following:

Give thought to how you dress. At a party held after work, while some people will change into dressier clothes, both men and women usually wear the clothes they've worn all day. If unsure about appropriate dress, check with a colleague who's attended similar events in the past or with the event coordinator. In general, conservative is better than flashy.

Wear your name tag if the function calls for them. At business functions attended by people from other departments or other businesses—and at conferences and conventions, for that matter—name tags are both necessary and useful.

Behave professionally. The proverbial employee who wears a lampshade on his head and dances on the table might be an exaggeration, but he does serve as a reminder of the potential of forgetting to keep things in check. Have a good time, but avoid drinking too much or making too personal comments or jokes. (See "One-Drink Rule," page 445.)

Thank the hosts or event planners. Be sure to seek out the hosts to extend your thanks upon leaving. If the party is at someone's home, a follow-up note is always appreciated, and a good move if the host is your boss. (See "The Business of Thanks," page 446.)

After-Hours Activities

After hours, don't be too quick to let your hair down with coworkers. In a relaxed atmosphere, tongues are loosened and defenses are dropped, especially if alcohol is consumed. Don't make the mistake of believing that a conversation held off the premises is off the record. If you pass on a rumor, belittle or disparage an absent

---

where to wear your name tag

Name tags are usually worn on the right side because that's where most people look when they first greet each other with a handshake. Okay, so you're right-handed and you naturally reach over to your left side to place your name tag. Not a big deal, but once you learn the logic of your name tag on your right, placing it on the right is a good habit to get in to.

If pinning, clipping, or adhering a badge is likely to pull threads, cause puckering, or damage delicate fabrics, get creative: Consider attaching the badge to the waistband of your skirt or pants. Planners, take note: Necklace-style or magnetic ID tags are excellent alternatives.

---

coworker or boss, or reveal a workplace confidence, you can bet what you said will get back to the office, sometimes faster than you.

AT BUSINESS MEALS

All business meals have a measure of sociability over and above that of an office appointment. But as important as the fellowship is, your own behavior is equally so; how well you handle yourself reflects on you and your employer. (See also Chapter 6, "Table Manners," page 56; Chapter 9, "Dining Out," page 100.)

When You're the Host

If you're hosting a business meal—whether lunch, dinner, or even breakfast—taking a few steps beforehand will help make the event a success.

Time your invitation. Base when you extend the invitation on the situation, the particular guests, or the number of guests. It could be as soon as a day in advance for a casual lunch, or a week or more if you need to coordinate several schedules and book a popular restaurant.

What's their taste? If possible, find out if your guest(s) especially likes or dislikes certain foods or ethnic cuisines; you can either ask when extending the invitation or call the person's assistant. If you're hosting a group, choose a restaurant with a wide range of menu selections so that all the guests will find something to their taste.

Stick with the tried and true. Go with a place you know will have good food, service, and atmosphere—all conducive to a successful business meal. The unknown is too risky: The business meal isn't the time to try a new restaurant. The hottest new place in town may have bad service or be so noisy or cramped that it's hard to carry on a conversation. What's more, you might be disappointed in the food.

Reserve a table. There's no excuse for failing to make reservations.

Have a seating plan in mind before you arrive. It is the host's duty to indicate to guests where to sit. A polite host should see that guests take the better seats—those facing *away* from a wall, a waiters' station, the restroom, or the kitchen door. Always place the guest of honor to the right of the host and in the

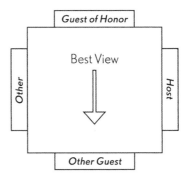

best seat—usually the seat facing out into the room. For a large number of people, draw up a seating plan ahead of time. Best of all, have place cards for each guest.

Be prepared to offer suggestions. Since you're familiar with the restaurant, you can offer ordering advice to your guest: "If you like prime rib, this place has the best."

Who pays? The person who does the inviting typically does the paying. The best time to clarify who pays is when the invitation is extended. "Will you be my guest for lunch?" If you've been invited out a couple of times and the invitee has paid, when he calls and invites you again, you can offer to pay, "Tom, that sounds great. You've paid the past couple of times, so this time lunch is on me."

Splitting the bill? If you and the other person see each other frequently and have developed a close working relationship, you might suggest, "How about if we split lunch next week?"

Is a specific item of business on the agenda? So that your dining partner can prepare and bring any pertinent materials, be specific about business topics you want to discuss and how deeply you'll be delving into them.

When should you discuss business? At a lunch or breakfast, business can be discussed anytime after the orders have been placed. At a dinner, business usually waits until after the main course has been cleared. As the host, it's up to you to initiate the conversation.

Reconfirm with both your guest and the restaurant. Call on the morning of a lunch or dinner; if you've scheduled breakfast, call the day before.

Be prompt. It's wise to arrive at least five minutes early so you can greet your guest after making sure everything is in order.

Paying the check. When you're the host, it's a good idea to let the maître d' or waiter know beforehand that the check should be given to you. This is especially important for women hosts, since even today many waiters automatically present the check to a man. Keep the check out of view as you look it over; it's not a guest's business to know what the meal cost—nor should you disclose it.

Alternatively, near the end of the meal, you can excuse yourself and give your credit card to the waiter and ask him to have the bill ready for you with a 20 percent tip added. Doing this ensures the check is never presented at the table.

Consider it your responsibility to pay your guest's coat check tab, but don't argue if he insists on paying it himself—something many guests will do.

When You're the Guest

Your first responsibility as a guest is to be on time. If you're running late, call the host on her cell phone or call the restaurant and ask that your host be told you're on your way. When you finally arrive, don't waste time by offering an elaborate excuse; a quick and sincere apology will do. If you arrive first, wait until your host arrives and go to the table with him.

Who Sits Where? If the host doesn't indicate where to sit, a guest should ask before seating himself.

During the Meal. Follow your host's lead. If she forgoes a first course or dessert, you should, too. If she doesn't order alcohol, you shouldn't, either.

To Drink or Not? Having alcohol at a business meal depends on the circumstances, the personalities and attitudes of the people concerned, and the degree

one-drink rule

If you're going to have alcohol, limit yourself to one drink. After a long day at work, especially when you haven't eaten anything for hours, a drink on an empty stomach can affect you very quickly. Even the person who thinks he can handle his liquor should take heed. Long before you feel the effects of alcohol, it can cause you to say and/or do things that you might regret the next day. Business social events are not drinking contests. They are an opportunity to meet people and showcase your skills at representing yourself and your company.

Better yet, by not drinking at all you give yourself the *best* opportunity to be successful.

of personal closeness. The days of the three-martini lunch may be over, but alcohol isn't automatically off-limits at a business meal.

Still, forgoing alcohol is the smartest route for hosts and guests alike. Ultimately, you know best how alcohol affects you, so weigh that against the importance of staying alert and poised. Again, take your cue from the host before ordering even one glass of wine; if he declines, you're wise to abstain as well.

Who Initiates the Business Conversation? If you're at a hosted meal, always wait for the host to bring up business. Your host may be interested in getting to know you better and business may not even be discussed. If you're with a group of colleagues, anyone may start the business conversation.

Repaying Invitations Does inviting someone to a business lunch, dinner, or breakfast mean it's tit for tat? Not necessarily. The rules governing the reciprocating of invitations vary from situation to situation.

- You're not expected to repay an invitation to a strictly business meal, no matter who issued the invitation—a customer, a vendor, or your boss. But reciprocating is a nice gesture if you continue to do business together.

- A client who is entertained by a salesperson or supplier isn't expected to return the invitation, even if his spouse or family was invited.

- Do return social invitations from coworkers and other business associates, whether it's to cement a business relationship or just because you enjoy one another's company. You needn't reciprocate in kind.

For instance, if your coworker included you in a fancy dinner party at her home, you can return the favor with an invitation to any gathering, including a backyard barbecue.

THE BUSINESS OF THANKS

A thank-you should always be offered. The method of thanking can be a note, face-to-face, phone, or email.

First-time meetings, especially at a lunch or dinner, usually call for a handwritten note, unless you know the person is from an email culture. When in doubt, choose the note. A prompt, sincere, handwritten one is always appropriate and is greatly appreciated by the recipient. It's also good business. Be sure to check spelling and grammar. If your handwriting is illegible, a typed note on your business stationery is fine.

When It's Okay to Send an Emailed Thank-you Note

- When you have lunch with an associate with whom you have a longtime business relationship and she picks up the tab, an emailed thanks is fine unless she's the kind who stands on tradition.

- When your host is someone with whom you exchange business correspondence via email two or three times a week, you can use email to express your thanks after a business lunch as you would in a handwritten note. If your host treated you to a business dinner, your better option would be to write and mail a thank-you note.

- When time is of the essence, use an emailed thank-you note as a prelude to a handwritten one. Send the email as quickly as possible and the note in one or two days.

When a Handwritten Thank-you Note Is a Must

- When you've been entertained at a business-related occasion that crosses from business to social—dinner, an evening out with your spouse, a weekend house party at the home of an employer or other business associate, or as guest of honor at an office party—send a handwritten note.

- When the occasion was purely social but was hosted by someone with whom you do business, address your note to your host and his or her spouse and send it to their home. Social thank-you notes are handwritten on either notepaper or personal stationery.

- When you receive a gift from a client, vendor, or associate, send a handwritten note if verbal thanks weren't given in person. Even if you did thank the giver in person, a follow-up note is always appreciated.

Less Formal Thank-yous

- When you're one of many at an office party or a restaurant where you share a meal while doing business, a face-to-face, phoned, or emailed thanks just after the event is sufficient. While it's never wrong to write a thank-you note, you can repeat your thanks in your next business correspondence instead.

- As a lunch guest of a host with whom you speak often, you can either express your thanks again the next time you talk or you can send an email.

- If you've lunched with someone you see regularly and he paid, saying thanks is fine. You would, however, mention the lunch in your next business communication: "Thanks again, Alfredo, for the lunch [or "for joining me for lunch" if you paid]. We really accomplished a lot, and I'll have that proposal to you by next week."

- The more expensive the entertainment, the more the need for a handwritten note.

SOCIALIZING OR TRAVELING WITH THE BOSS

It's generally up to your boss, not you, to initiate any socializing. That doesn't mean you can't suggest an occasional lunch together, but it does mean that you should do so only if you and your boss have established a comfortable rapport and your lunch invitation seems natural. You don't want to force your friendship on your boss. After all, you are not coequals. It can create an awkward situation when it's time for work assignments and evaluations. Nor is it a good idea to buddy up in an effort to become her favorite, a tactic that can be obvious to your boss and annoying to your workmates.

What about traveling with your boss? On the road, you may need to take on the role of personal assistant. Whether of the old school or new, you should stay respectful, as always. Regardless of your boss's gender, polite acts, such as offering the more comfortable seat, show you as courteous and considerate. Take charge of various tasks—hailing cabs, making restaurant or theater reservations, and tipping service providers—unless your boss insists on doing them. Stay on your toes in every way. You've been handed the opportunity to get to know your boss better and to make a lasting positive impression.

BARS AND BUSINESS

There may be good reason to do business in a bar, where the same host-guest rules for business meals apply. As a favor to everyone, choose a bar with comfortable seating and a low noise level. Only on purely social occasions should businesspeople meet in a typical good-time, packed-to-the-gills kind of place.

AT PRIVATE CLUBS

As private clubs go, the country club is an ideal place for business entertaining. Your meal won't be rushed, and usually you can linger at your table for a while. When recreational sports such as golf or tennis are intended as the main activity, lunch or after-game drinks are usually included to ensure there's plenty of time to talk.

Another advantage: If businesspeople who have country club memberships take turns hosting at their respective clubs, "who owes whom" stops being an issue.

Members-Only Clubs

Members-only social clubs are the descendants of the gentlemen's clubs of old. A modern example is the university club, with alumni and alumnae of a given college or university eligible for membership.

Because tradition is important, conducting business is usually prohibited in the public areas. Many clubs have bylaws specifying that business entertainment reimbursements from a member's company aren't allowed; all expenses, including dues, must be paid personally. Using an item of business paraphernalia (cell phone, laptop, mobile device) is generally off-limits in public areas.

Many members-only clubs have strict dress rules, so a guest should ask the host what to wear or call the club's office and find out what's expected. The host can volunteer the dress code information when the invitation is extended.

Two things for guests to remember: First, don't strike out on a tour of the club. Enter the library or lounge, for example, only when escorted by your host. Second, be on your best behavior. Your actions reflect not only on you and your company but also on your host.

AT SPECTATOR SPORTS

Spectator sports are a great way to build a relationship with a business associate. Both the host and the guest can take advantage of the opportunity to get to know each other on a personal basis. A host should:

golf or tennis, anyone?

If you've been invited to play a round of golf or a set of tennis with a business associate, don't say, "I'd love to" unless you know the rules of the game and you can actually play it. A mere acquaintance with the rules may not be enough; people who play regularly won't take kindly to your lack of skill and knowledge. Being honest about your limited abilities allows the host to decide whether to suggest another sport or to invite you to a meal instead.

If you feel comfortable participating in the sport, accept with enthusiasm. On the day of the game, make a point of arriving early; road conditions and traffic can be unpredictable, and you don't want to cause a late start. As a token of appreciation, you might bring a sleeve of golf balls or a can of tennis balls as a gift for your host. Guest players should offer to pay their own greens, caddy, or court fees.

Follow your host's lead: Let him suggest any beverage, snack, or a meal (although if you're thirsty, don't hesitate to have some water). If you need to load up on carbohydrates before you play, eat before you leave home.

Remember that loud talking or other distractions are particularly annoying during games that require concentration. Many clubs prohibit the use of cell phones at their facilities, so leave your phone or pager in your car. If you're going to be on call, you may have to decline the invitation. Otherwise, if the club will allow it, set your device to vibrate and alert your playing partners that you may have to step aside to take a call.

- Order tickets in advance.

- Make plans not only for the event itself but also for any before or after activities.

- Make plans for transportation and inform his guest.

- Give the guest information about any attire needs for before, during, and after the event.

- Be attentive to a guest's comfort: Point out where restrooms are located, ask if the guest would like something to eat or drink.

As a guest, consider the following:

- If your host doesn't clue you in, ask him what he's wearing so you'll know whether to choose jeans, khakis, or shorts. Business attire might be appropriate if you're going directly from the office or when you're entertained in a corporate or private box.

- Follow the host's lead in other ways: Order alcohol only if he does, and let him initiate small talk in case he's the sort who wants to give undivided attention to the game.

unfamiliar events

Whether it's a polo match, Sumo wrestling, or the opera, if you've been invited and are unfamiliar with the event or performance, do a little research ahead of time to familiarize yourself with what's expected and how to behave.

- Unless your hometown or favorite team is playing, root for the host's team. If your team is indeed playing and wins, offer commiseration and refrain from gloating.

- Volunteer to buy a snack and a drink for your host and any other guests.

- Excuse yourself only when there's a break in the action.

AT THE THEATER

An invitation to a movie, play, concert, opera, or ballet is an excellent choice when entertaining business associates—particularly when spouses or dates are included. Beginning or topping off the evening with dinner makes for an even more memorable occasion. Unless you're familiar with your guests' tastes, ask which kind of entertainment they prefer; people who are passionate movie buffs might be less than enthusiastic about the opera, and vice versa.

AT OFF-SITE BUSINESS VENUES

From time to time you may find yourself traveling off-site to a convention, trade show, seminar, or a training course. Often these off-site events are hosted in another city or a resort. There's no question that while you're there to do business or hone your skills, there's a social aspect as well. After hours, the entertainment ranges from receptions at hospitality suites to dinners at city restaurants, golf, or group outings. You're meant to have fun, but don't completely let your hair down. As a representative of your company in a larger public arena, focus on making sure that your actions reflect positively on you and your company. What happens in Vegas has a tendency to find its way back to the office.

When It's Your Booth

Your booth is your chance to introduce your company and your product to a targeted audience. In addition to a professional-looking booth, these pointers can help make a good impression:

- Dress appropriately. If your company hasn't specified a uniform—logoed polo shirts, for example—or a dress code, dress as if you were meeting an important client.

- Stand. At least one person should always be standing in order to greet visitors. If you are seated and a visitor approaches, stand to greet him.

- Greet each person with a handshake, smile, and warm welcome.

- Give each visitor your undivided attention.

- If another visitor is waiting to speak to you, acknowledge him and return to finish talking with your first visitor. "Hi, please have a look around. I'll be with you shortly."

As a Participant

Conventions, trade shows, seminars, and trainings are educational and your company is expecting you to take the opportunity to further your knowledge in your field. Here are ways to participate effectively:

- Arrive on time for classes, workshops, or speeches.

- Turn off your cell phone.

- Be a good listener.

- At the end of the session, don't usurp the speaker's time or monopolize the Q&A.

After Hours

When the work part of your day is done, it's expected that you relax and enjoy yourself. It's a great opportunity to get to know others from your company, whether they're coworkers or from another department or site. It's likely that you'll also run into prospects that you met earlier. Make sure you greet them. You can even spend some social time with them, but don't go back into "sell" mode. Above all—and we can't stress this too strongly—you still represent your company, even when you're off duty. Avoid the following:

- **Too much alcohol.** Getting drunk just plain makes you look undisciplined and immature, and it reflects poorly on your company. And when strangers—who could be prospects or even others from your company—overhear comments like, "Boy, was I wasted last night," they aren't impressed.

- **Adult entertainment venues.** They're just not the right atmosphere to foster a business relationship.

- **Airing dirty laundry.** Dishing company gossip or venting about your boss or coworkers doesn't raise your status in anyone else's eyes but your own. You're more likely to be perceived as a complainer or someone who can't be trusted.

---

name tags, part II

At large conventions, *everyone* wears a name tag, and for good reason. They make introductions and starting conversations a breeze. There's little worry about forgetting a name—it's right there in front of you. And the tag also includes the company name, city, and state, so you already have some vital information. All this and anything else a participant wants to share is encoded on the tag.

LIFE STAGES
AND
SPECIAL TIMES

PART VII
home and family life

CHAPTER 36 Today's Home and Family 457

CHAPTER 37 Pregnancy, Birth, and Adoption 473

CHAPTER 38 Children and Teens 478

CHAPTER 39 Living with Others 490

CHAPTER 40 People Who Work in Your Home 500

CHAPTER 41 Separation and Divorce 511

CHAPTER 42 Elder Etiquette 520

CHAPTER 43 Illness 531

CHAPTER 44 Loss, Grieving, and Condolences 539

36

today's home and family

Is there a difference between a home and a family? The people are the family and the where is the home, but the two are inextricably linked. Whether it's two in an apartment or twelve in a house, it's the intangibles—the connections, comfort, love, security, trust, and knowledge of belonging—that define both the family and the home.

[CREATING A CULTURE]

A home is a reflection of the people who live there and the culture they have created through the physical appearance of the home, the emotional atmosphere, the standards set, and the traditions kept. No two homes have an identical culture nor would we expect that. As you walk into a home, you learn a lot about its inhabitants and get clues as to what's expected there. Almost the first thing a visitor notices is the physical appearance. Is it impeccably neat or comfortably cluttered? Is the furniture casual or formal? Is this a home

where everyone removes their shoes upon entering? A visitor can sense the type of atmosphere from the welcome, which could be anything from whoops of joy and a hug, to a "hello" and a handshake. More subtly the culture can reflect traditions and values.

Setting Standards

"In our house we all help clear the table." "Here we don't use that language." "You can hang your coat on those hooks over there" or "Just put your coat on the back of that chair." The people who live in the home set the standards and a visitor should respect them. When the standards are based on the principles of etiquette—consideration, respect, honesty, courtesy, and kindness—the home atmosphere is both ordered and comfortable. Typically a family sets its own standards regarding greetings, style of communication, language (both the one spoken and the words that aren't allowed), timeliness, housekeeping standards, and what cooperative work is expected. There is no way to list all the standards that can be set in a home; suffice it to say that it is an etiquette imperative that everyone (guest or resident), by virtue of entering the home, makes an implicit agreement that they will abide by the standards.

Traditions

The residents also have the prerogative to establish the traditions that guide both everyday life and special events. In a sense, tradition drives respectful behavior. For example, people remove their baseball caps when they come indoors. It's an old, old tradition that dates back to the days of knighthood and helmets and visors. The guest removed his helmet and visor to reveal his identity and friendly intention. Now a baseball cap doesn't hide your identity but it's still respectful to remove it.

Traditions also give everyone in the household a sense of what to expect. The way you celebrate birthdays, say grace at the table, have dinner together three nights a week, and turkey with wild rice stuffing on Thanksgiving are all traditions. Everyone knows not only what to expect but what's expected of them.

Traditions and standards are an integral part of the culture of a home. Some may be decades old and some of your own creation. New or old they reflect the "family" who lives there and deserve respect from all who enter.

DEVELOPING A RESPECTFUL HOME LIFE

When the adults who head the family treat each other with respect, warmth, courtesy, and integrity, they set the tone for *all* their family relationships.

- **In private and public, they demonstrate respect for each other.** That means promoting your partner's best qualities, speaking positively of him or her, and avoiding put-downs. Don't discuss intimate matters with others. How you show respect (or disrespect) for each other is the model your children will carry into their adult relationships.

- **They recognize the other half of their partnership.** When speaking about shared relationships, responsibilities, and possessions, use "we" and "our" to express closeness and mutual respect: "*We* (not I) have three children."

- **They consult each other before making social arrangements.** When accepting invitations or hosting social occasions individually, talk with your spouse or partner and be sure your plans are okay. Anticipate conflicts: If your husband is an avid golf fan, avoid scheduling social events the weekend of the Masters Tournament.

- **They respect each other's privacy.** Don't open each other's mail; read each other's journal, diary, or private correspondence; or listen in on phone calls. Nor should you expect a spouse or partner to *automatically* share all of his or her opinions and attitudes. Her thoughts about a subject might be private, different from yours, and she might not want to share them.

- **They respect alone time.** Each partner's right to time alone is often a core value in successful relationships. Allowing each other time off and supporting individual interests reinforces the trust essential to an enduring partnership.

The home is where children learn the standards and traditions that are essential to becoming considerate, respectful, honest people. Parents of very young children begin the process by helping them understand that other people have feelings like their own. When reason kicks in, around age six, parents can explain the whys of considerate behavior and put thoughtful actions into context. Family life presents daily opportunities for lessons in thoughtfulness and consideration: "Remember, we all share in the cleanup." "Please turn the music down, so we can hear each other."

It's important for parents to be clear that their children must respect the standards and traditions in their own home and in the homes they visit. They learn this both from their own parents and from the people they visit.

Parents need to talk with their children about variations in home standards: "I know in our house we keep our shoes on, but at others' you may be asked to take them off. I expect you to respect the rules in other people's homes even if they are different than ours. However, if you think you're being asked to do something you think is disrespectful, then I'd like you to talk to me about it."

And when other children are visiting your home, you can help them learn your standards by telling your young visitors what they are. It's completely acceptable to expect children to meet your standards in your home. You can always say to a visiting child, "In our home, we don't jump on the furniture, so please stop."

As children grow older, the dialogue changes in both content and direction. In adolescence, many young people begin to pull away from the standards and traditions in their homes, and some seem to forget their manners overnight. This is an expected part of the process of growing up, though it tests virtually every parent's patience. Still, it's an excellent time to promote thoughtfulness by engaging teens in discussion and negotiation as often as possible, and letting them exercise their critical thinking skills. Respecting their opinions even when you disagree teaches them the value of tolerance and how to "agree to disagree." Not every family discussion will be a success, but don't give up. Through the respectful, considerate, and honest

disciplining other people's kids

While you can and should stop other people's children, including relatives' children, from engaging in negative behaviors or disregarding the standards in your home, you really don't achieve anything by punishing them. Let their parents know if they've been misbehaving. If the behavior doesn't improve, it is perfectly appropriate to say, "Russell is continuing to have a hard time behaving at our house. It might be best if you stay, too, when he's visiting here."

give-and-take of discussion, teens learn to value the needs and ideas of others and to think about the consequences of their own actions. Be alert to a young person's thoughtful deeds and be generous with your unconditional support and praise.

TODAY'S FAMILIES

As we enter the twenty-first century, there's a wide diversity in the family constellation. In some two-parent families, both adults are wage earners. A growing number of couples are waiting until they are older to marry and have children. Many children live in single-parent homes. Some people who don't marry make a deliberate choice to be single parents. You may know unmarried couples living together with or without children, married couples who have chosen not to have children, and people who are perfectly happy living alone. While some people count only their immediate family members, others widen their definition of "family" to include close friends and others with commonly held beliefs.

In practice, families are self-defining and seem almost infinitely varied in their size, structure, and complexity. Today's "ideal" family is found anywhere that

love grows, respect is nurtured, and kindness and consideration flourish.

FAMILY VALUES, FAMILY MANNERS

For all their diversity, today's American families share many basic values, including mutual affection and respect, commitment to the well-being of other family members, personal responsibility and integrity, and loyalty to the family unit. These values are passed on from generation to generation.

Respect for our own families should logically engender respect for other families, whatever their makeup. Yet different families may have different standards and practices. This chapter highlights some of the key etiquette issues created whatever these value structures might be. There are certain standards and behaviors that help create smooth interactions and promote solid relationships. The following recommendations can be applied when interacting with other families:

Be considerate of any parent's primary obligations. Working parents find it especially challenging to make time for their families in the face of their work obligations. It's important to respect parents' commitments and desires to be with their families whenever they can.

Be available to listen. Children sometimes turn to an adult other than a parent to talk about their feelings and problems. Don't push children into discussions, but be attentive to their cues. You may be able to offer suggestions, but don't be drawn into criticism of others in the family or taking sides.

Avoid saying or doing anything that casts doubt on a parent's competence or parenting skills. A casual remark such as "It's too bad your mother (or father) has to work and can't come to your ball games" is like salt in a wound for a child who already knows that his parent isn't as available as he'd like.

Don't criticize another parent around children—yours or others'. A seemingly inoffensive comment by an adult about another parent's lifestyle can be hurtful, and it could also easily turn into cruel teasing on the playground.

COURTESIES FOR TODAY'S MANY FAMILIES

While the following family structures aren't all-inclusive and often overlap in complex ways, the fundamentals of courtesy and consideration apply to all.

Stepfamilies

Stepfamilies are primarily the product of combining households through remarriage after divorce or the death of a spouse. The partnership of unmarried adults may also create a stepfamily-type relationship when one or both have children. Of course, stepfamilies also include any children the couple has together. Multiple remarriages can create a maze of relationships that are hard even for immediate family members to keep straight.

When a child's name changes after a divorce, remarriage, or the marriage of a single parent, it's not generally announced publicly. However, a parent may want to inform family and close friends of the change. It's also a good idea to tell the parents of the child's friends and ask them to explain to their children. Teachers and school officials, coaches, and health-care providers should be informed as soon as a legal change is made.

To achieve stable, loving, enduring relationships, stepfamilies need the support of other relatives and friends. Grandparents and close family members can be of great help by welcoming stepchildren wholeheartedly and treating all the children in the newly formed household equally. This isn't always easy, especially when the bonds between natural family members have been very tight. But caring adults are able to curb the impulse to show favoritism; they respect the individuality of each child.

It's equally important to respect both stepparents and biological parents, and to avoid comparisons between them. Children in stepfamilies often suffer from divided loyalties, and no adult should do or say anything that indicates or implies that one parent is "better" than another. Speak of and treat a new spouse (and his or her children if this is the case) respectfully—whatever the custodial arrangement. No matter what other family members may think of former in-laws and their new partners, it's unkind and uncaring to sow seeds of doubt in the minds of children.

Here are a few more recommendations for the family and friends of stepfamilies:

Be considerate of custodial and visitation arrangements. A child's need for time with a noncustodial parent overrides other family members' invitations and schedules. If your grandchild, niece, or nephew can't attend a family gathering because of a prearranged visit with his parent, confine yourself to a normal expression of regret. You don't want the child to feel that he or his noncustodial parent has caused a problem.

Include stepparents in family discussions. Stepparents should be involved in family discussions and decisions about the children. Whether it's something simple like asking for a child to visit or a major concern about discipline, try to include both parent and stepparent when you raise an issue.

Avoid overindulging children in stepfamilies. The stereotypical view of children in stepfamilies as fragile can lead others to indulge them out of misguided sympathy.

Single-Parent Families

Single-parent families may result from divorce, death of a spouse, or parental choice, so don't assume that every family has the same story. A single parent might be a grandparent or other relative, a legal guardian, an adoptive parent, or a foster parent.

Single-parent families can have more challenges than two-parent families, particularly when the adult must be both breadwinner and full-time parent. This dual role can cause stress as the competing demands of parenting and providing financial support can come into conflict. Support from family and friends can make a huge difference for both the single parent and the children.

Offer genuine and specific help. You may take a child to school, social events, or pick him up at daycare. Sometimes, just telling a parent that you're available in emergencies is the greatest assistance. You may never be called on, but your offer can bring peace of mind.

Don't expect tit-for-tat return of favors. Single parents may not have the time or resources to reciprocate for every nice thing you do, so don't be upset if they don't. If you feel a parent is imposing on you, have a conversation with him and let him know what you can or can't do. Whatever you do, don't complain to his child.

When she keeps saying no. Even if a single parent hasn't been able to accept social invitations in the past, friends should continue to ask. It may be the very next time that she would be able to accept, and she will surely be disappointed to be off your list.

Other Parent Figures

Sometimes an extended family member (grandparent, aunt, uncle, older sibling, or cousin) takes on the care and nurturing of children, becoming their parent figure. Depending on the circumstances, this may be a temporary or permanent arrangement. While there are no specific etiquette guidelines relative to this situation, friends and other family members may want to be especially sensitive during the early adjustment period. Also, the family member in the parental role should be afforded the same respect and credibility that would be given to the child's biological parent.

Families with Same-Sex Parents

Whatever their feelings about same-sex relationships, adults should never make negative comments to or around the child of a same-sex couple, other children, or anyone else, for that matter. If you are ever unsure about how to address a same-sex couple, pay attention when you are introduced and follow their lead. In general, you'll be okay referring to them as "Bobby's parents," "Bobby's moms," or "Bobby's dads."

Singles and Couples Without Children

People who live on their own and couples without children now constitute the largest number of households in the United States. Many have chosen their independent lifestyle: young adults in their higher education and career-forming years, older adults who are delaying marriage and children, and people who don't want to marry or become parents.

Some people still have trouble realizing that alone doesn't automatically mean lonely or searching for a mate. Single women now enjoy the social freedom once limited to men. It's no longer necessary to arrange a date for a single dinner companion, though it's fine to offer. Likewise, there's no reason to exclude singles and couples without kids from occasions that include children.

Expressing disapproval of a person's chosen lifestyle is presumptuous and rude. On the other hand, singles and couples without kids should try not to become defensive when subjected to thoughtless comments, such as, "Oh, I bet you miss having children." You may be able to use good humor to fend off a friend bent on matchmaking or promoting the virtues of parenthood. If you must be more direct, be kind and avoid getting into a lifestyle debate: "You and Andy have a great marriage, but marriage isn't the right choice for me, at least right now."

Older Parents

The trend toward delaying marriage and childbearing has produced couples who have children in their later thirties, and on into their forties and fifties. People may jump to the conclusion that a fifty-year-old woman with a five-year-old are grandmother and grandchild. To prevent such misunderstandings, older parents should introduce their children by name and relationship: "This is my daughter, Francesca." If you forget to clarify and the person you're meeting misinterprets, explain as quickly as you can: "Actually, Francesca is my daughter." It's likely that your friend will be embarrassed; give her a friendly smile and change the subject.

If you're the one who made the mistake, apologize when you are corrected but don't be too embarrassed. Just be careful not to compound the error by making remarks like "Was she a surprise?" that are prying and insensitive.

Grandparents

Whether they live in their grown children's homes or travel for hours to visit once a year, grandparents are a vital force in their grandchildren's lives. Children learn about their grandparents' histories; how to interact with elders; specific skills such as cooking, fishing, hunting, or storytelling; and perhaps even patience. It's

not always easy to listen to a grandparent telling the same story for the tenth time, but the lesson in patience is invaluable.

When grandparents visit, all the guidelines for being a good host and guest apply. Despite the urge to spoil the child, grandparents should respect the standards and limits set by the parents. Also, it's a breach of etiquette to be overtly critical of the parents' child-rearing styles.

However, this relationship is a two-way street. It's important that when your kids are visiting their grandparents, you coach them to respect and follow their standards. "Dan, I know you don't like to wear a jacket and tie, but Nana and Grampa G really care that you do. We show them our love and respect by wearing our dressier clothes when we have Thanksgiving dinner at their house."

INTRODUCTIONS AND NAMES—A FORM OF RESPECT

Respect means little unless it's demonstrated on a daily basis. The following etiquette issues involve common courtesies and consideration within families and also for outsiders. These basic courtesies might be tricky

Q: *I have four girls and my mother-in-law goes to extremes when it comes to Christmas and birthday gifts. I'm talking about thirty presents for each child! My children are losing the concept of why we celebrate in the first place. What can I do?*

A: Before you actually talk with your mother-in-law, strategize with your spouse. Decide on a gift limit that you think is reasonable. Working together, you'll be in a stronger position to make your case. Understand that much of the joy of grandparenting is giving gifts. You and your spouse should talk with her together. "It's great that you're so caring and generous with the kids, but we really want to tone down the *quantity* of gifts. Please, can you give the kids only a few gifts at Christmas and birthdays? Instead of the extra presents, perhaps you'd like to do something with Katie and Chris? They've been talking about wanting to go to the new water park for ages. We could help you plan an outing."

Here are some other suggestions:

- Let her know that you'll hold on to some of the gifts and give the rest on the kids' birthdays.

- Tell her that you may have to give some of the gifts away.

when family relationships are complicated. But respecting the preferences of the people involved and using common sense—plus tolerance on everyone's part when mistakes are made—will smooth the way.

Stepfamilies. Forcing a reluctant child to refer to steprelations as "mother/father," "sister/brother," and "grandmother/grandfather" can damage the growth of trust and affection. It's usually best to let children and teens decide how they want to introduce a stepparent, stepsibling, and other relatives. A child may be comfortable saying, "My stepmom, Bonnie" (*or* Bonnie O'Brien if the last names are different), or "my mother, Bonnie," or simply "Bonnie O'Brien."

However, children shouldn't be allowed to address or introduce any family members in a rude or disparaging manner. No matter how difficult relationships might be at any given time, introducing or speaking of a stepparent as "my father's other wife" or a stepsibling as "my mother's husband's kid" is unacceptable, especially when the tone makes it obvious that the words are intended to cause pain and embarrassment.

Grown children are often uncomfortable referring to an older parent's new spouse as their mother or father, even when the marriage itself is welcome. Conversely, older stepparents may be hesitant to call a spouse's adult children by any variant of daughter or son. It's common for adult children and their stepparents to address each other by first name. As long as an introduction is warm, it's respectful for an adult to say, "I'd like you to meet Louis Strayhorn, my mother's husband" or "Ginny Alvarez, my husband's daughter."

Adoptive families. Adopted children are introduced just as biological children are. Unless there's a specific reason (for instance, introducing the child to a health-care provider who will be taking a family medical history), there's no need to comment on the relationship. Adopted children generally call their parents by some form of "mother" and "father," though older children may prefer first names or nicknames.

Guardianships. Relationships need not be spelled out in introductions, but if you're the guardian of a relative, you would include the family relationship and your relative's last name if different from yours: "I'd like you to meet my niece, Cecelia Jernigan."

When introducing a child in foster care, consider the situation before announcing the relationship. Although there are times when an explanation is needed, as when introducing a child to school officials, always think of the child first. Should someone ask if the child is yours, you can respond, "No, Ricky is our foster son," if the child prefers. But it's just as easy to reply something like, "No, but we love having him with us."

Former spouses. When introducing a relative's former spouse, it's rarely necessary to mention the nature of the relationship. Simply leave the former relationship out of the introduction. "Maria, I'd like you to meet my good friend Gerry McMahon." If you do include a relationship, your former sister-in-law is just that, not your ex-sister-in-law.

Domestic partners. There are really no universally accepted terms as yet to denote intimate relationships outside marriage but most people today are comfortable using "partner." (See "Greetings," page 10, and "Introductions," page 15.) Consult the people involved about how they prefer to be introduced and then respect their wishes: "I'd like you to meet Jenna Mies and her partner/boyfriend/significant other Fred Stollins." You can always say, "I'd like you to meet Jenna Mies and Fred Stollins."

GOOD RELATIONS WITH IN-LAWS

When a couple marries, they gain "instant parents." What's more, two sets of relatives, who may be little more than strangers to one another, are brought together as extended family. Each family has its own customs, traditions, and expectations, which may differ widely. Even when family cultures are similar, they aren't the same, and everyone must be prepared to make adjustments.

Probably the best way to establish and maintain harmonious relationships is for couples and their in-laws to follow a policy of noninterference. In spite of the mother-in-law jokes, interference can come from both generations and genders. While a person may have good intentions, too much advice and criticism can fracture family relationships. In most instances, the wise course is to

◆ Be tolerant of and show respect for differences.

◆ Try to avoid reading hidden meanings into everyday remarks.

◆ Listen politely and respond noncommittally to unsolicited advice.

◆ Don't give unsolicited advice, opinions, or instructions.

◆ Clear up any major misunderstandings quickly and courteously.

◆ Don't hesitate to apologize when you're in the wrong.

◆ Make every effort to put a problem behind you.

◆ Don't carry a grudge.

Who Are Your In-Laws?

When a couple marries, each becomes a member of the other's family. Thus, your husband's or wife's relatives become your in-laws—mother-in-law, father-in-law,

Q: *My former sister-in-law and I have known each other since high school and remain good friends although she is now divorced from my brother. But we both wonder how we should make introductions to people who don't know our family history.*

A: Unless there's a reason to indicate the past relationship, simply introduce each other by first and last names. You might simply say, "This is my friend, Ashley McNamara." If your surnames are the same and someone asks if you're related, you can truthfully say, "No," or you can briefly describe the relationship: "We used to be in-laws, but we've always been friends." Using the term "former sister-in-law" is friendlier than "ex-sister-in-law."

brother-in-law, and so on. However, the husbands and wives of your in-laws are not technically related to you. Your husband's sister is your sister-in-law. Her husband is your husband's brother-in-law, but not yours: He's simply your sister-in-law's husband. Their children, on the other hand, would be your nieces and nephews.

Such technicalities can confuse even a genealogist, and most people just do what's comfortable. "In-law" is generally reserved for a spouse's nuclear family (parents and siblings) but rarely used for grandparents, aunts, uncles, and cousins. However, it can also be a term of family endearment, or to show closeness, so if you introduce your husband's sister's husband as your "brother-in-law," don't worry.

How to Address In-laws

Should you call your new mother-in-law "Mom" or "Christine" or "Mrs. Turner"? Will your father-in-law be "Dad" or "Pop" or "Bill"? The question often troubles engaged and newly married couples, but it needn't. If your parents-in-law haven't broached the subject, ask them how they want to be addressed, and then respect their decisions. The same consideration applies to grandparents, aunts, and uncles.

However, many people feel that intimate terms such as "Mom" or "Dad" should be reserved for biological or adopted family. If your new son- or daughter-in-law is uncomfortable with any variation of "mother" and "father," don't force the issue. These days, in-laws often address one another by first names, which is convenient and recognizes the adult nature of their intergenerational relationship.

Q: *My wife's parents invite us out for a nice restaurant dinner every two months or so. But they always pay, and this makes me feel awful because they live on a fixed income and both my wife and I are well-paid professionals. My wife says it's their choice, but I know that treating us is a sacrifice for them. Should I insist on picking up the check?*

A: Although the cost may be a strain on your in-laws' budget, they apparently enjoy treating you. Getting together seems to be worth the financial outlay. Since they issue the invitation, you are their guests and don't pay. You can always reciprocate by inviting them out at another time. You and your wife might also suggest a family meal at your home as an occasional alternative to a restaurant. Look for ways to share their company without challenging their independence or dampening their pleasure in being your hosts. When your in-laws do pay, show your gratitude and don't feel guilty.

In-law Intrusions

Two classic sticking points for newly marrieds and their in-laws are the first major holiday and the birth of the first grandchild. While a usually agreeable compromise is to share holidays (see Q&A, page 470), welcoming a new grandchild can be trickier. Which in-laws see the baby first; the baby's name; the choice of godparents;

bottle or breast-feeding—these are all subjects for unsolicited advice and potential hurt feelings: "But I'm your mother! Don't you want me in the delivery room?" Often new parents are caught in the middle between their old and new families. These are intimate family matters, and grandparents should always wait to be asked for their input. Even when asked for advice, be careful that it doesn't sound like criticism, demands, or expectations: "Well, I bottle-fed my son and he turned out just fine." Instead, "I didn't breast-feed, but I'd be happy to do some laundry while you're feeding Jamie."

GETTING ALONG WITH EXTENDED FAMILY

Are they coming to visit or just dropping by? The Golden Rule provides the basis for positive family visits:

- Use the same good manners you would use when visiting or hosting people who aren't relatives.

- Don't criticize or condescend to family members, gossip about them to others, or embarrass them by telling personal stories or sharing private information. There can be a fine line between friendly teasing and hitting a nerve.

- Always treat your spouse and children respectfully, especially in the presence of others.

- Give advance notice when you're planning to stop by.

- Ask, don't expect, relatives to babysit on the spur of the moment.

- Avoid borrowing money, cars, and other possessions; if you do borrow, always return items in the same—or better—condition as you borrowed them.

- Be on time.

- Don't treat family occasions as business opportunities or expect relatives to provide free professional advice, service, or goods.

- Always offer to help at family gatherings and accept family assistance when you are the host.

- Discipline your children when it's called for. Support the host family members in enforcing their house rules when your children visit their home.

- Never allow your child to tease or bully the children of other relatives.

- Avoid boasting excessively about your child or frequently comparing him to other children in the family.

- When the kids aren't invited, respect the host family's plan for a child-free, adults-only event.

Remembering Milestones

Birthdays, weddings, anniversaries, religious holidays, graduations—every family has its milestones and its own ways of observing them. These occasions celebrate both the event and the family, and it's worth the effort to attend if you can.

Giving gifts can be problematic, however. Some

those "once removed" cousins

Betty and Bob are sister and brother. But what are their children to one another and who is "once removed"? The answers lie in the generations. It begins with siblings. The children of siblings are first cousins because they are the first generation of cousins. The children of first cousins are second cousins to one another. And so on through the generations.

"Once removed" doesn't indicate that a cousin was ever banished from the family—just that the cousins are separated by a generation. So when your first cousin has a child, you and that child are first cousins once removed. Your children and your cousin's children are second cousins. The following chart diagrams the cousin relationships. By the time people reach grandparenthood, almost everyone will probably be introducing one another simply as "cousin," which is both polite and correct.

GENERATION	FAMILY MEMBER(S)	RELATIONSHIP TO . . .	FAMILY MEMBER(S)
First	Betty	sibling	Bob
Second	Betty	aunt	Bob's children
	Betty's children	first cousins (same generation)	Bob's children
Third	Betty	great-aunt	Bob's grandchildren
	Betty's children	first cousins once removed (one generation apart)	Bob's grandchildren
	Betty's grandchildren	second cousins (same generation)	Bob's grandchildren

family members can afford to send gifts for every holiday and birthday or make a splash with expensive presents, but overdoing can cause hurt, resentment, or confusion when others aren't so fortunate. Gift exchanges that began within the limits of a nuclear family can get out of control when the family grows to include dozens of sisters- and brothers-in-law, aunts, uncles, and nieces and nephews. People often have different ideas about the appropriate occasions for gifts. For example, in many families, Mother's Day and Father's Day are observed with calls, visits, cards, and gifts. Other families make little or no fuss. Be sure you know where your family stands.

When deciding when to give and what to select, consider the family norm. You don't have to do exactly what everyone else does, but do think about the wishes of the recipient and the general nature of the gifts from other family members. If a relative has made it clear

Q: *My husband and I married last June, and now my parents and his parents have invited us for Thanksgiving. Unfortunately, we all live hundreds of miles apart. We don't want to hurt their feelings, but to visit with both families means spending most of our holiday on the road. We both work and have only a few days off.*

A: This is a common dilemma when families are separated by distance. First, you and your husband must decide what *you* want to do. What can appear to be pressure is usually just an enthusiastic invitation. You might visit one family this year and the other next year. Another option is for you to host Thanksgiving for one set of parents this year, alternating with hosting the other parents next year. This option often moves to the top of the list once couples start having their own children. Or you might spend your first Thanksgiving on your own and visit with your families at less busy times. Since it's unlikely that either set of parents wants your holiday to be an endurance test, they should be sympathetic to your decision when they know your situation and your feelings. If you decide not to travel, call your parents on Thanksgiving at a time when you can have more than a hurried conversation.

that he or she doesn't want birthday gifts, respect the request and consider alternatives—a card, a personal note, or perhaps a donation to her favorite charity.

If gift giving within the family has gotten out of hand, the adults need to consult one another about options, such as drawing names and setting spending limits; restricting annual gift exchanges to one holiday; or giving gifts to children only. When family members agree to limitations, everyone should stick to the deal.

Staying in Touch

Your mom and dad have moved to a retirement community in the Sun Belt. Your daughter, her husband, and children live in the East. Your son is at college on the West Coast. Siblings are scattered across the continent and around the globe.

Sound familiar? Today's family is likely to be far-flung, and maintaining family ties can seem difficult. Though some family members may see each other nearly every day, others often pass months or years between visits. But we live in an age when technology facilitates frequent contact, through texts, emails, Skype, Facebook, Instagram, FaceTime, and the time-honored cards and letters:

REARRANGING YOUR NEST

For many modern families, the actual dynamic of which family members live in the home changes over time: A couple lives together, marries, and has children. The children become adults and move out, leaving the

couple on their own again. Today, that may not be the end of the story, as adult children or parents of adults move back to the nest.

Empty Nesters. Parents whose children have grown and left home make up a rapidly expanding portion of American households. It was once believed that it was a sad time for parents when their kids left home. But today's empty nesters are more likely to feel a renewed sense of personal freedom.

The adjustment can be hard, however, in the early weeks when parents often feel "homesick" for their children. Rather than constantly bemoaning your circumstances (even close friends will tire of it), focus on positive things you can do with your new independence—all those things you haven't had time for in the last twenty or so years!

Return to the Nesters. Sometimes that empty nest fills up again. Children graduate from college, change jobs, break up with a significant other, or move back to town. They have nowhere to go except the one place that always holds a welcome—home. However, things have changed. The kids are now adults in their own rights; the parents have adjusted to a new, childless lifestyle. While on their own, the kids have established their own "house rules" and ways of doing things. But back home, doesn't Mom still deal with the grocery list and Dad pay the electric bill? There's much to learn about living together again, and it can be a rocky road until new ground rules are negotiated. Some basic etiquette skills and good communication can help. Here are the top issues that should be discussed, preferably prior to the "return to the nest":

- ◆ **Schedules.** Both adult children and parents are used to coming and going as they please. They should let each other know of any schedule changes that will affect the others.

- ◆ **Guests.** They should let each other know when they're planning to have guests over so everyone is aware the shared living spaces may be tied up. Set up a procedure for dealing with schedule conflicts.

- ◆ **Responsibilities.** Have a respectful but candid discussion about household chores and financial contributions. If the back-to-the-nester is short on funds, she may run errands, provide lawn care, cook, clean, or do laundry to help out. If rent is being paid (a good idea if possible), agree on a due date.

- ◆ **Food.** Agree on fridge rules—what's available to be eaten and what's off-limits.

- ◆ **Quiet times.** A note to parents: You may still work 9 to 5 and sleep from 10 to 6, but your daughter's waitressing job may be from 6:00 PM to midnight and her sleep hours 3:00 AM to 11 AM. You'll both require peace and quiet time.

- ◆ **Messages.** Even if they seem trivial to one person, messages may be important to another. Whatever the message, it should be legible and left where it's easily seen.

- **Respect shared spaces.** Bathrooms, living or family rooms, and kitchens are everyone's responsibility. Clean up after yourself and leave spaces as neat as you would expect to find them.

- **Privacy.** Closed doors should be respected. Knock before entering. Mail, journals, and computer files should be treated as private.

- **Respect other's belongings.** Do not "borrow" without asking. If you break something that belongs to someone else, be prepared to replace it.

When Parents Come to Live in Your Nest. In a more mobile society, with young adults moving away to different cities and states, the elderly become more dependent on nursing homes, long-term care or assisted living facilities, and hired help in their own homes. However, some do move in with their children. This can be quite an adjustment for both children and their parents—especially as the elderly experience some of the frailties common with aging.

If your elderly parent has physical disabilities, you may need to make changes to your home. Ramps, stair climbers, railings, and carpeting (as opposed to scatter rugs) may be necessary to prevent falls and help your parent cope with increasing weakness or loss of balance. While you can't force your parent to use a cane or walker, you may find yourself employing gentle nagging (just as they did with you when you were young). You may also need to make adjustments to shopping and meal preparation to meet special dietary needs.

If your elderly parent is experiencing dementia—memory loss or confusion—there are several things you can do to make life easier:

- Establish a routine and stick to it.

- Keep things in the same place. Don't move furniture around.

- Make sure there are night-lights in all the rooms your parent can access.

- When friends arrive, tell your parent their names and who they are. Link them to an event from the past that your parent might remember.

- If your parent can be a little combative, let your friends know in advance so they don't take it personally or get drawn into an uncomfortable discussion.

If you have friends with elderly parents living in their homes, you can help them out by offering to spend an evening so your friend can go out to dinner, or take their parent out for a car ride so your friend can have some time in the home alone. Ask if you can bring a meal over (check about any special diets first), or be clear with your friend that you're available to offer a hand. As with any offer of help, it's more useful to be specific: "Would you like me to take your mother for her hair appointment this week?"

37
pregnancy, birth, and adoption

he time has come. You're planning to extend your family, and the decision to have a child brings with it a set of questions concerning your relationships with family and friends. Who do you tell what when? How much information do you share? How do you respond to personal questions? What, if anything, do you do about showers? And what's the etiquette for announcements? In this chapter we'll begin at the beginning with the decision to grow your family.

WHO TO TELL AND WHEN

The choice about who to tell and when is definitely influenced by your relationships. Most people tell immediate family first. Be intentional about sharing the news. You might not want the grandmother-to-be to hear the news from someone down the street or on your Facebook page, so once you've decided to go public, let those in your close family circle know first.

It's sometimes more difficult to decide when you'll tell people rather than whom. Some couples let people know that they're trying. Many share the news once the pregnancy is confirmed or the adoption papers filed. Others wait until the first trimester is well in hand or until they've been accepted as an adoptive family and it's simply a matter of time. In either case, the wait for the baby's arrival can be long and some couples don't want the primary focus of every conversation to be on the still-impending event. The key etiquette issue here is that it is the parents' prerogative to decide when to tell. It is not up to family and friends to continually ask about the couple's baby-to-come status.

> Q: *I'm happily expecting my first baby. I'm anxious about telling my best friend, who has been trying to get pregnant for years. Should I tell her?*
>
> A: Yes. She's sure to want to share your joy and she'd likely be hurt if she didn't hear it from you. Then take care not to overdo it by talking about your pregnancy and nothing else. Do continue to do things with her as you always have. The most important thing is to preserve your friendship with her.

⟨ PREGNANCY ⟩

The good news is out and physically it's evident that you're going to have a baby. There are definite guidelines to help both the pregnant couple and those around them know what's appropriate and what isn't.

Some Tips for the Pregnant Couple

- While your friends and relatives are happy for you, keep in mind that there are other things going on in the world besides your pregnancy.

- Be discreet about sharing pictures of your beautiful belly or ultrasound pictures of the baby.

- Let people know if you need to avoid certain foods and beverages during your pregnancy.

- If you don't want to answer inappropriate or personal questions such as "How much have you gained?" you can laugh and say, "You really don't want to know," and leave it at that. You are under no obligation to answer personal questions.

Some Tips for Those Around the Pregnant Couple

- Tell the couple how happy you are to hear their good news.

- Offer to help out when you can, especially as it gets closer to the baby's arrival.

- Avoid asking personal questions that may put the mother or the couple on the spot:

  - Have you been trying long?
  - You look quite big. Is the baby due soon?
  - Aren't you worried you're too old to be having a baby?
  - Do you know who the father is?

- Don't push alcoholic beverages, even if you believe one little glass won't hurt.

- Don't regale the couple with stories of horrendous birth experiences.

---

caution!

Don't just assume someone is pregnant and ask, "When are you due?" It's an impossible recovery if the woman says, "I'm not pregnant." Foot in mouth, for sure.

Q: *I'm so excited to be pregnant with my first baby and I'm eight months along. However, I'm not sure how to handle it when people come up to me and touch my belly, especially complete strangers. What can I say or do?*

A: Some women enjoy sharing the joy of their pregnancy with close friends and family and see the belly rub as part of that sharing; others, like yourself, do not—no matter who it is. After all, who would touch the belly of a nonpregnant stranger? If someone asks (and some do), you can definitely say, "Thanks for asking, but I'd really rather you didn't." If they just reach out to touch you can say, "I know it's tempting but please don't touch," while you do either of the following:

- Clasp your hands firmly over your stomach or gently stop their touch.

- Simply take a step or two back, out of their reach.

For those who are tempted to touch, *always* ask first and be respectful of the mom-to-be's wishes.

ADOPTION

Many families grow through the process of adoption. Decisions about who and when to tell carry the same weight as the ones surrounding the birth of a baby. The anticipation is great and the joy even greater when the child is welcomed to the family. There is no difference in the etiquette surrounding the arrival of a new child through adoption. Keep in mind that children who are adopted have exactly the same status as biological children and should always be treated as such. The following points will help guide other family members, friends, and acquaintances:

Realize that adoptive parents are parents, not saints. Adoptive parents want children for the same reasons as biological parents. When others imply that adoptive parents are unusually selfless or have somehow "saved a child," it can place an especially heavy burden on the parents: They're not "saints"; they're parents.

Understand that adoption is a process that is usually lengthy and can be disappointing. Respect the feelings of adopting parents as they go through the process. Unless you've had a similar experience, don't be too quick to give advice or to criticize the system. If the adoption isn't completed, the hopeful parents will need time to grieve. Comments such as "You can always try again" trivialize their loss.

Wait for the adoptive parents or child to discuss their individual adoption story. Just as it would be thoughtless to ask about a biological child's conception and birth, it's rude to ask for the details of individual adoptions (for example, whether the adopting parents were present at the birth of the child). The choice to share personal information is theirs alone.

Don't inquire about a child's biological parents. This is a private matter and shouldn't be broached by others. If the subject is raised by the adoptive parents or child, avoid using the term "real parents," which implies that the adoptive parents are not true parents. "Birth parents," "biological parents," and "genetic parents" are all correct; in conversation, you can usually pick up the term preferred by the family.

Most adoptive parents are happy to provide information about the adoption *process* to people who are genuinely interested. If you're considering adopting or want information for a family member or friend, it's fine to ask procedural questions like how to begin, what's involved in a home visit, what kind of lawyer to hire, and so forth.

⟩ SHOWERS ⟨

It's hard not to make a fuss over a new baby, even before the little bundle of joy arrives. That's why we "shower" parents-to-be with presents. Not only will these gifts make their lives easier and provide for the new member of the family, but they also help family and friends feel connected to the big event. (For information on hosting a shower, see "Baby Showers," page 320.)

Q: *We adopted our only child three years ago, when he was one, and he's the joy of our life. He is of a different race, and I'm getting really sick of people who make obnoxious comments. The other day, I ran into a friend whom I hadn't seen in years, and when she saw Tommy, she asked me, "Whose little boy is this?" I said that he is my son, and then she asked if I have any children of my own! I try not to get upset, but my child now understands what people are saying, and I worry about his feelings.*

A: Your friend obviously spoke without thinking, and there's little you can do except hold your temper and make a polite reply, "No, we don't have other children. Tommy's our only child and our greatest joy." Your son's feelings are your most important concern. You can't shield him from tactless people, but you and your husband will be his models for handling other people's ignorance and lack of common sense.

Introduce him as soon as you meet people who are unfamiliar with your family. "I'd like you to meet our son, Tommy" will satisfy most people's curiosity. If someone persists with inappropriate remarks, you may have to be firm: Matters such as your child's background are personal and not open to discussion.

ANNOUNCEMENTS

Want to spread the word about your new baby? Announcements are a great way to let others know about her arrival and to share your joy. Family and friends, near and far, should be on your list, but skip business associates and casual acquaintances. Announcements carry no obligation for gifts, so don't hesitate to send them for first babies and every new addition to the family. If someone does send a gift, be sure to send a note of thanks.

Announcements include the parents' and baby's names, the baby's birth date, some indication of the baby's sex if the name isn't obviously male or female, and the baby's birth weight and length, if you wish. You might include a photo. If you have a website devoted to the baby, you can add the Internet address to the announcement.

Birth and adoption announcements can be worded in formal, third-person style, or more informal and personal language. Commercial fill-ins, printed cards, or cards you design yourself are all popular options. Announcements can also be made by personal notes written by Dad as well as Mom.

E-announcements from online card, invitation, and social network sites are another way to spread your happy news. It's easy to personalize your announcement and even add a photo. Keep in mind that some relatives and friends may not use a social network site or have access to the Internet. It would be important to send them a more traditional announcement through the mail.

Adoption announcements are usually sent soon after the legal proceedings are completed. As with birth announcements, parents can have cards printed, design their own, send handwritten notes to relatives and friends, or send e-announcements. Commercial card manufacturers also make cards and fill-in announcements specifically for adoptions.

Adoption announcements are appropriate for older children as well as infants, and when a stepparent adopts a spouse's biological child. Choose a style that suits the child's age; a card decorated with a stork is a better choice for a newborn than for a three-year-old. Include the parents' and child's name, the date of the adoption or when the child came to live with the family, and the child's age or birth date. When the child is adopted abroad, it's fine to add the child's country of birth.

thoughtful postings

Sharing the news and pictures of your new arrival on your social networking page is a great idea, but hold off until you've told your children, the grandparents, and other close relatives and friends who would want to receive the news personally. Be sensitive, too, about the pictures you post: Proud mom and dad holding their newborn is fine; save those of the birth itself for sharing privately with closest friends and family who have expressed a specific interest in seeing them.

children
and teens

TEACHING MANNERS AT EVERY STAGE

"When can I teach my child manners?" There's no single answer to this question other than to say that the teaching is ongoing from the time your child is born. But we can say that while teaching manners to children and teenagers may not seem easy, it can be done more easily than many parents realize. And the lifetime benefits are nearly limitless. Just as children go through physical developmental stages, they also experience distinct stages of social development. Throughout each stage children learn increasingly complex skills, which build, one on the other, until they are able to manage a variety of social interactions.

The manners children learn throughout each social stage can be sorted into three areas:

Communication: "Magic words," greetings, introductions, word choice, thank-you notes, speech, and written and electronic communications.

Table manners: Mechanics of eating, table settings, and social aspects of mealtimes.

Out and about: School, travel, shopping, movies and theaters, car rides, sports events, image, and special events like parties, weddings, and funerals.

know what to expect . . . and then expect it!

The lessons begin when your baby arrives and continue throughout childhood. In order to effectively teach manners, parents should know what to expect from children in given age ranges. Then they need to think about each child's individual personality. The following basic progression can serve as a guide to teaching children etiquette year by year.

These are some of the basic manners you can expect from children and teens at different social development stages. Consider your child's manual dexterity, personality, maturity, and experience as you decide which manners to focus on at any given age. It's never too late! If your child is older and you haven't taught these manners, start now. Select the manners you think are most important and work on them, one or two at a time. If you demonstrate and teach consistently every day, your child will develop the habits that will serve him well today and in the future.

BIRTH TO ONE YEAR

During their first year babies will absorb the climate you create, so it's very important to treat those around you respectfully and considerately, using good manners all the time.

Communication

Magic words. Use them every day with everyone. When you use the word *please*, you change a demand into a request. The whole tone changes. Babies hear that tone and react accordingly. If you develop the habit of using "magic words," your child will be more likely to develop the same habit later on.

Greetings. A smile every time you greet your baby helps her learn that smiling is an essential part of every greeting. It also contributes to the climate of respect that you're building. Your ten-month-old can learn to

wave "hi" or "bye" long before she speaks; they're some of her first interactive communications.

Speech. Even in their first year babies hear the tone, pitch, and volume of every voice. By the way you speak, you're teaching them how voice communicates meaning—even before they can understand the actual words you use.

Table Manners

Bibs are first napkins. By wiping babies' hands before they eat, parents teach that every meal begins with a hand wash. When a ten-month-old baby holds his plastic spoon, he's learning that spoons are utensils for eating. Turn off the television, shut down the computer, ignore the phone, and spend ten or twenty minutes with your baby when you're feeding him. Talk to him. It will be his first lesson that mealtime is also a social event.

Out and About

You'll take your baby to many public places during her first year—the doctor's office or clinic for checkups, stores, parks, and restaurants. Right now, it's up to you to see that each out-and-about occasion is easy for your child, comfortable for you, and not an imposition on others.

breast-feeding on the go

It's best for both your baby and you when feedings are calm and free of anxiety. If people around a breast-feeding mother and child are uncomfortable, the mother is likely to be tense and the feeding may not go well. The ideal is to find a balance.

Some people still regard breast-feeding as a private activity. If your baby becomes hungry or your schedule dictates that you must breast-feed in a public place, try to find a quiet spot for a relaxed feeding. A baby blanket or shawl carefully draped over your shoulders is an easy way to cover up while the baby is nursing and allows you to nurse anywhere.

Plan ahead. Pack your baby bag with the things *you'll* need while you're away from home. It's also a good idea to plan for quick escapes. If you're going to an unfamiliar place, it pays to explore a bit as soon as you arrive—locate the changing rooms, rest areas, and exits. And if your baby is really fussy, then it's time to go home, regardless of whether or not you've completed what you set out to do.

Visiting friends. It's your responsibility to bring your own baby supplies. Keep the visit short, and be ready to leave if your baby (or your friend's baby if it's a baby date) gets cranky.

] ONE TO THREE YEARS [

Toddlers develop physically at a rapid rate, learning to walk and run with confidence. And they begin to inter-act "socially" with other toddlers, even if it's simply parallel play. They develop their first verbal skills, many of which are associated with manners. First sentences, interest in books, and first scribbles on paper make up communication skills. At this age children eat at the table with the family.

Communication

Magic words. Among the first words you teach your toddler are the classic magic words *Please* and *Thank you.* Children will tell you years later that saying "please" is the first manner they learned.

Greetings. Toddlers may hide behind your knee, but even the shyest can learn to say a clear "hello" with a smile. This skill takes practice, so help them along.

Conversation. Read books, go to different places, watch television together, and listen to music. Then talk about what you've just done together. Even if they have a small vocabulary, toddlers can respond to things you hold in common especially as they approach three years old.

Table Manners

The children in this age group can manage a meal last-ing twenty or so minutes.

- While they're at the table with you, be sure to include them in the conversation.

- Give them soft foods they can manage with a spoon.

- Bibs are still their napkins.

- Food is for eating. Throwing or playing with food is a definite cue that they've reached their limit and you need to end their meal. Be firm, and help them leave the table. They can still play in the same room.

Out and About

- During visits to the doctor or dentist for their checkups, children learn to wait. Read them a book or play a quiet game to show them strategies for waiting.

- Demonstrate courteous behavior with service people everywhere. Children learn by watching you.

- Be firm about car seats.

- Keep a small bag of activities that your toddler can do while riding in a car.

- Yelling, screaming, crying, kicking—pull over and park. Begin driving only when your child has calmed down.

⌠ THREE TO FIVE YEARS ⌡

Kids in this age group are developing manual dexterity and confidence as they take on increasingly complex skills. They interact with peers and adults in structured play groups or daycare.

Communication

Magic words. Children this age can be expected to *say* "thank you." They'll need reminding often, but don't give up. By the time they're four or five, they can also add "excuse me" and "you're welcome" to their list of magic words. This is also the time children begin to "write" their own thank-you notes: A child tells his parent what he likes about the gift, the parent writes the short thank-you note, and the child adds a drawing or "signs" his name.

Conversation. At this age children are learning the fundamental skills of good conversation. You can help by reminding them to

- Speak slowly and clearly.

- Not interrupt unless it's an emergency.

- Take turns talking.

Phones. While some three- to five-year-olds have a difficult time on the phone, it's time for them to try at least a simple hello. At first it's helpful if the person on the other end is someone they see and speak to often—Dad or Grandma, for example. When they are only three or four, kids may simply look at the phone and refuse to say anything. Encourage them to say hello but if they don't, gently take back the phone and try again another time. Webcams, Skype, and FaceTime may make phone visits easier and more user-friendly.

Table Manners

This is a building time—a perfect time to teach manners at the table. Children this age can

- Add forks to their repertoire of eating utensils.

- Put napkins on their laps (definitely by the time they are five).

- Chew with their mouths closed.

- Participate in table conversation, so be sure to include them.

- Ask to be excused when finished eating, especially if others plan to stay longer at the table.

- Help with simple table setting and clearing.

Out and About

At this age children are with you throughout the day as you do your errands and daily activities.

- Encourage them to help load the grocery cart and unload small bags at home.

- Lunch at a fast-food restaurant provides the opportunity to work on basic line manners, early restaurant manners, and clearing the table.

- This is a time to reinforce basic manners with service people in a variety of venues—shops, restaurants, banks, or post office—and with people who provide service to you at home.

When out and about, you can help your child learn from what he observes. Point out and talk about examples of good manners and bad behavior. "That lady was so nice to the checkout person when she said 'Thank you'" or (out of earshot) "Did you notice how that man let the door slam on the woman behind him?"

SIX TO TEN YEARS

Time to emphasize school manners: Six- to ten-year-olds are at school, away from their parents for an extended time, and require some reinforcement to help them remember good manners. They have a well-developed sense of empathy, understand that kind acts are important, can tell the difference between tactful comments and brutal honesty, and can comprehend the importance of consideration and respect in their relationships.

Communication

Six- to ten-year-old children can handle increasingly complex ideas as their vocabulary grows and they're better able to express themselves.

Magic words. They may require fairly constant reminders to use the magic words but this is a reasonable expectation! At this stage most children can and should write their own thank-you notes: when they receive gifts, and after an overnight or extended visit to family or friends.

Greetings. By age six, children can perform a correct greeting: standing up, saying "hello," shaking

lunchroom manners

When your kids start having meals at school, remind them of these special manners for the school cafeteria:

- Make room for others at your table, even if they aren't your best friends.
- Hold your food tray with both hands.
- Do not take or touch food on someone else's tray without permission.
- Don't offer to trade food. This can be awkward if you ask someone who doesn't want to trade or who has allergies.
- Don't make comments about another student's food.
- Follow the directions of the adult in charge, even if he isn't your teacher.
- Follow basic "line" manners.
- Be respectful of the servers in the cafeteria line and say "Thanks."
- Clear your place at the table and take your tray to the drop-off station when you leave.

Table Manners

You continue to build on the table manners already established. By now:

- They can manage all the basic table manners.
- They have the manual dexterity to hold utensils properly, so you can now add the knife.
- Setting the table is a reasonable expectation.
- They absolutely can chew with their mouths closed and not talk with their mouths full!

At school. When kids are eating in a school cafeteria, some of the standard table manners don't apply. For example, often there's a limited time to eat so kids should begin as soon as they sit down and shouldn't wait until everyone else is seated.

Out and About

You can expect six- to ten-year-olds to manage their behavior when they're out in public. However, they may still need your instruction about the manners that demonstrate respect and consideration for those they meet. Here are some everyday manners to practice:

- A six- to ten-year-old can stand next to you on the bus in order to make room for an elderly person, or a pregnant woman, or a person with a disability.
- Car safety trumps everything else. Insist on seat belts and booster seats (if required), quiet voices

hands, looking a person in the eyes, and smiling. It may take practice, but every child can and should learn this important skill. By eight or nine, they can make simple introductions and introduce themselves.

Phones. Sixes can answer phones, make calls, and, as they get a little older, take messages. As they approach ten years old, some children have cell phones. If they do, review cell phone manners and be firm about expectations for following all standards you have estab-

and activities, and no fighting, whining, or arguing. Adults can and should expect safe and mannerly behavior in the car.

- ◆ Teach children in this age group the fundamentals of being a good host and a good guest, basic party manners, and audience manners.

- ◆ Six to tens are involved in competitions of all sorts. It's a perfect age to learn the basics of good sportsmanship:

  - Follow the rules of the game.

  - Congratulate the winner.

  - Thank the loser for a good game.

  - Thank and compliment team members.

  - Listen to and show respect for the coach, referees, and umpires.

ELEVEN TO FOURTEEN YEARS

Pre- and young teens are going through physical, emotional, social, and cognitive changes at a rapid rate. They often feel completely out of control, so anything you can do that gives them a sense of control is helpful. Manners can do just that. They can understand that manners are a reflection of their attitudes toward others. They also value things like privacy, honesty, respect, tradition, and relationships. If you can show them how manners can help them build and strengthen relationships in all phases of their lives, help them know what's expected of them and what they can expect of others, and make them more likable, you will help them to develop self-confidence in everything they do.

addressing adults

Even in these casual times, children should learn to call adults by their title and last name: Mrs. Swenson, Dr. Singh, Rabbi Levine. Many adults believe it's the respectful thing for children to do and, in fact, *expect* children to use titles. It's up to the adult to say if he wishes to be called by his first name. When an adult makes this request, let your child know if this exception is okay, and that she can go ahead and call Mr. Grant "Fred." A few other points to be made regarding this potentially delicate issue:

- ◆ If a parent prefers that their child address adults more formally by using titles and last names, and an adult asks to be called by her first name, the child can simply say, "My parents really want me to call grown-ups Mr. or Mrs." The adult should respect the parent's wish so the child doesn't get caught in the middle.

- ◆ There are variations, some regional, to how children address adults respectfully:

  - By title and first name (Miss Cindy, Mr. Joe).

  - As "Sir" or "Ma'am."

- ◆ Children call some close family friends by terms often used for relatives. A parent's closest friend may be "Aunt Rosa," even though she's not a family member.

teaching kids communication skills in a tech world

General communication etiquette continues to be essential to helping kids build and strengthen their relationships. How do you transfer your understanding of communication etiquette to your kids so they can and will use it in the world of electronic communication?

- Explore the communication world your kids inhabit. Become familiar with the various technologies that your kids know so well.

- Teach them the specifics. As these new forms of communication have evolved, new manners have also evolved. Help your kids link these manners to the fundamental principles that form the foundation for all our relationships: consideration, respect, and honesty.

Communication

This is the time to stress the importance of body language. Kids are well aware of the impact of shrugs, rolling eyes, sneers, slouching body posture, and lack of eye contact. Cognitively, they can handle an abstract thought in one moment and only a concrete one the next. While their ability to think abstractly is developing, they can be surprisingly literal at the same time. It requires patience and care as you engage them in conversation.

Because young teens often lack the verbal and social skills to express their feelings and thoughts gracefully, back talk and sassing are common at this age. While you don't want to tolerate back talk, you should look for opportunities to teach the art of disagreeing without being disagreeable. When you negotiate privileges or sibling disputes, for example, model consideration by giving children time to make their points and listening carefully to their thinking. Present your own ideas in a respectful manner, keeping the discussion focused on the primary issue and ending the conversation pleasantly. If your child becomes angry or frustrated, you can always stop the discussion and return to it later, without recriminations for the child's earlier behavior.

Tech Manners Basics for Kids

The following manners related to new communication tools can be shared with kids of all ages:

- **Phones**
  - The people you're with in person come first. If you must make or take calls when you're with others, excuse yourself, keep it short, and return as soon as you can.
  - Keep your volume low. Talking loudly forces everyone around you to listen in, whether they want to or not.
  - There are some times when you turn off *the ringer*. If you're expecting a call and are in a

public place—store, waiting area, library—or on public transportation, put your phone on vibrate.

- There are other times when you turn your phone *off*: church, concerts, theaters, and anywhere else your phone call or text might disturb those around you. Also, in places where you are required to have your phone off—as in school.

◆ Email and texting

- Read everything over once before clicking "send." There's no way to get it back and you might offend someone without meaning to.

- Write only what you're willing to have all the world see. Once it's sent, it's out of your control.

- Respect others' privacy. Don't forward messages sent to you in confidence.

---

cyberbullying and sexting

Bullying is an unfortunate fact of middle school life and it's not limited to the playground. Cyberbullying is using a social network site, Twitter, email, texts, or voice mail to intimidate or malign another. Sexting is posting or texting sexually explicit material about or to someone. Both forms of harassment can have dire consequences for the victim. It's never okay or cool to contribute to, visit pages, or forward messages that make fun of a classmate or acquaintance. Be sure your kids know that if they experience or are aware of cyberbullying or sexting, they should let a responsible adult know immediately.

- If you're angry about something, wait until you've calmed down before writing about it. You're less likely to say something you regret later.

◆ Social networking

- Be careful what you post. On some sites, your Web page and your friends' pages can be viewed by *anyone,* including the family you babysit for, your teachers, and your own family.

- If you want to post photos of others, ask their permission first.

- Don't accept friend requests from people you don't know.

- It's all right to ask others to remove a photo or comment about you from their page. And if for any reason you don't like a comment or image left on your page by someone else, it's okay to delete it.

- It's never okay or cool to contribute to or visit pages that make fun of a classmate or acquaintance.

◆ Music players

- It's all about earbuds—take *both* of them out when you're in a conversation or dealing with a service person—clerk at a store, librarian, or office staff at school.

- Be aware when using earbuds when you're biking, skiing, or running. Someone might need to get your attention.

- Keep the volume down in public places (even with earbuds the person sitting next to you might be bothered by your music).

◆ Portable games. The two most important manners for these devices are

- Do NOT play games while you're in a conversation with others.
- Earbud manners for music players apply to portable game devices, too.

Table Manners

Having learned most of the basic table manners, it's time to tackle tricky mealtime situations. Talk with your kids about what to do when they spill something, have to cough or sneeze, find something in the soup or their mouths that shouldn't be there, need to leave the table, burp, or their food is hotter or spicier than expected. (Since these manners are the same as for adults, see Chapter 6, "Table Manners," page 56.)

Out and About

Good manners aren't just for family and friends. All of the manners that kids have acquired by this point can and should be applied in every setting beyond home and school. Eleven- to fourteen-year-olds *are* out and about in malls, at fast-food restaurants, the movies, miniature golf, and more. Suggest they think about "mall manners" and then talk about how they can be respectful, considerate, and responsible. Remind them to

- Make room for the other people who are walking in the mall, keeping it to two or three abreast at most.
- Watch their language. Swearing is offensive, and a poor example for younger children.
- Watch their volume. "Just keep it down!"
- Use only the tables and chairs they need in the food court. Avoid spreading packages and backpacks over extra chairs and tables. Kids need reminding to clear their trash, put tables and chairs back where they found them, and wipe off the table if something has spilled.
- Use all their basic manners: Say "Good morning," "Please," and "Thank you" to store clerks; open the door for others; say "Excuse me"; put things back on the shelves and racks as they found them; introduce friends and family if they don't already know each other; and, most important, smile.

FIFTEEN TO EIGHTEEN YEARS

As they emerge from childhood, older teens will be choosing the image they want to project and the person they want to be. Reminders and encouragement to use good manners continue to be an important part of helping them mature. Since you won't be there most of the time, the task now is to help them make the best choices they can and to make the manners they've learned an integral part of the adult they are growing to be. In addition, there are new skills to learn that will be relevant as they transition to adulthood.

making the difference

You've made the proverbial short list. Timely thank-you notes are definitely a smart move and might be just the thing to make you stand out from the others who also made it. If you have the interviewer's email address, send a brief, well-written email note, followed by a handwritten one. Two important tips to make these work for you:

1. Send your email right away and your follow-up note within a day or two so the interviewer receives them while you are fresh in her mind.

2. Keep your notes short. Three or four sentences is enough. This is a thank-you, not a note to restate your talents.

Dear Mrs. Jackson,

Thank you very much for taking the time to meet with me yesterday. It sounds like you have a great team working at The Fitness Space, and I would love to be on it. Please let me know if you need any other information from me.

I'm looking forward to hearing from you.

Thank you again.

Sincerely,

Ramon Zeno

Communication

All the manners already mentioned for electronic communication continue to be important. Magic words are still magic and it's helpful to continue to encourage their use. Choice of words has a great impact on image. While it's clear that some words may not be offensive to your teen or her friends, they may be to other important people in her life. The point for teens to consider is the effect their words may have on grandparents, advisors, bosses, or younger children.

Interviews. Teens are apt to be interviewing for jobs and colleges. Going over basic manners for an interview may help them rise to the top when competition is great:

- Be early!
- Be ready! Have all the pertinent information about yourself available.
- Be prepared! Do some research about the college, the job, or company. Think in advance about the important questions you want to ask.
- Dress appropriately! If the job is in a local clothing store, you might choose one outfit; if it's with a pool cleaning company, you might choose another.
- Speak clearly!
- Shake hands twice: when you arrive and when you leave.
- Say "Thank you" twice: once verbally when you leave and once again in a short handwritten note.

Table Manners

During their high school years, many teens go out to a fancy restaurant on their own for the first time, say, before a prom or other school dance. Beyond the basic table manners they've learned at the thousands of meals they've had, there are a few other "table manners" you can help them with. When they're going to a restaurant with a date or a group of friends, suggest they

◆ Make a reservation.

◆ Plan who will be paying the bill and how they will pay it before they go out.

◆ Arrive five minutes before the reservation time.

◆ Thank the maître d' or whoever takes them to the table.

◆ If they're planning on separate checks, discuss this with the waiter before he takes the order.

◆ Those paying together should order together.

◆ Be considerate of other diners by speaking at a normal volume.

◆ If there's a problem with the meal (it's cold or it's not what was ordered), gesture to the waiter to come over and then quietly tell him what the problem is.

◆ When paying the bill, tip the waiter 15 to 20 percent. Practice calculating a tip at home. (For how to calculate a tip, see "Restaurants," page 166.)

◆ If there's a coatroom attendant, tip him or her $2 for the first coat and $1 for each additional coat when they pick up their coats.

Out and About

Sometime between fifteen and eighteen, most kids start driving. A major focus, of course, is learning the rules of the road, prepping for the tests, and managing the car. However, the manners associated with driving and being a passenger are important also. (See "In Your Car," page 91, and "Road Trips," page 121.) Review all these manners with your teens and stress their importance in making the drive safer and more pleasant.

This is a time when teens are challenging and exploring beyond their family's norms. They may be trying out these behaviors and personae when they are out in public or hanging out with friends. Let them know they are still expected to use all the in-public manners they have learned. Using conversations about consideration, respect, and honesty is a great tool to emphasize ways to treat the people they come in contact with on a daily basis—shop clerks, bus drivers and passengers, school personnel—with courtesy.

39
living
with others

t some point during your life, you may be sharing living spaces with others: a cabin at summer camp, a dorm room in college, barracks in the military, an apartment or a house. Regardless of how you got into sharing your living space, it takes some effort on everyone's part to make it a good experience.

A roommate or housemate can be both your best friend and your worst enemy. In one week you can go from "Bill is the best! He cleaned the whole place" to "I can't believe he can't get a rent check in on time!" Living together is a mixed bag. On the one hand, you have others contributing to bills, supplies, rent, chores, and companionship. On the other, you're managing all those things with another person. Many friendships are both born and ended via the roommate relationship.

[KNOWING LIFESTYLES: YOURS AND YOUR ROOMMATES']

You *must* be honest about your lifestyle and habits when considering living with others. It would be very unfair if you cosigned a lease only to find out later that your roommate isn't okay with your frequent guests or 6:00 AM workout routine. Even little things like your cleaning habits and bill-paying system could be deal breakers. This is why it's so important to know yourself and what you want out of a living situation. Only then can you be honest with someone you're considering as a roommate.

When Choosing Your Roommates Isn't an Option

When you don't get to choose who you live with (summer camp, a college dorm, military housing), you can feel trapped. These are the times when the most common courtesies can be especially helpful. Large or

a good roommate

Before you begin any shared living arrangement, a self-evaluation is a must. A good roommate . . .

- Is honest about his own lifestyle and living habits.
- Understands and is honest about his expectations for others and himself.
- Is willing to handle problems in an effective and reasonable manner.
- Allows consideration, respect, and honesty to be his guide as opposed to emotion, assumption, and an iron fist.

unsafe problems should be handled via a counselor, an RA (residential assistant), or housing coordinator in a college setting. However, for smaller issues, it's important to establish a good dialogue with your roommates.

THE THREE Cs

Living with others means coping with their personalities, their possessions, their guests, their work schedule, and their LIFE! And *that* means mastering the three Cs of living with others: **communication, compromise,** and **commitment**.

Consideration, respect, and honesty are the three fundamental principles of building successful relationships (and good etiquette). Adding the three Cs lets you put these principles into action. They're self-explanatory and may even seem simplistic; but when you're in the thick of it with a problem at home, it's clear that com-

munication, compromise, and commitment can really help illuminate the situation for what it is. They help you avoid blame, get to the root of the problem, and come up with an effective solution. Be sure to talk about the problems, come up with possible solutions, agree on one, and commit to trying it out.

Communication: Your Way to Peace

When the room, apartment, or house gets out of hand, how are you going to handle it without offending each other? Together, decide that you'll always bring up an issue or problem when it occurs or plan a regular meeting to talk over any household issues. What would work best for both of you?

Meetings and talks should be times for looking at yourselves not as individuals, but as roommates who have a *responsibility to be good roommates to each other*. This is of course very difficult when you feel you've upheld your end and your roommate hasn't.

Effective communication can heal most wounds, and timing is everything. For example, if you come home every day and your roommate hasn't lifted a finger to clean, you could

a) Ignore your roommate's lapse and suffer silently, regretting ever having agreed to live together.

b) Get angry but not tell her why. You figure that sufficient silent treatment or terse remarks will do.

c) Clean everything yourself and lay a hefty guilt trip on your roommate by pointing out all that you do.

d) Talk reasonably about the problem.

Obviously, d) is the way to go.

roommate checklist

Use this checklist for yourself first and then use it when interviewing friends and others you might like to live with:

FINANCIAL

☐ What kind of a budget is she on?

☐ Can he be relied on to share the monthly bills for basic expenditures like rent, electric, water, phone, and heating/AC?

☐ Is she interested in contributing for extras such as cable or Internet fees?

LIFE SCHEDULE

☐ Is he a student?

☐ Does she work during the day or at night?

☐ Is she away for most of the day or at home all the time?

☐ Is he social or antisocial?

☐ Does he have houseguests often? (This can be a big issue for some people, especially if it's family members who visit often.)

PERSONAL LIFE CHOICES

☐ Drinking/smoking/drugs

☐ Sex life: abstinent/partner/one-night stands

☐ Vegan/vegetarian/local/kosher

☐ Religious beliefs

☐ Living green

HOUSEHOLD RESPONSIBILITIES

☐ How does he deal with dishes—right away or let them sit?

☐ Is she willing to pitch in with cleaning: vacuuming, mopping, tidying, trash, and recycling?

☐ Will she share in buying household supplies?

SLEEPING HABITS

☐ Is she sensitive to sound when she is sleeping? (This can be a serious issue, especially in a place with thin walls.)

☐ Is he asleep during the day and awake at night?

SIGNIFICANT OTHERS AND MORE . . .

☐ Does he have a significant other?

☐ Does the significant other have her own place?

☐ How often is she likely to be staying overnight at your place?

☐ Are one-night stands okay? Safe?

PERSONAL PREFERENCES

☐ TV: Does he watch a lot, a little, or none? Does he mind if you watch a lot, a little, or none? HD? DVR? Cable or streaming?

☐ Music: Type of music? How loud? When does she like to listen to it?

☐ Does he prefer to go out or stay in? A roommate who stays in more may have his friends over a lot.

☐ Pets: all, some, or none? What does your lease say? Would you expect your roommate to watch your pet if you go on vacation?

How you *choose* to communicate is just as important as communicating in the first place. Blame, anger, sarcasm, and avoidance won't help you. Instead, try taking these steps:

- **Establish that you're both on the same team.** "We both want to feel comfortable in the house and living together."

- **Identify the problem.** "The state of the house (dust, dishes, clothes, and stuff everywhere) isn't helping us feel good about where we live."

- **Identify the breakdown.** "Why aren't we able to make this happen?" Look at yourself, not just at your roommate: "My work schedule has changed . . ." or "got a girlfriend and spend less time here . . ."

- **Start making a plan to move forward.** "Okay, let's see how we can make this work for both of us . . ."

Setting a straightforward, no-blame atmosphere for these meetings will go a long way toward having an effective communication process for your household. When communicating, it's important to

- Ensure everyone has a chance to be heard.

- Keep the focus on the problem and how to solve it, not on who is causing it.

- Watch your message: Body language, tone, and choice of words can alter the way an entire conversation is perceived.

Compromise: Your Own Roommate Peace Treaty

It's in everybody's best interest. Sometimes the chore splitting just evolves: You always take out the trash and your roommate always deals with the recycling. Most of the time, however, you'll need to talk about what needs to be done and come to a compromise.

Compromises need to be reasonable, realistic, openly discussed, and agreed upon. It makes no sense to come up with a compromise that only one person can uphold. The key is to find common ground, and then arrive at an accommodation everyone can live with.

Compromise by nature is give and take. Think about where you are *able* to budge (maybe not willing, but able). If you take a moment to step back, often you can see places where you can give a little, be a little more flexible, and contribute to the solution rather than the problem.

Commitment: Where You Make It or Break It

Now that you and your roommate have discussed the issues, come to a compromise, and agreed to make it work, all that's left is to stick to the bargain. It's not always simple. The plan will only work if you commit to *making* it work. It might take a week or two for your new responsibilities or routines to become second nature, but once they do, your home life will run like clockwork. Just be sure to check in with each other from time to time to ensure that the commitment is still being met and the solution is still working for everyone.

when your housemates are your family

Whether they're your parents or your young adult children who've come back to your nest, it's even more important to agree to boundaries and expectations *before* you start living together. Just as with any housemates, use communication, compromise, and commitment, plus a hefty dose of consideration, to establish a healthy and harmonious household. (For more on living with relatives, see "Rearranging Your Nest, page 470.)

And if it's not working? Plan A didn't work, so you'll need to formulate a Plan B. You may have to try out several solutions but the more you try the closer you'll get to a system that works for you and your roommate.

Remember, the issue isn't whether or not the living room should be vacuumed every week or whether the dishes should be done right away. What's important is that you and your roommate are comfortable with the levels of effort being exerted in taking care of the space and items you share together.

SETTING BOUNDARIES

It's important to stand up for your personal boundaries and establish them early on. Some issues might arise after living together for a few months and others might be on your roommate checklist right from the start.

The important thing is to be assertive without being demanding. Requesting will get you much further, and allows for constructive conversations to occur: "Jim, I've noticed lately that guests have been coming by the house after 11:00 PM. With my morning schedule as it is, I'm not comfortable having people over this late. Do you think that on weeknights we could close our doors to guests after 11?" The following are common boundary issues:

- ◆ Borrowing
- ◆ Private spaces
- ◆ Noise
- ◆ Cleanliness
- ◆ Entertaining
- ◆ Houseguests
- ◆ Language
- ◆ Food

WHEN PROBLEMS OCCUR

Your roommate left dirty clothes all over the apartment or forgot to pay the electric bill—*again*. Naturally, you're upset—but before you lose it, consider these tips:

- **Give problems some time to settle.** When something really bothers us, it's often because a lot of other things are bothering us as well. Before you sit down with your roommate for a big discussion, let the issue settle for a day or two. By then, you'll be better prepared to talk it over calmly and constructively. The less emotion your roommate has to react to, the more he or she can focus on the problem.

- **Don't let things fester.** While it's a good idea to wait a day or two, waiting any longer can also cause resentment to build so that by the time you do discuss the problem you're ready to explode.

- **Approach the problem with an open mind.** If you go into a house meeting or roommate discussion with the idea that everything will go your way, you may be disappointed. Just as you have your reasons for feeling upset, your roommate might have legitimate reasons for handling things the way she did.

- **Think about options.** Before you talk things over with your roommate, come up with two or three possible solutions and be ready to present them. Of course you'll still want to wait and hear what she has to say—but having some ideas ready will show her that you're thinking actively about how to make things better for everyone and that you are open to more than one solution.

- **Pick a good time to talk.** Choose a time when everyone is relaxed and comfortable. If your roommate has just gotten home from a long day at work or a tough class, it's probably *not* a good time to discuss household issues. Schedule a time when you can sit down and talk together about the problem. That way, it won't seem like you're springing it on him out of the blue.

---

those little notes

It's pretty annoying to arrive home to an apartment plastered with sticky notes: "Use your own conditioner" "Who ate my leftovers?" "It's your turn to _____." When your roomie takes the passive-aggressive route, it's time to be direct and ask to have a chat. "Deb, I shouldn't have used your conditioner without asking, and I'm sorry for that. However, next time something bothers you, please come talk to me directly."

MEETING NIGHT

Many households have a regular meeting to check in with each other, talk about how things are going, or bring up problems. Here are some ways to organize a successful house meeting:

- Pick a time when everyone can make the meeting.

- Show up: Don't make other plans once the meeting time is set.

- Have a clear agenda. Housemates keep a running list of topics on a whiteboard or in a notebook, or check in on the same topics at each meeting.

- Make sure everyone has a chance to speak.

- Restate all decisions and compromises clearly to make sure that everyone is on the same page.

The goal is for each housemate to leave the meeting with an understanding of how problems will be handled and what he or she is responsible for around the house.

MOVING FORWARD

It's important to remember how to move on from trouble spots in your roommate relationships. Once issues have been discussed and worked out, it's time to let go. Try to have a positive, welcoming attitude toward your roommates after working something out.

Sometimes you were the problem and your roommates let you know what was bothering them. Let's face it: That feels lousy, but you've also worked through the issues and have a plan to help it not happen again. It is time to show them you're responsible and want to make the household a good place for everyone.

If it has gotten really ugly, apologies are necessary all around. Regardless of whether you have been the offender or not, it's always great to say, "Hey, I'm really sorry this happened and I'm glad we've found a way to move forward."

THE THREE WAR ZONES

Every home has hidden landmines just waiting to explode. In particular, there are three war zones you'll need to watch out for:

+ The kitchen
+ The bathroom
+ The living room

These make up the common spaces in your home. And in any common space, things can get messy—either you're making the mess and leaving it for your roommates, or you find yourself cleaning up your mess and theirs. The trick is to keep molehills from turning into mountains, so put the three Cs into action.

The Kitchen

Messy kitchens are one of the most common sources of roommate conflict. Cooking and eating means cleaning up dishes and food, so trouble starts right at the kitchen sink.

Dishes. Dirty dishes can be an extremely sore subject between roommates. Some people can tolerate them; others can't. Establishing—and committing to—sink rules is the best way to avoid a dish war.

Equipment. Decide ahead of time what equipment—food processor, microplane, your really expensive sauté pan—is open to all for use and what you'd

---

four ways to avoid the blame game

SUGGEST: "It might be a good idea if . . ." or "When I have trouble with _____, I try to _____."

SHOW CAUSE AND EFFECT: "When you _____, I feel _____."

OFFER TO HELP: "I'm good at organizing things; maybe I could give you a hand with that."

TAKE PREVENTIVE MEASURES: "I see that next week we'll both be really busy. Let's talk about how to handle house stuff when we have crazy schedules."

---

taming the kitchen cleanup

When you and your roommate cook meals together, try cleaning up as you go during the meal prep. Then you both help out with the rest of the dishes after you've eaten. It's so simple!

rather not share. If it is shared, who is responsible for repairs? It's important to establish these boundaries at the outset.

Food. The leftovers you planned for lunch are missing. If you share refrigerator or cabinet space it's a good idea to label your food. As a household decide whether you'll share everything, keep items separate, or just share staples. Then respect the decision. Note: Saying you'll replace something and actually doing so are two different things. Make it a priority to replace what you borrow of a roommate's food.

Shopping for groceries. Shopping together all of the time works well if you and your roommates have similar eating styles and budgets. But even if you have divergent tastes or decide to keep food separate, consider sharing expenses for foods or household supplies that you all use: kitchen staples (flour and sugar, for example), spices, condiments, paper towels, and cleaning supplies.

The Bathroom

It's a private space that we're not eager to share with people we know, let alone people we don't know. In a perfect world, we'd each have our own. In all likelihood you share a bathroom, not only with roommates, but also with guests who come to visit. Special care should be taken to leave the bathroom in reasonably good condition for the next person. In a two-gender household, that also means putting the toilet seat *and* lid down after using it.

Your bathroom doesn't necessarily have to be sparkling clean all the time, but when it is a shared space, it needs to be kept at a level of cleanliness that everyone feels comfortable with. If everyone agrees on a standard and sticks to it, you should have no problem.

The bathroom is also a place where you share resources and time constraints. Be aware of how much time you spend there, particularly during the morning "rush hour." Hot water is also a limited resource, so be considerate of others showering after you. Be respectful of medicine cabinets—no snooping through prescription labels—and don't help yourself to a roommate's toiletries or medications.

The Living Room

The living room may look harmless, but it's full of hidden dangers. Watch out for

The trail. Your things don't always make it back to your room, and if someone is having guests over and you're not around, chances are they'll have to deal with your stuff. Therefore, keep in mind how important it is to put away your things so they won't be in the way. Clutter can be tamed by designating areas for keys, jackets, mail, sunglasses, and anything else you typically grab or set down on your way in and out.

The thermostat. Your housemate's idea of bliss is a tropical 85 degrees and you like fresh air, even in winter. How to compromise? You might give her a cozy sweater or two and she might agree to a fifteen-minute daily airing. What could bring you both into the temperate zone is your skyrocketing heating bill.

Having guests over. Set standards ahead of time for having friends or significant others come to hang out at your place. It could be an open-door policy that says friends can drop by whenever or one that says all roommates have to agree when it's okay to have people over. You might have a combination: weekdays, ask your roommates first; weekends, anyone anytime. Or maybe you have set hours, such as after 11 PM the living room is closed so the house is quieter. It's important that you and your roommates acknowledge each other's comfort levels and expectations for having visitors to your home space.

Bandwidth. With so many people using the Internet to stream their favorite movies and TV shows, the issue of hogging the TV remote has been replaced with the issue of hogging bandwidth and using or sharing streaming accounts. First and foremost, you should make sure that you get an Internet plan that accommodates the number of users who will be online in your home. Then, establish clear-cut boundaries with your streaming accounts and who pays for what.

Shared furniture. When you first move in, it's best to set expectations and understandings when it comes to larger items in the house that will be shared. Couches can easily become stained, coffee tables scratched, and rugs ruined. Be clear with your roommates about how you expect any larger items you put in your home to be used and also repaired or replaced if they are damaged or ruined.

⸤ PARTING WAYS ⸣

There comes a time in most roommate relationships when one person leaves. A new job in another city, a new relationship, and a change in economic circumstances are all typical reasons for ending the roommate relationship. If it's time to part ways, be businesslike. The departing roommate gives notice in advance, with enough time for the other roommates to find a replacement or a new place. All possessions and items should be returned to their owners. Finances (bills, rent, and security deposits) should be settled. The spaces you've occupied should be cleaned and checked for damages so that there are no surprises when asking for the return of the deposit. Alert friends, family, and the post office of your change of address so that mail can be forwarded properly. That's the ideal.

Other times, the relationship ends because it's just not working: Your roommate is always late with her rent; he consistently breaks the house rules regarding overnight guests. Sometimes even best friends just can't live together. Whatever the reason for the parting of ways, harping on past issues won't help your relationship. Anger and resentment can also interfere with resolving the practical aspects, such as finalizing finances. A roommate who walks out slamming the door may owe money that she'll probably never pay. Patience, politeness, and keeping your cool can go a long way to ending the roommate relationship as positively as possible, and perhaps to maintaining the friendship going forward. "I'm sorry that this didn't go better, but I hope we'll still be friends." A little time and space can mend the relationship.

people who work in your home

the relationship between employers and those who work in their homes is every bit as complex as the employer/employee relationship in the traditional workplace. Sometimes people employed by housecleaning and maintenance services may rarely see the people in whose homes they work. Other times, employer and employee may develop genuine friendships, and employees are valued as family members. Whatever the nature of the relationship, people tend to get to know a lot about one another when the workplace is a home.

No matter how friendly an employer and in-home employee may become, employment is still a business relationship for both parties. Problems can arise when employers fail to regard their household employees as *individuals* with their own homes and families. A conscientious employer begins by respecting the people he or she employs. Consideration and open communication are the foundations of trust, loyalty, and *mutual* respect.

[YOUR RESPONSIBILITIES TO EMPLOYEES]

As an employer, your first responsibility is to be honest in your dealings. That means knowing your state's labor and wage laws and following them. If this is your first hiring experience, ask yourself what *you* would expect of an employer. If you've employed household workers before, analyze your past experience and consider what improvements you might make.

The ABCs of Hiring

There are good employment agencies and recruitment firms that specialize in domestic hiring, or you may conduct your own search. No matter how urgent your need for help may seem, try not to rush through the process. Finding and hiring the right worker requires the same professionalism, attention to details, and good manners as in business.

Develop a comprehensive job description for the position. Spell out an employee's duties in detail, and be honest about your expectations.

Determine wages, benefits, and conditions, including hours of employment and time off. Since compensation can vary regionally, consult other employers as well as your state employment department to determine what's legal, fair, and reasonable in your area.

Conduct the search ethically. Often the best way to find a good employee is to ask people you know for recommendations. But don't attempt to "steal away" a worker. If you want to compete for the worker, talk to the current employer first and proceed only if you both feel good about your doing so.

Be prepared for interviews. Prepare your questions in advance and try to anticipate questions that applicants will have. Schedule enough time for each interview, including a house or grounds tour if you want.

If the applicant's work qualifications aren't adequate for your needs, or if it's obvious that she won't be hired, it's fine to tell her, "I'm sorry, Ms. Salas. We're looking for someone with at least two years' experience."

Follow up by contacting references. Even if an applicant has been referred to you by someone you know well, call other references, including past employers, before you make any final offer.

Get permission for background searches. It's not unusual for employers to go beyond checking references (a must) and conduct more thorough background investigations of potential employees. If you plan to do so, consult an attorney about obtaining the proper signed releases.

When making an offer, notify applicants and agencies as soon as possible. Promptly contact the person you hope to hire. If other applicants are waiting for your decision, notify them as quickly as you can after the position has been filled. Some may ask why they weren't selected. Give business reasons but avoid any personal or biased comments.

Trial Periods

You may decide to hire for a trial period to be sure that there's a good fit. If so, determine the length of the trial in advance and inform applicants of this requirement. At the end of the period, sit down with your new employee and discuss his or her performance and future. Make it a two-way conversation; this is an excellent time to evaluate any problems and possibly revise your own expectations as well as your employee's. Even if you don't have a trial period, most employees appreciate the occasional opportunity to talk about the job and their performance.

Clear Expectations and Open Communication

Employers need to be clear and open with new employees about their duties. Ideally, you'll be available in person during the first day or days to explain more thoroughly what you want done. If you can't be on hand, leave a number where you can be reached and don't be put out by calls during the initial settling-in period. Once you and your employee are comfortable with the work arrangement, you can schedule regular times to check in.

From the first day, you and your employee are building a relationship that will work well if it's grounded in respect and trust. Ongoing communication is essential, and the employer should set the standard. The most common mistakes are being too lax or too rigid. The goal should be a reasonable amount of flexibility on both sides. For example, if a daily worker agrees to stay late to assist with a party, a considerate employer would not only pay overtime but also try to give him the next morning off.

One temptation when employing household workers is to increase their responsibilities without consulting them. This can happen unconsciously. An hour or two of watching the children each week turns into daily child minding. All alterations in job responsibilities should be discussed and agreed to by both parties. If new duties require more time or heavier labor, it's usually necessary to relieve the worker of other responsibilities or increase work hours and renegotiate salary or wages accordingly.

Considerate Treatment at All Times

The relationship between employer and domestic employee can be complex, but the glitches that inevitably occur can be greatly eased with consideration and good manners.

"Please," "thank you," and more. An employer should always observe the common courtesies they would with anyone who comes into their home.

Forms of address. Employers and employees should start a working relationship by addressing each other by title and last name until one or both request to be called by their first names. The employer might take the lead by saying, "Please call me Susan instead of Mrs. Jones," and ask the employee how he or she prefers to be addressed. Teach children and teens that it's respectful to address an adult employee as Mr., Mrs., Ms., or Miss, unless the adult prefers to be called by the first name.

Introductions. Introduce your employees by their first and last names when you have visitors. Or, without making formal introductions, referring to your employees by name lets guests know how to address them.

Transportation. Thoughtful employers offer to pick up and return employees to bus or train stops that aren't within easy walking distance and when the weather is bad. If an employee needs to take a taxi because she has to stay late into the night or work on a holiday when public transportation is limited, you should pay for the cab.

When an employee uses his or her vehicle as part of the job, you should reimburse the current per-mile government-established rate. Be sure that use of a personal vehicle is in the job description, and have your employee keep a mileage record so you can calculate the reimbursement.

Meals and breaks. Normally an employer provides meals for a domestic employee who works full days. Whether you provide the meals or the worker brings his own food, be sure that he receives time for a meal, a couple of personal breaks, and access to a restroom.

Part-time or contract workers generally bring their own meals, but should be afforded a personal break if they work three or four hours a day, or longer. It's kind to offer drinks, especially in very hot or cold weather and when the work is physically demanding.

Giving Effective Criticism

One of the marks of a good employer is the ability to give *constructive* criticism. Evaluate any problem carefully before talking with your employee. Did you give clear instructions? Did you expect your employee to handle a task that exceeded his or her authority or capability?

Don't hesitate to raise troublesome issues, as little worries can build into big ones. An employer has the right to expect things done in his or her way, but an employee has an equal right to know exactly what is expected.

One technique that's effective when giving criticism is called "the compliment sandwich," in which you

◆ Start with a compliment: "Lauren, overall you are doing a great job."

"good boss" behaviors

The following "good boss" behaviors describe bosses who are thoughtful, considerate, and respectful:

A GOOD BOSS . . .

. . . KEEPS UP BETWEEN VISITS. No employee should have to confront days' worth of food-encrusted dishes or dirty clothing scattered everywhere.

. . . GIVES CLEAR INSTRUCTIONS. No one can know where things belong or how chores are expected to be done without clear instruction.

. . . PROVIDES SUPPLIES AS AGREED UPON. Unless it's clear from the start that the worker or service will provide cleaning products, mops, and brooms, the boss should stock up on materials.

. . . IS CIVIL. It takes very little effort to greet an employee courteously, speak in a pleasant tone of voice, and converse and discuss rather than bark orders.

. . . CRITICIZES CONSTRUCTIVELY. Most employees respond to criticism when it's clear, calm, and leavened with some well-earned compliments and positive suggestions for improvement.

. . . DOESN'T CONSTANTLY EXPECT OVER-TIME. Workers should be *asked* in advance to work extra hours, and their decisions respected. It goes without saying that they should be compensated fairly.

. . . PAYS ON TIME. It's wrong to expect an employee to wait for wages because the boss "ran out" of checks or "forgot" to stop at the bank.

- State the criticism: "However, the floors just aren't as clean as I would like."
- Conclude with a compliment: "I'm really happy about the way the bathrooms are looking."

Another similar technique is "praise, concern, suggest."

- Start with praise: "Lauren, overall you are doing a great job and I enjoy having you work in my home"
- State your concern: "However, even though you've vacuumed, the kitchen floor still has crumbs and doesn't look clean."
- Suggest a solution: "Could you alter your routine and vacuum the floor after you have cleaned the counters? Thank you."

Discuss problems calmly and privately, and give your employee the opportunity to explain. Be quick to take responsibility for any role you played in creating the problem. Keep your discussion focused on the issue at hand: no personal attacks and no threats of firing unless you really mean it and have clear reasons for dismissal. Try to resolve any problem situation in a mutually satisfactory way. (See also "Dismissing an Employee," page 509.)

Tipping and Gifts

In general, household workers don't receive tips from employers. A raise or a bonus is the appropriate way to recognize outstanding work. Guests in your home shouldn't tip your employees without consulting you first, and then only when they've received extra service, such as doing a load of your houseguests' laundry. (See also Chapter 22, "Houseguests," page 261.)

Q: *My husband and I have two school-age children, and we both work full-time, so I hired a part-time housecleaner. We pay her more than the average in our city, but she's been so helpful that I'd like to do more. She has children several years younger than ours, and I've thought about giving her some of our children's outgrown clothes and toys. But I'm afraid she might take my offer as an insult. What should I do?*

A: Base your decision on the relationship you have with your housecleaner. Have you talked about your children and families? If your relationship is strictly business, then the sudden offer of hand-me-downs may seem like "charity," and she might be offended. But if you're friendly, the offer will probably be taken in the spirit you intend. Present the idea in person so you can judge her reaction. You might offer just the toys first, which are less personal than clothing. If she seems pleased about the toys, ask if she'd like to see the clothes. In either case, the toys and clothing should be in good condition.

Used clothes, toys, and household items aren't really gifts in the true sense. Thus, also think of other ways to show appreciation—a family Christmas gift perhaps, or an end-of-year bonus in her paycheck.

It's customary to give gifts to household employees for birthdays, holidays, and special occasions such as a retirement. While you might give money or gift certificates, items that reflect an employee's interests show that a gift was specially chosen. Use discretion and avoid gifts that are too personal, such as lingerie or perfume. When giving money, present it with a personally signed note or card in an envelope addressed to your employee. Be cautious about giving used clothing and household items; some employees may be understandably sensitive to the assumption that they need castoffs.

Gifts are rarely given to contract workers, such as those who work for a lawn or pool care service; however, you might consider giving an end-of-season or annual tip. Ask the contracting employer about any policies for tipping and gifts. You don't want to put a contract worker in the awkward position of having to refuse or return your gift. (See Chapter 13, "Tipping," page 165.)

CHILD-CARE PROVIDERS

When choosing a child-care provider, look for someone whose child-rearing philosophy is very similar to yours. Talk with applicants about their approach to child care and discipline and be forthright about your goals for your child. Discuss lifestyle issues. Do you run your home on a well-defined schedule or is your style more relaxed and spontaneous? Define the caregiver's authority in your absence. Child-care experts recommend that you interview perspective caregivers at least twice before offering the position. Do take the time; chil-

dren are most likely to benefit when parents and caregivers are consistent in their methods and messages.

Nannies

Nannies may be full- or part-time employees. They normally work without supervision and aren't expected to do housework that isn't child-care related. A nanny's typical duties might consist of caring for a child or children's physical needs, including meal preparation, baths, and dressing; laundry and other child-specific housekeeping; organizing and supervising play and outings; and transportation, including drop-off and pickup at preschool and school. Whether or not a nanny lives with a family, she is a key part of the family structure. Often she joins the family at meals and accompanies them on vacation. The nonprofit International Nanny Association (INA) provides in-depth information about all aspects of nanny employment at www.nanny.org.

Au Pairs

The French term *au pair* means "on equal terms." Au pairs—usually women between ages eighteen and twenty-six but sometimes older—travel to another country and live with host families for a specified time period. The au pair receives a private room, board, and a stipend or allowance, in exchange for assistance with household work that may include helping with the host family's children. An au pair is unlikely to have formal child-care training and may not be qualified to care for infants or young children beyond routine babysitting.

Families considering an au pair arrangement must understand that *au pairs are not employees*, and hosts have certain responsibilities, including taking a semi-parental interest in their young visitors: accommodating language differences, acclimating the au pair to American customs, and seeing that the au pair is included in family activities and also has reasonable personal time for rest, recreation, and study.

Babysitters

A babysitter's role is to care for children when a parent or parents aren't present. In most cases, a babysitter doesn't do housework except as it relates to the children, such as serving their meals and putting away toys. Be clear and specific about your house rules, including if and when a sitter may have a guest. Provide everything the sitter will need to care for your children. Discuss use of the fridge, phone, TV, and audio equipment. Do keep sitters abreast of any changes in a child's behavior, a change in house rules, or any particular challenges your child is currently experiencing.

Arrange transportation for the sitter to and from your home. If a sitter is expected to drive your children, be certain she's licensed and has a good driving record. Always leave phone numbers where you can be reached and emergency numbers. For everyone's sake, don't expect an unqualified person to care for sick children or administer medication.

etiquette for outside-the-home daycare

Out-of-home daycare options include full-time group centers, work-site daycare, after-school programs, and home care, when the provider cares for a number of children in her own home. Regardless of the care you select, the following considerations will help make your child's and your provider's lives easier:

◆ Be sure that you understand and accept all of the provider's policies and rules. Don't expect a provider to make exceptions for you and your child.

◆ Carefully observe the provider's drop-off and pickup times and always have a backup plan.

◆ Immediately notify providers of any change in your address, phone number, or status (such as a relocation, divorce, or marriage). Also, give adequate advance notice if your child will be leaving the daycare provider.

◆ Inform the provider if you suspect a serious problem, such as an incompetent child-care worker or a danger in the physical environment. Be sure that you've gathered your facts first. If nothing is done within a reasonable time, you can remove your child entirely and report the situation to the appropriate authorities. Reporting is an act of concern for the well-being of other parents and children.

◆ *Always* keep a sick child at home. Inform the provider about the illness, and don't let your child return until the possibility of contagion has passed.

◆ Follow the provider's policies for gift giving and tipping. Parents often pool together or give individual holiday gifts to daycare providers.

A Family Vacation Including a Nanny, Au Pair, or Babysitter

If you take a nanny, au pair, or other child-care provider along on the family vacation, make it very clear ahead of time if you expect them to be working or if this is a vacation for them, too. In many cases it is a bit of both—work and some child-care duties. Work out a vacation schedule just as you do your home child-care schedule. Don't expect your sitter to work limitless hours while you bask in the sun. Tagging along to your vacation destination isn't fair compensation for excessive overtime or duties beyond your provider's job description. You should pay for your sitter's travel expenses: transportation, meals, and lodging as well as for his or her hours on duty.

HOUSEHOLD STAFF

Before you seek household help, evaluate your needs, your time, and your budget. Consider carefully whether you need a full-time, part-time, or live-in employee and the impact that will have on your household.

Housekeepers and Butlers

In addition to the duties you normally associate with housekeepers and butlers, they may also handle budgeting, bill paying, and hiring and supervising staff and outside contractors. Because of their responsibilities, they often command high salaries and excellent benefits, and competition for their services can be stiff. Finding the right person can be time-intensive, so using a reputable recruitment or employment agency may be your best bet. Usually, housekeepers and butlers live in but don't join the family for meals as nannies do. While they may be "on call" 24/7, they are otherwise accorded privacy in their accommodations.

Clothing and Uniforms

Domestic employees normally choose their own work clothing. Comfort and appropriateness for the job are considered more important than style, though employers may want to set general dress standards. Be sure to inform prospective employees of any dress requirements, and provide them with a comfortable place to change and store their clothing and shoes.

The employer is responsible for furnishing uniforms. Whether or not you require uniforms, you should supply aprons and other cover-ups as necessary. If you want employees to wear particular clothing—expecting a chauffeur to wear business suits, for instance—you should bear the expense.

Live-in Help

A live-in worker should have private quarters (at least a bedroom and separate bath, ideally with a sitting room) and be provided with all meals when in residence. A live-in couple often has homelike quarters, such as an attached apartment or guesthouse.

House Rules for Live-in Help

You should discuss the following issues with anyone who lives in your home, making your guidelines clear:

Privacy. Everyone should respect everyone else's privacy. Live-in workers generally receive house keys and keys to their rooms.

Cleanliness. An employee's quarters are normally off-limits to others, but you can require basic standards of cleanliness and care of property.

Kitchen privileges. If the live-in employee's quarters don't include a kitchen, then he or she should have access to the main kitchen. Provide some food storage space in the kitchen or pantry.

Smoking and candles. If you want a nonsmoker, say so in your initial employee search. If you allow smoking, be clear where it's permitted and insist on safe use. The same applies to burning candles and incense.

Guests. A live-in worker needs company, so determine places for guest visits other than his or her bedroom. You have the right to know who will be visiting and when, especially if they will use a room shared with your family.

Use of alcohol and drugs. Discuss your policy about alcohol consumption with your employee and establish appropriate guidelines. You may ban alcohol outright, particularly if your employee is under age twenty-one. Use of controlled substances should be grounds for immediate dismissal.

Noise levels. Both you and your employee should agree to quiet hours and to lower the volume when requested.

Telephone. Many employees have their own cell phones. An employer may limit their use for personal calls during work hours. If employees use your phone, agree on the procedure for the payment of any of their personal long-distance calls.

Transportation. If an employee has access to your car for personal use, be precise about scheduling and costs for gas and maintenance. If the employee keeps her own vehicle at your home, reimburse costs incurred when she drives for you.

GUIDELINES FOR OTHER WORKERS IN YOUR HOME

There are other people who may work in your home but who aren't live-in domestic workers. Many have special qualifications and are employed (or volunteer) to perform well-defined tasks and services. All should be respected for their skills. Whether they are cooks, cleaners, chauffeurs, home health-care providers, paid companions, volunteers, personal assistants, maintenance workers, repairpersons, or contractors, keep the following in mind:

◆ Be considerate of workers' time by not engaging in excessive chitchat. Many have several clients to see each day and can't socialize for long.

◆ Consider carefully what they were hired to do before asking them to perform other or additional duties.

◆ Check references as you would for any employee.

◆ Before tipping a worker who comes from an agency or contractor, check for any policies their employer may have in place.

- When the work is done, be prepared to pay as arranged.

WHEN AN EMPLOYEE LEAVES

When an employee leaves, it's part of an employer's responsibility to make the departure as pleasant as possible. Begin by reviewing and honoring all legal and contractual obligations, including severance payments if you let the employee go, and transfer of any pension funds or insurance plans. Even if there was conflict, be sensitive to other members of your family who may have good relations with the employee. Children often need help understanding why a person they like or depend on is going away.

Accepting a Resignation

When a valued employee resigns, you may want to make an alternate offer—a pay increase or continued service but fewer hours. Give the employee some time to consider. If he or she doesn't take your offer, accept the final decision graciously: "Molly, you've done an excellent job for us and we're sorry to see you go." If an employee gives "personal reasons" as the cause for a resignation, don't pry or continue to ask questions if they don't offer specifics.

Dismissing an Employee

Theft, dishonesty, violation of confidentiality agreements, cruelty to children or others in an employee's care, serious negligence, drunkenness, and drug use

---

when something goes wrong

The washing machine that was repaired yesterday broke down again today. The basement is flooded because the new pump failed. Frustrating things happen, but getting angry often makes the problem worse.

STEP ONE is to calm down.

STEP TWO is to get in touch with the contractor or service company and explain the situation clearly. In a genuine emergency, be firm that you expect quick service.

If you have a complaint about a contractor's employee, report the problem to his or her employer or supervisor. You can do this in person, by phone, or in a business letter (emailed or mailed), but stick to facts.

Whatever the issue, if you call, ask to speak to a supervisor or someone in charge. It's both inconsiderate and pointless to expect the person who answers the phone to solve the problem or authorize restitution.

---

are all grounds for instant dismissal if an employee is caught in the act. But be very cautious about accusing a worker of illegal or negligent behavior based only on suspicions or circumstantial evidence. Be sure the facts support your action.

It's more likely that an employer will dismiss a household worker for poor job performance or general incompetence. In most cases an employee should receive a warning before being fired and have a chance to correct the problem. Good employers also review the

how much notice?

An instant dismissal should be for just cause. Otherwise, two or three weeks' notice is generally appropriate when a domestic employee resigns or an employer lets a worker go. However, if an employee who resigns is determined to leave sooner, it's usually best to agree.

job conditions and decide whether their own expectations are out of line. Since no one is perfect, you might want to put up with minor annoyances in order to keep an employee whom you and your family really like.

If the issue involves a clash of personalities or work philosophies, then it may be time to part ways. There are also situations when an employee is simply no longer needed. The kids have grown up and left the nest. The family may be moving. Changes in an employer's finances may necessitate a dismissal. In such cases, honestly and tactfully explain the reason for the job termination, give adequate notice, and respect your contractual obligations.

Giving References . . . or Not

You wouldn't give written references to anyone who's been fired for just cause. But if the employee resigned, or the reason for terminating the position didn't relate to the employee's character or performance, you should give a reference and, if practical, offer to help with the worker's job search. Even if a job ends on a less than high note, you can still provide a reference. Be fair: An

Q: *My school-age children want to have a farewell party for their nanny, who is leaving after five years to take another job. We all adore Virginia, but my husband thinks that a party would be unprofessional, and we should simply include a generous bonus in her final check.*

A: Why not do both? Your husband's concern about appearing unprofessional should be relieved when he understands how important this occasion is to your children. Five years is a long time to kids, and their involvement in a special farewell may help ease the parting. A generous bonus is an appropriate way to honor a valued employee and colleague. But a bonus wouldn't allow your children to participate in a way that's meaningful to them. In an important way, the party will be a gift to your children as well as to Virginia—a valuable life lesson in expressing love, respect, and gratitude to someone who has been one of the guiding forces in their lives.

honest employee whose work was up to par shouldn't be penalized for personality reasons.

When someone calls for more information, be as forthright and positive as possible. Stick to facts, and say nothing that could be taken as slander or a violation of the former employee's legal rights.

41
separation
and divorce

When Emily Post was writing her ground-breaking *Etiquette* in the early 1920s, divorce occurred in one out of six marriages. Today, it's more like one out of two. This increase in the occurrence of divorce has not made marital breakups any easier for the participants, but divorce and separation no longer carry the social stigma they did in Emily's day. Still, the decision to end a marriage is perhaps the most difficult one a couple can make, and the process can be heartbreaking for everyone. Good manners may seem like a minor concern, but attending to important details and taking time to nurture relationships with friends and other family can truly help during this difficult transition.

SEPARATION

A separation may be either a legal decision, spelled out in writing, or a private, less structured choice made by a married couple. In either case, often the goal is to live apart while working out problems. In some cases a separation allows the couple to reconcile their differences and resume their marriage on a new footing. In others, the couple decides to divorce. Sometimes they simply continue to live apart as a separated but not divorced couple for years.

Usually one spouse moves out of the family home, although there are situations when separated spouses continue to live under the same roof, or keep the children in the same house but trade on and off. Generally, the person leaving takes his or her personal belongings, but the couple's home and possessions aren't altered except by mutual agreement.

If there are children, the couple will need to make decisions concerning where the children will live and what visitation plans will be in place during the separation. Parents shouldn't encourage false hopes, but they need to be clear that this is a separation and not a divorce. (For more on helping children deal with separation and divorce, see "Divorce," page 512.)

The Etiquette of Separation

The following etiquette questions frequently arise during a separation:

When and how do I tell others? A separation isn't announced publicly. A couple should explain the situation to children and family first, then to close friends, and word will spread. If the couple reunites, there's no public announcement.

Do I keep my married name, and should I wear my rings? A wife may continue to use her husband's name (Mrs. Jeffrey Annin), and both spouses usually continue to wear their wedding rings.

Should we accept social invitations addressed to both of us? Usually, you don't attend social engagements together as a couple. If you do go to the same social or business functions, behave as normally—and as cordially—as possible. Most people make accommodations for separated couples by not inviting them both to the same social events. So don't get upset if mutual friends fail to include you in a party to which your spouse has been invited. Chances are, the friends aren't choosing sides but are trying to avoid a difficult situation for everyone.

] DIVORCE [

Divorce is an emotional earthquake; the shock waves extend far beyond the couple at the center and may continue for a long time. A divorce affects family, close friends, and the social world the couple shared together. The upheaval can even extend to the workplace. Sometimes individuals who are divorcing become introspec-

dating during a separation or divorce

There's no one-size-fits-all answer here, as circumstances can vary greatly. While separated or during the process of divorcing, spouses are free to carry on their social lives. Dating and serious relationships, however, should be carefully considered. It's especially important for couples to be respectful of each other and attuned to their children's feelings and concerns.

tive, forgetting about the impact of their decision on the people who love and care about them. Making an intentional effort to think about and reach out to others can be a kind of release that opens a path toward healing. Calling a former friend who may not be sure you're open to doing things together can let her know that you want to continue your relationship, even though your former spouse is no longer a part of the group.

While divorce challenges close relationships with family and friends, most people genuinely want to be helpful. They need guidance from the divorcing spouses, however. Consideration for other people includes not speaking disparagingly about your former spouse at social gatherings, not overburdening them with your problems, showing an interest in *their* lives, and not expecting them to choose between you and your spouse. Despite your best efforts, one of the unfortunate side effects of divorce is that some friendships may not survive.

When There Are Children

A divorce is an upheaval and is likely to be traumatic for the entire family, but children must come first. The secure world they have always depended on is no longer dependable. Together, if possible, parents need to explain what's happening before one parent leaves the home. Be clear with children, but avoid involving them in issues they can't understand. Never expect a child of any age to act as a go-between or to favor one parent over the other.

An extremely important first step is to make careful, clear decisions about living arrangements and visitation plans for the children. Try to maintain as normal a schedule as possible; the absent spouse shouldn't be an absentee parent. A child's ties with grandparents and other close adults can be especially important and should be nurtured. Divorcing parents also need to be alert to other changes in their child's life that may be occurring during the separation or divorce. A family breakup is likely to be doubly stressful for a child who is entering daycare, first grade, or a new school, or for a teenager who is applying to or preparing to leave for college.

When Unmarried Partners Break Up

The end of a relationship between unmarried partners or couples can be every bit as difficult as the end of a marriage. If children are affected, they will feel the same painful emotions and need the same loving attention as children in a divorce. A partner may not be a biological or adoptive parent, but if the bond between that adult and a child is strong, the loss of that person and that relationship is no less traumatic. The breakup should be handled much like a divorce in terms of explaining to children and telling others. There are no rules, but a relationship that began in love ought to end with as much mutual respect as possible.

wedding rings and gifts

Spouses do not continue to wear wedding rings after a divorce, and many remove their rings prior to the divorce when it's clear that the marriage cannot be saved or when legal proceedings are initiated. Once married, a woman's engagement ring belongs to her. A divorced woman may wear the engagement ring on her right hand or have the stones reset and worn in other jewelry. Often engagement rings are stored away and later passed on to children. Divorced couples do not return wedding gifts. However, wedding gifts should be returned if a marriage is annulled early on and the couple has never lived together.

INFORMING OTHERS

Whenever possible the people who matter most to you should be told in person. These conversations can sometimes be difficult, but you'll be glad you made the effort. Family and good friends can provide invaluable support, encouragement, and counsel during a divorce and later, when you face the world on your own.

Tell the Children First

Children of any age must be the first to hear of their parents' separation or divorce, and the news should come directly from the parents. Loving parents will not delegate this responsibility to anyone else. It's best if the couple can talk with their children together and reassure them that Mom and Dad love them as much as ever—and always will. One conversation won't be enough. Young children, teens, and even adult children need preparation for a breakup and plenty of time to adjust. Parents must answer their questions as fully and honestly as possible. Even young children may already have a sense of the friction between their parents and need lots of opportunities to talk about their feelings and fears. Don't just ask, "Are you okay?" More specific questions will help your child open up to you: "Are you afraid of anything?" "Do you have questions?" "How do you feel about what's going on?"

Parents should also inform anyone who cares for their child, including relatives, child-care workers, teachers, and the parents of their child's friends. People in frequent contact with a child or adolescent can often spot problems (depression, acting out, and other uncharacteristic behaviors) that parents who are dealing with their divorce might miss.

Telling Parents and Family

Although parents and close family members are often aware of trouble within a marriage, they need to be told of concrete changes such as a separation or impending divorce.

when older couples divorce

While the average age for first divorces in the United States is the early thirties, older couples divorce as well. The etiquette is the same. One issue deserves special attention: telling grown children. No matter how old they are or how far away they live, children should be directly informed by a parent or parents first—in person, if feasible. A couple with grandchildren should then consult with the parents about the best way to tell younger generations. Even when relations between older parents and grown children are not close, the news of a divorce can be disturbing and saddening, and regardless of age, a child shouldn't be the last to know.

Generally, husband and wife will each speak to their own relatives. Your family may immediately come to your defense, or they may be more circumspect. A person who is divorcing wants allies, but it's wrong to set family members against the other spouse or to turn what is a personal decision between two people into a family feud or worse.

The spouse with physical custody of children should make sure that the children's relationships with the other spouse's grandparents and close relatives are maintained. Feelings between spouses and in-laws are often strained during and after a divorce, but children need the comfort and security of extended family when their nuclear family is broken.

Talking to Friends

Very good friends should hear the news from you—not through the grapevine or on Facebook. Usually this means a conversation in person, but you might call or write friends who live elsewhere. Everyone needs sympathy at such a painful time, and you very well might spill all with your closest confidante. With anyone else, try to avoid going into intimate details or a full-blown account of all the dirty laundry, and don't expect friends to take sides. Someday, you and your friends may look back and regret things that were said if discussions become unnecessarily negative.

Q: *After my divorce six months ago, I moved to a new city. I haven't seen my former in-laws, with whom I was quite close, since the divorce. But we communicate fairly often by phone and email, and I want to keep my relationship with them. Is it appropriate for me to send them birthday and Christmas gifts this year?*

A: Yes. Since you remain friendly with your former in-laws you can send gifts if you want. If your former in-laws don't seem to expect to exchange gifts, then cards with personal messages are appropriate. Staying on good terms with former in-laws is wonderful, so long as you and they understand that the relationship is now different and that the pattern of your contacts will probably change over time.

forget the party

A growing trend is to celebrate a new divorce in a public way by holding "independence parties" and sending "funny" divorce announcements and greeting cards. Many people, friends and family included, feel quite sad when a divorce is final. While some proponents claim that celebrating a new beginning can be healing, it should be done respectfully, if at all. If you do celebrate, make the focus your gratitude for the support of friends and family, and not an attitude of "I'm finally free." Having a party whose purpose is to treat an ex-spouse as an object of ridicule is in bad taste.

When a friend or acquaintance hears about a divorce, the natural first response is "I'm sorry." Take the remark in stride. The person may mean that she's sorry your marriage failed, but it's just as likely she's expressing regret that you have gone through a difficult experience. Instead of becoming defensive, you can say something like, "Thank you. It was for the best, and I'm getting on with my life." A reasonably sensitive person will follow your lead and not pry.

You can ask close friends to tell others about the breakup and then let the news travel. Even so, not everyone will hear. When meeting someone who doesn't know, you may have to tell with tact. When asked, "How's Laura?" you might answer along these lines: "We're divorced now, but I talked to her recently, and she's doing well." Saying, "Didn't you know? We're divorced," (or worse) can make an acquaintance feel bad because he didn't know.

Coworkers and Business Associates

Tell those to whom your divorce will make a difference. Your employer and any immediate supervisor should probably know. You might also tell a few close coworkers and ask them to discreetly inform other colleagues, if this approach makes sense in your situation.

Discretion is the better part of valor in the workplace. If someone asks a tactless question, try to keep your responses neutral and brief, especially if fellow employees also know your spouse. Don't test other people's loyalties or spend work time dwelling on your personal situation.

Very difficult or messy divorces can affect a person's productivity, and even amicable breakups may require taking extra time off for meetings with lawyers and court appearances. Plan carefully for your absences so that you don't create extra work for your coworkers.

] THE PRACTICALITIES OF MAKING CHANGES [

The practical aspects of divorce include making some necessary changes.

Names and courtesy titles. Women have various options. A divorcée may keep her former husband's last name but not his first name. Mrs. Thomas Bronson would be Mrs. Andrea Bronson. Today, many divorced women opt for the courtesy title "Ms." Some will return to using their maiden name. Others, particularly when there are children from the marriage, prefer to retain

---

responding to the news of a divorce

Though there's no all-purpose response to the news, try to say something that shows concern without prying. Some things you can say:

- "Thank you for telling me. I know it's not always easy."
- "I'm sorry to hear that" or "Thanks for letting me know."
- "I wish you the best" or "I hope things get better for you soon."
- "Let me know if there's anything I can do to help. I'd be glad to watch the kids if you have to be at meetings or just need a little time to yourself."

A few things *not* to say:

- "Oh, no wonder you look so stressed and tired!"
- "I really feel bad for your children. It's going to be awful for them!"
- "I always thought he (she) was a jerk."
- "I thought this was coming."
- "I'm surprised it lasted this long."

How should a divorced or separated person reply to thoughtless comments? With a large grain of salt. Without being rude, you can ignore or defuse the remark—"It's all for the best" or "I really don't want to discuss it"—and turn the conversation in another direction.

"Mrs." and their husband's last name. When a marriage is annulled, the ex-wife always resumes her maiden name because an annulment signifies that the marriage never existed. The following chart indicates the most common options:

Married last name	Ms. (Mrs.) Andrea Bronson
Maiden name only	Ms. Andrea Jane Sloan
Maiden and married last names	Ms. (Mrs.) Andrea Sloan Bronson
Hyphenated maiden and married last name	Ms. (Mrs.) Andrea Sloan-Bronson

Men don't change their names unless they adopted a double, hyphenated surname during the marriage. Mr. Jacob Sloan-Bronson may keep the double name or go back to Mr. Jacob Bronson.

Professional titles. Professional, religious, and academic titles do not change, although a woman may keep her married surname or resume her maiden name: Dr. Sarah Schwartz or Dr. Sarah Fletcher.

Addresses. Mailing addresses, phone numbers, and email addresses reflect alterations in living arrangements. When one or both of the couple move from the former family home, they should be sure that the address and name changes are registered with the U.S. Postal Service and phone company as soon as possible. To head off email foul-ups like receiving an ex's personal communications, close any joint accounts and start over individually with new user names. You'll also want to have any shared stationery, social cards, business cards, and checks reprinted as soon as you can.

Other notifications. There are numerous people and institutions that must be told about your change of status, whether it's a new name, new address, or both. Some of these include your landlord or leasing agent; banks, credit card companies, and other financial institutions; health-care providers; insurance companies; your children's schools; and your place of worship. Often, notification is a simple matter of filling out change-of-address forms or making a few quick calls.

POST-DIVORCE ETIQUETTE

There's a saying that divorce never really ends. Months, even years, after a marriage has been dissolved, situations arise that require former spouses and their families to communicate and cooperate with tact, courtesy, and sensitivity. For some couples, time serves as a healer: New relationships are formed, planning for children's events goes more smoothly, and the community becomes familiar with how the former couple now socializes. Some divorced couples avoid attending the same social events; others develop a new way of interacting so that they can attend the same events without discomfort for anyone.

It's important to spell out the exact nature of post-divorce relationships and stick to the limits you set. (No "dropping by" unexpectedly or constantly calling an ex-spouse for help when the water heater breaks.) Honor any custody and visitation arrangements regarding children. Show consideration for your ex-spouse by having children ready for visits and returning from visits on time. Discuss any necessary schedule changes well in advance.

Sometimes, despite the healing that comes with time, situations occur that have the potential to create problems. In circumstances like the following, the goal is to do what's right—not to open old wounds or replay the past.

An Ex-spouse Who Won't Move On

When one spouse was a reluctant participant in a divorce, he or she may harbor thoughts of reconciliation. Ex-spouses are sometimes guilty of sending mixed signals—telling a former mate that he or she must "move on" while continuing to initiate contact (other than necessary ones regarding the children). The only option is to be firm, set limits, and stick to them.

When an Ex-spouse Remarries

If you are invited to a former spouse's wedding, to attend or not is a personal decision, although it's usually better to regret the invitation. In either case, be sure to reply. Even when relations are cordial, the presence of an ex-spouse may make family or other guests feel uncomfortable. If you are invited, be sensitive, too, with your selection of a wedding gift; choose it as thoughtfully as you would for any couple. (For information about the roles of divorced parents when their children marry, see Chapter 47, "Planning Your Wedding," page 572, and Chapter 51, "The Big Day," page 634.)

However you feel personally about your ex-spouse's new wife or husband, keep your remarks positive, especially with your children. If there is competition or jealousy between former and current spouses, children are bound to be caught in the middle. The adults should work together to keep that from happening. A typical issue involves how children should address a stepparent. A more serious concern relates to authority—when and how a stepparent should discipline. How well the adults resolve such questions will profoundly affect their children's happiness. (See Chapter 36, "Today's Home and Family," page 457.)

The Death of a Former Spouse

Even people who have been divorced for many years can feel grief and sadness when a former spouse dies. Expressing those feelings requires delicacy and consideration, particularly when the person's survivors include a current wife or husband and children. It's considerate on the part of the deceased's family to contact

Q: *My ex-husband brings his new girlfriend to my son's soccer games, and it makes me very uncomfortable. My son doesn't mind, but should I be subjected to this woman's presence? Isn't my ex being disrespectful of my feelings?*

A: Whatever your former husband's motives, it is your son's feelings that particularly matter. His father is taking an active role in his life, and whether your ex-husband attends games on his own or with a date, he is *involved* with his child. You may be uncomfortable, but for your son's sake, you should keep your feelings to yourself.

Life goes on and sooner or later, divorced parents must accept the fact that their former spouses may form new romantic attachments. If the current situation really is intolerable for you, you and your ex might agree to attend games alternately if this won't disappoint your son. For one-time special events such as a championship game or school play, both of you should make the effort to attend (with or without dates) and to behave with dignity. You can sit separately and focus on your child's participation in the event.

a former spouse and let them know of the death and any arrangements regarding services.

Generally, a divorced spouse stays in the background. It's appropriate to send a sympathy note, but include an offer of help only if you know it will be welcome. A donation to the deceased's designated charity may be preferable to sending flowers. It's usually best not to attend the visitation or grave site unless you've been specifically invited.

A divorced spouse may attend the funeral or memorial service as long as his or her presence won't cause discomfort for the family. If the service is private, a former spouse doesn't attend unless invited. A former spouse doesn't sit with the family unless asked to. If the divorced couple has young children, then it's kind to let the surviving parent sit with them—if doing so is the best thing for the children. The decision about whether the remaining parent sits with the children—and if so, where—ideally is worked out respectfully among the former spouse and the deceased's family members before the service. If graveside services are limited to family, a former spouse shouldn't attend unless specifically invited.

Rarely does a divorced person give a speech or take on an active role at an ex-spouse's funeral or memorial service. However, doing so would be appropriate if the deceased had no other living family, if his or her survivors make the request, or if it was the deceased's wish. An ex-spouse shouldn't attempt a eulogy unless he or she can pay genuine tribute to the deceased. (See "When the Family Has Been Split," page 548.)

42 elder etiquette

It's a twenty-first-century reality that people are living longer than ever before. Actuaries are predicting that children born today should plan on living into their nineties. So what is life like today for those over seventy-five? Are they all retired? Where do they live? When they need care, who gives it? How can they make decisions when confusion increases? Is there any special etiquette advice that pertains to age?

Both family members and friends have questions stemming from their relationships with elders. Many of the answers can be found in the principles that underlie all our social interactions: respect, consideration, and honesty. The challenge is to utilize these principles in the face of the significant health, emotional, cognitive, and social changes that may accompany the aging process.

In addition to living longer, today's elderly are more active than their predecessors, a result of major medical advances, better nutrition, and plenty of opportunities for social, mental, and physical activities. While these advances in health and lifestyle choices are positive, the elderly also have unique needs and problems that must be acknowledged by the seniors themselves and recognized and addressed by others. In general, our senior population can always use considerate help and extra doses of understanding and respect.

[LIVING ARRANGEMENTS]

The need for support varies from person to person. Some sixty-year-olds need more help than some eighty-year-olds. Regardless of age but depending on their physical and cognitive condition, different

seniors require different living situations that provide different levels of support. Some will move back in with adult children and others will need a care facility. (See "When Parents Come to Live in Your Nest," page 472.) For each situation there is etiquette that can improve interactions.

Independent Living— In the Community

Many people continue to live on their own throughout their senior years. They often rely on family members or neighbors to assist with things they can no longer do for themselves: transportation, shopping, or cleaning. Sometimes, all that is needed is assurance that the basic activities of daily living can be met. To that end, here are tips for

The Senior

- ◆ **When you need help, ask rather than expect.** "Is there any chance that you could drive me to the doctor's office on Friday?"

- ◆ **"Thank you" goes a long way to strengthening a relationship.** Whether the assistance came from a family member or paid caregiver, don't assume the person "knows" you appreciate their efforts on your behalf. Be sure to say so.

- ◆ **Find opportunities to do something for others.** If you're making your special jams or jellies, make an extra jar for the neighbor who always brings in your mail.

- ◆ **Invite others over.** You may not be able to offer a formal dinner but soup and sandwiches make a great meal to share with family and neighbors.

- ◆ **Be a joiner.** Join a book club, a bridge club, a game club, a health club, or a golf club. Keeping active—socially, mentally, and physically—will keep you alert and healthier. And all the relationships you develop will make your life more vital.

The Family Member, Neighbor, or Caregiver

- ◆ **Don't be a martyr.** The needs of your senior will probably be ongoing and it's important to be honest when you're not able to help.

- ◆ **Offer to help when you can.** Sometimes the senior in your life feels like all he ever does is ask for "favors." If you see something that needs doing, just offer.

- ◆ **Make an offer before helping.** Your elderly neighbor may not want you to shovel the walk. If you just do it, it takes it out of his control.

- ◆ **Make a little extra.** Soup, stew, macaroni and cheese—make an extra portion or two and offer it to the senior in your life.

- ◆ **Make suggestions for getting together.** "I'm going to the craft fair this weekend; why don't we go together?"

Independent Living— In a Retirement Community

All the tips for independent living in the community apply to independent living in a retirement community. There are, however, some etiquette tips unique to this style of living. Whether you are a senior, family member, or friend, here are some special considerations:

- When you greet anyone, say your own name. We all forget names once in a while, but as we get older, it becomes more of an issue. Seniors will tell you this form of memory loss is the most frustrating. The frustration can be almost eliminated if people *always* say their name when greeting others: "Hi, it's Cindy. How have you been?"

- When you entertain seniors, consider the various disabilities that can be a part of aging.

  - If one of your guests uses a walker, make sure there's room for her to maneuver.

  - Since many seniors experience hearing loss, lower the volume of any background music.

  - Ask guests if they have any dietary restrictions, then plan your menu accordingly.

  - Keep portions modest and then offer seconds. Elderly people often have decreased appetites and an overloaded plate can be unappetizing.

  - Make sure there is enough seating for everyone.

  - Follow the etiquette guidelines for great entertaining, such as welcoming your guests and making every effort to make them feel comfortable.

- If you can't make a scheduled appointment or class at an activity center, call and cancel so someone else can use your spot.

- If you know a couple (or one half of a couple) in the assisted-living level of your community, remember to invite them to your home, to join you in the community dining room, or to go out to special activities.

- Visit your friends who have moved to the assisted-living facility or the nursing home in your community. Keeping in touch can mean a lot to them.

- Most retirement communities have established rules and standards. Familiarize yourself with them, preferably before you move in. If some seem cumbersome or unnecessary, participate in the governance of the community so that you might be able to affect change.

Assisted Living

Whether the senior you know is in a stand-alone assisted-living facility or one that is part of a retirement community, your care and support will go a long way toward making it a successful living arrangement. Seniors move into assisted-living facilities because they need help with their activities of daily living. Help is available to them when it is needed, in a way that strives to allow seniors to retain much of their independence. Sometimes their special needs are related to physical changes and sometimes they need assistance because of some form of memory loss. (See also "Courtesies for People with Disabilities," page 30.)

Whether it's a problem with memory or mobility or both, the senior in an assisted-living residence is likely to need to do everything at a slower pace. From walking to talking, the processing and activity itself are slowed with age. Your patience will make things easier and less confusing or discouraging. Here are some tips for helping the senior when he or she moves into an assisted-living facility:

- Understand that downsizing is usually necessary. The new resident probably has to leave larger living quarters to move into either a studio or one-bedroom apartment. Help her grasp the reality that her scaled-down apartment can actually make daily living easier.

- Assist your senior with decisions about what to bring—and what to leave behind. Encourage her to select meaningful items to help her feel as much at home as possible from the very beginning.

- Help your senior settle in as quickly as possible. Ask the residence administrators for their move-in checklist and seek their insights on assimilating a new resident into the facility's daily routines.

- Be available. Especially in the first days and weeks, visit or phone as often as logistics and your schedule will allow. Even after she settles into her new environment, keep in touch on a regular basis.

- Be alert for signs of disorientation and sadness. It takes time to adjust to new living quarters at *any* age.

- Encourage and allow as much independence for your senior as possible.

  Here are tips for the senior to enhance the assisted-living experience from the very beginning:

- Give the change a chance. Your new home will feel strange at first, but over time, it will become more familiar and, hopefully, more enjoyable.

- Make an effort to meet and get to know people. Introduce yourself to other residents. Some conver-

sation starters could be, "How long have you lived here?" "Where did you move from?" "Do you have children, grandchildren?" "How's the food here?"

- Learn to accept help from the staff. Sometimes, this will require patience on your part as you learn to work together.

- Try out some activities. Most facilities offer a full array of activities, such as games, outings, music, movies, and exercise classes. Participating in some of these activities can enrich your days.

- Understand and try to accept the communal nature of your assisted-living home. Meals are eaten with other people and the living rooms and television areas may be shared. Sometimes that means compromising on the choice of a television show, or waiting to use the living room if another resident is visiting with his family.

- Help newcomers. Once you've settled in, try to welcome those who move in after you. In addition to introducing yourself, you might invite your new neighbor to join you in doing a puzzle or taking an exercise class.

Nursing Home or Care Center

Seniors in a nursing home require more intensive physical care than what is provided in an assisted-living residence. They may need assistance with walking, eating, bathing and dressing, toileting, and/or taking medications. This level of residential care has yet another set of unique etiquette tips:

- **Communicate in various ways.** If someone has had a stroke, he might be unable to speak but may be able to understand what you have to say, so say it. If he understands, you've had a communication; and if he doesn't, you've gained a few moments with him where the gentleness of your voice and the effort you make may actually be soothing.

- **Find activities you can do together.** Maybe you could go for a short walk and a visit on the outdoor terrace, play a card or board game, listen to music, or watch a TV show together. It may even be possible to take short outings off campus. The companionship is a benefit to you both and a way to strengthen your relationship during this stage of life.

- **Share a meal.** If your senior can't get out for a dinner date, bring it in—a favorite home-cooked meal or call out for take-out. It's a nice change from institutional cooking. Check for any dietary restrictions first and then choose a meal that fits.

- **Respect the need for privacy.** If the nurse or other medical personnel arrive during your visit, offer to go out and wait in the hall.

Dealing with Dementia

A visit to a senior who is experiencing memory loss or confusion calls for some special etiquette:

- ◆ **Be very clear.** Speak clearly and check frequently for comprehension. You may need to rephrase your question or information a few times until he can understand it.

- ◆ **Be patient.** It may take a few repetitions for something to be clear. Or your senior friend might forget what you just said ten minutes before. It's not a lack of attention or caring; it may just be a symptom of his dementia.

- ◆ **Be understanding of her repetitions.** She might have told you that story yesterday, and she is likely to tell it again tomorrow. It may be the one thing she remembers and she may not remember she has already told you. The most caring thing you can do is listen to it again.

- ◆ **Bring photos.** If your elder is surrounded with pictures of family and friends, it will be easier for him to remember them.

- ◆ **Introduce yourself when you visit.** When necessary, remind the senior you are visiting who you are and how you know each other. "Hi, it's Cindy; you and I worked together at the elementary school."

- ◆ **Avoid questions that call for recollections.** "Do you know who I am?" "Do you remember where we went on your birthday?" She may not, and it can be frustrating for her.

- ◆ **Speak to the senior as an adult.** Even if you have to simplify and break a conversation down into smaller units, do *not* talk to your elder friend or relative as if he were a child or, worse yet, in baby talk. When an elder is present, don't refer to him in the third person or talk to others as if he wasn't there or can't understand.

WORKING WITH PROFESSIONAL CAREGIVERS

Whether it's a home health aide in the home, a caregiver in an assisted-living residence, or a nurse in a nursing home, pay attention to your interactions with professional caregivers. Greet them when you arrive for a visit. While you don't need to socialize, take care to acknowledge their presence cordially. Offer to share any treats—cookies, donuts, muffins—that you might bring.

If your elderly family member isn't able to show appreciation to his caregivers, it's important that you do so for him. Check with the facility or agency about their policies regarding gifts or gratuities and then respect those policies. It can put a caregiver in an uncomfortable position having to refuse or return a gift if they're not allowed to accept one.

There are other things you can do to show appreciation if the caregiver's employer has restrictions on gifts. A heartfelt verbal thank-you is always a good thing. Be specific: "Thank you so much for all you do for Dad. He appreciates the care you take when you wash his sore feet." Or send a card adding the same sentiment in a personal note. A note to the head of the facility or the caregiver's employer expressing your gratitude for a job well done is a wonderful way to show your support and appreciation.

Of course, if the senior is able to express appreciation herself, as a family member you're in a position to remind her how important her thanks really are. Sometimes dealing with new and different living situations and being confined to a residence with people from all walks of life and different backgrounds can cause stress. Grumpiness can overshadow the basics of civil interaction. It's not the caregiver's fault; it's not the resident's fault. Your encouragement to the elder to make a few gestures of appreciation can go a long way to improve relationships.

Sometimes a senior resident bosses the caregivers around, complains about care, and makes disparaging comments. Friends and family members can help change that dynamic by interacting positively with staff and reminding their elder to show the respect the caregivers deserve. Start by choosing a time when there is some privacy and the caregivers aren't present. Mention some positive attributes and in a firm but gentle way let your family elder know that it's not okay to be disrespectful. Periodically remind him to thank his caregivers.

VISITING A CARE FACILITY

It's important to build good relationships in the particular community where your senior friend or relative is living. When visiting a residence, pay attention to everyone. A cheerful "good morning" when you pass a resident sitting in the hallway or see a staff member might just make their day. If you're waiting, talk to the other residents. You might discover someone who has experiences to share and is appreciative of someone to talk to.

If a resident needs assistance, offer to get one of the caregivers. If you notice someone has dropped something out of reach, give them a hand. The many small gestures of kindness that you make have the potential to brighten someone else's day. It's this spirit of con-

sideration that can enrich an assisted-living or nursing home experience.

SENSITIVE CONVERSATIONS

Wherever they live, seniors and their families may be faced with a variety of *"What to say?"* delicate conversations, such as when a parent should give up driving. Often, these conversations require multiple approaches from several angles. Once you've broached the subject of a major change, it might take some time for it to sink in, and finding the best solution can often involve various attempts and perhaps some compromise.

It's extremely important that a senior and her family or caregiver work in tandem to address issues head-on. It's common for an adult child to feel anxious about a parent's eventual need for a change in living arrangements and care and all that may entail, but denying or ignoring the problem is far from helpful. Part of the difficulty and sensitivity of these conversations stems from the fact that an elderly parent might

- ◆ Understandably resist relinquishing his role of authority or control to his grown child.
- ◆ Be anxious about the need for an upcoming change. The fear of the unknown is not something you outgrow.

The parent-child roles reverse when the parent is no longer able to think clearly and his adult child steps in to guide him. The wise adult child in the caregiver role learns to accept this reality and offers clear advice and crucial moral support. The necessary decisions and changes are more readily made when the parent accepts the help being offered. Solutions are achievable when the adult child empathizes with his parent and works through the awkward and sensitive conversations gently and diplomatically. There are no second chances. No one is getting any younger and the conversations are likely to become more difficult further down the road.

Certain issues call for a "big conversation" between the adult child and the senior parent. Below are some typical awkward situations when the family caregiver often wonders, "What do I say when . . ."

. . . it's time to stop driving? Having a conversation with an elderly parent about the need to stop driving is one of the most difficult moments experienced by many adult children. When a parent becomes mentally or physically unable to manage the wheel, the goal is to work through his fear of giving up independence in exchange for reliance on others to take him places. You'll need to be firm and not back down because your parent gets angry. Emphasize that because you love him, his safety and the safety of others is your main concern. "Dad, it's not that you don't know how to drive a car, but when you get disoriented you may cause an accident and hurt yourself or someone else." It's often helpful to enlist the help of other family members and his physician.

. . . my parent is having difficulty with financial and administrative responsibilities? Your mother is having difficulty balancing her checkbook and can't remember what bills she's paid. Even if she has no apparent difficulty, many seniors worry about outliving their money. One way is to approach the issue from a more general concern for her overall financial picture. Let her know that you want to plan ahead with her. "Why don't you and I review your finances to see how your savings and investments are looking for the future? I'd like to help you so you won't worry." With assurance, children can help parents manage this concern.

It is also a good idea to speak with your parent about allowing you to gain access to her locks and safes, computer passwords, and home security codes. If your parent uses the Internet, make sure she is aware of scams that target seniors. Whether over the phone or the Internet, remind your parent not to share confidential information such as checking account or Social Security numbers with strangers, no matter what the "emergency."

This may be the time for your parent to give power of attorney for accessing bank and credit card accounts, insurance, and medical permissions in case of sudden incapacity. Most seniors are relieved that their adult child, someone they trust, is overseeing and perhaps even managing their financial affairs and administrative tasks. Speak with their attorney or an eldercare professional to determine the best ways to assist your parent.

. . . living arrangements aren't working? Your father is no longer able to manage daily routine tasks. He isn't eating well, his laundry piles up, he's slacked off on grooming, and you're concerned about his safety. Perhaps he has become isolated and hardly gets out. These are all signs that help is needed and it's time to step up. "Dad, I'm worried about you falling on the stairs. Have you thought about moving to the down-stairs bedroom?" A more serious conversation is the one that suggests a complete change in living arrangements, especially if it involves moving to an assisted-living facility or a nursing home.

Most people in their senior years know that a change of some sort is usually inevitable. Some look forward to a lessening of domestic responsibilities and others fear that they are losing independence and the comfort of their surroundings, routines, and possessions. Before you have this important conversation, set the stage with a series of conversations that begin to outline your parent's needs and how they may be met given the family's resources. It's a delicate balance between respecting a parent's wishes and meeting the reality of his care needs. Other professionals, such as a doctor, pastor, or social worker, can help you advise your parent as to the best course of action. But if there is a downright refusal, know that in all cases safety trumps etiquette. Your parent's health and welfare are the primary concerns.

When there's a move involved—even one that's anticipated positively—the change is likely to be traumatic, especially initially. Don't be a disappearing caregiver. Visit often to see that your parent is adjusting to his new home.

. . . visits to the doctor are stressful or confusing? Taking care of one's health can be overwhelming at any age. Seniors may experience a variety of concurrent minor or major health issues. There might be numerous doctor and lab appointments, confusing medical terms to understand, and multiple prescriptions to manage. Can you be sure he is remembering to take his medications as prescribed? Offer your parent moral support and help, whether it's reviewing medical bills and insurance claims or picking up prescriptions. Offer to join him at his next visit to his physician. It can be helpful to have an advocate or a second pair of ears. Even if he's fortunate to be relatively healthy, he'll probably welcome your interest and support.

If you do join him on medical visits, allow him to retain his privacy and dignity. The two of you, along with his doctor, can determine how you may best be of assistance.

. . . we need to discuss end-of-life wishes? Even though death is a natural part of life, the topic is uncomfortable for many people. Issues related to death are particularly tough to face when you're dealing with your own parent's mortality. However awkward, now is the time to find out about your parent's end-of-life plans—*before* she might become incapacitated.

One option is for the senior to designate a health-care proxy or agent who can make medical decisions on her behalf if she's no longer able to make them. Talk about trust! Yet, the conversation and advance plans are extremely important. Without such planning, on-the-spot decisions, often in the throes of a medical emergency, are even more difficult. When your parent has stipulated her end-of-life choice, she has spared the family from the agony of guessing what she would have wanted at the end. It would also be wise to speak with your parent about her funeral and burial preferences.

senior dating

Some widowed seniors continue through the rest of their years solo. Others find a new soul mate, whether they remarry or not. Senior romances and weddings of those in their eighties and nineties aren't unusual. Most adult children regard a new romance as a plus: Their parent is loved by a new partner. Being in a close relationship is apt to lead to happiness— and even good health.

Yet there can be concerns. Children might regard the new sweetheart as a bad fit for their parent. Maybe the adult child can't get beyond her own sadness and accept her father being happy with someone other than her mother. And there are some adult children who see a parent's new relationship as a threat: That "new woman" is just after his money.

These are all legitimate concerns and it's prudent to be cautious, but at a certain point it's your parent's decision and should be respected. In terms of etiquette we encourage you to focus on your parent's happiness and on keeping a positive relationship. "Mom, I like the man you introduced me to the other day, and I think he likes you. I want you to be happy. It would be wonderful if you start seeing each other . . . whenever you're ready, of course!" Your parent will know when and if it feels like the right time to start dating. (See also Chapter 29, "Dating," page 370.)

PEACEFUL FAMILIES: PEACE AMONG SIBLINGS

Much of etiquette is based on caring about, understanding, and communicating clearly with others. If you have siblings, make every effort to decide *together* how to care for your elderly parent. Hold regular family discussions. Siblings might not agree on the issues, and sometimes family members may even deny that their parent needs help. If disagreements arise, try to resolve them promptly and *without* allowing them to upset your parent.

Once you all have listed what needs to be accomplished, each of you can be responsible for tasks that match up with your individual strengths and availability. The sibling who's a whiz at math could take care of Dad's finances. The organizer might keep track of appointments or schedule home health aides. There's no one-size-fits-all answer for dividing up caregiving duties. The key is to be willing participants and to communicate with each other regularly and clearly.

CARE FOR THE CAREGIVER

Adult children caring for elderly parents are often referred to as the sandwich generation. Research shows that nearly 50 percent of Americans between the ages of forty-five and fifty-five have children under the age of twenty-one and are also caring for aging parents or in-laws. Caught between two demanding family scenarios, these men and women carry heavy loads. Both their children and their parents need physical, mental, and emotional attention. Often, there is little time or energy left for work, household chores, or leisure. Maybe one spouse must spend time and money to travel frequently to visit his elderly parents. His absences might lead to an unpaid leave from a job, or his family finds his absences difficult. The caregivers who take care of their children *and* their aging parents truly find themselves "sandwiched."

Q: *Our mother is selling our family home and moving into an assisted-living facility. One of my sisters thinks that she is entitled to first dibs on the furniture because she's been the one spending the most time with our mother. The rest of us don't live nearby, but do help our mom in other ways from afar. How can we convince our sister to be fair?*

A: For starters, talk to your mother to see if she has any plans. After all, it's her furniture. Perhaps she wants each of you to receive certain items, or perhaps she's planning to sell it all for extra income. If she does intend to pass them along to you and your siblings, you could propose that all of you get together with your mother and work it out. Some families take turns picking items; others try to make sure the value of the items is evenly distributed.

Whether it's a family member or paid professional, any discussion of caregiving would be incomplete without mentioning the importance of taking good care of the caregiver. There's no shortage of stressful issues: needs that can't be met, a grumpy elderly person, a senior with dementia, worry about finances, little or no time off, and more. It's vitally important to guard against burnout.

Caregivers need to make these their top priorities:

◆ Get plenty of sleep.

◆ Ask for help.

◆ Take breaks.

And others need to be sensitive to the caregiver:

◆ Offer help and support.

◆ Step in and give relief when you're able.

◆ Provide time to talk and take part in planning.

◆ Be careful not to isolate either the senior or the caregiver.

43

illness

Any etiquette surrounding a minor illness is fairly straightforward. We know to be careful not to spread anything contagious—the common cold included—and whenever we're in the company of someone who's under the weather, we offer sympathy: "Sorry to hear you've been down with the flu. I hope you're feeling better."

A more serious illness, including the recovery period after an operation, calls for a get-well card or note, flowers, or perhaps a visit. But dealing with a debilitating or terminal illness makes more demands on loved ones and friends, all of whom want to make such difficult days as comfortable for the patient as possible.

[WHEN YOU'RE THE ONE WHO IS ILL]

Until science finds that elusive cure, the one illness no one can escape is the common cold. Running a close second is influenza, or the flu.

If you're like most people, you go about your routine activities when you come down with a cold—but if that includes shopping and going to work, you're not doing the people around you any favors. Colds are contagious during the first few days of infection, and it's common sense to stay home as much as possible during that period. To lessen the risk of passing on a cold, you should wash your hands frequently, as hand contact passes the virus to anything you touch. Sneeze into a handkerchief or tissue. Think of a sneeze as an aerosol spray of infection, so if you don't have a tissue, the next best thing is to sneeze (or cough) into the inside crook of your elbow.

You'll also need to wash your hands after sneezing or nose blowing. Since children may be less attentive to hand washing, wiping their noses, or covering their mouths when they cough or sneeze, you might keep them home and out of contact with others for a longer period than you would an adult.

A case of flu generally confines you to bed for a few days, but can still spread easily. Flu is infectious for three to five days after symptoms first appear, so isolate yourself for as long as necessary.

Serious Illnesses or Major Surgery

Colds and the flu pale in comparison to an extended illness, an injury, or major surgery of any kind, be it a recovery from persistent infection, a bout with mononucleosis, a knee replacement, or something much more serious. When you'll be incapacitated for a few weeks or more, there's more to consider.

It's very likely that you'll need your own space, both literally and figuratively, during your illness or recovery. Talk with your caregiver(s) and see what can be arranged, whether it's a separate room or a designated space that's set aside for you. Explain to family members and friends that there will be times when you need to be alone and other times when you feel like being sociable. Stress that no one should be offended when you want privacy; at times, solitude can be just the right medicine.

Because the primary caregiver in your family will often deal with health-care professionals, good communication is essential to prevent conflicts or misunderstandings between you, the caregiver, and any other

a caregiver could be

your spouse ✦ your parent
another family member ✦ a friend
a paid helper ✦ a professional care provider

care providers. So there won't be mixed signals, make sure your caregiver fully understands your wishes. Write everything down, including notes on discussions with doctors, which medications and other treatments have been prescribed, and any questions you'd like to ask your doctors.

While you're laid up, other family members will need to take over your household tasks. Be flexible; no one who's helping you will ever do things exactly the way you do, whether it's choosing groceries or putting away the dishes. If you tend toward perfectionism, make a concerted effort to be both grateful and gracious. You'll have plenty of time to straighten out cupboards when you're back on your feet.

When you start to feel well again, be aware of how your transition can affect your family. Do things gradually. If you're resuming certain responsibilities that have been taken on by others, be considerate as you take back your tasks and be thankful for the efforts made by others.

ADVICE FOR CAREGIVERS

When caring for someone with a prolonged illness, it's extremely important to let that person feel as independent as possible. Everything he needs should be close at hand—a telephone, radio, television remote, reading material and a good light, and so on. If the person is confined to bed, provide a bell or some other way of calling when help is needed; shouting takes precious energy. An important note: Take care not to hover over someone who's ill. There's such a thing as being *too* solicitous.

So the patient can follow his own schedule, he should have a room or area away from where his spouse or partner sleeps. If he's having trouble sleeping at night, he'll be able to read, watch television, or do whatever he wants without disturbing someone else. A separate space also gives him a place to get away to rest during the day.

Screening phone calls for a person who is ill or recuperating is a good idea when he doesn't feel like talking. Use the answering machine or have another person in the home take messages and field calls with a prearranged line like "I'll check to see if he's awake" or "Sam's resting right now; would you like to try back around six? Thanks, and I'll tell him you called."

Debilitating Diseases

Family and friends alike may struggle for the right words when someone has been diagnosed with a debilitating or terminal disease, such as cancer, severe cardiovascular disease, or Alzheimer's. No matter how you word it, an "I'm here for you" will reassure the person of your love and support. Just listening can be therapeutic. It can give her the opportunity to express her own fears and concerns.

Acts of kindness can range from shopping to bookkeeping to tidying up. When a terminally ill person lives alone and is still ambulatory, close friends might band together to stage periodic "evenings with Jenny." The patient and friends arrange a schedule and a different friend arrives with a meal (easily available through takeout these days), ready for an evening of camaraderie. Even after the illness worsens, rotating visits could consist of sitting with your friend and talking, reading, or just holding her hand.

care for the caregiver

If the caregiving falls on one family member, a friend or relative might give her a periodic break. This respite care will allow the caregiver time for herself—perhaps to run errands, take care of personal business, or visit friends. Health-care professionals say that respite care is vitally important for the mental health and effectiveness of the caregiver and the family as a whole.

When a person's mental abilities have declined severely, as they do with Alzheimer's and other forms of dementia, it's important to understand that mood swings, verbal or physical aggression, and combativeness are completely out of the person's control. Instead of taking these behaviors personally, accept them as part of the disease and try to stay calm, patient, and flexible. Always acknowledge requests and then act on them if you can. When helping with activities (eating, taking a walk, playing cards, and so forth), minimize distractions and focus on the person's enjoyment, not on how much she can or cannot achieve.

When you arrive to visit with someone with memory loss, say who you are. She might not recognize you and be wondering who this stranger is: "Hi, Lucy, it's Maria." She may say, "Of course, I know that," even if she didn't. What really matters is that now she does know who you are and you've saved her a potentially embarrassing moment.

Don't let the tenderness you feel toward anyone with a debilitating disease lead you to treat her as a child. Speak to her as an adult, as you normally do. Be alert to her cues as to whether she can hear you or if you're speaking too fast. Give a person who is bedridden notice of what you're going to do, whether it's turning or moving her, getting her out of bed, or getting her a drink of water.

Choose Your Words Well

Sometimes even the best-intentioned words can cause discomfort or be slightly offensive to a person who is ill. Things *not* to say include:

> Q: *Through a third party, I just learned that a friend of mine has cancer. She'll be at a party I'm attending next week, and I'm not sure what to say. Or should I say nothing?*
>
> A: Because your friend will doubtless be working through the emotions of dealing with her illness, she may not be ready to discuss it with anyone just yet. So wait until she broaches the subject. If and when she does, say you're always ready to offer support and lend an ear. If her illness has become public and you know for sure that she's talking about it with others, you can take the initiative: "I just heard about your diagnosis from Linda. You know I'm here for you, so please let me know whenever I can help you in any way." You might offer a few specific ways in which you'd be able to help: "I'd be happy to pick up some groceries for you or take you to your doctor's appointment next week."

- "I know how you feel" (no one knows exactly how another person feels).

- "You're going to be fine" (this is especially inappropriate for someone who knows he is terminally ill).

- "It's not that bad" (often said to help the speaker himself feel more comfortable).

It's not up to you to play psychologist and talk someone who is ill out of feeling morose or blue. It's far better to listen to what he has to say, accept and acknowledge the situation and his feelings about it, and make empathetic statements he can react to. Some appropriate responses: "It must be tough" or "I'm so sorry you're going through this." If his chances for recovery are slim, steer clear of remarks that sound either too optimistic or pessimistic and stick to the middle ground.

If the visit is to a fellow member of your house of worship or to anyone else who's receptive to prayer, praying together is appropriate and can be a comforting way to show your support.

Professional Home Care

Professional nurses and hospice caregivers can make a wonderful difference for a seriously ill person and her family. A skilled professional nurse will not only tend to the patient's needs but also provide practical advice regarding care and bolster the morale of everyone concerned as they cope.

When nothing more can be done to save a patient in the last stages of cancer, Alzheimer's, AIDS, or other chronic diseases, hospices and hospice care agencies provide emotional support, pain relief, and, if requested, spiritual guidance. This professional help allows families to find their own way (and at their own speed) as they struggle to come to grips with the terminal illness of a loved one.

In the end stage of a terminal illness, hospice caregivers often become temporary live-ins, providing twenty-four-hour care, making their interpersonal skills and bedside manner all the more important. A good hospice caregiver is pleasant and personable but also

understands that he should let family members initiate and take the lead in conversations.

Caregivers usually develop close relationships with the people they care for, so when a patient dies, make certain you tell the caregiver how much his service meant to his patient and to you. Inform him of all funeral arrangements so that he has the opportunity to attend, if he wishes. If you think it appropriate, a small gift with a personal note will underline your appreciation. If the caregiver's agency prohibits their employees from accepting gifts, a donation to the agency would be a thoughtful alternative.

VISITING THE SICK AT HOME

When planning to visit someone who is ill at his home, always call first. *Never* arrive unannounced. Likewise, start a phone call by asking if it's a good time to talk; if the person isn't feeling well, he may not be up to it.

Unless you're visiting a close relative or friend who's indicated he would like you to linger, plan on about a half-hour visit. While you're there, it's important to be in the sick person's "zone" and let him guide the conversation. People who are ill may show less enthusiasm for the things that usually interest them or become irritable or overly excited. Such reactions are usually temporary, and changing the subject can be an effective way to restore calm.

It's very important not to patronize or speak condescendingly. Just because a person is bedridden or using a wheelchair doesn't mean his mental faculties aren't sharp. Above all, when other people are present, don't talk about the sick person as if he weren't there. Likewise, don't talk "over and around" him; the conversations should always include the person you are all there to see.

Although running errands for friends who are ill and bringing food when you visit are welcome in most cases, you should always ask before doing any favors. Patients may feel that friends and family members are going too far out of their way, and could feel guilty or overwhelmed.

HOSPITAL VISITS

Visiting someone in the hospital requires some forethought, especially when the illness is serious. Always check to see if and when the patient can have visitors. When you arrive on the floor, be courteous toward nurses and the other hospital personnel. Avoid asking for special attention from anyone who is obviously busy. (Your friend or loved one isn't the only patient on the floor.) Check with the nurse before you bring food, even if the patient has asked for it; she may be on a special diet and certain foods may be off-limits.

It's okay to take a patient's hand gently, but avoid hugging, especially if surgery was involved. Keep conversations upbeat. The news that her son is failing math or the family car was involved in a fender bender will hardly improve her mental outlook. Your job as a visitor is to cheer her up, not weigh her down with more worries. The best approach is to be yourself and take your

cues from her about what she wants to talk about. It's perfectly fine to ask someone you're close to about her illness, pain, or feelings if you feel comfortable doing so. She might actually be relieved to have an opportunity to talk about what she has been going through. She might welcome news about daily routines, such as what you and others are doing. Day-to-day happenings might actually present a great diversion from constant attention to her situation and illness.

When you've been asked to sit with the patient for a few hours, let her know that she needn't chat or entertain you. Take reading material along, attend to simple tasks or requests as needed, sit where she can see you, and let her know that you're quite happy to have an hour or two in which to quietly enjoy being with her. Assure her that you're content with your book or magazine whenever she wants some quiet time while you're there.

If relatives are present, you'll want to shorten your visit to give the family more privacy. Introduce yourself, if necessary, leave your present if you've brought one, and wish your friend a quick recovery. Then, unless you're asked to stay, say, "It was so nice to meet all of you," and make your exit.

You should also leave sooner if other visitors arrive so the patient doesn't get overtired. Trying to follow a

caring hospital visits

Whether the patient is an acquaintance or a member of your immediate family:

Do check the hospital's visiting procedures and keep your visit within the bounds. Some hospitals have flexible visiting hours; others have clearly defined ones. Some ask you to limit your visit time; others don't. Even if the policies don't specify it, do wear shirts and shoes!

Do keep any cold or contagion you have at home. Hospital patients are especially vulnerable and even using a tissue and washing your hands may not provide enough protection.

Don't wear perfume or cologne. Scents can smell stronger, even nauseating, to someone who is ill.

Don't sit on the edge of the bed, unless invited. While you may think it shows personal concern, it may cramp or cause pain for the patient.

Do position yourself within easy range for the patient to see and hear you. Try to sit or stand within roughly three feet and face her when speaking. Speak clearly and loudly enough (no shouting, though) for her to hear you. Be aware of noises, such as the TV or sounds from the hall, and offer to turn down the volume or close the door.

Don't forget who's listening. If doctors or other health professionals are in the room, don't talk to them as if the patient weren't there or refer to her in the third person.

Do keep your visit brief and cheerful, and leave the patient rested and encouraged. In most cases, make up your mind before you arrive that you'll stay no more than fifteen or twenty minutes, then stick to it.

Do be a gracious advocate for the patient, as needed. Perhaps she would like some ice water or a brief visit from the nurse. Be her "messenger" by relaying her needs on her behalf. Just be respectful and aware of the demands placed on the nursing staff, and be sure to thank them afterward for their help.

---

conversation conducted by people seated on all sides of the room can be exhausting. When two or three people are present, either stand or put your chairs on the same side of the bed.

Flowers and Other Gifts

Giving flowers sends the message that you care. Just be sure a floral arrangement is of a manageable size and comes with its own container, as vases or other suitable containers are very difficult to find in hospitals. Potted plants can be a better alternative to cut flowers because they're easy to care for, last longer, and can be taken home by a family member if the room starts to look like a flower shop.

When choosing a gift other than flowers or plants, be guided by the severity of the illness and the length of the hospital stay. Light reading matter (both in weight and content), podcasts, audiobooks (which don't have to be held and can be listened to with eyes shut), music, DVDs, and e-books are good choices for almost all patients. If the patient may be hospitalized for some time, a new robe, pajamas, or bed jacket can be a real day brightener. As for food, make sure it's allowed on the patient's diet.

While touches from home (a favorite pillowcase, framed family pictures) aren't gifts, they'll be gratefully received. For some patients, news of friends and family may be the best gift of all; a lengthy hospital stay is an isolating experience.

Semiprivate Rooms and Wards

If the hospital patient doesn't have a private room, be sure to consider the other people who will be affected by your visit. First and foremost, keep your voice low so you won't disturb other patients who may badly need their rest. If the patient is able, you could go to a communal room for your visit. In some instances, you might draw the curtains between the beds for privacy and quiet. On the other hand, if the person you're visiting and her roommate have become friendly, the roommate may enjoy being included in the conversation. At the very least, be cordial and greet the roommate and her visitors if there's an opportunity to do so.

Many hospitals now have small receivers and speakers that can be set on the patient's pillow for individualized television and radio. Even so, the volume needs to be kept low so as not to disturb a roommate in a semiprivate room.

Phoning a Hospital Patient

When calling a landline phone in the patient's room, three or four rings is long enough for the patient to reach and answer the phone, but not so excessive that it would disturb others. The cell phone actually comes in handy for helping patients receive calls in a relatively nonintrusive way. It allows them to keep the phone nearby and to manage the ring and voice mail. However you make phone calls to a hospital patient, be considerate and try to determine when phone calls would be most convenient for her, such as just before meals, when she is apt to be awake.

loss, grieving, and condolences

s they have in every culture from the beginning of time, the rituals observed after the death of a loved one or friend salve our grief. Respect for the person who died, combined with kindness, consideration, and compassion for the mourners, underlies all the rituals, words, and outward signs of mourning. It is in this context that the etiquette surrounding death and mourning becomes most meaningful. In recent years the focus of funerals and memorial services has shifted from being solely a standardized service to mourn the deceased, to one that celebrates his life, highlighting his personality, interests, and accomplishments. More and more, families decide the nature and style of their loved one's funeral or memorial service, and then take an active part in planning it. Once rare, cremation is almost as common a choice today as the traditional burial with a casket, and services are adapted for the interment or scattering of ashes. Funeral directors and clergy are willing to see that the family's wishes are fulfilled. The choices everyone will find the most meaningful—from the songs to the clothing for burial or cremation to the tone of the service itself—can provide comfort. While the style of the service and even what to wear to it may have changed in recent years, other elements have stayed the same: deciding who to notify first about the death and the particulars of the service, enlisting the participants, and offering and accepting condolences.

NOTIFYING OTHERS

As difficult as it is, informing others of the death is the first duty of the bereaved. It starts with telling family members—a job for someone who can keep her composure and break the news in person or by telephone as soon as possible and in the gentlest way. An alternative is to start a chain of calls, with the original caller asking the first person she tells to call another family member, and so on. If the funeral or memorial service arrangements have been made, share this information as well. It's helpful to make a list—prioritized if needed—so that

---

posting on a social network page

Is it okay to post the death of a family member on your social network page? Yes, with certain caveats. It is critical that a family member tell other family and close friends personally as soon as possible after the death. A few days later, or once the obituary or death notice has appeared in the newspaper or online, the news may be posted on your social network page. The reason for the delay is to avoid the hurt that might be felt by a relative or close friend who receives the news in a less personal way.

---

vides information at 800-228-6332 or www.nfda.org.) If the family has no affiliation with a place of worship, the funeral director can recommend someone to officiate or will offer funeral home staff to preside.

Newspapers. Most obituaries appear in both a newspaper's printed and online versions. A standard obituary includes the name of the deceased, date and place of death, date and place of birth, town or city of residence, and the names of immediate family and various relatives. It can be expanded to include information on the deceased's education, civilian or military career, club or organizational affiliations, and hobbies. It's also the norm to include the location of the service, where friends may call on the family, and give specifics about flowers or charitable contributions. The submission form for an obituary varies from paper to paper—so check with yours. Obituaries may be written and submitted by family members or by the funeral home. In either case, the paper will call the funeral home to verify the death. A funeral home staff member can write the obituary for you, but check first to see if they charge a fee for the service.

key family members are included: spouse, parents, children, and siblings. It is also a courtesy to inform an ex-spouse.

Others to notify include:

Funeral director and clergy. Family member(s) need to discuss and make arrangements with the funeral director or member of the clergy concerning burial versus cremation; the type of service and the date, time, and place; clothing for the deceased, open or closed casket, if there is one; eulogies, music, and how traditional or personalized they wish the service to be. (The National Funeral Directors Association pro-

It's important to check with the newspaper regarding the cost of an obituary. Most charge a per-word or a per-line fee and it can be expensive, especially if a photo is included. The online version, when it's offered, is optional, a choice for the family to make. Some papers use an online service, such as www.legacy.com. The online version of the obituary usually includes a guestbook where people can leave comments or notes of sympathy and where families can post a general thanks or updates regarding the service.

Memorials online. In recent years, the Internet has played a growing role in bereavement and death, enabling people anywhere in the world to contribute to online guestbooks, sharing their memories, and offering tributes and condolences. Websites, including www.legacy.com, www.mem.com, and www.memorialsonline.com, make it possible to celebrate a loved one's unique life story with photographs, souvenirs, mementos, awards, or anything else that captures the person's essence. In addition, the family can post thanks and updates. Be aware that some services charge a fee to download or access the memorials.

Charities and other organizations. If the family names a charity or organization to receive donations memorializing the deceased, a family member should call the organization to set the process in motion and get the necessary mail or email address for contributions. Be sure to ask to be notified of any contributions so that donors can be thanked.

MAKING ARRANGEMENTS

As hard as it may be for a family to make decisions immediately after a loved one's death, planning the services may actually help them cope with their loss. One of the first major decisions concerns burial versus cremation. If the deceased had not made her wishes known before her death, the family can enlist the help of the funeral director or clergy to make that decision.

Another decision is whether to have a memorial service, a funeral, or simply a service at the graveside or where the ashes will be interred or scattered. These core decisions drive many of the other arrangements that follow. In addition to the type of service, the family will need to decide on the location, who they will ask to participate, and if they will have visitation hours.

TYPES OF SERVICES

A Funeral Service

A funeral service is typically held in a house of worship or at the funeral home, and the casket is present during the service. The family must decide whether to have the casket opened or closed. The funeral director or clergy from the family's church can help with this decision. The family must also decide on the clothing for the deceased, and whom to ask as pallbearers.

Clothing for Burial

The deceased may have left instructions about burial clothing, but if not, the family chooses it: A suit; a uniform; a favorite, brightly colored dress; sports clothes; and even a well-worn gardening outfit are some of the choices made today.

Pallbearers

If the coffin will be carried during the funeral, the family chooses close friends, relatives, and sometimes coworkers or business associates to be pallbearers. Do take into consideration whether a person is physically up to the job before asking. Professional pallbearers provided by the funeral home could also perform the duty.

Honorary pallbearers also participate by escorting (not carrying) the coffin, though in some cases they may push it on a trolley during the processional and recessional. The family appoints the honorary pallbearers (usually no more than eight) from those who were close to the deceased. A phone call is the appropriate and simplest way to request that someone act as a pallbearer.

A Memorial Service

A memorial service—a service without the presence of the body—is designed by the family, and usually consists of verses, prayers, hymns, and a eulogy delivered by a member of the clergy and sometimes by one or a few family members or close friends. They are most often held when the family prefers to have a celebration of life rather than a funeral, following a cremation, when a funeral has taken place far from the home community, when the deceased died overseas, or when the burial will occur later in the year when the ground thaws.

A Graveside Service

Some families prefer to have the service and the burial occur at the same time in the cemetery. Many of the decisions are the same ones that families must make when they decide on a funeral or a memorial service: who will officiate, how the family will arrive and depart from the service, and how the family may actually participate. If the deceased was a veteran, the local military unit may be asked to participate. The funeral director can help the family with those arrangements.

Services for Cremations

The service preceding or following a cremation differs in some ways from that for a funeral or memorial service. Whether the family accompanies the body to the crematorium before or after the service is a matter of choice. If they do, a very short service is held there as well. Following cremation, the ashes, in a container, are later delivered to the family to be kept, interred, or scattered in accordance with the wishes of the deceased.

Many families choose to have the ashes present at a memorial service and follow it with interment in a special section of the cemetery or placement of the urn in a memorial building. In that case the officiant may incorporate the burial prayers into the memorial service, thus eliminating the need for a service at the crematorium.

A Personalized Service

Whether it's a funeral, a memorial service, or a graveside service, each ceremony can be as unique as the life it celebrates. Many people find that planning a personalized service for their deceased loved one is therapeutic. Friends find it beneficial as well because it provides a comfortable way to talk about the deceased with her family.

A personalized service can include an arrangement or display of items set up where the service is held. The tableau for an avid sportsman might include his fishing gear; for a gardener, her tools and pots of her favorite plants. Whatever the theme, photographs of the person at every stage of his life can be placed around the room where the service or reception is held.

Even cremation urns can be personalized. An engraving of a military emblem, the insignia of a fraternal organization, a symbol of a favorite activity or hobby, or anything else that reflects the deceased's interests and personality is appropriate.

IMPORTANT CONSIDERATIONS

Ushers

The family chooses the men and women who will serve as ushers, greeting attendees, handing out programs, and assisting with seating, if needed. Although funeral homes will supply personnel, it's preferable to enlist members of the extended family or close friends who will be more likely to recognize those who attend. The guests can then be seated according to the closeness of their relationship to the family. Contact those you would like to have serve as ushers early on in your planning.

Bulletins or Programs

For a funeral or memorial service, the name of the deceased and his date of birth and death are usually printed on the cover of a bulletin or program; a photo-graph is also a nice addition. The order of service and any other information relative to it, such as aspects of a religious service that may be unfamiliar to those attending, are printed inside. The bulletin may include additional information regarding the burial or interment of ashes. If it follows the service, list this information and include the address if it is at another location. If the burial is private, say so in the bulletin; otherwise it is expected that all who are at the service may also attend the burial. When the service follows the burial, list the date in the program: "Interment took place at Oaklawn Cemetery on June 14."

Reproducing the obituary or death notice on the back cover is a nice idea because some of the attend-ees may have missed seeing it in the paper. Programs can also include an invitation: "Following the service, all are invited to join the family for lunch at 142 Northwood Boulevard, Colorado Springs."

Some bulletins include a separate sheet for remem-brances, which might read, "If you have any memories of Jamie you wish to share with the family, please write them below and place in the basket at the rear exit. They will be most welcome."

Eulogists and Readers

Family members or friends may be asked to deliver a eulogy. This should be done in the early stages of plan-ning the funeral or service. Because of the personal nature of the request, ask in person or by phone if pos-sible. Limit eulogists to no more than three, since the officiant will also be speaking.

Family and friends may also be asked to be readers at the funeral or service. As with a eulogist, make the request personally and, unless the person is free to choose the reading, provide her with a copy, preferably in large type, ahead of time so that she can practice.

Honorariums

A contribution is generally given to the officiant who presides at the service. Because customs differ from place to place, rely on your funeral director or the sec-

retary at your house of worship to suggest the proper honorarium, since anything from $100 to $300 or more could be appropriate. The check is presented after the service, either by you or the funeral director. Accompanying the check with a personal note of thanks will express your appreciation all the more.

Any professional musicians who play at the service may also be due an honorarium. Consult whoever is planning the service for the appropriate amount.

when you're asked to give a eulogy

Friends are often asked to give one of the eulogies at a service, and whether to accept is a personal decision. If you decline because you're too upset, be honest with the family and explain why you don't think you can do it.

If you accept, approach the task with great sensitivity and caring for the deceased and his family. You might ask the family if there is anything they feel should be mentioned—or not mentioned. It's also fine to ask others to share their memories. Relate stories that show the deceased in a positive light, and handle any humor with care. If you like, include a poem, passage, or anything else you feel reflects your friend's life.

Remember that the subject of your eulogy is the person's best qualities, not your feelings. And the more eulogies to be delivered, the shorter yours should be—no less than two minutes but no longer than eight or ten. It's wise to have a friend read over your eulogy before you finalize it and to practice delivering it several times.

BEFORE THE SERVICE: VISITS AND VISITATIONS

Visiting customs vary from region to region. Families may choose to receive visitors at home or at a funeral home. In some areas, it's customary to visit only during the hours noted in the newspaper. In others, visitors pay their respects at any time during the funeral home's visiting hours. The visit needn't last more than a few minutes, but it's important to sign any guest register—legibly—so that the family will know you were present. An official visitation (also called a wake or calling hours) is when family members are present to receive visitors and to accept expressions of sympathy. The hours should be included in the death notice in the newspaper.

If the casket will be open at the funeral, it will also

be open at the funeral home. Generally, visitors pass by the coffin before making their way to the family members and offering sympathy. If a kneeling bench is placed beside the coffin the visitor may kneel and say a prayer, although he could simply stand in front of it for a moment instead. Anyone who feels uncomfortable viewing the body may bypass the coffin and go directly to greet the family. It goes without saying that phones should be silenced during the time of the visitation and no photos taken unless with the express permission of the family.

Greet as many family members as you can. It's a kindness to introduce yourself and include your relationship to the deceased: "Hello, I'm Anna Soren. I worked with Victor at the bank." While acquaintances and casual friends can simply say, "I'm so sorry" or "He was a wonderful person," closer friends may offer a more personal message: "We're going to miss Victor so much" and offer to help in some way. Refrain from asking about the details of the illness or death. If a family member brings up the subject, offer as much comfort as you can as you talk about the deceased's last days. Being a good listener can be a great comfort to family members who may wish to talk about their loved one.

As soon as you've expressed your sympathy to each member of the family and spoken for a moment or two with those you know well, how much longer you stay is your choice.

Signing the Guest Register

The guest register at the funeral home or visitation, usually placed by the door, tells the family who stopped by to pay their respects. Visitors should sign it using their full name, including any title: "Dr. and Mrs. Michael Grizzardi" or "Ms. Deborah Hall." Full names and titles are a favor to anyone who might write a note acknowledging the visit. This isn't the time to hastily scribble your usual signature; take the time to write legibly so family

---

what and what not to say

Apprehension often accompanies a conversation with the bereaved because you're not sure what to say. The following suggestions will help ease your mind:

DON'T SAY . . .	SAY INSTEAD . . .
"He's in a better place."	"I'm so sorry for your loss."
"Call me if there's anything I can do."	"May I bring you dinner tomorrow night?"
"It's God's will."	"She was an extraordinary person."
"I know how you feel."	"Please know that I am thinking of you."
"Now you're the man of the house."	"Your father was an example for us all."

members aren't trying to decode the scrawl. If no family member is present and you haven't been able to express your sympathy in person, your visit alone can properly take the place of a sympathy note, although a note is always welcome, especially if you knew the person well.

⎧ AT THE SERVICE ⎫

If ever there were a place for decorum to be maintained, it is at a funeral, memorial, or graveside service. A processional accompanied by a Dixieland band may be a time to joyfully celebrate the life of the deceased, but the service itself requires a respectful presence.

It's simple: Silence your phone and other electronic devices. Sit quietly, and don't get up during the service. The exception is when you have a cough that won't stop or you have to quiet a crying or unruly child; in both cases, quickly go to the vestibule or lobby. If a eulogy or tribute to the deceased is sprinkled with humor, it's fine to laugh, though not raucously.

Clothing

Because the nature of funerals and memorial services varies so widely today, attire isn't limited to just black or dark gray. The exception may be when you're a pallbearer or honorary pallbearer, in which case a dark suit is the usual attire unless the family requests something else. Remember, though, that it is a serious occasion and your clothing should reflect that, especially if you are participating in the service. At the very least it should be clean, neat, and pressed as for any other important occasion.

Arriving

When attending a service, be on time and enter the house of worship or location where the funeral will be held as quietly as possible. If there are no ushers, remember that the seats closer to the front should be taken by very close friends, with acquaintances seating themselves in the middle or toward the rear.

If you arrive late, enter a row from a side aisle, not the center aisle. If a processional has begun, wait outside instead of trying to squeeze past those who are a part of the cortege and are waiting to walk down the aisle.

Processionals

At some funerals, the coffin is brought in as part of a processional. The officiant and the choir (if any) lead the funeral procession. Directly after come the honorary pallbearers, two by two, preceding the coffin, brought by assistants from the funeral home, or the pallbearers carry the coffin. Unless they have chosen to be seated beforehand, the family comes next, chief mourner(s) first, walking with whomever he or she chooses. Close friends may follow, completing the procession. The family and pallbearers occupy the front rows, with friends filling vacant places on either side. The service begins when everyone is seated.

At memorial services and at a funeral where the coffin or urn is already present, there is no processional. In these cases, the service starts after the family and officiant enter, usually from a front or side door.

> Q: *At a funeral I recently attended, I was startled to see several women wearing brightly colored dresses. I've always thought you were supposed to wear black or another somber color to funerals. Were they out of line?*
>
> A: While you'll never go wrong with black or subdued colors, bright colors are considered appropriate today as long as the clothing is in good taste. This change is in line with thinking of the funeral as a celebration of the deceased's life. We know of a woman who wore a red dress to her best friend's funeral because it was her friend's favorite color. Women might wear pants and turtlenecks if any part of the service is outside in the colder months. It simply boils down to being respectful. When in doubt, it's safe to dress conservatively and use color as an accent.

Children

Children should be encouraged to attend the ceremonies surrounding the death of a family member or close friend to whatever degree they find comfortable. Those exposed to the rituals learn that death is a natural part of life and that rites are observed when someone dies.

Always consider a child's age before taking her to a funeral, memorial service, or prolonged visitation. Because very young children can become restless or have trouble staying quiet, you might choose to have them stay home with a sitter, or bring a sitter who can take them home if needed.

Older children should sit with their family, closest to whoever can give them the most comfort. The children should wear clothing that's age appropriate and similar in style to that worn by adult family members. Generally, children do not wear black.

Recessionals

A recessional ends the service, whether a processional took place or not. As a rule, the officiant leads the honorary pallbearers, followed by the coffin (carried or guided by the pallbearers), and then members of the immediate family. At a memorial service the officiant leads the family out through the same door they entered. The immediate family leaves first, followed by the other relatives.

It's common practice for one or more of the relatives to stop at the back of the church or outside to briefly thank those who have attended the service, with perhaps a special word to close friends.

If the deceased is to be buried following the service, the site of the interment will be announced. Unless the grave site is on the place of worship's grounds, a processional of cars will form to drive to the cemetery. Everyone attending is welcome to follow the family to the graveside service unless the burial is private—that is, attended by immediate family only—but no one is obliged to attend. As the casket is lifted into the hearse, the family enters cars or limousines waiting immediately behind. The after-service protocol for a cremation or mausoleum interment is the same as that for a burial.

The coffin is usually placed graveside at the cemetery, with flowers that were sent to the funeral home or house of worship placed around it. The officiant says the prayers common to the rite of burial, and a eulogy may be given as well. At the end of the service, no cortege is formed, so attendees leave as they wish.

YOUR ROLE AS A FRIEND

Don't feel that getting in touch with someone who's just lost a loved one is an intrusion. It's the support of friends and acquaintances that helps ease the pain of the bereaved. Give them your condolences and offer specific ways in which you might help, such as assisting with meals, child care, notifications, or answering the phone.

If you are a very close friend of the deceased or someone in his family, you could pay a visit. Just be sure to ask permission beforehand, since some people prefer to be with family members only in the first days after the death.

FLOWERS AND CONTRIBUTIONS

With their beauty, color, and scent, flowers serve as grace notes during the mourning period, whether at the visitation, the funeral service, the graveside, or the home of the bereaved. While roses, lilies, carnations,

when the family has been split

The protocol for a survivor who was divorced from the deceased is fairly straightforward:

- If cordial relations have been maintained with the family, the former wife or husband attends the funeral or memorial service but doesn't sit with the family, unless invited. When the surviving former spouse shares or has custody of the children, it is gracious to invite him or her to sit with the family.

- If the deceased had sole custody of the children, the ex-spouse should ask the family, or the older children, whether it would be comforting or disruptive if he or she attends, and then do as they wish.

- If there was ill feeling between the ex-spouse and the deceased, the ex usually doesn't attend the service, unless invited by the family. Regardless, it would be thoughtful to write a sympathy note to an immediate family member.

In an age when more and more families are "blended," funeral directors and clergy members are equipped to answer questions you might have, so don't hesitate to ask for help with any problems that arise. (See also "The Death of a Former Spouse," page 518.)

and other traditional choices have never gone out of style, arrangements that are more personalized or colorful are increasingly common. The family usually provides flowers for the altar or dais, where other gifts of flowers may be displayed as well.

The etiquette considerations of sending flowers largely involve who sends what:

Floral baskets and living plants. Friends, coworkers, and relatives may choose to send flowers. Flowers can be sent to the bereaved's home, workplace, or to the funeral home.

Floral wreaths, crosses, and sprays. These are often sent by a group. They are also a good choice for companies or associations that want to honor the deceased. They may be displayed at the funeral home, or on the altar or dais at the service.

Floral tributes. Good friends or family members often choose to send this type of arrangement to the location where the service will be held. Sometimes floral tributes are personalized designs based on the deceased's occupation, clubs, hobbies, or even his personality.

Casket arrangements. Family members—siblings, children, or grandchildren of the deceased—may supply lid sprays for the coffin. Smaller arrangements, also provided by the family, can be placed inside the casket by the funeral director.

There are no rules for timing the delivery of flowers, but it's good to get them to the bereaved as soon as possible—either at home, to the house of worship, or to the funeral home in time for the visitation or funeral. However, some close friends send flowers to the home over the course of a few months as a reminder of their love and concern.

A group of people may pool their resources for an arrangement. If the list of names on the enclosure card is long, the senders can be identified as a group: "The Murchison Family," "The Sixth Street Book Club," or "The Copyediting Department, Sun-Light Publishing." Later, a card can be signed by the individuals who chipped in and then be sent to the bereaved.

It's necessary to record the receipt of flowers so that the givers can be thanked. Someone at the funeral home or house of worship should make a record of any flowers sent there, while a family member or close friend can keep track of flowers sent to the home of the bereaved or elsewhere.

"In Lieu of Flowers"

When the notations "in lieu of flowers" or "contributions to . . . would be appreciated" appear in an obituary, you can send both flowers and a charitable contribution. If you wish to send only one expression of sympathy, however, follow the family's wishes and choose the contribution:

◆ Consider giving at least what you would have spent on a flower arrangement.

◆ When you make a donation include a note saying whom it memorializes. Also add it on the notation line of the check itself: "In memory of Rowan McGuire." Include your address in the note so the organization and the family will know where to send an acknowledgment. You may want to confirm with the charity that they will notify the family of your donation.

- If you do as the notice advises and send a contribution to "your favorite charity," choose one that might mean something to the family as well. Include the deceased family's address so the charity will know where to send an acknowledgment.

- Ordinarily, cash isn't sent to the family in place of flowers or a charitable contribution, but exceptions can be made. For example, if the bereaved person is having financial difficulties, a group (fellow employees, club or lodge members, neighbors) might take up a collection or set up a scholarship fund for the deceased's children.

If you want to be sure that the bereaved knows of your contribution, it's fine to mention it in person or in your sympathy note: "We've remembered Maria with a contribution to The Benevolent Society."

AFTER THE FUNERAL OR MEMORIAL SERVICE

A luncheon or reception is often held after the service, either at the house of worship, a club or hall, or at the home of the deceased or a relative. If it's held at the home of the immediate family, other relatives and friends usually provide the food.

The spirit of these gatherings ranges from solemn to exuberant and celebratory. It's up to the family to decide the tone for the event; whatever would most please their loved one and give the family the most comfort are the determining factors.

RELIGIOUS CUSTOMS

Different religions take different approaches to funeral services, and customs vary not only from denomination to denomination but from region to region. Anyone who is attending a funeral for someone of another faith—whether it's Islam or Buddhist, Unitarian or Baha'i—should ask knowledgeable friends or the funeral director to give them a general idea of what to expect.

Christian Funerals

While the funeral services of each Christian denomination and even each church may be unique, there are common features, which include prayers, readings from scripture, a eulogy or message from the priest or minister, as well as eulogies from friends or family. The services can last from fifteen minutes to over an hour.

Catholic funerals are almost always held at a church, not at a funeral home, and may include a Mass and communion. Non-Catholics would not receive communion. Protestant funeral services can be held at a church, a funeral home, the graveside, or at another location.

Music is an important part of many Christian services although it's not essential. The family may ask the local organist, the choir, a soloist, or professional musicians to be a part of the service.

Jewish Funerals

Jewish funerals generally take place early in the day in the funeral home, rarely in a synagogue. They're also held as close to death as possible (ideally within twenty-four hours), since embalming the body is forbidden and prompt burial is considered a mark of respect. However, exceptions are made when close family need time to travel.

At Orthodox and some Conservative services, no flowers are placed on or around the casket or in the room. Instead of ordering flowers, friends and relatives make a donation to a charity in the name of the deceased. Reform congregations, however, permit flowers. (If you're unsure whether flowers are permitted and the newspaper notice doesn't specify, call the synagogue or funeral home for guidance.) At Orthodox and Conservative Jewish funerals the coffin is closed so there is never a viewing of the body. The Reform ritual sometimes permits viewing.

In all congregations, the service includes a reading of Psalms by the rabbi, a eulogy by the rabbi or a close friend or relative, and the recitation of the memorial prayer. After this prayer, the family leaves the funeral home first, directly behind the coffin as it is carried to the hearse for the burial service. Usually, only close friends go with the family to the cemetery.

At the graveside, the first memorial prayer, or *kaddish*, is recited. Male mourners drop a handful of earth into the grave, followed by all other men (and women, if it is the family's wish) who wish to participate. It is customary to stay at the site until the coffin is covered.

For seven days following a Jewish burial, mourners follow the custom of sitting *shivah* (Hebrew for "seven"). The period begins the moment the family returns home from the cemetery. Friends will have set out food and drink, and the memorial candle, which will burn for seven days, is lit. Only close relatives sit *shivah* for the first three days, with friends making condolence calls in the days thereafter, except on the Sabbath. Visits usually last for a half hour or so. Most people pay calls in the afternoon or evening or on the Sunday of the week of the death, although regular meal hours should be avoided. Mourners usually sit on a low stool, but friends paying a condolence aren't expected to do so. Mourners will wear black and pin a scrap of cloth on their clothes to show that they are in mourning. Some cover mirrors as well.

Usually, religious services called a *minyan* and that last from ten to twenty minutes are held twice a day (morning and evening) and might occur when friends are visiting. Ten people are required for these services. Non-Jewish visitors should stand when others stand during the service. In Conservative and Orthodox traditions, mourners say *kaddish* for a whole year after the death. Specific prayers are listed for people who lost a parent, sibling, or a child.

When calling on an Orthodox household, one should knock and enter, not ring the doorbell. The door is usually left unlocked so that no one needs to attend it. It is appropriate to bring a meal if visiting someone who is sitting *shivah*.

Islamic Funerals

Although the funeral and burial practices of American Muslims vary from culture to culture, locale to locale, and even mosque to mosque, some Islamic traditions hold fast. First, Islamic burials should take place within twenty-four hours of the death if at all possible. Second, in preparation for the burial the eyes are closed, and the body is ritually washed (*ghusl*), males by a male relative and females by a female one, and wrapped in a simple white shroud (*kafan*). While in Muslim countries the body is always prepared at home or at a mosque, in the United States the preparation must take place at a hospital, funeral home, or some other site that meets health department codes.

To Muslims, saying the funeral prayers (*Salaat ul Janaazah*) is considered a community obligation. Led by an imam, the funeral prayers are recited by family and members of the community, preferably outside the mosque. In some cultures and mosques, only men attend the service.

Muslims are never cremated and are traditionally buried without a coffin. However, in the United States, cemetery codes require the body to be placed in one. The deceased is placed in the grave or coffin lying on his right side. Because ostentation of any kind is discouraged, a plain pine casket is preferred. The coffin bearing the deceased is driven to the cemetery, after which mourners take turns reverently carrying it to the grave site. After the coffin is lowered and positioned so that the face of the deceased is toward Makkah (Mecca), members of the family shovel earth into the grave; they then recite a verse from the Qur'an (Koran). Graves are not adorned with headstones or flowers.

Three days is the generally prescribed mourning period. While a time of sadness for family and friends, it is also a time of reflection. Weeping is permitted, but other overt displays of emotion are frowned upon. Condolences may be offered anytime following a death, but the focus should not be on loss, but on the unimportance of this life and the gracious acceptance of the will of Allah.

Non-Muslim friends of the deceased are welcome to attend the funeral. They should dress conservatively, stand still when the funeral prayers and verses from the Qur'an are recited, and keep their emotions under control. Sending flowers to the bereaved is not a part of Muslim tradition, but they will be respectfully received. However, most Muslims would prefer that a donation be made to a humanitarian cause.

THE DAYS AND WEEKS AFTER

How long should close relatives of the deceased wait before resuming an active social life? The answer is up to the individual. Some people deal with grief by plunging into their regular activities, while others spend time with close friends but otherwise keep to themselves as they adjust to their loss. Some follow mourning rituals prescribed by their religion or cultural tradition.

Widowers or widows may start to date when they feel ready, but it is considerate to take into account the feelings of in-laws, children, and others close to them. One year was generally considered the appropriate "waiting period" before remarrying, but if a couple believes they are ready, then there is no reason not to marry sooner.

Observant Jews restrict work, social, and recreational activities after the burial of a close relative—most assiduously during *shivah*, the first seven (or, for many

Reform Jews, three) days of the monthlong mourning period. During this time, they generally remain at home and receive condolence calls. The restrictions are significantly relaxed during the next twenty-three days, but some remain in effect even then—and a few until a year after burial. If you want to extend a social invitation to a Jewish mourner or express your sympathy in person, it's best to ask for guidance from one of her relatives or close friends or, after the first week of bereavement, the mourner herself.

Children

Many people are uncertain about whether children who have lost a parent should participate in their usual activities. The answer is yes, as much as they wish. Older children, however, may not feel up to going to purely social events for a period of time after the death of a parent.

Offering Condolences as Time Goes By

Be understanding of the changes a friend is going through in the weeks and months after the loss of a loved one. Don't take it personally if she seems moody or doesn't return phone calls right away. Do stay in touch.

Friends and relatives of the deceased often wonder whether they should make a gesture to one or more of the survivors on the first anniversary of the death. It's never wrong to show that you care about someone who has suffered a loss, but each person grieves differently. Let the person's state of mind and personality be your guide, judging whether a condolence would comfort or only serve as a sad reminder. In most cases, a card or handwritten note, a home-cooked meal, an offer to spend some time together, or a telephone call would be very much appreciated.

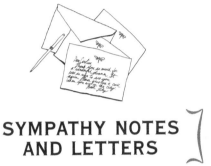

SYMPATHY NOTES AND LETTERS

Because condolence notes and letters are too personal to follow a set form, one simple rule should guide you: Say what you truly feel. A single sincere line expressing the genuine feeling you had for the deceased is all you need to write. If you have a specific memory about the deceased to include in your note, it will be a welcome addition, but this is completely optional.

As you write, don't dwell on the details of an illness or the manner of death. Nor should you suggest that the loss is a "blessing in disguise." It is appropriate to ask if there is something you can do to help, even suggesting something specific, such as "Please let me know if I can help by babysitting."

The following is an example of a short sympathy note:

Dear Vanessa,

Ken and I were so very sad to hear of Robert's death. He always greeted us with kind words and had a wonderful way of making us feel special. If we can help by shopping, running errands, or doing anything else for you, please do call on us. In the meantime, you are in our thoughts and prayers.

With deepest sympathy,

Carolyn

Whom to Address

When you send condolences in writing, it's sometimes hard to know to whom you should address your note. Some guidelines:

- If you knew the deceased well, but not the family, address the note to the closest relative—usually the widow, the widower, or the oldest child. You can also add "and family" if you wish.

- If you didn't know the deceased but do know one of the relatives, write to that person.

- If it's a friend whose parent has died, write to the friend.

- Address letters to children who have lost a parent on separate lines: Miss (Ms.) Renée Wynn (the daughter), with Mr. Charles Wynn (the son) underneath. The salutation reads "Dear Renée and Charles."

Emailing Condolences

If you're certain that a bereaved friend uses email fairly frequently, you can precede a phone call or written condolence with an email—an immediate and nonintrusive way to show him that you are thinking of him. Follow an emailed message with a handwritten note and, whenever possible, attendance at the funeral or visitation.

Online Condolences

Many newspapers and funeral homes offer the opportunity on their websites for people to post sympathy or condolence messages. The postings can be extensive and some families receive pages of emailed condolences. The family may respond with one note that can be published on the website thanking the senders for their support. It's not necessary to send individual responses to each comment that is posted, but do send a note to anyone who follows up with a handwritten note.

timing for sending condolences

Under most circumstances, a note or letter of condolence is sent within a week or so after learning of the death. But that doesn't prohibit you from writing weeks or even a few months later.

If you put off the note because you felt you couldn't find the right words, your sentiments will be welcome anytime. In a handwritten note, just say you've held the family in your thoughts and prayers and will continue to think of them.

Acknowledging Expressions of Sympathy

Handwritten condolence notes, flowers, Mass cards, contributions to charities, and acts of kindness should always be acknowledged (by the recipient, if possible). The exception is when the writer asks that her note not be acknowledged—a thoughtful thing to do when writing a close friend or when someone you know well will receive a great number of condolences. Preprinted cards with no personal message, emailed notes of condolence, online sympathy notes, and visits to the funeral home or the service don't need to be acknowledged in writing. Letters of thanks are customarily written to pallbearers, honorary pallbearers, ushers, eulogists, and readers.

If the list of acknowledgments is so long that the recipient isn't up to the task, a family member or a close friend may write for him or her: "Mom asks me to thank you for your beautiful flowers and kind message of sympathy."

Following is a sample response:

Dear Paige and Will:

On behalf of my family, I want to thank you for your expression of sympathy after the death of my sister, Louise. The beautiful floral wreath meant all the more to us because it came from lifelong friends.

Sincerely,

Fred

A personal message on a note card is preferable to any printed card, and it takes only a moment to write "Thank you for your beautiful flowers" or "Thank you for your note. Your kind words have been a comfort." If you use the printed acknowledgments given to you by the funeral director, add a personal message. When the list of condolences is long, these printed cards can serve as an intermediary thanks until more personal acknowledgment notes can be written.

PART VIII
weddings

CHAPTER 45 The Engagement 559

CHAPTER 46 Trends and Traditions 567

CHAPTER 47 Planning Your Wedding 572

CHAPTER 48 Wedding Invitations
and Announcements 597

CHAPTER 49 Wedding Attire 613

CHAPTER 50 Wedding Registries, Gifts,
and Thank-yous 624

CHAPTER 51 The Big Day 634

CHAPTER 52 Remarriage 654

CHAPTER 53 A Guide for Wedding Guests 662

45 the engagement

n engagement may last only a few days or weeks, or extend over several years. While the average period is about fourteen months, however long the engagement, it's always a busy, exciting time.

You might want to marry at a specific time of year or on a certain date. If you have a special location in mind, you may need to reserve wedding and reception sites as much as a year to eighteen months in advance. Religious requirements can also factor into the equation. And sometimes an engagement is shortened or prolonged by outside circumstances such as school, military service, or work commitments.

This exciting time also includes being attentive to the feelings and needs of the *other* key people in your life. There's much to do and many decisions to be made. Just remember to take some time off from planning your wedding to enjoy each other and the other people in your life.

TELLING FAMILY AND FRIENDS

Before informing the world of your engagement, consider the people closest to you. Usually, people know when romance is in the air and marriage is a possibility, but family and good friends deserve your special attention, and there is a thoughtful order to the telling.

Children. If one or both of you have children, be sure to tell them before anyone else. This is critically important for children and teens—as well as for adult children—whose lives will be dramatically changed by the addition of a stepparent and perhaps stepsiblings. (See Chapter 41, "Separation and Divorce," page 511, and Chapter 52, "Remarriage," page 654.) Your children

may be thrilled, but they're just as likely to be doubtful, reluctant, and even frightened or resentful. It takes love, honesty, and patience to transform individuals into a family, so respect every child's need to question your decision and seek your reassurance. Your ex-spouse should also be told, especially if there are children from that marriage. Even if you did not have children but are on friendly terms, it's kind to inform your ex.

Parents. After children, parents deserve priority. Couples can inform their own parents or speak as a couple with each set of parents. If your parents don't know your fiancé(e), it's your responsibility to introduce them. If parents live at a distance, you can make introductions by phone, but also plan to visit as soon as you can. Nothing is better than getting together in person.

In the event that the engagement will be a total surprise, the couple should be considerate of his or her own parents and talk privately with them first. This allows parents to ask questions that they may be hesitant to ask with their future son- or daughter-in-law present.

In the past, the suitor spoke first with the father of the young woman in order to declare his intentions and obtain the father's consent before proposing. Although this tradition is obsolete, it's still a sign of respect for a prospective spouse to meet with future in-laws and discuss career and life plans. This conversation might take place before the engagement, when the couple tells parents of their engagement, or soon thereafter—whenever seems most appropriate.

When parents are separated or divorced, the news is conveyed to each—in person if possible or by the most convenient means. Even if a parent and child are estranged, it's more considerate for the parent to hear the news directly instead of from others.

Engaged couples should think carefully about their family structures and have realistic expectations. In the best of all worlds, everyone will receive the news of the engagement with joy, but don't expect your upcoming wedding to heal old wounds caused by divorces, remarriages, and other complicated family arrangements.

Close family and friends. When and how you spread the word is up to you, so long as you're sensitive to people's feelings and thoughtful of what's going on in their lives.

Be careful not to make promises before you've planned your wedding. For example, some couples find themselves with a much larger wedding party than they wanted because in the euphoria of becoming engaged, they ask too many people to be bridesmaids and groomsmen. Or they risk hurting the feelings of people they care about by having to rescind such invitations. The same can occur if you initially invite more people to your wedding than you ultimately want to have on your guest list. Be forewarned: Stop and think before inviting.

Colleagues and coworkers. You may want to inform a boss or supervisor first as a matter of courtesy. The easiest way to spread the news among the people you work with is to tell one or two people and ask them to tell others. At some point, meet with the person in charge of employee compensation and make the necessary alterations in benefit, insurance, and pension plans effective following your wedding date.

If parents or children disapprove. When parents or children disapprove, it's natural to feel hurt, sadness, or disappointment. Many parents have some initial anxiety because they worry whether their child is making the right decision. That anxiety usually disappears once wedding plans are under way and they get to know their son or daughter's fiancé(e). But if the tension increases or a parent clearly voices objections, then the problem must be addressed openly.

- First and foremost, *stay calm* and approach any discussion as adult to adult.
- Second, be willing to listen to parental concerns and to take them seriously. Address those concerns as best you can.
- Third, try to remember that your happiness is important to your parents, and don't let minor disagreements get out of hand.

If you can't overcome their objections and still decide to marry, don't sever family ties. Make sure they know when and where the wedding will be and how much it would mean to you to have them there.

When children disapprove, especially adult children, family relationships can become quite strained. If time and communication can't bridge the gap, or basic civility and politeness have been abandoned, then professional counseling should be initiated to help the entire family understand one another's feelings.

] THE FAMILIES MEET [

A wedding isn't just the joining together of two people, it's also the joining together of two families—and sometimes more in the case of remarriages.

Traditionally, the parents of the groom contact the bride's parents soon after they've all learned of the engagement. But nowadays, it really doesn't matter who makes the first move, though the bride's parents might want to wait a few days to give the groom's family a chance to honor the custom. If they don't, the bride's parents should make the contact. A phone call is generally the easiest way, but either a handwritten note or an email would suffice, too. The key is that the parents get in touch with each other in the spirit of friendship. Ideally, they can plan to meet in person, along with the newly engaged couple, to celebrate the news. If it's impossible for the parents to get together at this point, a meeting over the phone or a video chat is a good second best.

The bride and groom are best positioned to know when a meeting will be convenient for everyone and what kind of gathering is most likely to help put everyone at ease. Who actually hosts the occasion is a matter of preference more than tradition. A casual event, such as a barbecue or informal supper, is often most comfortable. But if one set of parents has a more formal lifestyle than the other, a good compromise might be a dinner or weekend brunch at a good, midrange restaurant.

When parents are divorced and when there are stepfamilies to consider, a couple will often plan several separate get-togethers so that everyone involved has a chance to meet.

Q: *My partner and I wish to marry. What's the best way to plan and tell others of our decision?*

A: Each situation is personal and unique—so let your knowledge of the people involved guide you. Reactions may range from delight to outright rejection. Be patient and give those who have a negative reaction time to assimilate the news.

As with any engagement, a partner's children should be told before the couple's parents. Still, some gay and lesbian couples prefer to tell their supportive friends even before parents or children. Receiving their positive, joyful reaction can be a morale booster prior to potentially difficult family discussions.

Not all negative reactions are based on prejudice. As with concerns regarding a heterosexual engagement, your friend or relative may have the traditional doubts about your choice of partner and future together: Is he right for you? Will you be financially stable? Do you have to move far away? Take the time to listen carefully.

THE ENGAGEMENT RING

A new sparkler on a woman's left hand can be the only clue needed for people to realize a wedding is in her future. An engagement ring, however, isn't essential for you to be officially engaged, and many couples choose to put the money toward other purposes. Some couples postpone purchasing an engagement ring until later in the marriage when they can afford it (a romantic way to celebrate a special wedding anniversary). Some women simply don't like to wear rings. Or another type of jewelry might be substituted. The only true rule is that an engagement ring isn't worn until the divorces for either of the couple are finalized.

Engagement rings can be new or antique, bought from the showcase or custom designed. Rings may be passed down in a family, and heirloom stones might be reset in a more contemporary style. Traditionally, the man selects and purchases the ring on his own, but today's couples often make this decision together and may even share the cost.

If you select a diamond or other precious gem, the wisest course is to do your homework before you purchase. Online research or working with a reputable and knowledgeable jeweler, preferably certified by the American Gem Society, is recommended. If possible, do some comparison shopping.

wearing the ring

Most American women follow the centuries-old European style of wearing engagement and wedding rings on the third finger (next to the pinky) of the left hand. According to the ancient Greeks, this finger contained the "love vein," which ran directly to the heart. Since cultural and religious practices vary, however, there's no single correct way to wear an engagement ring.

must she wear the family heirloom ring?

No. If the bride is uncomfortable accepting the family heirloom, she may decline graciously. "John, your grandmother's ring is beautiful, but I'm not sure that it fits my style. I'd love to look into what our options could be." Whether resetting the ring is an option is something the groom should speak to his parents about.

Turning down the ring is especially awkward if it's the groom's family making the offer. While they may be focused on honoring a family tradition by passing along an engagement ring, they may be putting the bride in an awkward position. If she refuses, she may seem ungrateful; if she accepts, she may feel resentful.

It's best if parents make the offer to their son *before* the rings are chosen. They should also let him know that they understand completely if the couple chooses a different ring or creates a new setting.

AN ENGAGEMENT PARTY

An engagement is definitely something to celebrate, and a party may be the perfect way for family and friends to toast the future bride and groom. Modern engagement parties may be as formal or informal as you like—and are by no means mandatory.

Hosts. Although the bride's parents usually host any engagement party, another family member, friend, or group of friends may do so. When the couple's families live in different parts of the country, the parents of the bride and groom each might host parties in their hometowns—an alternative to the more traditional posthoneymoon party given by the groom's family to honor their new daughter-in-law.

What kind of party? Cocktail parties and dinners are popular, but there's no standard party format. From a casual brunch to a formal reception, there are many possibilities. Sometimes, engagements are announced at surprise parties. Whatever suits the hosts, the couple, and the guests is just fine.

Guests. Generally the guest list is limited to the couple's relatives and good friends. It can be as short or long as you want. However, it's taboo to invite someone to an engagement party who will not be on the wedding guest list.

Q: *I've attended a number of engagement parties, and I still can't figure out the etiquette of gifts. Some people bring presents, others don't. Do I need to bring a gift to an engagement party?*

A: It depends. In the past, engagement gifts were not obligatory or expected and this is usually still the case. However, in many parts of the country, bringing a gift to an engagement party has become the norm. Gift instructions aren't included on invitations, so if you're not sure, it's fine to call the hosts and ask. Couples who are conscious of taxing their friends' budgets will have told their hosts that they prefer "no gifts."

Ultimately, your decision whether or not to give an engagement gift depends on local custom, your relationship to the couple, and your budget. Often close friends and family members do give a gift.

An engagement gift is really a good-hearted gesture of affection, and it needn't be expensive or elaborate. Simple things such as a cookbook or good bottle of wine—intended to help the couple establish a collection—make great engagement gifts.

Invitations. Written or printed invitations are normally sent, but for a small intimate gathering, phoned or emailed invitations are acceptable also.

The announcement. Whether the news will be a surprise or is already known among the guests, traditionally the host, often the bride's father, makes the official announcement and leads a toast to the couple. At a large party with guests who already know about the engagement, the couple and their parents might compose an informal receiving line to welcome guests and make introductions. A word to the wise: When the engagement news is intended as a surprise for party guests, be sure to coordinate with any publication that will be running an announcement.

Gifts and thanks. If all the guests don't bring gifts, the gifts are set aside and opened afterward. If gifts are given by *everyone*, the couple can open them at the party (if there's time) and express their appreciation personally. Follow-up thank-you notes are necessary, regardless of whether gifts were opened and the givers were thanked at the party.

NEWSPAPER OR FACEBOOK ENGAGEMENT ANNOUNCEMENTS

Most newspapers provide information forms for couples to complete online. Announcements are generally brief and follow a set format. If you choose to announce your engagement on Facebook, hold off until you've told family and close friends personally.

WHEN THE ENGAGEMENT DOESN'T WORK OUT

One of the underlying purposes of a period of engagement is to give a couple time to test their commitment, and not every engagement ends in marriage. When an engagement is broken, it can be a time of great sadness, confusion, and all too often, ill will. But whatever the feelings of the people involved, they shouldn't be embarrassed about taking a difficult step that prevents future and even greater unhappiness.

There are important dos and don'ts associated with a breakup—some grounded in respect and consideration for others and a few practical matters, too.

Do tell close family as soon and as tactfully as possible. Your children and your parents should be the first to know. When children are involved, particularly if they have developed a good relationship with the person you were engaged to, they can feel an intense loss. Explain the breakup as best you can without demeaning the other person.

Don't expect family and friends to choose sides. A broken engagement shouldn't be a declaration of war by either party. Some people will instantly rally around you, but many don't want to be drawn into your very personal decision, no matter how sympathetic they feel.

Do inform everyone involved in the wedding as soon as you can. A family member or friend may be able to help you out by getting in touch with people who have been contracted for services (caterers and the like), but you should personally speak with the officiant, attendants, and others who agreed to participate in the planned wedding. Remember to contact anyone who has planned a social event in your honor.

Do return all engagement, wedding, and shower gifts, including monetary gifts. Return gifts as soon as possible. This is generally the woman's responsibility since gifts are traditionally sent to the bride-to-be, but there's no reason why the man cannot return gifts given to him and his former fiancée by his personal friends. Accompany returned gifts with a brief note such as the following:

Dear Samantha,

I am sorry to have to tell you that Josh and I have broken our engagement. I'm returning the beautiful wineglasses that you were so thoughtful to send.

Love,

Jessica

Q: *My ex-fiancé and I have just broken off our engagement. Our decision was mutual, so I hope we can be friends again someday. But what should I do with my engagement ring? He hasn't asked for it, and my friends say I should keep it.*

A: It's best to return the ring even though in most states you don't have a legal obligation to do so. The ring was given as a token of a pledge to be fulfilled. Since the pledge was broken, do you really want to keep a constant reminder of the broken promise? Returning it shows that you place value on the relationship that you once had and not on its material symbol. The decision is yours, and your conscience is a much better guide than the opinions of friends.

If the ring is an heirloom from the groom's family, there's no question: It should be returned along with any other jewelry you received while engaged. However, if you and your fiancé bought the ring together, then it should be sold and the proceeds split proportionally; if one person wants to keep the ring, the other should be reimbursed for his or her share.

If you return a gift directly to the store or over the Internet, make sure the giver's account is credited and indicate this in your note.

Inform invited guests. When an engagement is broken after invitations have been mailed and there is sufficient time, you can send a printed card or make phone calls. (For more information, see Chapter 48, "Wedding Invitations and Announcements," page 597.)

If One of a Couple Dies

When one of an engaged couple dies, the survivor is unlikely to be able to handle many obligations. It's good for relatives and friends to help out with certain painful but necessary tasks, including notifying members of the wedding party, the officiant, the wedding location, anyone hired for services, and the guest list if wedding invitations have been sent.

The bereaved bride-to-be can certainly keep her engagement ring if she wishes. Returning gifts is a personal decision and only the most insensitive people would complain if gifts are not sent back or are returned after weeks or months. A note should be included with a returned gift, and family members can handle this task if the bereaved partner isn't up to it.

46 trends and traditions

Weddings are full of traditions inherited from families, cultures, and convention. At the same time, personalization is one of the most visible trends in contemporary weddings. Brides and grooms now enjoy the freedom to fashion weddings that are unique to them. They have the best of both worlds—new and novel ideas and timeless traditions. Couples of different ethnic, national, and religious heritages are likely to plan weddings that blend and honor their individual cultures. Personal interests can provide inspiration for wedding themes and elements of the ceremony and reception. This chapter provides an overview of such trends as well as ways to adapt wedding plans with sensitivity to the feelings of the wedding party, family members, guests, and wedding professionals. Couples who are true to the underlying principles—respect for one another, consideration for others, and honesty in all their dealings—should have little difficulty achieving the wedding of their dreams.

WEDDING TRENDS

Trends don't always become traditions, but the following current wedding customs seem to have real staying power:

Personalized weddings. Today's marriage ceremonies often blend elements that have special meaning for couples, and perhaps their families, with traditional religious and secular vows. Many couples make concerted efforts to fight the hype of the wedding industry by planning their weddings as expressions of their personal interests. Intimacy and individualization are at the heart of this trend, along with a strong desire to express who they are as a couple.

Sharing the costs. Wedding expenses are no longer the exclusive responsibility of the bride's parents but frequently are shared by the couple, and sometimes the groom's parents. More and more couples pay most or all of the expenses. With wedding costs so high, it's no wonder that "Who pays?" and "How much is available?" are some of the first conversations that engaged couples have.

Weddings and high tech. The Internet plays a major role in registries, gift selection, finding vendors, and shopping for wedding supplies; wedding blogs and websites enable couples around the world to share information and advice. Most couples create their own wedding websites and use online wedding planning companies, though thank-you notes should still be handwritten.

Green weddings. Acting with consideration and respect for others is only a small step away from treating our environment similarly. Green weddings seek to have a low negative impact on the environment. Couples can "go green" on a few aspects or the whole process. To throw a green wedding, look for vendors or products that are local, organic, natural, fair trade, sustainable, carbon neutral, recyclable, or low consumption.

Encore and family weddings. Nearly 40 percent of today's weddings are encore events, meaning that the bride, groom, or both have been married before. More remarrying couples with children are hosting family weddings that actively involve their children in the ceremony. (See Chapter 52, "Remarriage," page 654.)

Involved grooms. Grooms are as likely as brides to be active participants in wedding planning and decision making. Couples often take mutual responsibility for everything from financing to registry creation to writing thank-you notes.

Celebrating different religious traditions. Interfaith marriage services often combine elements from both faiths. Couples of different faiths—or the same faith—may ask several officiants to perform the service. Help guests who may be unfamiliar with traditions of another faith by describing all aspects of the ceremony in the wedding program and by supplying them with necessary information ahead of time, such as any religious restrictions or dress requirements.

Including parents. Mothers as well as fathers can escort their daughters in the processional, and more brides are asking both parents to accompany them on the walk down the aisle. Many mothers are now also making speeches in honor of the couple at the reception as well.

Honor attendants. It's not unusual for a bride to have a male friend as one of her attendants or a groom to include a female friend as one of his. When these friends fill the roles of "best woman" and "man of honor," they are known as "honor attendants." Women who serve as honor attendants to grooms sometimes wear outfits in muted colors—gray, silver, navy blue, black—that reflect traditional formal and semiformal male attire, or they might wear traditional bridesmaid's dresses. Male honor attendants to brides wear the same or a similar suit as the groomsmen, but may feature a tie in the same color as the bridesmaids' dresses. Their boutonniere uses the colors of the bridal party's flowers, but they don't carry a bouquet.

More wedding attire choices. Modern brides increasingly express their individual taste and style in their attire. Wedding dresses, shoes, and accessories can include colors, designs, and fabrics that reflect the bride's culture or ethnic heritage. Attendants' outfits are often chosen with consideration for future use, and many brides have their bridesmaids select dresses in the same or coordinating colors but different cuts to flatter them, or the same cut, but different colors. Black is no longer "out" for bridesmaids or female guests, and white can be acceptable as well. (See also Chapter 53, "A Guide for Wedding Guests," page 662.)

Variations in color. Traditional white still reigns, but color is blooming not only in bouquets and floral arrangements but also in brides' and grooms' attire, invitations and announcements, reception decorations and table linens, wedding cakes, and gift wrappings.

Destination weddings. More couples are choosing distant locations for their big day. Destination weddings are typically small. Send save-the-date announcements as soon as possible to allow guests time to book flights and plan vacation time. For many couples a destination wedding is a dream come true, but for attendants, family, and guests, finding the necessary time and money to attend may be an insurmountable challenge. Be sensitive to a guest's limitations, especially if the wedding is scheduled during a holiday weekend, when it can be more difficult and expensive to travel. Couples should be prepared to accept graciously the likelihood that some of their hoped-for family and friends will be unable to join them.

TRADITIONS IN NEW CONTEXTS

Most guests will enjoy unconventional weddings, but their enjoyment will be greater if they know what to expect. The objective should be a pleasant surprise for guests—not a shock. The ceremony program is a good place to include explanations of customs and rituals that are likely to be unfamiliar. The officiant or members of the wedding party can also explain specific rituals to the guests during the service.

Discuss the inclusion of religious rituals and/or readings from other religious texts with your officiant. Some faiths do not allow deviation from their standard services, but it may be possible to include other elements either before or after the ceremony or at the reception.

Unity candle. A fairly recent addition to many marriage services, the lighting of a single candle symbolizes a couple's unity. The ceremony can take place at any point in the service, but if more than the couple are involved, it's often staged after the exchange of vows. Usually, the bride and groom each hold lighted candles and light a third candle together. The individual candles can then be extinguished, but some couples keep them lit throughout the service as a sign that they remain individuals within their union.

The unity candle ceremony is easily adapted. Family members may be included, and parents and stepparents can participate if everyone agrees. Sometimes the bride's and groom's mothers light the candle. Lighting a unity candle is also a good way for an encore couple to involve their children in the service.

Customs from other faiths and cultures. In religious and secular services, today's couples may adopt and adapt elements from faiths other than their own. One example is the Jewish tradition of having mothers and fathers in the processional. Some couples have adapted the Greek Orthodox crowning, or wreath, ceremony (see "Wedding Customs in Many Faiths," page 672) as a symbol of their unity. Another gracious addition to some American weddings is the Chinese tea ceremony, during which the couple offers cups of sweet tea to each other's families. Native American ceremonial sand painting has inspired sand-blending rituals to signify the mingling of two individuals and their families into a single family.

Secular readings. Including nonreligious poetry and prose readings in marriage ceremonies enables couples to express their commitment in words that have special significance for them—and also allows personalization of the service by couples who don't compose their own vows. Couples may ask family members and friends to be readers. Religious and secular officiants might suggest sources for readings, and an Internet search will yield many ideas. Appropriateness and brevity are important, so discuss your options with the officiant early in the planning process.

Music. Maybe you'd like to open your ceremony with the ringing of a Tibetan gong, walk up the aisle to the sound of Scottish bagpipes, or include Balinese dancing at your reception. Music provides innumer-able ways to personalize (and internationalize) wedding celebrations. Ask your officiant about any restrictions on secular music. Musical selections are usually listed by title and composer in the ceremony program, and a very brief explanation can also be included to help guests understand why you made a particularly meaningful choice.

Jumping the broom. This custom, most often associated with African American weddings, is done to honor the slaves who weren't allowed to marry legally, but who did marry and form strong families. The ritual is said to symbolize the establishment of a new household and is usually performed just after the wedding service or at the reception. The broom (a regular house broom is fine) is decorated with ribbons, flowers, and perhaps special trinkets. The broom is laid on the floor, and guests gather round. On the count of three, the newlyweds, hand in hand, jump over the broom and into their new life as husband and wife. (In the pre–Civil War era, the broom was held above the floor, behind the couple, and they jumped it backward!)

Handfasting. A custom most associated with pagan Celtic tradition, handfasting is now being included in some religious as well as secular services. During the service, the couple's hands are ceremonially tied with rope or ribbon to symbolize their union. Though the Celtic handfasting ceremony probably originated as a contract between a couple to stay together for a year and a day (if the arrangement worked, the contract was renewed), handfasting today signifies the enduring nature of the marriage commitment. It may be the source of the phrase "tying the knot."

The shared cup. In many traditions, both religious and secular, the bride and groom share a cup of wine during the wedding ceremony—a custom unrelated to Christian communion services. In Chinese tradition, the couple drinks wine and honey from goblets tied together with red string. In Japan, couples who wed in the Shinto tradition take nine sips of sake, as do their parents, to symbolize the new bonds of family.

Sharing a wedding cup is also a reception custom in many cultures. French couples drink wine from a *coupe de mariage,* or double-handled cup (also called a "loving cup"). Irish guests gather round the newlyweds, and toasts are made over cups of mead.

Marrying to a Theme

Themed weddings can carry personalization into nearly every aspect of planning, from the look of invitations to the shape of the wedding cake. Themes should be meaningful to both of the couple—and not so far out that guests won't get the idea. A theme shouldn't be an imposition on guests, such as requiring them to dress in period costume. It's also important to consider budget; a themed wedding complete with costuming for the wedding party and staff at the reception, elaborate decorations, and complicated menus can be very costly.

But themes—whether carried through the entire occasion or just the reception—can be great fun and a satisfying outlet for creative thinking. The following categories and examples are provided as idea starters for themes that are both practical and memorable:

- **The season or the month of the wedding.** An October wedding might be the inspiration for autumn colors, country dances, even a hayride to the reception site.

- **A favorite place.** A couple who met in Paris, Nairobi, or Hong Kong might theme their reception around the foods and music typical of those cities.

- **A historical period or era.** The spectacle of ancient Egypt, the romance of medieval courts, the sleek style of 1930s art deco—history is a treasure trove of decorating ideas.

- **A shared interest.** A mutual love of Shakespeare might suggest an Elizabethan theme with sonnets as guest favors. A couple devoted to water sports or camping could create a nautical or outdoors theme.

- **The wedding location.** A floral theme might be perfect for a wedding in a beautiful garden. The reception for a beach or lakeside wedding could be just right for a clambake, luau, or barbecue.

47
planning your wedding

the perfect wedding . . . a beautiful bride, a beaming groom, elegant attendants, and a happy complement of family and friends. The realization of this lovely image has more to do with nuts and bolts than romance. You and your partner will need to be in agreement about the major elements of your wedding.

A wedding involves planning two events. The wedding itself is often a religious ceremony, while the reception is a social event. Even the simplest of ceremonies and receptions require time, effort, and major doses of the "three Cs" of wedding planning—*consideration*, *communication*, and *compromise*—to make the dream come true.

PRIMARY DECISIONS: TURNING DREAMS INTO REALITY

Start by separating your primary decisions from those that can wait awhile. You'll find that once you've made the big decisions, the secondary decisions will fall into place. First decisions—the foundation for the other choices you make—include

- ◆ guest list
- ◆ budget
- ◆ date and time
- ◆ location of your ceremony and reception
- ◆ your ceremony officiant
- ◆ a professional wedding consultant
- ◆ style and formality
- ◆ attendants

The Guest List

Beginning with the guest list may seem a little odd. Isn't budget more important? It is rare that a couple is so wedded to the food, invitations, dress, or flowers that these dictate the budget more than who will be invited. It is sometimes the case that a particular location is so special to the couple that they choose to work with its limits or its price tag. But at the end of the day, many couples decide that what matters the very most isn't the location or the formality or the special details, but the people that they share this very special moment with. This is why we suggest that you start your wedding planning by developing your guest list.

Your budget priorities and other major decisions will depend on the number of people you invite. In the long run, it's easier to modify spending than to leave out people who really matter to you. Also, by starting with a preliminary guest list, you'll be better able to pare it down if you have to cut costs.

Traditionally, with the bride's family hosting, the guest list was divided equally between the bride's and groom's families and friends. As couples today often host their own weddings or involve the groom's family, guest lists may split differently. Certainly the bride and groom will seek input from their families, but it's up to the couple—whose wedding it is—to make the final choices. This process calls for tact and compromise. The ideal guest list is a magical number of family and friends that

- ◆ Suits the size of your ceremony and reception sites.
- ◆ Corresponds with the level of intimacy desired for the wedding.
- ◆ Can be accommodated within your budget.

It's helpful to think about your list in terms of categories—relatives, friends, business associates—and tiers of closeness—first cousins, close friends, coworkers. For example, if numbers are limited you could invite all aunts and uncles, but not cousins. There's less chance for hurt feelings than if you invite one or two cousins and not the other twelve. Consider the following categories when creating the list:

The must-haves. These are your close family and good friends, without whom the wedding day would be incomplete. This list includes immediate family: parents, siblings, grandparents, the couple's own children, if any.

Extended family. These are relatives who may not be as close, but are important to you and your parents: aunts, uncles, cousins, nieces, nephews.

The bride's and groom's friends. In varying tiers of closeness—childhood friends, friends from school, new friends, work friends.

Acquaintances and friends of the couple's families. These are parents' friends, and perhaps some of their business associates.

Be sure to include . . . The spouse, fiancé(e), or live-in partner of each invited guest (even if you've never met); the person who performs your ceremony and his or her spouse; and the parents of ring bearers and flower girls.

guest list discretion

Your standby list is for your eyes only. You might
have a standby list—people you will gladly
invite if circumstances allow—but other than
you and intimate family who are involved in
developing the guest list, no one should know
who is on your lists or how your decisions were
made. Even hinting that someone was on a secondary list can cause hurt feelings and destroy
friendships. Keep your standby list relatively
small and put people in logical categories. For
example, "second cousins" could move as a
group onto a primary list. Try to send secondary
invitations within a week or two of sending the
original invitations. A last-minute invitation is
a sure sign that the invitee was an afterthought.

Maybe include . . . Plus-ones and children of
guests. You have to decide if you want single guests
to bring dates and parents to bring their children.

Once you've combined the original lists, you'll
likely have two lists: 1) must invite and 2) maybe invite.
Though you'll probably add or trim names before the
invitations go out, you now have a preliminary estimate
of the number of guests. It's time to discuss costs and
begin your preparations.

Establish the Budget

Traditionally, the bride's family paid for the wedding but
that's no longer the reality today. Brides and grooms
are generally older (in their 30s rather than in their
early 20s) and financially independent by the time they

marry. It's common today for brides and grooms to host
and pay for a portion or all of their own weddings, or for
the couple's parents to pool resources and host the
wedding together.

Even though many families are willing to share the
costs of a wedding, it should never be assumed that
they are expected to do so. Before approaching parents
to discuss the wedding budget, couples should agree
on and have a clear picture of what they would like to
accomplish. Any conversation about money should
be respectful and candid. If they ask for financial help,
the couple must also be willing to compromise, listen
to others' ideas, and be appreciative of whatever their
parents can contribute.

Careful and Considerate Budgeting

The first rule of budgeting is to be realistic; the second
is to be considerate. With your preliminary guest list and
overall budget amount, you'll be able to establish per-
person spending limits for the reception and decide if
you need to adjust your plans. As you gather estimates,
be sure they include all applicable taxes and tips or gratuities. If your budget is limited, decide what takes priority: a big, glamorous wedding with a shorter guest list,
or a larger guest list and a more toned-down reception.
This is the time to communicate extra carefully and find
compromises: Shorten the guest list; decide to marry
at a time of year or time of day when costs are less; or
choose a more affordable reception site. The variations
are endless.

There are other practical matters to consider, too.
The costs of some items are fixed—such as the wed-

ding license, any required medical tests, officiant's fee, postage, and fees for your ceremony and reception sites. Before signing any contracts, read them carefully and look for hidden costs. Don't think that you have to sacrifice quality to cut costs. With creative thinking and smart planning, you can have your dream wedding without breaking the bank. The Wedding Budget Planning Chart (page 696) can help you determine which elements are essential for you.

Set the Date

June is the most popular wedding month, followed by October and the summer months, July through September. Rates are usually highest and wedding and reception sites can be difficult to reserve. Obviously, most weddings are held on Fridays, Saturdays, or Sundays—scheduled around regular religious services and other holy day observances. A weekday wedding is an option and usually the case if you're having a civil ceremony, but work commitments may make it difficult for guests to attend.

Find the Location

If you want to be married in a house of worship, make inquiries as soon as you have an approximate wedding date. It may be possible to make a tentative reserva-

tion and then confirm the day and time when you have reserved your reception site.

When selecting both your ceremony and reception sites, be certain there's adequate space for your guests, including parking. Aside from a house of worship, your choices for the ceremony and/or reception might include a home, a hotel, a wedding hall, a restaurant, a club, city hall, an historic or cultural facility, and even a beach.

Choose Your Officiant

The person who performs your marriage service may be a religious or secular official. If it's important that a specific person officiate, then his or her availability will be a factor in your choice of day and time. Policies regarding guest clergy vary among religions and sects, so plan early if you wish to invite an officiant from another congregation or faith. If you're planning to ask a friend to become legally qualified to officiate, review the state law, as the qualifications differ across the country.

A Professional Wedding Consultant

While it isn't necessary to use a wedding consultant, their services can benefit couples who work full-time or are staging a large wedding. Wedding consultants save their clients time and money. In general, a wedding consultant:

◆ Listens carefully and understands your wedding vision, then is your advocate to realize that dream in the best way possible.

◆ Helps you set a budget and stick to it.

- Helps locate and reserve ceremony and reception sites.

- Helps select and hire reputable suppliers and vendors: florist, caterer, musicians, photographer.

- Advises on the selection and wording of invitations, announcements, and other communications.

- Draws up a timeline to keep everyone on schedule, both pre-wedding and on the wedding day.

- Serves as a referee, friend, budget advisor, etiquette expert, shopper, detail manager, and organizer.

- Coordinates your rehearsal with your officiant.

- Supervises all the last-minute details of your wedding day.

When selecting a wedding consultant, choose someone who has experience and preferably is a member of a professional consultants' association. Equally important is choosing someone who has good chemistry with you—who's a good listener and someone you're comfortable confiding in.

Your Wedding Style

When determining the style of your wedding, you're really deciding on how formal or informal you wish it to be. There are three categories of weddings—formal, semiformal, and informal. The formality is related to the location of the ceremony and reception, and the time of day. Evening weddings and those in a place of worship tend to be formal or semiformal; afternoon, at-home, or beach weddings are generally informal. Any combination is possible, though, so choose what suits your circumstances.

Family Matters

If your family or families are complicated by divorce, remarriage, step relationships, or family feuding, address these issues as early in the planning process as possible.

Unfortunately, divorced parents aren't always friendly. Although well-mannered adults will lay their differences aside for a wedding, you should avoid putting them in awkward and uncomfortable situations. Asking divorced parents and their spouses to the same social events, or seating them together at the ceremony or reception, isn't always feasible and might be stressful for everyone, including other guests. (See Chapter 51, "The Big Day," page 634.) Don't wait until the last minute to make these decisions. Speak to those involved well ahead of the event so that when the time comes, everyone knows what's expected.

Choosing Your Attendants

For many couples, the choice of attendants is easy—sisters, brothers, and dearest friends—but if you have a large family or a wide circle of good friends (or both!), the decision can be difficult. Asking siblings or your fiancé(e)'s siblings certainly promotes family unity, but it's not a requirement; you have many options for choosing your attendants in both considerate and logical ways.

- There is no required number of attendants. You can include as many or as few as you wish, and even a big, formal wedding with just one or two attendants on each side is perfectly acceptable.

- It's unnecessary to have an equal number of bridesmaids and groomsmen or ushers: One groomsman can easily escort two bridesmaids in the recessional, or bridesmaids can walk alone or in pairs. Since ushers have the practical responsibility of seating guests at the ceremony, the general rule is one usher for every fifty guests, though you may have more.

- You can have two maids of honor, a maid and a matron of honor, or two best men. Though not so common, two chief attendants may be the right solution when you don't want to choose between siblings or close friends. The attendants can share the duties—and the fun!

- It's fine to ask a friend who is pregnant to be a bridesmaid. Just be considerate of her needs and capabilities. For instance, you can see that a chair is placed near the altar area so that she can sit during a lengthy service.

When to Ask

This is one of your first wedding decisions to make after your engagement is announced. Once you've decided whom you want in your wedding, ask them right away so they can organize their calendars, purchase clothing, arrange transportation, and plan any parties they might wish to host.

It's always nice to ask in person, but if you can't, then call, write, text, or email your invitation—whatever is the easiest way to get in touch. Supply as many of the basic plans as you can: the wedding date (even if you aren't sure of the time), the location, and some sense of the formality of the event. The person may accept immediately, but don't push for an instant reply. Even the closest friend may need a few days to consider.

It's a great honor to be asked to be in a wedding, but people have other obligations and accepting may not be possible. Don't be offended or expect a detailed explanation if someone turns down your invitation. A refusal is often based on important family, job, or financial concerns, so be sensitive. Express your disappointment without any hint of disapproval. Rather than jeopardize a relationship, assume that the person has made a conscientious decision and is doing what he or she thinks is best for everyone.

Attendants' Responsibilities

Attendants have a special duty to assist the bride and groom and to see that the wedding and the reception run smoothly. They're expected to be gracious and visit with guests, assist the elderly and anyone else who needs help, be attentive to any young children in the wedding party, be available for picture taking, and generally help out whenever needed. If there's a receiving line, the maid/matron of honor will be asked to stand in line, but it's optional for the best man and bridesmaids; ushers and groomsmen are exempt. In addition, attendants

- Pay for their wedding attire and any alterations, shoes, and accessories (excluding flowers).

- Arrange and pay for their own transportation.

- Attend the rehearsal and rehearsal dinner.

- Attend other pre-wedding events when possible.

smartphone, smart couple

Communication is essential to a well-planned wedding. Your wedding website and social network page, texts, tweets, email, and even good old-fashioned phone and voice mail are great tools to help you plan your wedding and keep your team and your guests up to speed. Given that not everyone will use all of these ways of communicating, your information strategy might involve a combination of high and low tech. Here are ways the e-world can assist:

WEDDING WEBSITE: Is it a must? No, but it sure can be convenient to have an info central, and it's free on sites such as theknot.com. More and more guests automatically look to a couple's website not just for registry links but also for information regarding the ceremony, attire, directions, links to local accommodations and places of interest, and even to RSVP. Having all of this information on your site can also be a lifesaver, such as when a guest forgets to bring her invitation, and while en route to the wedding can't remember the name of the place where the wedding's being held—smartphone to the rescue! It's also the perfect place to share pictures and stories of your engagement, and wrap it up with wedding and honeymoon pictures and a group thank-you to all your guests.

What to avoid:

* Out-of-date information—keep your site current.
* Heavy emphasis on your gift registry—those links shouldn't be the first or only thing a guest sees.
* Skimping on showing appreciation—a general thanks on your site doesn't take the place of individual handwritten notes for wedding gifts.

SOCIAL NETWORK PAGE: It's a great place to share the news and photos of your engagement and upcoming wedding with all your friends. But put away your phone and honor your guests and each other by being fully present at your ceremony and reception.

What to avoid:

* The rush to gush—make sure that you've told your big news to your most important relatives and friends before you tell the world.
* TMI—no outrageous photos of the bacholor(ette) party.
* Hurt feelings—not all your social network friends will be coming to your wedding, so keep planning chatter to a minimum.

EMAIL AND TEXTING: These are planning lifesavers for the busy couple, and it's hard to imagine life without them. Coupled with a smartphone you can keep everyone up to speed wherever you are. Make an email group that includes the members of your wedding party, so that sending out occasional emails isn't such a chore and you won't inadvertently overlook anyone. When making plans with vendors, keep a thread open as plans develop and you'll have a running record of decisions made. Emails can be great for save-the-date notices as well as informing guests of any last-minute changes to the date or venue.

What to avoid:

- ◆ Overwhelming the wedding party with constant updates and changes.
- ◆ Discussing sensitive issues—do this face-to-face, or at least in a phone call.
- ◆ Assuming that all intended recipients of your emails and texts have received important information. A "please confirm" request will alert you to contact any stragglers.

- ◆ Give an individual wedding gift to the couple or contribute to a joint gift from all the attendants.
- ◆ Arrive at specified times for all wedding-related events and follow instructions.
- ◆ Possibly host or cohost a pre-wedding party, such as a shower or bachelor(ette) party; however, *this is by no means mandatory*.
- ◆ Understand their specific responsibilities.

Specific Attendant Responsibilities

In addition to the general duties mentioned above, there are a few unique duties for the following attendants:

Maid or Matron of Honor

- ◆ Helps the bride select bridesmaids' attire.
- ◆ Is available to be the bride's "right hand," helping with communications with other attendants and with wedding professionals if requested.
- ◆ Coordinates a shower or bachelorette party, *if the bridesmaids decide to host one*.

- ◆ Organizes the bridesmaids' gift to the bride, if one is given.
- ◆ Holds the groom's wedding ring and the bride's bouquet during the ceremony.
- ◆ Witnesses the signing of the marriage certificate.
- ◆ Helps the bride during the reception (gathering guests for cake cutting, dancing, the bouquet toss).

Junior Bridesmaid

Junior bridesmaids are between eight and fourteen years old. They attend the rehearsal and, depending on the individual's age and maturity, the rehearsal dinner and other pre-wedding parties, if invited. Her parents pay for her dress and accessories. She may give a separate gift to the couple or be included in her parents' gift.

Q: *Help! I'm a maid of honor and the bride is insisting that her bridesmaids treat her to a long weekend at a fancy hotel in Las Vegas. Most of us can't afford to do this. What do we do?*

A: The bachelorette party has become so popular that many brides think it's now a "must do." It's not. Being an attendant can be costly. You're responsible for purchasing your clothing, paying for your transportation to and from the wedding, contributing to a bridesmaids' gift for the bride, purchasing a shower gift if there's a shower, and purchasing or contributing to a gift for the couple. For many attendants, that's stretching the budget already. There's no requirement for you to host a shower or a bachelorette party as well.

Talk with the bride and explain the circumstances. As much as you'd like to grant her wish, you just can't afford it. Be kind, but firm. Try to find out what she really wants to get out of the weekend—time with friends, a wild night at a bar, the chance to stay at a terrific hotel—and see if it can happen another, less costly way.

Best Man

- Organizes the bachelor party for the groom, if there is one.

- Coordinates the groomsmen and ushers' gift to the groom, if one is given.

- Delivers prearranged payments to officiants, assistants, and musicians and singers at the ceremony.

- Sees that groomsmen and ushers are properly attired and arrive on time.

- Instructs ushers in the correct seating of guests (if there is no head usher).

- Hands the bride's wedding ring to the groom during the ceremony.

- Witnesses the signing of the marriage certificate.

- Drives the bride and groom to the reception if there's no hired driver; has a car ready for the couple to leave after the reception and may drive them to their next destination.

- Offers the first toast to the bride and groom at the reception; dances with the bride, mothers, maid of honor, and other single female guests.

- Gathers and takes care of the groom's wedding clothes, returning rental items on the next business day.

Groomsmen and Ushers

Groomsmen stand with the groom during the ceremony. Ushers help prepare the wedding site for the ceremony and escort guests to their seats before the ceremony. Groomsmen may also serve as ushers, and this is fairly common at small to medium-size weddings. At large weddings or when the bridegroom has only a best man and perhaps one other attendant, additional ushers are often needed. As a general guide-line, plan to have one usher for every fifty guests.

In addition to the attendant responsibilities mentioned above, groomsmen/ushers' duties include learning any special seating arrangements prior to the ceremony; greeting and escorting guests to their seats; arranging and removing the aisle runner, if one is used; and helping guests who need directions to the reception site.

Honor Attendants

"Honor attendant" is the name for an attendant, such as a maid of honor, of the opposite sex. Today, many brides and grooms pay tribute to their closest friends or broth-ers and sisters of the opposite sex by including them as attendants. Honor attendants perform the same duties as the maid of honor, best man, bridesmaid, or grooms-man position that they represent. Some responsibilities are altered as necessary: For example, a male honor attendant wouldn't help the bride get dressed.

Flower Girl

A flower girl, usually between the ages of three and seven, precedes the bride down the aisle, carrying flowers or a flower basket. During the ceremony she stands with the bridesmaids or sits with her parents or other adults. A flower girl's parents pay for her dress and accessories (excluding flowers). She attends the rehearsal and is invited to the rehearsal dinner with her parents. There may be more than one flower girl, and this can be a nice way to include children of close friends or relatives.

Ring Bearer

The ring bearer, a three- to seven-year-old boy, walks down the aisle before the flower girl and carries the wedding rings on a small cushion. (If there's a worry that the rings could get lost, the best man holds the actual rings and the ring bearer carries token rings.) He stands with the groomsmen or may sit with his parents or other adults during the service. His outfit is provided by his family. He attends the rehearsal and is invited to the rehearsal dinner with his parents. A flower girl and ring bearer sometimes enter and exit together.

Special Helpers

Some couples ask close family members and friends to assist at the wedding and the reception. Though not strictly attendants, these helpers perform special func-tions, such as participating in the ceremony as read-

children at the rehearsal dinner

It's a courtesy to invite the flower girl, ring bearer, and their parents to the rehearsal din-ner. The children will likely see your wedding as a huge occasion in their lives, too. Do talk to the parents ahead of time. It's not mandatory for children to attend the dinner, and, if it's going to be a late night, parents may choose to decline the invitation or let the children attend for a short while and then have a sitter on duty. Either way, the goal is to have the children well rested for the wedding.

ers, soloists, cantors, or altar assistants. They might be asked to hand out ceremony programs, oversee the signing of a guestbook, or greet guests. These helpers are usually honored with corsages and boutonnieres. They're included in some wedding photographs, and their names and responsibilities are often listed in the wedding program.

PRE-WEDDING CELEBRATIONS AND PARTIES

As soon as an engagement is announced, friends and family start thinking about parties. Showers, bridesmaids' parties, bachelor and bachelorette gatherings, and a rehearsal dinner are all traditional celebrations. None of these parties are "musts" or "have-tos," but most couples are feted in some manner before the wedding takes place. Pre-wedding parties don't have to be gift-giving occasions. It's perfectly acceptable for the bride and groom to suggest a "gift-free" gathering when someone offers to host a party for them.

Showers

A shower is an intimate gathering of friends and family, given to extend good wishes to the bride and to "shower" her with gifts. Today, showers are just as likely to include the groom and his male friends. A shower may have a theme that indicates the type of gifts expected. Opening the presents is usually the high point of the party, but the real purpose is to bring good friends together to celebrate the upcoming marriage. As gifts are opened, the host or someone else keeps a list of gifts and who gave them. The bride and/or groom is expected to write thank-you notes for *each* shower gift, even when guests were thanked in person.

A shower can be held in any way the hostess or host chooses—a brunch, an afternoon tea, an evening get-together—and is more often casual than formal. The ideal timing is from two months to two weeks before the wedding—after the couple has firmed up their wedding plans. Unless the shower is a surprise, the honoree is consulted about the date, time, theme, and guest list, but party planning is up to the hostess or host.

Who hosts a bridal shower? While an engaged couple shouldn't throw themselves a shower—a direct "ask" for gifts—it's fine for anyone else to host, including the bride's mother or sister. If the bride is visiting her future in-laws and the groom's mother wants hometown friends and family to meet her, she may host a shower, reception, or engagement party. Sometimes several of the bride's friends or relatives host the shower together. Individual circumstances guide the decision.

Who's invited? The guest list usually includes close friends, family members, and attendants. Anyone invited to a shower must be invited to the wedding. The one exception is a workplace shower to which a large number of coworkers contribute, knowing that the couple is unable to invite them all.

How are invitations issued? Shower invitations are usually informal, so notes or preprinted fill-ins are standard. It's also fine to invite by phone, email, or e-vite. It's okay for the hostess to include the theme or gift registry sources, but never specific gift requests or suggestions.

How many showers? There's no specific rule here, but common sense and consideration should guide you. Multiple showers are fine, but invite different guests to each party. If someone is invited to more than one shower, they need not take a gift to more than the first shower.

Bachelor and Bachelorette Parties

The basic idea for these events is to treat the groom or bride to one last night out as a single person. The guests are good friends, the atmosphere is relaxed, and there's no reason not to have a great time—so long as everyone is willing to exercise self-control. Whatever entertainment is planned, it should not embarrass, humiliate, or endanger the honoree or any of the guests. It's wise to hold a bachelor or bachelorette party a week or more before the wedding, so everyone can rest after what will probably be a late night. Today, camping trips, a spa day, a sporting event, and group adventures are popular alternatives.

Bridesmaids' Luncheon

A luncheon or brunch is traditional, but it could be a dinner or cocktail party instead. Usually held a day or two before the wedding or even on the morning of the wedding, this event is often hosted by the bride's aunt(s), mother's friends, or by the bride and her mother as a thank-you to the bridesmaids. It's a good time for the bride and bridesmaids to exchange their gifts for one another.

Rehearsal Party

Traditionally, the dinner following the wedding rehearsal was hosted by the groom's parents, but today, just about anybody may host. The party needn't be a seated dinner; you could follow a daytime rehearsal with a brunch or an afternoon rehearsal with a cocktail buffet. A post-rehearsal party isn't obligatory, but it's an excellent opportunity for the couple's families to come together and get to know one another better. The party can be held at a home, restaurant, or club. The guest list normally includes all attendants and their spouses or

Q: *My fiancée's parents think that we should include all of the out-of-town guests at the rehearsal dinner. Is this true?*

A: In a nutshell, no, you're not obligated to include out-of-town guests at the rehearsal dinner, and most guests know that they're on their own except for the wedding and reception. Inviting all the out-of-town guests to the rehearsal dinner has the potential of being as large and lavish as the wedding day festivities, stealing the thunder of the big day. Alternatives for out-of-town guests include providing a list of local restaurants or arranging for friends to host a dinner, barbecue, or cocktail party.

partners, the parents of young attendants, the couple's close relatives, and special guests, such as the officiant and his or her spouse.

SECONDARY DECISIONS: THE DETAILS

With the big decisions made, you're ready to tackle the details. The size and style of your wedding will determine your exact "to do" list, but the following checklist will give you a general idea of how to proceed with your plans:

- Check with local government officials about requirements for a marriage license.

- Speak with your officiant about any requirements if you're having a religious ceremony.

- Choose the wedding dress and accessories for the bride, and clothing for the groom and attendants.

- Shop for wedding rings.

- Plan the reception menu and interview caterers, if one isn't provided at the reception site.

- Discuss music for the ceremony and reception. Interview/listen to musicians and DJs.

- Interview florists.

- Interview photographers and videographers.

- Investigate sources of rentals for any necessary equipment such as tents, awnings, chairs, tables, outdoor lighting, etc.

- Order invitations, enclosures, announcements, and other printed material.

- Make decisions about your wedding gift registries.

- Discuss your honeymoon and consult with travel planners as necessary.

LINING UP HELP

For many couples, their wedding is their first experience organizing a major social event from start to finish. Unless your wedding is very small or very casual, you'll need assistance. Before calling on others, however, evaluate your own time and limitations. Be honest. Knowing what *you* can reasonably do will help you better allocate your resources and delegate responsibilities to others.

Whether you're working with hired professionals or family and friends who volunteer their time, trust them to do what you ask. Successful delegation requires sensitivity to other people's lives and schedules, and gratitude for their efforts on your behalf. Talented family members and friends may be delighted to help with the preparations. Be open to offers of assistance.

Contracting for Services

Chances are, you'll be working with suppliers and vendors, either directly or through a wedding consultant. Be clear about what you want, but also be open to suggestions. Experienced wedding suppliers can often help you avoid common problems and pitfalls.

Review contracts so that there are no misunderstandings about responsibilities. When you make agreements well in advance of the wedding, call back closer to the day and confirm times, delivery schedules, directions, site access, and other critical details.

If you don't have a wedding coordinator, it's smart to have a point person on your wedding day—someone whom suppliers can go to with problems and questions. This might be a parent, honor attendant, or a good friend or family member who is thoroughly acquainted with your plans.

Help from Friends and Family

Talented family members and friends may be delighted to help with the preparations, so be open to offers of assistance. But should you pay? You'll have to use good judgment. If a friend takes on a major task such as catering the reception, then it's appropriate to bring up payment. If they won't accept reimbursement, give a nice gift along with your note of thanks. If someone offers to help and you don't want to accept, be gracious when you decline and avoid implying that the person isn't capable. You might ask the person to do something else.

Showing Appreciation

Whether receiving help from a professional or a friend, here are some fundamental courtesies for bride and groom to remember:

- Always say "thank you" for favors large and small.

- Keep requests reasonable.

- Treat suppliers, vendors, and their employees with respect.

- Take responsibility for your own mistakes.

meals for vendors

If you're serving a meal to your guests, then you should feed photographers, videographers, DJs, musicians, and other hired professionals as well. Many reception sites have a separate area where your crew can eat. Often the caterer will serve them a less expensive meal, or the same meal at a discount. Be sure that vendor meals are part of your catering contract, and plan the best time during your reception for musicians and photographers to take a half-hour meal break. Caterers generally arrange meals for their employees, but check to be sure.

write it down

It can be a special book just for weddings, a plain spiral notebook, your computer, or smartphone, tablet, or app, but a planner is a must. Whether your wedding is large or small, you'll have a lot to keep track of, and lists are more trustworthy than memory. Couples often keep separate planners and compare notes. If you use your computer, be sure to print out lists to take to meetings and have some way—either electronically or on paper—to jot down ideas and questions whenever they occur.

CEREMONY PLANS

Once you've decided on the location, make an appointment to meet with the officiant to confirm the ceremony date and time. Here are some points to review:

- **Length and format of the ceremony.** Civil ceremonies are usually relatively short, but the length of religious services can vary. Inquire about specifics, such as personalizing the ceremony with readings, music, or your own vows.

- **Number of guests and seating arrangements.** How many guests will the site hold comfortably? At a place other than a house of worship, discuss the general organization of the room or outdoor setting.

- **Site facilities.** Ask about dressing areas, flowers and decorations, music, photography, videotaping, handicap access, guest parking, and vendors' access.

- **The names you want used in the ceremony.** How do you want the officiant to address you during the ceremony? Full names? Nicknames?

- **The rehearsal.** Reserve the site and set the time for your rehearsal. Rehearsals are usually held on the day or evening before the wedding.

- **Any requirements you must fulfill.** Different religions and sects have different traditions, so ask for clarification if you have any questions. If premarital counseling or instruction is required, make your appointments now. Ask about any documents you must provide, such as baptismal certificates. If you want an officiant from another congregation or faith to participate in or perform the service, or you will marry in a house of worship other than your own, ask about any special requirements.

- **Clothing restrictions.** Are there any restrictions on dress for the wedding party: hats, long sleeves, long skirts?

- **Fees.** Discuss amounts and methods of paying the site fee, officiant's fee, and fees for other participants (organist, musicians, sexton, altar boys, choir director) provided through the place of worship.

RECEPTION PLANS

Choosing the Reception Site

Along with an at-home wedding, there are many options for the reception site. Consider the following:

Hotels, private clubs, and reception halls. Food, beverages, and staff are generally provided by the site. The location may offer complete wedding packages, so ask about all the possibilities.

Sites that offer space only. A wide variety of places—most houses of worship, reception or private meeting halls, civic or historic sites, galleries, or museums—offer physical space, but you must provide everything else and also arrange access for your suppliers and vendors.

Restaurants. Restaurant options include reserving space in the main dining room, renting a private room, or renting the entire facility. The focus here is on the food, beverages, and service, but not necessarily on other reception elements such as photography, music, and the cake. If these are important to you, check with the manager to see what's possible.

Military facilities. When one or both of an engaged couple are on active duty, they may have access to base facilities, including chapels and officers' clubs, for their ceremony and/or reception. The principal advantages are price (often lower than comparable off-base locations), convenience for guests who are also in the service, and flexibility. Base clubs will generally accommodate scheduling changes when a groom or bride is reposted—without charging extra.

Outdoor sites. An outdoor service and/or reception might be held at home; a club, restaurant, reception hall, or place of worship with outdoor facilities; a park or beach; or a historic site that is available for entertaining. Plan for:

- **Weather.** Whatever the general climate, the weather on your wedding day is greatly unpredictable. Check into historical weather trends at the site you're considering.

- **A plan B.** You must have a fallback plan that includes an alternate indoor site and a plan to notify guests of the change in the event of inclement weather.

- **Fees, permits, and restrictions.** Some sites, such as public parks or beaches, may charge a fee or require a permit. Before choosing, be sure any restrictions on hours of operation, vehicular access, or use of fire (candles, cooking) won't affect your plans. Consider purchasing insurance.

- **Access.** Consider your suppliers and guests. The caterer and florist will need access for their vehicles. Where will guests park? Will walking at the site be difficult?

- **Directions.** Include maps and detailed directions in your wedding invitations and on your wedding website.

Finalizing Your Choice

Whichever site you select, have at least one guided tour before signing an agreement. Reconfirm the day and time of the reception and your space requirements. Finalize your contract, and make the required deposit payment. Rented facilities often charge substantial cancellation fees, so read the contract thoroughly and ask about anything you don't understand.

RECEPTION DECISIONS

Once the site has been selected, there are several more decisions for the bride and groom:

- What's your menu?

- Will you hire a caterer?

- What type of beverage service will you offer?

- How will you handle seating arrangements?

- How will you get from the ceremony to the reception, and is there guest parking?

- Is there vendor access to the site for musicians, florists, cake maker, and photographer?

Planning the Wedding Food

Choosing the menu is one of the most enjoyable parts of planning the wedding for many couples. Your favorite foods, dishes that celebrate the region, or seasonal flavors may impact your decisions. Keep your budget in mind, as food is one of the most costly wedding expenses.

Do You Need a Caterer?

If the reception will be small and you have family and friends to help, you may not need professional catering. Hiring a caterer is recommended for receptions of more than thirty people. Food preparation and service is a major undertaking and can be exhausting. Using a professional caterer can relieve stress and allow friends and family to enjoy themselves as guests.

Meet with your caterer or the site manager early and discuss your options. Be ready with the information the caterer needs—the number of people to be served (guests, wedding party, plus musicians, photographers, etc.); the date, time, and style of the reception; location details, including the size of the space and its kitchen facilities; your general food preferences; and your budget. You should also talk about beverage and bar service. Schedule a food tasting before you finalize the deal; pay attention to the quality of the service as well as the food you sample.

Be sure you understand all costs. Is breakage insurance included or extra? Are gratuities and taxes included in the caterer's estimate? How will you be charged for any overtime? (See also "The Catered Party," page 306.)

Types of Service

Passed-tray service is ideal for afternoon and cocktail receptions when a full meal isn't provided. Servers circulate among the guests and offer hors d'oeuvres from trays. Finger foods are the general rule, and cocktail napkins are provided. Sometimes the food trays are supplemented with crudités, cheeses, and fruit served from a buffet table or tables. If sauced or dipping foods are served, small plates, napkins, forks, skewers, and other utensils can be placed on these tables.

Buffet service adapts to any wedding style and is particularly well suited for brunch and luncheon receptions. Guests serve themselves or are served by staff standing behind the buffet table. With buffet service, you can serve a varied menu from which most people will find things they like.

Guests sit at dining tables, which may or may not have assigned places. These tables can be large or small, though circular tables seating more than ten may impede cross-table conversation. Normally, places are set with tableware, glasses, and napkins, but at a casual buffet, guests might pick up their own utensils and napkins. Drinks can be served from a separate service table(s) or at the dining tables by waitstaff.

At a **seated meal**, guests usually have assigned places and are served by waitstaff. Generally, a seated wedding meal has three courses—soup, salad, or appetizer; entrée (or entrée choices) with vegetables; and dessert—but can be more lavish. Whether you offer a choice of entrées, the food items are predetermined so it's easier to estimate quantities than for a buffet. Per-

person cost may actually be less than for a buffet, but the primary deciding factors will be the food itself and the number of waitstaff required.

There are several variations on seated service, including:

- **Plated service.** The food is already arranged on the plates when they are set before the guests at the table.

- **Russian service.** Empty plates are on the tables, and the waitstaff serve each course from platters. There may be more than one waiter; one serves the meats, another the vegetables, and a third might serve salad.

- **French service.** One waiter holds the serving platter while another serves the plates. French service can be very efficient when guests are offered a choice of entrées.

You can also mix these styles—perhaps having plated salad and dessert courses and Russian or French service for the main course.

What to Drink?

You will provide beverages, but you don't have to serve alcohol if you don't want to or have religious or moral reasons not to. Some couples and their families don't drink alcohol themselves but do provide alcoholic drinks for their guests. Others restrict alcohol to wine, wine and beer, or just champagne for toasting. Budget is always a consideration, but people also limit or eliminate liquor for health and safety reasons.

If you serve liquor, carefully estimate the amount of alcoholic drinks likely to be consumed. If you serve a seated dinner, plan for drinks for the cocktail hour *and the meal*. The methods of charging for beverage service include:

Open bar. The hosts pay a flat fee for drinks served during a specific time period—either during the cocktail hour or for the entire event.

Consumption bar. Drinks are charged at a per-drink rate, and a running tab is kept for the time the bar is open. The hosts are charged for what is actually served.

The word *bar* doesn't have to be taken literally. Whether you offer liquor or not, beverage service may mean that drinks are passed on trays, served at drink stations, or from the buffet table. At a seated dinner and often at a buffet, wine is poured at the dining tables. For a very casual outdoor reception, drinks might be kept in ice coolers so guests can serve themselves.

There are many nonalcoholic beverage options. Juice-based punches are traditional, but not everybody wants sugary drinks, so it's a good idea to provide several choices: Sparkling and still waters, natural juices, fruit spritzers, sodas, tea (plain and sweet), coffee—just think about your guests' tastes. Any bubbly beverage can be substituted for champagne.

Assigned Seating

For sit-down dinners and formal buffets, the couple usually determines the seating arrangements. Deciding who sits with whom requires tact, consideration, and a sense of fun, so it's smart to begin your plan once you've received most of the guests' replies. Get an exact diagram of table placement from your reception site manager. You may want to make copies, as you're unlikely to nail the perfect seating plan on your first try. Colored sticky notes, with a guest's name on each, make the process easier.

Place cards are recommended for seated dinners and formal buffets with more than twenty guests. At larger receptions, tables are usually numbered. The number of each guest's table is written on his or her card. On entering the reception area or after going through the receiving line, guests pick up their cards at a small table near the reception entrance; the cards are arranged alphabetically by last name. For small receptions with only a few tables, put a card at each guest's place or guests can seat themselves as they wish.

If you don't use assigned seating, whether the reception is large or small, it's a good idea to have tables reserved for the wedding party, the officiant, the parents, and elderly guests.

Parents' tables. Customarily, each set of parents has their own table, hosting family members, close friends, or both. If the number of people involved is small, the bride's and the groom's families can be seated together. However, it's probably best to seat divorced parents and their families at different tables. The divorced parents may be amicable, but their separate entourages of family and friends are often too large for a single table.

The bridal table: the bride and groom, plus attendants. The bridal table is generally rectangular or U-shaped and set at one end of the room. The newlyweds sit at the center, facing all the guests, and no one is placed opposite them. The bride sits to the groom's right. The best man sits next to the bride, and the maid or matron of honor is seated next to the groom. Bridesmaids and groomsmen then alternate places. If there's enough room, spouses and partners of wedding party members can be included.

The "sweetheart" table. This variation has the bride and groom seated on their own at a table for two. A separate table is set for the rest of the bridal party. This can be charming and romantic, and give the bride and groom an opportunity to have some private conversation. However, some couples might find it awkward to be the center of attention while they eat their first meal together. They may prefer to dine with their attendants and save "twosome" time for later.

Informal bridal party seating. Some couples opt not to have a formal bridal table, choosing instead to move about the room and visit with guests during dinner. Still, a table should be reserved for their attendants, even though they may not all eat at the same time. At a buffet, the couple can go to the buffet table with their guests or a waiter can bring filled plates to them wherever they're seated.

THE WEDDING CAKE

Among the oldest wedding traditions is the cake—probably because wheat and other grains are universal symbols of fertility.

Wedding cakes are still the visual focal point of many receptions. There's no real limit on the size, shape, color, and style. Cakes often reflect the color scheme or general theme of the wedding. Some couples prefer sheet cake to tiers, and others skip the cake cutting and serve individual iced cakes or cupcakes to their guests. Another option is to display a frosted "faux" cake, with slices of real cake plated and served from the kitchen.

FLOWERS AND DECORATIONS

Whatever the season, flowers add beauty and romance to any wedding. The kinds and number of flowers are your choice, and the following guidelines can help you plan your floral scheme:

- In general, the more formal the wedding, the more formal the floral arrangements and bouquets. White is the traditional color for very formal weddings.

- Flowers can provide a unifying visual theme. You might work with a limited color palette (reds and pinks, for instance) for both the ceremony and reception.

- Locally grown seasonal flowers are usually fresher, last longer, and are less expensive than flowers shipped from distant suppliers.

- Choose flowers and greenery that complement the architecture and decor of the wedding and reception site. For example, a high ceiling calls for taller arrangements and plants, and flowers can soften the space and add romance to a reception under a tent.

- Scents should be subtle. Strongly scented flowers in a small or enclosed space can be stifling, but intense fragrances will dissipate in an outdoor setting.

Even if your budget is small, you may want to work with a florist. A florist can advise you about which seasonal flowers are available and may be able to get lower prices on fresh flowers purchased in bulk. He or she may also have rental services for vases, live or artificial greenery, and silk flower arrangements for the altar.

Selecting a Florist

If you don't have a florist in mind, get recommendations from friends, caterers, local nurseries, and managers of your ceremony and reception sites. When you interview possible choices, look at each florist's portfolio and describe your taste in flowers and floral designs. You might bring photos of favorite flowers with you. After making your choice, discuss specifics with the florist, including:

Your flower budget. Everything from choice of flowers to numbers and types of arrangements will depend on how much you can spend. Be prepared to discuss your priorities: An experienced florist can stretch the budget if he knows what matters most to you.

The overall theme of the wedding and details of the location(s). The florist needs to know the time and style of the wedding, wedding theme if you have one, your color preferences, and the decor and sizes of the ceremony and reception sites. Provide the names and phone numbers of ceremony and reception site managers, caterer, and anyone else whom the florist may need to consult.

Installation and delivery. Do you want the florist to install all or some of the floral decorations, or do you need only delivery? Will flowers be delivered to one or several locations? When should deliveries arrive? As soon as you can, provide the florist with complete delivery information: dates and times; address and directions to the site(s); precise information about site access and parking; names, addresses, and all telephone numbers for site managers, wedding coordinators, and anyone who will supervise deliveries and installations for you.

Other floral needs. You may want your florist to handle floral gifts for wedding helpers, table arrangements for the rehearsal party, thank-you flowers for shower and party hosts, flower girl flowers, flowers on the wedding cake, and welcome flowers for out-of-town guests staying at hotels. These items and delivery schedules should be included in your plans.

The contract. Before signing a contract, discuss financial arrangements, including initial deposits and other payment deadlines. Be sure there are no hidden costs, such as taxes, delivery charges, and gratuities.

Flowers for the Ceremony

If your ceremony will be held in a house of worship, ask your officiant about any restrictions or limitations on the use of floral arrangements, greenery (including decorating the chuppah, or canopy, for Jewish ceremonies), and candles. Many religious sites are inherently

decorative and need little embellishment; others can benefit from arrangements that reflect their simplicity.

Flowers for the Reception

What suits the site? The following pointers can be useful as you plan your reception flowers:

- Centerpieces should be above or below eye level so that guests can see across dining tables.

- The bride's and attendants' bouquets can substitute for centerpieces on the bridal table(s). In addition to cutting reception costs, this charming custom lets guests get a closer look at your flowers. Bouquets can also be placed around the wedding cake.

- Seasonal greenery can expand your decorations, add volume to flower arrangements, and stretch the budget.

- Potted plants can make attractive dining and service table arrangements, and hanging baskets add bursts of color both indoors and out.

After the wedding, you can offer arrangements to family, guests, or attendants; or arrange to have them delivered to a hospital or care center.

Other Decorative Ideas

Lighting and linens are also a part of your decorating options.

Indoors or out, you can supplement the basic lighting with romantic touches—twinkling fairy lights strung in trees and shrubs, or hanging lanterns. Lights in the reception hall can usually be adjusted to create the right mood. Be sure to have adequate lighting, especially outside: Rough ground, steps, and terraces can be hazards when poorly lit. Colorful fabrics and table linens are increasingly popular, and can carry out the color scheme of the wedding.

MUSIC AND MUSICIANS

Though music isn't a must, it can play several important roles: setting and maintaining the mood of the occasion, and giving cues for specific ceremony and reception activities (the processional, the cutting of the wedding cake) and transitions (from cocktails to dinner, for instance). If your budget is really tight, creating your own playlists for ceremony and reception music is a popular option. If that's the case, have someone in charge who knows when to "press play."

Music for the Ceremony

If you plan your ceremony in a house of worship, check with the officiant and/or music director about any restrictions on music. Some don't allow secular music, such as Mendelssohn's "Wedding March." The house organist or other musicians affiliated with the site may be the best choice since they're already familiar with the acoustics, the organ or piano, and the timing of religious services. Visiting organists and other musicians may need to coordinate practice time at the wedding site.

Apart from specific religious requirements, the music is up to you. There's a wide variety of choices; the typical ceremony components are as follows:

Prelude. A program of music that begins a half hour before the wedding, the prelude can be played by an organist, a single musician, or an ensemble, and can include a choir or vocal soloist.

Processional. This music signals the beginning of the ceremony, starting when the bride's mother is seated, the groom and best man enter, and the rest of the wedding party is ready to enter. The same piece can be played throughout the procession, but many brides process to a different piece.

Ceremony. Some couples include one or two hymns or songs in the ceremony. These might be solo or choral performances or sung by all the guests.

Recessional. The music played as a couple exits the ceremony site reflects the joy of their new union and might be accompanied by trumpets or ringing bells.

Postlude. Played as the guests leave the ceremony site, the postlude is a piece or short program that continues the joyful mood of the recessional.

Music for the Reception

When hiring musicians for the reception, audition before you make a commitment. If possible, you should see and hear the musicians—whether a soloist, a band, or a DJ—in a live performance. At the very least, ask for a CD or a site where you can listen to or download the music. Check that the performers are the ones who will actually appear at your wedding. Review the playlist, and number and duration of breaks. Ask for and check references, and carefully review the contract, clarifying all costs and payment terms before signing.

Music, whether live or recorded, enhances the festive mood of any reception. The following guidelines can help you select music and musicians tailored to your occasion:

A midday or afternoon reception. When dancing isn't planned, keep the music low-key, so guests can talk. A single pianist, harpist, violinist, guitarist, a small ensemble, or even recorded music will add to the mood without being obtrusive.

A cocktail reception. Go for lively, but not so loud that it drowns out conversation. A pianist, instrumental combo, or classical or jazz group are popular choices.

A dinner dance. Your choices range from a dance band to a full orchestra to a disc jockey or MP3 player. Select musicians or a recorded program that changes as the evening progresses from cocktail to dinner hours and then to dancing.

PHOTOS AND VIDEOS

When interviewing a photographer and/or videographer, couples need to consider their budget and preferred visuals, as well as the following:

- Study the portfolios carefully. Ask to see a recent job of a complete wedding online, not just a sampling of "best shots." You don't have to be an expert to see when pictures and tapes are poorly framed, badly lighted, or fuzzy. Also listen to the audio on a sample video to evaluate the sound quality.

- Check references and confirm who will actually be shooting the wedding.

- Ask about wedding packages and what's included: number and size of prints, options such as fewer but larger prints, extra prints, or videos. Some photographers charge a fee to shoot your wedding, and then deliver all the discs or footage to you. You

---

the first dance

Many couples choose a romantic tune for their first dance as husband and wife, but there's no reason not to cut loose on the dance floor. Just be sure that your selection fits the occasion and that, if you have a live band, they can play the piece well.

own the materials and can print as many copies as you wish.

- Get all the details about costs, including taxes, overtime charges, and fees/expenses for travel time and pre-wedding inspection of the site.

- Will you receive a completed album or can you select photos from an online gallery or proof book? Ask about copyright restrictions.

- Discuss the style. Do you want color or black and white, traditional or photojournalistic, or a mix?

- Tell your photographer/videographer if photos are prohibited during the service. You can probably stage photographs before or after.

Professional photographers and videographers know to be unobtrusive. Still, their work will be easier when you are clear about:

- What photos or scenes you want and the settings you prefer for posed shots.

- Whom to include. Provide a list of people you want in candid shots and assign an attendant or family member to help the photographer spot them. Also, let him know if there are any sensitive family situations, such as divorced or separated parents.

- The schedule of events, and approximate times of special activities (cutting the cake, first dance, etc.).

} TRANSPORTATION {

Unless the ceremony and reception are held at your home, getting from one place to another requires planning. It isn't necessary to hire limos; you might do noth-ing more than spruce up the family car or cars. What matters is that everyone involved in the wedding gets where they need to be on time.

Generally, the bride's family organizes transportation for the bridal attendants to the wedding and reception. The best man and/or head usher coordinates for the groomsmen and ushers. The best man usually drives the groom to the ceremony site, sometimes drives the newlyweds to the reception, and often organizes transportation for the couple when they leave the reception.

Attendants may arrange their own transportation, but they must know scheduled arrival times. If wedding participants drive themselves, you may need to reserve convenient parking for them—even for home weddings. Children in the wedding are usually brought to the ceremony site by their parents; they may go to the reception with the other attendants or the bride's parents, but it's fine if they want to ride with their families.

Be sure that wedding attendants have a ride home or back to their lodgings after the reception. Ask the best man or reliable relatives to see that every attendant has a safe ride and to stop anyone (attendants and guests) from driving if they have overindulged.

Limousine Service

Interview reputable rental services as soon as your ceremony and reception sites are confirmed—limousine companies are often booked many months in advance for peak times.

The traditional complement of hired cars comprises:

- A car to the ceremony site for the bride and her father or escort.

- Cars from the ceremony to the reception for 1) the bride and groom, and 2) the bride's mother or both parents, any children in the wedding party, and/or bridesmaids. You'll need more if you provide transportation for special guests, grandparents, and other family members. You may want only one limo for the bride and groom's drive to the reception. When you arrange rentals, be precise about locations and exact times that drivers will be needed, and provide detailed directions to unfamiliar sites.

Horse and Buggy—and Other Modes of Transportation

Maybe you want to arrive at the reception in a romantic horse-drawn carriage. Perhaps a caravan of hay wagons, classic cars, or motorcycles is just the thing to set the tone for the celebration. Sometimes it's necessary to transport guests from parking areas to the ceremony and/or reception sites. Vans, buses, trolleys, and even golf carts can do the job. Arrangements to hire these vehicles and other novelty transportation must be made well in advance, just as for limos. And be sure to check the drivers' qualifications before making a reservation.

wedding invitations and announcements

Your wedding invitation asks those most special to you and your families to share the celebration of your marriage. Your invitation will not only tell guests when and where you will marry, but also convey the style and tone of your wedding. It will indicate the religious or secular nature of your service, and the formality or informality of the occasion.

Traditional invitation style and wording evolved to give invitees all the details in an instantly recognizable format. Not a traditionalist? Your invitation is yours alone and you may word and design it to fit your circumstances. Yet from the most formal to the most casual—even when phoned or emailed because a couple decides to marry on very short notice—all wedding invitations should provide the information guests need to plan their schedules, send their replies, make travel arrangements if necessary, and select their attire for the big day.

TIMING FOR ORDERS AND MAILING

Wedding invitations are usually mailed six to eight weeks before the wedding date. To place your invitation order in time, count backward from your mailing date. As a general rule, plan at least three to four months for printing and delivery of formal engraved or printed invitations, enclosures, and envelopes. Your stationer will give you a time frame based on your invitation choice. Even if you decide to laser-print or hand-write your invitations, you'll still need time to select paper and develop the design. Schedule an additional two weeks to address, assemble, and double-check them. A few "just in case" days added into the schedule can make a big difference if there's some unexpected delay.

Some Invitation Tips

Here are some ideas to make the invitation process proceed smoothly:

- Ask your supplier to deliver invitation envelopes to you as early as possible, so you can start addressing them.

- Mistakes happen, so order at least a dozen extra invitations and envelopes or just envelopes. Also order extras as keepsakes for yourself and your family.

- Establish a system for recording all replies and gifts.

- For addressing, you need the full names and titles for all guests; be certain that spellings are correct. Make note of relationships ("Sue is Mom's best friend," "Linda's fiancé") as you assemble your list. These details can be helpful when you greet guests whom you don't know personally, arrange table seating for the reception, and write your thank-you notes.

WHAT'S YOUR STYLE?

Stationers and printers can provide catalogs and samples, and you'll have an almost endless variety of papers, shades and colors, designs, typefaces, and extras to choose from. Whatever you select, the style of the invitation should reflect the nature of your ceremony and reception—the more formal the occasion, the more formal the invitation. (For information about engraving and other printing styles, see "A Printing Primer," page 201.)

wedding e-vites

They sound so practical, thrifty, and green—and they are. If those were the only criteria for sending electronic wedding invitations, they'd be used by more couples. If you're intrigued by the concept, consider these points:

- *Do all your guests use email and check it regularly?* This may be the case for your younger guests, but not for your great-aunt Sadie. Some services also require Internet access to view and respond to the invitation. You may end up having to print some invitations and mail them, which could cut down on the convenience factor.

- *Will it get delivered?* While posted snail mail has been known to go astray, emails can fall victim to misspelled addresses and spam blockers.

- *Is it personal and special enough?* A wedding invitation is one of the most personal invitations issued, and an electronic version may not convey that sentiment. Its ephemeral nature doesn't give it keepsake status.

- *Will it make responding easier or more timely?* Not necessarily. The good guest will respond right away, no matter how the invitation is issued. But for the rest of the world, unless you set up reminders (and don't set them for two days before the wedding!) once the email notice falls below the screen, it may be out of sight, out of mind. Follow-up phone calls are likely.

On the plus side, their fun factor makes them great for a wedding shower or attendants' party. Also, when there's no time for a printed wedding invitation, by all means send the prettiest electronic one you can find.

INVITATION ESSENTIALS

All wedding invitations should convey the following:

- Who is hosting: the parents of the bride or couple, the couple themselves, others.

- The purpose of the event: a marriage, a commitment ceremony.

- Who is being honored: the names of the bride and groom, or couple.

- When the event will take place: the date and time.

- Where the event will take place: a house of worship or other location.

- Reception information and an RSVP (or separate reply card): Add these when all the guests are invited to both the ceremony and the reception.

Traditional Formal Invitations

The most formal and traditional invitations are engraved on ivory, soft cream, or white heavy paper, usually 5½ by 7½ inches either as a flat single sheet or a folded double or single sheet, with or without a raised border. The typeface is classic and conservative, such as a

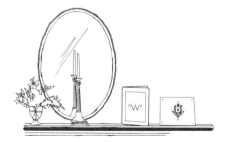

Roman serif. Engraving is the most formal printing style, but thermography and letterpress are popular alternatives.

Traditional Wording for a Wedding Invitation

Third-person wording is the rule for formal invitations:

DOCTOR AND MRS. JAMES STUART EVANS, JR.

REQUEST THE HONOUR OF YOUR PRESENCE

AT THE MARRIAGE OF THEIR DAUGHTER

KATHERINE LEIGH

TO

MR. BRIAN CHARLES JAMISON

SATURDAY, THE TWENTY-EIGHTH OF MAY

TWO THOUSAND SEVENTEEN

AT HALF AFTER THREE O'CLOCK

FIRST CONGREGATIONAL CHURCH

SPRING HILL, MINNESOTA

AND AFTERWARD AT THE RECEPTION

SPRING HILL GOLF CLUB

425 OAK DRIVE

RSVP

The wording and spelling are governed by the following conventions:

- The hosts of the wedding are listed first. When there are multiple hosts, as when a divorced couple or divorced and remarried couples host, each is listed on separate lines with their names and titles in the following order:
  - the bride's mother (and spouse)
  - the bride's father (and spouse)

- the groom's mother (and spouse)
- the groom's father (and spouse)

◆ No punctuation is used except for the abbreviations *Mr.*, *Mrs.*, *Ms.*, *Jr.*, or *Sr.*, or when a phrase requiring a comma occurs on the same line as in the date: Saturday, the twenty-eighth of May.

◆ Abbreviations aren't used, except for *Mr.*, *Mrs.*, and *Ms.*; *Jr.* and *Sr.* are preferably abbreviated or else written out, lowercase; *Doctor* and military titles (*Major*) aren't abbreviated unless the person's name is particularly long and wouldn't fit on one line. (When addressing the envelope, titles such as *Doctor* or *Major* may be abbreviated.)

◆ Use the full names and titles of those extending the invitation. It's okay to omit a middle name by choice or if the name is too long for one line, but don't use an initial.

◆ When a wedding is held in a house of worship or is a religious ceremony held in another location, the phrase "request the honour of your presence" is used. Note the traditional spelling of "honour" with a *u*. The same traditional spelling is used for the word *favour* in "The favour of a reply is requested."

◆ Invitations to a purely civil ceremony or to the reception only are worded "Mr. and Mrs. James Stuart Evans / request the pleasure of your company . . ."

◆ When a Roman Catholic Mass is part of the ceremony, the phrasing is "request the honour of your presence / at the Nuptial Mass uniting their daughter / Katherine Leigh / and / Mr. Brian Charles Jamison." If there is no Mass, use the standard invitation wording.

◆ While traditional invitations use the phrase "*at the marriage of*," it's correct to alter the wording to make grammatical sense in a less formal invitation. For example: "invite you *to* the wedding of" or "hope you will join us *for* the wedding of . . ."

◆ The bride is listed without her title or her last name, unless her last name is different from the hosts': Katherine Leigh. The groom's full name and title is used: Mr. Brian Charles Jamison.

◆ In the Jewish faith, men and women are joined by marriage, so the word *and* replaces the word *to*: Deborah Leah / and / Mr. David Jacob Posen.

◆ Dates on wedding invitations may include the year, spelled out, using lowercase: "two thousand seventeen." The full date of the wedding, including year, is always used in a wedding announcement.

◆ Numbers in the date of the wedding are spelled out: "the twenty-eighth of May."

◆ Long numbers in the street address mentioned on the invitation are written in numerals: "425 Oak Drive." One-word numbers are spelled out: "Thirty Oak Drive."

◆ Half hours are written as "half after three o'clock" (not "half past three" or "three-thirty").

◆ When the invitation is to the wedding ceremony only, it doesn't include an RSVP. The invitation to the reception only or a combined ceremony-reception invitation does request a reply—either RSVP or "The favour of a reply is requested."

◆ Replies are sent to the return address on the invitation envelope. If they are to be sent elsewhere, the address is written below the RSVP line.

When the couple issues their own formal invitation, the wording is as follows:

THE HONOUR OF YOUR PRESENCE
IS REQUESTED AT THE MARRIAGE OF
Ms. Katherine Leigh Evans
TO
Mr. Charles Stuart Jamison

or

Ms. Katherine Leigh Evans
AND
Mr. Charles Stuart Jamison
REQUEST THE HONOUR OF YOUR PRESENCE
AT THEIR MARRIAGE

Past Traditions

For the most traditional of formal invitations, the names of invited guests are written by hand:

Doctor and Mrs. James Stuart Evans, Jr.
REQUEST THE HONOUR OF THE PRESENCE OF

Mr. and Mrs. Thom Nguyen

(HANDWRITTEN)
AT THE MARRIAGE OF THEIR DAUGHTER

Another lovely tradition is the handwritten note but it's only practical when you are inviting a small number of guests. Be sure to include all the necessary information:

Dear Aunt Mary and Uncle Jim,

Charlie and I will be married at 3:30 on Saturday, May 28th at The First Congregational Church in Spring Hill. It would mean the world to us if you could be there.

Love,

Kitty

please save the date

Save-the-date cards, giving advance notice of an upcoming wedding, can be very helpful to guests who must make travel plans, when a destination wedding is planned, or when the wedding will be held at a busy time such as a holiday weekend.

Since save-the-date cards are chosen long before the wedding invitation, they can be fun and informal, even if the wedding and invitation are formal. They're mailed any time from four to six months prior to the wedding depending on circumstances. *Everyone who receives a save-the-date card must receive an invitation.* Now's the time to look at your list and only send them to the guests who are closest to you, the friends and family whom you want to be sure have every chance to make the wedding. Other guests can receive just an invitation. This way, you haven't committed yourself to any but your most important guests.

Contemporary Invitations

There's the formal invitation, and then there's everything else. While no less elegant, many couples opt for invitations that are more personal and reflect the style of their wedding. The information is the same as with a formal invitation, but can be written in the first person. The paper and design might incorporate the theme of the wedding, and stationery manufacturers now offer a wide variety of color schemes, borders, designs, colored inks, and contemporary typefaces to choose from.

The following samples illustrate wording for contemporary invitations:

An informal invitation from the parents of the bride:

MR. AND MRS. SAMUEL RILEY
[or LUCILLE AND SAM RILEY]
INVITE YOU TO SHARE OUR JOY
AS WE CELEBRATE THE MARRIAGE OF OUR DAUGHTER
BRIE ANNE
TO
MR. MARTIN JOSÉ DIEGO
ON FRIDAY, THE FIFTEENTH OF OCTOBER
TWO THOUSAND SEVENTEEN
AT FOUR O'CLOCK
ST. XAVIER'S CATHOLIC CHURCH
NASHVILLE, TENNESSEE
PLEASE JOIN US AFTER THE CEREMONY
FOR THE RECEPTION
FOX HILL COUNTRY CLUB
231 CENTENNIAL AVENUE

RSVP

An informal invitation from the couple to their at-home ceremony and reception:

ELIZABETH PATTON AND DAVID KIM
INVITE YOU TO CELEBRATE OUR MARRIAGE
ON
SATURDAY, APRIL TWENTY-FOURTH
AT ELEVEN O'CLOCK
118 CEDAR CREEK DRIVE
BELLINGHAM

RSVP

When the groom's parents are included:

SHARON AND ELLIOT KAUFMAN
AND
HELEN AND JOSHUA POSEN
WOULD BE HONORED TO HAVE YOU SHARE
IN THE JOY
OF THE MARRIAGE OF THEIR CHILDREN
ETC.

From the couple and their parents—often the simplest solution when parents have been divorced and/or remarried:

TOGETHER WITH THEIR FAMILIES
DEBORAH LEAH KAUFMAN
AND
DAVID JACOB POSEN
ETC.

rsvp etiquette

An RSVP or the phrase "The favour of a reply is requested" obligates invitees to accept or regret an invitation. The notation of the RSVP goes in the lower left-hand corner of the invitation. RSVP notations are included on reception-only invitations, combined ceremony-reception invitations, and enclosed reception cards. They're not included on a ceremony-only invitation. Usually, replies are mailed, either by returning the response card or by a handwritten reply. Today, adding an email address for replies is also an option.

INVITATIONS TO THE RECEPTION

When all guests are invited to both the ceremony and the reception, you can combine the invitations as in the example on page 599. When the ceremony is small and private and a larger reception follows, the invitations to the wedding are generally issued orally or by personal note, and the printed invitation is to the reception only. A traditional reception invitation is worded as follows:

Mr. and Mrs. Roland Benjamin
request the pleasure of your company
at the wedding reception
for their daughter
Amy Claire
and
Mr. Mark Jerome Heinrich
Friday, the fourth of June
two thousand seventeen
at seven o'clock
The University Club
719 Eastside Boulevard
Cedar Rapids
RSVP

When a reception card is included with a wedding invitation, the RSVP goes on the card, not the invitation:

Reception
immediately following the ceremony
⌈or at five o'clock⌉
The Demeter Club
518 Lafayette Street
Lincoln, Nebraska
The favo(u)r of a reply is requested
⌈or RSVP⌉

WORDING FOR SPECIAL SITUATIONS

Although invitations are traditionally sent by the bride's parents, family situations vary so widely that alternate wording may be necessary. The guiding principle is that the invitation is issued by the host or hosts of the wedding and reception. This may be a parent, parents and stepparents, the couple themselves, other family members, or friends. The examples in this section illustrate how formal invitations can be worded to reflect individual circumstances.

When the Bride Has One Living Parent

The invitation is issued in the name of the living parent.

Mrs./Mr. James Prentiss Driscoll
requests the honour of your presence
at the marriage of her/his daughter . . .

If the bride very much wishes to include the name of her deceased parent, it's important not to use wording that implies that the deceased is issuing the invitation. The special wording of this type of invitation overrides the issue of who is hosting the wedding:

DOREEN LOUISE MICHAELS
DAUGHTER OF MRS. MARVIN GADSDEN MICHAELS
AND THE LATE MR. MICHAELS
AND
ROGER LEONARD SIMPKINS
SON OF MR. AND MRS. HORACE SIMPKINS
REQUEST THE HONOUR OF YOUR PRESENCE
AT THEIR MARRIAGE . . .

The same form is used if the groom wishes to acknowledge his deceased parent on the invitation, with his late parent listed below his name: "Roger Leonard Simpkins / son of Mr. Horace Simpkins and the late Mrs. Simpkins . . ."

When the Bride's Parents Are Divorced

If divorced parents are friendly, they may share wedding expenses and act as cohosts. The wedding invitation is usually issued in both names, with the mother's name (and her current husband's if she has remarried) appearing first, and the bride identified by her full name.

MR. AND MRS. BRYANT INMAN
AND
MR. RICHARD COUSINS
REQUEST THE HONOUR OF YOUR PRESENCE
AT THE MARRIAGE OF ⌈THEIR DAUGHTER⌉
COURTNEY MARIE COUSINS . . .

When the Bride Has Stepparents

When the bride has been raised by a parent and stepparent, and her other natural parent is not cohosting the wedding, the appropriate wording is as follows. The bride's full name is used if her last name is different from her stepfather's.

MR. AND MRS. KENNETH CUMMINGS
REQUEST THE HONOUR OF YOUR PRESENCE
AT THE MARRIAGE OF HIS ⌈ OR HER ⌉ DAUGHTER
OLIVIA CAROL ⌈or OLIVIA CAROL STEIN⌉ . . .

When the bride has been legally adopted by a stepparent or she regards the stepparent as if he or she were a natural parent, the invitation reads "their daughter."

When the Couple's Parents Issue the Invitation Together

In some religious and cultural traditions, it's customary for both sets of parents to issue the invitation. These days, joint invitations are increasingly sent when the groom's family shares a major part of the wedding expenses. The traditional wording of the invitation would be as follows, with the bride's parents named first:

MR. AND MRS. ANTHONY COHEN
AND
COLONEL AND MRS. MARSHALL GOODMAN
REQUEST THE HONOUR OF YOUR PRESENCE
AT THE MARRIAGE OF
SHERYL LAURA COHEN
AND
LEWIS ALBERT GOODMAN . . .

five invitation mistakes to avoid

Before anything is printed, check for the following:

- Check, double-check, and have others check the wording. Be particularly attentive to spelling, the correct names and addresses of ceremony and reception sites, and dates.

- Avoid any mention of gifts or listing of gift registries. Also, don't include a notation such as "No gifts please." Keep the entire focus of the invitation on the person you are inviting, not on any implied obligation to bring a gift.

- If you don't want children, don't invite them. Never add "No children" or "Adults only" to an invitation.

- Dress notations aren't included on a wedding invitation unless the ceremony and reception invitations are combined. If it's essential to indicate "black tie" or "white tie," the notation is printed on the lower right corner of the reception invitation.

- References to food and alcohol service aren't included on invitations, although food choices may be listed on reply cards. (See "Reply Cards," page 609.)

Invitations to Same-Sex Ceremonies

The formats for traditional wedding and reception invitations—and announcements—can easily be adapted for same-sex ceremonies and celebrations, though the wording should reflect the nature of the union. The invitation may be from the couple, from friends, or from one or both sets of parents. When from the couple or jointly from their parents, there is no set etiquette as to whose name comes first. It could be listed alphabetically or decided by a coin toss.

USING TITLES CORRECTLY

Professional titles are written in full when used. It's also acceptable for people to use only their social titles if they wish.

- Physicians, veterinarians, and dentists use "Doctor" and clergy use their religious titles.

- Educational degrees, professional certifications, and business titles, such as Esquire, aren't used in wedding invitations and announcements; social titles are used instead.

- People who are customarily addressed by titles in daily usage may also use them in invitations—Judge *or* Justice Judith Wade, Mayor Angelo Bentonni, or Senator Rachel Waggoner.

- A person who may be referred to as "the Honorable" doesn't use the title to refer to himself.

- When a woman holds a professional/elected title and her husband uses a social title, the wording for invitations and addresses is Senator/Doctor/Reverend/Judge/Colonel Marilyn Wentworth and Mr. Russell Wentworth.

(For more on the use of titles, see Chapter 17, "Social Names and Titles," page 215; Chapter 15, "Official Life," page 179; and Resources, "Names and Titles," page 676.)

Military Titles

When the bride and/or groom and/or parents are members of the armed services or serving on active duty in the reserve forces, their military rank or rating is used in invitations. All military titles are written in full—never abbreviated—on invitations and announcements and for mailing addresses. For the correct use of titles for military personnel of another nation, contact one of that country's consular offices or their embassy in Washington, D.C.

When the Groom Is in the Military

◆ For officers ranked captain or higher in the army, air force, and marines or lieutenant, senior grade, or higher in the navy, the rank appears on the same line as the name, with the service branch below:

> CAPTAIN ARTHUR O'MALLEY
> UNITED STATES ARMY

◆ For junior personnel, rank and branch of service are printed below their names.

> NEIL PROCTOR ARMSTRONG
> ENSIGN, UNITED STATES NAVY

◆ Some military personnel, if they prefer, may use their titles (chaplain, doctor) instead of rank or rating on social invitations with no indication of service branch:

> DOCTOR MICHAEL MARTIN ORTIZ

◆ Members of the reserve forces on active duty *only* follow the same rules regarding rank and rating but add "Reserve" to the second line: United States Army/Naval/Air Force Reserve.

When the Bride Is in the Military

When the bride is on active duty, both her rank or rating and the branch of the military are included on the invitation. Her first and middle name appear on one line with her rank or rating and service branch on a separate line following:

> . . . MARRIAGE OF THEIR DAUGHTER
> MARIE CLAIRE
> LIEUTENANT, UNITED STATES ARMY

When One or Both Parents Is in the Military

◆ When a parent is a member of the armed forces, either on active duty, a retired officer, or retired after many years of service, the military rank and rating may be used. The service branch or "retired" isn't used since a civilian spouse cannot be included in the military designation:

> GENERAL AND MRS. HERMAN WRIGHT

◆ If both parents are in the military, the higher-ranked officer is listed first:

> COMMANDER JOHN OAKS AND
> MAJOR BRENDA OAKS
> REQUEST THE HONOUR . . .

◆ In a traditional invitation to a military wedding hosted by the bride's parents, like the following example, only the bride's first names—with her rank and service—are used unless her last name differs from her parents':

> GENERAL AND MRS. BENJAMIN JOHN HODGES
> REQUEST THE HONOR OF YOUR PRESENCE
> AT THE MARRIAGE OF THEIR DAUGHTER

VICTORIA SUSAN
LIEUTENANT, UNITED STATES MARINES
TO
COLONEL ISAAC HALLIWELL
UNITED STATES MARINES . . .

ENVELOPES AND ENCLOSURES

The traditional formal wedding invitation is sent in two envelopes, and the paper and printing match the invitation. The outer envelope is addressed using full names and titles. It also carries the return address. The inner envelope includes only the names of the people for whom the invitation is intended.

Although inner envelopes aren't required (it's perfectly correct to enclose everything in a single, outer envelope), they can serve a useful purpose. The names on the inner envelope make it absolutely clear who is being invited.

Addressing Outer Envelopes

Address the outer envelope using the guest's full name and title, just as you would for any other invitation: *Mr. and Mrs. Ashok Singh*; *Doctor Susan Bartlett and Mr. Henry Bartlett*. *Mr.*, *Mrs.*, and *Ms.* are abbreviated; *Dr.* and *Rev.* are abbreviated if there isn't enough room on the line. It's fine to use middle names, but if you do, they're written out in full and an initial isn't used. (For more examples, see Resources, "Names and Titles," page 676; and Chapter 17, "Social Names and Titles," page 215, for a full discussion.)

Q: *My friend's wife is deployed overseas. Do I address my wedding invitation just to him or to the couple?*

A: Definitely address the invitation to the couple just as you would if she were home. Enclose a short, personal note: "Dear Holly and Jim, We wish you both could be here on my special day! Holly, even though you're overseas, Sam and I want you to know that there's a place for you, even if it's last minute! Jim, we hope to see you on the 25th. Love, Melissa."

In the address lines, words like *Street*, *Avenue*, *Boulevard*, and *Post Office Box* are also fully written out. Either write out the state name—most formal—or use the two-letter postal code.

While the U.S. Postal Service prefers that return addresses on all first-class mail be written or printed in the upper left corner on the front of the envelope, you can have the return address embossed or printed on the back flap. Names aren't used, but do use the address where you would like guests to send gifts and replies.

Because of their personal nature, wedding invitations are usually addressed by hand. Laser printing is

Before you make a final selection, take samples
of your invitation, enclosures, and envelopes
(printers and stationers can supply sample
sheets in the right sizes and weights) to your
post office. Have the postal clerk check the
size and bulk of your entire invitation package.
Consult about postal regulations if you plan to
use a large, small, or oddly shaped envelope or
to enclose anything other than flat and folded
papers. Look over the current stamp catalog.
Many post offices don't keep large inventories
of special stamps on hand, but they will order
them for you with advance notice.

check with the post office

acceptable; just don't use stick-on labels for guest or return addresses—it's too impersonal.

Addressing Inner Envelopes

If used, inner envelopes are addressed using titles and surnames only: *Mr. and Mrs. Singh*; *Doctor and Mr. Bartlett*. There are some exceptions:

Close family and friends. It's fine to address *inner* envelopes with familiar names and titles for close family members and good friends: *Aunt Sara and Uncle Doc*, *Gran and Pops*, *(Cousin) Sally*.

Married couples with young children. Address the outer envelope to the parents only. If you know the children, you can address the inner envelopes with their first names. Otherwise, use children's full names without titles:

Lisa and Bobby [*or*]

Lisa Adair

Bobby Adair

If there are several siblings in the household, you can address the inner envelopes to *The Misses Adair* (two or more sisters), *The Messrs. Adair* (two or more brothers), or both.

Teenagers in the home. Children aged thirteen and over really should receive individual invitations. If this isn't possible, include them in their parents' invitation as above. When courtesy titles are used, teenage girls are *Miss* before age eighteen; afterward use *Ms.* Young boys use no title until they turn eighteen, when they are *Mr.*

Couples who live together. Couples or partners who live together at the same address receive a joint invitation. Address the inner envelope to *Ms. Rasmussen and Mr. Colwell*, or *Ms. Davis and Ms. Lucas*.

An invitee and guest. If you use an inner envelope, address the outer envelope to your invitee and write *Ms. McKay and Guest* (or the guest's name, if you know it) on the inner envelope.

If you use only one envelope, address it only with the invitee's name: Ms. Penelope Denise McKay. Do not write ". . . and Guest" on the outer envelope. Wedding invitations are very personal, so let your guest know by including a separate note, jotting a note on the reply card, or calling to let her know that you'd like for her to invite a guest.

People with military and professional titles. On inner envelopes, treat military and professional titles as you would social titles, written in full: *Admiral and Mrs. Jernigan*; *Judge Sims and Mr. Sims*.

Enclosures

There are a number of extra cards that can be enclosed with a wedding invitation. These are placed in the inner envelope, or the outer envelope if you use only one. Reception cards and ceremony cards are discussed beginning on page 599. You may also need

Reply cards. Although handwritten replies are always correct, printed reply cards and envelopes are now the norm. Reply cards are actually just for the reception—to give you an accurate guest count—not the ceremony. They're printed in the same style as your invitation. Reply cards should include a space for invitees to write their names and a space to indicate whether they will or will not attend.

M _____

_____ accept(s) [or *will attend*]

_____ regret(s) [or *will not attend*]

The favour of your reply is requested [or]

Please respond by the twenty-ninth of May

The *M* precedes the space where the guest writes in his or her title and name: Ms. *Phyllis Reynolds* or Mr. and Mrs. *Matthew Iorio*. If children were included in the invitation, then their names should be written on the reply card, too—at the bottom is fine. If it was an "and Guest" invitation, the invitee should write in the name of his or her guest as a courtesy.

Since a reply card is meant to be convenient, make it as simple and easy to use as possible and include a *preprinted, stamped envelope*.

Pew cards. Small cards printed with the words "Pew Number ____" or "Within the Ribbon" are sometimes included in invitations to family and friends who

guests gone bad

Your replies start to come in and it's so exciting to see the list of "yeses" grow. But wait, Mr. John Doe has added a Ms. Mary Smith and the Deans are plus their four little darlings. It's galling when some guests assume that they may include others when you did not write "and guest" or add the names of the kids to the envelope. It's rude to you and to the plus one, who probably has no idea she's an uninvited guest. How do you handle it graciously?

You might choose to avoid a potentially unpleasant situation and accommodate these unwanted extras. But if you don't have the room or these extras will cause bad feeling among guests who correctly did not bring their kids or a date, then a firm, polite "no" is the right answer. Here's a time when only a face-to-face or phone conversation will do: "John, we're so glad you can come to our wedding, but I'm afraid we can't accommodate extra guests. We hope you understand and we look forward to seeing you on our big day." "Claire, I just received your reply and I think there is a mistake. We're not inviting children, but I hope you and Neil can still come to our wedding."

If you get pushback, stand firm: It wouldn't be fair to other guests with children; your guest list is limited. The superbully may threaten not to come, as if you are the unreasonable one. "John, I'm sorry it doesn't work for you— we'll miss you." Remember the rudeness is his, not yours.

WHEN THE ENVELOPE IS OPENED, *the guest should see the addressed inner envelope, or the face of the invitation and any enclosures.* **TO STUFF THE INNER ENVELOPE:** *1) Insert the wedding invitation face up; the left or folded edge goes in first. 2) Face up and in size order, place the reply card and any other enclosures on top. Enclosures are stacked with the largest one on the bottom, the smallest on the top. 3) Insert the unsealed inner envelope, addressed side up, bottom edge first, into the outer envelope. Note: If you don't use an inner envelope, follow the above steps to place the invitation and enclosures directly into the outer envelope.*

are to be seated in reserved areas. Guests with cards simply show them to the ushers.

Pew cards can also be sent separately, after acceptances and regrets have been received and the exact number of reserved seats needed has been determined.

Maps and directions. Maps and directions to the wedding and reception sites are helpful for guests unfamiliar with your area. You can include them with your invitations or send them later, when you receive acceptances. It isn't necessary to send directions to guests who already know the way. They don't have to be expensively printed, but try to keep them small and in the style of the invitation.

Tissues. In the past, tissue papers were included with invitations to keep engraving ink from smearing. Today's printing technology makes tissues unnecessary, but you can use them if you want. It's a matter of choice.

Stuffing the Envelopes

Use the following guidelines to put each item in its correct place:

When using an inner envelope:

1. Insert the invitation face up, left or folded edge first.

2. Slip the reply card under the flap of its envelope so the card is face up and the addressed side of the envelope is face down.

3. Stack the enclosures—reception or ceremony card, directions or other information, reply card with stamped, addressed envelope—face up, in size order, largest piece on the bottom.

4. Insert all the enclosures, face up, into the envelope on top of the invitation. If using tissues, place them between the invitation and the enclosures.

5. The inner envelope is not sealed, nor is the flap tucked in. Turn it address side up, and place it in the outer envelope, so the name of the invitee is visible when the envelope is opened.

If you're only using one envelope, follow the above directions to insert the pieces into the outer envelope, and then seal it.

POSTPONEMENT, CHANGE OF DATE, OR CANCELLATION

Many things can happen—an illness or death, an unexpected military deployment, even a serious business crisis—that force a change of wedding date after invitations have been printed. Reprinting the invita-

tions is very costly, and there may not be time. If you haven't mailed the invitations and know the new date, you can either

- neatly cross out the old date on the invitation and write the new one in ink, or

- include a small printed or handwritten card with the message "The date of the wedding has been changed from April eighteenth to May sixteenth."

If the wedding invitations have already been mailed and there's no time to print and mail announcements, the couple can notify invited guests by telephone or email.

When the wedding is postponed after the invitations have been mailed and there's time for additional printing and mailing, you can send a printed announcement.

Cancellation

When a wedding is called off, invited guests must be notified as quickly as possible.

When there's time, the family can send printed cards. Cancellation notices should be sent to all invitees whether they have responded to the wedding invitation or not.

MR. AND MRS. ROY KENNON

ANNOUNCE THAT

THE MARRIAGE OF THEIR DAUGHTER

MADISON GRAY

TO

MR. THOMAS CHOU

WILL NOT TAKE PLACE

This saves the bride, groom, and their families from having to answer questions when they are undoubtedly upset.

If time is too short to send an announcement, then phone your guests. Have a prepared message: "I'm sorry to tell you that Tom and Madison's wedding has been called off." It isn't necessary to go into details, but if the cancellation is caused by the death of one of the couple, do tell people, since they may not yet have heard the sad news. Attendants, family, and good friends can make these calls to spare the couple and their families from having to explain again and again.

WEDDING ANNOUNCEMENTS

Wedding announcements aren't obligatory, but they're a nice way to share your happy news with people who weren't included in your guest list—faraway friends, distant relatives, acquaintances, and business associates. Announcements aren't sent to anyone who received a wedding invitation. Gifts aren't expected, though some people may send them; this is strictly their choice. Announcements are usually mailed a day or a few days *after* the wedding.

A traditional announcement follows the style of the wedding invitation (typeface, paper, printing method), and the envelopes are addressed in the same manner as the invitations. The variations in circumstances, names, and titles follow the conventions for wedding invitations, except that the year is always included on an announcement. Announcements are sent by the bride's family, the bride and groom's family, or the couple.

MR. AND MRS. FRANK WILLIAMSON
HAVE THE HONOUR OF
ANNOUNCING THE MARRIAGE OF THEIR DAUGHTER
AMY SUE
TO
MR. PIERRE MICHELE DUMAS
SATURDAY, THE SEVENTEENTH OF JANUARY
TWO THOUSAND SEVENTEEN
OAKLAND, CALIFORNIA

MR. AND MRS. FRANK WILLIAMSON
AND
MR. AND MRS. LOUIS DUMAS
HAVE THE HONOUR OF
ANNOUNCING THE MARRIAGE OF
THEIR CHILDREN . . .

Newspaper Wedding Announcements

Today, wedding announcements are often included in a newspaper's online edition as well as in the physical paper. Since the policies and requested information vary paper to paper, check several weeks—even months— in advance if you'd like your wedding announcement posted. Policies, deadlines, and the information forms vary. Inquire, too, about a photograph. Today, a picture of the couple is the norm.

wedding attire

before you dash off to the stores to buy your dream dress, first determine how formal or informal your ceremony and reception will be, when and where they will take place, and how much money you're prepared to spend. Religious and cultural considerations can affect your selections, too. So will the choice of attendants, since bridesmaid's dresses should be chosen with the women who will wear them in mind.

Most brides purchase new wedding gowns, and it's smart to begin shopping as soon as the critical planning decisions are made. If you're having your dress made, you'll need plenty of time to work with your designer or seamstress. Even purchased dresses require time to order and alter, so factor in fittings as part of your and your attendants' busy pre-wedding schedule.

Men's clothing is easier to select, but don't wait until the last minute. Many men rent formal, and sometimes informal, wedding attire. Because formal-wear rental stores can run out of stock at certain times during the most popular wedding months (June through September), prom season (May), and holidays (December), you should investigate rental sources and place orders well in advance.

This chapter applies primarily to traditional American wedding attire, but the basic guidelines and etiquette of selecting clothing for the wedding party are applicable to virtually every culture.

THE WEDDING GOWN

White is just one of a rainbow of colors worn by today's brides, though it has been "the color" since the 1800s, when Queen Victoria donned a white gown and orange blossoms at her 1840 wedding. By the late twentieth century, white came to signify joy rather than virginity (though traditionalists may hold to the older symbolism) and is now considered appropriate for all brides, including those marrying again. Other colors—especially those drawn from non-European cultural traditions—are equally acceptable. Although white, in all its many shades and pastel tints, is still the conventional choice for long, formal, and semiformal bridal gowns, the ultimate decision about color belongs to the bride.

Fabrics and Styles

As a general guide, the more formal the wedding, the more formal the fabric of the wedding dress. Select fabrics with both the season and the weather in your area in mind. While most people think of silk, satin, lace, and peau de soie as gown material, today's designers offer a much wider range.

Think about your comfort, and don't be guided by looks alone. Lace is beautiful but can be itchy over bare skin. Ball gowns of multilayered or bead-encrusted fabrics can literally weigh a bride down after several hours. Since formal gowns may be boned and often require more structured undergarments than women today are used to, try on the dress with the correct undergarments to get a sense of its weight and ease of movement.

Your choice of style, or silhouette, is a matter of what is most flattering to you and most appropriate to the formality of the wedding. Style, length, and color may also be determined by the couple's cultural heritage. Many brides, grooms, and their attendants wear full ethnic and national ensembles or adapt elements such as the Japanese marriage kimono, Turkish tunic, African *bubah*, or Indian sari.

Neckline, sleeves, and back. Brides often ask how revealing their gowns may be. Your personal comfort is a good guide, but it's also important to think about where and in what tradition the wedding will be held. For a religious ceremony, ask your officiant about any dress restrictions or expectations:

- Are bare shoulders and arms acceptable?
- Is a face veil required?
- Do dress rules differ for religious services in a house of worship versus at a secular location?

For an interfaith or inter-sect service, there may be several traditions to observe, so talk to each officiant.

There may be more freedom of choice for secular ceremonies, but issues of good taste and consideration for others still apply. If you'll be married in a judge's chambers, for instance, respect both your officiant and the solemn civil office he or she holds by dressing appropriately.

something rented, something borrowed

The average cost of today's new wedding gown plus fittings, headpiece, shoes, and undergarments is between $1,000 and $1,800, with designer gowns running into the multiple thousands. But brides have less expensive options, including renting, borrowing, or purchasing a preowned dress. These routes are acceptable and sensible, especially if you want to save money or feel no real need to preserve the dress. After all, you'll always have the photos!

Think about your guests. What's acceptable to your contemporaries—a backless dress, say—may make older guests uncomfortable. While it's tempting to say "my wedding, my way," a gracious bride should never shock or discomfort the people invited to share her wedding day.

Train. A train adds visual interest to the back of a floor-length gown, but it's by no means necessary. Trains may be sewn into the dress, and many sewn-in trains can be "bustled," or gathered up, at the back, so the bride won't need to carry her train after the ceremony. Detachable trains are easily removed for the reception.

Accessories

You have many options, from regally elaborate to stately simplistic. Accessories are best selected to complement your gown and the formality of the wedding, but, again, your comfort is essential.

Veil and headdress. Veils and headdresses may be a matter of religious custom but otherwise are strictly personal choices. Many of today's brides prefer nothing more than flattering hairstyles, perhaps enhanced with flowers, hair combs, or elegant barrettes.

Veils can be worn over the face or trail from the top or back of the head and are usually attached to or draped under a headdress. They come in a variety of lengths and semitransparent materials, including lace and tulle.

A face veil, worn for the processional and during the ceremony, is usually about a yard square and may be detachable. Sometimes the father lifts the veil when he presents the bride. Other times, the bride wears the veil until the end of the ceremony, when it's either removed or lifted by the maid of honor when she returns the bride's bouquet, or lifted by the groom or the bride herself. Traditionally, the blusher veil, a short veil worn over the face that may fall just below the shoulders, is reserved for young, first-time brides.

Bows, headbands, tiaras, and floral wreaths can be worn with or without a veil. Fashion hats and headbands, with or without short veils, make attractive accessories with informal attire such as a wedding suit.

Undergarments. Your dress shop or dressmaker should be able to recommend bras and other undergarments to support the "architecture" of your dress. You should wear these for your fittings and make sure they complement your gown. Since women today aren't used to wired, boned, or strapless bras, or waist-length and full-torso undergarments, "practice" by walking around, bending, moving your arms, dancing, and generally getting comfortable in all new undergarments.

Shoes. The bride's shoes are traditionally satin (with a satin gown) or peau de soie, dyed to match her gown. Then again, brides have been known to go barefoot, or wear flip-flops, sneakers, colored shoes, and cowboy boots. Whatever the style, shop for comfort! It's hard to smile with sore feet. Bring your shoes to fittings to ensure a correct hem length.

Gloves. Wearing gloves can often enhance the look of a wedding dress, but is optional even at very formal weddings. A short, loose glove can easily be removed by the bride and handed to the maid of honor when rings are exchanged. Tight or long gloves are trickier. When it's difficult to remove a glove, you can snip open the seam on the underside of the ring finger before the ceremony and then slip off only that finger of the glove when you receive your ring. Fingerless gloves are another way to solve the ring finger problem. Rings aren't worn over gloves.

Jewelry. Traditional bridal jewelry is classic in design and neutral in color, such as a pearl or diamond necklace and earrings, or simple gold ornaments. Colored stones are fine, too, and brides often wear heirloom family jewelry that is the gift from the groom. Very ornate jewelry can distract from the bride's overall look.

] BRIDESMAIDS' ATTIRE [

Because attendants generally pay for their own dresses, alterations, and accessories, the bride should carefully consider the cost of their outfits. It's also important to think about your bridesmaids' height, figures, and coloring, and look for styles that will be as flattering as possible for everyone.

Though the maid or matron of honor traditionally assists in the selection of bridesmaids' attire, try to consult with all your attendants. Unless someone requests that you order her gown, it's best to respect your attendants' privacy and not ask for sizes and measurements.

Q: *My mother has always hoped that I'd be married in her wedding gown. It's really beautiful and I'd love to wear it, but my mom is 4 inches shorter than I am, and she's petite while I'm more full figured. She's offering to have her dress altered for me, but I'd rather get something new that really fits. How can I get out of this without hurting her feelings?*

A: Wearing an heirloom gown is a wonderful tradition, when it's practical. Based on the differences you describe, however, your mother's dress would probably need to be completely remade. When you talk with your mother, be sure she knows that you think it's a beautiful gown and you'd wear it if you could. Be respectful, but also be clear that you won't feel comfortable in a dress that doesn't work for your measurements. You might also talk with a seamstress or tailor who can explain to your mom how extensive the changes would be. Then involve your mother in your dress selection; seeing you in a beautiful new gown is likely to cure her disappointment. If it's feasible, incorporate something from her gown (some lace or her veil) in your outfit or bouquet—a loving way to show how much you appreciate her.

Try to let your attendants do their own ordering. Alterations are usually handled by the store where the gown is purchased, but inform your attendants if you have better sources.

Appropriateness

Bridesmaids' dresses should match the bride's dress in formality, though not necessarily in style or fabric. As long as the dresses are complementary, the bride can wear a long gown while bridesmaids' dresses can be a shorter length. At very formal weddings, however, both the bride and her attendants traditionally wear floor-length gowns.

Attendants' dresses don't have to match each other exactly, so brides may offer their bridesmaids a range of styles—dresses in the same fabric and color (or range of colors) but of different cuts. Another option is to ask attendants to select their own dresses within general guidelines for fabric, length, color, and degree of formality. Maid or matron of honor's dresses and flowers may be of a different color and style than the other attendants'. Virtually all colors are acceptable today, including black and shades of white. If choosing white, just be careful that attendants won't look like the bride.

Whatever you decide, the goal is to create a look for the entire wedding party that is harmonious and suitable for the occasion. Before selecting attendants' outfits, however, be sure to check with your officiant about any dress requirements.

Accessories

Attendants' shoes are usually the same type and color but don't need to be exactly the same shoe. Dyed fabric shoes are one choice. Tip: Collect all the bridesmaids' shoes and have them dyed at the same time to assure that the colors are a perfect match. Or you can ask your bridesmaids to wear dressy black or white shoes in a similar style. When attendants are wearing street-length or midcalf-length dresses, you'll want to coordinate the color of panty hose—if only for photographs.

Although the bride selects any headdress for her attendants, she should never dictate hairstyles. If you expect attendants to wear matching jewelry, you should provide it, perhaps as your bridesmaids' gifts. Otherwise, discuss jewelry with your attendants but leave the final choice to them.

Young Attendants

When children are included in the wedding, their parents are expected to pay for their outfits. The bride and groom or their families provide all the necessary accessories, including flowers, baskets, and ring cushions.

Junior bridesmaids wear the same clothing as their adult counterparts, but adapted so that it's suitable for their age and size. A ten-year-old, for instance, could wear a strapped version of the bridesmaids' strapless dresses. A **junior usher** dresses like his elders, usually in a tuxedo or dark suit and tie.

A **flower girl** traditionally wears a white or pastel dress of midcalf length, white socks, and party shoes like Mary Janes. The dress may be similar to the bridesmaids' gowns but appropriate for a young child. Head-

Q: *I'll be a bridesmaid in a couple of months, but the bride is making all her attendants crazy with her instructions. She sends us lists with the color and brand of lipstick, eye shadow, and nail polish we have to wear. We're all supposed to have our hair and nails done at one very expensive salon. She's even asked one bridesmaid to have her ears pierced and another to get her hair highlighted. Is this normal? What can we do?*

A: It's understandable that brides want their wedding days to be perfect, but some get carried away and obsess about details. Your situation could be worse. There are brides who have told attendants to lose weight, have teeth capped, hold off getting pregnant, or undergo skin treatments before the wedding—all of which are wrong to ask!

You and the other attendants should meet with the bride now and talk about your issues. Be as kind as you can (she may not realize that her instructions are excessive), but let her know that you're united. Explain your objections clearly and rationally. Look for some compromises. You'll be glad to discuss makeup and hairstyles, but the final choice is up to each of you. You might bring up costs, but don't make it your main issue; if the bride says she'll pay, you'll be back to square one.

If she still insists on having her way, you have two choices: Go along graciously or get out (though hopefully, it won't come to that point). Should you decide to "resign," avoid blaming or saying anything that could end your friendship. Good people can do very foolish things under stress, and your friend may someday regret her overbearing behavior.

dresses include wreaths of real or artificial flowers, or ribbons or flowers braided in the child's hair. Do a test run—if headwear makes a child uncomfortable, it's better to skip it. Flower girls carry a small bouquet or a basket of flowers, but scattering petals before the bride is discouraged because they easily become slippery when stepped on.

Very young boys who are **ring bearers**, **train bearers**, or **pages** wear white Eton-style jackets and short pants with white socks and shoes. Older boys usually wear dark suits with matching socks and black shoes, and a boutonniere.

THE GROOM AND HIS ATTENDANTS

Though formal and semiformal attire for grooms, groomsmen, and ushers hasn't changed significantly for a century (aside from updating lapels and trouser cuts), grooms do have more fashion choices, especially for informal and casual weddings. Even the traditional black tuxedo can be paired with a modern shirt or tie and cummerbund in colors other than black. Clothing from other cultural or religious traditions can be worn for any degree of formality.

It's best to select outfits for yourself and your attendants that are appropriate to the style of the wedding and the solemnity of the marriage service. The chart on page 683 will give you the specifics of dress for traditional formal and semiformal wear, but the general guidelines are as follows:

Formal daytime. A black or Oxford gray cutaway coat and black or gray striped trousers, pearl-gray waistcoat, stiff white shirt, stiff fold-down collar, and black-and-gray four-in-hand tie or dress ascot is worn for a wedding and/or reception before 6:00 PM.

Formal evening. Wear white or black tie when the wedding and/or reception is after 6:00 PM.

Semiformal daytime. Gray, dark navy, or black suit, soft shirt, and four-in-hand tie.

Semiformal evening. Semiformal evening attire usually calls for a dark suit, but it's fine for the wedding party to wear black tie. A white dinner jacket and black cummerbund can be substituted in hot-weather seasons or climates.

Informal day or evening. Lighter-weight suits or jackets and trousers, collared dress shirts, and four-in-hand ties in a dark, small pattern are suitable. In warm weather, grooms and attendants might wear dark blue or gray jackets or blazers with white trousers, with dress socks and shoes. In hot climates, white suits can be worn.

Groomsmen's attire can be organized in two ways: The groom might tell his attendants what he will wear and ask them to rent or purchase the same, or it may be more convenient for the groom or best man to ask for sizes and measurements and then order all the outfits and accessories from a single rental source. Formalwear rental stores may offer discounts for multiple orders and normally provide alteration service. Plan fittings as far in advance as possible in case alterations need to be made. Dress shoes can also be rented, and this is a good way to assure that everyone wears the same style.

Except for boutonnieres (supplied by the groom), attendants are responsible for their rental, alteration, and/or purchase costs. It's normally the duty of the best man or head usher to see that everyone is dressed appropriately.

Don't forget comfort when selecting attire. Coats

should lie smoothly across the back but give you freedom of movement—especially for dancing. Coat sleeves should reveal a half-inch of shirt cuff when your arms are straight at your sides. Trousers are hemmed to where the heel meets the back of the shoe and then angle up slightly to break in front, so the hem rests on the shoe.

PARENTS OF THE WEDDING COUPLE

This will be your children's day, but you have the right to shine, too. Parents and stepparents should choose clothing in keeping with the style of the wedding. Comfort matters as well, since you're likely to be busy for the entire event, so select outfits that feel good, fit well, and look great.

Mothers

Mother-of-the-bride or -groom outfits should correspond with the style of the wedding, and brides can be very helpful by encouraging "the moms" to work together in choosing their outfits. Tradition and courtesy say the bride's mother gets first choice, but that doesn't mean that the groom's mother is limited to beige—unless that's her color. Matronly is out—fashionable and age appropriate is in. Here are some other tips for the mothers of the bride and groom:

- Try not to wear the same or very similar colors as the bridesmaids—you won't stand out.

"best woman" and "man of honor"

When a man is the bride's "maid of honor" or a woman serves as the groom's "best man" they are called honor attendants, but what do they wear? A male honor attendant simply wears the same attire as the groom and groomsmen, but perhaps chooses a tie coordinating with the bridesmaids' dresses, or a boutonniere using the bridesmaids' color or flowers.

A woman may wear a dress in the same color family as the bridesmaids, or she can choose a dress in black, gray, or whatever the main color worn by the groomsmen. Her attire is in keeping with the formality of the wedding. She can even wear a tuxedo or suit like the groomsmen. A woman usually wears a corsage featuring the same flowers in the groomsmen's boutonnieres.

- Wear different colors from each other. Variations on the wedding color scheme are fine as long as each mother's dress color is distinct.

- The length of your gown or dress is your choice, even for formal weddings. Long dresses and skirts are fine for weddings from noon on.

- Mothers of the bride and groom don't have to wear the same length, though many do, feeling that it creates a more harmonious look, especially in wedding photos.

Fathers

When they participate in the ceremony, fathers and/or stepfathers almost always wear the same outfits as the groomsmen. This is also the case for any man who escorts the bride down the aisle.

When the father of the groom doesn't have an active role, he can either match the formality of the male attendants or "dress down" a bit—choosing a tuxedo or dark suit instead of more formal attire. But if the groom's father is to be in a receiving line, he might opt to dress like the bride's father and the groomsmen.

THE MILITARY WEDDING PARTY

In general, brides and grooms in the service may wear either civilian clothes or their uniforms, as may their colleagues who serve as attendants. Depending on the formality of the occasion, everyday and dress uniforms are equally correct, since young and noncareer personnel often don't have dress uniforms. For commissioned officers, evening dress uniforms are the equivalent of civilian white tie, and dinner or mess dress is the same formality as a tuxedo. Noncommissioned officers can wear dress or everyday uniforms for formal and informal ceremonies.

Regulations vary by service branch, but as a rule, only commissioned officers in full uniform wear swords. Hats and caps are carried during an indoor ceremony, and gloves are always worn by saber or cutlass bearers. Flowers are never worn on uniforms, but brides in uniform may carry a bridal bouquet. Service members not in uniform and nonmilitary members of the wedding party dress as they would for any service. (For more on military weddings, see "Reception Plans," page 586, and Chapter 51, "The Big Day," page 634.)

FLOWERS FOR THE WEDDING PARTY

Though not technically attire, the flowers that you and your wedding party wear and carry will be your most striking accessories. It's a good idea to wait until you've chosen your and your attendants' attire before selecting flowers, but begin interviewing florists as early as possible. As a rule, flowers that are in season locally are less costly than flowers ordered from distant suppliers, so ask about readily available flowers and greenery that are appropriate to the style and formality of your wedding. Even if you or your friends will arrange your wedding flowers, it's a good idea to discuss ideas with a professional florist. (For more about hiring and working with a florist, ceremony and reception flowers, and who pays for the flowers, see "Flowers and Decorations," page 591.)

Attendants' flowers can be of a different color or colors than the bride's, and styles can differ as well. For example, bridesmaids might carry sprays while the bride carries a traditional nosegay. The maid or matron of honor might have a different color bouquet, or all the attendants' bouquets could vary across a color range—lighter to darker shades of pink, for instance.

In addition to the color scheme and style of the wedding and wedding attire, consider the size of the bouquet in proportion to your attendant: An 18-inch-diameter bouquet might overwhelm a petite bridesmaid. More important, ask attendants about any allergies they may have; if there's a problem, you can substitute silk flowers.

The bride's bouquet. Traditionally, formal bouquets are all white—including ribbons or trims—and can include one type of flower or several. The flowers are usually formal varieties, including roses, gardenias, lilies, calla lilies, stephanotis, and lily of the valley. Though usually shaped as a nosegay or cascade, they can be as simply elegant as a single calla lily or white rose. If not going the traditional formal route, brides choose any color or style that pleases them or holds special significance.

Tossing bouquets. If a bouquet toss is included in the reception plans, the bride's bouquet can be designed to include a "breakaway" bouquet that's removed from the main bouquet for tossing, or a separate tossing bouquet that's similar to but not as elaborate as the bridal bouquet.

Flower girl's flowers. Since scattered rose petals can be slippery, flower girls today usually carry small bouquets or baskets filled with firmly secured blossoms.

Flowers for the hair. Fresh flowers make charming adornments, whether pinned or braided in the bride's and attendants' hair, worn as a crown or head wreath, or attached to a headpiece. When a veil is gathered into fresh flowers, consult your florist about the best way to attach the flowers to the veil.

Boutonnieres. Boutonnieres are supplied for the groom, all groomsmen and ushers, the couple's fathers, stepfathers, and grandfathers, and perhaps for special male guests and helpers. A boutonniere is usually

practice makes perfect

It's customary for a bride to hold a faux bouquet at her wedding rehearsal, but bridesmaids also need a chance to practice. Use paper and tape to make fakes in the size and shape of the real bouquets. A line of attendants look best when their bouquets are held at approximately the same level, which may be at the waistline for shorter attendants and slightly below the waist for taller women. With a little practice, everyone should become comfortable carrying their flowers.

A FEW TIPS: When bridesmaids enter or exit in pairs, they hold arm bouquets on the outside arms, toward the guests. When bridesmaids are escorted from the ceremony by groomsmen, bouquets are carried in the free, outside hand—not the hand looped through the man's arm. Stems remain directed downward, and to prevent stains, neither stems nor blossoms should be pressed against dresses.

a single bloom or a small spray of a variety like stephanotis that doesn't crush or wilt easily. It can be wired with greenery, so long as it doesn't appear to be a corsage. The groom's boutonniere is traditionally a flower featured in the bride's bouquet. Boutonnieres for other male members of the wedding party needn't match the groom's in color or variety but should be complementary. They're worn on the left lapel, so they won't get crushed when dancing. Boutonnieres are completely optional.

Corsages. Corsages may be given to the couple's mothers, stepmothers, and grandmothers, and sometimes to siblings who aren't in the wedding and to special female guests. When family or friends assist at the reception, the women often receive corsages both as gifts of appreciation and for the practical purpose of distinguishing them from other guests. Corsages complement the flowers of the wedding party, but don't need to be the same color or flowers.

50
wedding registries, gifts, and thank-yous

There's a long history regarding wedding gifts. In ancient cultures, whole communities celebrated weddings as times of renewal and hope for the future. Each union was greeted as the beginning of a new family, and families assured the survival of the community. Wedding couples were showered with symbols of fidelity, fertility, and prosperity. In many cultures, household items were given to help newlyweds establish their home and prepare for children.

Today, the tradition of wedding gifts is as deeply ingrained as ever. Even though some people complain that wedding gifts have become overly extravagant, the sentiment of giving gifts to marrying couples is an excellent one. Gifts are a tangible representation of love and support, a generous offering to help a bride and groom get a good start on their new life together. Wedding gifts may be practical or fanciful, moderate or over-the-top expensive, but each one represents the giver's happiness for the couple.

WEDDING GIFT REGISTRIES

Gift registries have been around for nearly a century as a means of helping guests select gifts that the bride and groom will enjoy. In addition to the traditional choices of china, crystal, flatware, and linens, today's brides and grooms are just as apt to register for hardware, garden supplies, or sporting goods. And couples who already have most of their household items may opt for charity, honeymoon, or financial registries instead.

Today's gift registries remain a convenience for guests, especially those who don't know a couple's tastes, have little time for shopping, or are unable to shop at a couple's local stores. But many guests enjoy shopping for gifts and take pleasure in selecting a surprise for the couple. It's important to note that guests are *not* obligated to choose a gift from the couple's wedding registry.

When, What, and How to Register

Register as soon as you can. Most couples set up their registries early in the planning process, shortly after they become engaged and months before their wedding invitations are mailed. You can register for almost anything these days, but most people consider a wedding present to be something valued and lasting, something that will be cherished by the couple for its significance or sentiment. Register even if you're marrying on a short schedule, so guests can shop after the wedding. The following suggestions should help you select registry items wisely and with consideration for your guests:

Think about what you really need. A registry is a "wish list" but should be based on your real needs and lifestyle. If your style is casual, you may not be interested in fine china and silver. On the other hand, you may look forward to the time when your life is more formal and want to register for these more traditional gifts.

Register as a couple. Registering can be a fun and effective way to plan together. In fact, many grooms play an active role in selecting gifts these days. Couples often need to compromise on selections; and there is usually room on the lists to accommodate their individual choices.

Know that it's a guest's prerogative to choose your gift. A guest doesn't have to select a gift from your registry; in fact, surprises are often the best gifts of all.

Register items in a variety of price ranges. Just as guests have varying budgets, your list should contain items in different price ranges. Also, it's a good idea to include choices for more moderately priced shower gifts.

Include some national chains and/or catalog services registries when possible. This makes gift selection easier for out-of-town guests. They can order through catalogs, local stores, or use a chain's website or toll-free number.

Getting the Word Out

The tried-and-true method of telling people about your gift registry is word of mouth. Once you've registered, provide your parents, attendants, and anyone else who is close to you with a list of your registry sources. Guests often ask a couple's close family and friends about registries. Or they find out about registries by asking the couple directly where they're registered or checking the couple's wedding website. In fact, it's a great idea to show registry links on your website, as long as the links aren't the first thing guests see when visiting.

Do *not* include gift registry lists in your wedding invitations. Some retailers encourage couples to send registry lists with their invitations. Although such enclosures might seem practical, they easily offend recipients by putting the emphasis on gifts instead of on the invitation to the wedding. Don't do it.

If guests ask you directly where you're registered or what you would like, assure them that the choice of gift is up to them. You may certainly say where you're registered (just be sure that *you* aren't the one to bring up the subject), then add, "But *whatever* you choose would be special. Thanks for thinking of us!"

It is okay to include registry information with a shower invitation. Unlike a wedding, the purpose of a shower is to "shower" the honoree with gifts. Your shower host may either enclose a registry list or tell guests about your wish list if they ask.

Do include registry information on your wedding website. It's convenient for your guests and, in fact, wedding guests now expect to find gift links there. Make sure, though, that they're not the first things a guest sees when visiting your site. Guests might take offense, thinking you're more interested in receiving their gifts than in sharing your wedding news.

Registry Alternatives

Not every couple is comfortable registering, and not everyone needs or wants tangible items. Alternatives, like the following, can fulfill your wishes, help your guests with gift selections, and may even spread your happiness in unexpected directions.

No registry. Couples don't have to register for gifts. If you plan an intimate wedding or your guests are all family and friends who know your tastes and needs, there may be no reason to register. In most cases, however, there will be some guests who prefer to give a tangible gift, and having a small registry will be helpful to them.

Charitable gifts. Couples who don't want gifts might steer guests to special charities and nonprofit services. Give close family and friends a list of the causes you consider worthwhile and ask them to inform other guests. You could also encourage guests to give to their favorite charities in lieu of their gifts to you. Established charities will notify you of donations made in your name. It's advisable to avoid suggesting political or highly controversial causes. Also, some people may not hear about your desire or may prefer to give more traditional gifts, so be gracious if you receive traditional or tangible items.

Combination gift and charity registries. This creative type of gift registry enables you to assign a certain percentage of the value of each gift you receive to one or more charities of your choice. Couples can find this unique registry directly at www.idofoundation.org or they can link to the foundation through www.weddingchannel.com.

Financial registries. Check with your bank or investment house about financial gifts; some now have registries for savings accounts, stocks, bonds, and other investment vehicles. There are even registries for couples who are saving for down payments on houses or automobiles. One caveat: If you want monetary gifts, let your family and friends tell others. Don't initiate discussion about your desire for funds or imply that money matters most to you.

Cash and checks. Cash gifts are perfectly acceptable, *if* the guest feels comfortable with the idea. (Although cash gifts are traditional in some areas and cultures, some people just don't like to give money, and that's their prerogative.) If asked, a couple might say, "We're saving for living room furniture, so if you like the idea of giving a check as a gift, that's how we will use it. Whatever you decide would be terrific!"

Honeymoon registries. Now available through many travel companies and agents, these registries allow guests to contribute to a couple's honeymoon trip fund.

⌈ ALL ABOUT GIFTS ⌉

A gift is, by definition, voluntary. Although gifts are customarily expected for some occasions, including weddings, this is a matter of social convention, and no one should regard a gift as an entitlement. Local and cultural traditions may influence gift choices and methods of delivery or presentation, but the following guidelines will help couples know when gifts are considered appropriate, what types suit specific occasions, and how to receive every gift with grace and gratitude:

Engagements

Except when part of a couple's culture, no gifts are expected, regardless of whether there is an engagement party. Engagement gifts, if given, are generally tokens of affection (for example, a picture frame, a guestbook or photo album, a bottle of good wine, a set of guest towels) and not too expensive. If some guests bring presents to an engagement party, the gifts should be opened later so that guests who didn't bring gifts aren't embarrassed. Only if *everyone* brings gifts to an engagement party (in some locales, gifts have become the norm) is it okay for the couple to open them at the gathering.

Showers

Gifts fit the theme of the party (kitchen, bath, linen, etc.) and shouldn't be too elaborate or very costly. A group gift, often organized by the host, is a popular way to give a more elaborate present, but no one should be forced to participate, and no other present is expected from people who do contribute. People who can't attend aren't obliged to send a shower gift, though sometimes close friends or relatives do.

Conscious of the financial burden that shower gifts plus wedding gifts can place on friends, considerate couples (through their hosts) are coming up with clever, low-cost ideas such as the following:

Entertainment showers. Books, games, movies, music, and sports make great themes for showers for a couple. A DVD shower might be perfect for movie lovers.

Recipe showers. An old custom revived, the presents are favorite recipes, usually written on standard recipe cards and collected in a recipe box or file. Online recipe services such as www.tastebook.com can create printed, personalized recipe books that can be added to in the future.

Pantry showers. For couples who already have well-equipped kitchens, guests bring useful and often exotic pantry supplies—spices, condiments, coffees and teas, paper products, bamboo skewers, and the like.

Stock-the-bar showers. Guests needn't buy expensive brands to help a couple acquire the basic bar components, including items such as measures, bottle openers, swizzle sticks, cocktail napkins, bottled garnishes, and tins of fancy nuts.

Best wishes showers. Instead of things, guests bring sentiments—original writings, favorite quotations, humorous sayings. These expressions can be written on pages supplied by the host before the party, read aloud at the party, and then collected in an attractive notebook for the couple.

Your Wedding Gifts

As every child knows, receiving gifts is a thrill, and that childhood pleasure will bubble up again when your wedding gifts begin to arrive. It's especially delightful when couples open their gifts together, but circumstances don't always cooperate, as when you and your fiancé(e) live some distance apart. Don't put off opening gifts; delays will hold up your thank-you notes and may cause red faces when you run into a friend whose unopened package you've stashed away. Being organized about receiving and acknowledging gifts is a must.

When are gifts sent? Be prepared. Gifts may be sent as soon as the wedding invitation arrives, and some may come earlier if people know for certain that they'll be invited (like your grandmother). Most guests send gifts before the wedding, but gifts may arrive afterward, particularly when the wedding is held on short notice. In some cultures and communities, the gifts are brought to the wedding.

How are gifts delivered? Guests send gifts by mail or delivery service to the RSVP address, so when you craft your invitation be sure that this address is where you want both your replies and gifts delivered. After the wedding, guests usually send gifts to your home address.

If it's customary for guests to bring their gifts to the wedding ceremony or reception, then you should plan to have a table set up for them. You're not expected to open the gifts during the reception, but you should arrange to have someone oversee the packages and transport them to a safe place afterward.

How are gifts acknowledged? When gifts are mailed or shipped, a quick call or email to let the giver know that the item arrived is a nice touch. Whether you call or not, *every wedding gift must be acknowledged with a handwritten personal thank-you note*. A guest who doesn't receive a thank-you note after a reasonable time—usually three months after sending the gift—may (rightly) contact you to learn if the gift was delivered. (See "The Importance of 'Thank You,'" page 630.)

Is record keeping really necessary? Yes, absolutely. Gift cards can easily be lost or mixed up, and it's hard to remember who gave what. Keeping a record helps you associate specific gifts with the givers, so you can personalize and keep track of your thank-you notes.

Most couples keep a written or computer log, recording information as soon as gifts arrive. This information should include

- **Date the gift is received.** Also note how it was shipped in case there was damage or breakage.

- **A clear description of the item or items.** Writing "platter" won't help much if you receive three or four. Be specific: "18-inch pottery platter, sunflower design." Include the quantities of multiple items ("4 monogrammed pillowcases, pale blue").
- **Source of gift.** Store, catalog service, etc., if known.
- **Name of the giver or givers.** Save gift cards to double-check spellings.
- **Notation of when your thank-you note is sent.**

It's also a good idea to number the gifts in your log and attach the same number to the gift. If gifts are going to several addresses, be sure that everyone who might take delivery knows to jot down the date, delivery service, and other pertinent information and to attach a note securely to the package.

Wedding announcements. Sent soon after the marriage to inform people who weren't invited to the wedding, announcements are a courtesy and carry no obligation for a gift, although some people may send them.

Other Gifts

Gifts are often exchanged among members of the wedding party, and gifts from the bride and groom to their attendants are considered especially important.

Bride and groom's gifts. It's traditional for the bride and groom to give a special gift of appreciation to each attendant. Usually the bride chooses the gift for her bridesmaids and the groom for his groomsmen and/ or ushers, but a couple might give the same gift to everyone. (Glassware, picture frames, engagement books, and decorative boxes are typical of gifts that cross gender lines.) Gifts needn't be expensive but should be a meaningful commemoration of the occasion.

If you have children in your wedding, personal and age-appropriate gifts will be a special treat for them.

Gifts to attendants are usually presented at the rehearsal dinner, the rehearsal if there is no dinner, or at any bridesmaids' and groomsmen's parties.

Gifts from attendants. Wedding attendants may present gifts to the bride and groom, though this isn't an absolute. The expense of being in a wedding can put a serious strain on an attendant's budget, and couples need to be sensitive. If attendants host a pre-wedding party or give shower presents in addition to their individual wedding gift, a considerate couple will be clear that no other gifts are expected. (You might tell your maid of honor or best man, and ask them to speak to the other attendants.) A group gift—bridesmaids to bride, groomsmen/ushers to groom, or all attendants to the couple—can be the ideal way to express love and best wishes at the least expense for each attendant.

Attendants' gifts are usually presented at bridesmaids' and groomsmen's parties, the rehearsal, or rehearsal dinner.

Gifts to each other. Though not essential, couples often give each other personal engagement and wedding gifts, in addition to their rings. Gifts can range from jewelry engraved with the wedding date or a special sentiment to fun items to share in your new life together.

Gifts for guests. Welcome bags are a popular and thoughtful gesture for out-of-town guests. Wedding favors are also a nice touch, but be assured that both of these are completely optional.

THE IMPORTANCE OF "THANK YOU"

There are two fundamentals of expressing gratitude. First, every gift—whether a tangible item, money, a social event in your honor, or a gift of time or talent—should be acknowledged in writing. And second, your acknowledgment should be prompt.

Personal, handwritten thank-yous remain the gold standard of courtesy in this age of texting, email, and instant messaging. Written notes demonstrate that the writer cares enough about the giver to compose an individualized message and put the words on paper. (See also Chapter 16, "Notes and Letters," page 197.)

Respond in a timely fashion. Ideally, you'll write within a few days of receiving a wedding gift. If you put off all note writing until after the wedding, it can truly become a chore. For couples stymied by the large number of notes to be written, a good suggestion is to set a daily goal. Completing three or four notes each day doesn't seem nearly as impossible as writing a hundred notes within a month. The accepted standard: Your thank-you notes should be written and sent *within three months* of receipt of each gift.

Share the responsibility. The days when thank-yous were the sole duty of the bride are over. Today's brides and grooms share the responsibility, which greatly decreases the time involved, and each writes to the people he or she knows best. This makes it easier to tailor notes to the individual givers.

Include your fiancé/fiancée or new spouse in the thanks. Though you sign your notes with your own name, your message expresses gratitude from both of you. (See "The A+ Note," page 632.) There may be exceptions (when someone does a favor or entertains specifically for you), but in general, people are giving to you as a couple.

Don't take shortcuts. Simply signing store-bought cards shows very little consideration. If you have a Web page, you might put up a general thanks to everyone for sharing your special day, but this isn't an acceptable substitute for personal notes.

Whom to Thank

As you write notes, remember that not all gifts come wrapped in pretty paper. The following categories include both gift givers and the people who make a wedding special through their efforts and goodwill:

Everyone who gives you a wedding present. This includes people who literally hand you a present, no matter how effusively you thank them in person. You should write to each person or couple who contributed to a group gift. The one exception is a group gift from more than four or five coworkers, in which case you can

---

what kind of stationery?

There's no single stationery required for thank-you notes, though you'll probably use a standard one-sided card or single-fold note and matching envelope. The paper can be plain or bordered, white, ecru, ivory, or a pastel color. Use ink that's easy to read; black is always legible.

Brides sign with their maiden names before the wedding, married names afterward. Monogrammed notes sent by the bride before the wedding have her maiden name initials; post-wedding notes have her married initials or the couple's last name initial. (For more about monograms, see "All About Monogramming," page 356.)

Notepapers printed with "Thank You" or a short quotation or verse are fine, so long as you write your own note; but it's unacceptable to use a card with a preprinted message. Some photographers offer note cards printed with a photo from your wedding. These can be great souvenirs for guests, but don't delay note writing while you wait for these cards to arrive.

write one note to be shared among them. (See "People who entertain for you," right.)

Note: Thank-you notes are expected for shower gifts even though you thanked the giver in person when presents were opened. Written notes must also be sent to anyone who couldn't attend the shower but sent a gift.

Anyone who gives you money—cash, checks, contributions to savings and investment accounts, donations to designated charities. You can mention amounts if you want, and doing so assures givers that

currency arrived intact. Always include some indication of how you plan to use a monetary gift.

Your attendants. In addition to thank-you notes for wedding presents, be sure to attach a card or note with a personal sentiment to the gifts you give your attendants: "Thanks for everything, baby brother. You really are the *best* best man I could ask for. Love, Mitch."

People who entertain for you. When there's more than one host for a shower or party, write to each person or couple. These notes should go out no later than two days after the event. The one exception is when a large number of people in your office or workplace host a shower or party in your honor and give a group gift. While it's preferable to thank everyone with an individual note, it is acceptable to write to the organizer or organizers only. Be sure your note includes your appreciation for everyone's participation. The person who receives your note should forward it to coworkers or post it in a common area. But if individual presents are given, write individual notes.

People who house and/or entertain your guests. When family and friends invite out-of-town guests or attendants to stay in their homes, write notes to the hosts and send thank-you gifts. The gift, with your card or note attached, might be an item for the home such as a potted plant or a basket of soaps, or a book by their favorite author. Friends who entertain your visitors—inviting them to dinner, taking them shopping, showing them the sights—deserve a note from you.

People who do kindnesses for you. The neighbor who accepts delivery of your gifts when you're at work, the cousin who supervises guest parking at your reception—anyone who assists you during your preparations, the wedding itself, and after the big event should be graciously thanked. It's also nice to send notes to your officiant and others (the organist or music director, for instance) who worked with you on the ceremony, even though you've paid them the customary fee.

Suppliers and vendors. You don't have to write everyone you hire for services, but anyone who exceeds your expectations will appreciate a courteous note of thanks.

The A+ Note

While there's no formula for the perfect thank-you note, the notes people remember are the ones that express real feeling. Think about the people you're thanking before you write anything. How would the conversation go if you were thanking them in person? Another hint: Look at the gift when you prepare to write; it may provide inspiration.

The first two examples illustrate the difference between a note that gets the job done adequately and one that expresses thanks for a gift and real interest in the givers.

A simple note:

Dear Mr. and Mrs. Gresham,

Thank you so much for the lovely silver candy dish. It was so nice of you to think of Phil and me on our wedding day. I'm sorry you couldn't be with us, but we hope to be back in St. Paul at Christmas and maybe we can all get together then.

Thanks again for thinking of us in such a nice way.

Love,

Courtney

A livelier and more personal note:

Dear Mr. and Mrs. Gresham,

I'm looking right now at the lovely silver candy dish you sent and imagining how pretty it will be on our Thanksgiving table next month. (We're hosting Phil's family for the first time!) It really is one of our favorite things, and Phil and I are so grateful to you.

We were both sorry that you couldn't come to the wedding, but I know your trip to New Zealand must have been amazing. If all goes according to plan, we will be in St. Paul for Christmas, and we'd love to see you and the girls and hear about your travels.

Again, thank you so much for the candy dish and for the beautiful thoughts in your note.

Love from both of us,

Courtney

ten dos and don'ts of thank-you notes

Do personalize your notes and make reference to the person as well as the gift.

Do be enthusiastic.

Don't send form letters or cards with printed messages and just your signature; don't use email or post generic thank-yous on your website in lieu of personal notes.

Don't mention that you plan to return or exchange a gift, or indicate dissatisfaction in any way.

Don't tailor notes to the perceived value of gifts. No one should receive a dashed-off, perfunctory note.

Do refer to the use you will make of monetary gifts. Mentioning the amount is optional.

Don't include wedding photos or use photo cards if this will delay sending notes.

Do promptly acknowledge receipt of shipped gifts, either sending your thank-you within a few days or calling or emailing the sender and following up with a written note.

Don't use being late as an excuse not to write. If you're still sending thank-you notes after your first anniversary, keep writing.

Do remember that a gift should be acknowledged with the same courtesy and generous spirit in which it was given.

There's no reason for a note to be stuffy and formal. Write from your heart and the words will come—as they did in this warm and humorous example:

Dear Uncle Jim,

Well, you really saved the day—the Big Day—when my car conked out. If it weren't for you, I'd probably still be standing in front of Bartlett's, hanging on to my tux bag and trying to hail a cab in that downpour. Meg considers you our personal guardian angel. First you get me to the church on time, and then we arrive in Antigua and discover that you've treated us to three days of our trip! I hope you enjoyed the photo I texted so you could see the incredible view of the ocean from our hotel.

We can't thank you enough for everything you've done. And I promise never to leave home without my jumper cables again.

Much love from your grateful, if forgetful, nephew,

Peter

51
the big day

After so many weeks and months of planning and preparation, *the big day* has finally arrived! It would be unrealistic to say that a wedding day won't be stressful to some degree, but excessive stress is often the result of unrealistic expectations of perfection. When couples keep the real meaning of the occasion firmly in mind; put the "three Cs" of consideration, compromise, and communication first; and genuinely appreciate the efforts others make on their behalf, they're likely to achieve a kind of perfection that has little to do with dresses, decorations, and seating arrangements. Adding two more Cs—calmness and creativity—should get you over any hurdles. As the hour approaches, take a deep breath and relax. The day is yours to savor.

⟦ GETTING READY ⟧

The Bride and Attendants Get Ready

Dressing: The bride generally dresses at home, and if room permits, the bridal attendants can dress there as well. Many wedding sites offer rooms where the entire bridal party can dress for the ceremony, and some brides rent hotel rooms so that they and their attendants can dress together. After they dress, the bride and her attendants should all assemble at least an hour before they're scheduled to leave for the ceremony. The bride's mother and maid of honor help the bride with the finishing touches. Sometimes a professional hairdresser and makeup artist are on hand to help prepare the bridal party for the wedding. If desired, pictures of the bride and her attendants getting ready may be taken.

The maid of honor and bridesmaids check that the bride is wearing "something old, something new, something borrowed, something blue," according to the long-standing tradition. The maid of honor makes sure that an emergency kit of pins, makeup, tape, and other essentials is nearby and ready to go.

Bouquets: If the bride's attendants will be at the house, their bouquets should be delivered there; otherwise have them delivered to the gathering place at the ceremony site. Similarly, deliveries should be made for the flower girl's nosegay or basket, the bride's mother's corsage, and the bride's father's boutonniere.

Transportation: The bridesmaids usually travel together. The bride's mother may go with them or she may accompany any children who are in the wedding party and/or the bride's children from a previous marriage. The bride usually rides with her father. If the groom has children from a previous marriage, they're taken care of by the groom's parents or other family members. The flower girl and ring bearer ride with the bride's mother, or they're taken directly to the pre-ceremony gathering site by their parents.

The Groom and Best Man Get Ready

Dressing: The groom should be dressed and ready to go at least an hour before the ceremony; he can then spend the time before he leaves for the ceremony with his best man.

Arrival: The groom and his best man should arrive at the ceremony site at least fifteen minutes before the hour of the ceremony. Once there, the best man drops the groom off in a private room, such as the vestry or officiant's study. At this point he also makes sure that

---

the best man's last-minute duties

The best man makes sure that all the necessary papers are together and (if there is no ring bearer) that the bride's wedding ring is safe in his pocket. If the couple will be leaving directly from the reception for their honeymoon, the best man checks that all bags are packed and "going away" clothes are ready. Traditionally, the best man also arranges for the newlyweds' transportation from the reception.

---

he and the groom have their boutonnieres, pinning them on their left-side lapels, stem down. The best man waits with the groom until the signal that the ceremony is about to begin.

Ushers on Duty

Arrival: The ushers should arrive at the ceremony site about an hour before the ceremony is to begin. If a head usher is appointed—and it's a good idea to do this because the best man has other duties—it's his job to see that all the ushers have transportation to and from the ceremony.

Flowers: The bride provides a list of those receiving flowers to the head usher, who then parcels out the tasks among the other ushers. Boutonnieres for the ushers and the bride's father, plus any others, say for the groom's father or the couple's grandfathers, are distributed and pinned on—left side, stem down. Ushers are also responsible for presenting corsages to those designated to receive them, such as mothers, grandmothers, and any special friends helping out.

Programs: If there are ceremony programs, the ushers are usually responsible for handing them to guests as they seat them; however, this job can also be given to special appointees of the bride and groom who don't have another part in the ceremony.

Pew cards: If pew cards have been sent to relatives and close friends, they should be presented to the ushers upon arrival. It should be determined ahead of time if certain ushers will escort particular guests who hold pew cards. If the groom's brother is an usher, for example, he would escort his grandmother and mother, just as the bride's brother would escort his own grandmother and mother.

The aisle carpet: Some couples like to have a white carpet rolled out before the bridal attendants and bride come down the aisle. At the rehearsal, confirm when and how it's rolled out and how many ushers are required to place it successfully. It is a good idea for the ushers to practice this maneuver. The head usher designates which ushers will be responsible for rolling out the aisle carpet. After the ceremony, he sees that it is rerolled.

Last-minute details: A last-minute check is made by the ushers. If the room is stuffy or hot, they can open windows. They can make sure that pews are clear of papers or other clutter. They should also familiarize themselves with where the restrooms are, should a guest ask.

Escorting guests: The ushers show all guests to their seats. They should ask any guests they don't immediately recognize whether they wish to sit on the bride's side—the left—or the groom's—the right. If a guest doesn't have a preference, the ushers should try to keep the seating even between the two sides.

In taking guests to their seats, an usher offers his crooked *right* arm for the women guests to hold on to, while their escorts walk behind them. Or the usher may lead a couple to their seats. When a single male guest is escorted, the usher should walk on his left. Ushers don't need to be somber. This is a happy occasion so they should smile warmly and exchange a few quiet remarks as they escort the guests.

SEATING FAMILY

Seating parents: The parents of the bride always sit in the first pew or row on the left, facing where the ceremony will be held; the groom's parents sit in the first row on the right. If the site has two aisles, the congregation sits in the center section. The bride's parents sit on the left side of the center section and the groom's parents on the right.

Seating widowed parents: Widowed parents of either the bride or groom may prefer to have someone by their side during the ceremony, and it is perfectly correct to do so. Their companion is treated as an honored guest.

Seating divorced parents: When either the bride or groom's parents are divorced the seating needs to be planned carefully and the ushers need clear instructions. It can be tricky: Divorced parents may or may not get along, or the bride may be close to one parent and not the other. Tact and diplomacy will be critical for keeping the peace.

In the lucky event that all the parties get along, there's no reason why the divorced parents cannot share the front row. But when there is strain or outright bitterness, it's necessary to use a careful, well-thought-out alternative plan that keeps the parties separated.

When divorced parents sit separately, and using the bride's parents as an example, her mother (and stepfather, if Mom has remarried) sits in the front row. Members of her mother's immediate family—the bride's grandparents, any siblings who aren't attendants, and aunts, uncles, and their spouses—sit immediately behind in the next one or two rows. The bride's father, after escorting his daughter up the aisle and presenting her to her groom, sits in the next row behind the bride's mother's family—usually the third or fourth—with his wife and their family members. This protocol is followed even if the bride's father is hosting the wedding. (If the bride is estranged from her mother, her father and his family would sit in the first rows.)

When the groom's parents are divorced, they're seated in the same manner. The groom's mother, accompanied by close members of her family, sits in the first row (or rows) on the right side of the aisle. The groom's father and family sit in the next rows behind the groom's mother's family.

---

smoothing the way

If you need to make decisions regarding divorced parents or stepparents, make them early on in your planning and don't wait until the rehearsal. It's important to speak to those involved well ahead of the actual event, so when the time arrives everyone knows what's expected. Listen with an open mind to others' concerns and ideas. You can be confident with your final decisions, but keep the conversation sensitive and respectful.

Seating immediate family: Behind the front rows, several rows on either side of the center aisle are reserved for the immediate families of the couple. These guests may have been sent pew cards to show their usher, or the usher may keep a list of guests to be seated in the first few rows.

THE CEREMONY

While this section describes the traditional Christian order of seating, ceremony, processional, and recessional, many secular weddings use the same format.

Places, Everyone

The guests have arrived and been shown to their seats and it's about two minutes before the starting time on the invitation. Before the procession begins, the ushers seat the immediate family of the bride and groom, a signal that the wedding is about to begin. While it's usually just the bride and groom's parents who are escorted

Q: *I have a problem deciding who should walk me down the aisle. Naturally, my father would be the logical choice, but my stepfather helped raise me and is an important part of my life. What do I do?*

A: Choosing between parents may be one of the hardest decisions a bride has to make. If they're cordial to each other, you could ask both to escort you down the aisle—it's rare, but not unheard-of. Or, your biological father could walk you halfway and meet your stepfather, who then escorts you to the altar. But if you really think your stepfather should be the one, you'll have to have a heart-to-heart with your biological father and gently tell him your plan. If neither of these solutions solves your dilemma, you could ask your mother to escort you, choose to walk alone, or ask a brother, uncle, or grandfather to do the honor.

to their seats, the grandparents may be escorted just before them, with the groom's grandparents followed by the bride's grandparents.

The groom's parents enter: The groom's mother and father are the next-to-last people to be seated before the bride's mother is seated and the ceremony begins. Once they're seated, the bride's mother is escorted to her seat.

The bride's mother enters: This is the signal that the wedding procession is about to begin. After the bride's mother is escorted to her place, no guest may be seated from the center aisle. If guests arrive after the bride's mother is seated, they must stand in the vestibule, go to the balcony, or slip into a pew from the side aisles. The ushers may assist them.

Aisle runner: Once the bride's mother is seated, it's time to place the aisle runner, if one is being used. Two ushers pick up the runner, place it at the head of the aisle, and carefully draw it all the way to the rear.

The countdown begins: The bride and her father (or other escort) arrive at the precise moment for the wedding to start, and the procession forms in the vestibule or entrance at the back. As soon as the attendants have taken their places, a signal is given—usually the opening bars of the wedding march—and the officiant enters, followed, in order, by the groom and the best man.

The groom and the best man take their places at the right side of the head of the aisle or, in some churches, at the top of the steps to the chancel. The best man stands to the groom's left and slightly behind him, and they both face the congregation. As soon as they reach their places, the procession begins.

The Traditional Processional

1. The ushers can lead the procession, walking two by two, the shortest men first. Junior ushers follow the adults. In a more modern version, the bridesmaids lead the procession while the ushers stand with the groom and the best man.

2. Junior bridesmaids come next.

3. The bridesmaids follow, walking in pairs or singly. The space between each couple or individual should

ALTAR OR DAIS

Groom

Officiant　　　　*Best Man*

Groomsmen

Bridesmaid

BRIDE'S FAMILY　*Bridesmaid*　GROOM'S FAMILY

Maid of Honor

Ring Bearer

Flower Girl

Father of the Bride　*Bride*

TRADITIONAL PROCESSIONAL *Alternatively, the groomsmen wait at the altar or dais with the groom and best man.*

be even and approximately four paces long. A slow, natural walk is more graceful than the old-fashioned hesitation step.

4. The maid or matron of honor follows the bridesmaids.

5. The ring bearer comes next, followed by the flower girl.

6. The bride enters on her father or other special person's right, her left arm looped through his (or her) right arm.

At the Altar or Dais

The arrangement of the attendants at the front of the altar or dais varies. The ushers may divide and stand on either side, as may the bridesmaids, or the ushers may line up on the groom's side and the bridesmaids on the bride's. You and your officiant will help determine what looks best during the rehearsal.

◆ The maid of honor stands to the bride's left and below or behind her.

marching to a different drummer

There are many variations to the traditional procession, some made by practical necessity and some by creative whimsy. Groomsmen could escort the bridesmaids, or enter with the groom and best man from a side door. The entire wedding party has danced down the aisle or been preceded by the family pups in beribboned collars. And there's a world of music beyond the wedding march. However you choose to make your entrance, let it be in keeping with the venue and let the bride—and perhaps her groom—star. Two-year-olds dressed to the nines and pulled in a wagon may be adorable, but they could upstage the bride.

♦ The best man remains in the same position, but, because he turned to face the altar as the bride and her father arrived at the steps, he should now be on the groom's right.

♦ Usually, the flower girl stands next to the maid of honor, while the ring bearer stands next to the best man. (Children too young to stand for the entire ceremony sit with their parents, who should be seated close by so the children can join them.)

The Ceremony

When the bride reaches the groom's side, she lets go of her father's arm, transfers her flowers to her left arm, and gives her right hand to her groom. He puts it through his left arm, and her hand rests near his elbow. If the bride isn't comfortable this way, they may stand hand in hand or merely side by side. The officiant faces them.

The bride's father remains by her side or a step or two behind until the officiant says, "Who will support and bless this marriage?" or "Who represents the families in blessing this marriage?" The bride's father says, "Her mother and I do," or something similar. He then turns and takes his seat.

If there are children from the bride or groom's previous marriages, the officiant could ask, "Who will support this new family with their love and prayers?" In this instance, the bride, groom, children, and often the guests may answer together.

Just before the bride receives her wedding ring, she hands her flowers to her maid of honor.

At the conclusion of the ceremony, the officiant may say, "I now pronounce you husband and wife." The bride and groom kiss. In some ceremonies, the officiant announces the newly married couple by name.

The Recessional

1. The maid of honor hands the bride back her bouquet and straightens her gown and train for her before she starts down the aisle.

2. The flower girl and ring bearer walk together behind the bride and the groom, followed by the maid of honor and the best man.

3. The other attendants step forward and recess behind the couple either singly or side by side, depending on their number. They may walk together as they entered, groomsmen with one another and brides-

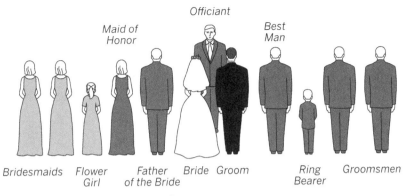

Officiant

Maid of Honor

Best Man

Bridesmaids   Flower Girl   Father of the Bride   Bride   Groom   Ring Bearer   Groomsmen

CONGREGATION

AT THE ALTAR OR DAIS

ALTAR OR DAIS

Officiant

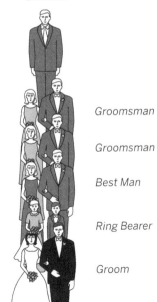

Bridesmaid	*Groomsman*
Bridesmaid	*Groomsman*
Maid of Honor	*Best Man*
Flower Girl	*Ring Bearer*
Bride	*Groom*

TRADITIONAL RECESSIONAL

maids together, or bridesmaids may pair up with groomsmen. Each member of the wedding party should know how to fall in line, since this recessional will have been practiced during the rehearsal.

4. Family and guests follow the processional row by row, starting with those in the front rows.

THE JEWISH WEDDING

A Jewish wedding is rich in tradition and symbolism. While many people may be familiar with the ceremony that takes place under the chuppah, or canopy, there are other parts of the ceremony that they might know less about.

Before the Procession

The Ketubah: Presenting the Marriage Contract. This beautiful, ornately decorated document is traditionally written in Aramaic and is a record of the promises the groom makes to his bride. It is signed by the groom before the marriage ceremony, and given to the bride. It will hang in a place of honor in the couple's home. Today, a *ketubah* may include promises made by both the bride and groom, and may be signed by them or by two witnesses, depending on the tradition followed.

Bedeken: The Veiling of the Bride. Before the ceremony begins, the groom places the bride's veil over her face. This custom recalls the biblical story of Jacob, who was tricked into marrying the elder veiled Leah, thinking her to be the younger Rachel.

The Conservative or Traditional Jewish Processional

The ceremony begins with the procession to the chuppah. Both parents accompany their children. The bride's parents do not "give her away"; rather the two families join when their children marry.

1. The processional for a traditional Jewish ceremony is led by the rabbi and the cantor.

2. The groom's attendants—groomsmen, then best man—follow.

3. Then the groom is escorted by his parents, his father on his left and his mother on his right.

4. The bridesmaids process, followed by the maid of honor.

5. The bride is escorted by her parents, her mother on her right and her father on her left.

6. The bride's and groom's grandparents may also be included. They follow the rabbi and cantor and are seated in the front rows as the rest of the party approaches the ceremony area.

Under the Chuppah

The bride, groom, their parents, maid of honor and best man, and perhaps the rest of the wedding party gather under the chuppah, or canopy. At the rehearsal, the rabbi will determine how many of the wedding party can fit under the chuppah. The bride stands to her groom's right. The ceremony now begins.

Erusin: The Betrothal. The first of two parts of the wedding ceremony, it begins with the reciting of a

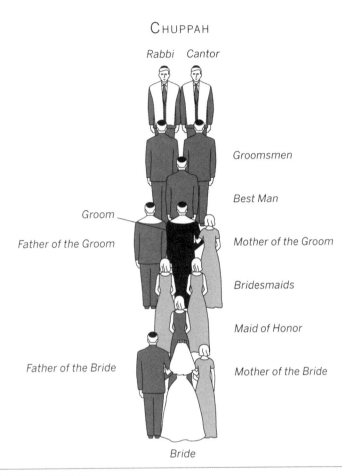

CHUPPAH

Rabbi *Cantor*

Groomsmen

Best Man

Groom

Father of the Groom *Mother of the Groom*

Bridesmaids

Maid of Honor

Father of the Bride *Mother of the Bride*

Bride

TRADITIONAL JEWISH PROCESSIONAL

blessing after which the bride and groom drink from the same cup of wine, symbolizing that they will share everything that life brings them. The groom places the ring, a simple band in precious metal with no stones, piercings, or engravings, on the bride's right forefinger—the finger with the most direct line to the heart. Now the *Ketubah* is read, concluding the betrothal ceremony.

Nisuin: The Nuptials. This is the actual wedding ceremony, which begins with the chanting of *Shiva Brachot*, or seven blessings. At the end of the blessings, the couple drinks from a second cup of wine. At this point the bride may give the groom a ring. The groom breaks a glass with his foot and the entire congregation shouts "*Mazel Tov!*"—"Congratulations" or "Good luck."

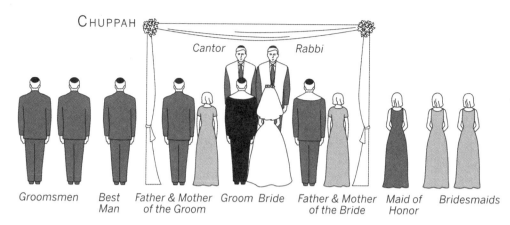

CHUPPAH

Cantor   *Rabbi*

Groomsmen   *Best Man*   *Father & Mother of the Groom*   *Groom*   *Bride*   *Father & Mother of the Bride*   *Maid of Honor*   *Bridesmaids*

CONGREGATION

UNDER THE CHUPPAH

CHUPPAH

Rabbi   *Cantor*

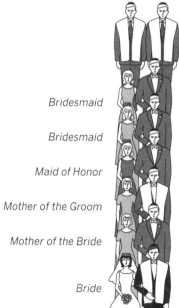

Bridesmaid	*Groomsman*
Bridesmaid	*Groomsman*
Maid of Honor	*Best Man*
Mother of the Groom	*Father of the Groom*
Mother of the Bride	*Father of the Bride*
Bride	*Groom*

TRADITIONAL JEWISH RECESSIONAL

The Recessional

The recessional is led by the newlyweds, followed by the bride's parents, groom's parents, attendants (men and women in pairs), the rabbi, and finally the cantor. Women are on the men's right.

After the Recessional

Yichud: Seclusion. Immediately following the ceremony, the bride and groom retire alone to enjoy the first moments of their new life together and to share the first bites of food as a married couple.

Simcha: Celebration. Tradition holds that on their wedding day, the bride and groom are king and queen. Their guests celebrate them with food and dancing to bring them joy.

THE CELEBRATION BEGINS!

Photographs and Videos

Now is the time for the photographer or videographer to take pictures. If allowed by the place of worship, they may record the bride and groom as they recess; otherwise, they'll take pictures as the couple exits the ceremony site. The bridal party may then gather for a

formal wedding party portrait. If certain aspects of the ceremony are to be re-created for the photographer, the wedding party quickly reenters the building for pictures to be taken *as quickly as possible*. The guests either wait, taking their cue from the parents or ushers, or depart for the reception if it's suggested they do so.

Ceremony Receiving Line

If a receiving line isn't planned for the reception, the bride, groom, their parents, and the maid of honor (and sometimes the bridesmaids) may form a receiving line and greet guests as they exit the ceremony site. If either the bride or groom has children, they may want to stand in the receiving line, too, as a part of the new family.

Bubbles and Rose Petals

If part of the festivities, rose petals or bubbles will be distributed to guests. Once any photography is completed, the wedding party heads to their waiting cars and may be showered with rose petals or bubbles by the guests. (See Q&A, page 646.)

Transportation to the Reception Site

Cars taking the wedding party to the reception should be waiting near the entrance of the ceremony site. The bride and groom are helped into the first car by the best man and are the first to leave for the reception. The bride's parents ride together, and the maid of honor and bridesmaids depart in the same cars in which they arrived. The flower girl and ring bearer may travel with their parents, or they may ride with either the bride's parents or the bridal attendants.

Q: *We're debating whether to be "showered" as we leave for the reception. Any advice?*

A: If you're set on being showered with rose petals or some other celebratory symbol, first ask if this option is allowed— and if it is, you should take responsibility for cleanup, which may mean hiring someone. Many sites ban guests from throwing anything at the bride and groom as they leave the ceremony for the reception, because cleanup is too costly.

All the traditional materials have their drawbacks: Rice can be dangerous for birds if ingested; birdseed can sprout weeds in unwanted places; rose petals are notoriously slippery; and even bubbles can stain a gown. Instead you might distribute colored flags or streamers for guests to wave as you leave. It beats assigning someone the nearly impossible task of trying to recover grains and seeds from grass and flower beds.

AT THE RECEPTION

No matter how large or how small, your reception is a celebration, and you and your family are the hosts. You are there to welcome guests, feed them, enjoy their company, and thank them. Make sure that you greet all your guests, either with a receiving line or by visiting each table to let each person know how happy and pleased you are that they are there to celebrate with you.

From Here to There

The reception hosts and the bridal couple should get to the reception as soon as possible. Since photographs may cause delays, plan the photo session so that the shots including parents, other family members, and attendants are taken first, both at the wedding and reception sites.

People do expect some delay, but any longer than thirty to forty-five minutes becomes excessive, unless your invitation included a later starting time for the reception. If there's a long lag between the arrival of guests and the wedding party, arrange to have special helpers at the reception site ready to greet guests, make introductions, and see that guests are offered drinks and hors d'oeuvres. It's nice to have music (live or recorded) to set the mood. It's not acceptable for the wedding party to disappear, whatever the reason, while reception guests are left to wonder when the reception will begin.

signing the papers

At some point during the proceedings, the bride and groom must sign their wedding papers, witnessed by the maid of honor and best man. If this hasn't been done before the ceremony, then it should be done before they leave for the reception.

when to schedule formal photos

If taken before the reception starts, keep the session as brief as possible. Organize carefully in advance so that everyone in the photos knows exactly where to go and what pictures will be taken. Other options include taking photos before the ceremony or after the receiving line is finished; or taking some shots before the receiving line and finishing the photo shoot later during the reception. Be sure that your photographer and wedding coordinator are aware of the schedule. Don't leave guests hanging while you pose for endless pictures.

THE RECEIVING LINE

A receiving line is a traditional and efficient way for the wedding party to greet guests, either after the ceremony or upon their arrival at the reception. Whether you decide to have a receiving line is simply a matter of choice. It's certainly not required.

When is a receiving line recommended? It's helpful to have a receiving line for a large wedding, when there are seventy-five or more guests. It's an effective way to greet and thank your guests since you may not have the chance to speak personally with everyone during the course of the day.

When is it best not to have one? If the combination of picture taking and receiving line means guests could be left hanging for an hour or more with little to do, it's better to skip it. Just be sure that you greet each guest at some point during the reception. Also, have the DJ or bandleader introduce the bridal party and the bride and groom's parents so that guests will know who's who.

When do you schedule it? If a receiving line is planned, it can be done at the ceremony site immediately following the service. After the line is completed, the couple takes their formal pictures and then continues on to the reception site. The receiving line can also take place as soon as the couple reaches the reception site—after the wedding party completes any formal photographs at the ceremony site.

Where should it be? When the receiving line is at the reception site, the ideal location permits guests to have refreshments while they wait their turn or one that flows into the reception area. If you choose the latter, position a waiter at the end of the line with a tray of beverages (including champagne, if you wish) to offer to guests.

Where to put the cocktail? See that a small table for used glasses, plates, and napkins is placed near the beginning of the receiving line. No food or beverages

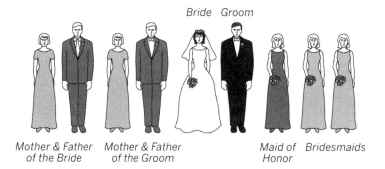

Bride Groom

Mother & Father   Mother & Father   Maid of   Bridesmaids
of the Bride   of the Groom   Honor

RECEIVING LINE, LEFT TO RIGHT: *Mother and Father of the Bride, Mother and Father of the Groom, Bride, Groom, Maid of Honor, Bridesmaids. Line up so guests greet the mother of the bride first.*

should be carried by guests while greeting the hosts and wedding party.

Who stands in the receiving line? The reception's hosts are first in the line. The traditional order is the bride's mother, the bride's father, the groom's mother and father, the bride and groom, the maid or matron of honor, and one or two bridesmaids. When the receiving line is at the reception site instead of at the ceremony site, fathers aren't required to stand in line—they can circulate among the guests—but if one father participates, the other should as well. In a military wedding, it's protocol for a groom in uniform to stand before his bride.

If the line is short, the best man and groomsmen can be included. Sometimes the children of the couple participate, if they're willing and mature enough to greet people. Ushers, flower girls, and ring bearers aren't included, nor are siblings who aren't members of the wedding party.

If people other than parents host (the adult children of the bride, for instance, or an aunt and uncle), they would be first in the receiving line—before the bride's

parents or the couple. If the bride and groom host their own wedding, they may be first in line or give that honor to their parents, if they wish.

Where do divorced parents stand? Divorced parents don't stand together in the receiving line. Usually the parent and stepparent who host the reception, or are closest to the bride or groom, stand in the line. More important than the lineup, however, is how everyone feels about it. Individual situations vary so much that the arrangement should be the one that is most sensible for your family. Plan early with your parents to determine who stands where. Sometimes the fathers circulate among the guests simply to make things easier, but if there's serious discord between parents and stepparents, it may be best to forgo the formal receiving line altogether.

When relations between divorced parents and their current spouses are amicable, they may all be in the line—but separated by the other set(s) of parents to prevent confusion or embarrassment for guests. When all the parents are divorced and remarried, the order can be 1) bride's mother and stepfather, 2) groom's mother and stepfather, 3) bride's father and stepmother, and 4) groom's father and stepmother. If that's the case, excuse the bridesmaids—the line is long enough!

The same alternating order can be followed for single divorced parents. If a widowed or divorced parent is engaged, his or her partner may stand in the line if this is comfortable for everyone. To avoid a very long line, the different sets of parents might take turns standing in line.

---

navigating the receiving line

As a guest, move through the receiving line as quickly as possible, pausing only long enough to be greeted by the host and hostess, wish the bride happiness, and congratulate the groom. Close friends and family often accompany their congratulations with a kiss. Before going through the line, get rid of any plates or glasses. Start by extending your hand and introducing yourself to the first person in the receiving line, who will greet you and then introduce you to the next person in line before greeting the next guest. This eliminates the need for the guest to have to introduce himself repeatedly, and makes the process more personal.

No one should tie up the line with extended conversation. If a guest is talkative, it's up to the parents or the bride and groom to gently break in and say, "We're so glad you're here—let me introduce you to . . ." to help move that person along.

⌠ TOASTS ⌡

Toasting the happy couple at the wedding reception is one of the event's most cherished traditions. The customary toasting drink is champagne. It's fine to toast with plain water, but consider offering something more festive for your guests who don't drink alcohol: Ginger ale, sparkling water, or fruit spritzers are all great options.

Pouring the champagne. At a sit-down reception, champagne is poured as soon as everyone is seated. At a cocktail reception where guests are either seated at small tables or standing, it's poured after everyone has gone through the receiving line or after the couple has entered the reception and been introduced. If champagne isn't being served (or some guests don't want any), toasts are then made with whatever beverage guests have in front of them, whether water, soft drinks, punch, or juice.

Getting the guests' attention. The best man attracts the attention of the guests, either from his table or from the microphone, and proposes a toast to the bride and groom.

What's the order of the toasts? Traditionally, the best man gives the first wedding toast to the bridal couple. It's perfectly fine for his to be the only one offered. The fathers of the bride and groom may each follow with a toast or speech of their own, welcoming guests and saluting the newly married couple. It's perfectly fine for mothers to toast as well. Then it's the groom's turn to toast his bride, and the bride may reciprocate with a toast to the groom. The maid of honor and other members of the bridal party may propose toasts, and both the bride and groom may toast and thank their parents and new parents-in-law. After that, anyone may propose a toast.

Who stands, who sits? Everyone should rise for the toasts to the newlyweds except the bride and groom, who remain seated. If a toast is directed to the bride only, the groom rises; if it is directed to their parents, both the bride and groom rise. If there's no seating and everyone is standing, those toasted just smile and say, "Thank you."

When the bride and groom toast together. When making a toast together, the bride and groom don't speak in unison, but rather stand together while one speaks or take turns speaking.

How should the bride and groom respond to a toast? When toasted, the bride and groom don't stand. They smile appreciatively and when the toast is finished acknowledge it with a "thank you."

---

making a good toast

Wedding toasts are best prepared ahead of time as you may be more nervous or emotional than you might expect. Keep what you say short and sweet—one to two minutes, three at the most. It can be a very simple salute to the couple: "To Jessica and Kyle—two very special people. May you always be as happy as you are today." Resist the urge to monopolize the microphone with a long, rambling story or to regale guests with tales of either the bride or groom's single life.

There are entire books devoted to the subject of wedding toasts, so pick one up if you're really struggling with what to say. Don't be intimidated. It's more important for wedding sentiments to be heartfelt than eloquent.

Sample Wedding Reception Toasts

Best Man or Maid or Matron of Honor to the Couple

- After a brief speech, propose something along the lines of "To Jane and Ben, may they enjoy happiness and prosperity in their life together."

Groom to Bride; Bride to Groom

- "All my life I've wondered what the woman I'd marry would be like. In my wildest dreams, I never could've imagined she would be as wonderful as Keisha. Please join me in drinking to my beautiful bride."

- "I'd like you all to join me in a toast to the man who's just made me the happiest woman in the world. To Michael!"

Parents to Couple

- "We're thrilled you're now a part of our family, and we know that Matt's (*or* Sherry's) life will be blessed and enriched by having you as his (her) wife (husband). Matt and Sherry, we wish you health, wealth, and lifelong happiness as you set off on your greatest adventure."

- "As long as I've known Sherry, she's kept the perfect man in her mind's eye. And the first time I met Matt, I knew immediately that she had found him. You were no doubt meant for each other, and I want to wish you a long and happy life together."

(For more on toasts, see "Toasts and Toasting," page 258.)

BLESSING THE MEAL

If your reception includes a meal, saying a blessing beforehand is certainly appropriate. Here is a wonderful opportunity to honor a relative or friend by asking them to participate. No matter who gives the blessing, you should be sure to ask him or her ahead of time, so that they can prepare.

all a-twitter

Guest, host, bride, groom—who are you tweeting? People who weren't invited? This is one time when the people you want to connect with are right here with you. So, enjoy the reception and share the comments and the photos later.

If you have a DJ or bandleader, ask him to request everyone's attention, at which point the person giving the blessing goes to the microphone. If there is no microphone, the best man calls for quiet and introduces the person saying the blessing. After the blessing is given the best man thanks the person, signaling to guests that the meal should begin.

Guests who aren't religious or who are of other faiths can simply lower their heads and remain respectfully silent during the blessing.

DANCING

Dancing is often an essential element of the reception and almost every culture has a traditional dance: polka, line dance, jig, tarantella, the dollar dance, the *kalamatianos*, and the hora. While there are many types of dances and a wide variety of customs, here are a few general guidelines for dancing at the wedding reception:

When does the dancing start? If there is dancing, it usually follows dessert at a seated dinner, but at a buffet reception, it might start after the receiving line or photo session. That's not to say that the dancing couldn't begin when guests are seated for the first course and continue between courses throughout the meal and afterward. At an afternoon reception when the meal is served later, guests might dance before the bridal party goes to their table.

Who dances first? The bride and groom dance the first dance, while guests watch and applaud.

Who dances next? For the second musical number, the bride dances with her father and the groom dances with his mother. To keep everyone on their toes, either midway through this dance or beginning with the third dance, the groom's father cuts in and dances with the bride. The bride's father cuts in and dances with the groom's mother, while the groom asks the bride's mother to dance. After that, the dancing is open to everyone.

When do the bride and her father dance? While the above scenario gets everyone dancing, a simpler version features a special father-daughter dance. The groom and his mother may do the same. The bride and groom may want to select special songs in advance for their respective parents. They may either dance the entire song alone or be joined by the bride's mother and the groom and the groom's father and the bride. They may change partners halfway through the song and join their respective spouses, and the other guests may join them on the dance floor.

Stepparents and blended families. When family relationships are more complicated, everyone can join the couple after their first dance. The newlyweds should then make a point to dance with all parents and stepparents at some time during the reception.

> # TRADITIONAL CLOSING ACTIVITIES

In bygone eras, guests would wait for the bride and groom to make their grand departure before leaving. Today, cutting the cake is the signal that guests may take their leave. However, it's much more likely that the bridal couple will see some of their guests off and then continue the celebration. As a courtesy to elderly guests and those with young children, consider cutting the cake earlier in the reception so that guests are free to leave when they're ready.

Cutting the Cake

At a seated dinner, the cake is cut just before dessert is served. At buffets or passed-tray receptions, the cake cutting usually takes place nearer the end of the reception. Be sure to give your caterer or site manager and your photographer an approximate time for the cutting. Remember, too, that it takes a while to cut, plate, and serve the cake, so don't leave it to the very end.

Typically, the person acting as master of ceremonies announces the cake cutting, at which point the bride and groom proceed to the cake table and their attendants gather round.

The bride places her hand on the knife handle and the groom puts his hand over hers. It's easier to cut the bottom layer of a tiered cake. Pierce the cake with the knife's point, then carefully make two cuts, removing a small slice onto a waiting plate with two forks.

◆ The groom *gently* feeds the bride the first bite, and she feeds him the second. No smushing!—it's tacky, messy, and requires makeup repair!

- The couple may share a kiss.
- It's a lovely gesture for the bride and groom to cut slices for their parents, with the bride serving the groom's parents and the groom serving the bride's.
- The cake is whisked away and cut so guests can be served.
- Many couples save the top layer of the cake for their first anniversary. If that's the case, be sure to tell the caterer in advance so it's not served.

Tossing the Bouquet

Just before the couple leaves the reception, the bride or her maid of honor gathers the bridesmaids and all single women guests together, often at the foot of a stairs, in the center of the dance floor, or by the door. The bride then turns her back and throws her bouquet over her shoulder. (If she wants to keep and preserve her original bouquet she can throw a "tossing bouquet," a breakaway piece of her bouquet or a small replica.) Tradition has it that whoever catches the bouquet—and gets to keep it, by the way—will be the next one married.

Throwing the Garter

In some places, the garter toss is traditional. The bride wears an ornamental garter just below her knee so the groom can remove it easily. The best man and the ushers gather, and the groom throws the garter over his shoulder. According to tradition, the man who catches the garter will be the next to marry. The throwing of the garter should never be done in a tasteless manner, with the groom fondling the bride's leg for all to see, for example. This can be embarrassing for both the bride and the guests.

Both throwing the garter and tossing the bouquet are completely optional activities, and you can do one without doing the other. Or, the bride could give her bouquet to the couple married the longest or to her maid of honor. Plan in advance whether or not you'd like to include these traditions, so that your DJ or bandleader will be prepared.

Away They Go!

The bride and groom may leave in their bridal finery or change into "going away" clothes. If they decide to change, the maid of honor and the best man generally attend to the bride and groom in their separate changing rooms and collect the wedding clothes. At some point, parents and relatives join them for a good-bye.

Sometimes, the ushers decorate the departure vehicle with "Just Married" written in shaving cream or something similar that is (hopefully) easy to clean. When the newlyweds are ready to go, the attendants and the other guests form a corridor and the happy couple dashes through it to a waiting car, limo, boat, plane, or horse-drawn carriage while being showered with birdseed, rose petals, bubbles, or other such biodegradables. (See Q&A, page 646, about "showering" materials.) Make sure to have someone record the moment, in photographs or videotape, when you make your grand leap into your new life.

52 remarriage

n encore wedding—when one or both of the couple has been married before—is almost, but not quite, like a first wedding. Gone are the days when couples were expected to celebrate second (or third or fourth) marriages with as little fanfare as possible. Today, couples celebrate their unions in whatever style they like, and encore weddings range from the classic and traditional to highly personal and creative events. Indeed, many brides wear white and ask their fathers to walk them down the aisle. Couples register for gifts, have engagement parties, and even ask their "best person" to attend them at the altar again.

Encore couples, however, do have to consider how their wedding will affect other people and the impact their marriage will have on the lives of those they love. When one or both of the couple has children, the marriage is the joining not only of two people but also of preexisting nuclear family units. The wedding marks the beginning of a new family and brings changes to the children's established relationships and routines. Other family members, former spouses, and former in-laws will also be affected.

This time around, an encore couple is likely to be responsible for all wedding planning and expenses, especially if both of them were previously married. Encore brides and grooms have certain advantages based on the perspective gained through past experiences. Having been through it all before, they're usually familiar with some of the essentials of wedding etiquette and are often better prepared to anticipate the decisions they need to make and to take any glitches in stride.

The decision to marry again is a powerful commitment to the ideals and values of love and family, and it deserves to be celebrated. Honoring responsibilities to others is a major part of that commitment, but it's also important for couples to make time for themselves and share the satisfaction of planning a wedding that expresses their love for each other and their hopes for the future.

TELLING THE CHILDREN

Before telling anyone else that you're getting married, inform your children—whatever their ages—from previous marriages. Ideally, each parent will talk with his or own children privately and in person (or via phone, as necessary). Your one-on-one talks can give your children the opportunity to be candid, and also give you insights into any concerns they might have.

In some families, remarriage is indeed good news for all involved, without fears and worries beyond what's normally associated with a major change. But the news might still be unsettling, particularly for younger children and teenagers. No matter how fond they are of a future stepparent, children often feel torn, seeing the remarriage as a test of their loyalty to their other biological parent. They may be sad that there's an end to any hope of their parents reuniting. They may also worry about how their new family will function, especially sharing their parent with stepsiblings, and how much control the new stepparent will have over their lives. Very young children may not know how to react and will need your help to understand what's happening.

No matter how your children take the news of your remarriage, the engagement period can be a time to build. It's a great opportunity to lay the solid foundations of mutual respect, understanding, and affection upon which to construct your new family.

Also be sure to tell your former spouse, especially if he or she is in regular contact with the children. You might even want to inform your ex before talking with your children, so he or she can be prepared to react appropriately. When divorced couples are on reasonably good terms, the first concern should be helping their children adjust to the new family arrangement.

After you tell the children, inform your parents, siblings, and other close relatives before making a public announcement. Though you may no longer be dependent on the people who raised you, make the effort to tell them of your plans before they hear it from someone else.

A PRENUPTIAL AGREEMENT

The idea of a prenuptial agreement can be awkward to raise, but if you feel one is needed, discuss it as soon as possible after you decide to marry. A prenuptial agreement (prenup) can be very important for an encore couple who has children from former relationships and who wants to ensure that certain assets will be legally passed on to their children. The agreement can also define the future custody of minor children.

While a prenup may be a sensitive topic, its purpose is to protect a couple. Be clear with your fiancé(e) that you aren't expecting your marriage to fail, but that you must protect yourself or your children in case you die or divorce. You might suggest that he or she have a similar

ten guidelines for encore weddings

The following list can help couples plan and stage encore weddings that become happy memories for the bride, groom, and those they care about. While many of these basics apply to any wedding, some are specific to encore weddings.

- Work together; the decisions about your wedding should be shared.
- Keep it simple; don't let the details take over.
- If you have children, tell them first—no matter what their ages.
- Be realistic about your budget—in all likelihood it's just the two of you footing the bill.
- Plan your celebration around traditions and themes that are significant to you and have positive associations for your children, family, and friends.
- Talk with your officiant about ways to include your families, especially children. Review the wording of traditional services and texts for appropriateness.
- Make sure that you have put closure to your first marriage, legally, financially, and emotionally. Put away engagement and wedding rings from past marriages; you can save them for the next generation or have stones reset into other jewelry.
- Register for gifts if you want. Even if you don't expect gifts, many guests will want to give them. Registries are helpful to those trying to select something a couple would like to have. Be sure to register in a range of prices.
- Thank-you notes never go out of style. Send a written note within three months for every gift you've received. And remember: Grooms can write notes, too!
- Thank everyone—in person or by note—who helped make the wedding a success.

agreement as well. Then assure your fiancé(e) that you want both of you to continue focusing on building your life together, and put the agreements behind you.

PLANNING AN ENCORE WEDDING

For a number of reasons, including respect for the new spouses, the remarrying couple will want to avoid an exact duplication of their earlier celebrations. However, if the bride hasn't been married before, she may want a traditional wedding. This is a time to consider all your options and be open to doing things differently with the mutual goal of sharing a joyous occasion.

Fortunately, the options are plentiful and since today's weddings focus on incorporating elements that have personal meaning, encore couples can create their own unique celebration. This can mean anything from writing your own vows and including your children in the ceremony to hosting your wedding at your dream destination. (For more ideas, see Chapter 46, "Trends and Traditions," page 567.)

Whom to Invite

The guest list may be especially significant in determining the size and style of your encore wedding. The size of the guest list is up to you (and your budget), but whom to invite can be problematic if a previous marriage ended in discord and you retain mutual friends with your former spouse. If friends sense that attending the wedding means choosing sides between you and an ex-spouse, they may legitimately feel trapped between a rock and a hard place. In this instance, you might decide on an intimate wedding with only close family and friends in attendance. Another option might be a small ceremony and a larger, informal reception.

If you include guests who attended your first (or most recent) wedding, it's usually best to plan a ceremony and reception that won't invite comparisons.

Instead of the formal, evening, church wedding you had last time, you might host an informal midday service and brunch reception at home.

Inviting your former spouse and in-laws? It's usually not a good idea to invite your former spouse or in-laws to your encore wedding. Your family and friends could feel awkward celebrating your new marriage when your ex is there. Most important, consider your new spouse and any children you both bring to your marriage. It can be difficult and confusing for them to celebrate your new family if your ex is there.

Even if you and your ex are friendly, it's generally best to leave him or her out of the festivities, but circumstances vary. Let yours be your ultimate guide as to whether to invite your ex and/or former in-laws. If you and your fiancé(e) both feel good about doing so, you may certainly bend the general rule.

Widowed people who remain close to their former in-laws may certainly invite them. Again, be conscious of their feelings; your new marriage may be bittersweet for your former spouse's parents. It's a good idea to talk with them personally and tell them how much you would like them to attend, but also let them know that you understand if they choose not to.

Invitations

Like first-time weddings, invitations to encore weddings reflect the nature of the occasion—formal, semiformal, informal, or casual. Invitations to small weddings are often made by phone calls or personal notes.

Parents may issue the invitation, especially if the bride is young, or the invitation can be sent in the names of both sets of parents, with the bride's family listed first. These options are correct even though parents may not be paying for the wedding.

When the couple has been living independently, they often issue the invitation themselves. The following example is a traditional invitation from the couple, though the use of social titles is optional:

THE HONOUR OF YOUR PRESENCE IS REQUESTED
AT THE MARRIAGE OF
[MS.] CLARA MILLER O'CONNOR
AND
[MR.] ARNOLD NEUMEYER
FRIDAY, THE TWENTY-SEVENTH OF AUGUST
AT HALF AFTER FOUR O'CLOCK
FIRST PRESBYTERIAN CHURCH
SAN ANTONIO
AND AFTERWARD AT THE RECEPTION
THE CITY CLUB
43 ANGEL BOULEVARD
RSVP

For more examples of wedding invitations, see Chapter 48, "Wedding Invitations and Announcements," page 597.

When adult children host. It's particularly nice when grown children host their parents' wedding and/or reception. On the invitation, the children (and their respective spouses) are listed as hosts with the bride's children named first. Each set of children is listed according to age, from eldest to youngest.

MAKING IT A FAMILY AFFAIR

The following are some ways that today's encore couples are reaching out to make their weddings into genuine family affairs:

Children as attendants. This is practical when there aren't too many children or children too young to take an active part. To avoid any appearance of favoritism, if one younger child or teen is included, all should be. If the bride wants her teen daughter to be a bridesmaid, then it's advisable to ask the groom's teen daughter as well.

If the bride has more than two children, it's usually best not to have them all escort her down the aisle. Since girls as well as boys can be ushers, this can be a responsible role for older children. Children who are comfortable before an audience might present a reading. Just be sure that each child is happy with his role, whatever it may be.

A family addition to the service. After the couple is pronounced husband and wife, the children can be asked to come forward to join them. The officiant then addresses a special message to the children. A family prayer is often included in religious ceremonies. This brief part of the service usually emphasizes the creation of a new family, and the children are mentioned by name.

A candle-lighting ceremony. After the ceremony, the children and perhaps the parents of the bride and groom join the couple. Candles are lit by everyone as an expression of the union of the families.

Special remembrance gifts. The couple might present all the children with something unique to the occasion such as an engraved medallion, picture frame, or photo album.

Wedding photos. Include the children in wedding photos. Be sure your photographer knows who they are and gets them in plenty of candids as well as formals.

Flowers. Small tokens can mean a great deal. Whether they take part in the ceremony or not, be sure that each child has a boutonniere or flower. Corsages are fine for girls, but a small nosegay, a miniature version of the bride's bouquet, can be particularly meaningful and memorable.

---

when future stepsiblings meet

If you both have children from previous marriages, you'll want to get them together before the wedding, but try to make first meetings as casual as possible. A ball game or a movie-and-burgers night makes for a lot less stress at first meetings than a formal family dinner or an engagement party. Divide your attention equally among all the children and avoid remarks such as "I know you're going to be great friends" or "Isn't it wonderful that you're going to have a big brother now?" Kids are naturally curious about and wary of new stepsiblings, so let them take early meetings at their own pace.

Adult children also need some attention. Give your grown children opportunities to meet before the wedding, if possible, but don't try to force relationships. Adult stepsiblings may never become close, but they should always treat one another—and you—with respect and courtesy.

A Few Family Dos and Don'ts

As you and your fiancé(e) move forward with your plans to marry, the following guidelines can help you build family harmony:

Do consult each child individually to determine if he or she would like to be in the wedding. Avoid simply expecting them to participate. Respect the wishes of a child or teen who doesn't want to participate, but also leave the door open for a change of heart.

Don't question your future spouse's children about their other parent. Your interest may be benign, but questioning children may be seen as prying and can undermine the children's trust in you.

Do answer children's questions about your previous marriage. You can be honest without being explicit.

Do speak respectfully about a former spouse. This is the time to create a positive, respectful atmosphere.

Do consult your former spouse to schedule events involving the children, especially if wedding activities may conflict with regular visits. Set the pattern now for cooperation with ex-spouses.

Don't use wedding-related activities as an excuse for missing your regular visits and special events with the children.

ENCORE QUESTIONS ABOUT . . .

. . . Attire

No longer are encore brides advised to wear a pastel suit or off-white gown. White is a color of joy and celebration for encore and first-time brides alike. Our

children and the honeymoon

Sooner or later young children are likely to ask, "What's a honeymoon?" followed by, "Can we go?" Whether they raise the subject or you do, be very sensitive to their feelings.

An encore wedding followed immediately by a honeymoon trip can be difficult for children. The disappearance of their parent and new stepparent right after the wedding may be confusing for very young children. Older children may feel hurt or angry at being excluded, especially if they worry that your remarriage will relegate them to second place in your affections.

Children tend to live in the present moment. They may not really grasp why you're going away after the wedding—no matter how well you explain. If children are genuinely troubled or upset, there are alternatives that couples might consider:

- Dividing the honeymoon into two parts—for example, several days devoted to the children followed by time on your own as a couple.

- Delaying the honeymoon. Give the children some time to settle into their new family life (and perhaps new home) and to adjust to the idea that you and your new spouse will be going away on a trip by yourselves. This adjustment period could be several months, or more than a year, depending on the circumstances and the ages of the children.

- Planning simultaneous trips. Arrange for the children to spend special time with their other parent or perhaps their grandparents. If you all return from your trips at the same time, the children are likely to see their time with relatives as something special. You can all share your stories about your trips.

---

advice? Choose a dress, suit, or gown that's appropriate to your age and figure. The same advice applies to a veil, if you wear one. Choose one that suits your outfit, but forgo the blusher veil that's more appropriate for a very young or first-time bride.

. . . Attendants

While your wedding shouldn't be a replica of your first wedding, it's absolutely fine to include people who remain near and dear to you, whether they were attendants in your previous wedding or not. Sisters, brothers, best friends . . . all are eligible, but just make sure that whoever you ask is comfortable with the idea.

. . . Showers

Here's a place where second-time couples should exercise some tact and good judgment. A shower is okay only if it's carefully planned. Other than close friends and relatives, the guest list shouldn't include people who came to a shower for your first wedding. If friends plan to invite people who have already "showered" you, a luncheon or afternoon tea—sans gifts—would be a better way to go.

Often theme showers work well because they allow the couple to be specific about what they need. For example, a monogram shower has lots of possibilities, from notepaper and luggage tags to towels and linens.

. . . Gifts

Technically, gifts aren't obligatory for encore weddings, and many couples don't want them, as they may already own china and silverware and may even have a surplus of kitchen appliances after combining their two households. However, guests who weren't invited to a previous marriage—and some who were—often want to express their best wishes with gifts. So how do you tell people "no gifts, please"?

First, make no mention of gifts on your wedding invitation or enclosures. Instead, rely on word of mouth, mentioning your wish to attendants, relatives, and good friends and encouraging them to pass the word. While adding "no gifts" to the invitation may seem thoughtful, even the smallest mention of gifts puts the emphasis on material items. If someone sends a gift anyway, receive it graciously and acknowledge it with a thank-you note.

Q: *After my divorce, I kept my ex's last name and all the monogrammed wedding gifts including the sterling flatware. Now I'm remarrying, and I wonder what to do with these things.*

A: Many encore couples dispose of monogrammed items like towels and table linens—either giving them away or passing them on to children from their earlier marriages—but something as costly as sterling flatware can be another matter entirely. You might sell the sterling and replace it with a set you both choose. Or if your future husband agrees, you could continue to use it. Nowadays, people collect silverware that has been engraved with many different initials, so setting the table with your monogrammed flatware may hardly be noticed. Just be sure to discuss the options with your fiancé and make the decision together.

New friends who've never given you a wedding gift before may want to give you something, so it's thoughtful to register for gifts. Registering at one or two stores can be helpful for guests. If you decide to register, think about your interests: Sporting goods, hardware, garden tools, books, music, and movies—you can register for items that are both useful and inexpensive. (See also Chapter 50, "Wedding Registries, Gifts, and Thank-yous," page 624.)

53
a guide for wedding guests

wedding isn't just another party. It's a piece of history—cemented in ceremony and recorded in law—and being a part of its celebration is an honor that entails some obligations. The bride and groom are the stars of the event, but guests also have a role to play: to witness the formation of a new family and to celebrate that union joyously, graciously, and with the utmost consideration for others. Unlike most parties, a wedding usually brings together people of several generations, and it's important to be understanding and respectful of people whose view of "proper" conduct may differ from your own. A wedding may be your introduction to a tradition or culture, and good guests adapt to and respect customs that are new to them.

Whether the wedding is held in a cathedral or a backyard, whether the guest list includes a mere handful or several hundred, every guest should behave in a way that will make the day happy for everyone—an obligation that actually begins with the arrival of your invitation.

[PROMPT RESPONSES]

A guest's first duty is to respond promptly to any wedding invitation that includes an RSVP request or a reply card. Check your schedule and consult with anyone else included in your invitation, then make your response as soon as you can. The reasons for a prompt reply are simple: The hosts of the wedding need the most exact count of guests in order to plan for catering, guest seating, and so on. If you regret promptly, the couple will have time to invite someone in your place if they wish.

Many wedding invitations come with a reply card and preaddressed return envelope. Fill in your name(s), indicating whether you'll attend. (See also Chapter 48, "Wedding Invitations and Announcements," page 597.)

are my children included?

If your children's names are on the invitation's envelope(s) or it says, "The Smith Family," then they're in. If their names are not listed, then they're **not** invited. No one should ever ask the couple or the hosts to include children—or anyone else—who haven't been specifically invited. It's rude to ask a couple to make an exception for your children or to subject them to the embarrassment of having to say "no" to such a request.

Occasionally, children are invited to a ceremony but not to the reception or vice versa. Whether children are excluded altogether or included in only one of the wedding day activities, the invitation will arrive in more than enough time for you to arrange for child care on the wedding day.

When the invitation is addressed to you "and guest," you must decide if you want to bring someone. When you accept, let the hosts know if you'll be bringing a guest. Ideally, write the name of your guest on the reply card or include the name in your written response. If you don't yet know who that will be, accept for yourself "and guest" ("Ms. Jenna Abernathy and guest"). Once you know whom you'll bring, it's thoughtful to let the hosts know your guest's name—prior to the wedding day, if possible. If you reply only for yourself, don't show up at the wedding with a date or companion.

Written Responses

When an invitation includes an RSVP but no response card, be guided by the information on the invitation.

In some cases, there may be an address and an email address, and you can reply either in writing or by email.

If there's an address below the RSVP notation, write to the hosts at that address. When there is no address on the invitation itself, respond to the return address on the mailing envelope. Responses are handwritten, normally on plain or bordered notepaper or monogrammed stationery. When you regret, excuses aren't included, but in a personal note, you might explain your absence if you want. There are three basic types of response, illustrated below:

Formal response. Written in the third person, this reply follows the wording of a formal invitation:

Mr. and Mrs. Harold McGowan
accept with pleasure
[or *regret that they are unable to accept*]
your kind invitation for
Saturday, the nineteenth of June

Personal note. Usually written to hosts you know well, a personal note should be brief but sincere:

Dear Ann and John,

Rob and I are delighted to accept your invitation to attend Margaret and Tom's wedding on June nineteenth.

Yours sincerely,

Brittany Ellis

Dear Agatha,

I am so sorry that I can't join you and Max for your wedding. I have to be in Chicago on business, but you two will be first in my thoughts on your special day.

Love to you both,

Dottie

Cancellations

If something unforeseen happens and you cannot attend a wedding after you've accepted the invitation, you should call the hosts immediately. This is very important because the hosts will, in most cases, be held financially responsible for all or a substantial percentage of any catering expenses for no-shows. Also, alerting the hosts that you can't come may give them time to invite someone else.

CHOOSING AND SENDING GIFTS

You've heard it many times before, but the saying still holds true—"It's the thought that counts."

Gift selection isn't really about buying, nor is it a competition. Choosing a gift is a matter of *deciding* what you believe will give pleasure. Thinking about someone else is one reason why people often enjoy shopping for

destination weddings

Guests to a destination wedding are invited months in advance, particularly if the location requires making travel arrangements. This can be a problem if your schedule is uncertain or if you're unsure that you can afford the trip. A long weekend of wedding festivities in Barbados may sound fantastic, but take some time to consider before accepting. Guests pay for their own transportation and lodging. Can your budget bear it? Also, will you be able to get the time away from your job? If children aren't invited, can you make child-care arrangements? Do you have other obligations that must be honored—military reserve service, for example? What you want to avoid is a last-minute cancellation that disappoints your hosts and costs you financially.

others. Still, guests do have questions about gifts, and these are the most frequently asked:

Do I have to choose something from the bridal registry? No. The registry is a convenience for guests, not a mandate. However, checking a couple's registries may give you a better idea of their taste and needs, even if you purchase off-registry.

Am I supposed to buy a gift that costs as much as what the hosts spend on each person at the wedding? No. This modern myth causes considerable anxiety for guests, but it is simply untrue. The amount you spend is strictly a matter of your budget, how close you are to the bride or groom, and what you think is an appropriate gift. Even if you're aware of how much is being spent on the wedding, you are under no obligation to spend more than you can afford.

Is it tacky to send money? Not at all. Wedding gifts of money have been around for quite some time and are perfectly acceptable *if* the guest feels comfortable with the idea. Cash gifts are often just right for couples who have already established their households or are saving for something special. In fact, some couples set up financial gift registries, such as savings or house-down-payment accounts, as well as honeymoon registries. (For more about financial gifts, see "Registry Alternatives," page 626.)

How do I give the couple a gift of money? A monetary gift is sent either directly to the couple with a personal note, or into the financial gift registry. When a gift is sent to a financial institution or a travel agency where the couple has registered, the couple receives a notification of the gift and its amount. In some cultures, a gift of money is brought to the wedding and presented to the bride and groom.

Can I send something I already own? Yes, but only as long as it is in good condition—*not* a castoff—and you're confident that the couple will like the item. A pre-owned wedding gift is usually an heirloom piece and one that has been in the bride's or groom's family, like a silver tray or an antique valued for its age and history. Heirloom jewelry is often passed on in families also. As with any gift, choose something you truly think the couple will be happy to receive.

Don't I have up to a year after the wedding to send a gift? No. This is another myth. Gifts should be sent before the wedding or as soon after the wedding date as possible. But late is better than never, so if you have an unavoidable delay, send your gift when you can.

Can I take my present to the wedding? You can, but *only* if this is the tradition in the couple's culture or community. In most cases, it's best (and safest) to send or hand-deliver gifts to the bride's or the couple's home, or the return address on the invitation. If you're sending a gift from one of the couple's registries, it will be clearly listed where the gift is to be sent.

May I send a group gift? Married couples and nuclear families generally send one gift, as do couples who live together. If you receive an "and Guest" invitation, you're responsible for a gift but your guest or date isn't. Group giving, when guests pool their resources to purchase a more elaborate gift, is also fine.

Is a gift necessary for a destination wedding? Technically, whether you attend the destination wedding or not, you should send a gift to the couple's home instead of bringing one, as doing so would require the couple to coordinate shipping it home. As the cost of attending a destination wedding is often high, it is perfectly fine to choose a less expensive gift. That said, it is a gracious gesture when the couple spreads the word that "your presence is your present."

What do I do if I don't receive a thank-you note? Give the couple a reasonable amount of time to send their thank-you—usually three months postwedding. After that time, you're free to ask if the gift was received. You can check with the couple or with one of their parents, if you know them well. Be sure to inquire in a tone of concern, not annoyance.

Q: *I've received a wedding invitation from someone I knew in high school. She was a friend back then, but I haven't seen or heard from her in fifteen years. She lives halfway across the country, and I have no intention of going to the wedding. Would it be terribly rude not to send her a gift?*

A: Since you have really lost touch with each other and it's unlikely that you'll be reviving your friendship at this point, your situation is a reasonable exception to the traditional gift-giving "rule." Send your regrets immediately, but instead of simply checking a reply card or writing a formal response, it would be thoughtful to include a personal note, saying how nice it was to hear from her after so many years and wishing her your very best. Even if you don't want to renew the friendship, thank her for thinking of you at this very special time in her life. Your prompt, gracious note of regret will be an acceptable substitute for a wedding present.

What if I learn that my gift was returned or exchanged? Say nothing. Once you have given any gift, the recipients may do as they like with it. Returns and exchanges are common when a couple receives duplicate items.

[GUEST ATTIRE]

Despite the general trend toward casual attire, many people see weddings as an opportunity to dress up and look their very best. But a wedding is different from a gala party or opening night at the theater. Guests' clothing should be appropriate to an occasion that is, at its heart, a serious ceremony and also often one that takes place in a house of worship.

Suitable for the Occasion

The wedding invitation and the time of the wedding will be your best guide to its formality or informality. A formal invitation to an evening wedding indicates that you'll definitely dress up. An informal invitation to a noon wedding tells you the affair is either informal or casual.

Other factors will influence your dress choice:

The nature of the service. Is it secular or religious? Does the religion or the culture of the bridal couple require head coverings? Would bare shoulders and arms or open-toed shoes be offensive? Note: If head coverings for women and/or men are required, they will usually be provided at the site for people who do not have them.

Local custom. Some parts of the country are more conservative than others. For instance, in some areas, men wear tuxedos to formal weddings after six o'clock regardless of whether women wear long or short dresses.

The listing on the next page includes general rec-

FORMAL	DAYTIME	EVENING
WOMEN	Cocktail or afternoon dress; gloves optional. Hats or head coverings optional (unless required).	Depending on local custom, long evening dress or dressy cocktail dress; gloves optional. Hats or head coverings optional (unless required).
MEN	Dark suit; conservative shirts and tie.	Tuxedo (required if invitation states "Black tie") or dark suit.
SEMIFORMAL	DAYTIME	EVENING
WOMEN	Short afternoon dress, dressy pantsuit or cocktail dress. Hats or head coverings optional (unless required).	Cocktail dress, very dressy pantsuit. Hats or head coverings optional (unless required).
MEN	Dark suit; dark blazer, dark pants.	Dark suit.
INFORMAL	DAYTIME	EVENING
WOMEN	Afternoon dress. Hats or head coverings optional (unless required).	Afternoon or cocktail dress. Hats or head coverings optional (unless required).
MEN	Dark suit; dark blazer, light or dark pants (depending on season).	Dark suit.

These guidelines also apply to teenagers. Younger guests wear traditional "Sunday best" or party clothes to formal and semiformal weddings: Dress or skirt, blouse and jacket or sweater for girls; pants, sport jacket, dress shirt, and tie for boys are appropriate for informal and casual weddings.

ommendations for formal, semiformal, and informal guest attire, but if you're unsure, check with someone who knows—parents, wedding attendants, good friends of the couple, or the couple themselves. (The information in Chapter 49, "Wedding Attire," page 613, may also help with your clothing choices.)

Guest Fashion Faux Pas

Even for the dressiest wedding, it's usually best to err on the conservative side when selecting attire. Out of respect for the bride, groom, and their families, guests should have no difficulty avoiding the following fashion blunders:

- ◆ Clothing that's too skimpy or overtly provocative. (Save the plunging necklines, miniskirts, and bare backs for other occasions.)
- ◆ Costumes, except when you've been expressly asked to dress to the wedding theme.
- ◆ Blue jeans (unless the wedding is very casual and you *know* that the groom and his attendants will be in jeans) and T-shirts.
- ◆ Any jewelry that calls attention to your own faith when attending a service of another faith.
- ◆ Baseball or sports caps; large fashion hats that block other guests' view of the ceremony (they should be removed for the ceremony).

women in white? black? pantsuits?

In the past, no female guest would dare to wear white—the bride's traditional color. Today, that rule is no longer in effect, and you may wear white, with caution. Whatever the shade of white, the outfit should in no way distract from the bride's gown. A creamy white, street-length sheath or tailored silk suit might be just fine, but not a full-skirted white evening gown. If you have any qualms, wear another color. Black is also acceptable, as long as your outfit is in keeping with the formality of the wedding, and in no way looks like mourning attire. You might want to add a bright accessory to either white or black outfits if you're concerned that you would otherwise look too bridal or too somber.

Pantsuits are also acceptable, and nowadays, women of every age may be seen in dressy trousers with jackets or soft, flowing tops. But be conscious of local customs; if wearing a pants outfit will make you stand out like a sore thumb—or violate any religious restrictions—then wear a dress.

- ◆ Casual shoes or boots with formal or semiformal outfits.
- ◆ Sunglasses worn indoors (except for a legitimate medical reason).
- ◆ Boutonnieres or corsages unless supplied by the hosts (to avoid being confused with members of the wedding party or immediate families).

ON THE WEDDING DAY

Anyone who has ever planned a wedding knows how quickly their hard work can seem for naught if guests (including members of the wedding party) behave badly. The stereotypical "bad guest" is one who drinks too much and becomes loud and unruly, but other small discourtesies, like arriving late for the ceremony or shifting a few place cards in order to sit next to a friend at the reception, can be just as rude.

Wedding guest etiquette isn't very different from the manners for any social occasion. The information that follows will, however, alert guests to some manners specific to weddings today.

At the Ceremony

Punctuality is essential. A wedding usually begins at the time stated on the invitation, and you should arrive at least twenty minutes early. It's fine to greet other guests in the lobby or vestibule of the ceremony site, but it's best to hold off on much talking until after the ceremony.

Let an usher show you to your seat. At a casual wedding, guests might seat themselves, but remember that the front two or three rows are usually left free for family and special guests. If a program is provided, look it over and familiarize yourself with the order of the service. Programs may include helpful instructions for guests of other faiths and traditions.

After you're seated, quiet chatting is permissible, but when the mothers of the bride and groom are escorted to their seats, it's the customary signal for guests to wrap up their conversations.

Observe these other basics of good ceremony manners:

◆ Avoid loud greetings.

◆ Silence phones, beepers, and any other electronic devices that can disrupt the service.

◆ Be conscious of people with physical problems and make room for them to take aisle seats.

◆ Don't save seats for other guests once it becomes obvious that the space is needed.

◆ Don't take pictures with your phone unless the couple has given their okay.

◆ Stay where you've been seated throughout the service. (If you must leave early, take an aisle seat in an inconspicuous location near the rear.)

◆ If your children become disruptive in any way, leave immediately and don't return unless they are calm and quiet.

◆ Respect traditions that are unfamiliar to you.

Late arrivals. If you arrive to see that the wedding party is already assembled in the foyer, stay out of the way. Hopefully, there will be an usher to assist you, and there may be a side door you can enter quietly. Don't

bride's side or groom's side?

Strict seating rules are not so often observed these days, but family members are generally seated on the bride's or groom's side of the sanctuary, or room, and specially assigned seating areas are usually marked off with ribbons. Usually, the bride's side is on the left and the groom's side is on the right. Ushers will ask other guests if they prefer one side. If you're a friend of both the bride and groom or if you see that one side of the room is emptier than the other, you can leave the seating choice up to the usher. Be willing to sit on either side if you're asked to help to even out the seating.

enter during the processional or a prayer. If there's no usher present, wait until the service has begun; then slip in as quietly as possible and take a seat at the rear.

Standing and kneeling. There are usually points in a religious service when the congregation stands and perhaps kneels. As a general rule, guests of other faiths stand at the appropriate times but are not expected to kneel. You don't have to say prayers, refrains, or creeds outside your faith. If communion is offered, it may be limited to those of the service's religion or open to the entire guest company, but you don't have to participate if this rite is not part of your faith.

The end of the service. It may be marked with a kiss or an introduction of the newlyweds to their guests. Some couples now conclude the service with their own ritual, such as the lighting of a unity candle. Whatever is done, guests should be observant and not make a move to leave until it is clearly time.

Clapping. Religious and secular ceremonies sometimes end with the guests clapping for the couple when the officiant introduces them to the guest assembly. The applause should be initiated by someone who knows the couple's preference, and the guests can follow that lead. Otherwise, don't clap.

The recessional. In a traditional wedding, the bride and groom lead the recessional, followed by the wedding party and family members. Then guests depart by rows, the rows closest to the front of the room emptying first. But the etiquette of departing really depends on the situation. In a variation on the traditional reces-

the arch of steel

Undoubtedly the most romantic sight at a military wedding is the raising of sabers or cutlasses to form an arch under which a couple passes at the end of the service. The formation varies slightly by service branch and is a tradition rich in history and meaning, symbolizing the couple's safe entry into their new life together. It may be performed inside or outside the ceremony site, sometimes both. Whether formed by commissioned officers who are members of the wedding party or a special honor guard, a command will be given ("Draw swords" or "Arch sabers"). Only the couple and perhaps their attendants participate. All other military guests should stand at attention, and civilian guests honor the tradition by standing still and being quiet.

the long wait

Usually for scheduling reasons, guests may be forced to take a lengthy break between a ceremony and the reception. There's always some delay, particularly when the reception is at a different location, but what do you do if the ceremony ends at three-thirty and the reception doesn't start until six o'clock? You'll be able to tell from the invitation that there's going to be a break, so plan ahead. If you live in the same locality as the wedding, you can just go home and put your feet up. You might even invite some of the out-of-town guests to join you. Other possibilities include enjoying a bit of sightseeing or shopping.

sional, at a small wedding the newlyweds might stop at each pew or row of seats to greet guests. (In this case, guests should limit their comments to offering best wishes and not delay the couple with conversation.) Wait until the wedding party has exited before leaving. At informal and casual weddings that don't take place in a house of worship, there may be no formal recessional, and guests simply disperse, often going forward to speak to the couple and their families.

The receiving line. If there's a receiving line after the ceremony or at the reception, go through quickly; introduce yourself to the first person in the line if necessary and keep all comments brief and complimentary. Unless you can't attend the reception, you'll have plenty of time to speak more with the newlyweds later on. If wedding photos are also being taken at this time, be sure to keep out of camera range.

On to the Reception

It's time to celebrate! There may be some lag time before the reception gets under way, and this is a good chance to greet friends, meet guests you don't know, and sign the guestbook if there is one. Hors d'oeuvres and drinks may be served immediately, but if not, don't ask.

The following fundamentals are specific to wedding receptions, but if you want to brush up on your party manners and dining etiquette, you can refer to Chapter 6, "Table Manners," page 56, and "Start-to-Finish Guidelines," page 106.

- Move quickly through a receiving line, and don't monopolize anyone's time. Don't carry plates or drink glasses while in the line.

- When there's no receiving line, be sure to greet the couple and their families at some time during the festivities to offer congratulations and say thank you to your hosts.

- As you mix and mingle, introduce yourself to guests you don't know.

- Never move place cards if there's a seated meal. Respect your hosts' seating arrangements, and don't ask anyone to change places with you.

- Be gracious to guests at your table. Be sure to greet everyone and introduce yourself to anyone you don't know.

- Ask guests without partners to dance. (This isn't a requirement, just a very nice gesture.) Customs vary, but generally the first dances are reserved for the couple and their parents.

Q: *This is really embarrassing to admit, but I made a fool of myself at my best friend's wedding last weekend. Too much champagne. My friend's new wife will probably never forgive me. Is there any way to make amends?*

A: You behaved irresponsibly at the wedding, but at least you admit it and want to make amends now. Your friend and his wife may never raise the subject, so it's up to you to own up to your actions. It's best to make amends in person, if you can. If you're unable to see them, a phone call and perhaps even a short "I'm so sorry" note and a thoughtful little gift would be in order. Your heartfelt apology, made without excuses (after all, *you* drank the champagne), will probably earn forgiveness. Your friendship may require some extra-special nurturing for a while, but isn't it worth it for your best friend and his wife?

- Pay attention to the needs of elderly or infirm guests. Also, be attentive to children—just a smile and a few words can make them feel special.

- If asked to make a toast, be prepared and keep it brief, clean, and appropriate to the occasion—no embarrassing anecdotes about the newlyweds. (See "Toasts," page 649.)

- Participate in activities if you can. No matter what your feelings about a bouquet toss, for instance, don't leave the bride standing alone.

- Don't overwhelm the band or DJ with special requests.

- Don't take centerpieces, favors, or anything else that isn't clearly yours. If the hosts give you a centerpiece or decoration, take it only after tables have been cleared or at the end of the reception. And don't ask for a doggie bag for leftover food.

Respecting reception customs. These days, you're more likely than ever to be invited to weddings celebrated in traditions outside your own. Even the most traditional wedding may include innovative customs with which you're unfamiliar. A mannerly guest observes others and goes with the flow. It's fine to ask necessary questions, but rude to make negative remarks or comparisons.

When to leave. It's customary for guests to remain at a reception at least until the couple cuts their wedding cake or after their first dance, if there's dancing.

Many guests remain until the bride and groom depart. When there is dancing, the party may go on very late, with the newlyweds staying to the end; in this case, guests may leave when they think it's appropriate. In any event, don't exit without thanking the couple and their parents or any other host(s). If you haven't done so already, also take a few moments to offer congratulations to grandparents and other family members before leaving.

The type of reception will give you a sense of its probable duration. An evening or midday reception that includes a seated meal or full buffet is likely to last longer than an hors d'oeuvres–and-cake affair. An afternoon reception is often briefer, but guests should probably plan on at least a three-hour commitment even for very intimate weddings and receptions.

Tipping. Guests have no need to tip anyone because gratuities are usually included in wedding costs.

---

wedding customs in many faiths

The following brief list is intended to point out some major differences you may encounter, but it is by no means definitive. For detailed information, you can call the house of worship where the ceremony will be held or speak with someone of the faith.

CHRISTIAN. The traditional Protestant ceremony is described in Chapter 51, "The Big Day," page 634. There are many variations among denominations, and traditional services may include elements specific to the couple's national and ethnic origins, as well as local customs.

ROMAN CATHOLIC. Traditional Roman Catholic weddings may include a nuptial Mass with communion; this precedes the final prayer and nuptial blessing. Generally, non-Catholics do not take communion. In Italian tradition, the priest may greet the couple and their families at the church door.

ORTHODOX (EASTERN ORTHODOX). The service consists of two parts: the betrothal and blessing of the rings followed by the ceremony at the altar. During the latter, crowns or garlands joined by a white ribbon are exchanged three times over the couple. There are no vows said during the service. Female guests should wear clothing that covers their arms, with hems below the knee. The reception following a Greek Orthodox service may include the traditional breaking of plates, symbolizing happiness and endurance, and in which guests usually participate.

CHURCH OF JESUS CHRIST OF LATTER-DAY SAINTS (MORMON). If the marriage is held in one of the church's dedicated temples, only members of the faith may attend. This is called a *wedding ceremony*, or "sealing ordinance," and is for couples of great faith. Mormons may also marry in a *civil ceremony*. This ceremony is simple and sacred, and is usually held in a church or a home with a bishop of the church officiating. The civil ceremony may be attended by anyone. Typically, a reception takes place after both types of ceremonies, usually later in the evening. Guests often bring their gifts to the reception, but sending gifts is fine.

QUAKER. The simplest of the Christian services, a Quaker wedding is conducted as a regular meeting and may be held in the meeting house, at home, or in another location. There is no officiant; the bride and groom exchange their vows and sign a wedding certificate, which is read aloud. Guests are asked to sign the certificate as a pledge of their support of the marriage. The reception might include light refreshments or a full meal and may be a potluck; no alcohol is served. There may be music and dancing. Some couples request that gifts be in the form of charitable contributions.

JEWISH. The traditional Jewish wedding is described in Chapter 51, "The Big Day," page 634. The couple says their vows under a canopy, or chuppah, which symbolizes the home they will build together. Male guests wear a yarmulke or *kippah* (head coverings, often supplied at the site for non-Jewish guests). Head coverings may also be required for female guests. In Orthodox tradition, attire should be conservative and modest. Only male Jewish guests wear a prayer shawl. Otherwise, wedding attire is often very festive, depending on the formality or informality of the event. At Orthodox and Hasidic weddings men and women are separated—both at the ceremony and the reception. Foods served at Jewish wedding receptions will most likely be kosher.

ISLAMIC. Marriage is a sacred contract, but not a sacrament. The contract (*aqd-nikah*) is signed in the presence of witnesses and then publicly announced. The officiant can be any practicing Muslim and may be an imam (prayer leader). The bride and groom sit apart during the ceremony and at the reception. The service often takes place in a mosque but may be held in the bride's home, and the officiant delivers a sermon. The postceremony banquet (*walima*) is hosted by the groom, his family, or the couple. It is a festive event, but alcohol isn't served. There may be dancing if the *walima* does not take place in a mosque. Female guests should wear clothing that covers the arms, hems below the knees, and a head scarf. Gifts are often presented at the banquet. By tradition, women congratulate the bride, and men congratulate the groom.

HINDU. A Hindu wedding is a holy sacrament. A priest officiates and may provide explanations of rituals during the ceremony. The most important rite is the Seven Steps—seven rituals symbolizing food, strength, wealth, fortune, children, happy seasons, and friendships. The ceremony may take place in a temple, house, or an outdoor site under a *mandap*, or canopy. Shoes are not worn in a temple or under the wedding canopy, and guests may be seated on the floor, so comfortable dress is recommended. Receptions, at which traditional Indian foods are served, may begin before and continue after the ceremony. Gifts are often brought to the wedding.

BAHA'I. There is no standard marriage service or officiant. The couple says their vows in the presence of two witnesses (who are approved by the local spiritual council). The wedding may be as simple or elaborate as the couple desires, at a location of their choosing. No alcohol is served at receptions, but there may be music and dancing.

BUDDHIST. There is no standard wedding ceremony, and some Buddhist weddings are similar to Protestant ceremonies. The service is generally brief, with a minister or priest presiding. The service can be held in a temple or outdoors, and seating may be on meditation cushions. (Guests should dress comfortably if this is the case.) Guests should never enter the ceremony during meditation. Usually, wedding gifts aren't expected. No alcohol or meat is served at the reception.

SIKH. The ceremony is called the *arnand karaj* (ceremony of bliss) and may be performed at a temple (*Gurdwara*) or the bride's home. Shoes are removed while in the temple. Women typically wear bright colors, and should have a long scarf or shawl to cover their heads while in the temple. Men wear a head covering as well, using one provided at the temple or carrying a large handkerchief with them. The ceremony is often scheduled before noon. The officiant may be a priest or any Sikh approved by the families. During the ceremony, guests sit around a central platform on which the Holy Book is placed. Men sit to the right and women to the left of the Holy Book. After the couple is married, the ceremony ends with prayer, a hymn, and the sharing of sweet food by all the guests.

NATIVE AMERICAN. There is no single marriage service in Native American culture, but traditionally, a wedding is a community event. It may be religious or secular in nature, and the service and reception often integrate modern customs with ancient tribal rituals. The reception may include a full meal, and gifts may be presented at the reception.

RESOURCES

NAMES AND TITLES

SITUATION	OPTIONS/NOTES
ADDRESSING A MAN	
Given name	Mr. George Wilkes *Boys use the title "Master" until age 6 to 7; then no title until age 16 to 18 years, then "Mr."
ADDRESSING A WOMAN	
Maiden name	Ms. Jane Johnson Miss Jane Johnson* * "Miss" is used until age 16 to 18, then "Ms."
Married, keeping maiden name	Ms. Jane Johnson
Married, uses husband's name socially	Mrs. John Kelly Mrs. Jane Kelly Ms. Jane Kelly
Separated, not divorced	Mrs. John Kelly Mrs. Jane Kelly Ms. Jane Kelly
Divorced	Mrs. Jane Kelly Ms. Jane Kelly Ms. Jane Johnson (maiden name)
Widowed	Mrs. John Kelly* *If you don't know the widow's preference, this is the traditional and preferred form. Mrs. Jane Kelly Ms. Jane Kelly
Addressing a Person Who Prefers Not to Specify Gender or Identify as Male or Female	Mx. Sam Weathers
ADDRESSING A COUPLE	
Married, she uses her husband's name socially	Mr. and Mrs. John Kelly

NOTE: *Traditionally, a man's name preceded a woman's on an envelope address, and his first and surname were not separated (Jane and John Kelly). Nowadays, the order of the names—whether his name or hers comes first—doesn't matter and either way is acceptable. The exception is when one member of the couple "outranks" the other—the one with the higher rank is always listed first.*

Married, she prefers Ms.	Mr. John Kelly and Ms. Jane Kelly Ms. Jane Kelly and Mr. John Kelly *Do not link Ms. to the husband's name: Mr. and Ms. John Kelly is incorrect.
Married, informal address	Jane and John Kelly John and Jane Kelly

SITUATION	OPTIONS/NOTES

Married, she uses maiden name	Mr. John Kelly and Ms. Jane Johnson
	Ms. Jane Johnson and Mr. John Kelly
	
	If you can't fit the names on one line:
	Mr. John Kelly
	    and Ms. Jane Johnson
	      *Note the indent; either name may be used first.

Couples or partners living together	Ms. Jane Johnson and Mr. John Kelly
	    *Note: Write the names on one line, using "and." Either name
	    may be used first.
	If you can't fit the names on one line (see above):
	Mr. John Kelly
	    and Ms. Jane Johnson

Individuals living at the same address	Ms. Jane Johnson Mr. John Kelly *Note: Use two lines and do not use "and."
A woman who outranks her husband: elected office, military rank	The Honorable Jane Kelly and Mr. John Kelly If you can't fit both names on one line (note indent): The Honorable Jane Kelly and Mr. John Kelly
A woman who outranks her husband: professional or educational degree	Dr. Jane Kelly and Mr. John Kelly
Both are doctors (PhD or medical) and use the same last name	The Doctors (Drs.) Kelly (omit first names) Drs. Jane and John Kelly / Drs. John and Jane Kelly Dr. John Kelly and Dr. Jane Kelly / Dr. Jane Kelly and Dr. John Kelly
Both are doctors (PhD or medical); she uses her maiden name	Dr. Jane Johnson and Dr. John Kelly Dr. John Kelly and Dr. Jane Johnson

BUSINESS

Woman	Ms. is the standard form of address, unless you know positively that a woman wishes to be addressed as Mrs.
Professional designations—use only for business	Jane Kelly, CPA; George Wilkes, CLU

NOTE: *Do not use Ms. or Mr. if using a professional designation such as CPA.*
Socially, drop the professional designation and use Mr., Ms., or Mrs.: Ms. Jane Kelly.

Esquire: Attorneys and some court officials	Jane Kelly, Esquire; George Wilkes, Esq.

NOTE: *If using Esquire, do not use Ms. or Mr.*

In conversation or socially, "Esquire" is not used; use Mr. or Ms.: Ms. Jane Kelly, Mr. George Wilkes.

Attorney at Law	Ms. Jane Kelly Attorney at Law This is an alternative to "Esquire" for attorneys. Use Mr. or Ms. and use two lines with no indent.

OFFICIAL FORMS OF ADDRESS

OFFICIAL	LETTER ADDRESS	SALUTATION	SPOKEN GREETING	FORMAL INTRODUCTION
US GOVERNMENT				*If abroad, "of America" follows "United States"
The President	The President The White House	Dear Mr. / Madam President:	First: Mr. / Madam President Then: Sir / Ma'am	The President of the United States (of America—abroad) The President President Last Name
Former President	The Honorable Full Name Address	Dear Mr. / Mrs. / Ms. Last Name:	First: Mr. Vice President Then: Mr. / Mrs. / Ms. Last Name	The Honorable Full Name, the former President of the United States*
The President's Spouse	Mr. / Mrs. / Ms. Full Name The White House	Dear Mr. / Mrs. / Ms. Last Name:	Mr. / Mrs. / Ms. Last Name	Mr. / Mrs. / Ms. Last Name
The Vice President	The Vice President The White House Address	Dear Mr. / Madam Vice President:	First: Mr. / Madam Vice President Then: Sir / Ma'am Mr. / Mrs. / Ms. Last Name	The Vice President of the United States* The Vice President Vice President Last Name
Cabinet Members	The Honorable Full Name Secretary of (Department) Department of ____ Address	Dear Mr. / Madam Secretary:	Mr. / Madam Secretary Secretary Last Name Mr. / Mrs. / Ms. Last Name	The Honorable Full Name, The Secretary of ____ of the United States* The Secretary of ____
Attorney General	The Honorable Full Name The Attorney General Address	Dear Mr. / Ms. / Madam Attorney General:	Mr. / Ms. / Madam Attorney General Mr. / Mrs. / Ms. Last Name	The Attorney General
The Chief Justice	The Chief Justice of the United States The Supreme Court Address	Dear Chief Justice:	Mr. / Madam Chief Justice Mr. / Mrs. / Ms. Last Name	The Honorable Full Name, The Chief Justice of the United States* The Chief Justice Chief Justice Last Name
Associate Justice	Justice Last Name The Supreme Court Address	Dear Justice Last Name:	Mr. / Madam Justice Justice Last Name	The Honorable Full Name, Associate Justice of the United States Justice Last Name
Federal Judge	The Honorable Full Name U.S. Court of ____ Address	Dear Judge Last Name:	Justice or Judge Last Name Madam Justice or Judge Last Name	The Honorable Full Name Mr. / Madam Justice Last Name Judge Last Name
Senator	The Honorable Full Name United States Senate Washington, DC or district office address	Dear Senator Last Name:	Senator Last Name Then: Senator, Sir / Ma'am	The Honorable Senator Last Name, Senator from State Senator Last Name

OFFICIAL	LETTER ADDRESS	SALUTATION	SPOKEN GREETING	FORMAL INTRODUCTION
Representative	The Honorable Full Name House of Representatives Washington, DC or district office address	Dear Mr. / Mrs. / Ms. Last Name:	Mr. / Mrs. / Ms. Last Name	The Honorable Last Name, Representative from State Congressman / Congresswoman Last Name
DIPLOMATIC				
American Ambassador	The Honorable Full Name Ambassador of the United States American Embassy Address	Dear Mr. / Madam Ambassador:	Mr. / Madam Ambassador	The Honorable Full Name, Ambassador of the United States of America (at post) (When not at post add: to Country) Mr. / Mrs. / Ms. Full Name, Ambassador of the United States of America American Ambassador (When no foreign nationals are present, add: to Country) Ambassador Last Name, United States of America
Foreign Ambassador	His/Her Excellency Full Name The Ambassador of _____ The Embassy of _____ Address	Excellency: or. Dear Mr. / Madam Ambassador:	Excellency Mr. / Madam Ambassador	His / Her Excellency, the Honorable Full Name, Ambassador Extraordinary and Plenipotentiary of _____ The Ambassador of _____
STATE				
Governor	The Honorable Full Name Governor of State Address	Dear Governor Last Name:	First: Governor Last Name Governor Then: Sir / Ma'am	The Honorable Full Name. Governor of the state of _____ Governor Last Name The Governor
State Legislator	The Honorable Full Name Address	Dear Mr. / Mrs. / Ms. Last Name:	Mr. / Mrs. / Ms. Last Name	Mr. / Mrs. / Ms. Last Name
Mayor	The Honorable Full Name Mayor of City Address	Dear Mayor Last Name:	Mayor Last Name Mr. / Madam Mayor Your Honor	The Honorable Full Name, Mayor of City (or. of the city of _____) Mayor Last Name
RELIGIOUS DIGNITARIES				
Protestant Clergy	The Reverend Full Name Name of church Address	Dear Reverend Last Name:	Reverend Last Name	The Reverend Full Name
Protestant Clergy, with doctorate	The Reverend Full Name, D.D. Name of church Address	Dear Dr. Last Name:	Dr. Last Name	Dr. Full Name The Reverend Doctor Full Name

OFFICIAL FORMS OF ADDRESS (CONTINUED)

OFFICIAL	LETTER ADDRESS	SALUTATION	SPOKEN GREETING	FORMAL INTRODUCTION
Episcopal Bishop	The Right Reverend Full Name (academic degrees) Bishop of _____ Address	Dear Bishop Last Name:	Bishop Last Name	The Right Reverend Full Name, The Bishop of _____
The Pope	His Holiness, Pope Papal Name Vatican City, Italy	Your Holiness: Most Holy Father:	Your Holiness Most Holy Father	His Holiness, Pope _____ The Holy Father The Pope The Pontiff
Cardinal	His Eminence, First Name Cardinal Last Name Archbishop of _____ Address	Your Eminence: Dear Cardinal Last Name:	Your Eminence Cardinal Last Name	His Eminence, Cardinal Last Name
Roman Catholic Bishop	The Most Reverend Full Name Bishop/Archbishop of _____ Address	Your Excellency: Most Reverend Sir: Dear Bishop/Archbishop Last Name:	Your Excellency Bishop/Archbishop Last Name	His Excellency, Bishop/Archbishop Last Name
Monsignor	The Right Reverend Monsignor Full Name Address	Reverend Monsignor: Dear Monsignor Last Name:	Monsignor Last Name Monsignor	Monsignor Last Name
Roman Catholic Priest	The Reverend Full Name Address	Reverend Father: Dear Father Last Name:	Father Last Name Father	The Reverend Last Name Father Last Name
Roman Catholic Mother Superior	The Reverend Mother Full Name, initials of order Address	Dear Reverend Mother (Last Name):	Reverend Mother	Reverend Mother Last Name
Roman Catholic Nun	Sister Full Name, initials of order if used Address	Dear Sister Name / Last Name:	Sister Name / Last Name Sister	Sister Name Last Name
Roman Catholic Brother	Brother Given Name (Last Name), initials of order, if used Address	Dear Brother Given Name:	Brother Given Name Brother	Brother Given Name
Mormon	Mr. Full Name President of _____ Temple Address	Dear Mr. Last Name:	Mr. Last Name	Mr. Last Name, the President of _____ Temple
Imam	The Imam Name Address	Dear Imam Name:	Imam Name	The Imam of the _____ Mosque/Islamic Center
Rabbi	Rabbi Full Name (academic degrees) Address	Dear Rabbi Last Name: Dear Rabbi:	Rabbi Last Name Dr. Last Name (if holds a degree) Rabbi	Rabbi Last Name, of Name of Temple/Congregation
Cantor	Cantor Full Name Address	Dear Cantor Last Name:	Cantor Last Name	Cantor Last Name, of Name of Temple/Congregation

OFFICIAL	LETTER ADDRESS	SALUTATION	SPOKEN GREETING	FORMAL INTRODUCTION
CANADIAN OFFICIALS	*Note that Honourable is correctly spelled with a u.*		**Do not use Mr. or Madam in front of a person's job title.*	
Governor General	His/Her Excellency the Right Honourable Full Name, C.C., C.M.M., C.O.M., C.D. (add other postnominal letters, e.g., P.C., Q.C., here) Governor General of Canada Rideau Hall 1 Sussex Drive Ottawa, Ontario	Excellency:	First: Your Excellency Excellency Then: Sir / Madam	His/Her Excellency, the Right Honourable Governor General of Canada, Full Name, (post-nominal letters)
Spouse of the Governor General	Her/His Excellency Full Name C.C. Rideau Hall 1 Sussex Drive Ottawa, Ontario	Excellency: Dear Mr. / Mrs. Last Name	First: Your Excellency Excellency Then: Sir / Madam	His/Her Excellency Full Name
Prime Minister	The Right Honourable Full Name, P.C., M.P. (add other postnominal letters here) Prime Minister of Canada Langevin Block Ottawa, Ontario	Dear Prime Minister: **Mr. / Madam Prime Minister is incorrect.	First: Prime Minister Then: Mr. / Mrs. / Ms. / Miss Last Name	The Right Honourable Prime Minister of Canada, Full Name, (post-nominal letters)
Chief Justice	The Right Honourable Full Name, P.C. Chief Justice of Canada Supreme Court of Canada Address	Dear Chief Justice:	First: Mr. / Madam Chief Justice Then: Sir / Madam Mr. / Mrs. / Ms. / Miss Last Name	The Right Honourable Chief Justice of Canada, Full Name, (post-nominal letters)
Lieutenant Governor	His/Her Honour The Right Honourable Full Name, (post-nominal letters) Lieutenant Governor of Province Address	Your Honour: My Dear Lieutenant Governor:	First: Your Honour Then: Sir / Madam Mr. / Mrs. / Ms. / Miss Last Name	His/Her Honour the Honourable Lieutenant Governor of Province, Full Name, (post-nominal letters)
Premier of a Province	The Honourable Full Name, M.L.A. or (M.P.P., M.N.A., or M.H.A.) Premier of Province Address	Dear Premier: **Mr. / Madam Premier is incorrect. Last Name	First: Premier Then: Mr. / Mrs. / Ms. / Miss	The Honourable Premier of Province, Full Name, (post-nominal letters)
Senator	The Honourable Full Name, Senator *or, if member of the Privy Council:* Senator the Honourable Full Name, P.C., M.P. The Senate of Canada Address Ottawa, Ontario K1A 0A4	Dear Senator Last Name:	Senator Last Name	The Honourable Senator Full Name, (post-nominal letters)

OFFICIAL FORMS OF ADDRESS (CONTINUED)

OFFICIAL	LETTER ADDRESS	SALUTATION	SPOKEN GREETING	FORMAL INTRODUCTION
Member of the House of Commons	Mr. / Mrs. / Ms. / Miss Full Name, M.P. *or, if member of the Privy Council:* The Honourable Full Name, P.C., M.P. House of Commons Parliament Buildings Ottawa, Ontario K1A 0A6	Dear Mr. / Mrs. / Ms. / Miss Last Name:	Mr. / Mrs. / Ms. / Miss Last Name	Mr. / Mrs. / Ms. / Miss Full Name, (post-nominal letters). Member of Parliament
Mayor of Area Municipalities	His/Her Worship Full Name Mayor of _____ Address	Dear Sir / Madam: Dear Mr. / Madam Mayor:	First: Your Worship Then: Mayor Last Name	His/Her Worship the Mayor of _____, Full Name. (post-nominal letters)

* Sources: Peggy Post, *Emily Post's Etiquette* 17th edition, HarperCollins, 2004.
Cherlynn Conestco and Anna Hart, *Service Etiquette*, 5th edition, Naval Institute Press, 2009.
Letitia Baldrige, *Letitia Baldrige's Complete Guide to Executive Manners*, Rawson Associates, 1985.
U.S. Department of State Foreign Affairs Handbook, Volume 5, Handbook 1 (5 FAH-1 H-420).
www.cftech.com: Forms of Address.
The Government of Canada's Cultural Heritage Website: www.pch.gc.ca.

DRESSING FOR THE OCCASION

OCCASION	MEN	WOMEN
WHITE TIE	• Black dress coat (tailcoat), matching trousers with a single stripe of satin or braid in the US; two stripes in Europe or the UK • White piqué wing-collared shirt with stiff front • Braces, to ensure a good fit • Shirt studs and cuff links • White vest • White bow tie • White or gray gloves • Black patent shoes and black dress socks	• Formal (floor-length) evening or ball gown • Long gloves (optional)
BLACK TIE	• Black tuxedo jacket and matching trousers • Formal (piqué or pleated front) white shirt • Shirt studs and cuff links • Black bow tie (silk, satin, or twill) • Black cummerbund to match tie, or a vest • Dressy braces to ensure a good fit • No gloves • Black patent shoes and black dress socks • *In summer, in the tropics, or on a cruise:* White dinner jacket, black tuxedo trousers plus other black-tie wardrobe	• Formal (floor-length) evening gown • Dressy cocktail dress • Your dressiest "little black dress"
CREATIVE BLACK TIE	• Tuxedo combined with trendy or whimsical items, such as a black or other colored shirt, or matching colored or patterned bow tie and cummerbund	• Formal (floor-length) evening gown • Dressy cocktail dress • Your dressiest "little black dress" • Fun or unique accessories
BLACK TIE OPTIONAL	• Tuxedo (see "Black Tie" above) • Dark suit, white dress shirt, and conservative tie • Leather dress shoes and dark dress socks	• Formal (floor-length) evening gown • Dressy cocktail dress • A "little black dress" • Dressy separates

OCCASION	MEN	WOMEN
SEMIFORMAL	◆ Dark business suit ◆ Matching vest (optional) ◆ Dress shirt ◆ Tie ◆ Leather dress shoes and dark dress socks	◆ Short afternoon or cocktail dress ◆ A "little black dress" ◆ Long dressy skirt and top ◆ Dressy separates
FESTIVE ATTIRE (USUALLY FOR HOLIDAYS)	◆ Seasonal sport coat or blazer in color of choice and slacks ◆ Open-collar shirt, or dress shirt ◆ Tie—festive or with a holiday theme	◆ Cocktail dress ◆ Long dressy skirt and top ◆ Dressy pants outfit or separates ◆ A "little black dress" ◆ Feature holiday colors
BUSINESS FORMAL*	◆ Dark business suit ◆ Matching vest (optional) ◆ Dress shirt ◆ Conservative tie ◆ Leather dress shoes and dark dress socks	◆ Suit ◆ Business-style dress ◆ Dress with a jacket ◆ Stockings (optional in summer) ◆ Heels, low or high
BUSINESS CASUAL*	◆ Seasonal sport coat or blazer with slacks or khakis ◆ Dress shirt, casual button-down shirt, open-collar or polo shirt ◆ Optional tie ◆ Loafers or loafer-style shoes, and socks	◆ Skirt, khakis, or pants ◆ Open-collar shirt, knit shirt or sweater (no spaghetti straps or décolleté) ◆ Dress
DRESSY CASUAL	◆ Seasonal sport coat or blazer, and slacks ◆ Dress shirt, casual button-down shirt, open-collar or polo shirt ◆ Optional tie	◆ Dress ◆ Skirt and dressy top ◆ Dressy pants outfit ◆ Nice jeans and dressy top
CASUAL	◆ Khakis or good jeans (clean, no holes) ◆ Cargo or Bermuda shorts—depending on occasion and climate ◆ Plain T-shirt (no slogans), polo shirt, turtleneck ◆ Casual button-down shirt, and/or sweater ◆ Loafers, sneakers (with or without socks), sandals	◆ Sundress ◆ Long or short skirt ◆ Khakis or nice jeans ◆ Shorts (depending on occasion and climate) ◆ Plain T-shirt (no slogans), polo shirt, turtle-neck ◆ Casual button-down blouse

*Always check and abide by your company's dress code.

SAMPLE INVITATIONS AND ANNOUNCEMENTS

Typical wording for a printed or handwritten informal shower invitation:

MOLLY JENKINS, PAULA KLEEMAN,
AND JENNIFER WU
HOPE YOU'LL JOIN US
AT A LUNCHEON AND BABY SHOWER HONORING
CHRISTY DIANGELO
SATURDAY, OCTOBER 9
11:30 A.M.
305-B WEST 69TH STREET
PLEASE REPLY TO JENNIFER, 202-555-0945,
TEXTS WELCOME

A formal printed or engraved invitation to a bar mitzvah and reception:

MR. AND MRS. JACOB KENNETH ROSEN
JOYFULLY INVITE YOU
TO WORSHIP WITH THEM
AT THE BAR MITZVAH OF THEIR SON
DAVID STEVEN
SATURDAY, THE SEVENTEENTH OF JULY
TWO THOUSAND SEVENTEEN
AT TEN O'CLOCK
AT CONGREGATION BETH ISRAEL
4205 OCEAN DRIVE
AND TO CELEBRATE WITH THEM
AT A LUNCHEON IMMEDIATELY FOLLOWING
COMMODORE COUNTRY CLUB
RSVP
1219 WILLOW ROAD
ST. PETERSBURG, FLORIDA 33733

A sample invitation to a quinceañera, which includes an invitation to a Mass and a reception; the invitation to a religious service does not include an RSVP, but the invitation to the reception does:

MR. AND MRS. JORGE DELGADO
REQUEST THE HONOUR OF YOUR PRESENCE
AT A MASS CELEBRATING
THE FIFTEENTH BIRTHDAY
OF THEIR DAUGHTER
ANA THERESA
ON SATURDAY, THE TWENTY-FIRST
OF FEBRUARY
TWO THOUSAND SEVENTEEN
AT HALF PAST FOUR O'CLOCK
SAINT BONIFACE CATHOLIC CHURCH

The reception card:

PLEASE JOIN US AFTERWARD
FOR THE RECEPTION
THE PACIFIC CLUB
902 BAYSIDE ROAD
RSVP
11106 NAUTILUS CRESCENT
SAN DIEGO, CA 92138

An informal invitation to a birthday party given by adult children for their mother:

LOUISA PENSKI ISAACS AND ROBERT PENSKI
PLEASE JOIN US
TO CELEBRATE THE 60TH BIRTHDAY OF OUR MOTHER
HELEN TATE PENSKI
AT DINNER
WEDNESDAY, NOVEMBER 10
7 O'CLOCK
742 FERNBANK TERRACE
ALMAVILLE
RSVP
LOUISA: 879-555-1212

A formal invitation issued by a couple celebrating their wedding anniversary:

1992–2017

MR. AND MRS. ARTHUR EDWARD LaGRANGE
REQUEST THE PLEASURE OF YOUR COMPANY
AT A RECEPTION
HONORING
THEIR SILVER WEDDING ANNIVERSARY
ON SUNDAY, THE TENTH OF OCTOBER
AT FOUR O'CLOCK
THE CENTURY CLUB

RSVP
15 PRINCE ROAD
WILMINGTON, DELAWARE 19899

A formal invitation for an anniversary party issued by the adult children of the honorees:

THE CHILDREN OF
ANNA AND GREGORY HOFFMAN
REQUEST THE HONOR OF YOUR PRESENCE
AT THE
FIFTIETH ANNIVERSARY
OF THE MARRIAGE OF THEIR PARENTS . . .

[or]

MR. AND MRS. GREGORY HOFFMAN, JR.
MR. AND MRS. JAMES LEE DAUGHERTY
AND
MS. CHRISTINA HOFFMAN REED
REQUEST THE PLEASURE OF YOUR COMPANY
AT A RECEPTION
HONORING
THE FIFTIETH ANNIVERSARY
OF THE MARRIAGE OF THEIR PARENTS
MR. AND MRS. GREGORY HOFFMAN . . .

A sample baby announcement:

MARY LOU AND BRENDON O'DWYER
ARE HAPPY TO ANNOUNCE
THE ARRIVAL OF
MARY KATHERINE
SEPTEMBER 28, 2017
7 POUNDS 8 OUNCES

A sample adoption announcement:

MR. AND MRS. DANIEL SHELTON
JOYFULLY ANNOUNCE
THE ADOPTION OF
DANIEL IVAN
BORN JULY 7, 2009 IN BAKU, AZERBAIJAN
AND WELCOMED INTO OUR HOME
ON OCTOBER 10, 2017

GUIDE TO FOOD AND DRINK

We've all faced unfamiliar or hard-to-eat foods, or wondered whether the way we eat a particular food at home "isn't done" in public. What you do depends on the situation. With friends, don't be embarrassed to say, "I've never eaten escargots before. Please show me how." If you're at a formal function or among strangers, just delay eating until you can take a cue from your host or the other diners. Reviewing the guidelines below will help keep you from wondering how to serve or how to eat "tricky" foods. (See also Chapter 6, "Table Manners," page 56, and visit www .emilypost.com for videos showing how to eat tricky foods.)

Artichokes

Artichoke leaves are always eaten with the fingers. Pluck off a leaf on the outside, dip its meaty base into the melted butter or sauce provided, then place it between your front teeth and pull forward. The idea is to use your teeth to scrape the meat off the leaf. Continue leaf by leaf, placing discarded leaves on the edge of your plate (or on a plate provided for the purpose), until you've reached the artichoke's thistlelike choke or the leaves are too small or meatless. Use your knife at a 45-degree angle to remove the remaining leaves and the fuzzy, thistlelike choke, exposing the artichoke heart below. Then cut the heart into bite-size pieces and eat it with a fork, dipping each forkful into the sauce.

Asian Dishes

Chinese, Indian, Japanese, Thai, Vietnamese, and Korean cuisines are well established in America. While there's no real need to follow the eating traditions from each country, it doesn't hurt to know a bit about them. For instance, at a Chinese or Japanese meal it's fine to hold the rice bowl close to your mouth; in Korean custom the bowl is left on the table. And then there are chopsticks: While fun to master, they also have their own etiquette.

Many Asian meals are communal, with dishes being shared. Ordering is a group effort, too, with each diner having a say. Courtesy and Chinese custom say that the elderly should be served first. Take your fair share from the platters and, near the end of the meal, don't take the last serving of food left on a platter without offering it to the other diners first. It's also nice to follow the Asian custom of serving tea to your fellow diners before you fill your own teacup.

Since food is communal, take care in using your chopsticks when serving yourself. Ideally, ask for another pair of chopsticks that can travel with the communal bowl. Alternatively, you can reverse your chopsticks and use the wide end to choose food from the communal plate. Don't rummage around in the communal bowl to find what you like and never eat directly from a communal dish. Instead, choose a piece close to you and transfer it to your plate or bowl. Once you've touched a piece of food you must take

it. And don't pass food from chopsticks to chopsticks—always transfer food to a plate. Transferring directly recalls the Japanese custom of passing bones as part of a funeral rite. Sauces are for dipping and aren't poured over the food. As with Western etiquette, double-dipping in a communal bowl is a no-no.

Sushi and sashimi. In Japan, the assorted raw fish dishes called sushi are eaten with chopsticks or the fingers. Whichever method you choose, there's a correct way to dip a piece of sushi into the accompanying soy sauce. So that the sticky rice won't break up, only dip the fish side into the sauce. Then bring the piece to your mouth and eat it in one bite (or two bites if the piece is too large). If you skip tradition altogether and use a fork, cut any pieces that are too large to eat in a single bite with your knife and fork.

A typical Japanese meal begins with sashimi—thinly sliced, raw, boneless fish served without rice. Before eating sashimi, mix a dollop of the green horseradish mustard called wasabi into the dish of soy sauce that is provided. The fish is then dipped into the sauce with chopsticks or a fork.

Asparagus

It's fine to pick up unsauced, firm asparagus with your fingers, one stalk at a time, and dip them in butter or sauce—but look to your hostess or dining companions first to see if knives and forks are the order of the day. Always use a knife and fork at a formal meal, at a restaurant, when the asparagus has been sauced, or when you're in doubt.

Avocados

Avocado slices are cut and eaten with a fork. When an avocado is served halved, hold the shell to steady it and scoop out each bite with a spoon. When tuna salad or any other mixture is served in an avocado half, it's fine to hold the shell steady while eating the contents—this time with a fork.

using chopsticks

The secrets to mastering chopsticks will hardly come as a surprise: patience and practice. Use the broad end to pick up food from a communal serving plate, use the narrow end to pick up food you are eating. Once used, the small end of chopsticks should never touch any bowl or platter used by others. A few other pointers:

- Just as you don't play with your fork, don't play with your chopsticks. Waving them, pointing them at someone, tapping them, and using them to move plates or dishes are all impolite.

- It's impolite to spear food with your chopsticks, except in rare instances. You can use them to tear apart larger items, such as vegetables. In an informal setting, you can spear a cherry tomato or a fish ball, but purists would frown.

- It's okay to bite in half any dumplings and other small items that are a little too large to eat, holding the piece firmly in your chopsticks as you carefully take a bite.

- Rest the pointed end of your chopsticks on a chopstick rest or place them on your plate, not directly on the table. Also, make sure they don't point toward anyone else at the table. If you're using disposable chopsticks, you can fold the paper covering to make a chopstick rest.

- In Japan, crossing your chopsticks symbolizes death; in Vietnam, leaving your chopsticks in a V position is a bad omen; and in Korea, setting chopsticks to the left of the spoon is done only as part of a funeral ritual.

- Don't stick your chopsticks vertically into a bowl of rice. In many Asian cultures this is only done during funeral rites.

Breads

Bread and rolls are served either on individual bread plates or passed around the table in a basket, in which case diners take one piece, place it on their plate or bread plate, and pass it on. Use your fingers to break off a smaller piece. Butter and eat that piece before breaking off and buttering and eating another. Toast should be cut in half before it's served. Toast and hot biscuit and muffin halves can be buttered all over at once so the butter has a chance to melt in.

Fried or flat bread. Naan, pappadam, and puri from India and pita bread from the Middle East are brought whole to the table on plates or in flat baskets. Break or tear off a fairly sizable piece with your fingers and transfer it to your plate, then tear off a smaller piece to eat.

Whole loaf breads. When a whole loaf is served on a cutting board, use the accompanying bread knife to cut the loaf into slices for everyone at the table. Grasp the bread with a clean napkin (ask for one if it isn't provided) while you're cutting it. Cut a round loaf in slices rather than wedges. Start by cutting the loaf in half; then turn the loaf 90 degrees and, beginning at one side, cut into thin slices.

Butter

To transfer butter to your own plate, help yourself. Using the serving utensil, place the butter either on your dinner or butter plate, then use your own dinner or butter knife to butter the bread. If no communal utensil was provided, use your own clean butter knife, knife, or fork to serve yourself. When individually wrapped squares or small plastic tubs of butter are served in a restaurant, leave the empty wrappings or tubs on your bread plate or on the edge of your dinner plate, not on the table. (See also "The Table," page 57.)

Caviar

Caviar is traditionally served in a crystal or glass bowl on a bed of cracked ice. Use the accompanying spoon to place the caviar on your plate. Caviar is rare and expensive, so take a dime-size portion. With your own knife or spoon, place small amounts of caviar on toast triangles or blini—tiny pancakes. If chopped egg, minced onions, or sour cream are served, spoon these toppings sparingly onto your caviar.

Cherry Tomatoes

The trick to eating a whole cherry tomato is to use your knife or the edge of the salad bowl to hold the little tomato steady as you stick a fork into it. Gently push the tines of your fork against the tomato until they puncture it. If the tomato is large, cut it in half by using the holes you just made with the fork as the spot to begin cutting. If the tomato is small enough to fit in your mouth whole, do so. Be very careful to keep your lips closed as you bite gently . . . they're notorious squirters! When they're part of a crudités platter, it's fine to use your fingers and pop the whole tomato in your mouth, remembering to practice squirt prevention.

Condiments

From salt and pepper to bottled sauces to relishes—condiments have their own etiquette guidelines.

Salt and pepper. In the United States when someone asks for the salt or pepper, pass both. These items travel together, so think of them as joined at the hip. Even a saltcellar is passed with the pepper. If the shakers are opaque and you can't tell one from the other, the pepper shaker is the one with the larger holes or just one hole.

At formal dinners, a saltcellar—a little bowl with a tiny spoon—sometimes takes the place of a shaker. You can use the spoon to sprinkle salt over your food as needed or you can fall back on the old tradition of placing a small mound of salt on the edge of your plate and then dipping each forkful of food into the salt. If no spoon comes with the cellar, use the tip of a clean knife; if the cellar is for your use only, it's fine to take a pinch with your fingers. Salting or peppering your food before tasting it assumes that the dish wasn't seasoned properly and could be insulting to the chef.

Ketchup and sauces. Pouring steak sauce or ketchup directly onto your food is fine in an informal setting. At the dinner table or in a fine restaurant, use the serving utensil to spoon some sauce onto your plate next to the food it will accompany. Leave the serving utensil in the dish once it's been used. If there is no utensil, it's okay to use a clean one of your own—once.

Other condiments. As international cuisines are now more prevalent in the American culinary scene, you're more likely to encounter several separate condiment dishes on the table, such as chutneys or salsas. Spoon a small portion of the sauce or condiment onto the edge of your dinner plate or butter plate, replenishing it as needed. Never dip food directly into a communal condiment dish, and don't take anything from the condiment bowl directly to your mouth; it goes onto your plate first.

Corn on the Cob

Corn on the cob, eaten with the hands, is served at family or informal dinners and is a staple at summer barbecues and seafood bakes or boils. At a formal dinner party corn should be cut off the cob and served in a dish. Perhaps the only rule to follow when enjoying corn on the cob is to eat it as neatly and quietly as possible—no noisy, nonstop chomping up and down the rows. Providing corn holders makes the job a lot less messy and can save burned fingers. Insert the prongs into each end of the corn and use the "handle" to hold on. To butter the corn, put pats or a scoop of butter on your dinner plate, then, using your knife, butter and season only a few rows of the corn at a time. There is another school that says rolling the corn in a communal stick of butter is the way to go. In either case, try not to get your fingers greasy and do make frequent use of your napkin.

Desserts

What do you do with a dessert fork and spoon when you find them in your place setting? Depending on what you're eating, these utensils are often interchangeable, but the idea is to match the utensil to the job at hand. The fork is for piercing, the spoon for scooping, and both work as a pusher or for cutting.

In general, use your spoon to eat desserts with lots of sauce or juice or soft desserts such as custards, mousse, or ice cream. Cakes, pies, crepes, or other pastries usually call for a fork, but if they're served à la mode—with ice cream—they may be eaten with either or both of the utensils.

Escargots

Escargots (French for "snails") are usually baked or broiled and can be eaten in a number of ways. Shelled snails served on toast are eaten with a knife and fork. Escargots in their shells are served on snail plates along with special tongs that grip the shell to steady it. Squeeze the tongs to open them, place around a shell, and gently release to hold the shell. Use a pick, oyster fork, or two-pronged snail fork to remove the snail and eat it. The garlic butter that remains in the shells can be poured into the snail plate and sopped up with small pieces of bread on the end of a fork.

Fish

As an entrée, fish is often served as a fillet and eaten with a knife and fork. At a restaurant, if a fish is presented whole, it's fine to ask the waiter to prepare it for you, either tableside or in the kitchen. More daunting is a whole fish you must fillet for yourself. If so, you should be provided with a fish knife and fish fork, tools designed for the job.

To fillet a fish, first anchor it with your fork and remove the head, placing it on a plate for discards. Then, holding your knife parallel to the fish, use the tip to cut a line down its center, from gill to tail, just above the bones running down the middle of the body. Next, you can either eat the flesh directly from the fish; or, lift the top half of the flesh with the knife and fork, put it on the plate, and then remove the skeleton.

If you detect a fish bone in your mouth, work it to your lips unobtrusively; then discreetly remove it with your fingers and place it on the side of your plate. (Fish bones can be too tiny to maneuver onto a fork for removal.)

Frogs' Legs

Frogs' legs, which are similar to little chicken drumsticks, can be eaten with either the fingers as a passed hors d'oeuvre or a knife and fork at the table.

Fruit

Most fruit should be prepared in the kitchen and presented so that it can be eaten with a spoon or fork. Small fruits, such as grapes, plums, apricots, figs, and cherries, can be eaten with your fingers. Peel a whole orange, but a grapefruit should be served halved and prepared so it can be eaten with a spoon or serrated grapefruit spoon. Berries are eaten with a spoon.

Hors d'Oeuvres

Typically, hors d'oeuvres are finger foods and intended to be eaten in one or two bites. At parties, you may be choosing hors d'oeuvres from platters set on a table or taking them from a passed tray. In either case, plenty of napkins should be available. Take small portions from tables and trays. When taking two or more items, use one of the small plates provided; a single can be held on a napkin. A napkin also goes under any plate you're holding in case you need it.

There's usually a small receptacle on the table or tray for used food skewers and toothpicks. If not, hold any items such as shrimp tails and toothpicks in your napkin until you find a wastebasket. Don't place used items on the buffet table unless there's a receptacle for the purpose.

When crudités (raw vegetables) or chips and dip are offered, spoon some of the dip on your plate. If a communal bowl is used instead of individual plates, don't double-dip.

Lemons

When squeezing a lemon section over a dish or into tea, shield other diners from squirts by holding a spoon or your cupped hand in front of it as you squeeze. After squeezing, place the lemon on the edge of the plate (or saucer) or drop it into your iced tea.

Meats

With a few exceptions, meat is eaten with a fork and cut with a knife or a steak knife for more robust cuts. Cut and eat one piece at a time. When meat is served "on the bone," as is the case with chops and ribs, there are times when it's okay to pick up the bones in your fingers.

Chops. At a dinner party or relatively formal restaurant, pork, lamb, and veal chops are eaten with a knife and fork. The center, or eye, of the chop is cut off the bone, and then cut into two or three pieces. If your host or hostess invites you to "pick up the bones," then it's fine to do so.

Among friends at an informal occasion or at home, you can hold the chop and bite off the last juicy morsels of pork, lamb, and veal. But if a chop is too big to be picked up with only one hand, it should stay put on the plate.

Grilled meats. At an informal barbecue, it's fine to eat hamburgers, hot dogs, ribs, and pieces of chicken with your fingers, but use a knife and fork for sausages without buns, fish, steak, and other meats served in large portions.

Olive Oil

Pour olive oil from a cruet onto your bread plate. If it's served in a dish, either spoon a small pool of oil onto your bread plate or dip a bite-size piece of the bread into the communal bowl. Spooning is preferable as it reduces the chance for drips on the tablecloth. If you dip in the communal bowl, be sure not to double-dip.

Olives

Eat olives from an antipasti platter with your fingers; you also use your fingers to remove the pit from your mouth while cupping your hand as a screen. The pit goes into a small dish provided, or on the side of your plate.

When olives come in a salad, eat them with your fork. Remove a pit from your mouth either with your fingers or by pushing it with your tongue onto your fork; then place the pit on the edge of your dinner plate.

Poultry and Game Birds

At a formal dinner, no part of a bird—chicken, turkey, game hen, quail, or squab—is picked up with the fingers. The exception is when a host encourages his guest to use fingers for eating the joints of small game birds served without gravy or sauce.

When eating the breast or leg of a bird, use your knife and fork to cut as much meat as you can from the bone, working parallel to the bones, and then leave the rest on the plate.

If you're served a small, whole bird, such as a quail, cut the bird in half, head to tail, through the center of the breast. Then separate the wings and leg from the body, using your fork to hold the leg or wing and your knife to cut through the joint.

The no-fingers rule doesn't always apply, such as when you're dining at home or in a family-style or informal restaurant. It's fine to eat fried chicken with your fingers and to do the same with the wings, joints, and drumsticks of other poultry. When eating a turkey drumstick, however, start with a knife and fork to eat the easily cut pieces of meat before you pick up the drumstick and eat the rest.

In some parts of the United States, notably in the South, fried chicken is almost always eaten with the fingers, but take a cue from your host to be sure.

Salad

Large pieces of lettuce or other salad greens can be cut with a knife and fork. However, don't make a beautiful salad into coleslaw by cutting it up into small pieces all at once.

Sandwiches, Wraps, and Wrap-Style Foods

Sandwiches are almost always finger food and should be served cut into halves or quarters.

Empanadas. Empanadas, which range in size from very small to quite large, are Mexican or Spanish turnovers filled with meat and vegetables. Small empanadas served as appetizers are finger food, while larger ones are eaten with a knife and fork.

Fajitas. Fajitas (flour tortillas with a choice of fillings) are filled and rolled by the diner, then eaten with the fingers. To keep things neat, spread any soft fillings (usually refried beans, guacamole, sour cream, or melted cheese) onto the tortilla first; then add the strips of beef, chicken, or seafood and top with any garnishes. Roll up the tortilla and eat it from one end. Your fork is used only to eat any filling that falls to the plate.

Quesadillas. When served as an appetizer, a quesadilla—a flour tortilla topped with a mixture of cheese, refried beans, or other ingredients and then folded and grilled or baked—is cut into wedges and eaten with the fingers. When served whole as a main course, it is eaten with a fork and knife.

Tacos. Crisp tacos are eaten with the fingers, since cutting the crisp shell with a knife and fork will leave it cracked and crumbled. Do use a fork, however, for any filling that falls to the plate. Soft tacos, which are often topped with a sauce, are eaten with a knife and fork.

Wraps. Burritos, gyros, and other sandwiches in which the filling is wrapped in thin, flat bread (usually tortillas or pita bread) are most easily eaten with the fingers. Cut wraps in half if they're long. Any filling that falls to the plate is eaten with a fork.

Seafood Stews

Seafood stews, such as bouillabaisse, are made with varying combinations of fish, octopus, shrimp, and scallops, as well as clams, mussels, and crab legs, often in their shells. You'll need not only a soupspoon but also a seafood fork, a knife, and sometimes a shellfish cracker. A large bowl should be placed on the table for discarded shells. If no receptacle is provided, place empty shells on the plate under your soup bowl.

Shellfish

By their very nature, shellfish call for special implements to get to the meat inside the armor plating.

Crab legs. Use crackers to open the leg and a pick or seafood fork to remove the meat, then eat it using the small fork.

Soft-shell crab. A soft-shell crab is eaten shell and all, whether it's served in a sandwich or on a plate, in which case cut the crab with a knife and fork down the middle and then into bite-size sections.

Lobster (whole). A large paper napkin or plastic bib is provided for the lobster eater. Be sure to wear it, since handling this shellfish usually results in more than a few squirts and splashes. You'll also be given a shell cracker, a small fork, a knife, and a pick.

Holding the lobster steady with one hand, twist off the claws and place them on the side of your plate. Using the cracking tool (a shellfish cracker or nutcracker), crack each claw (slowly to reduce squirting) and pull out the meat with a fork or lobster pick. You'll need to remove the meat from the tail (often already cut into two solid pieces) and cut into bite-size pieces.

Spear each piece of meat with your fork and dip it into the accompanying butter or sauce before eating. True lobster lovers get an additional morsel out of the legs by break-

ing them off one at a time, putting them into the mouth broken end first, and squeezing the meat out with the teeth.

A large bowl or platter should be provided for the empty shells. Finger bowls with hot water and lemon slices are often put at each place as soon as the meal is finished, or, in less formal settings, premoistened towelettes are provided. Remove the bib before dessert—the person clearing the table will dispose of it.

Lobster tail. When just the tail is served—baked, broiled, stuffed, or lobster salad in the shell—use a fork and knife, if necessary.

Mussels. When eating whole mussels served either in a broth or sauce, use a fork or spoon to remove the mussel from its shell and eat it in one bite. If you need to, you can steady the mussel with your fingers. Don't eat any mussels that haven't opened at least halfway—they may be spoiled. Anywhere but at a formal dinner, it's fine to pick up the shell and a little of the juice, then eat the mussel and juice directly off the shell. The juice or broth remaining in your bowl can either be eaten with a spoon or sopped up with pieces of bread speared on your fork. Empty shells are placed in a bowl or plate provided for discards, on the edge of your plate, or left in your bowl.

Oysters and clams on the half shell. When served raw, oysters and clams are usually opened, the top shell removed, and served on cracked ice, arranged around a container of cocktail sauce and garnished with a lemon wedge or two. Hold the shell with the fingers of one hand and a shellfish fork (or smallest fork provided) with the other hand. Spear the clam or oyster with the fork, dip it into your sauce or squeeze on a spritz of lemon, and eat it in one bite. If there's a communal bowl of sauce, spoon some onto your plate or onto the shellfish. Never dip raw food into a communal sauce.

At a picnic, an oyster or clam bar, or a raw bar, it's fine

to pick up the shell with your fingers and eat the meat and juice right off the shell.

Shrimp. For shrimp cocktail, use your fork if the tails are off. It's okay to use your fingers if the tail has been left on. The traditional utensil is an oyster fork, although any small fork will do. If the shrimp are bigger than one bite's worth, just spear each shrimp with your fork and cut it on the underplate on which it's served.

Shrimp served as a main course are eaten with a knife and fork. Shrimp can also be served unpeeled, as in a shrimp boil, in which case they are finger food. Pick up the shrimp, insert a thumbnail under the shell at the top end (the opposite end from the tail) to loosen it, then work the shell free and eat the meat. An extra plate should be provided to hold the discarded shells. If not, arrange them on the edge of your plate.

Shrimp served as an hors d'oeuvre are eaten with the fingers. Hold a shrimp by the tail and dip it into cocktail sauce, if you like—just be sure not to double-dip.

Steamed clams, aka steamers. Steamers are finger food. Don't eat any steamed clams that haven't opened at least halfway; they may be spoiled. Open the shell fully, holding it with one hand. Then slip the skin off the neck with your fingers and put it aside. Holding the neck in your fingers, dip the clam into the broth or melted butter (or both) and eat it in one bite.

If no bowl is provided for empty shells, deposit them around the edge of your plate. In a more casual setting, it's okay to drink the broth after you've finished eating the clams. If you're a guest, follow the host's lead.

Shish Kebab

Shish kebab (chunks of meat, fish, and vegetables threaded onto skewers and then broiled or grilled) are eaten directly from the skewer only when they're served as an hors d'oeuvre. When eating shish kebab as a main course, lift the skewer and use your fork to push and slide the chunks off the skewer and onto your plate. Place the emptied skewer on the edge of your plate and use your knife and fork to cut the meat and vegetables into manageable pieces, one bite at a time.

Soup

Dip the spoon sideways into the soup at the near edge of the bowl, then skim from the front of the bowl to the back. Sip from the side of the spoon, being careful not to slurp. If the soup is too hot, it's okay to blow gently over the soup in the spoon before you put it in your mouth. If you want a bite of bread while eating your soup, don't hold the bread in one hand and your soupspoon in the other. Instead, rest your spoon, then have a bite of bread. To retrieve the last spoonful, slightly tip the bowl away from you and then spoon away from you as well to reduce the chance of spilling in your lap.

Where do you leave your spoon when you're pausing or finished? If the bowl is shallow, leave it in the bowl; if the bowl is deep or the soup is in a cup, leave the spoon on the underplate or saucer.

French onion soup. This tricky-to-eat soup requires a few pointers. That's because it's topped with a slice of French bread covered with melted cheese (notorious for stretching from bowl to mouth in an unbroken strand). To break through to the soup, take a small amount of cheese onto your spoon and twirl it until the strand forms a small clump. Then cut the strand off neatly by pressing the edge of the spoon against the edge of the bowl; or, you could use a knife for cutting. Using your spoon, and knife if necessary, cut and eat the bread (called a crouton). Eat the cheese and bread and then enjoy the soup. If any strands of cheese trail from your mouth, bite them off cleanly so that they fall back into the bowl of the spoon.

Spaghetti and Other Long Noodles

The traditional method for eating spaghetti, linguine, fettuccine, and tagliatelle is to place your fork vertically into the pasta at its edge until the tines touch the plate, then twirl it, catching a few strands, until the strands form a fairly neat clump. The resulting "package" should be small enough to fit into your mouth. If it's not, then start over.

The alternative is to hold the fork in one hand and a large spoon in the other. Take a few strands of the pasta on the fork and place the tines against the bowl of the spoon, twirling the fork to neatly wrap the strands.

For those who haven't mastered the art of twirling pasta strands, there's the simple cutting method. Just be sure not to cut the whole plateful at one time; instead, use your knife and fork to cut small portions.

Tea

Brewed. Either the hostess pours and passes the cups, or the pot is passed and each person serves herself. Strong tea can be diluted with hot water poured from a second pot.

Tea bags. After steeping, let the bag drip briefly into the cup as you remove it and place it on a saucer or plate (no squeezing it with your fingers or the string). Some restaurants serve a selection of tea bags with a small pot of hot water. It's less messy to put the tea bag into the pot, let it steep, and then pour the tea into your cup.

WEDDING BUDGET PLANNING CHART

ITEM	MANDATORY	OPTIONAL	COST
ATTENDANTS			
Accommodations			
Bridesmaids' luncheon (if hosting)			
CEREMONY FEES			
Officiant's fee			
Site fee			
Organist's fee			
Cantor/vocalist/instrumentalist fee(s)			
FLOWERS			
Ceremony			
Reception			
Bridal bouquet			
Bridal attendants' flowers			
Corsages			
Boutonnieres			
GIFTS			
Engagement ring			
Bride's gifts for attendants			
Groom's gifts for attendants			
Bride's gift for groom			
Groom's gift for bride			
People who host parties or do special favors for you			
HONEYMOON COSTS			
Transportation			
Accommodations			
Meals			
Incidentals			
INVITATIONS/ANNOUNCEMENTS/STATIONERY			
Save-the-date			
Invitations/enclosures			
Announcements			

ITEM	MANDATORY	OPTIONAL	COST
Calligraphy			
Postage			
Thank-you notes			
Ceremony program			
LEGALITIES			
Marriage license			
Health/physical/blood test fees			
MUSIC FOR RECEPTION			
Musicians/DJ/MC/MP3			
PHOTOGRAPHY			
Engagement photographs			
Wedding photographer			
Wedding videographer			
RECEPTION			
Location fee			
Food/beverage expenses (per-person cost)			
Reception favors (per-person cost)			
Wedding cake			
REHEARSAL DINNER			
Location fee			
Food/beverage expenses (per-person cost)			
TRANSPORTATION/PARKING			
Limousines for bridal party			
Traffic officials at ceremony, reception			
Valet parking			
Travel costs for ceremony officiant, if necessary			
Guest transportation to lodging postreception			
WEDDING ATTIRE			
Bridal gown			
Bridal accessories			
Groom's outfit			
Bride's ring			

ITEM	MANDATORY	OPTIONAL	COST
Groom's ring			
Beauty costs (hair, nails, makeup)			
WEDDING CONSULTANT FEES			
MISCELLANEOUS			
Telephone bills related to planning			
Trips home during planning if you live away			
Wardrobe costs for wedding-related events			
Tips (if not included in above costs)			
Taxes (if not included in above costs)			
TOTALS			

WEDDING BUDGET CATEGORIES FOR ATTENDANTS

ITEM	MANDATORY	OPTIONAL	COST
ATTIRE			
Purchase or rental of attire			
Shoes			
Accessories			
Hair, nails, makeup, etc.			
GIFTS			
Individual or group gift to bride and groom			
Bridesmaids' individual or group gift to bride			
Groomsmen's individual or group gift to groom			
Shower gift			
ENTERTAINING			
Shower			
Bachelor(ette) party			
Bridesmaids' luncheon			
Bachelor dinner			
TRANSPORTATION			
To and from the wedding			
To and from showers or other parties			
TOTALS			

index

A

abbreviations (online), 385
academic titles, 184, 517, 677
accessories, 50–51
    bridesmaids', 617
    men's, 52–53
    wedding gown, 615–16
    women's, 54–55
accidents
    automobile, 94–95
    host's coping with, 251
    spills, 73–74, 111
acknowledgment cards, 365
addiction, talking about, 44
address, forms of. *See* names and titles
adoption, 475–76
    announcements, 477, 686
    interracial, 476
    introductions, 465
    shower for child, 322
adult entertainment venues, 451
adventure travel, 135
African American weddings, 570
AIDS/HIV, 377
air kiss, 14
air travel, 122–26
    with babies and children, 125
    boarding the plane, 123
    carry-ons and overhead bins, 123
    cell phone use, 122–23, 232
    chatting with other passengers, 124
    check-in, 122
    disembarking, 126
    at the gate, 122–23
    preparation for, 122
    seat etiquette, 124–25
    security, 122
    switching seats, 123
airbnb, 128
airports
    routine at, 122–23
    tipping personnel, 169

akikah, 337
alcoholic beverages
    business events and, 445–46, 451
    cocktail party selection, 310–11
    eating garnishes, 312
    excessive drinking, 252, 306, 671
    at formal parties, 316–17
    home employees' use of, 508
    one-drink rule, 445
    at performances, 164
    refraining from, 257
    at wedding receptions, 589
    as wedding shower gift, 628
    See also champagne; wine
allergies, 65, 256, 257, 297, 351, 376
ambassadors, 180, 182, 183, 679
American (zigzag) style of utensil use, 66, *67*, 68
"and guest"
    on formal invitations, 281–82
    gifts and, 326
    on wedding invitations, 608, 663
anniversary parties, 330–32
    gifts, 331, 350
    invitations, 278, 331, 686
    reaffirming marriage vows, 332
    at restaurants, 332
    traditional elements, 330–31
announcements, 289–91
    adoption, 477, 686
    birth, 477, 686
    business, 290
    engagement, 564, 565
    graduation, 329
    legal name change, 220
    samples, 686
    wedding, 612, 629
    See also newspaper announcements
annulment, 513, 517
anonymity, online, 238, 384
anonymous notes, 417
apartment dwellers, 82–83
apologies, 9
    "I'm sorry," 8, 9
    notes and letters of, 207
appetizers
    at restaurants, 104, 107
    utensils for, 57, *62*
applause, 159–60, 161, 670
appointments, workplace, 420

appreciation. *See* "thank you"
aqd-nikah, 673
arch of steel, 670
archbishop, addressing, 184
arenas, 162–63
arm, offering, 27, 636
arnand karaj, 674
artichokes, eating, 686–87
Ash Wednesday, 344
Asian dishes, 687
asparagus, eating, 70, 687
assisted living, 522–23
associate justices of Supreme Court, 180, 678
attachments, email, 241
attire. *See* dress; grooming; wedding attire
Attorney General, 180, 678
attorneys, "Esq." used by, 219, 605, 677
au pairs, 361, 505–6, 507
autograph seekers, 161
automobiles, 91–96
    accidents, 94–95
    attention while driving, 92
    backseat drivers, 93–94
    carpooling, 95–96
    cell phone use while driving, 232
    children in, 483–84
    driving don'ts, 92–93
    holding door of, 26
    horn use, 93
    at intersections, 94
    merging, 92
    parking, 94
    passengers, 93, 95, 121–22
    road rage, 92
    rubbernecking, 94
    safety and, 92, 483–84
    senior parents giving up driving, 526
    signaling, 92
    speed limit, 92
    tailgating, 92
    teen drivers, 489
    U.S. flag on, 189
avocados, eating, 687

B

babies
    air travel with, 125
    breast-feeding, 425, 480
    See also birth ceremonies

baby showers, 320–22
    gifts, 321, 350, 354, 362, 421, 476
    honorees and hosts, 321
    invitations, 321, 685
    for subsequent births, 321
    thank-you notes, 321–22, 362
    time and place, 320–21
    workplace, 421
babysitters, 506, 507
    tips/gifts, 173
bachelor party, 580, 583
bachelorette party, 579, 580, 583
background
    searches, 501
    talking about, 41
bacon, eating, 70
baggage checkers, tipping, 169
Baha'i weddings, 674
ballet, 161
balls. See dances and balls
banks, 98
baptisms, 334–35, 350
bar, 316–17
    business conducted at, 448
    at weddings, 589
bar mitzvah/bat mitzvah, 339–40
    the celebration, 339
    gifts, 340, 350
    invitations, 278, 340, 685
barbecues, 308
barber shops, 98–99, 172
bartenders, 311, 316
    tipping, 168, 317
baseball caps, 52–53
basketball hoops, 84
bathrooms. See restrooms/bathrooms
beaches, 152–53
beauty salons, 98–99, 172
bed-and-breakfasts (B&Bs), 128
bedeken, 642
bellman, tipping, 171
benefits, invitations to, 282–83
best man, 577, 640, 642, 648, 649, 650
    last-minute duties of, 635
    responsibilities of, 580
    witnessing wedding paper signature, 647
best wishes showers, 628
beverages
    manners for, 68
    nonalcoholic, 300
    ordering at restaurants, 104

    at performances, 160
    spilled, 73–74, 111
    wedding reception, 589
    See also alcoholic beverages
bicycling
    basic rules and courtesies for, 146
    mountain biking, 147–48
    on the sidewalk, 28
bigotry, 42, 90
birdseed, throwing (wedding), 646, 653
birth announcements, 477, 686
birth ceremonies, 334–37
    Christian, 334–35
    Islamic, 337
    Jewish, 335–37
birthday parties, 322–25
    for adults, 324
    for children, 322–24
    gifts, 323–24, 325, 350, 363–64, 421
    invitations, 278, 322–23, 324–25, 685
    party favors, 324
    quinceañera, 325–26, 685
birthstones, 325
bishop, addressing, 184, 680
black tie, 317, 319, 326, 619, 667
    creative, 683
    optional, 683
blessing, pre-meal, 64, 304, 651
blind dates, 371
blindness or vision loss, 32–33
block form (address), 202
blusher veil, 615
boating, 148–51
    at the boat launch, 150
    flag etiquette, 150, 189
    hosting guests, 150–51
    at the marina, 149
    on the radio, 150
Bodhi Day, 344
body language, 37, 133, 419, 485
body odor, 48, 49
body piercings. See piercings
bonds, as gifts, 351
borrowing and lending, 85, 86
boss
    gifts and, 423
    going over the head of, 433
    good, 415, 503
    socializing or traveling with, 447–48
bouquets. See wedding flowers

boutonnieres, 53
    prom, 328
    wedding, 568, 622–23, 635
box seats, 156–57
bravo!, 161
bread, 106, 688
bread (or butter) plate, 58, 59, 60, 65, 102
breakfast
    midnight, 318
    party, 307–8
breast-feeding, 425, 480
breath, bad, 48
bridal showers. See wedding showers
bridal table, 590
bride
    bouquet toss, 622, 653
    escorting down the aisle, 568, 638, 639
    getting ready, 634–35
    in military, 606, 621
    toasts by, 650
    unreasonable demands by, 618
bridesmaids, 577, 583, 621–22, 634–35, 638–39, 640–42, 645, 648
    unreasonable demands on, 618
    wedding attire, 616–18
bris (Brit Milah), 335–36, 350
brit bat or brit hayyim, 336–37
Brit Milah. See bris
brother, Catholic, 184, 680
brunch, 308
bubbles, "showering" wedding couple with, 645, 646, 653
Buddhism
    holy days, 344
    religious services, 347
    weddings, 674
budget. See money
buffets, 64, 65
    cocktail, 296, 310
    hors d'oeuvre, 317
    restaurant, 115, 167
    table setting, 301–2
    tipping, 167
    wedding, 588
bullying, 10, 486
burgee, 150
busboys, tipping, 169
buses
    cell phone use, 232
    charter/tour, tipping driver, 170

common courtesies on, 29
courtesy/hotel shuttle, tipping
    driver, 169
travel guidelines for, 126–27
business announcements, 290
business associates
    divorce, telling about your, 516
    gifts and, 360, 366, 423
    tips for good relationships with, 439
    See also coworkers
business cards, 419, 440–41
business casual attire, 684
business email, 214, 238, 242–43
business formal attire, 684
business letters, 212–14
    of commendation, 213
    of complaint, 213–14
    of reference and recommendation,
        213
business meals, 443–46
    conversation, 446
    guests, 445–46
    host, 444–45
    reciprocating, 446
    thank-you, 446–47
butlers, 507
butter, 59–60, 65, 106, 689
butter knife, 58, *60*, 62, *62*
butter plate. *See* bread (or butter)
    plate
BYOB/BYOF invitations, 277, 296

C

cabinet members, U.S., 180, 183, 678
cafeterias, 115
caller ID, 223
calling cards. *See* social cards
call-waiting, 225–26
cameras, on mobile devices, 233, 436
camping, 148
Canadian officials, 681–82
cancellations, 99, 611–12
candle-lighting ceremony, 658
candles, 60, 301, 315
    home employees using, 508
    unity, 569–70
cantors, 184, 642, 645, 680
captain's table, 130
car services, tipping, 30, 170
"Card of Thanks" (newspaper), 365
cardinal, Catholic, 183–84, 680
care facilities (senior), 523–24, 525–26

caregivers
    advice for, 533–35
    care for, 529–30, 533
    communication with, 532
    family members as, 521, 529–30
    professional, 524–25, 535
carpooling, 95–96
cars and driving. *See* automobiles
cash bar, 317
caskets
    flowers on, 549
    open or closed, 541, 544–45, 551
    U.S. flag on, 189
casual attire, 684
casual dining, 115–16
casual invitations, 278
casual parties, 278
catered events
    parties, 306–7
    weddings, 588
Catholicism. *See* Roman Catholic
    Church
cats, 84–85
caviar, eating, 689
CC&Rs (covenants, conditions, and
    restrictions), 88
cell phone, 230–35
    air travel and, 122–23, 232
    cameras, 233, 436
    children and teens, 485–86
    don'ts, 232
    driving and, 232
    on the golf course, 140–41
    at meetings, 236, 419
    at performances, 158
    in public, 24, 231
    on public transportation, 29, 126,
        232
    in restaurants, 101, 113, 231–32
    ring tones, 232
    shopping and, 96, 97
    smartphone, 230–32, 436
    take-care zones, 231–32
    turning off, 113, 144, 231, 232, 255,
        407, 485–86, 545
    at yoga class, 144
centerpieces, 60, 315, 592, 672
ceremonies, 334–41
    See also birth ceremonies; coming-
        of-age ceremonies
certificates of deposit, as gifts, 351
chain letters, emailed, 240

chairs, holding, 26–27, 63, 102, 375
champagne
    glasses, 63, 103, *299*
    uncorking, 297
    at wedding reception, 649
Chanukah, 345
chaplain, addressing, 185
charger. *See* service plate
chauffeurs, 507
    See also limousine service
cheese course, 108
chemo caps, 23
cherry tomatoes, eating, 689
chewing food, 71–72
chicken, eating, 70, 692
Chief Justice
    Canadian, 681
    court of appeals, 180
    U.S., 180, 183, 678
chief of staff, 181
child-care providers, 505–7
    See also au pairs; babysitters;
        daycare; nannies
children, 478–89
    addressing adults, 17, 484
    age-appropriate expectations of,
        478
    birth to one year, 479–80
    birthday parties for, 322–24
    bringing along uninvited, 254
    care providers, 505–7
    cell phones and, 485–86
    correcting other people's, 20, 459
    criticizing parents around, 461
    custodial arrangements, 462, 514,
        518
    in daycare, 506
    death in the family and, 547, 553
    divorce of parents and, 217, 513, 514,
        518, 519
    eleven to fourteen, 484–87
    email and, 486
    engagement of a parent and,
        559–61
    in foster care, 465
    in the home, 459–60
    home office and, 426
    of houseguests, 265
    illness in, 506, 532
    introductions and, 17
    invitations to, 277
    listening to, 460–61

children (*cont.*)
    moving back home as adults, 471–72
    name changes, 461
    neighbors and, 83–84
    one to three years, 480–81
    online interactions, 485–87
    parental dating and, 374, 379–80,
        519
    at performances, 160
    phone answered by, 427, 481, 483
    remarriage of parent and, 518, 568,
        655, 656, 658–59, 660
    at restaurants, 113, 116–17
    school lunchroom manners, 483
    separation of parents and, 511
    shopping with, 96–97
    six to ten years, 482–84
    social networks and, 486
    sports participation by, 137–38
    stationary for, 199
    in stepfamilies, 461–62, 465, 518,
        659
    thank-you notes from, 364
    three to five years, 481–82
    travel with, 121–22, 125
    of unmarried mothers, 217
    visitation arrangements, 462, 511,
        518
    wedding invitations to, 608, 663
    in wedding party, 581, 629 (*see also*
        flower girl; junior bridesmaids;
        junior ushers; ring bearer)
    at the workplace, 424–25
    See also adoption; teens
Chinese tea ceremony, 570
chops, eating, 691
chopsticks, 688
christenings, 278, 334–35, 336
Christian religions
    birth ceremonies, 334–35
    coming-of-age ceremonies, 337–39
    funeral and burial services, 550
    holy days, 344
    weddings, 672
    See also individual religions
Christmas, 344
chuppah, 642–43, *644*, 673
churches. *See* religious services
circumcision. *See* bris
city comptrollers, 181
city council members, 181
city council president, 181

city government protocol, 181
clams, eating, 693–94
classical music performances, 161–62
clergy, 541
    addressing, 183–84, 218–19, 348,
        679–80
    death and, 540
    gifts to, 361
clients. *See* customers and clients
clothing stores, 98
coat-check attendant, 101, 169
cocktail hour, 294–95, 315
cocktail parties, 310–12
    buffet, 296, 310
    hired help for, 311
    invitations, 278, 310
    juggling plates and glasses, 311
    mingling at, 311
coffee, 59, 109, 304, 316
coffee shops, 116
coffeehouses, 162–63
cologne. *See* perfume and cologne
colors (U.S. flag), 189
coming-of-age ceremonies, 337–41
    Christian, 337–39
    Jewish, 339–41
coming-of-age parties, 325–27
commendation, letters of, 213
commitment
    to customers, keeping, 440
    roommates and, 491, 493–94
common areas, apartment or condo, 82
communication
    with caregivers, 532
    with children, 479, 480, 481, 482–83,
        485–87
    dating and, 371
    with the elderly, 523–24
    with home employees, 502
    with roommates, 491–93
    with teens, 485–87, 488
    See also names and titles; notes
        and letters; online interactions;
        personal communication
        devices; telephone
communion, 342–43, 669
    See also First Communion
complaints
    customer, 438–39
    letters of, 213–14
    in restaurants, 117–18
    workplace, 430–32

compliment sandwich, 503–4
complimentary close, 212, 241
compliments, 43, 255, 433
compromise
    with roommates, 491, 493
    workplace, 429
comptrollers, 180, 181
computers, 244–46
    bandwidth sharing, 498
    public use of, 245–46
    sharing, 245
    See also online interactions
concierge, tipping, 171
condiments, 59, 65, 108, 689
condolences
    acknowledging, 555
    emailing, 554
    gifts or contributions, 350, 363,
        421–22, 541, 544
    notes and letters of, 553–55
    offering, 44, 548, 553
    online, 554
    timing for, 555
    what and what not to say, 545
    from the workplace, 421–22
condom use, 377
condominium dwellers, 82–83
conference calls, 235
"Confidential" (envelope notation),
    203
confirmation, 350
    Christian, 338–39
    Jewish, 340–41
conflicts, workplace, 429–30
congratulations
    gifts or cards, 363
    notes and letters of, 206–7
consideration, 6, 8, 255
consumption bar, 589
contact lenses, 51
Continental (European) style of utensil
    use, 66, *67*, 68
contributions. *See* donations and
    contributions
conversation, 35–45
    on airplanes, buses, and trains, 124,
        126
    audience, 39
    body language, 37
    at business meals, 446
    children and, 481
    compliments, 43

controversial topics, 40, 72, 73, 380
correcting others, 39
criticism, 42
on a date, 375
dinner party, 304
disagreements, 41–42
extracting oneself from, 41
eye contact, 36, 37, 38
foreign phrases, 39
gossip, 42
host's responsibilities, 251
humor and jokes in, 42–43
inflection, 39
interrupting (*see* interruptions)
during introductions, 17
listening, 36, 39
official titles in, 182–86
opinions, 39
personal information, 40–41
personal space, 36
pitfalls, 40–42
practicing, 39–40
repetitive, 38–39
safe topics, 72–73
slang, 39
small talk, 39–40, 414–16
stoppers of, 45
at the table, 72–73, 109
talking too much, 38
thoughtfulness, 35–36
three tiers approach, 40
vocabulary, 38
voice volume, 37–38
what to say when, 43–44
whispering, 39
workplace, 414–16
about yourself, 40
copiers, workplace, 413, 416
corn on the cob, eating, 690
correspondence cards, 198, 199, *199*
corsages, 319
prom, 328
wedding, 623, 635
coughing, 75, 158, 227
county commissioners, 180
couples
addressing, 217–18, 676–77
invitations to, 277
separation of unmarried, 513
wedding invitations to, 608
See also partners, domestic

courses
five-course meal place setting, *60*
in restaurants, 107–8
three-course meal place setting, *59*
two-course meal place setting, *58*
cousins, once removed, 469
cover letters, 398, 399, 400–402
coworkers
complaining about, 431–32
divorce, telling about your, 516
engagement announced to, 560
gifts to and from, 360, 423
interacting with, 434
wedding gifts from, 421, 630–31
See also business associates
crab legs, eating, 693
creative black tie, 683
cremation, 542, 552
criticism, 42, 461, 503–4
cross-country skiing, 154
crowning or wreath ceremony (Greek Orthodox), 570
crudités, 691
cruises, 128–31
captain's table, 130
crewmembers, 130
dress, 129
meals and entertainment, 130
meeting others, 129
noise and, 130
recreational activities, 129
tipping staff, 130–31, 170–71
cummerbund, 53
cups and saucers, 59, 316
customers and clients
dealing with, 438–39
email support for, 214
home office and, 426
keeping commitments to, 440
cutting food, 66, 71
cyberbullying, 486
cycling. *See* bicycling

D
dances and balls
debutante, 318–19, 326–27
dress, 317–18
presentation, 283
proms, 327–28
dancing, 164, 317, 594, 651–52, 671

dating, 370–82
arriving at a date's home, 374
asking for/responding to, 372–73
blind dates, 371
breaking a date, 374
breaking up, 378
bringing along an uninvited date, 254
building a relationship, 382
children and, 374, 379–80, 519
conversation, 375
dining, 375–76
after divorce, 380, 512
ending a date, 41, 376
follow up, 376
getting back to, 379–80
gifts and, 377
going to the door, 374–75
meeting people, 371–72
online, 380–82
paying for, 373–74, 376, 381
punctuality, 374
reviewing plans, 375
safe sex, 377
safety in, 382
self-appraisal and, 370–71
seniors and, 528
during separation, 512
transportation, 375
by widows and widowers, 552
workplace, 376–77, 436
daycare, 506
deafness. *See* hearing loss or deafness
death and mourning, 539–55
children and, 547, 553
clergy and, 540, 541
condolences (*see* condolences)
cremation, 542, 552
in divorced or "blended" families, 518–19, 548
engaged couple and, 566
flowers and, 548–49
funeral directors and, 540, 541
funeral services (*see* funeral services)
making arrangements, 541
memorial services, 542
mourning duration, 552–53
notifying others, 539–41
obituaries, 540, 543
social network postings, 540
sympathy notes and letters, 553–55
visits and visitations, 544–45

debutante parties and balls, 318–19, 326–27
delicatessens, 116
dementia, 472, 524, 534
demitasse spoon, *62*
depression, talking about, 44
deputy mayor, 181
dessert, 108–9, 304–5, 690
dessert fork, 58–59, *60, 62*, 63, 109, 316
dessertspoon, 58–59, *60, 62*, 63, 109, 316
destination weddings, 569, 664, 665
dietary restrictions, 65, 256, 257, 297, 376
diners, 116
dining out. *See* restaurants
dinner fork, 57, 61, *62*
dinner knife, 57–58, 62
dinner parties, 294–306
    ambience, 299–303
    clearing the table, 305
    conversation during, 304
    after dessert, 304–5
    dining format, 295–96
    dinner is served, 303–4
    ending the meal, 304, 316
    farewells, 305–6
    formal, 314–16
    host/hostess gifts, 257, 303
    inebriated guests, 306
    invitations, 278, 296
    menu, 296
    place cards, 303, 315
    preparing the house for, 299–300
    seating plan, 302–3
    starting to eat, 304
    table, 300–302
    wine, 296–98, 315–16
dinner plate, 57
diplomatic corps, 183, 679
disabilities, 30–34
    hearing loss or deafness, 31–32, 227–28, 522
    mental, 33–34
    service dogs, 32, 33
    speech impairments, 33
    vision loss or blindness, 32–33
    wheelchair use, 33
distress signal flag, 150
district attorney, 181

divorce, 512–19
    children and, 217, 513, 514, 518, 519
    dating after, 380, 512
    ex-spouse relations, 465, 518, 560, 655, 657
    ex-spouse's death, 518–19, 548
    "independence" parties, 515
    informing others of, 513–16
    multiple, 216–17
    name and courtesy titles after, 216–17, 356, 461, 516–17
    post-divorce etiquette, 517–19
    response to news of, 43, 516–17
    rings and, 513
    wedding gifts and, 513
    wedding invitations and, 604
    wedding receiving line and, 648–49
    wedding seating and, 637
    See also remarriage; separation
Diwali, 344
Do Not Call registry, 223
doctors. *See* Dr., use of title
dogs
    aggressive or annoying behavior in, 84
    allergies to, 256
    hiking with, 147
    neighbors and, 84
    service, 32, 33
    travel with, 127
    walking, 28
    See also pets
domestic partners. *See* partners, domestic
donations and contributions
    for baptisms or christenings, 335
    condolence (*see* condolences, gifts or contributions)
    in lieu of flowers, 549–50, 551, 552
    in lieu of gifts, 351–52, 626
    at the workplace, 423–24
doorman, tipping
    hotel, 171
    residential, 173
doors
    holding, 25–26, 375
    women preceding men through, 27
    in the workplace, 413
double-booking parties, 258
Dr., use of title, 184, 185, 210, 218, 605, 677

dress
    akikah, 337
    appropriate, 46–47
    baptism or christening, 335
    bar/bat mitzvah, 339
    at the beach, 152
    black tie, 317, 319, 326, 619, 667, 683
    black tie optional, 683
    for burial, 541
    business casual, 684
    business formal, 684
    casual, 684
    confirmation, 338
    creative black tie, 683
    on cruises, 129
    at dances and balls, 317–18
    at debutante ball, 319
    dressy casual, 684
    festive, 684
    First Communion, 338
    formal, 53, 317–18, 667, 683
    at funeral and memorial services, 546, 547
    golf attire, 140–41
    for home employees, 507
    for home office, 425–26
    informal, 667
    invitations and, 55, 274–75, 605
    for job interviews, 404–5
    for men, 51–53, 683–84
    monogrammed, 358
    at office parties, 443
    for papal audience, 193
    at performances, 159
    for religious services, 342, 343, 346
    semiformal, 667, 684
    tennis attire, 143
    white tie, 317, 319, 326, 619, 683
    for women, 53–55, 683–84
    workplace, 411, 443, 684
    See also accessories; grooming; wedding attire
dressy casual attire, 684
drinks. *See* alcoholic beverages; beverages
drug use, by home employees, 508
Duhsera/Durga Puja, 344
dutch treat, 114

E

earbuds, 236, 486
Easter, 344

Eastern Orthodox Church, 343, 673
eavesdropping, 413
'Eid al-Adha, 345
'Eid al-Fitr, 345
elbows on the table, 70–71, 109
elder etiquette, 520–29
    assisted living, 522–23
    caregivers, 521, 524–25, 529–30
    dating, 528
    dementia or memory loss, 472, 524,
        534
    divorce in older people, 514
    doctor visits, 527–28
    driving, need to stop, 526
    end-of-life wishes, 528
    financial responsibilities, 526–27
    independent living, 521–22
    living arrangement problems,
        527
    nursing home or care center,
        523–24, 525–26
    parents living with adult children,
        472
    retirement community, 521–22
    sensitive conversations, 526–28
    sibling relations, 529
electronic brick wall, 238
elevators, 25–26
email, 238–43
    address line, 239
    attachments, 241
    autofill and autocorrect features,
        239
    automatic signature, 240
    business, 214, 238, 242–43
    Cc and Bcc features, 239, 241
    chain letters, 240
    checking, 239
    children and teens, 486
    condolences, 554
    customer support, 214
    dating and, 381
    emoticons and emojis, 239
    falling into the wrong hands, 240
    holiday greetings, 209
    invitations via, 273, 275, 286, 598
    length of, 239
    out of office/auto reply feature,
        242
    privacy, 238
    reliability, 238
    reply all feature, 241, 242
    responding to, 241–42
    return receipts, 241
    send delay feature, 239
    sentence case, 239
    spam, 239, 240
    subject line, 239
    thank-you notes, 210, 267, 406,
        446–47
    tips for exemplary, 238–42
    wedding invitations via, 598
    wedding planning, 578–79
embossing, 201
emoticons and emojis, 239
empanadas, eating, 692
empathy, 6, 7
employment agencies, 399–400
enclosures, 275–76, 288–89, 609–10,
    611
encore weddings. See remarriage
end-of-life wishes, 528
engagement, 559–66
    announcements, 564, 565
    breaking off, 565–66
    death of one of the couple, 566
    disapproval of, 560–61
    families meet, 561
    gifts, 350, 564, 565–66, 627
    parties, 563–64
    response to news of, 43
    telling family and friends, 559–61
engagement ring
    divorce and, 513
    heirloom, 563, 566
    options and selection, 562
    returning, 566
    wearing, 563
engraving, 201, 356
    See also monogramming
ensign (U.S. flag), 150, 189
entertaining at home. See parties
entertainment showers, 627
envelopes, 200–203
    addressing, 202, 517, 607–8
    linings, 200
    seals, 203
    wedding invitation, 607–11, 610
    See also enclosures
Episcopal bishop, 680
errands. See shopping and errands
erusin, 642–43
escalators, 27
escargot, eating, 690
Esquire, use ot title, 219, 605, 677
eulogies, 543–44
e-vites, 273, 275, 286, 598
"excuse me," 8, 9, 28
ex-spouse
    death of, 518–19, 548
    engagement news and, 560
    introducing, 465
    remarriage of, 518, 655, 657
    who won't move on, 518
eye contact, 22–23
    in conversation, 36, 37, 38
    cultural differences and, 133
    in greetings, 13
    in introductions, 18
    wandering eye problem, 38
eyewear, 51

F
Facebook
    invitations via, 274
    linking Twitter to, 388
    overview of, 387
facial expressions, 37
fajitas, eating, 692
families, 460–72
    adult children living with, 471–72
    changing dynamics in, 470–72
    childless, 463
    divorce, telling about your, 514
    elderly relatives and, 521, 529–30
    empty nesters, 471
    of engaged couple, meeting, 561
    engagement, telling about your,
        559–61
    extended, 468–70
    gatherings, 309
    gift-giving, 464, 468–70
    as houseguests, 269, 270
    introductions, 17, 464–66
    listening in, 460–61
    older parents living with, 472
    as roommates, 494
    separated by distance, 470
    single-parent, 462
    stationary for, 199
    staying in touch, 470
    talking about, 40–41
    values and manners in, 460–61
    wedding arrangements and, 576,
        585
    wedding invitations to, 608

families (*cont.*)
  wedding seating and, 636–38
  See also adoption; children;
    grandparents; in-laws; parents;
    stepfamilies; teens
family style service, 64, 295
fast-food restaurants, 116
father of the bride, 568, 621, 635, 638,
  639, 640, 648, 649
father of the groom, 621, 648, 649
festive attire, 684
fidgeting, 37
fillers, verbal, 38
fill-in invitations, 278, 279, 282
finances. *See* money
financial registries, 626, 665
finger bowls, 73, 108, 316
First Communion, 337–38, 350
first dance, wedding, 594, 651, 671
First Lady, addressing, 192, 678
fish, eating, 690
fish fork, 61, *62*
fish knife, 62, *62*
fishing, 152
fist bump, 15
fitness center, 143–45
flag, U.S., 186–90
  angled staff, 188
  on automobiles, 189
  on boats, 150, 189
  care of, 187
  on caskets, 189
  crossed staffs, 189
  displayed by foreigners, 191
  displaying, 188–89
  in displays with other flags,
    189–90
  flying upside down, 188
  folding, *187*
  half-mast or half-staff, 188, 189
  in house of worship, 188
  illuminating, 188
  as lapel pin, 189
  on Memorial Day, 188
  mounted, 189
  other names for, 189
  in processions, 190
  raising and lowering, 188
  retiring/destroying, 188,
    189
  saluting, 188
flattery, 10

flatware, 57–63
  monogramming, 358
  at restaurants, 102
flower girl, 581, 617–18, 622, 635, 639,
  640, 645, 648
flowers
  bereavement and, 548–49
  contributions in lieu of, 549–50, 551,
    552
  at debutante ball, 319
  gifts of, 351
  for hospital visits, 537–38
  ushers presenting, 635–36
  See also boutonnieres; corsages;
    wedding flowers
fold-over note cards, 198, *199*, 199–200,
  200
food
  allergies, 65, 256, 257, 297, 351, 3
    76
  arriving at different times, 107
  bones in, 74
  chewing, 71–72
  cutting, 66, 71
  dietary restrictions, 65, 256, 257,
    297, 376
  eating while on the phone, 227
  on face, 111
  foreign objects in, 74, 110–11
  gifts of, 351
  gristle in, 74
  guide to eating, 686–95
  passing, 64–65
  at performances, 160
  picking up/using fingers for, 70, 71
  pits in, 74, 691
  pushing, 66–68, 71
  roommates and, 497
  seasoning, 71
  sending back in restaurants, 107,
    113
  take-out deliveries, 172–73
  tasting one another's, 107
  on teeth, 74–75
  too hot or spoiled, 74
  wedding reception, 587–89
  See also meals
food stations, 317
foreign phrases, 39
forks
  dessert, 58–59, *60*, *62*, 63, 109, 316
  dinner, 57, 61, *62*

at end of course, 68, *69*, 107
fingers *vs.*, for specific foods, 70
fish, 61, *62*
holding, 66
luncheon, *62*
order of, 61
oyster, 61, *62*, 107
resting, 68
salad, 57, *60*, 61, *62*, 63
FOrKS (mnemonic), 57
formal attire, 53, 317–18, 667, 683
formal dinner parties, 314–16
formal greetings, 11
formal invitations, 280–84
  adding "and guest" to, 281–82
  appearance and style, 280–81
  fill-in, 282
  from groups/organizations,
    282–84
  from multiple hosts, 287–88
  recalling, 289
  replying to, 286–88
  to the White House, 191–92
formal parties, 316–18
formal table setting, *60*, 60–63, *62*
foster care, 465
French fries, eating, 70
French onion soup, eating, 694
French service, 589
frogs' legs, eating, 690
fromager/fromagère, 108
fruit, eating, 108, 690–91
funeral directors, 540, 541
funeral homes, 544–46
funeral services
  arrival at, 546
  behavior and ceremonies at,
    546–48
  bulletins or programs, 543
  clothing for burial, 541–42
  described, 541–42
  dress for, 546, 547
  eulogists and readers, 543–44
  graveside services, 542
  honorarium for officiant, 544
  pallbearers, 541–42, 546
  personalized services, 542–43
  post-service receptions, 550
  processional, 546
  recessional, 547–48
  religious customs, 550–52
  ushers, 543

G

gag gifts, 358–59
game birds, eating, 692
gaming
    online, 388–89
    portable devices, 486–87
garter toss, 653
gender non-specific address, 676
genuflection, 342
gestures, 37, 133
get-well cards, 421
get-well gifts, 350, 363, 537–38
ghosting, 378
ghusl, 552
gift certificates, 351
gift receipts, 359
gift registry, 276, 353–55
    baby shower, 321, 354
    wedding, 353, 354, 624–27, 661, 664
gifts, 349–69
    akikah, 337
    anniversary, 331, 350
    announcements and, 290, 477, 629
    awful, 366
    baby shower, 321, 350, 354, 362,
        421, 476
    bar/bat mitzvah, 340, 350
    birthday, 323–24, 325, 350, 363–64,
        421
    bris, 336, 350
    brit bat or brit hayyim, 336–37
    broken or damaged, 365–66
    christening or baptism, 335, 336, 350
    to clergy, 361
    condolence (*see* condolences, gifts
        or contributions)
    confirmation, 338–39, 341, 350
    cost of, 350, 354, 361–62, 366
    for daycare providers, 506
    for debutante, 319, 327
    declining, 422
    discontinuing exchange of, 360
    donations in lieu of, 351–52, 626
    duplicate, 366
    enduring, 350
    engagement, 350, 564, 565–66, 627
    exchanging, 368
    in families, 464, 468–70
    favors as, 352
    First Communion, 338, 350
    food, wine, and flowers, 351

gag, 358–59
    get-well, 350, 363, 537–38
    gift certificates, 351
    gift receipts, 359
    graduation, 329, 350
    group, 352–53
    from guests of guests, 326
    holiday, 174, 350, 363–64
    for home employees, 173, 361,
        504–5
    host/hostess, 257–58, 268, 303,
        350, 359
    housewarming, 257, 313, 350, 355
    inappropriate, 366–67, 422
    of money, 351, 363, 505, 626, 631,
        665
    "no gifts, please," 331, 332, 359–60,
        605, 661
    for nurses, 360–61
    occasions for, 350
    ordination or profession of vows, 350
    overly expensive, 366
    overseas customs, 134
    personal, 350
    personalizing, 355–56
    pidyon haben, 337
    for professionals, 173, 360
    quinceañera, 326
    receiving and acknowledging, 362
    reciprocating, 368
    regifting, 367–69
    retirement, 333, 350, 421
    returning after broken engagement,
        565–66
    sending to the office, 377
    for service providers, 350, 361
    for teachers, 354, 361
    temporary, 349–50
    thank you for, 362–65
    as thank you for favor, 350, 365
    tips to simplify giving, 354
    wedding (*see* wedding gifts)
    wedding shower, 350, 362, 565–66,
        627–28, 631
    welcome, 90
    what not to give, 358–59
    to the White House, 192
    workplace and, 353, 360, 421–23
    wrapping, 359
glasses, drink, 58, *60*, 63, 103
    champagne, 63, 103, *299*
    etiquette of, 304

    upside down, 105, 304
    wine, *60*, 63, 103, 105, 298, *299*
gloves, 54–55, 319
    bridal attire, 616
    removing, 14, 55, 318
godparents, 336
golf, 140–42, 449
Good Friday, 344
good-bye, 15, 255, 305–6
gossip, 42, 375
    in letters, 211
    neighbors and, 85
    workplace, 433, 451
government
    addressing officials, 678–79
    precedence and rank of officials,
        180–81
governor, 180, 183, 679
governor general (Canadian), 681
graciousness, 6–7, 17, 371
graduation, 328–30
    announcements, 329
    gifts, 329, 350
    invitations, 278, 328–29
    parties, 329–30
grammar, 385
grandparents, 463–64
    divorce of, 514
    wedding seating, 638
graveside services, 542
gravy
    serving, 65
    sopping up, 71
Greek Orthodox Church, 343, 570,
        673
green weddings, 568
greeting cards, 208
greetings, 10–15
    by children, 479, 480, 482–83
    eye contact in, 13
    formal, 11
    four steps to, 13
    from the host, 251
    hugging and, 14, 15
    informal, 11
    in job interviews, 405
    kissing and, 14–15
    to neighbors, 81
    standing during, 11–12, 13
    touch and, 14
    See also handshaking;
        introductions

groom
    garter toss, 653
    getting ready, 635
    involvement in wedding plans, 568
    in military, 606
    toasts by, 650
    wedding attire, 619–20
grooming, 47–50
    for job interviews, 404–5
    for men, 51–53
    in public, 24, 55
    at the table, 109–10
    wardrobe care, 49–50
    for women, 53–55
groomsmen, 577, 580–81, 619–20, 640,
        642, 648
group tours, 131
groups
    formal invitations sent by, 282–84
    gifts to and from, 352–53
    introducing members of, 17
guardianships, 465
guest books, 212, 265, 331
guest lists, 249, 274, 293, 573–74, 657
guest of honor
    baby shower, 321
    gifts and, 257
    invitations on behalf of, 274
    at official functions, 181, 182
    thank-you notes from, 206
guest register, 212, 545–46
guest room, 262
guests, 253–58
    bar/bat mitzvah, 339–40
    on boats, 151
    bringing uninvited people, 254
    at business meals, 445–46
    engagement party, 563
    general guidelines for, 254–56
    of home employees, 508
    inebriated, 252, 306
    reciprocating hospitality, 258
    rehearsal party, 583
    reneging on acceptance, 253–54
    at restaurant, 112–13
    roommates and, 498
    thank-you notes from, 204–5, 256
    toasts by, 258
    wedding shower, 582
    See also host; houseguests; wedding
        guests
gum chewing, 24, 227, 407, 435

H

hair
    facial, 53
    in food, 74, 110–11
    men's, 53
    taking care of, 48
    women's, 55
Hanamatsuri Day, 344
hand kissing, 14–15
handfasting, 570
handkerchiefs, 52, 53
handshakes, 12–14
    exceptions to, 13–14
    with individuals in wheelchairs, 33
    overseas travel and, 133, 134
    removing gloves for, 14
    sneezing and, 15
hats
    baseball caps, 52–53
    chemo caps, 23
    men's, 52–53
    at performances, 158
    religious services and, 23, 50
    removing, 22–23, 50, 52, 63, 158,
        190, 191
    women's, 54, 63
    yarmulkes, 336, 339, 346, 673
headhunters, 399–400
heads of state, foreign, 180
health, talking about. See illness
health-care proxy, 528
hearing loss or deafness, 31–32,
        227–28, 522
help, offers of
    to host, 255
    to neighbors, 80, 83
    to seniors, 521
    at the workplace, 414
high five, 15
high school graduation night parties,
        330
high school proms, 327–28
hiking, 147
Hinduism
    holy days, 344
    weddings, 674
Holi, 344
holiday newsletters, 208–9
holidays
    double-booking parties, 258
    dress, 684

gifts, 174, 350, 363–64
    party invitations, 278
    tipping, 166, 174
holy days, 344–45
home employees, 500–510
    alcohol and drug use by, 508
    background searches, 501
    child-care providers, 505–7
    clothing and uniforms, 507
    communication with, 502
    considerate treatment of, 502
    criticizing effectively, 503–4
    dismissal of, 509–10
    employer responsibilities to,
        500–505
    expectations, clarity of, 502
    gifts to, 173, 361, 504–5
    "good boss" behaviors, 503
    guests of, 508
    hiring, 501
    household staff, 507–8
    introductions, 502
    kitchen privileges, 508
    live-in help, 507–8
    meals and breaks, 503
    noise level guidelines, 508
    offering hand-me-downs to, 504,
        505
    overtime, 503
    paying on time, 503
    privacy for, 508
    references, 501, 510
    resignation of, 509
    smoking and candle use by, 508
    telephone use by, 508
    tipping, 173, 504–5
    transportation, 502–3, 508
    trial periods, 501
    vacations including, 507
home life, 457–60
    adults and, 458–59
    children and, 459–60
    courtesy, 21–22
    culture, 457–58
    setting standards, 457–58
    teens and, 459–60
    traditions, 458
home office, 425–27
    children and, 426
    clients and, 426
    dress, 425–26
    gloating about, 425

meetings at, 425
neighbors and, 426
pets and, 427
work creep and, 425
homeowners, neighbors and, 83
homeowners' associations, 87–89
honesty, 6, 10, 400
honeymoon, 660
honeymoon registries, 627
honor attendants, 568, 581, 620
"honorable," use of, 183, 184, 605
honorary degrees, 218
hors d'oeuvres, 295, 310, 317, 691
horseback riding, 147
horse-drawn carriage, 596
hospice care, 535
hospital visits, 536–38
host, 249–53
    accidents and, 251
    baby shower, 321
    on the boat, 150–51
    at business meals, 444–45
    cocktail party, 310–11
    cohosting, 253
    contingency plans, 252
    conversation responsibilities, 251
    dinner party, 303–6
    ending the event, 253
    engagement party, 563
    flexibility, 251–52
    general guidelines, 249–50
    gifts to, 257–58, 268, 303, 350,
        359
    greetings and introductions, 251
    inebriated guest, 252, 306
    office party, 443
    rehearsal party, 583
    at restaurant, 101, 102, 111–12,
        332
    restaurant employee, tipping,
        167–68
    toasts by, 250, 258, 259
    wedding shower, 582
    See also guests
hot towels, restaurant, 108
hotels, 127–28
    room service, 128, 171
    tipping staff, 127, 171–72
    wedding receptions at, 586
House of Commons member (Canada),
    682
house tours, 301, 313

houseguests, 261–70
    bed linen and, 267
    bringing along uninvited, 254, 269
    children of, 265
    departure of, 265
    extended visits by, 269–70
    family members as, 269, 270
    gifts for host, 268
    guest book, 265
    guest room, 262
    guidelines for, 265–66
    making the visit easy, 264–65
    meals for, 264
    overstaying by, 266
    replying to invitations, 266
    schedules and routines, 263–64
    setting a date, 261–62
    sleeping arrangements, 262–63
    time out from, 267
    welcoming, 262
housekeepers, 507
housekeeping staff (hotel), tipping,
    171–72
housemates. See roommates
housewarmings, 80, 257, 278, 313, 350,
    355
hugging, 14, 15
humor, 42–43

iced-tea spoon, 62, 63
illness, 531–38
    caregivers, 532, 533–35
    in children, 506, 532
    colds, 531–32
    debilitating, 533–34
    flowers for patient, 537–38
    get-well cards, 421
    gifts, 350, 363, 537–38
    home visits, 535–36
    hospital visits, 536–38
    major surgery, 532–33
    in oneself, 531–33
    response to news of, 43–44
    serious, 532–33
    talking about, 41, 534–35
    things not to say, 534
"I'm sorry," 8, 9
imam, addressing, 680
indented form (address), 202
inflection, 39
informal attire, 667

informal greetings, 11
informal invitations, 192, 278–79
informal table setting, 57–60, 58, 59
in-laws, 466–68
    addressing, 467
    divorce and, 515
    former, remarriage and, 657
    intrusions by, 467–68
Instagram, 388
instant messaging (IM), 243–44
International Code flags, 150
Internet. See online interactions
internships, 177
interruptions, 18, 36, 38, 226
introductions, 10–11, 15–19
    children and, 17
    excessive deference to one party, 18
    eye contact in, 18
    of family members, 17, 464–66
    forgotten, 18
    of group members, 17
    gushing during, 18
    of home employees, 502
    by the host, 251
    interrupting to make, 18
    making, 16–17
    making someone wait for, 18
    mistakes in, 17, 18, 19
    names and titles in, 15–16, 17, 19
    official titles in, 182–86
    order of, 16
    receiving, 17
    self-introductions, 18–19
    too-personal comments in, 18
    See also greetings
invitations, 271–89
    addressing, 276–77
    anniversary party, 278, 331, 686
    baby shower, 321, 685
    bar/bat mitzvah, 278, 340, 685
    basic elements of, 271–72
    birthday party, 278, 322–23,
        324–25, 685
    to business meals, 444
    BYOB, 277, 296
    BYOF, 277
    casual, 278
    clarity in, 249
    cocktail party, 278, 310
    confirmation, 338
    to debutante ball, 327
    dinner party, 278, 296

invitations (*cont.*)

    dress instructions on, 55, 274–75,
        605
    by email, 273, 275, 286, 598
    enclosures, 275–76, 288–89,
        609–10, 611
    end times on, 275
    engagement party, 564
    e-vites, 273, 275, 286, 598
    Facebook, 274
    fill-in, 278, 279, 282
    First Communion, 338
    formal (*see* formal invitations)
    gift registry information, 276, 354,
        625
    graduation, 278, 328–29
    guest of honor's name on, 274
    to houseguests, 266
    informal, 192, 278–79
    by mail, 273, 286
    to meetings, 418
    from multiple hosts, 273–74,
        287–88
    name or title mistakes on, 288
    by phone, 224, 272–73, 284, 286
    potluck, 277, 296
    quinceañera, 326, 685
    recalling, 289
    received too late, 285, 286
    regrets only, 276, 284, 286
    replies to, 253, 266, 276, 284–88
    reply cards (*see* reply cards)
    rescinding, 323
    RSVP, 253, 276, 284, 286
    samples, 685–86
    to separated couples, 512
    by text, 273
    wedding (*see* wedding invitations)
    wedding shower, 583, 626
    when to send, 277–78
    to the White House, 191–92
Isar an Mi'raj, 345
Islam
    birth ceremonies, 337
    funeral and burial services,
        551–52
    holy days, 345
    imams, 680
    mosques, 134, 346–47
    religious services, 346–47
    travel courtesies, 133, 134
    weddings, 673

J

Jet Skis, 151
jewelry
    basic rules for wearing, 50
    bridal, 616
    at job interviews, 404
    men's, 52
job interviews, 403–8
    confidence in, 405
    dining with the interviewer, 408
    dos and don'ts, 406–7
    dress, 404–5
    for home employees, 501
    interviewer follow up, 406
    people skills in, 405
    preparation for, 405
    punctuality, 403–4, 405
    questions, answering, 406
    questions, asking, 407
    questions, inappropriate, 407–8
    responding to a rejection, 408
    responding to an offer, 408
    salary discussion, 407
    teens and, 488
    thank-you notes, 405–6, 408,
        488
    waiting for results of, 408
job search, 395–402
    employment agencies and
        headhunters, 399–400
    honesty in, 400
    networking, 395–97
    online, 398–99
    references, 402
    resumés and cover letters, 398, 399,
        400–402
    salary discussion, 401
    starting out cold, 397–98
    thank-you notes, 397, 398
joggers, 28
jokes, 42–43
Judaism
    birth ceremonies, 335–37
    clergy, 184
    coming-of-age ceremonies, 339–41
    funeral and mourning customs,
        550–51, 552–53
    holy days, 345
    religious services, 346
    weddings, 642–45, *643, 644,* 673
    yarmulkes in, 336, 339, 346, 673

judges, 678
jumping the broom, 570
junior bridesmaids, 579, 617, 638
junior ushers, 617, 638
justices, U.S., 183
    associate, 180, 678
    Chief (*see* Chief Justice)

K

kaddish, 551
kafan, 552
keep right, pass left rule, 27–28, 147
ketchup, 689
ketubah, 642, 643
kindness, 6–7
kippah, 673
kissing, 14–15
    air kiss, 14
    double or triple, 14
    hand kissing, 14–15
    resisting, 15
    right cheek to right cheek, 14
kitchen
    guests keeping clear of, 255
    home employees' privileges,
        508
    roommates and, 496–97
    workplace, 416
kitty
    travel funds, 120–21
    for workplace celebrations,
        424
knives
    butter, 58, *60,* 62, *62*
    dinner, 57–58, 62
    at end of course, 68, *69,* 107
    fish, 62, *62*
    luncheon, *62*
    order of, 62
    resting, 68
    salad, 62, 63
    steak, 58, 62
Krishna Janmashtami, 344

L

language
    offensive, 232, 432, 436
    online, 385
    overseas travel and, 132–33
    "people first," 90
    sensitivity in, 31
    speaking in foreign, 434

teens and, 487
　workplace, 432, 434, 436
laser printing, 201
Laylat al-Qadr, 345
leftovers, 108, 305
lemons, squeezing, 691
letter sheet, 199
letterpress, 201
letters. *See* notes and letters
lieutenant governor
　Canadian, 681
　U.S., 180
lighting, outdoor, 83
limousine service
　common courtesies, 30
　for prom, 328
　tipping driver, 30, 170
　for weddings, 595–96
linens
　monogramming, 356–58
　table, 60, 61, 300, 315
lines, 24–25, 115, 155–56
LinkedIn, 387–88, 395, 399
listening
　active, 438
　to children, 460–61
　in conversation, 36, 39
　to customers, 438
　during introductions, 17
　at meetings, 419
　at the workplace, 412
lithography, 201
littering. *See* trash disposal
living room, sharing with roommates, 497–98
lobster, eating, 693
love life, talking about, 41, 375
luncheon fork, *62*
luncheon knife, *62*
luncheons, 278, 307, 583
lunches, business, 442

M

"Ma'am," use of, 185, 220
"magic words," 8–9, 31
　birth to one year, 479
　one- to three-year-olds, 480
　six- to ten-year-olds, 482
　three- to five-year-olds, 481
　See also "excuse me"; "I'm sorry";
　　"please"; "thank you"; "you're
　　welcome"

maid or matron of honor, 577, 580,
　621–22, 634–35, 639, 640, 642,
　645, 648, 650
　responsibilities of, 579
　witnessing wedding paper signature,
　　647
maiden name, 216, 217, 356, 440, 516,
　517
maître d', 101, 167–68
makeup, 55
market prices (M.P.), 104
marriage
　reaffirming vows, 332
　response to news of, 43
　See also wedding
Master, use of, 215, 676
matron of honor. *See* maid or matron
　of honor
Maundy (Holy) Thursday, 344
mayor
　Canadian, 682
　U.S., 180, 181, 679
meals
　business, 443–46
　on cruises, 130
　home employees, 503
　for houseguests, 264
　job interview, 408
　with seniors, sharing, 524
　for vendors, 585
　See also food
meats, eating, 691
meetings, 417–20
　agenda, 418
　cell phone use, 236, 419
　contradicting others in, 419
　expectations and follow through,
　　419–20
　home office, 425
　invitations, 418
　lengthy, 419
　listening, 419
　organizer's responsibilities,
　　417–18
　participants' responsibilities,
　　418–20
　planning, 417
　positive demeanor in, 419
　punctuality, 418
　purpose and goals of, 417
　with roommates, 495
Memorial Day, flag display on, 188

memorial services, 542
memorials, online, 541
memory loss, 472, 534
men
　addressing, 215, 676–77
　dress and grooming, 51–53, 683–84
　at formal dinners, 315
　holding chair for woman, 26–27, 63,
　　102, 375
　offering arm to woman, 27, 636
　seating at official functions, 181
　stationary for, 198
　suffixes used by, 215–16
　wedding attire, 667
　women preceding through doors, 27
mental disabilities, 33–34
menu
　dinner party, 296
　restaurant, 104, 113
midnight supper or breakfast, 318
military academy students, 186
military titles, 185, 606–7, 608
military weddings
　arch of steel, 670
　facilities for, 586–87
　invitations to, 606–7
　receiving line, 648
　wedding party attire, 621
minyan, 551
miscarriage, response to news of, 43
Miss, use of, 215, 676
mistakes
　in introductions, 17, 18, 19
　on wedding invitations, 605
　at work, 431
monarch sheet, 198
monarchs, 180
money
　cost of gifts, 350, 354, 361–62, 366
　gifts of, 351, 363, 505, 626, 631, 665
　party budget, 293–94
　paying for a date, 373–74, 376, 381
　paying the restaurant check, 104,
　　112, 113–15, 332, 444, 445, 467
　prom budget, 327–28
　seniors and, 526–27
　talking about, 41, 42, 375
　wedding budget (*see* wedding
　　budget)
monogramming, 356–58
　clothing and personal items, 358
　creating, 357

monogramming (*cont.*)
    flatware, 358
    stationary, 356
    wedding gifts, 356, 661
monsignor, addressing, 184, 680
Mormons
    clergy, 680
    weddings, 673
mosques, 134, 346–47
mother of the bride, 568, 620, 635, 638, 648, 649
mother of the groom, 620, 648, 649
Mother Superior, 680
mountain biking, 147–48
movies, 162, 234
moving walkways, 27
Mr., use of, 215, 676, 677
Mrs., use of, 216, 516–17, 676
Ms., use of, 215, 216, 516, 676, 677
municipal government protocol, 181
music
    anniversary party, 330–31
    classical concerts, 161–62
    for funerals, 550
    tipping musicians, 168
    for weddings, 570, 593–94
music players, 236, 486
Muslims. *See* Islam
mussels, eating, 693
Mx., use of, 676

N

nail care, 48, 55
name tags, 19, 246, 443, 451
names and titles, 215–20, 676–77
    academic titles, 184, 517, 677
    on bride's stationary, 631
    on business cards, 440–41
    children's use of, 17, 484
    couples, 217–18, 676–77
    divorce and, 216–17, 356, 461, 516–17
    forgetting a name, 19
    getting titles wrong, 19
    home employees and, 502
    honorary degrees, 218
    individuals at the same address, 218
    in introductions, 15–16, 17, 19
    on invitations, 280, 288
    legal name changes, 220
    military academy students, 186
    military titles, 185, 606–7, 608

misspelled or incorrect, 288
    on notes and letters, 202
    official titles (*see* official titles)
    overseas customs, 134
    professional titles, 184, 218–19, 517, 605, 608
    religious officials, 183–84, 218–19, 679–80
    separation and, 512
    on social cards, 210
    social titles, 215–18, 605
    suffixes, 215–16
    on wedding invitations, 605–7, 608
    at the workplace, 411, 429, 677
naming ceremonies, 336–37, 350
nannies
    farewell party for, 510
    gifts for, 173, 361
    responsibilities of, 505
    vacations with, 507
napkins
    avoiding leaving stains on, 71
    blotting lips with, 68
    dropped, 110
    at end of meal, 64, 73, 106
    formal dinner party, 315
    formal setting, 61
    informal setting, 57
    at restaurants, 103, 106
    using, 64
    wet, 73
national anthem, 52, 134, 158, 190
Native American weddings, 570, 674
neckties, 52
neighbors, 79–90
    apartment and condo, 82–83
    awareness and, 89
    borrowing and lending by, 85, 86
    boundaries and, 80
    children and, 83–84
    diversity and, 89–90
    gossip and, 85
    greeting, 81
    help offered to, 80, 83
    home office and, 426
    homeowners, 83
    homeowners' associations, 87–89
    liability issues and, 84
    new, 79–81
    noise and, 83, 84
    parties and, 86
    peacemaking and, 90

pets and, 84–85
    privacy of, 82
    property of, 82
    resolving issues with, 87, 89
    soliciting, 85–86
    with special expertise or talents, 81
    thanking, 80, 82
    visiting, 81, 82
    welcome gifts, 90
    yard sales, 85
networking, 395–97
    See also social networks
newspaper announcements, 290–91
    engagement, 565
    obituaries, 540
    wedding, 612
newspaper "Card of Thanks," 365
Nirvana Day, 344
nisuin, 643
"no"
    to a date request, 372–73
    saying courteously, 9–10
"no gifts, please" request, 331, 332, 359–60, 605, 661
"no more than three" rule, 61, 63
nodding, 37
noise
    on cruises, 130
    during golf games, 141
    home employees and, 508
    neighbors and, 83, 84
    at performances, 158–59
    at the workplace, 435
noodles, eating, 695
nose blowing, 75, 532
notepapers, 198
notes and letters, 197–214
    angry, 211
    of apology, 207
    best left unwritten, 211
    body of, 210–11
    complimentary close, 212, 241
    of congratulations, 206–7
    ending, 211
    folding, 203
    gossip, 211
    on greeting cards, 208
    handwritten, 203–4, 362–63
    holiday newsletters, 208–9
    home address and date, 210
    "personal" and other notations on, 203

personal letters, 210–11
social cards, 209–10
sympathy/condolence, 553–55
tell-all, 211
woe-is-me, 211
wording of, 206
See also business letters; envelopes; stationary; thank-you notes
nun, addressing, 184, 680
nurses, gifts to, 360–61
nursing homes, 523–24

O

obituaries, 540, 543
obscene phone calls, 223
official life. *See* protocol
official titles, 182–86, 678–82
academic, 184, 517, 677
Canadian officials, 681–82
military, 185, 606–7, 608
in other countries, 185–86
on place cards, 182
professional, 184, 218–19, 517, 605, 608
religious officials, 183–84, 218–19, 679–80
U.S. officials and dignitaries, 182–83, 678–79
older people. *See* elder etiquette
olive oil, 60, 691
olives, eating, 691
one-drink rule, 445
online interactions, 237–46, 383–89
abbreviations, 385
anonymity misconception, 238, 384
children and teens, 485–87
commenting, 388
condolences, 554
content choice, 385
dating, 380–82
electronic brick wall, 238
gaming, 388–89
grammar, 385
how you communicate, 237, 385
human contact *vs.*, 237
images, 385
instant messaging, 243–44
job search, 398–99
memorials, 541
politeness in, 384
public and permanent nature of, 237, 384

punctuation, 385
sentence case, 239, 385
spelling, 385
video calls, 233, 244, 426
wedding planning, 568, 578–79, 626
what you communicate, 237, 384–85
word choice, 385
See also computers; email; social networks
open bar, 589
open house parties, 312–13
opera, 161
ordination or profession of vows, 350
Orthodox Christian Church, 343, 570, 673
outdoor performances, 160–61, 162
outside-in rule, 57, 61, 63, 102
overseas travel, 131–34
basic courtesies, 133–34
basic research for, 131–32
body language, 133
language, 132–33
regional sensitivities, 134
oyster fork, 61, *62*, 107
oysters, eating, 693–94

P

pages (wedding attendants), 618
pallbearers, 541–42, 546
pantry showers, 627
parades, 163–64
"pardon me," 9
parents
criticizing around children, 461
criticizing competence or skills of, 461
of debutante, 319
divorce, telling about your, 514
engagement, telling about your, 560–61
father of the bride, 568, 621, 635, 638, 639, 640, 648, 649
father of the groom, 621, 648, 649
living with adult children, 472
military wedding invitations and, 606–7
mother of the bride, 568, 620, 635, 638, 648, 649
mother of the groom, 620, 648, 649
older, 463
other family members as, 462
same-sex, 463

single, 462
sports event etiquette, 137–38
unmarried mothers, 217
wedding attire, 620–21
wedding ceremony seating, 636–38
wedding invitations and, 603–4, 606–7
wedding involvement by, 568
wedding reception seating, 590
wedding toasts by, 651
working, 460
parties, 292–313
bachelor, 580, 583
bachelorette, 579, 580, 583
barbecues, 308
breakfast, 307–8
brunch, 308
budgeting money and time, 293–94
catered, 306–7
christening, 335
clean up, 305–6, 309
coming-of-age, 325–27
date and time, 292–93
divorce ("independence"), 515
double-booking, 258
engagement, 563–64
formal, 316–18
graduation, 329–30
guest list, 293
housewarmings, 80, 257, 278, 313, 350, 355
late supper, 308
luncheons, 278, 307, 583
neighbors and, 86
office, 442–43
open house, 312–13
picnics, 308
potluck, 277, 296, 309–10
pre-wedding, 582–83
size of, 293
tailgate, 137
tipping hires, 174
ultracasual, 312
wedding rehearsal, 581, 583–84
See also anniversary parties; birthday parties; cocktail parties; dinner parties
partners, domestic
addressing, 218
engagement of, 562
introducing, 465–66
as parents, 463

partners, domestic (*cont.*)
    wedding invitations from, 605
    wedding invitations to, 608
    See also couples
party favors, 324
Pascha, 344
passed-tray service, 317, 588
passing others, 27–28, 147
Passover, 345
pepper. *See* salt and pepper
performances, 155–64
    applause, 159–60, 161
    arenas, 162–63
    audience etiquette, 157–61
    ballet, 161
    box seats, 156–57
    bravo!, 161
    children at, 160
    classical music, 161–62
    coffeehouses and clubs, 162–63
    coughing during, 158
    dress, 159
    exiting, 157, 161–63
    heckling, 160
    intermission, 157
    late arrival, 156, 162
    movies, 162, 234
    noise at, 158–59
    open seating, 157
    opera, 161
    outdoor, 160–61, 162
    parades, 163–64
    photography at, 159
    punctuality, 155
    row seating, 157
    seating, 156–57
    smoking at, 159, 160, 164
    street, 163–64
    talking at, 157–58, 163
    theater, 161, 450
    ticket line, 155–56
perfume and cologne, 48, 144, 404, 435,
    537
"Personal" (envelope notation),
    203
personal cards. *See* social cards
personal communication devices,
    230–36
    See also cell phone; earbuds; music
      players
personal information, 40–41
personal space, 36, 133

personal trainers, tipping, 145
personalized services, 542–43
pets
    as gifts, 359
    home office and, 427
    houseguests and, 267
    neighbors and, 84–85
    at performances, 160
    travel with, 127
    See also dogs
pew cards, 609–10, 636
pharmacies, 98
photography
    cell phone cameras, 233, 436
    at funerals and visitations, 545
    at performances, 159
    at religious services, 341
    at weddings, 594–95, 645, 647,
      659
picnics, 308
pidyon haben, 337
piercings, 50–51, 404
Pilates, 144–45
pizza, eating, 70
place cards
    dinner party, 303, 315
    switching, 255, 671
    titles on (official functions), 182
    wedding reception, 590, 671
place mats, 60, 61, 300
place settings, 57–63
    See also table setting
plated service, 64, 295, 315, 589
plates
    bread or butter, 58, *59, 60*, 65, 102
    dinner, 57
    salad, 58, 102
    service, 61, 102, 315
"please," 8, 71, 502
Pledge of Allegiance, 190, 191
pointing, 37
politics, talking about, 41–42, 375
pools, 84
Pope
    addressing, 680
    audience with, 193
pornography, email transmission of, 243
porters, tipping, 169
Postal Service regulations, 198, 202,
    608
postlude (wedding music), 593
posture, 37, 158

potluck, 277, 296, 309–10
poultry, eating, 692
power of attorney, 527
"praise, concern, suggest" technique,
    504
predinner hour, 294–95
pregnancy, 473–75
    assuming, 474
    of bridesmaid, 577
    responding to news of, 43
    tips for tactful behavior, 474
    touching the mother's belly, 475
    who and when to tell, 473
prelude (wedding music), 593
premier (of Canadian province), 681
prenuptial agreement, 655–56
presentation balls, 283
President, U.S.
    addressing, 182–83, 678
    former, 180, 678
    meeting, 192
    in order of precedence, 180
    spouse of, 192, 678
    widows/widowers of, 180
President Pro Tempore of Senate, 180
priest, Catholic, 183, 184, 680
Prime Minister (Canadian), 681
printers, workplace, 416
privacy
    the elderly and, 524
    email and, 238
    at home, 458, 472
    for home employees, 508
    neighbors and, 82
    workplace, 413
private clubs
    business at, 448
    tipping at, 172
    wedding receptions at, 586
processionals
    funeral or memorial service, 546
    wedding, 593, 638–39, *639*, 640,
      642, *643*
profanity, 24, 137, 436
professional designations, 219, 677
professional titles, 184, 218–19, 517, 605,
    608
professionals, gifts for, 173, 360
proms, 327–28
Protestantism
    baptisms, 335
    clergy, 183, 184, 218, 679

confirmation, 338
First Communion, 337
funeral and burial services, 550
religious services, 343
weddings, 672
protocol, 179–93
city, municipal, and town governments, 181
national anthem, 190
official titles, 182–86
for people of other nationalities, 191
place cards, 182
Pledge of Allegiance, 190, 191
precedence and rank, 180–81
seating at official lunch or dinner, 181–82
state government, 180
U.S. flag, 186–90
White House etiquette, 191–92
prying, 413
public advocates, 181
public displays of affection, 24
public places
cell phone use in, 24, 231
children in, 479–80, 481, 482, 483–84, 487
common courtesies in, 24–25
computer use in, 245–46
teens in, 487, 489
public transportation, 29, 126–27, 169–70, 232
punctuality, 22
dating and, 374
by guests, 254–55
for job interviews, 403–4, 405
for meetings, 418
for performances, 155
for religious services, 341
for sports and games, 139, 141
workplace, 411
punctuation, 385
Purim, 345

Q

Quaker weddings, 673
quesadillas, eating, 692
questions
job interview, 406, 407–8
nosy, 44
quinceañera, 325–26, 685

R

rabbis, 184, 642, 645, 680
Ramadan, 345
receiving line, 54
formal party, 318
President and First Lady, 192
wedding, 645, 647–49, *648*, 670, 671
reception cards, 603, 685
recessionals
funeral or memorial service, 547–48
wedding, 593, 640–42, *641, 644,* 645, 670
recipe showers, 627
recommendation, letters of, 213
recreation. *See* sports and recreation
redcap, tipping, 169
redemption of the firstborn, 337
referees, 138
references
home employees, 501, 510
job, 402
letters of, 213
regifting, 367–69
registry. *See* gift registry
"regrets only," 276, 284, 286
rehearsal party, wedding, 581, 583–84
religion
holy days, 344–45
talking about, 41–42, 375
tourist visits to sacred sites, 347
U.S. flag in house of worship, 188
See also individual religions
religious officials, 183–84, 218–19, 679–80
religious services, 341–47
Buddhist, 347
hats and, 23, 50
interfaith weddings, 568
Islamic, 346–47
Jewish, 346
at one's own house of worship, 341
Orthodox Christian, 343
of other faiths, 342–47
photographs, 341
Protestant, 343
punctuality, 341
Roman Catholic, 342–43
seating, 341
singing, 341
standing or kneeling at, 669
weddings, 568, 570, 586

remarriage, 654–61
attendants, 660
attire, 659–60
children and, 518, 568, 655, 656, 658–59, 660
after death of spouse, 552
of ex-spouse, 518, 655, 657
family dos and don'ts, 659
gifts, 656, 661
honeymoon, 660
invitations, 657–58
name change and, 216–17, 461
prenuptial agreement, 655–56
showers, 660–61
wedding guidelines and planning, 656–58
reply cards, 276, 278, 286, 288–89, 609, *610*
representatives
state, 180, 181
U.S., 180, 183, 679
reservations, restaurant, 100–101, 112, 444
residential building staff, tipping, 173
respect, 6, 8
dating and, 371
in families, 458–60
for neighbors, 82, 90
response cards. *See* reply cards
restaurants, 100–118
anniversary parties at, 332
appreciation for service, 118
arrival at, 101–2
bread and butter, 106
buffet, 115, 167
business meals, 443–46
cafeterias, 115
cell phones in, 101, 113, 231–32
children at, 113, 116–17
coffee shops, 116
complaints, 117–18
consideration for other patrons, 113
conversation, 109
dates at, 375–76
delicatessens, 116
dessert, 108–9
diners, 116
disposing of litter, 116
dropping things at, 110
dutch treat, 114
excusing oneself from the table, 109
fast-food, 116

restaurants (*cont.*)
    finger bowls, hot towels, and
      towelettes at, 108
    first courses, 107
    food arriving at different times, 107
    food on face alert, 111
    foreign objects in food, 110–11
    fruit and cheese courses, 108
    grooming at the table, 109–10
    guests, 112–13
    hosts, 101, 102, 111–12, 332
    knocking over a drink, 111
    leftovers, 108
    main courses, 107–8
    napkin, 103, 106
    no-nos at, 111
    ordering at, 103–6
    parties at, 294
    paying the check, 104, 112, 113–15,
      332, 444, 445, 467
    premature removal of plate, 111
    reservations, 100–101, 112, 444
    running into friends at, 110
    seating, 101–2
    self-service, 167
    sending food back, 107, 113
    separate checks, 104
    service at, 106
    sharing plates, 107–8
    side dishes, 107
    splitting the bill, 114–15, 444
    table setting, 102–3
    tasting one another's food, 107
    teens at, 489
    tipping at, 115, 116, 166–69
    unclean utensils at, 110
    waitstaff, 103, 167
    wedding receptions at, 586
restrooms/bathrooms
    airplane, 124
    excusing oneself to use, 109
    phone calls from, 227, 233
    roommates and, 497
    workplace, 417
resumés, 398, 399, 400–402
retirement
    celebrating, 332–33
    gifts, 333, 350, 421
retirement communities, 521–22
Reverend, use of title, 218–19
revolving doors, 25, 27
rice, throwing (wedding), 646

ring bearer, 581, 618, 635, 639, 640,
    645, 648
road rage, 92
road trips, 121–22
rollerblading, 28
Roman Catholic Church
    baptisms and christenings, 335
    clergy, 183–84, 680
    confirmation, 338
    First Communion, 337, 338
    funeral and burial services, 550
    papal audience, 193
    quinceañera, 326
    religious services, 342–43
    weddings, 672
room service, 128, 171
roommates, 400–499
    assigned, 490–91
    avoiding blame, 496
    bathrooms and, 497
    boundary setting, 494
    characteristics of good, 491
    checklist, 492
    commitment and, 491, 493–94
    communication and, 491–93
    compromise and, 491, 493
    family members as, 494
    kitchen and, 496–97
    living room and, 497–98
    meetings with, 495
    moving on from problems, 496
    notes left for, 495
    parting ways, 498–99
    problems with, 494–95
rose petals, "showering" wedding couple
    with, 645, 646, 653
Rosh Hashanah, 345
RSVP, 253, 276, 284, 286, 602
rudeness, 19–20, 21, 238
rumors, 433
running, 146
Russian service, 589

S

Salaat ul Janaazah, 552
salad, 316, 692
salad fork, 57, *60, 61, 62, 63*
salad knife, 62, 63
salad plate, 58, 102
salary discussion, 401, 407
salespersons, 97
salt and pepper, 59, 65, 315, 689

same-sex parents, 463
sandwich generation, 529
sandwiches, eating, 692
sashimi, eating, 687
sauces, 689
save-the-date cards, 601
scarves, 52
scent. *See* perfume and cologne
seafood stews, eating, 693
seals, envelope, 203
seated meals, 588–89
seating
    on airplanes, 123, 124–25
    business meal, 444, 445
    dinner party, 302–3
    at official functions, 181–82
    at performances, 156–57
    at religious services, 341
    restaurant, 101–2
    at the table, 63
    train and bus, 126
    wedding ceremony, 636–38,
      669
    wedding reception, 589–90
Secretary General of the U.N., 180
Secretary of State, 180
self-respect, 6
self-service restaurants, 167
semibuffet style, 295
semiformal attire, 667, 684
senators
    Canadian, 681
    state, 180, 181
    U.S., 180, 183, 678
sentence case (online), 239, 385
separation, 511–12
    children and, 511
    dating during, 512
    informing others of, 512
    invitations and, 512
    rings and, 512
    of unmarried couples, 513
    women's names and titles, 216,
      512
    See also divorce
served meals, 64, 295, 315
service dogs, 32, 33
service plate (charger), 61, 102, 315
service providers
    common courtesy toward, 25
    gifts for, 350, 361
Seven Steps, 674

sex
    safe, 377
    talking about, 41, 42
sexting, 486
sexual harassment, 377, 436–37
sexually transmitted diseases (STDs), 377
shared cup, 571
shellfish, eating, 693–94
shish kebab, eating, 694
shivah, 551, 552–53
shoes, removing, 134, 312, 346, 674
shopping and errands, 96–99
showers, 278
    See also baby showers; wedding showers
shrimp, eating, 70, 694
siblings
    elderly parents and, 529
    step-, 659
side dishes, 107
sidewalks, sharing with others, 27–28
signature
    email, 240
    on greeting cards, 208
    on letters, 211–12
Sikh weddings, 674
simcha, 645
single-parent families, 462
singles, 463
"Sir," use of, 185, 220
skateboarding, 28
skiing, 153–54
skycap, tipping, 169
Skype, 426
slang, 39
small talk, 39–40, 414–16
smartphone, 230–32, 436
smiling, 13, 21, 37, 405
smoking, 24, 152
    by home employees, 508
    at performances, 159, 160, 164
sneezing, 15, 75, 227, 531–32
snot rockets, 145
snowboarding, 153–54
social cards, 209–10, 329, 396
social diary, 259
social networks, 385–88
    announcements on, 477
    children and teens on, 486
    choosing a site, 386
    death notices on, 540

managing your space, 386
newborn photos posted on, 477
popular sites, 387–88
unfriending, unfollowing, and ignoring, 386–87
wedding information on, 578
social skills
    in job interviews, 405
    online, 238
social titles, 215–18, 605
soft-shell crab, eating, 693
soliciting
    neighbors, 85–86
    telephone, 223
soup, 107, 694
soup spoon, 58, *60, 62, 63,* 107
spaghetti, eating, 695
spam (online), 239, 240
spas, 99, 172
Speaker of the House of Representatives, 180
speakerphones, 235–36, 435
speech impairments, 33
spelling, 385
spills, 73–74, 111
spitting, 24, 145
spoons
    demitasse, *62*
    dessert, 58–59, *60, 62, 63,* 109, 316
    at end of course, 68, *69*
    holding, 66
    iced-tea, *62, 63*
    order of, 63
    resting, 68
    soup, 58, *60, 62, 63,* 107
    tea, 58, *62, 63*
sports and recreation, 136–54
    beach activities, 152–53
    bicycling (*see* bicycling)
    boating (*see* boating)
    with business associates, 448–50
    camping, 148
    fishing, 152
    fitness center, 143–45
    golf, 140–42, 449
    hiking, 147
    horseback riding, 147
    mountain biking, 147–48
    parental behavior at events, 137–38
    personal trainers, 145
    pickup games, 139–40

    referees and umpires, 138
    regular league or team games, 139
    rehydrating and, 146
    running, 146
    sharing the road, 145–46
    skiing and snowboarding, 153–54
    spectator etiquette, 136–37
    tailgate parties, 137
    tennis, 59, 142–43
    water skiing and personal watercraft, 151–52
    yoga and Pilates, 144–45
sportsmanship, 139–40, 389
stairs, sharing with others, 27
standard (U.S. flag), 189
standing
    during greetings, 11–12, 13
    for toasts, 259, 650
    workplace protocol, 412–13
"Star Spangled Banner." *See* national anthem
state assemblymen, 181
state government protocol, 180
state legislators, 679
stationary, 197–200
    for children and teens, 199
    correspondence cards, 198, 199, *199*
    for families, 199
    fold-over note cards, 198, *199,* 199–200, *200*
    informals, 198, 279–80
    letter sheet, 199
    for men, 198
    monarch sheet, 198
    monogramming, 356
    postal service regulations on size, 198
    printing options, 201
    for thank-you notes, 631
    for women, 199
    writing on, *199,* 199–200
    See also envelopes
steak knife, 58, 62
steamed clams, eating, 694
stepfamilies
    children in, 461–62, 465, 518, 659
    first meeting of stepsiblings, 659
    introductions, 465
    stepfather as bride's escort, 638
    wedding dancing and, 652
    wedding invitations and, 604
    wedding receiving line and, 649

stocks, as gifts, 351
stock-the-bar showers, 628
straw, drinking, 68, 71
street fairs and performances, 163–64
subways, 29
suffixes, name, 215–16
suits, men's, 52
Sukkot, 345
sunglasses, removing, 51
supper
    late, 308
    midnight, 318
Supreme Court
    associate justices of, 180, 678
    Chief Justice of, 180, 183, 678
surfing, 153
sushi, eating, 687
"sweetheart" table, 590
swimming pools, 84
sympathy notes and letters, 553–55
synagogues, 346

T

table
    brushing crumbs from, 316
    clearing, 73, 305
    decorations, 301
    dinner party, 300–302
    linens, 60, 61, 300, 315
table manners, 56–57, 63–75
    beginning the meal, 65–66
    blessing, 64, 304, 651
    chewing food, 71–72
    children and, 479, 480–82, 483, 487
    before coming to the table, 63
    conversation, 72–73, 109
    cutting food, 66, 71
    elbows on the table, 70–71, 109
    ending the meal, 73
    food that is too hot or spoiled, 74
    foreign objects in food, 74, 110–11
    leaving the table, 71
    during the meal, 68–72
    mishaps and, 73–75
    refusing a dish, 65
    seasoning food, 71
    seating, 63
    serving the meal, 64–65
    spills and, 73–74, 111
    teens and, 487, 489
    wayward food and, 74–75
Table of Precedence, 180

table setting, 57–63
    five-course meal, *60*
    formal, *60*, 60–63, *62*
    at formal dinner party, 315
    informal, 57–60, *58*, *59*
    at restaurants, 102–3
    three-course meal, *59*
    two-course meal, *58*
tablecloths, 61
tacos, eating, 70, 692
tact, 6
tailgate parties, 137
take-out deliveries, tipping on, 172–73
talking
    knowing when to stop, 38
    at performances, 157–58, 163
tallit, 339–40, 346
tattoos, 50–51, 404
taxis
    common courtesies in, 29–30
    holding door of, 26
    tipping driver, 30, 170
tea, 316
    invitations to, 278
    serving, 59, 109, 695
tea spoon, 58, *62*, 63
teachers, gifts for, 354, 361
teens, 484–89
    cell phones and, 485–86
    communicating with, 485–87, 488
    dress and, 47
    driving and, 489
    email and, 486
    high school graduation night parties, 330
    in the home, 459–60
    invitations to, 276–77
    job interviews and, 488
    online interactions, 485–87
    prom, 327–28
    quinceañera, 325–26, 685
    social networks and, 486
    stationary for, 199
    table manners, 487, 489
    wedding invitations to, 608
telephone, 221–29
    answering, 222
    answering calls for someone else, 222
    caller ID, 223
    call-waiting, 225–26
    children and, 427, 481, 483

conference calls, 235
    dating and, 381
    dropped calls, 224, 226
    eating and, 227
    ending calls, 227
    faux pas on, 227
    gum chewing and, 227
    home employees' use of, 508
    home office calls, 426–27
    hospital patient, calling, 538
    interruptions, 226
    invitations via, 224, 272–73, 284, 286
    mechanical glitches, 226
    offensive calls, 223
    placing calls, 224–25
    returning calls, 229
    sneezing or coughing into, 227
    solicitors, 223
    speakerphone, 235–36, 435
    timing calls, 225
    TTY/TDD, 32, 227–28
    using someone else's, 225
    voice mail, 228–29, 235
    workplace, 435
    wrong numbers, 222–23, 224–25
    See also cell phone
temples
    Buddhist, 347
    Jewish, 346
tennis, 142–43, 449
text messaging, 92, 158
    by children and teens, 486
    guidelines for, 233–35
    invitations via, 273
    responding to, 233
    sexting, 486
    wedding planning, 578
text speak, 235, 385
text telephones. *See* TTY/TDD phones
"thank you," 8, 9
    for birthday gifts, 324
    to customers, 438
    gifts as, 350
    to home employees, 502
    to host, 255, 256
    to neighbors, 80, 82
    for prom assistance, 328
    to references, 402
    for restaurant service, 165
    from seniors, 521
    at the table, 71
    for wedding help, 585

thank-you notes, 204–6
  acknowledgment cards, 365
  for baby shower gifts, 321–22, 362
  for bar/bat mitzvah gifts, 339–40
  for birthday gifts, 363–64
  for business meal, 446–47
  computer-generated, 367
  dos and don'ts of, 633
  by email, 210, 267, 406, 446–47
  for engagement gifts, 564
  gifts warrenting, 362–65
  for graduation gifts, 329
  from guest of honor, 206
  from guests, 204–5, 256
  for holiday gifts, 363–64
  to host, 256, 267
  for job interviews, 405–6, 408,
    488
  in job search, 397, 398
  for quinceañera gifts, 326
  sample notes, 204, 205, 364,
    632–33
  tips on writing, 363
  for wedding gifts, 363, 628, 630–33,
    665
  for wedding shower gifts, 362,
    631
  whom to address, 204
theater, 161, 450
themed weddings, 571
thermography, 201
thermostat, disagreements over,
    498
"Three Block Rule," 160
ties, 52
time. See punctuality
tip jars, 166
tipping, 165–74
  airport personnel, 169
  at barber shops, 172
  bartenders, 168, 317
  at beauty salons, 172
  busboy, 169
  coat-check attendant, 169
  coupons and, 167
  cruise staff, 130–31, 170–71
  daycare providers, 506
  digital, 170
  gratuity included, 167
  guidelines, 165–66
  holiday, 166, 174
  home employees, 173, 504–5

host/hostess (restaurant employee),
    167–68
  hotel staff, 127, 171–72
  less, 166
  limousine driver, 30, 170
  maître d', 167–68
  musicians, 168
  party hires, 174
  personal trainers, 145
  private club, 172
  problem with, 167
  professionals, 173
  residential building personnel,
    173
  restaurant, 115, 116, 166–69
  for room service, 128
  ski instructors, 153
  at spas, 172
  street performers, 164
  on take-out food deliveries, 172–73
  taxi drivers, 30, 170
  tip jars, 166
  tour guides, 131
  travel and, 169–70
  valet parking attendant, 101, 169
  washroom attendant, 169
  at wedding receptions, 672
  wine steward, 105, 168
titles. See names and titles
toasts, 250, 258–60
  prepared, 259
  spur-of-the-moment, 259–60
  wedding, 649–51, 671
toothpicks, 75, 110, 311, 691
touch, 14, 133
tour guides, 131
towelettes, 73, 108
town government protocol, 181
train bearers, 618
trains, 29
  cell phone use, 232
  tipping personnel, 169
  travel guidelines for, 126–27
trampolines, 84
transportation
  dating and, 375
  for home employees, 502–3,
    508
  wedding, 595–96, 635, 645
  See also public transportation
trash disposal, 24, 82, 83, 141, 152, 159,
    160–61

travel, 119–35
  adventure, 135
  with boss, 447–48
  with children, 121–22, 125
  with friends, 120–21
  group tours, 131
  with pets, 127
  pretrip meeting, 121
  pretrip preparations, 119–20
  road trips, 121–22
  tipping and, 169–70
  See also air travel; buses; cruises;
    overseas travel; trains
TTY/TDD phones, 32, 227–28
Twitter, 385, 388, 651

U

ultracasual parties, 312
umbrella manners, 29
umpires, 138
unfriending and unfollowing, 386–87
unity candle, 569–70
ushers, 638, 648
  funeral service, 543
  wedding, 577, 580–81, 635–36, 639
utensils
  American (zigzag) style of use, 66,
    67, 68
  Continental (European) style of use,
    66, 67, 68
  holding, 66–68, 67
  order of, 57, 61, 66, 102
  placement when finished, 68, 69, 71,
    73, 107
  at restaurants, 102, 107, 110
  resting, 68, 107
  unclean, 110

V

vacation, with child-care provider, 507
valet, tipping, 172
valet parking attendant, 101, 169
veil, wedding, 615
vendors, 585, 632
vest, 53
Vice President, U.S., 180, 182, 678
video calls, 233, 244, 426
videos
  of performances, 159
  of weddings, 594–95, 645
vision loss or blindness, 32–33
vocabulary, 38

voice
    conversational, 37–38
    in public places, 24
    telephone, 221–22
voice mail, 228–29, 235
volunteering, 175–78
    on a board, 178
    finding a good match, 175–76
    internships, 177
    on the job, 176–77
    signing up, 176
    working with a supervisor, 177

W

wai, 133, 134
waitstaff
    restaurant, 103, 167
    room service, 128, 171
    tipping, 167, 169, 171
    train, 169
wakes, 544–45
walima, 673
wallets, 52
washroom attendant, 169
water skiing, 151–52
wedding, 559–674
    cancellation of, 611–12
    contracting for services, 584–85
    date, 575
    date change/postponement, 611
    destination, 569, 664, 665
    getting ready, 634–36
    green, 568
    handfasting, 570
    help for, 584–85
    jumping the broom, 570
    location, 575
    music and musicians, 570,
        593–94
    officiant, 575, 639, 640, 658, 670
    personalized, 567
    photos and videos, 594–95, 645,
        647, 659
    planner for, 585
    primary decisions, 572
    receiving line, 645, 647–49, *648*,
        670, 671
    rehearsal party, 581, 583–84
    religious customs, 672–74
    secondary decisions, 584
    secular readings at, 570
    shared cup, 571

"showering" couple, 645, 646,
        653
    signing of wedding papers, 647
    style, 576
    themed, 571
    traditions in new contexts, 569–71
    transportation, 595–96, 635, 645
    trends, 567–69
    See also military weddings;
        remarriage; wedding *headings*
wedding announcements, 612, 629
wedding attendants, 576–82
    at altar or dais, *639,* 639–40, *641*
    best man (*see* best man)
    bridesmaids (*see* bridesmaids)
    budget categories for, 698
    choosing, 576–79
    flower girl, 581, 617–18, 622, 635,
        639, 640, 645, 648
    flowers for, 621–23, 635
    getting ready, 634–35
    gifts to and from, 629
    groomsmen, 577, 580–81, 619–20,
        640, 642, 648
    honor, 568, 581, 620
    junior bridesmaids, 579, 617, 638
    junior ushers, 617, 638
    maid or matron of honor (*see* maid
        or matron of honor)
    pages, 618
    processional and, 638–39, *639,* 642,
        643
    recessional and, 640–42, *641, 644,*
        645
    remarriage, 660
    responsibilities, 577–82
    ring bearer, 581, 618, 635, 639, 640,
        645, 648
    thank-you notes to, 631
    train bearers, 618
    ushers, 577, 580–81, 635–36, 639
    when to ask, 577
wedding attire, 613–23
    bride (*see* wedding gown)
    bridesmaid, 616–18
    flowers, 621–23
    groom/groomsmen, 619–20
    guests, 666–68
    honor attendants, 620
    military weddings, 621
    more choices in, 568–69
    parents of the couple, 620–21

remarriage, 659–60
    young attendants, 617–18
wedding budget
    careful and considerate spending,
        574–75
    establishment of, 574
    fees for ceremony participants, 586
    for flowers, 591
    planning chart, 696–98
    sharing costs, 567–68
wedding cake, 590–91, 652–53
wedding ceremony, 636–42
    aisle runner, 636, 638
    altar or dais positions, *639,* 639–40,
        641
    applause following, 670
    escorting bride down the aisle, 568,
        638, 639
    flowers for, 592
    guests at, 668–70
    interfaith, 568
    music, 593
    planning, 586
    processional, 593, 638–39, *639,* 640,
        642, *643*
    programs, 636
    recessional, 593, 640–42, *641, 644,*
        645, 670
    seating, 636–38, 669
wedding consultants, 575–76
wedding flowers
    bouquet, attendants', 635
    bouquet, bride's, 622
    bouquet toss, 622, 653
    boutonnieres, 568, 622–23, 635
    for ceremony, 592
    corsages, 623, 635
    flower girl, 622, 635
    for reception, 592
    remarriage, 659
    selecting a florist, 591–92
    usher presenting of, 635–36
    for the wedding party, 621–23
wedding gifts, 350, 627–33
    acknowledgment of, 363, 365, 628,
        630–33
    announcements and, 612
    to and from attendants, 629
    choosing, 664–66
    couple's gifts to each other, 629
    from coworkers, 421
    delivery, 628

for destination wedding, 665
divorce and, 513
for ex-spouse, 518
for guests, 630
money, 626, 631, 665
monogramming, 356, 661
"no gifts, please" request, 360, 605, 661
non-attendees and, 666
record keeping of, 628–29
registries, 353, 354, 624–27, 661, 664
remarriage, 656, 661
returning after broken engagement, 565–66
sending, 628, 664–66
wedding gown, 613–16
accessories, 615–16
color, 569, 613–14
fabrics and styles, 614–15
heirloom, 616
more choices in, 568–69
rented or borrowed, 614
shoes, 615
train, 615
undergarments, 615
veil and headdress, 615
wedding guests, 662–74
attire, 666–68
bringing uninvited people, 609
at the ceremony, 668–70
choosing and sending gifts, 664–66
encore weddings, 657
gifts for, 630
guest list, 573–74, 657
informing of broken engagement, 566
at the reception, 671–72
religious customs and, 672–74
responding to invitation, 662–64
seating, 636
wedding invitations, 597–612
adding "and guest" to, 608, 663
cancellation of wedding, 611–12
cancelling acceptance to, 664
contemporary, 601–2
date change/postponement, 611
envelopes and enclosures, 607–11, 610
e-vites, 598
gift registry information not included, 354, 625

mistakes to avoid, 605
pew cards, 609–10
postal service regulations, 608
to reception, 603
remarriage, 657–58
reply cards, 609, 610
responding to, 602, 662–64
RSVP, 602
to same-sex ceremonies, 605
save-the-date cards, 601
style, 598
timing for orders and mailing, 597–98
tissue paper in, 610, 611
titles on, 605–7, 608
traditional formal, 599–601
when to send, 278
wording, 599–601, 603–4
wedding reception, 646–53
beverages, 589
blessing the meal, 651
bouquet toss, 622, 653
cake cutting, 652–53
catered, 588
dancing, 594, 651–52, 671
decisions, 587–90
delay in arrival at, 646, 670
departure of couple, 653
first dance, 594, 651, 671
flowers for, 592
food, 587–89
garter toss, 653
guests at, 671–72
invitation to, 603
music, 594
place cards, 590, 672
planning, 586–90
seating, 589–90
site, 586–87
toasts, 649–51, 671
types of service, 588–89
wedding rings, 643
best man and, 635
divorce and, 513
ring bearer and, 581
separation and, 512
wedding showers, 579, 582, 626
gifts, 350, 362, 565–66, 627–28, 631
number of, 583
remarriage, 660–61
types of, 627–28

wheelchair attendant, tipping, 169
wheelchair use, 33
whispering, 39, 416
white
"tennis whites," 143
wedding gown, 569, 613–14
wedding guests in, 668
when to wear, 54
White House protocol, 191–92
white tie, 317, 319, 326, 619, 683
widows/widowers
dating after death of spouse, 552
former spouse's parents, 657
of former U.S. presidents, 180
names and titles, 217, 356
weddings and, 636, 649, 657
Wi-Fi, public, 246
wine
choosing and serving, 296–98, 315–16
decanting, 298
gifts of, 351
glasses, 60, 63, 103, 105, 298, 299
holding the glass, 298
ordering, 105, 112
pouring, 298
red and white, 60, 63, 103, 105, 297, 298, 299
temperature, 297–98
uncorking, 297
wine steward, 105, 168
wish lists, 353–55
women
addressing, 216–17, 516–17, 676–77
divorced, 216–17, 356, 516–17
dress and grooming, 53–55, 683–84
at formal dinners, 315
holding chair for, 26–27, 63, 102, 375
husband outranked by, 192, 605, 677
monograms and, 356
offering arm to, 27, 636
preceding men through doors, 27
professional titles used by, 218, 605, 677
seating at official functions, 181
separate worship area for, 346
separated, 216, 512
single parent, 217
stationary for, 199
suffixes used by, 215
wedding attire, 667, 668

workplace, 395–451
    after-hours activities, 412, 443
    angry callers, 439–40
    anonymous notes, 417
    appointments, 420
    bars and business, 448
    breast-feeding at, 425
    business cards, 419, 440–41
    business letters, 212–14
    business meals, 443–46
    children at, 424–25
    collections at, 423–24
    complaints, 430–32
    compliments, 433
    conflicts at, 429–30
    conversations and small talk,
        414–16
    cubicle courtesies, 412–13
    dating and, 376–77, 436
    door open or shut, 413
    dress, 411, 443, 684
    email, 214, 238, 242–43
    embarrassing moments, 420
    firings and layoffs at, 44, 435
    first day at the office, 411–12
    gifts and, 353, 360, 421–23
    gifts sent to, 377
    gossip and rumors, 433, 451
    instant messaging, 243
    kitchen, 416
    listening, 412
    lunches, 442
    mistakes at, 431
    names and titles at, 411, 429, 677
    noise in, 435
    odors at, 435–36
    offensive language or comments in,
        432, 436
    off-site business venues, 450–51
    parties, 442–43
    privacy problem, 413
    private clubs and business, 448
    punctuality, 411
    rank and, 429
    requesting and offering help, 414
    restrooms, 417
    sexual harassment, 377, 436–37
    sharing space and equipment at,
        245, 416–18
    social side, 442–51
    sports and business, 448–50
    standing for greetings, 412–13
    theater invitations to associates,
        450
    the welcoming office, 413
    See also boss; business associates;
        coworkers; customers and
        clients; home office; job
        interviews; job search; meetings
wraps, eating, 692
wreath or crowning ceremony (Greek
    Orthodox), 570
wrong numbers (telephone), 222–23,
    224–25

Y

yard sales, 85
yarmulkes, 336, 339, 346, 673
yichud, 645
yoga, 144–45
Yom Kippur, 345
"you're welcome," 8, 9

Z

zip code placement, 202

Emily Post, 1872 to 1960

Emily Post began her career as a writer at the age of thirty-one. Her romantic stories of European and American society were serialized in *Vanity Fair*, *Collier's*, *McCall's*, and other popular magazines. Many were also successfully published in book form.

Upon its publication in 1922, her book, *Etiquette*, topped the nonfiction bestseller list, and the phrase "according to Emily Post" soon entered our language as the last word on the subject of social conduct. Mrs. Post, who as a girl had been told that well-bred women should not work, was suddenly a pioneering American career woman. Her numerous books, a syndicated newspaper column, and a regular network radio program made Emily Post a figure of national stature and importance throughout the rest of her life.

"Good manners reflect something from inside—an innate sense of consideration for others and respect for self."

—Emily Post